American Indian Religious Traditions

American Indian Religious Traditions

An Encyclopedia

VOLUME 3 R–Z

Suzanne J. Crawford and Dennis F. Kelley

A B C  C L I O

Santa Barbara, California   Denver, Colorado   Oxford, England

Library of Congress Cataloging-in-Publication Data
Crawford, Suzanne J.
   American Indian religious traditions : an encyclopedia / Suzanne J. Crawford
and Dennis F. Kelley.
       p.   cm.
   Includes bibliographical references and index.
   ISBN 1-57607-517-6 (hardback : alk. paper)—ISBN 1-57607-520-6 (ebook)
   1. Indians of North America—Religion—Encyclopedias.   I. Kelley, Dennis F.
II. Title.

E98.R3C755   2005
299.7'03—dc22

                                                           2004028169

08   07   06   05   04   10   9   8   7   6   5   4   3   2   1

This book is also available on the World Wide Web as an e-book. Visit
abc-clio.com for details.

ABC-CLIO, Inc.
130 Cremona Drive, P.O. Box 1911
Santa Barbara, California 93116–1911

This book is printed on acid-free paper.
Manufactured in the United States of America

Editorial Board

These volumes are dedicated to the memory of my mentor and friend, Professor Howard Harrod, who passed away February 3, 2003. We are blessed to be able to include his work in this project. Howard first introduced me to the study of American Indian religious traditions and encouraged me to continue. Without him, this work would never have come into being.

—Suzanne J. Crawford

I would like to dedicate my efforts in this work to the women and men who strive to maintain their Native cultures and languages so that subsequent generations of American Indians can know who they are, and from where they have come. With this knowledge, they can know where they are going.

—Dennis F. Kelley

The editors have directed that proceeds from the sale of these volumes go to benefit the American Indian College Fund. Information about this important organization can be found at http://www.american-indiancollegefund.org.

Contents

Contributors and Their Entries

Jeffrey D. Anderson
Colby College
Waterville, Maine
    Ceremony and Ritual, Arapaho

Tasiwoopa ápi
Educational Fundamentals
    Religious Leaders, Southwest

Juan A. Avila Hernandez
UC Davis
Davis, CA
    Yoeme (Yaqui) Deer Dance

Karren Baird-Olson
California State University
Northridge, California
    Retraditionalism and Revitalization
        Movements, Plains

Martin Ball
University of California
Berkeley, California
    Kachina and Clown Societies
    Spiritual and Ceremonial
        Practitioners, Southwest

John Baumann
University of Wisconsin
Oshkosh, Wisconsin
    Ecology and Environmentalism

Tressa Berman
University of Technology
Sydney, Australia
    Art (Contemporary), Southwest

Lydia Black
University of Alaska (emerita)
Fairbanks, Alaska
    Missionization, Alaska

Josiah Blackeagle Pinkham
Nez Perce
    Ceremony and Ritual, Nez Perce

John H. Blitz
University of Oklahoma
Norman, Oklahoma
    Mounds

Colleen E. Boyd
Wesleyan University
Middletown, Connecticut
    Oral Traditions, Northwest Coast

Jeane Breinig
University of Alaska
Anchorage, Alaska
    Oral Traditions, Haida

Martin Brokenleg
Vancouver School of Theology
Vancouver, British Columbia
    Ceremony and Ritual, Lakota
    Christianity, Indianization of
    Kinship

Jovana J. Brown
Evergreen State University
Olympia, WA
    Fishing Rights and the First
        Salmon Ceremony

Raymond A. Bucko, S.J.
Creighton University
Omaha, Nebraska
    Sweatlodge

Donna Cameron-Carter
Syracuse University
Syracuse, New York
    Tekakwitha, Kateri

Alex K. Carroll
University of Arizona
Tucson, Arizona
    Boarding Schools, Religious
        Impact
    Cry Ceremony
    Dance, Great Basin
    First Menses Site
    Ghost Dance Movement
    Oral Traditions
    Puhagants
    Religious Leadership, Great Basin

James Taylor Carson
Queen's University, Kingston
Ontario, Canada
    Dance, Southeast
    Retraditionalism and Revitalization
        Movements, Southeast

Mary Jane McDermott Cedar Face
Southern Oregon University
Ashland, Oregon
    Mourning and Burial Practices

(Kanaqlak) George P. Charles
University of Alaska
Anchorage/Fairbanks, Alaska
    Oral Traditions, Yupiaq

Ward Churchill
University of Colorado
Boulder, Colorado
    Sovereignty

Brian Clearwater
University of California
Santa Barbara, California
    Art (Traditional and
        Contemporary), Northeast
    Oral Traditions, Northeast
    Religious Leadership, Northeast
    Retraditionalism and
        Revitalization, Northeast

Walter H. Conser, Jr.
University of North Carolina at
    Wilmington
Wilmington, North Carolina
    Missionization, Southeast

Julianne Cordero-Lamb
University of California
Santa Barbara
    Datura
    Healing Traditions, California
    Herbalism
    Power, Barbareño Chumash

Charlotte Coté
University of Washington
Seattle, Washington
    Whaling, Religious and Cultural
        Implications

Suzanne J. Crawford
Pacific Lutheran University
Tacoma, Washington
    Angalkuq (Tuunrilría)
    On the Academic Study of
        American Indian Religious
        Traditions
    Ceremony and Ritual, Yup'iq
    First Salmon Rites
    Giveaway Ceremonies
    Guardian Spirit Complex
    Kennewick Man
    Masks and Masking
    Menstruation and Menarche
    Missionization, Northeast
    Missionization, Southwest
    Powwow
    Religious Leaders, California
    Religious Leaders, Plains
    Religious Leaders, Plateau
    Religious Leaders, Pueblo
    Sacred Sites and Mountains, Black
        Hills

Elizabeth Currans
University of California, Santa Barbara
Santa Barbara, California
    Gender and Sexuality, Two Spirits

Richard Dauenhauer
Sealaska Heritage Institute
Juneau, Alaska
    Oral Traditions, Tlingit

Aaron Denham
University of Idaho
Moscow, Idaho
    Spiritual and Ceremonial
        Practitioners, Plateau
    Spirits and Spirit Helpers, Plateau

Walter R. Echo-Hawk
Native American Rights Fund
Boulder, Colorado
    Law, Legislation, and Native
        Religion

Clyde Ellis
Elon University
Elon, North Carolina
    Missionization, Kiowa-Comanche-
        Apache Reservation
    Sun Dance, Kiowa

Phyllis Ann Fast
University of Alaska
Fairbanks, Alaska
    Potlatch, Northern Athabascan
    Religious Leaders, Alaska
    Women's Cultural and Religious
        Roles, Northern Athabascan

Donald L. Fixico
Arizona State University
Tempe Arizona
    Termination and Relocation

Rodney Frey
University of Idaho
Moscow, Idaho
    Ceremony and Ritual, Coeur
        d'Alene
    Ceremony and Ritual, Nez Perce
    Dance, Plateau
    Oral Traditions, Plateau

James Garrett
Colorado State University
Fort Collins, Colorado
    Buffalo/Bison Restoration Project

Joel Geffen
University of California, Santa Barbara
Santa Barbara, CA
    First Salmon Rites
    Retraditionalization and
        Revitalization Movements,
        Columbia Plateau

Joyzelle Godfrey
Lower Brule Community College
South Dakota
    Deloria, Ella

Chris Goertzen
University of Southern Mississippi
Hattiesburg, Mississippi
    Song

John A. Grim
Bucknell University
Lewisburg, Pennsylvania
    Power, Plains
    Sun Dance

Andrew Gulliford
Fort Lewis College
Durango, Colorado
    Sacred Sites and Sacred Mountains

Dixie Ray Haggard
Valdosta State University
Valdosta, Georgia
    Power, Southeast
    Religious Leaders, Great Lakes
    Religious Leaders, Southeast

Jane Haladay
University of California
Davis, California
    Basketry

Michael Harkin
University of Wyoming
Laramie, Wyoming
    Power, Northwest Coast
    Sacred Societies, Northwest Coast
    Spiritual and Ceremonial
        Practitioners, Northwest Coast
        and Southeast Alaska

Howard L. Harrod
Vanderbilt University—The Divinity
  School
Nashville, Tennessee
    Bundles, Sacred Bundle Traditions

Dennis Hastings
Omaha Tribal Historical Research
  Project
    Sacred Pole of the Omaha

C. Adrian Heidenreich
Montana State University,
Billings, Montana
    Missionization, Northern Plains
    Oral Traditions, Western Plains
    Sun Dance, Crow

Louis A. Hieb
University of Washington
Seattle, Washington
    Architecture

Michael Hittman
Long Island University
Brooklyn, New York
    Native American Church
    Power, Great Basin

Tom Holm
University of Arizona
Tucson, Arizona
    Warfare, Religious Aspects of

Erica Hurwitz Andrus
University of Vermont
Burlington, Vermont
    Drums

Lee Irwin
College of Charleston
Charleston, South Carolina
    Dreams and Visions
    Vision Quest Rites

Connie A. Jacobs
San Juan College
Farmington, New Mexico
    Erdrich, Louise

M. A. Jaimes-Guerrero
San Francisco State University
San Francisco, California
    Feminism and Tribalism
    Hopi Prophecy
    Identity

James B. Jeffries
Colgate University
Hamilton, New York
    Manitous
    Missionization, Great Lakes

Jennie R. Joe
University of Arizona
Tucson, Arizona
    Health and Wellness, Traditional
      Approaches

Marilyn E. Johnson
Anishnawbe Health
Toronto, Ontario
    Women's Cultural and Religious
      Roles, Great Lakes

Aldona Jonaitis
University of Alaska Museum of the
  North
Fairbanks, Alaska
    Art (Traditional and
      Contemporary), Northwest
      Coast
    Totem Poles

Sergei Kan
Dartmouth College
Dartmouth, New Hampshire
    Potlatch

Linda K. Karell
Montana State University
Bozeman, Montana
    Mourning Dove

Dennis F. Kelley
University of Missouri, Columbia
    On the Academic Study of
       American Indian Religious
       Traditions
    Academic Study of American
       Indian Religious Traditions, Ishi
    American Indian Movement (Red
       Power Movement)
    Ceremony and Ritual, California
    Giveaway Ceremonies
    Missionization, California
    Oral Traditions, California
    Retraditionalism and Identity
       Movements
    Retraditionalism and Revitalization
       Movements, California
    Spiritual and Ceremonial
       Practitioners, California

Clara Sue Kidwell
University of Oklahoma
Norman, Oklahoma
    First Foods Ceremonies and Food
       Symbolism

Benjamin R. Kracht
Northeastern State University
Tahlequah, Oklahoma
    Dance, Plains
    Sacred Societies, Plains
    Spiritual and Ceremonial
       Practitioners, Plains
    Yuwipi Ceremony

Frank LaPena
California State University, Sacramento
Sacramento, CA
    Art (Traditional and
       Contemporary), California and
       the Great Basin

Luke Eric Lassiter
Ball State University
Muncie, Indiana
    Kiowa Indian Hymns

Cynthia Lindquist Mala
Cankdeska Cikana (Little Hoop)
   Community College
Fort Totten, North Dakota
    Hoton Ho Waste Win . . . Good Talk
       Woman: Dakota Spirituality: My
       Perspective

Karen D. Lone Hill
Oglala Lakota College
Pine Ridge, SD
    Black Elk
    Religious Leaders, Plains
    Sacred Sites and Sacred
       Mountains, Black Hills

Denise Low-Weso
Haskell Indian Nations University
Lawrence, Kansas
    Chief Seattle

Nora Marks Dauenhauer
Sealaska Heritage Institute
Juneau, Alaska
    Oral Traditions, Tlingit

David Martínez
University of Minnesota
Minneapolis, Minnesota
    Ceremony and Ritual, Pueblo
    Kiva and Medicine Societies
    Oral Traditions, Pueblo

Joanna Mashunkashey
University of Kansas
Lawrence, Kansas
    I^n-Lo^n-Skah

Carter Meland
University of Minnesota
Minneapolis, Minnesota
    Tricksters

Jay Miller
Seattle, WA
    Ceremony and Ritual, Northwest
    Dance, Northwest Spirit Dances
    Healing Traditions, Northwest
    Religious Leaders, Northwest
    Religious Leadership, Northwest
    Sbatatdaq (Sqadaq)

Catherine Murton Stoehr
Queen's University
Kingston, Ontario, Canada
    Jones, Peter
    Sacred Societies, Great Lakes

Larry Nesper
University of Wisconsin
Madison, Wisconsin
    Clowns and Clowning

Alexandra Witkin New Holy
Montana State University
Bozeman, Montana
    Mother Earth
    Parrish, Essie

Jennifer Nez Denetdale
University of New Mexico
Albuquerque, NM
    Native American Church, Peyote
        Movement

Pamela Jean Owens
University of Nebraska
Omaha, Nebraska
    Beloved Women, Beloved Men,
        Beloved Towns
    Trail of Tears

Donald Panther-Yates
Georgia Southern University
Statesboro, Georgia
    Ceremony and Ritual, Southeast
    Mourning and Burial, Choctaw
    Oral Traditions, Southeast
    Spiritual and Ceremonial
        Practitioners, Southeast

Jordan Paper
York University, Toronto
University of Victoria, Victoria, British
    Columbia
        Ceremony and Ritual, Anishnabe
        Female Spirituality
        Sacred Pipe
        Tobacco, Sacred Use of

Nancy J. Parezo
University of Arizona
Tucson, Arizona
        Ceremony and Ritual, Diné
        Sandpainting

Raymond Pierotti
University of Kansas
Lawrence, Kansas
        Hunting, Religious Restrictions
            and Implications
        Owens, Louis

Annette L. Reed
California State University
Sacramento, California
        Indian Shaker Church

James Riding In
Arizona State University
Tempe, Arizona
        Repatriation, Spiritual and Cultural
            Implications

Robin Ridington
University of British Columbia
    (Emeritus)
        Dreamers and Prophets
        Sacred Pole of the Omaha

Mike Ring
        Art (Traditional and
            Contemporary), Plains

Aleta M. Ringlero
Arizona State University
Tempe, Arizona
        Art (Traditional and
            Contemporary), Southwest

Mary V. Rojas
University of California
Santa Barbara, California
        Scratching Sticks

James Ruppert
University of Alaska
Fairbanks, Alaska
        Oral Traditions, Northern
            Athabascan

Greg Sarris
University of California, Los Angeles
Los Angeles, CA
        McKay, Mabel

Ananda Sattwa
University of California
Berkeley, California
        Green Corn Ceremony

John Scenters-Zapico
University of Texas
El Paso, Texas
        Momaday, N. Scott

Siobhan Senier
University of New Hampshire
Durham, New Hampshire
Winnemucca, Sarah

Theresa S. Smith
Oral Traditions, Ojibwe

Carolyn M. Smith-Morris
Southern Methodist University
Dallas, Texas
Mourning and the Afterlife,
Southwest

Richard W. Stoffle
University of Arizona
Tucson, Arizona
Ghost Dance Movement
Power Places, Great Basin
Puhagants
Religious Leadership, Great Basin

Dale Stover
University of Nebraska
Omaha, Nebraska
Symbolism in American Indian
Ritual and Ceremony

Linea Sundstrom
Day Star Research
Shorewood, Wisconsin
Petrographs and Petroglyphs

Inés Talamantez
University of California
Santa Barbara, California
Ceremony and Ritual, Apache
Female Spirituality, Apache

Coll Thrush
University of Washington
Seattle, Washington
Missionization, Northwest

Deward E. Walker, Jr.
University of Colorado
Boulder, Colorado
Religious Leadership, Plateau

Frances Washburn
University of Arizona
Tucson, Arizona
Literature, Religion in
Contemporary American Indian
Literature
Oral Traditions, Lakota (Teton)

Nakia Williamson
Nez Perce
Dance, Plateau

Joseph Winter
Native American Plant Cooperative
Prison and Native Spirituality

Christopher Wise
Western Washington University
Bellingham, Washington
Brave Bird, Mary (Crow Dog)
Crow Dog, Leonard

Gary Witherspoon
University of Washington
Seattle, Washington
Emergence Narratives

Michael Yellow Bird
University of Kansas
Lawrence, Kansas
    Reservations, Spiritual and
        Cultural Implications

Larry J. Zimmerman
Indiana University-Purdue University
Indianapolis, Indiana
    Archaeology

Michael J. Zogry
University of Kansas
Lawrence, Kansas
    Ball Games

Introduction

Welcome to *American Indian Religious Traditions: An Encyclopedia*. These volumes are the culmination of an enormous amount of effort from many different corners of both academia and Indian Country. Our goal in creating this reference work was to compile a set of articles that would help to define the academic study of American Indian religious traditions as it is undertaken at the beginning of the twenty-first century and to create a reference work both sensitive to and reflective of the political and ethical concerns of the Native communities upon which these volumes depend. The entries in these volumes, therefore, do not approach religion as an isolated experience but as an integral part of cultural, political, economic, and social lives, placing their individual topics within the wider social and political context. These volumes are made up of entries by Native academics and community members, as well as non-Native scholars who have demonstrated themselves sensitive to the concerns of Native communities and aware of the political implications of their work. We are proud to present entries written by the top scholars in the field, whose scholarly endeavors are a testimony to their ethical commitment to Native cultural survival. We have worked to ensure that Native voices are respected in these volumes, encouraging our authors to consult with elders, community leaders, and tribal cultural resource managers whenever possible. And we are encouraged that more than half of the entries in these volumes are written by scholars who are themselves of Native descent.

For much of its early history, scholarship on Native communities was done by non-Native authors who had little knowledge of the internal workings of Native communities and cultures. Interpreted from the perspective of outsiders, much of this early work misrepresented Native religious life. This encyclopedia seeks to rectify this problem by presenting Native spiritual traditions as they are understood by people within the communities themselves.

This project stands apart from other reference works in a number of ways. The authors in these volumes have been allowed to maintain their own voice, perspective, and position. We have not dictated the focus, content, or style of entries, but provided guidelines within which our authors have creatively worked. The reader may therefore notice the use of the first person and the citation of individual Native elders as authoritative sources, methods not often found in reference works. Rather than a series of brief, definitional paragraphs, defining specific ceremonies or individuals, readers will find more general entries that place the specific within a broader context.

In an era when much of Native religious life is at risk because of threats to sacred land, repressive laws, or misappropriation by New Age religious groups, it is extremely important that these traditions be presented to the wider public in a way that both informs them of the true nature and context of Native religious life and is simultaneously respectful of Native privacy and intellectual property rights. Our overall intention for this project is to provide students with research and learning resources that are both reliable and respectful. The entries and suggestions for further reading set their topics within a historical context as well as a contemporary setting; it is our hope that students, as well as interested individuals in the wider population, will find this a valuable resource as they begin their own research into American Indian cultural life.

Rather than brief dictionary-style entries we have chosen to include longer entries that demonstrate the complexity and context of the issues involved. To lead the reader through the complex web of culture, experience, and history that makes up American Indian religious life, the entries are intentionally linked, via cross-references. Longer, chapter-length entries are devoted to broad topics such as Dance, Ritual and Ceremony, and Religious Leadership.

How to Use These Volumes

If you have a specific term, ceremony, individual, or tribal nation in mind that you would like to study, we recommend that you first turn to the index. At the end of the book you will find an index of tribal nations and key terms that will lead you to relevant entries. Keep in mind that some tribal nations are known by more than one name: for instance, many people think of the Native nation living in the four corners area of the Southwest as the Navajo. They refer to themselves, however, as the Diné. In this project, we have chosen to use the names for Native nations that they themselves prefer to use. The index will help readers find the nations that might be listed in the volumes using an unfamiliar name.

Each entry is followed by suggestions for further reading and research. These include scholarly works cited within the entry and other works that the contributor recommends as reliable resources. Many students undertaking the study of American Indian religious traditions are confronted by the difficult task of weeding through reliable and unreliable sources. It is our hope that these references will help to point students toward solid scholarship that has been conducted with careful sensitivity to the concerns and needs of the Native communities.

A Brief Word on Terminology

As many people from within Native American communities can confirm, the language that is used with regard to

American Indian culture is contested and highly politicized. Mainstream culture and New Age writing frequently refer to "The Indian," suggesting that there is a single identity and experience that defines the Native people of this country. With over 500 federally recognized tribes (not to mention the hundreds of tribes recognized at only the state level), this is clearly not the case. Each nation possesses a unique culture, language, history, and sense of identity. The tendency in the dominant culture to take these multiple and complex topics as parts of a single whole has added to the kind of rhetoric against which Native people now find themselves struggling. At the outset, these volumes set themselves apart from such homogenizing by reference to the plurality of American Indian religious traditions. The entries in this volume avoid broad generalizations and focus on specific, grounded examples of individual Nations. Throughout these volumes the reader will find names and terminologies in their original indigenous language. This is done in an effort to demonstrate tribally specific phenomena as they are perceived from within the indigenous community. It will therefore be necessary for the reader to contend with terms presented in their appropriate indigenous language as well as with the creative use of English terms that come closer to the communities' own understanding than other more commonly-used words. One important example of the latter is the use of the word "shaman." In many non-Native

publications, the term "shaman" refers to any and all spiritual leaders among any and all indigenous populations. We have worked to avoid the use of the "shaman" label in these volumes, as we feel it negates the distinct differences existing among indigenous spiritual leaders, healers, and counselors. To introduce readers to these distinctions, these volumes offer extensive entries on spiritual and ceremonial practitioners, providing examples from throughout Indian Country of many distinct and unique religious practitioners. Some contributors may choose to keep the problematic term "shaman," but they do so in a way that situates them locally.

Many readers will be familiar with the debate over the use of the words "Indian," "Native," and "First Peoples" to refer to the indigenous people of this hemisphere. The term "Indian" is the familiar self-reference that most Native communities use among themselves and its use here is intended to convey the internal-community-to-external-audience nature of this work. The use of the term "Indian" here is reflective of the intimate relationship with Native communities within which the entries were created and therefore does not advocate its broad use among non-Native people—it is a recognition of its use and importance among indigenous communities.

What's Here and What's Not
Perhaps the most difficult part of a project such as this is deciding what will be included and what will be excluded.

Given a limited amount of space, we quickly realized that much would necessarily be left out. We have tried to include those topics that are most likely familiar to students and that they are most likely to be researching in a reference work. Although we recognize the impossibility of including every tribal nation and every tradition, we have done our best to give students a sense of the vast diversity of American Indian cultures. We encouraged our authors to provide general overviews, along with a few detailed, grounded examples of the traditions that they were discussing. We decided that offering a few specific examples dealt with carefully and at length, would better serve our student readers than entries that discussed large numbers of traditions without nuanced descriptions or adequate contextualization. The volumes thus address broader topics and ideas, rather than specific minutia. The entries include tribally specific examples of these broader ideas and hopefully succeed in demonstrating the diversity of traditions. Still, we must readily admit that these entries are nowhere near exhaustive. They are meant to provide a brief introduction to the complexity and diversity of experience and to point our readers in the direction of more detailed information.

Because of the limited space and our desire to adequately cover those areas we did include, we made the difficult decision that we would not seek to extensively discuss tribal nations in Hawaii, Mexico, or Canada. However, we drew these national boundaries with extreme flexibility. We worked to construct these boundaries as Native nations do: nations and cultures oftentimes transgress political borders. For this reason, we encouraged authors whose topics crossed political borders to do so as well. Entries discussing nations from the Pacific Northwest Coast thus include nations from British Columbia, and entries on northern Alaska include information on Inuit and Northern Athabaskan communities in Canada. Entries on Native cultures from the Great Lakes and New England likewise cross the Canadian divide. And, some entries discussing the American Southwest freely cross over into northern Mexico. We knew we could not possibly do justice to the complex tribal and cultural diversities within Canada, the Pacific, and Mexico. And yet, we also did not want to laboriously draw our borders along these political lines. Hence, the contributors were encouraged to make reference to communities in these areas when appropriate.

And finally, many subjects were intentionally left out. Many religious traditions for Native communities are extremely private and not meant to be discussed in print. Some people may argue that we have gone too far with what we did include. Some might insist that it is never appropriate to discuss religion in print. We hope that the entries represented here demonstrate our concern to respect the values and wishes of the Native communities they discuss. Some traditions, such as detailed information regarding secret societies, details of ritual activity, sacred songs and prayers, and images of sacred objects are not meant to be represented outside of their specific ritual and ceremonial context. Although much has been published about these subjects elsewhere, we chose not to do so. By way of example, the Huadenasaunne (or Iroquois) Six-Nation Confederation has requested that no reproductions or images of False Face masks be publicly available. For this reason, no images of False Face masks appear in these volumes.

The editorial board and we volume editors have made every effort to produce this work with honor and any shortcomings will hopefully be tempered by the knowledge that these efforts guided this project.

We would like to thank our editorial board for their gracious support and guidance. Each member of the editorial board assisted with overall editorial guidance of the book, and each also offered guidance with materials covering the specific regions with which they had particular expertise. Inés Talamantez (Mescalero Apache), University of California, Santa Barbara, advised us on traditions in the Southwest; Inés Hernandez Avila (Nez Perce/Chicana), University of California, Davis, advised us regarding Native traditions in Southwest and Plateau regions; George Charles (Yup'iq), University of Alaska, Fairbanks, advised us on traditions of Native Alaskans; Lee Irwin, College of Charleston, advised us on traditions of the Great Plains; Joel Martin, University of California, Riverside, advised us on traditions in the Southeast and on historical approaches overall; Ken Mello (Pasamaquoddy), University of Vermont, advised us on entries for the Northeast region of the country; and Michelene Pesantubbee (Choctaw), University of Colorado, Boulder, advised us regarding entries on the Southeast and on contemporary issues relating to gender, sovereignty, and intellectual property rights.

We would also like to thank our families and loved ones for their patient support through what has been a long and difficult project. Suzanne Crawford thanks Michael T. O'Brien for his faith, encouragement, and affection. And Dennis Kelley extends his thanks to his wife, Kate, and their son, Seamus, for their love, patience, and inspiration.

Suzanne J. Crawford
and Dennis F. Kelley

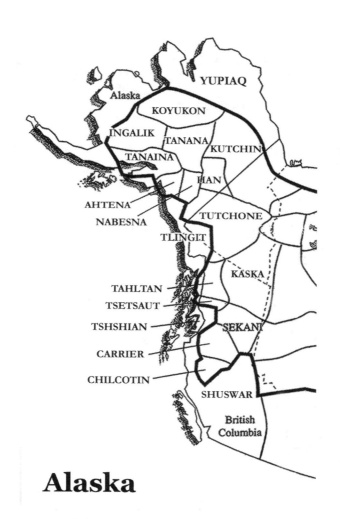

YUPIAQ

Alaska

KOYUKON

INGALIK

TANANA

KUTCHIN

TANAINA

HAN

AHTENA

TUTCHONE

NABESNA

TLINGIT

KASKA

TAHLTAN

TSETSAUT

TSHSHIAN

SEKANI

CARRIER

CHILCOTIN

SHUSWAR

British
Columbia

Alaska

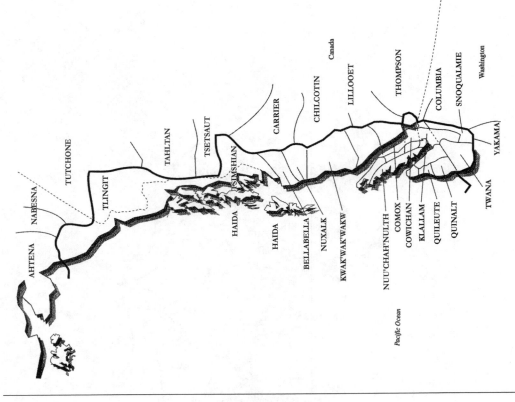

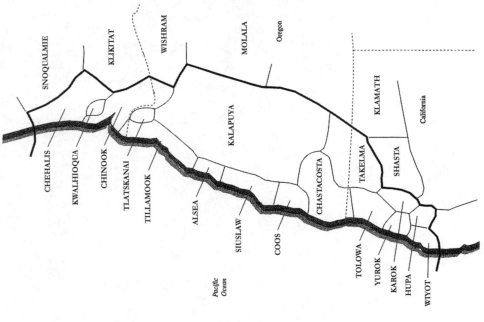

Northwest Coast

Northwest Coast and Alaska

The Northwest Coast culture area encompasses more than 2,000 miles of the Pacific coast, from southern Alaska to northern California. The width of this narrow coastal region varies from about 10 to 150 miles. It is cool, damp, and thickly forested and is cut by many rivers. The mountain ranges that run north-south along the eastern limits of the region include the Coast Ranges in Canada and the Cascade Range in the United States. The region is characterized by mild, wet winters and cool summers. Evergreen forests thrive where there is soil enough to support them, and huge trees form dense canopies that block out much sunlight. Springs and streams from mountain glaciers feed numerous rivers, which, along with the ocean at the coast, provide abundant fish, and the forests are home to abundant plants and animals, providing a wealth of foods and medicines for the Indian peoples of the region.

Northwest Coast peoples speak a variety of languages, with linguistic families ranging from Athapaskan and Penutian, to Salishan and Wakashan. The region is home to numerous and varied tribal traditions, as well, which can be divided into three basic groupings: those of the colder northern area, including the Queen Charlotte Islands of western British Columbia; those of the central region, in the vicinity of Vancouver Island and the mouth of the Columbia River; and those of the warmer southern region, who shared some cultural traits with peoples of the California culture area.

Social organization is primarily focused on extended-family village groups, with regular seasonal cooperative fishing and hunting camps for temporary dwelling. In the central and northern areas, multiple-family houses of cedar planks organized villages into collectives, which shared political connections prior to contact.

Canoes play an important role both culturally and religiously in the central and northern areas at the coasts. Large ocean-going canoes, carved out of single cedar trees, capable of carrying several individuals on fishing, hunting, or trading trips throughout the region were common.

Religious diversity abounds in the region, with southern tribal groups connected to the World Renewal ceremonial paradigm, a complex collection of dances that are key in the firming up and renewing of the earth for

continues

Northwest Coast and Alaska (continued)

the next cycle. People of the central areas and the central and northern regions participate in potlatch ceremonies. Potlatching, once actually outlawed in both Canada and the United States, provides opportunities for the celebration of significant events in the life of the community, such as marriages and births, as well as seasonal observations like solstices and equinoxes. At potlatch ceremonies, the significant aspect is a redistribution of wealth items, often in the form of gift-giving, but at times redistribution includes destruction of property.

The Northwest Coast is a diverse region that requires diverse approaches for the long-term maintenance of available resources, and for the ongoing continuity of tribal cultures. Much of the ceremonial activity in this region, therefore, focuses on both of these aspects, propitiating the spirit world for the continued gifts of fish, game, and plant resources and taking time to celebrate the communities that cooperatively manage these resources.

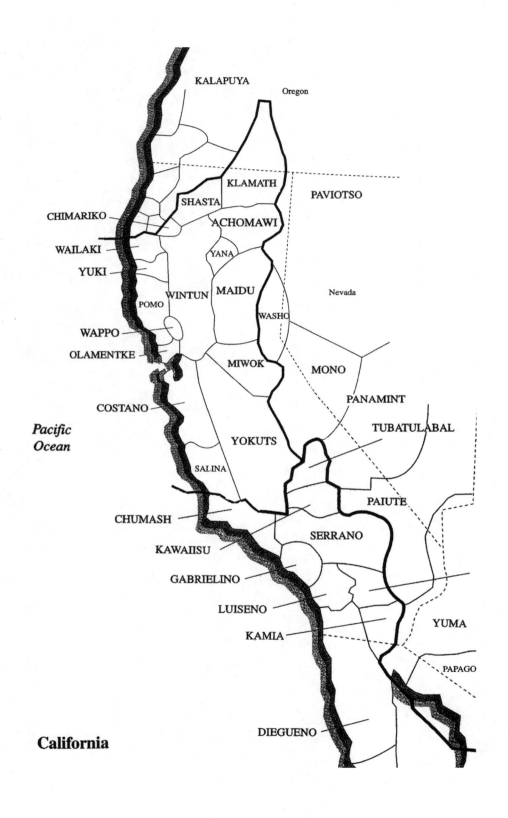

KALAPUYA

Oregon

KLAMATH

SHASTA

CHIMARIKO

ACHOMAWI

PAVIOTSO

WAILAKI

YANA

YUKI

MAIDU

Nevada

WINTUN

POMO

WASHO

WAPPO

OLAMENTKE

MIWOK

MONO

Pacific
Ocean

COSTANO

PANAMINT

TUBATULABAL

YOKUTS

SALINA

PAIUTE

CHUMASH

KAWAIISU

SERRANO

GABRIELINO

LUISENO

YUMA

KAMIA

PAPAGO

California

DIEGUENO

California

The California Indians, when taken as a whole, reside in a culture area that includes roughly the present-day state of California as well as the Lower California Peninsula, or Baja California. There are two mountain ranges that run north and south through the state of California: the Coast Ranges to the west and the Sierra Nevada to the east. The Coast Ranges drop off to coastal lowlands along the Pacific coast in most areas, but rocky cliffs and awe-inspiring vistas characterize the range to the north. Between the Coast Ranges and the Sierra Nevada, the San Joaquin and Sacramento Rivers form a basin known as the Central Valley. The climate is generally a mild, Mediterranean-style, with wet and dry seasons and many days of warm weather, especially in the south. Rainfall varies significantly throughout the state, with the forested regions in the north receiving the highest levels and the deserts in the south the lowest. Plant and animal life abound, and the region boasts a rich and varied ecology.

The Sierra Nevada mountain range has long provided a natural barrier to the movement of peoples. As a result, Native Americans east of the Sierra Nevada practice markedly different ways of life and are often included in the Great Basin or Southwest culture areas. Some Indian peoples just south of California's present-day northern border shared ways of life with peoples of the Northwest Coast culture area and the Plateau culture area further inland.

California was one of the most densely populated North American culture areas before European contact, with numerous tribes and bands speaking more than 100 distinct languages. Nearly all of the Indian language families in the lower forty-eight states are represented in California.

Much scientific evidence places the first human occupancy of California at the very end of the last ice age (approx. 10,000 years BP), but the rich nature of tribal sacred history reveals a continuous interaction between peoples, movements in and out of regions, and long-term stewardship of specific regions from time immemorial. It very well may have been that the California culture area was a melting pot of sorts, with tribal groups influencing one another through both trade and population movement.

continues

California (continued)

California once had abundant resources that supported large Native American populations without the need for agriculture before the arrival of Europeans. The dietary staple of most California Indians was the acorn, which was collected in the fall. Acorns can be pounded into flour and rinsed of the bitter-tasting tannic acid, creating an acorn meal that can be boiled into a soup or gruel or baked into bread. This complex carbohydrate, when augmented with protein from fish or meat, provides an extremely healthy diet.

Most Native Americans in the California culture area lived in villages of related families with descent and property ownership traced through the male's family. Permanent villages often had smaller satellite villages nearby, and the complex was presided over by one principal chief, acting much like the mayors of contemporary California. In addition, many regional groups made use of temporary hunting or gathering camps that they occupied for portions of the year.

Religiously, the region is far too diverse to accommodate here, but suffice it to say that the sometimes-fickle nature of California's weather patterns produced philosophical systems that took the uncertain nature of the universe into consideration, with the sacred beings often unconcerned about their human communities. Not relying on simple good versus evil scenarios, California Indian religions tend to view the world as it is. Religious professionals have the ability to sway spiritual matters in one direction or another, either through the employment of specific ritualized formulae, or through the constant monitoring of the movements of the cosmos. California Indian peoples also employed healing artists, people with knowledge of the workings of the human body, herbal remedies to aid in the body's repair, and propitiation of spiritual influences that may be causing physical harm from the spiritual realm.

California's diverse and varied climate, then, presides over a diverse human situation, as well, with many language groupings interacting with the physical landscape, producing religious systems that allow for the continuing interaction with territory both physical and sacred.

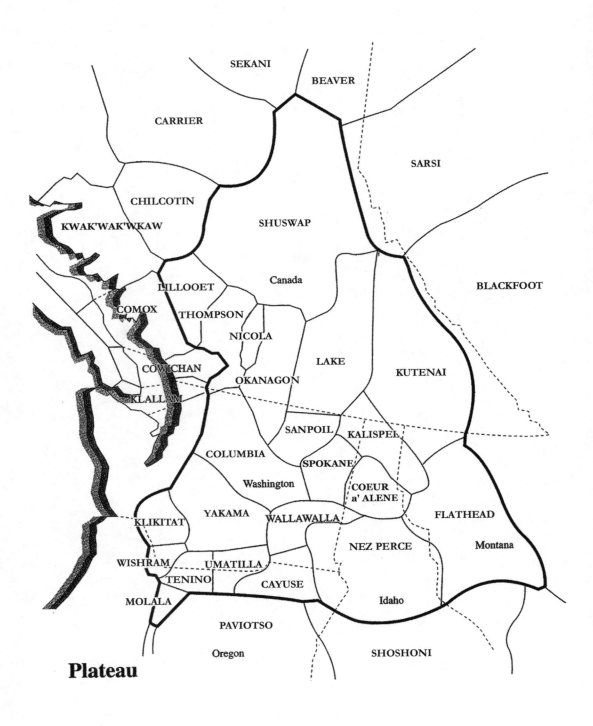

Plateau

Plateau

The native people of the Plateau are linguistically and culturally diverse. Many aspects of their lives are unique adaptations to the mountains and valleys in which they live. However, these people were strongly influenced by the Plains people to the east and the Northwest Coast people to the west prior to Euro-American contact. Most of the Plateau people lived in small villages or village clusters, with economies based on hunting, fishing, and wild horticulture.

The Plateau culture area is an upland region that encompasses the Columbia Plateau and the basins of the great Fraser and Columbia Rivers. The Columbia Plateau is surrounded by the Cascade Mountains to the west, the Rocky Mountains to the east, the desert country of the Great Basin to the south, and the forest and hill country of the upper Fraser River to the north.

The mountains bordering the Columbia Plateau catch large amounts of rain and snowfall. This precipitation drains into a great number of rivers and streams, many of which feed the Columbia River on its way to the Pacific Ocean. The mountains and river valleys have enough water to support forests of pine, hemlock, spruce, fir, and cedar, while the land between the mountain ranges consists of flatlands and rolling hills covered with grasses and sagebrush. The climate varies greatly depending on proximity to the ocean and the altitude. Game animals are generally small, except in the mountain areas. However, nutritious plant foods such as tubers and roots can be found in meadows and river valleys. Seasonal runs of salmon in the Columbia, Fraser, and tributary rivers significantly enhanced the region's available food supply, providing both a staple food and a key sacred symbol.

The Plateau was not as densely populated as the Northwest Coast culture area to the west before contact, yet many different tribes have called the region home. Two language groups are dominant: Penutian speakers such as the Cayuse, Klamath, Klickitat, Modoc, Nez Perce, Palouse, Umatilla, Walla Walla, and Yakama in the interior portions, and Salishan speakers, the Columbia, Coeur d'Alene, Flathead, Kalispel, Shuswap, and Spokane to the northwest.

continues

Plateau (continued)

More than two dozen distinct tribal groups inhabited the Columbia Plateau at the time of European contact. Ancestors of peoples speaking languages of the Penutian linguistic family probably settled the area more than 8,000 years ago. Over the centuries these groups have been influenced by the landscapes of the Plateau region in the development of their religious cultures, often centering on the sharing of the salmon runs. First Salmon ceremonies are fairly typical in the region, wherein the people celebrate and give thanks for the new salmon run with a religious ritual prior to partaking in the resource. This activity, while displaying an appreciation for the gift from the sacred beings that salmon represent, also ensures that adequate numbers of fish get to villages farther upstream, and that the strongest fish arrive at the spawning grounds, maintaining a strong genetic line for the future.

Localized variations on this ceremony abound, as well as region-specific rituals and ceremonies of thanksgiving and propitiation appropriate to localities. The extended-family group nature of the tribal system, along with the numerous tribes in the region, also point to the need for extended cooperative trade relationships and intermarriage.

The Plateau cultural area, like all of the cultural regions used to discuss Native American peoples, is really a diverse and varied one with linguistic, cultural, and religious differences from area to area within the region. However, there is enough ecological similarity in the region to inspire some common traits among the tribal groups. Groups of the region often sacralize these commonalities in regular intertribal gatherings for trade and intermarriage.

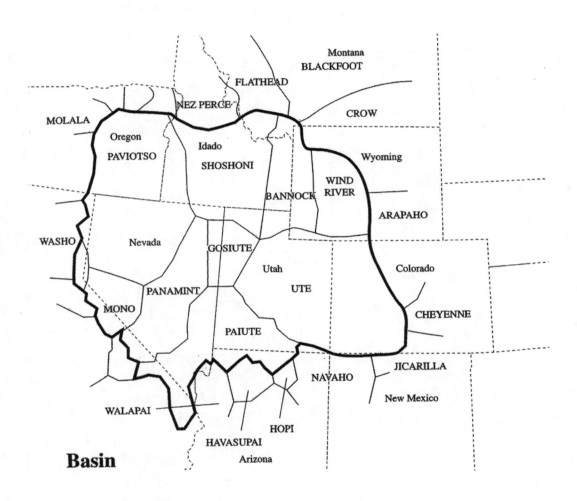

Montana
BLACKFOOT
FLATHEAD
NEZ PERCE
CROW
MOLALA
Oregon
PAVIOTSO
Idado
SHOSHONI
Wyoming
WIND
RIVER
BANNOCK
ARAPAHO
WASHO
Nevada
GOSIUTE
Utah
Colorado
PANAMINT
UTE
MONO
CHEYENNE
PAIUTE
JICARILLA
NAVAHO
WALAPAI
New Mexico
HOPI
HAVASUPAI
Arizona

Basin

Great Basin

The Great Basin culture refers to an arid inland region encompassing much of the western United States. Consisting of a vast natural basin, with occasional rocky uplands breaking up long stretches of mostly barren desert, the region is surrounded by the Sierra Nevada range on the west, the Rocky Mountains on the east, the Columbia Plateau on the north, and the Colorado Plateau on the south. The region includes the open expanse of the Mojave Desert in the southwest, which provides a stark exception to the general ecological makeup of the area.

The river systems of the Great Basin drain from the high country into the central depression and disappear into sinks and thus have no outlet to the oceans (hence the "basin" characterization). The mountains to the east and west block the rain clouds, leading to both low rainfall and high evaporation. The Great Basin once contained dozens of lakes, some quite large, as evidenced by their remnants, including Great Salt Lake. In the western part of the Great Basin is Death Valley, where temperatures in the summer often exceed 125°F. Sagebrush dominates the sparse vegetation throughout the Great Basin, with some piñon and juniper trees in the higher elevations.

This somewhat harsh environment produces more nomadic tribes than regions to the west, and these tribes speak variations of the Uto-Aztecan family. The one exception is the Washoe to the west who speak a Hokan dialect. The major tribal groups of the Great Basin are the Paiute, Shoshone, and Ute, each with various subdivisions and offshoots. Although dialects vary throughout the region, their similarities have made it possible for different groups to maintain diplomatic relations for trade and intermarriage.

Great Basin Indians adopted their nomadic lifestyles in order to fully exploit wild food resources as they became available. Social organization for this type of resource management tends to be smaller than that of more settled groups, with the extended-family group being the primary source for identity. Leadership is provided through "headmen," who are often capable and wise individuals who oversee the affairs of the family in trade negotiations and the like. Regular gatherings of these family groups, for practical purposes such as "rabbit Drives" (mass rabbit hunts requiring the labors of many), seasonal observations such as solstice and equinox

continues

Great Basin, (continued)

ceremonies, or weddings often doubled as the group's religious system, and the bands' spiritual advisors would preside over general rites of propitiation and thanksgiving.

The relatively difficult day-to-day circumstances lead to less overall time spent in philosophical pondering, but by no means should this fact be assumed to equate less religiosity. The daily gatherings and hunting done by the family group are accompanied by ritual activity, personal spiritual interaction, and the diplomatic interaction between the human and the other-than-human world.

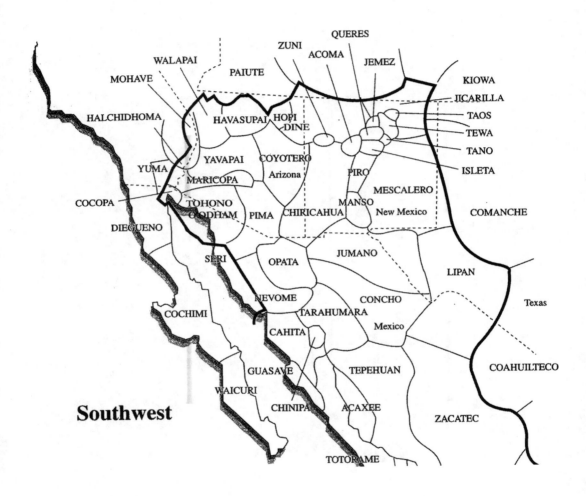

Southwest

Southwest

In the Southwestern portion of the United States, the tribal communities that maintain their connection to their homeland have done so more successfully than many other tribal groups in the United States. The arid region, relative isolation, and insular nature of the various communities therein are all factors, but in any case, it is important to note that the region boasts a high rate of language, culture, and religious retention despite the long history of colonial pressure, both from Spain and the United States.

The Southwest is one portion of Indian country where the intimate relationship between Native peoples and their lands can be seen most clearly. The Diné (Navajo), Hopi, Apache, and Pueblo communities, while distinct, have relatively similar lifeways owing to the nature of the landscape in what is now the Four Corners region. Despite the arid nature of the high deserts of modern-day Colorado, Arizona, New Mexico, and Utah, proper management of the available rainfall has yielded corn crops sufficient to give rise to the complex and ancient cultures that call this region home.

The Southwest culture area reaches across a great swath of arid country in what is now the southwestern United States and northern Mexico. It includes diverse terrain, from the high mesas and canyons of the Colorado Plateau in the north to the Mogollon Mountains of present-day southern New Mexico. Cactus-dotted deserts flank the Little Colorado River in present-day southern Arizona and the Gulf of Mexico in present-day southern Texas.

Few rains water the Southwest, and most rainfall occurs during a six-week period in the summer. Snowfall is infrequent except in mountain areas. Three types of vegetation are dominant, depending on altitude and rainfall: western evergreen in the mountains; piñon and juniper in mesa country; and desert shrub, cactus, and mesquite in lower, drier regions.

Among peoples in the Southwest, three language families predominate: Uto-Aztecan, Yuman, and Athapaskan. Uto-Aztecan speakers included the Hopi of Arizona and the Tohono O'Odham (Papago) and Akimel O'Odham (Pima) of Arizona and northern Mexico. Some Pueblo peoples, including the Tewa, Tiwa, and Towa in modern-day New Mexico, speak dialects of Kiowa-Tanoan, a language family related to Uto-Aztecan. The Cocopah,

continues

Southwest (continued)

Havasupai, Hualapai, Maricopa, Mojave, Yavapai, Yuma (Quechan), and other neighboring peoples in Arizona speak Yuman. The Apache and Navajo (Diné) of New Mexico and Arizona and the southern fringe of Colorado and Utah speak Athapaskan languages.

In the early historic period, four distinct farming peoples came to occupy the Southwest: peoples of the Mogollon, Hohokam, Anasazi, and Patayan cultures. The people of these cultures raised corn, beans, and squash. For each of these peoples, the adoption of agriculture permitted the settlement of permanent villages and the continued refinement of farming technology, arts, and crafts, especially pottery.

The Mogollon people of southeastern Arizona and southwestern New Mexico, who appeared about 2,300 years ago, built permanent villages in the region's high valleys and developed pottery distinct in its intricate geometric patterns. The Mimbres people, a Mogollan subgroup, are famous for painting pottery with dramatic black-on-white geometric designs of animals and ceremonial scenes. From about AD 1200 to 1400 the Mogollan culture was gradually absorbed by the then-dominant Anasazi culture.

The Hohokam people of southern Arizona first appeared about 2,100 years ago. Hohokam Indians dug extensive irrigation ditches for their crops. Some canals, which carried water diverted from rivers, extended for many miles. Hohokam people also built sunken ball courts—like those of the Maya Civilization in Mesoamerica—on which they played a sacred game resembling a combination of modern basketball and soccer. Hohokam people are thought to be ancestors of the Tohono O'Odham and Pima, who preserve much of the Hohokam way of life.

In the Four Corners region, where Arizona, New Mexico, Utah, and Colorado now join, the Anasazi Indians gradually emerged from older Southwestern cultures, and took on a distinctive character by about 2,100 years ago. Anthropologists refer to the Anasazi of this early era as Basket Makers because they wove fine baskets from rushes, straw, and other materials. Basket Makers hunted and gathered wild foods, tended fields, and lived in large *pit houses,* dwellings with sunken floors that were topped by sturdy timber frameworks covered with mud. By about 700 CE, the Basket Maker culture

continues

had developed into the early Pueblo cultural period. Over the next 200 years these peoples made the transition from pit houses to surface dwellings called *pueblos* by the Spanish. These dwellings were rectangular, multistoried apartment buildings composed of terraced stone and adobe arranged in planned towns connected by an extensive network of public roads and irrigation systems. At its peak, after about 900, Pueblo culture dominated much of the Southwest. From about 1150 to 1300 Pueblo peoples evacuated most of their aboveground pueblos and built spectacular dwellings in the recesses of cliffs. The largest of these had several hundred rooms and could house a population of 600 to 800 in close quarters.

The Patayan people lived near the Colorado River in what is now western Arizona, and developed agriculture by about 875 CE. They planted crops along the river floodplain and filled out their diets by hunting and gathering. Patayan Indians lived in brush-covered structures and had extensive trade networks as evidenced by the presence of shells from the Gulf of California region. The Patayan people are thought to be ancestors of the Yuman-speaking tribes.

During the late 1200s the Four Corners area suffered severe droughts, and many Pueblo sites were abandoned. However, Pueblo settlements along the Rio Grande in the south grew larger, and elaborate irrigation systems were built. Between 1200 and 1500 a people speaking Athapaskan appeared in the Southwest, having migrated southward along the western Great Plains. Based on linguistic connections, these people are believed to have branched off from indigenous peoples in western Canada. They are thought to be the ancestors of the nomadic Apache and Navajo. Their arrival may have played a role in the relocation of some Pueblo groups.

Two principal ways of life developed in the Southwest: sedentary and nomadic. The sedentary Pueblo peoples are mainly farmers who hunt and gather wild plant foods and medicines in addition to growing the larger part of their subsistence diet: corn. Squash, beans, and sunflowers are also grown in plots that range from large multifamily fields to smaller extended-family plots. A number of desert peoples, including the upland and river Yuman tribes and the Tohono O'Odham and Pima, maintain a largely agrarian way of life as well.

continues

Southwest (continued)

The religions of this region are as distinct as the cultures represented here, however, the presence of relatively sedentary communities from about 1500 CE on renders a similar "emergence" philosophy, in which the people are said to have come to their present place from lower worlds, and the role that agriculture plays for these cultures leads to a common emphasis on fertility, balance, and of course, rain.

The Hopi and other Pueblo cultures celebrate the presence of ancestral spirit beings, called *Katsinam*, for the majority of the year. These beings provide rain, fertility, and social stability through exemplary conduct used to teach the people how to live. Similarly, the Diné (Navajo) utilize the symbolism of corn and the cycles of the growing seasons to pattern both their ceremonial lives and their behavior toward one another and to the universe. Apaches likewise view their reliance on the seasonal cycles as indicative of their sacred responsibilities.

Though the region known as the Southwest culture area appears to be a dauntingly complicated landscape to maintain long-term communities in, the tribal peoples therein have not only managed, but also thrived. In addition, due to the stark nature of the Southwest, and the isolated nature of many portions within it, these tribal cultures have a level of cultural continuity that belies the harshness of the land.

Plains

Great Plains

The vast region known as the Great Plains culture area stretches from the Mississippi River valley west to the Rocky Mountains and from present-day central Canada to southern Texas. Dominated by rolling, fertile tallgrass prairies in the east, where there is adequate rainfall for agriculture, the landscape shifts to short grasses in the drier high western plains. Some wooded areas interrupt these vast fields of grass, mostly stands of willows and cottonwoods along river valleys, and in some places highlands rise up from the plains and prairies, such as the Ozark Mountains in Missouri, and the Black Hills of South Dakota and Wyoming. The region is remarkable, however, for the extent and dominance of its grasslands. For thousands of years tens of millions of bison grazed the grasses of the Great Plains.

Prior to the arrival of Europeans, most occupants of the Great Plains lived along rivers in the eastern regions. Predominantly farmers, these culture groups hunted bison and other game seasonally to augment their diets with dried meat and to make use of the hide, bones, and fat of these enormous animals.

The region is known for its diverse Native cultures, some of which have resided in the Plains region longer than others. The Hidatsa, and Mandan, both speakers of Siouan linguistic dialects, as well as Caddoan-speaking Pawnee and Wichita made use of the river banks for small-plot farming and they hunted in large cooperatives once or perhaps twice a year.

More hunting-oriented peoples eventually moved into the region and developed cultural and philosophical traditions based on the bison and warfare/raiding warrior cultures. These include the Algonquin-speaking Blackfeet from the north and the Uto-Aztecan-speaking Comanche from the northwest. After, and in some cases because of, the arrival of Europeans in North America, Eastern tribal groups such as Siouan-speaking Assiniboine, Crow, Kaw, Osage, Quapaw, and the various tribal groups often incorrectly glossed as "Sioux" (Lakota, Nakota, and Dakota) from the Great Lakes region moved to the region. From the Northeast came the Algonquin-speaking Arapaho, Cheyenne, and Gros Ventre. To be certain, this is an abbreviated list. The key issues are that movement into the region coincided with

continues

Great Plains (continued)

the entrance of horses to the Great Plains and the groups that call the Plains home have all participated in a development of regional, seminomadic cultural traditions that have come to be erroneously lumped together. This tragic loss of a sense of tribal diversity on the Great Plains has been exacerbated by the "Hollywoodization" of Indian issues, itself merely a continuation of nineteenth-century dime novels about the West.

After European contact, some Great Plains peoples continued to farm, and many groups hunted a variety of game, fished rivers, and gathered wild plant foods. However, with the spread of horses as a means of transportation to follow the seasonal migrations of bison herds over great distances, bison meat became the staple food.

Most Great Plains tribes consisted of bands of related families, often with several hundred members. Tribal leadership was typically divided between a peace chief and a war chief (or several war chiefs). Peace chiefs tended to internal tribal affairs. War chiefs, usually younger men, conducted warfare and led raids on enemies. The bands lived apart in smaller family groups most of the year, coming together in the summer months for communal bison hunts, ceremonies, or councils. In opposition to the idea that Indian people never owned land, tribal groups often took responsibility for particular regions, sharing hunting lands with friendly tribes, but protecting them from enemies.

Another myth is that all Indians of the Plains lived in tepees prior to contact. The tepee is a portable shelter that served its purpose for most groups for portions of the year. Earth and grass lodges were also frequently used dwellings before Euro-American arrival, providing large communal dwellings and ceremonial structures.

Religion among the Plains peoples is as diverse as the linguistic traditions represented there, however, there are also some similarities. With the important role that bison play in the lives of these tribal groups, it is no wonder that that animal would be an important spirit being and relative, as well. In addition, the migratory nature of bison, and consequently that of the peoples who rely upon them, support a seasonal and cyclical

continues

Great Plains (continued)

philosophical system wherein the circle is a key element. Plains Indian religious culture is often represented by circles, sun-wise directional prayers, and cyclical senses of time and space.

Major ceremonies include the Sun Dance, a regular gathering of bands for communal propitiation of the spirit beings, and the more recent religious innovation known as the Ghost Dance, wherein visions and ecstatic dancing propels the tribal culture forward in the face of the difficulties arising from modernity.

The Great Plains, often viewed as the exemplary Native American culture area, is far more diverse and multilingual than popular culture depicts, and the Plains peoples have many localized and territorial traditions that represent specific regional differences.

Ontario

Quebec

OJIBWA

OTTAWA

ALGONKIN

MENOMINI

SAUK

Wisconsin

WINNEBAGO
SANTEE

FOX

Michigan

POTAWATOMI

HAUDENAUSANEE

KICKAPOO

NEUTRAL

IOWA

HURON

MIAMI

ERIE

Illinois

ILLINOIS

Indiana

MOSOPELEA

MISSOURI

Kentucky

SHAWNEE

CHEROKEE

CHICKASAW

Great Lakes

ALGONKIN

Canada

OTTAWA

ABNAKI

PENNACOOK

Michigan

MASSACHUSET

New York

POTAWATOMI

HAUDENAUSANEE

MOHEGAN

MAHICAN

NEUTRAL

METOAC

Pennsylvania

DELAWARE

CONESTOGA

MIAMI

ERIE

Ohio

NANTICOKE

MOSOPELEA

MONACAN

POWHATAN

Northeast

Northeast and Great Lakes

As with most Native American groups, Northeastern tribal groups varied greatly. However, the region has a fairly unified cultural history, resulting in some important similarities across tribal groups.

Since 1000 BCE, the areas encompassing what are now the states east of the Mississippi River, north of the Mason-Dixon line, and bordered to the north by the Great Lakes and the east by the Atlantic Ocean have been occupied by relatively sedentary agricultural communities. Corn has been cultivated by the region's Native peoples from the Adena (1000 BCE–200 CE) and Hopewell (300–700 CE) periods of prehistory, to the arrival of Europeans to the area in the early 1500s. In fact, the United States owes much of its genesis to the interactions between the first European settlers and the Native peoples of the Northeast.

The mound-building Adena and Hopewell cultures contributed a regionally interactive collection of independent nation-states to the Native history of the area, culminating in the Mississippian influence, mostly limited to the southern portion of the area, in which hierarchical societies overseen by religious leaders dominated. From the north came more aggressive hunting cultures, which vied for control of the fertile and game-rich Mississippi and Ohio river valleys. This can be seen as a model for the Native history of the region: a tension between the tribal groups adhering to the more sedentary agricultural aspects of the southern influence and those that carried on the hunting traditions of their northern tribal cultures.

By the time European contact was made with the northeast region, Algonquin-speaking tribal groups were moving into the region and putting pressure on the more sedentary Iroquoian peoples, a situation that both the English and the French immigrants exploited for their own purposes. The Iroquoian tribes generally occupied the area that is now upstate New York and the lower Great Lakes, growing pumpkins, beans, squash, and corn in the extremely fertile soil. Algonquin speakers tended to settle near the coast in what is now New England, hunting and trapping inland and fishing at the coast. The arrival of Europeans increased the tendency for the Algonkin tribes to move west into Iroquoian regions, displacing those tribal

continues

Northeast and Great Lakes (continued)

groups and prompting the creation of what came to be known as the Iroquois Confederacy, a formal cohort of tribal groups in which each tribe had representation.

Religiously, the northern tribal groups tend to maintain an array of spiritual beings associated with the tasks of hunting cultures, with religious protocols, the proper behaviors dictated by the beings, dominating much of daily life. To the south, seasonal cycles associated with the agricultural needs of the people take precedence, owing to the need for continued fertility in the land. Both the Algonkin groups of the north and the Iroquoians to the south participate in annual or semiannual memorial ceremonies for important leaders who have died. These regular ceremonies serve to provide centripetal focus where the tendency is to favor difference and independence and to allow for the meeting of trade and potential marriage partners and the formation of other types of important allegiances.

The Native peoples who inhabited the region at the time of contact sustained perhaps the longest and most intense pressure to conform to the colonialist project, from the Plymouth colony and French fur trappers of the sixteenth century, to colonial law and French-English hostilities, to America's war for independence from England.

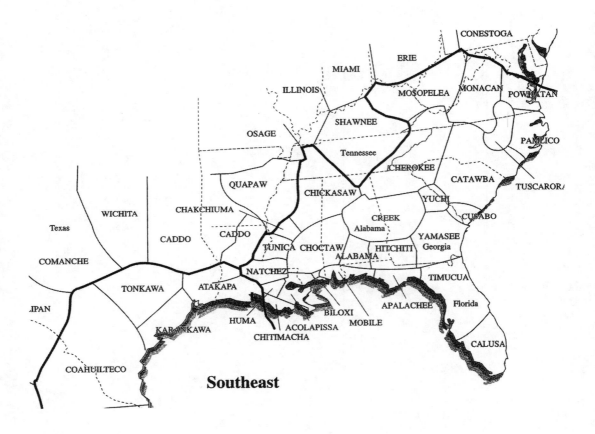

Southeast

The Southeast

The Southeast culture area is a region north of the Gulf of Mexico and south of the Middle Atlantic–Midwest region, extending from the Atlantic coast west to what is now central Texas. Semitropical in nature, the area is humid and wet. The terrain and vegetation of the Southeast culture area consists of a coastal plain along the Atlantic Ocean and Gulf of Mexico, with saltwater marshes, grasses, and large stands of cypress. Rich soil can be found in what are now Alabama and Mississippi, as well as along the Mississippi River floodplain. The region also includes the vast swamplands, hills, and the high grass of the Everglades in present-day Florida, as well as mountains of the southern Appalachian chain. At the time of early contacts between Native Americans and Europeans, much of the region was woodland, with southern pine near the coasts and more broadleaf trees further inland.

European incursion, initiated by the French from the Mississippi Valley, then the Spanish after the eighteenth century, found a region of the United States that was bordered by the Atlantic Ocean, the Gulf of Mexico, the Trinity River, and the Ohio River. The cultures of this region include the Catawba, Chickasaw, Choctaw, Creek, Cherokee, and Seminole Nations. Influenced by the earlier Mississippian cultures, characterized by monumental mound building and corn cultivation, later tribal groups tended toward sedentary village-based cultures, regional trade, diplomatic systems, and religious traditions that supported the agrarian lifestyle. Much of this lifeway is characterized by sacred activities oriented toward seasonal plant growth patterns.

One example of such sacred activity is the renewal festival, an annual ceremony oriented toward fertility of the soil in the coming year, recognition of the passing of the annual celestial cycle, and especially thanksgiving for the bounty of the previous year. Like many regional ceremonies throughout Native America, these festivals played important diplomatic roles because status issues were an important part of the process of planning and celebrating these festivals. The festivals provided opportunities for young people to meet potential mates outside their familial lineage group.

continues

The Southeast (continued)

In addition to agricultural production of corn, beans, and squash, pre-contact Southeastern tribal groups hunted game to augment the plant foods in their diet, and this practice also gave rise to certain rituals. Hunters all over Indian country are aware of the sacred nature of their endeavor, and this is certainly true among the peoples of the Southeastern United States. The propitiation of animal spirits and the need for respectful treatment of the physical beings associated with them require hunters to hunt in a respectful way; failure to do so runs the risk of going hungry.

Another aspect common throughout the region is the important role that games play in both the leisure and religious realms. Most notable among these is the ball game, in which a small leather ball is thrown, kicked, or advanced with playing sticks (depending on the tribal area) by two teams intending to score by advancing the ball past the opponent's goal, as in a combination of field hockey, soccer, and American football. This game has sacred as well as entertainment value.

Many traditions have similar regional manifestations, owing to the relatively unified early cultures extant before European inculcation, far too many for this brief introduction. Suffice it to say that, although the tribal cultures that call the Southeastern United States their place of origin differ greatly one from another, the tendency to maintain similar traits such as sedentary village life, clan and sacred society membership, and regular, important religious festivals remind the student of these cultures that the tribal differentiation which is now of great import in these communities developed out of a regionally aware collection of autonomous villages with much intervillage interaction and intellectual discourse prior to the arrival of Europeans.

The village served as the primary form of social organization among Indians of the Southeast prior to contact, and political organization also began at the village level. The people governed the affairs of a specific area, and village leaders, often led by a headman, met regularly to discuss matters of import to the entire community, such as the cultivation of fields owned by the community, or providing for defense of the village.

continues

The Southeast (continued)

Some Southeast tribes are organized into chiefdoms, defined as a society with an ultimate ruler with social rank often determined by birth. Some earlier Southeast chiefdoms encompassed many villages, and these tended to have powerful priesthoods, leading to stratification in those societies. The Natchez, Chickasaw, and the Creek Confederacy had well-developed hierarchies until the Euro-American political system undermined the authorities within them. Other Southeastern tribes such as the Cherokee and Choctaw, tended to be more democratic in their political organization and were less likely to be inundated with efforts by religio-political American authorities. Today, the village orientation continues in the region, albeit within the imposed Indian Reorganization Act (1934) system.

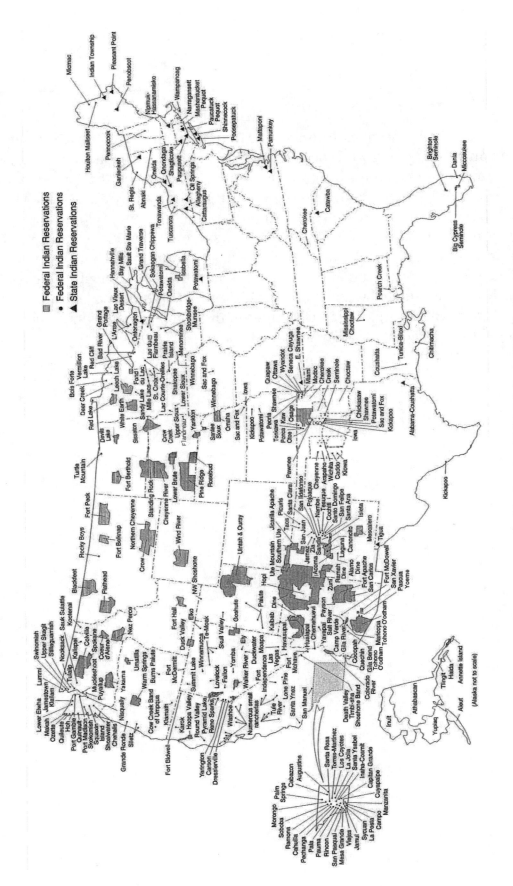

Reprinted from Duane Champagne, ed., Native America: Portrait of the Peoples. Visible Ink Press, 1994. Used by permission.

Red Power Movement

See American Indian Movement (Red Power Movement)

Religious Leaders, Alaska

With more than 200 Alaska Native nations and 20 major languages, cultural diversity and shortcomings in education often leave Alaska Natives uncertain about who qualifies as a spiritual leader. One element common to all customary definitions of Alaska Native spiritual leaders, however, is the notion of having a mission that goes beyond human endeavors. The men and women listed below represent only a fraction of those identified as spiritual through oral tradition, positions held, or election. They all conducted their lives and maintained religious traditions in a matrix of cultural theories, paradigms, ontologies, and epistemologies.

Ka-shishk (Tlingit)

One of the earliest Alaska Native spiritual leaders in recorded history is Ka-shishk, who is thought of as the greatest of the seven Tlingit men to inherit the title of Chief Shakes. He lived sometime in the sixteenth century, before Euro-Americans arrived in Alaska, as detailed by Tlingit oral tradition. The southern end of southeast Alaska has long been a trading, meeting, and war zone of the Tsimshian, Haida, and Tlingit nations. Several generations ago, at the end of a war in what is now British Columbia, the Nisq'a chief We-Shakes, in a move to avoid the humiliation of becoming a slave to the victorious Tlingit chief, removed his "killer whale" hat and placed it on his enemy's head—that of Tlingit chief Gushklin of the Stikine River near Wrangell. As he placed the killer whale hat on Nan-yan-yi Gushklin's head, the Nisq'a chief gave the Tlingit leader his own name, "We-Shakes." For unclear reasons, the title has since been shortened to "Shakes." The position maintains traditional Tlingit spiritual, military, and political dimensions.

This title has passed from Chief Shakes I to the present-day Chief Shakes

VI according to the customary laws of the Tlingit: through men of the maternal line. Chief Shakes I died in a smallpox epidemic soon after receiving the title. He was succeeded by his brother, Ka-shishk. Ka-shishk was renowned because of his benevolence and consideration for his people, thus living the paradigmatic life of Tlingit religious traditions as a "crystal person." He died after a long reign when he was killed by a falling tree on his return from a trading expedition on the Stikine River. Indicating his stature at the time of his death, many slaves were sacrificed at his funeral in order to serve him in the next world. (Excerpts from a pamphlet first printed in 1940 by the *Wrangell Sentinel* and written by E. L. Keithahn.)

While Ka-shishk and his successors met, or attempted to meet, expectations set on them as chiefs through ancient Tlingit notions of power, human morality, and the numinous, contemporary Tlingit spiritual leaders have had to face the challenges of postcolonial suppression of indigenous religious practices. Some of them, like Walter Soboleff, have combined formal Christian training with equally formal Tlingit customs in order to meet the spiritual needs of their followers. On the other hand, some spiritual leaders strive to meet the needs of justice beyond their own cultural boundaries. One such leader was Elizabeth Peratrovich. Still others, like Ethel Lund, have recognized the practical importance of Tlingit theories of spiritual power with respect to medicine, and

they use their roles as leaders to bring these important elements into the clinics and hospitals of southeastern Alaska.

Walter T'aaw Chán Soboleff (Tlingit)

Walter Soboleff was born on November 14, 1908, in Killisnoo, Alaska, to Anna Hunter Soboleff (Shaaxeidi Tláa), a Tlingit woman, and Alexander (Sasha) Soboleff, of Russian and German descent. Dr. Soboleff's common Tlingit name is T'aaw Chán, and his ceremonial name is Kaajaakwti. He is of the Aanx'aakhittaan house (People of the Center of the Village House) of the L'eineidi (Dog Salmon) clan in the Raven moiety. Perhaps inspired by his father, who was a Russian Orthodox priest, Dr. Soboleff pursued his interest in Christianity at the University of Dubuque in Iowa, where he received a bachelor of arts degree in 1937 and a bachelor of divinity degree in 1940. In that same year he was ordained as a Presbyterian minister, and he served at the Memorial Presbyterian Church in Juneau for twenty-seven years. In addition, he served as chaplain for the Alaska National Guard, achieving the rank of lieutenant colonel prior to his retirement. Dr. Soboleff received an honorary doctor of divinity degree from the University of Dubuque in 1952, and in 1968 he received an honorary doctor of humanities degree from the University of Alaska at Fairbanks. From 1970 to 1974 he headed the Alaska Native Studies Program in Fairbanks. At the age of ninety-five, Dr. Soboleff returned briefly to Fairbanks from his home in Juneau to be the 2003 commencement speaker at the graduation ceremony of the University of Alaska at Fairbanks.

Dr. Soboleff married Genevieve Ross, a Haida woman. Genevieve, born December 17, 1914, died on January 27, 1986. She and her husband had four children: Janet Soboleff Burke, Sasha, Walter Jr., and Ross. Dr. Soboleff married Stella Atkinson, Tsimshian, in 1997. For more information, consult Dauenhauer and Dauenhauer (1994).

Elizabeth Jean Wanamaker Peratrovich (Tlingit)

Although most would not consider Elizabeth Jean Wanamaker Peratrovich (1911–1958), whose Tlingit name was Kaaxgal.aat, a spiritual leader, her impact on Alaska has a strong spiritual component for all Alaskans. She was born and reared in Petersburg, in southeast Alaska, having been born to the Lukaax.adi clan in the Raven moiety and adopted in early childhood by Andrew Wanamaker of the Kaagwaantaan clan (Eagle moiety). She married Roy Peratrovich in 1931 in Washington state, and in 1941 they moved to Juneau, where they discovered that racial discrimination in Alaska prevented them from buying or renting certain homes and that "No Native" signs were often displayed in store fronts. Both Elizabeth and her husband initiated efforts toward an Anti-Discrimination Act in the Alaska Territorial Legislature in 1943, although Elizabeth is credited with the testimony that moved

legislators to pass the Anti-Discrimination Act on February 16, 1945, a day that has since been named Elizabeth Peratrovich Day by former Alaska state governor Tony Knowles. Although her life was relatively short (she died in 1958 of cancer), memory of her lives on in annual ceremonies, plays, stories, and other media events.

Ethel Aanwoogeex' Shtoo.aak Lund (Tlingit)

Another Tlingit leader whom many might not view as spiritual is Ethel Aanwoogeex' Shtoo.aak Lund. Lund was born in Wrangell, Alaska, to Carl Lund of Sweden and Maartha Ukas Lund of Wrangell. She is of the Tlingit nation, Raven moiety, Frog clan. Granddaughter of Thomas Ukas, a totem carver and Tlingit historian, Dr. Lund has three children: David, Diane, and Leah. Dr. Lund suffered with severe illness as a child, and she was not expected to survive to adulthood. But survive she did, and with determination to enter the health field. She attended the Good Samaritan School of Nursing in Portland, Oregon. Throughout her lifetime she has combined Tlingit cultural methods of healing with Western medicine. One of the founders and president of the Southeast Alaska Regional Health Consortium (SEARHC), she has overseen its regional operations, which include the Mt. Edgecumbe Hospital in Sitka, the outpatient medical facilities in Juneau, in Haines, and on Prince of Wales Island, and the village-based health programs in outlying communities. To retain Tlingit cultural doctrines of medicine, she established an elder's council as a management advisory group.

Dr. Lund served as chair of the Alaska Native Health Board from 1978 to 1981, and she developed a landmark Memorandum of Agreement with the Indian Health Service in 1978. She served as chair of the Alaska Tribal Health Directors and vice chair of the National Indian Health Board. In addition, she served on President Carter's Mental Health Commission. Dr. Lund served as grand president of the Alaska Native Sisterhood (ANS) Grand Camp, as well as local president of the ANS Camps 1 and 70. In 1984 she was selected Woman of the Year by the Business and Professional Women, Juneau Chapter, making her the first Alaska Native woman to receive that honor. In 2001 the University of Alaska, Anchorage, offered Dr. Lund an honorary doctor of laws degree. Dr. Lund has a life of service in the field of health care to Alaska Native people, and a commitment to retaining cultural input in present-day programs.

Maniilauraq, or Maniilaq (Inupiaq)

There have been many other Alaska Native spiritual leaders in other regions of Alaska, each following paths that meet the needs of both their times and their cultural traditions. One of the best known of Alaska's spiritual leaders is Maniilauraq, or Maniilaq as he was more commonly called, an Inupiaq man of the early 1800s. He came from the Upper Kobuk region of northwestern Alaska off Kotzebue Sound near a place called Qala. Born to an Inupiaq woman named Qupilguuraq and a father whose name has been lost, Maniilaq was the oldest of three children. He was celebrated as a great prophet, and the Maniilaq Association (a nonprofit agency sponsored by the Northwest Arctic Native Association [NANA]) is named for him. His many prophecies included the passing or change in the powers of the *agnatkut_* (the Inupiaq word for medicine people), as well as travel on water without the use of paddles and in boats through the air.

Maniilaq and his wife had two sons, Uqquutaq and Itluun, as well as a daughter, Piqpukpak. According to oral tradition, Maniilaq traveled throughout the Kotzebue Sound area telling people of his prophecies. Before the arrival of Euro-Americans in this region (1850s), he disappeared without a trace (Terry and Anderson 2001). Legends about his life and prophecies are still an important part of Inupiat education.

Dr. Della Puyuk Keats (Inupiat)

A half-century later, in 1906, the late Dr. Della (Puyuk) Keats was born near Maniilaq's homeland on the Noatak River, north of the Kotzebue Sound. Keats served the people of Alaska for more than sixty years as a bridge between modern medical techniques and traditional practices. Her hands were her primary diagnostic tool. By touching the area of pain on a patient, Dr. Keats could help by locating the trouble, describing it, performing a curative maneuver or prescribing herbal remedies, or by using massage or exercise. Her hands "were so strong they could move the powerful muscles of a man who worked all his life. They were delicate enough to feel the walls of an organ inside a person's body. They were so exacting they could move an umbilical cord wrapped around the neck of a baby inside a mother's womb" (Mauer 1986, B-1).

In the 1970s, Della Keats spent many hours recording stories by Inupiat elders along the Kobuk River in northern Alaska, as well as in the Senior Center in Kotzebue, where she was a board member. When she was in her seventies, she worked for Maniilaq Association (the nonprofit organization in Kotzebue named for the nineteenth-century Inupiaq prophet) as a healer and teacher. Her teachings led to the development of the Della Keats Summer Enrichment Program at the University of Alaska, Anchorage, a scholarly course designed to help Native students study for health-related professions. Della Keats received an honorary doctorate of humane letters in health sciences from the University of Alaska, Anchorage, in 1983. She died in March 1986 in Kotzebue.

Albert Edward Tritt (Chandalar Gwich'in Athabascan)

To the east and south of the Inupiat of northern Alaska are northern Athabascans, of which there are eleven language areas, and at least as many traditional nations. Near the Canada/Alaska border,

a well-known Chandalar Gwich'in Athabascan medicine man known as Albert Edward Tritt was born around 1880 near Smoke Mountain, in a place close to Vashraii K'oo, or Arctic Village. He was born about twenty years after the Canadian Anglican missionary Robert McDonald began translating the Bible into Takudh, an eastern Gwich'in dialect. McDonald finished his translation in 1898, when Tritt was very young. By carefully comparing the Takudh Bible with the King James version, Albert Tritt taught himself to speak English in what Robert McKennan (1965, 86) described as a "truly biblical manner"; he referring to women as "damsels" and "virgins" when McKennan visited him in 1962 (ibid.).

At some time in the early 1900s, Tritt converted to Christianity, and he brought copies of McDonald's Bible and hymnals from Gwichyaa Zhee (Fort Yukon) to Vashraii K'oo in order to teach Gwich'in children to read and write. One of his greatest projects was to ensure that the people of Vashraii K'oo had enough food; at that time they were enduring terrible epidemics, loss of viable hunters, and long periods of starvation. Tritt's project, which took several years, ended in 1914 with the construction of a long caribou fence at the base of one of the nearby mountains. The fence, built according to traditional Gwich'in standards, was used to snare caribou of specific sizes on their migration routes through the mountain passes. Traces of the fence are still in place. Besides the caribou fence, Tritt also had villagers construct a small chapel in Vashraii K'oo. The chapel was finished in 1922. Since trees of sufficient size are not abundant in the area, logs had to be hauled from as far away as twenty miles from the village. His last proposal, to cut a wide, straight road to Gwichyaa Zhee, met with too much opposition in the community; it was never completed.

Despite Albert Tritt's conversion to Christianity, many of his activities as a leader in northeastern Alaska followed traditional Athabascan religious traditions, insofar as he believed that his missions were directed by sacred forces. However, although he had many followers, other spiritual leaders in the community eventually withdrew their support of his visions and mandates. Tritt's legacy is carefully guarded by his descendants. He compiled an early Gwich'in lexicon, and he wrote the story of his life in several ledgers that are accessible for study only by the Venetie Tribal Government (IRA).

While Tritt's knowledge of Christianity was primarily self-taught and informed by prophecies and visions, other Gwich'in leaders of that era were educated, and often raised, by an Episcopalian missionary—Hudson Stuck. One such was John Fredson (1895–1945), whom Stuck hoped would become a future Native leader and missionary. Fredson, who came from a community a little to the south of Tritt's birthplace, became successful in creating public facilities, such as schools, a medical clinic, mail service, and finally a reservation. Hearing of new federal legislation to create reserve lands for Indians, Fredson recognized the potential and solicited support from Gwichyaa Zheh, Viihtaii, Vashraii K'oo, and Zheh Gwatsal. As a consequence of his efforts, the 1.8-million-acre Venetie Reserve was officially created in 1943 (MacKenzie 1985, 170). John Fredson died of pneumonia two years later in 1945, at the age of fifty. He is venerated in his community through oral tradition, schools, and other public facilities that bear his name, and in the ethnographies of Cornelius Osgood.

Chief Andrew Isaac (Tanacross Athabascan)

Chief Andrew Isaac was born in 1898 in Ketchumstock, Alaska, near the Canada/Alaska border, 70 miles south of the Yukon River and south of the Gwich'in nation. He lived there with his family until 1917, when an epidemic claimed the lives of many people in his family and community. The survivors moved to Mansfield Lake, now thought of as the spiritual home of the Tanacross Athabascan people, for whom Chief Andrew Isaac is a beloved ancestor. In 1942 the entire community moved to Tanana Crossing, now called Tanacross. Isaac learned English and worked for the U.S. military during the 1940s as a construction worker; later he worked in coal mines near Eagle and Chicken Creek and in gold mines at Fortymile.

In the years following World War II Andrew Isaac became a leader of the Tanacross Athabascans and traveled often to Washington, D.C., where he advocated for personal development and education. He became the chief of the United Crow Band (one of the six matrilineages of the Tanacross people), holding that position for fifty-nine years. In 1972 he was named a traditional chief of the interior Athabascans, a role that he maintained until his death in 1991 at the age of ninety-two. The Alaska Native medical clinic in Fairbanks is named for him. In 1979 he received an honorary doctorate in humanities from the University of Alaska, Fairbanks, and in 1990 he was named Citizen of the Year by the Alaska Federation of Natives.

Howard Luke (Tanana Athabascan)

Fairbanks, one of the three large population areas of Alaska, is home to the Tanana Athabascans, and now it is home to Howard Luke. Luke is one of the most influential spiritual leaders in interior Alaska. The Howard Luke Academy, an alternative public high school, is named after him. Born in Linder Lake, a Tanana Athabascan community near Fairbanks, Alaska, Howard was raised in a traditional subsistence way of life. Although he was unable to finish a Western education at St. Marks boarding school in Nenana, his mother taught him to read and write at home while she and other relatives taught him the Tanana Athabascan cultural ways.

Dr. Luke developed the Bear Child Gaalee'ya Camp on grounds of the original Old Chena Village, just outside the Fairbanks city limits. People from throughout Alaska, and some from other cultures and nations, go there to learn Athabascan ways as well as to refresh themselves spiritually. He is particularly attentive to the needs of children and has achieved remarkable results with alcoholic and drug-addicted children, as well as with the children of addicts. In acknowledgment of his work, he received the Alaska Social Worker of the Year Award in 1993, and an honorary doctorate of humane letters from the University of Alaska, Fairbanks, in 1996. In addition to his work at Gaalee'ya Camp, Dr. Luke volunteers in classrooms at all levels of education, teaching the Tanana Athabascan language and culture. His snowshoes, sleds, fish wheels, and other traditional tools form an important part of his lectures and discussions.

Less is known about southwestern precolonial Aleut spiritual leaders than those from anywhere else in Alaska, since Russian Orthodoxy has become the religion of choice throughout that extensive coastal and islandic region. Two linguistic regions compose the Aleut region, and within them are several smaller nations. The two languages are Unangan and Alutiiq (also known as Sugstun). The nations include the Unangan of the Aleutian Chain, the Unangan of the Pribiloff Islands, the Alutiiq of Kodiak Island, the Alutiiq of Prince William Sound, and the Alutiiq of Cook Inlet. Despite the devastating effects of history, Unangan religious traditions are known and taught to young people. These include respect for elders, recitation of

Northeast

As with most Native American groups, Northeastern tribal groups varied greatly. However, the region has a fairly unified cultural history, resulting in some important similarities across tribal groups.

Since 1000 BCE, the areas encompassing what are now the states east of the Mississippi River, north of the Mason-Dixon line, and bordered to the north by the Great Lakes and the east by the Atlantic Ocean have been occupied by relatively sedentary agricultural communities. Corn has been cultivated by the region's Native peoples from the Adena (1000 BCE–200 CE) and Hopewell (300–700 CE) periods of prehistory, to the arrival of Europeans to the area in the early 1500s. In fact, the United States owes much of its genesis to the interactions between the first European settlers and the Native peoples of the Northeast.

The mound-building Adena and Hopewell cultures contributed a regionally interactive collection of independent nation-states to the Native history of the area, culminating in the Mississippian influence, mostly limited to the southern portion of the area, in which hierarchical societies overseen by religious leaders dominated. From the north came more aggressive hunting cultures, which vied for control of the fertile and game-rich Mississippi and Ohio river valleys. This can be seen as a model for the Native history of the region: a tension between the tribal groups adhering to the more sedentary agricultural aspects of the southern influence and those that carried on the hunting traditions of their northern tribal cultures.

By the time European contact was made with the northeast region, Algonquin-speaking tribal groups were moving into the region and putting pressure on the more sedentary Iroquoian peoples, a situation that both the English and the French immigrants exploited for their own purposes. The Iroquoian tribes generally occupied the area that is now upstate New York and the lower Great Lakes, growing pumpkins, beans, squash, and corn in the extremely fertile soil. Algonquin speakers tended to settle near the coast in what is now New England, hunting and trapping inland and fishing at the coast. The arrival of Europeans increased the tendency for the Algonkin tribes to move west into Iroquoian regions, displacing those tribal

continues

Northeast (continued)

groups and prompting the creation of what came to be known as the Iroquois Confederacy, a formal cohort of tribal groups in which each tribe had representation.

Religiously, the northern tribal groups tend to maintain an array of spiritual beings associated with the tasks of hunting cultures, with religious protocols, the proper behaviors dictated by the beings, dominating much of daily life. To the south, seasonal cycles associated with the agricultural needs of the people take precedence, owing to the need for continued fertility in the land. Both the Algonkin groups of the north and the Iroquoians to the south participate in annual or semiannual memorial ceremonies for important leaders who have died. These regular ceremonies serve to provide centripetal focus where the tendency is to favor difference and independence and to allow for the meeting of trade and potential marriage partners and the formation of other types of important allegiances.

The Native peoples who inhabited the region at the time of contact sustained perhaps the longest and most intense pressure to conform to the colonialist project, from the Plymouth colony and French fur trappers of the sixteenth century, to colonial law and French-English hostilities, to America's war for independence from England.

usually shamanic oral traditions, and medicinal knowledge.

Anfesia Shapsnikoff (Aleut)

Among the Aleuts' many respected spiritual leaders is Anfesia Shapsnikoff (1900–1973), who was born at Atka. Her father, Avakum Lazarov, was from Atka, while her mother, Mary Prokopeuff, was from the island of Attu near the western end of the Aleutian Chain. When Anfesia was six her mother took her and her brother John to Unalaska, a large island near the mainland. Anfesia's mother died in 1919 during the flu epidemic, following her father's death in 1914. In that year Anfesia married the Russian Orthodox deacon Michael Tutliakoff, who died in 1934 during the wreck of the *Unmak Native*. A few years later she married Sergie Shapsnikoff. Anfesia learned to read and write English, Unangan, and Russian, highly prized skills in Unalaska as well as throughout the Aleut region. She was ordained a reader of the Orthodox Church and often conducted services when the priest was absent. Throughout her lifetime she taught and promoted Unangan culture, and she was called on to lecture in California, Arizona, Oregon, and the Yukon Territory of Canada. Her pattern for a child's rainproof *kamleika* (hooded jacket) made of young sea lion or seal intestine is included in *Unugulux Tunusangin* (Hudson 1992).

Peter Kalifornsky (Dena'ina Athabascan)

Like so many other Alaska Natives from Alaska's southern coastal area, Athabascan leader Peter Kalifornsky (1911–1993) would not have considered himself a spiritual leader, but he is included here because of his extensive knowledge about Dena'ina Athabascan philosophy and culture. He was born on October 12, 1911, at Kalifornsky Village on the Cook Inlet bluff on the Kenai Peninsula, in south-central Alaska, at a place he called Unhghenesditnu ("farthest creek over"). His mother, Agrafena Chickalusion Kalifornsky, died when he was two years old, and he was raised by his father, Nick, his aunts, and an uncle. Kalifornsky spent most of his life in Kenai, working at various construction- and fishing-related jobs, as well as subsistence hunting, trapping, and fishing. Although he attending public school only through fifth grade, he worked closely for almost twenty years with linguists Kari and Boraas to record and study his language and the oral traditions of his ancestors. In addition to his work on Dena'ina cultural traditions, Peter Kalifornsky was an accomplished poet in both English and Dena'ina. He was an inspiration to many generations of Athabascan people. For more information, see *K'tl'egh'i Sukdu, A Dena'ina Legacy: The Collected Writings of Peter Kalifornsky* (Kalifornsky 1991).

The Alaska Native spiritual leaders named in these pages are but a few of the hundreds of people who have informed the lives and history in every Alaskan community. Some, such as the nineteenth-century Inupiaq *agnatkut_* Maniilaq, never saw Euro-Americans but told of the cataclysmic changes that would occur because of their imminent arrival in northwestern Alaska. Another, Ethel Lund of southeastern Alaska, became a spiritual leader by virtue of her survival from a terrible illness in childhood and her frequent testimony to her belief in the extraordinary powers of traditional Tlingit medicine in combination with Western knowledge. Still others, such as Paul John, traditional chief of Tooksook Bay in southwestern Alaska, and Peter Kalifornsky of south-central Alaska, have devoted much of their lives to explaining the spiritual roots of their cultural practices. In so doing, they have become leaders in spirit, political action, public and traditional education, as well as language.

Phyllis Ann Fast

See also Ceremony and Ritual, Yup'iq; Missionization, Alaska; Oral Traditions, Haida; Oral Traditions, Northern Athabascan; Oral Traditions, Tlingit; Oral Traditions, Yupiaq; Potlatch; Potlatch, Northern Athabascan

References and Further Reading
Dauenhauer, Nora Marks, and Richard Dauenhauer. 1994. *Haa Kusteeyi, Our Culture: Tlingit Life Stories.* Seattle and London: University of Washington Press; Juneau, AK: Sealaska Heritage Foundation.

Fast, Phyllis Ann. 2002. *Northern Athabascan Survival: Women, Community and the Future.* Lincoln: University of Nebraska Press.

Hudson, Ray. 1992. *Unugulux Tunusangin: Oldtime Stories: Aleut Crafts and Traditions as Taught to Students at the Unalaska City School by Augusta Dushkin, Sophia Pletnikoff, Anfesia Shapsnikoff, Agnes Sovoroff, Sergie Sovoroff, Annie Tcheripanoff, and Bill Tcheripanoff.* Unalaska, AK: Unalaska City School District.

Kalifornsky, Peter. 1991. *K'tl'egh'i Sukdu, A Dena'ina Legacy: The Collected Writings of Peter Kalifornsky.* Edited by James Kari and Alan Boraas. Fairbanks: Alaska Native Language Center.

Mauer, Richard. 1986. "Death Stills Healing Hands. Tribal Doctor's Skill Known Statewide." *Anchorage Daily News,* March 13, 1986, p. B-1.

McClanahan, A. J. 1986. *Our Stories, Our Lives: A Collection of Twenty-Three Transcribed Interviews with Elders of the Cook Inlet Region.* Anchorage, AK: CIRI Foundation.

McKennan, Robert. 1965. "The Chandalar Kutchin." Technical paper 17. Toronto: Arctic Institute of North America.

Osgood, Cornelius. 1936. *Contributions to the Ethnography of the Kutchin.* New Haven: Yale University Press.

Terry, Steven B., and Jill K. Anderson. 2001. *Maniilaq: Prophet from the Edge of Nowhere.* Seattle, WA: Onjinjinkta Publishing.

Religious Leaders, Basin

See Winnemucca, Sarah

Religious Leaders, California

What constitutes "religion," and likewise, what constitutes a "religious leader," is an important question when discussing American Indian spiritual and cultural leaders. The individuals mentioned in this essay might not all be what many anthropologists would call shamans. Many of these people are doctors, writers, educators, political activists, basket weavers, mothers, and fathers. What they share is a common commitment to preserving the traditional lifeways and spiritual practices of their people. Spirituality takes many forms: prayers offered when collecting plants for weaving a basket, healing a sick child, or leading people into war. These individuals are important leaders because they have worked to maintain a continuity with traditional California Indian culture, and they carry those traditions into the present. What follows are a few brief biographies of some important cultural and spiritual leaders in Native California. This collection is by no means inclusive. Many, many more individuals should have been included. This is but a small selection of some of the central figures.

Elsie Allen (Pomo)

Born in 1899, Elsie Allen was a renowned Pomo basket weaver and cultural expert. She was active in the Pomo Women's Club, which worked to provide financial and social support for individuals and families within the Pomo community. She took up basket weaving at the age of sixty-two, having been trained by her mother. Her book *Pomo Basketry: A Supreme Art for the Weaver* was published in 1972. She was a primary consultant for the Warm Springs Cultural Resources Study, and she received an honorary doctorate of divinity for her work as a tribal scholar and basket maker. She was the first to teach the art of Pomo basket making to people outside the Pomo community, breaking with an older practice but ensuring that the art of this tradition would be known and respected throughout the country and the world.

Curly Headed Doctor (Modoc)

Born in 1890 on the Modoc Reservation, Curly Headed Doctor was a powerful spiritual leader among his community who played an instrumental role in the Modoc War of 1873. Curly Headed Doctor was believed to have the ability to protect his followers from death and injury, and to draw a line that the enemy could not cross. Through his instigation the Modoc pursued a course of war against the U.S. Army that ultimately failed.

During the 1860s the U.S. government was aggressively seeking the separation of Native people from their traditional homelands and their consolidation on reservations. The United States sought to place the Modoc on the Klamath Reservation along the California-Oregon border. The Modoc people at first refused to be separated from their ancestral homelands and the spiritual and cultural traditions that they contained. When they were later relocated, the Modoc found themselves as unwanted guests among the Klamath, who were themselves struggling to survive on a reduced land-

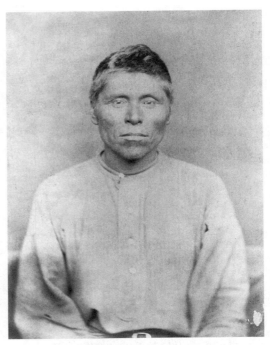

Curly Headed Doctor (Modoc) was a powerful spiritual leader whose followers believed he had the ability to protect them from death and injury. 1873. (Louis Heller/Library of Congress)

base with limited resources. Discouraged by reservation life, Captain Jack, a Modoc tribal leader, left the reservation and returned to Lost River near Tule Lake in the Modoc's ancestral homelands. Delegations from the U.S. Army, led by Superintendent Meacham, sought to convince them to leave. While Superintendent Meacham was speaking with Captain Jack, Curley Headed Doctor stood and announced that the Modoc would not go back to the reservation. At that sentiment shifted, and Captain Jack and the rest of the community likewise refused to leave Lost River. Captain Jack preferred to resist nonviolently, but Curley Headed Doctor advocated violent resistance and encouraged the Modoc to kill the army delegation.

Meacham and his party called for reinforcements, and the Modoc fled to the lava beds on the south shore of Tule Lake, where they established a stronghold. The army was unable to dislodge them. General R. S. Canby sought to establish peace, and he met with Captain Jack. At Curley Headed Doctor's instigation, Captain Jack killed Canby. The army responded by sending in fifteen hundred additional troops. Curley Headed Doctor told his followers that the army would be unable to cross a tule rope that he painted red and laid around the stronghold. He promised as well that none would be injured by gunfire. He then led the community in a night-long circle dance around a central medicine pole and medicine flag, in preparation for battle. On April 15, Curley Headed Doctor's power was discredited when the army crossed the threshold of the compound and a Modoc man was killed by a cannonball. Curley Headed Doctor surrendered on May 23, 1873, and soon after led the army to Captain Jack's hideout. He was exiled to Indian Territory in present-day Oklahoma, where he lived until his death in 1890.

Delfina Cuero (Diegueño Kumeyaaye)

Born around 1900 in the San Diego area in the Diegueno Kumeyaaye nation, Cuero was one of the few to survive the forced removal of her people. Having lived on the land for thousands of years,

her family's rights to ownership were denied with the arrival of the Spanish missions and later the Euro-American settlers. They were frequently forced to move as more and more settlers entered the area. Cuero moved with her family to Baja California, where she lived a difficult life. With the assistance of Florence Shipek, Cuero wrote her biography, preserving knowledge of the traditions and natural surroundings of her Kumeyaaye people. She also narrated the difficulties faced by Native women and children in a changing world characterized by poverty, inequality, wage labor, and abusive homes. She was able to establish her right to U.S. citizenship through the publication of her book, and she returned to live in the San Diego area. She died in 1972.

Doctor Charley (Modoc)

Born around 1880, Doctor Charley played an important role as a Modoc spiritual leader and healer, empowered by spirit powers of dog and frog. Through his spiritual abilities he was able to discern an illness affecting many Modoc infants. Children's hearts, he explained, were linked to an object in the supernatural realm. This caused their hearts to become irritated. A nightmare of either parent prior to the infant's birth could cause this ailment. Doctor Charley was able to cure the infant by means of a ceremony involving the infant's entire family, who grasped a cord representing that which bound the infant to the spiritual realm. During an era of rapid change characterized by reservations, disease and malnourishment, and the loss of traditional cultural practices, Doctor Charley's mode of curing met an important need. It enabled parents and families to come together to create healthy infants. Many California Indians during this time suffered from the spiritual and cultural trauma of changing ways of life. Doctor Charley's cure was a means of strengthening the bonds between families and communities during this difficult time.

Doctor George (Modoc)

Born in the mid-nineteenth century, Doctor George was an important spiritual leader and healer among his Modoc people. He was initiated as a healer during a traditional five-night ceremony attended by hundreds of people. Doctor George was widely known for his abilities to cure and also to change the weather. A local white cattle rancher asked him to pray for rain, and Doctor George was successful. The cattleman paid him for his services with money and food. He was a leader of the Dream Dance, a local variation of the 1870s Ghost Dance brought to the area from the Paiute. His wife, Sally George, who also served as a singer, as well as his son, Usee George, assisted him in all his ceremonial activities. (For more on the Dream Dance, see "Ghost Dance Movement," and "Dreamers and Prophets.")

Domenico (Luiseño)

Born in the mid-nineteenth century on the Rincon Reservation, Domenico was a powerful Luiseño spiritual leader and healer. He trained with his father, who was also a powerful healer, and began to receive power visions early in his life. Domenico was known to have the ability to hear conversations taking place miles away, to control the weather, and to be an effective and powerful healer. When healing his patients he would take on their symptoms, sharing in their suffering. He was able to communicate with powerful curing and disease-causing spirits and to effect cures through that communication. People of all ethnic and racial backgrounds sought out his assistance in curing physical, emotional, mental, and spiritual illnesses. He maintained an amiable relationship with Euro-American physicians and referred his patients to local doctors whom he trusted. He saw traditional and Western medicine as working cooperatively, and he had great success with his patients. He did not charge for his curing services, though appreciative patients often offered him gifts. He died in 1963.

Florence Jones, Pui-lu-li-met (Wintu)

Born in 1909 within the Wintu community, Florence Jones is widely known for her work as a doctor proficient in the Wintu tradition. In her early childhood Jones encountered powerful spirit powers, and at seventeen she entered her first trance. During such trances the spirit powers of animals, deceased relatives, and the powers inherent in sacred places would come and speak with her, teaching her songs and rituals for curing.

She was able to diagnose illness as these spirit powers worked through her hands, as well as locate lost objects. She was also a skilled herbalist. She trained several other Wintu in the traditional healing practices of her people. Florence Jones held public ceremonials at Mount Shasta for many years before retiring in 1995.

Ruby Modesto, Nesha (Desert Cahuilla)

Born in 1913 to her Desert Cahuilla father and Serrano mother, Modesto grew up speaking the Cahuilla language and learning the traditions of her father's people. She received her spirit helper, the eagle (Ahswit), when she was ten years old. As a young child she entered into a deep trance-sleep that lasted several days. It required the work of a traditional Cahuilla healer to bring her out of her sleep. She chose to devote her life to *pul*, the traditional spiritual practice of her Cahuilla people. As a healer she was widely known for her ability to cure people made ill by demonic influences. She was a teacher of her Native language and guest lecturer at colleges and universities. She also wrote a book, *Not for Innocent Ears: Spiritual Traditions of a Desert Cahuilla Medicine Woman.* Modesto lived on the Martinez Reservation until her death in 1980.

Julia Parker (Pomo)

Born in 1919, Julia Parker is widely known for her work as a Pomo basket weaver and cultural expert. She reared four children and helped to rear two granddaughters and seven grandsons. She worked as cultural demonstrator for Yosemite National Park, educating the public as well as future generations of Pomo children in the art of California Indian basketry. She studied with many well-known California Indian basket makers, including Carrie Bethel and Minnie Mike (Mono Lake Paiute and Southern Sierra Miwok); Mabel McKay (Cache Creek Pomo); Molly Jackson (Yokavo Pomo); Ida Bishop (Mono Lake Paiute); and Elsie Allen (Cloverdale Pomo). She has been instrumental in the preservation of Yosemite Miwok and Paiute traditions. Julia Parker has taught demonstration classes at national parks, museums, colleges, and the Smithsonian in Washington, D.C.

Somersal, Laura (Wappo/Pomo)

Born in 1892, Laura Somersal (Wappo and Dry Creek Pomo) grew to become a valued cultural expert, hand game player, and internationally known basket weaver and teacher among the Native communities of Sonoma County. Somersal was a linguistic expert, fluent in Wappo (her first language) and several other Indian dialects, as well as English, Russian, and Spanish. She began her training as a basket maker when she was only eight or nine years old, studying with her paternal uncle Jack Woho and later with her sister-in-law. During her lifetime she lectured on Pomo and Wappo cultural traditions and basketry techniques at colleges and universities throughout California. Her work as a cultural and linguistic expert made possible the preservation of the Wappo language, and she coauthored a Wappo-English dictionary. When the Army Corps of Engineers proposed to flood an area where Wappo people traditionally gathered basketry materials (present-day Lake Sonoma), Somersal led efforts to transplant those native plants to safer locations. Along with her brother George and her mother, Mary Eli, Somersal collaborated with Harold Driver to write *Wappo Ethnography* (Driver 1936).

Lucy Parker Telles (Miwok/Mono Lake Paiute)

Born around 1870, Lucy Park Telles would become a well-known expert in the art of California Indian basketry. By the time she was in her forties she had earned the reputation as the finest weaver in the Yosemite region. She introduced new designs, which other weavers soon began following. She worked for many years as cultural demonstrator and weaver for the Yosemite Valley National Park Service. She produced hundreds of baskets during her lifetime and was instrumental in passing on this important aspect of traditional California Indian cultural life.

Toypurina, Regina Josefa Toypurina (Gabrieliño)

Born around 1760 in the area of present-day Long Beach, California, Toypurina was an important spiritual and political leader for her Gabrieliño people. The daughter of a Gabrieliño chief, she was widely known and feared among her people as a powerful spiritual leader and ceremonial practitioner. Toypurina was believed to have the power to kill as well as to cure, and she was considered a powerful threat to the invading Spaniards. She was able to divine the future, protect her people through the use of a sacred bundle, as well as exert control over the weather. Through the use of datura, or jimsonweed, Toypurina was able to enter the supernatural realm, communing with spirits and gaining supernatural power. On October 25, 1785, when she was only twenty-five, she helped to lead a rebellion against San Gabriel Mission. As a spiritual authority acknowledged by her own tribe as well as other local tribes, she was sought out by tribal leaders and warriors for her protection and empowerment in their attack on the mission. By means of her spiritual power, Toypurina was to kill the soldiers and padres, returning local control to the Native people. She entered the mission compound along with a group of warriors, but news of the rebellion had already reached the mission fathers. The group was intercepted and arrested, and fifteen people were taken into custody, including two indigenous chiefs and Nicolas Jo'se, a newly converted neophyte. At her trial, Toypurina severely castigated the Spanish fathers, denouncing them for trespassing on land owned by and sacred to indigenous people. Jo'se likewise spoke out against the Spanish, their prohibitions against the practice of Gabrieliño religious traditions, and their coerced conversions of Native people. When called before the territorial governor, Pedro Fages, Toypurina reportedly kicked over a stool that had been offered her and proudly acknowledged her part in the rebellion and her anger at the invasive presence of the Spanish. Toypurina was held in custody at the mission until two years later, when she converted to Christianity and was baptized. Shortly thereafter she was pardoned and deported to San Carlos Mission in northern California, where she lived until her death on May 22, 1799, at the San Juan Bautista Mission. Jo'se was imprisoned along with two other rebellion leaders at the San Diego presidio.

Tsupu (Miwok)

Born in 1815 near Petaluma California, Tsupu was fluent in the language and cultural traditions of her Miwok people. She passed on her cultural and linguistic knowledge to her sons Tom and Bill Smith and their families. Thomas Comtechal (Tom Smith) would become an important Coast Miwok spiritual practitioner and healer. Because of her knowledge and successful transmission of that knowledge to her children and descendants, traditional Miwok cultural traditions survive to this day. Her granddaughter Sarah Smith Ballard was the last fluent speaker of Bodega Miwok, and she taught much of her knowledge to her grandson David Peri, Coast Miwok tribal scholar and anthropology professor at Sonoma State University. More than one thousand Native people can trace their ancestry to Tsupu, including David Peri; Bill Smith (former professor and director of American Indian Studies at Sonoma State University); Kathleen Smith (tribal scholar and artist); and Greg Sarris (professor of English, UCLA).

Suzanne J. Crawford

See also Basketry; Ceremony and Ritual, California; Datura; Dreamers and Prophets; Dreams and Visions; Ghost Dance Movement; Health and Wellness, Traditional Approaches; McKay, Mabel; Menstruation and Menarche; Missionization, California; Parrish, Essie; Power, Barbareño Chumash; Reservations, Spiritual and Cultural Implications; Spiritual and Ceremonial Practitioners, California; Termination and Relocation; Vision Quest Rites

References and Further Reading
Allen, Elise. 1972. *Pomo Basketmaking: A Supreme Art for the Weaver.* Naturegraph Publishing.
Bataille, Gretchen, and Laurie Lisa, eds. 2001. *Native American Women: A Biographical Dictionary.* New York: Routledge.
Cuero, Delfina. 1970. *Autobiography of Delfina Cuero: A Diegueno Woman.* Banning, CA: Malki Museum Press.
———. 1991. *Delfina Cuero: Her Autobiography: An Account of Her Last Years and Her Ethnobotanic Contributions.* Menlo Park, CA: Ballena Press.
Dillon, Richard H. 1973. *Burnt-out Fires: California's Modoc Indian War.* Englewood Cliffs, NJ: Prentice Hall.
Driver, Harold E. 1936. *Wappo Ethnography.* Berkeley: University of California Press.
Heizer, Robert F. 1978. *Handbook of North American Indians.* Vol. 8. Washington DC: Smithsonian Institution.
Johnson, Troy. 2002. *Distinguished Native American Spiritual Practitioners and Healers.* Westport, CT: Oryx Press.
Modesto, Ruby. 1989. *Not for Innocent Ears: Spiritual Traditions of a Desert Cahuilla*

Medicine Woman. Rev. ed. Cottonwood: CA: Sweetlight Books.

Sawyer, Jesse O. 1965. "English-Wappo Vocabulary." *University of California Publications in Linguistics* 43 (August): 1–128.

Religious Leaders, Great Lakes

Collectively known as the "Three Fires," the Odawa, Ojibway, and the Potawatomi have lived throughout the Great Lakes region since before the arrival of Europeans, and many of their communities still located in the region cling to traditional religious practices. At the same time, others of the Three Fires' communities have either adopted one form or another of Christianity or syncretized Christian and traditional elements together while maintaining their indigenous identity. In some cases, as they came into contact with new and different Native groups they merged spiritual elements from those other indigenous groups with their own. The best example of that occurred when, as members of the Three Fires moved west, they began to adopt religious traits from the Plains tribes. In general, the traditional religions of the Odawa, Ojibway, and the Potawatomi were not organized to any great degree, and they centered upon shamanism in which individual spiritual leaders chose and trained their successors based upon their individual areas of expertise and insights.

Odawa (Adawe, Odawe, Odawu, Ottawa, Outaouact)

Pontiac (ca. 1720–1769). A traditional Odawa military leader, Pontiac used the Delaware prophet Neolin's revitalization message to organize a military resistance to the British presence in the Great Lakes and Ohio River Valley region, and Pontiac's legacy continued to instill and inspire Odawa religious and cultural identification to the end of the twentieth century and beyond.

In the 1760s, Neolin, a Delaware prophet, began urging the Delaware to return to their traditional ways, which included restoring the proper exchange relationships within the Delaware community, with other tribes, with the natural world, and with their ancestors. He also preached a rejection of Anglo-American culture and urged Native people to resist Anglo-American settlement on ancestral lands. Pontiac took Neolin's message to heart and carried it back to his people. He used it to provide a spiritual foundation for an elaborate plan to unite all of the tribes in the Great Lakes and Ohio River Valley region to attack and destroy the British garrisons there and then drive Anglo-Americans back beyond the Appalachian Mountains. All but two of Great Britain's fortifications, Detroit and Pittsburgh, fell to Pontiac's alliance. However, since those two installations held out, the Native military alliance eventually disintegrated, and British expeditions into the interior re-established control in the region. A price was placed on Pontiac's head, and in 1769 he was

Ottawa chief Pontiac holding a wampum belt, in council. Hand-colored woodcut. (North Wind Picture Archives)

killed by a member of another tribe at Cahokia, Illinois. Despite the lack of a military victory by Pontiac and his alliance, his movement provided lasting inspiration to the Odawa people; along with the later revitalization movement of The Trout in the early nineteenth century, it created a culture and religious foundation for sustaining Odawa identity throughout the nineteenth and twentieth centuries.

The Trout (Mayagaway) (Early 1800s). A religious figure that sought to return the Odawa to traditional beliefs and life patterns, Mayagaway (The Trout) first began teaching the rejection of Anglo-American culture in 1807. The Trout seems to have been connected initially with the Odawa communities that lived in the

vicinity of Mackinac, and his home community was probably in that area. Eventually he came to have significant influence among the L'Arbre Croche community located on the northeast shore of Lake Michigan. Finally, after settling in Peoria, Mayagaway disappeared from the historical record.

Often associated with the Shawnee prophet Tenskawatawa, Mayagaway preached a rejection of Anglo-American materialism and alcohol, and he urged an Odawa return to ritual relationships with the natural world. Eventually this message embraced the complete, physical destruction of the Anglo-American presence in the western Great Lakes region. Along with Pontiac's military and spiritual crusade, Mayagaway's prophetic movement became a cornerstone for a continued, traditional Odawa identity and a revitalization effort that has lasted to the present day.

Ojibway (Chippewa, Mississauga, Saulteur, Saulteaux)

Copway, George (Kahgegagahbowh) (1818–ca. 1869). George Copway worked as a Christian missionary to Native people but gained fame as a lecturer and writer in the mid-eighteenth century. He was one of the earliest Native Americans to gain fame as an intellectual, speaker, and author.

Born at Rice Lake in Ontario, Copway's father served as chief and medicine man for the Rice Lake band of Ojibway. Both his mother and father converted to Methodism from their traditional Ojib-

George Copway (Kahgegagahbowh), 1860. Dopway was one of the earliest Native Americans to gain fame as an intellectual, speaker, and author. (Marian S. Carson Collection/Library of Congress)

Apostles into the Ojibway language, while working at the La Pointe Mission on Madeline Island. After that, Copway attended Ebenezer Manual Labor School in Jacksonville, Illinois, from 1837 until his graduation in 1839. From there he went back to Ontario, where he met and married Elizabeth Howell, an English woman. Her family did not approve of the marriage, but that did not deter the couple. Before and after the marriage, Copway worked at various missions for Native Americans in the United States and Canada. Several times during the 1830s, he performed his missionary duties with his cousins, John and Peter Marksman.

In 1846 the Saugeen Mission on Lake Huron and his own tribe accused Copway of embezzling funds, for which crime he was tried, found guilty, and served several weeks in prison. As a result of this scandal, the Canadian Conference of the Wesleyan Methodist Church expelled him. After his imprisonment, Copway published his life story, entitled *The Life, History, and Travels of Kah-ge-ga-gah-bowh (George Copway)* in 1847. Because of the success of his autobiography, Copway became a popular fixture on the lecture circuit. One of his favorite subjects for lectures was the need to use education and Christianity to improve the plight of Native Americans in both Canada and the United States.

In 1850, Copway published the *Organization of a New Indian Territory, East of the Missouri River,* in which he argued for a self-controlled Indian territory gov-

way beliefs on account of the missionary efforts of Peter Jones, among others. Copwell received his initial education at the mission school built for the Rice Lake Natives. Eventually, in 1830, George Copway also converted to Methodism, and at the age of sixteen, in 1834, he began to work as an interpreter at the Lake Superior Mission of the American Methodist Church along with his uncle and his cousin. A year later he assisted the Reverend Sherman Hall in the translation of the Gospel of St. Luke and the Acts of the erned by educated Native Americans that would one day join the United States as a state. Later, after touring Europe, he published an account of his travels called *Running Sketches of Men and Places* (1851). In the early 1850s, Copway remained a popular attraction on the lecture circuit, associated with the likes of James Fenimore Cooper, Washington Irving, and Henry Wadsworth Longfellow. However, before the end of the decade, he fell from celebrity because the novelty of his being an educated Indian had worn off. Interestingly, Copway was alleged to have been the model for Longfellow's poem *The Song of Hiawatha* (1855). He spent the last years of his life moving among the Native tribes in the northern territories of the United States and in Canada, fulfilling the duties of an itinerant healer. Finally, Copway worked as an interpreter for the Roman Catholic mission near Lake of Two Mountains in Canada. There he is said to have converted to Catholicism and died days later, on January 17, 1869, although some reports have him dying at Pontiac, Michigan, in 1863.

Sunday, John (Shahwundais) (ca. 1795–1875). John Sunday was a Mississauga Ojibway chief and a Methodist missionary to his people.

Born in New York state but a member of the Mississauga Ojibway in Upper Canada, Shahwundais became a leader of his people and fought in the War of 1812 before converting to Methodism in 1824. From that point forward he worked

to promote the spread of Christianity and education among Native people in the Great Lakes region of both Canada and the United States. Sunday toured Great Britain to raise funds for the Methodist missionary efforts in the Great Lakes area and even had an audience with Queen Victoria in 1836. He was effective at preaching to his people because he did so in their own language. Sunday was just as zealous in protecting Native rights as he was in converting his people to Christianity. He retired to Alderville, Ontario, in 1867 but remained active as a defender of Native rights and as missionary until he died, on December 14, 1875.

Steinhauer, Henry Bird (Shawahnegezhik) (1816–1884). Henry Steinhauer worked as an interpreter, missionary, and teacher among his people for more than fifty years.

Shawahnegezhik was born at Lake Simcoe in Ontario, and he converted to Methodism in 1828. For his initial education he went to the Methodist mission school located on Grape Island in the Bay of Quinte. While there he became known as Henry Steinhauer, after the Philadelphian that paid his educational expenses. Beginning in 1832 he continued his education for two years at New York's Cazenovia Seminary and after that attended the Upper Canada Academy at Cobourg, which is now known as Victoria College.

Steinhauer began work as a teacher in 1836 and as a missionary in 1840. For the rest of his life he made his living as an interpreter, missionary, and teacher, shifting from one mission school to the next every year or so as he was assigned. During this period, while working at Norway House, he helped James Evans translate the Bible into the Cree syllabary, and he helped establish a new mission known as the Oxford House at a Hudson's Bay Company post in 1850. Steinhauer married a Cree named Jessie Mamanuwartum in 1846. He toured Great Britain in 1854 to raise money and make presentations to various audiences. Finally, upon returning to Canada the next year, the Canadian Conference in London, Ontario, ordained Steinhauer. Although he continued his mission work and teaching in his later years, Steinhauer became an important fund-raiser for the Canadian mission effort among Native Americans. He died on December 30, 1884.

Jacobs, Peter (Pahtahsega) (ca. 1807–1890). Peter Jacobs served as an indigenous missionary to the Ojibway early in life, before suffering from poverty and alcoholism later in life. His autobiography continues to be a valuable primary source for the Mississauga Ojibway of the mid-eighteenth century.

Pahtahsega was orphaned as a young child, and as a result his early years were marked by poverty and lack of direction. Sometime around 1825, Pahtahsega began his education at Belleville, close to the Bay of Quinte, with the help of benefactors that covered the cost of his education. Later he attended the Credit Mission school. At some point while receiving his education, Pahtahsega took the name Peter Jacobs and converted to Methodism. Before he left the Credit Mission school, he served as an interpreter and led prayers. Jacobs continued his education under the guidance of the Dorcas Missionary Society in 1829. He began his own missionary work in 1836, and over the next two decades, Jacobs worked at and helped found several missions, primarily in upper Canada; eventually he was ordained in England in 1842. He wrote and published his valuable autobiography, *Journal of the Reverend Peter Jacobs, Indian Wesleyan Missionary,* in 1853, and throughout his missionary career, Jacobs assisted other missionaries with translations into and out of the Ojibway language.

Jacobs's first wife, Mary, was a member of the Credit Band of Mississauga Ojibway, and he had a daughter by her before she died in 1828. He remarried in 1831 to Elizabeth Anderson, and they had five children. Two of his sons by Elizabeth later became missionaries for the Church of England. Unfortunately for Jacobs, in 1858 the Methodist Conference dropped him for purportedly raising funds in the United States without the permission of the conference. Although he may have reconverted in 1867, this incident helped lead Jacobs down the path toward alcoholism and the poor house, which marred his last few years.

Marksman, Peter (Kahgoodahahqua or Madwaqwunayaush) (ca. 1815–1892).

Peter Marksman was an interpreter and influential missionary to Native Americans for the Methodist Episcopal Church in the Great Lakes area during the mid and late eighteenth century.

Born Khagoodahaqua in the Fond du Lac region in the western Great Lakes, Marksman's father was an Ojibway hereditary chief from Mackinac Island. His mother was also Ojibway. Because Marksman was a twin (his brother died at birth) and twins were seen as spiritual beings with special power, his parents prepared him to became a shaman in the Ojibway Midéwiwin religion. However, Marskman had different ideas after being introduced to Christianity as a child, and he finally converted in 1833. Throughout his life he worked as an interpreter, missionary, and teacher in the Great Lakes region, bringing the Methodist doctrine to the Ojibway and other Great Lakes tribes. In 1844, Marksman married Hannah Morien, who helped with his mission. The Potawatomi of the Upper Peninsula of Michigan were so grateful for the couple's work in their behalf that they named their town after Hannah, calling it Hannahville. After working almost his entire adult life as a missionary, Marksman died on May 28, 1892.

Gagewin (ca. 1850–1919). A practitioner of the Ojibway Midéwiwin religion, Gagewin became an important informant on the traditional Ojibway religion and culture for the ethnographer Frances Densmore in the early twentieth century.

Gagewin was a member of the White Earth Reservation band of Ojibway in Minnesota. He introduced Densmore to the Midéwiwin concept that living the correct way physically and spiritually led to a long life. Gagewin also provided information on how the young were instructed in the ways of the Midéwiwin by use of sacred scrolls. He died on October 23, 1919.

Fiddler, Jack (ca. 1820–1907). Of Cree-Saulteaux heritage, Jack Fiddler was a well-known shaman and leader of his people during the last half of the nineteenth and early twentieth centuries.

A member of the Red Sucker band, Jack Fiddler was the son of the shaman Porcupine Standing Sideways. The Red Sucker band as a group generally remained aloof from contact with Europeans and maintained traditional lifeways. As a leader of this group, Fiddler was noted for being a traditionalist, and as a shaman he built a reputation for his ability to heal, communicate with animals, and foretell the future. His family received their surname for their ability to play the fiddle. In 1907, Canadian authorities arrested Jack Fiddler and his brother, Joseph Fiddler, for the murder of Joseph's mentally ill daughter-in-law, Wahsakapeequay. The Fiddler brothers thought that she was a windigo. Windigos were feared spirits in the Algonquian belief system that ate human flesh, and according to tradition, they had to be eliminated to protect the people. The two brothers admitted to killing Wahsakepeequay, and Jack Fiddler admitted to killing fourteen other windigos during his lifetime. Later that year Jack Fiddler committed suicide because he could not face life apart from his people. One of as many as twelve children left behind when Jack Fiddler died was Adam Fiddler, who also became a spiritual leader of their people.

Fiddler, Joseph (Pesequan) (ca. 1856–1909). A mixed Cree-Saulteaux, Joseph Fiddler was a shaman and a leader of the Red Sucker band, located in northwestern Ontario.

Pesequan was the son of Porcupine Standing Sideways, and as a leader of the Red Sucker band he helped limit their contact with Europeans and urged them to follow traditional religious beliefs. With his brother, Jack Fiddler, Joseph was jailed and sentenced to be executed for the murder of his daughter-in-law Wahsakepeequay, whom the two believed to be a windigo. Later his death sentence was commuted to one of life imprisonment; Fiddler died in prison on September 4, 1909.

Mink, John (Zhonii'a Giishig) (ca. 1850–1943). An adherent of the Ojibway Midéwiwin religion and the Drum religion, John Mink was a local Medicine Lodge leader for the Lac Courte Oreilles Reservation in Wisconsin throughout most of his adult life. He was also an important informant for the ethnologists Joseph B. Casagrande and Robert Rittzenthaler in the early twentieth century. He did not begin seeking the ways

of a medicine man until two years after the death of his first wife in childbirth, when he had remarried. Through training and later through the process of fasting, Zhonii'a Giishing (the name given to him by his maternal grandmother) learned a multitude of medicines and sacred songs for healing the sick among his people. Mink became an important informant on Ojibway spiritual and healing practices late in his life. Casagrande wrote a short biography of Mink called "John Mink Ojibway Informant," which appeared in the book *In the Company of Man: Twenty Portraits of Anthropological Informants* (1960). After living more than ninety years, Mink passed away in 1943.

Gordon, Philip B. (Ti-Bish-Ko-Gi-Jik) (1885–1948). One of only a handful of Native American Roman Catholic priests in the country during the late nineteenth and early twentieth centuries, Philip Gordon used his position in the Catholic Church to improve the condition of Native Americans in the United States.

Born into a family with fourteen children in Gordon, Wisconsin, Philip Gordon went to the St. Mary's Mission School at the Bad River Reservation in Odanah, Wisconsin. After attending seminary, Gordon was ordained in 1913, and he later attended Catholic University in Washington, D.C. He then served at the Carlisle Indian School in Pennsylvania, worked for the Bureau of Catholic Indian Missions touring Indian schools and Indian agencies in the Midwest, and finally served at the Haskell Institute in Lawrence, Kansas. While in Lawrence, Gordon began to function as an activist to better conditions at Indian schools, missions, and reservations, because of what he had experienced at Haskell. In 1918 he began to assist his own people at the Lac Courte Oreilles Reservation in Wisconsin. Gordon worked with Sister Larush (also a converted Ojibway) to rebuild the Catholic church that had burned down there. Finally, in 1923, Gordon began work with the Committee of One Hundred, which was a reform group appointed by the secretary of the interior to help revise the federal Indian policy. After spending a lifetime serving the Catholic Church and half his life advocating reform of the federal Indian policy, Gordon died in 1948.

Fiddler, Adam (1865–1959). Continuing the family tradition, Adam Fiddler followed his grandfather (Porcupine), his father (Jack Fiddler), and his uncle (Joseph Fiddler) by practicing as a traditional medicine man or shaman for the Red Sucker band, but he also served as a Methodist lay minister in Ontario.

After experiencing a vision in 1901, Fiddler merged Christian elements with traditional Cree-Saulteaux beliefs. Inasmuch as he was the only person to introduce Christianity to his isolated people for a long period of time, he successfully led a syncretism of the two religions that was palatable to both Christians and traditional followers. Fiddler served his people as a religious leader until 1952. He died in 1959.

Larush, Sister M. Sirilla (Wayjohniemason) (1892–1976). Born on the Lac Courte Reservation in Wisconsin, Wayjohniemason converted to Roman Catholicism and served various missions as a nun for almost seventy years.

Given the name Fabiola at birth, Larush received her initial education at a mission school near her home, and she followed this up by later attending the Hayward Indian School. In 1908, Larush joined a convent in Milwaukee and later worked at a mission in Nebraska before returning to her reservation in 1925. Upon returning to her home, she restored the Catholic community and raised funds to rebuild the Church, which had burned down a few years earlier. In her later years, Larush served the Catholic community at missions in Chicago and Mississippi before she passed away in 1976.

Redsky, James, Sr. (Eshkwaykeezhik) (1890–?). James Redsky was a medicine man that practiced the Midéwiwin religion among the Canadian Ojibway at the Shoal Lake Reserve and eventually helped interpret many sacred scrolls of the Ojibway into English. He also wrote a biography of the Ojibway leader Misquonaqueb.

Born at Rice Bay in the Lake of the Woods region of Canada, Redsky started studying the Midéwiwin religion under the tutelage of his uncle (Baldhead Redsky) when he turned twelve. He also attended the Presbyterian mission school near his home. During World War I, Redsky served in the Canadian Infantry. After the war he finished his Midéwiwin education and eventually was given all of his uncle's sacred scrolls. Because the number of participants in the Midéwiwin religion was decreasing and he did not have an apprentice to whom he could pass on his knowledge, Redsky helped interpret and publish the scrolls in *Sacred Scrolls of the Southern Ojibway* (1975) with Selwyn Dewdney. Later Redsky converted and was ordained a Presbyterian elder in 1960, and afterward he wrote the biography of Misquonaqueb in *Great Leader of the Ojibway: Mis-quona-queb* (1972).

Reflecting Man, John (?–1956). A medicine man that practiced the Midéwiwin religion, John Reflecting Man carried on the traditions of his people on the Turtle Mountain Reservation in North Dakota until his death in 1956.

John-Paul (ca. 1900–?). The grandson of the legendary shaman Shawwanosway and a resident of the Birch Island Reserve in Canada, John-Paul became a shaman in his twenties and later in life turned to mysticism as his life's calling.

Mustache, James (Opwagon) (1904–?). The grandson of John Mink, James Mustache served his people as a traditional Ojibway religious leader and cultural preservationist.

Born on the Lac Courte Oreilles Reservation in Wisconsin, Opwagon was the grandson of a midwife, Iikwezens, and Midéwiwin medicine man, Zhonii'a Gishing (John Mink). Mustache was trained at an early age to be a spiritual leader, but he also received an Anglo-American education. He initially began his primary education at a Catholic mission school, but after attempts to convert him his grandparent transferred him to the Hayward Indian School in Wisconsin. Mustache went from Hayward to the Tomah Indian School, where he finished his Western education. He then enlisted in the military for four years and afterward served in the Indian Civilian Conservation Corps at Lac du Flambeau Reservation. At Lac du Flambeau he met and married the daughter of a spiritual leader, Rising Sun, which further strengthened his ties to traditional Ojibway culture. Eventually Mustache became civil and spiritual leader for the Ojibway and other tribes in the region, and he was a delegate to the National Congress of American Indians. Later in life he worked to use computer technology to record and teach Ojibway culture and language.

Jackson, Jimmy (ca. 1910–?). A traditional medicine man and religious leader, Jimmy Jackson became an important ethnographic informant when he was interviewed in the 1980s by Larry Aitken and Edwin Haller. Jackson used dreams to garner information and medicine for healing the sick.

Fortunate Eagle, Adam (ca. 1930–). An Ojibway from the Red Lake Reservation in Minnesota, Adam Fortunate Eagle worked as an activist, sociologist, and spiritual leader.

Fortunate Eagle received his initial education at the Indian boarding school in

Pipestone, Minnesota, and while still young he learned pipemaking and its ceremonial vestiges. After graduating from the boarding school, he continued his studies at the Haskell Institute in Lawrence, Kansas. After leaving Kansas, Fortunate Eagle moved to the Bay Area of California. In California he taught sociology at the University of California, worked with prison inmates, and for a decade was chairman of the Council of Bay Area Indian Affairs. In 1969, Fortunate Eagle participated in the American Indian occupation of Alcatraz to publicize the condition of Native Americans and how they were treated by the federal government. Finally, he became a pipeholder and ceremonial leader in 1972. As a religious leader, Fortunate Eagle conducted only ceremonies that he defined as intertribal. Later he moved to Fallon, Nevada, to run the Roundhouse Gallery.

Stillday, Thomas, Jr. (1934–). A leader of the Midéwiwin religion among the Ojibway on the Red Lake Reservation in Minnesota, Thomas Stillday became the first indigenous and non–Judeo Christian religious practitioner to become the official chaplain of the Minnesota legislature.

Stillday spent his childhood learning the traditional ways of his people before serving in the military for twelve years, which included a tour of duty in Korea. While in Korea he served as a "code-talker," in which he and other Native Ojibway speakers used a coded form of their language to protect their radio communications from the enemy. After leaving the military, Stillday studied elementary education at the University of Minnesota, Morris. As a traditional religious practitioner, he gradually rose to prominence in his community, which eventually led to his being appointed official chaplain of the Minnesota state legislature in the mid-1990s. Stillday's duties included providing the opening prayer for new sessions of the legislature. This was the first time that an indigenous religion had received official recognition in Minnesota.

Dowd, Donny (ca. 1940–). A spiritual leader among the Ojibway in the late twentieth century, Donny Dowd spent his early years seeking a direction for his life, and this led him to enlist in the military and participate as an activist with the American Indian Movement before finally finding his path within the Ojibway Midéwiwin religion.

Dowd grew up on the L'Anse Reservation in Michigan, although a portion of his childhood was spent in a Catholic orphanage. In his late teens Dowd dropped out of high school and enlisted in the U.S. Navy, where he pulled two tours of duty in Vietnam. Suffering from posttraumatic disorder after being discharged, he could not keep a job and suffered a failed marriage that produced two children. In the late 1960s, Dowd joined the American Indian Movement in Minneapolis. Eventually, after attending a Midéwiwin ceremony, he found his calling and sought training in this traditional religion. Finally, Dowd moved to a

Michigan reservation with a new wife and became a religious leader and cultural educator for the community.

Hascall, John (1941–). In the late twentieth century, John Hascall successfully syncretized traditional Ojibway beliefs with the tenets of Roman Catholicism to became a successful practicing medicine man and Catholic priest. He conducted Mass for Native Americans.

Potawatomi
Main Poc (ca. 1765–1816). Born without fingers on his left hand, which marked him as having special powers provided by the Creator, Main Poc used his gift to become a shaman and war leader among his people, and for a period of time in the early nineteenth century, he used his influence to resist Anglo-American encroachment.

Pokagon, Leopold (ca. 1775–1841). A charismatic leader of the Potawatomies during the era of removal, Leopold Pokagon worked to preserve a place for his band of Potawatomie to remain in Michigan, to maintain peace with their Anglo-American neighbors, and to convert his people to Roman Catholicism.

Shabona (ca. 1775–1859). Born of a Seneca mother and an Odawa father, Shabona became a leader among the Potawatomies through marriage. Prior to the War of 1812, he advocated joining Tecumseh's Native alliance against further Anglo-American encroachment and in rejection of Anglo-American culture, but after the war, Shabona advised accommodation of Anglo-Americans and peaceful coexistence.

Medicine Neck (early 1900s). A practicing Peyotist, Medicine Neck introduced peyote to the Menominee Reservation in Wisconsin during the early part of the twentieth century.

In 1914, Medicine Neck was arrested for bringing peyote and peyotism to Wisconsin, on charges of breaking a federal law that forbade the introduction of intoxicants to Native reservations. The judge eventually ruled that the law applied only to alcohol and set Medicine Neck free.

Negahnquet, Albert (1874–1944). Negahnquet was one of the earliest full-blooded Native Americans to be ordained by the Roman Catholic Church.

In 1874, Negahnquet was born in Topeka, Kansas, near St. Mary's Mission. Eventually he joined the Citizen Band of Potawatomi in Oklahoma and received his early education at the Sacred Heart Mission school located near the Potawatomi Reservation. From there he went to the College of Propaganda Fide in Rome and was ordained in 1903. Upon becoming a priest he returned to the United States to work with Native people in Minnesota and Oklahoma.

Dixie Ray Haggard

See also Ceremony and Ritual, Anishnabe; James, Peter; Manitous; Missionization, Great Lakes; Oral Traditions, Ojibwe; Women's Cultural and Religious Roles, Great Lakes

References and Further Reading
Aitken, Larry P., and Edwin W. Haller. 1990. *Two Cultures Meet: Pathways for*

American Indians to Medicine. Duluth: University of Minnesota Press.

Casagrande, Joseph B. 1960. "John Mink, Ojibwe Informant," Pp. 467–488 in *In the Company of Man*. Edited by Joseph B. Casagrande. New York: Harper and Brothers.

Clifton, James A. 1998. *The Prairie People: Continuity and Change in Potawatomi Indian Culture, 1665–1965*. Enl. ed. Iowa City: University of Iowa Press.

Hirschfelder, Arlene, and Pauletter Molin. 2000. *Encyclopedia of Native American Religions*. Rev. ed. New York: Facts on File.

Lyons, William S. 1996. *Encyclopedia of Native American Healing*. Denver, CO: ABC-CLIO.

Malinowski, Sharon, and Anna Sheets, eds. 1998. *Gale Encyclopedia of Native American Tribes*. Vol. I: *Northeast, Southeast, Caribbean*. New York: Gale Research.

Paper, Jordan. 1980. "From Shaman to Mystic in Ojibway Religion." *Sciences Religieuses/Studies in Religion* 9, no. 2: 185–199.

Pflug, Melissa A. 1998. *Ritual and Myth in Odawa Revitalization: Reclaiming a Sovereign Place*. Norman: University of Oklahoma Press.

Trigger, Bruce G., ed. 1978. *Handbook of North American Indians*. Vol. 15: *Northeast*. Washington, DC: Smithsonian Institution.

Religious Leaders, Great Lakes and Northeast

See Jones, Peter; Tekakwitha, Kateri

Religious Leaders, Northwest

The best known religious leaders in the Northwest for the past two and a half centuries have often blended their ancient beliefs in ways acceptable to imposed Christianity. Most have sought some kind of compromise or reformation satisfying to old and new beliefs.

Ivan Pan'kov (1770s–1850s)

On April 23, 1828 (the Feast of Alexander Nevsky), Ivan Pan'kov, Aleut leader (*toion, toyon*) in the Fox Islands of the Aleutian chain, arranged a remarkable meeting. For two years he had been working with Fr. Ioann Veniaminov (now St. Innokentii), a Russian Orthodox priest, on an Aleut (Unagan) translation of the catechism. At this meeting, Veniaminov listened carefully as Pan'kov translated the words to a famous shaman named Smirennikov. After serious reflection, the priest wrote his bishop that the sixty-year-old man seemed to be doing the work of God. Later, when he published the first ethnography of Native North America in 1840, Veniaminov continued to hold that there were both good and bad shamans, a sensitive admission for a extraordinary missionary, who later became supreme head of his church.

Even more significant is the contribution of Pan'kov in establishing literacy and trust in a new faith that has since become embraced by Aleutians in the succeeding century. Important in this process have been Creoles such as Iakov Netsvetov (1804–1864), mixed race clergy who used Native fluency to further indigenize Orthodoxy in Alaska.

Bini (?–1870s)

During the 1830s, at the south end of coastal Alaska, a Carrier prophet named

Bini ("mind") caused a stir along the Skeena River and the coast, preaching a blend of Catholic, Orthodox, and Native beliefs. He had been a successful hunter, shaman, and gambler until he lost everything by betting his goods, nephews, parents, and family. He went into the deep woods, where he dropped from exhaustion. He had a vision of a man dressed all in white who came from the Sky, charged Bini to take up preaching for a better world, and taught Bini something like the sign of the cross by touching his forehead, shoulders, and heart.

A search party found Bini's clothes and assumed he had frozen to death. Later they found him buried in snow, with barely a pulse. They carried him home, placed him beside a fire, and a shaman worked on him for two days. When he revived, Bini spoke an unknown language and taught new songs and dances. His feet were together and his arms outstretched, and he swayed his body as though crucified.

Bini's nephew spoke for him, as was appropriate for his heir. In this region, kinship was traced through mothers, so uncle (mother's brother) and nephew (sister's son) were very close. Bini predicted the advent of new things such as flour (dry snow) and horses, as well as special days like Sunday. People gathered and feasted at this house for several days. Some danced so strenuously that they ended by rolling on the floor. Then Bini preached five commandments: be faithful to one's home life,

avoid another's hunting grounds, do not murder, respect elders and chiefs, and stop war.

Bini left to visit far and wide. He continued to use an unknown language, and his nephew translated. Tsimshians learned his message and spread it to other coastal tribes when they took candlefish together on the Nass River. In this way, Bini's preaching went much farther than he actually did.

Before Bini several upriver women had received visions, as did his older brother. But Bini became a chief of the Beaver crest and thus earned prestige and respect for his message. He hosted a great potlatch and set up a carved pole to confirm his rank. After preaching for fifteen years, he installed aides and tried to introduce public confession and whipping. Too many hardships and fights followed from these disclosures, however, so he ended them. He died about 1870, perhaps from sipping poisoned water while trying to cure a woman.

His nephews and others, including at least one woman, assumed the Bini name and continued to preach until Catholic clergy arrived in the region and supplanted their efforts with mission churches.

Captain Campbell, Skagit, (c. 1850–c. 1880)

Just across the border from southern British Columbia, Upper Skagit Native villages were politically and religiously centralized through the efforts of Captain Campbell, the Skagit prophet who founded the present Campbell or Camel family. His father came from eastern Washington, supposedly fleeing a threat of sorcery directed against him. He moved across the Cascade Mountains and married a woman from the town at the mouth of the Snohomish River. The prophet was born and raised there before he married a woman from the village on Clear Lake on the Upper Skagit River. During one of his frequent visits to his Interior Salish relatives, he met Father Eugene Casimir Chirouse, an early and important oblate missionary active at the Catholic mission among the Yakama just before the 1855 Treaty War. Fr. Chirouse moved to the Tulalip Reservation in 1863, then ended his career among the Canadian Okanagans.

The prophet worked closely with Chirouse, particularly in translating liturgy into Lushootseed Salish. Apparently, the priest and the prophet communicated with each other using the Okanogan dialect of Interior Salish. The prophet established his own longhouse near Marblemount, at the junction of the Cascade and Skagit rivers, where he led Catholic services in the summer and Native spirit dances in the winter. His links with Chirouse expanded his basis of authority into Euro-American contexts.

When the prophet's first wife died, he married the daughter of Petius, who widened his political base, although she seems to have outranked him. This woman had assumed the chiefly name of a famous male relative and went everywhere with an escort of body guards and attendants who acted in her behalf.

John and Mary Slocum and the Shaker Church, 1882

Near Olympia, the capital of Washington territory, John Slocum, a man of chiefly family, died but soon revived to found the Indian Shaker Church. Brilliantly combining outward forms of Catholicism, Protestant hymns and notions of personal salvation, and core Native beliefs, several thousand international Shakers still worship from northern California to southern British Columbia.

John Slocum died and revived on October 20, 1882. Later, Mary received the healing trembling ("the shake") that distinguishes this faith—a manifestation akin to the trembling of the original Quakers and other ecstatic cults. Presbyterians, particularly in Olympia, were initially supportive, but relations cooled after Natives entered the state capitol in a Sunday-afternoon Christmas procession led by a man on a horse with his head bent and arms extended, followed by his wife, identified as either Mary or Eve. Their behavior and "strong fish smell" embarrassed the minister who had invited them, and he lost all sympathy with their beliefs.

Together, the Slocums revealed the word of the Christian God for Natives, protected by being legally incorporated in 1910 within Washington state. Its tenets strictly identify the church as an

Indian religion inspired by the Christian God and Jesus Christ, as well as another supernatural figure they address as the Spirit, who is compatible both with the Holy Ghost and the aboriginal immortals who acted as guardian spirits.

The Spirit enters members during public ceremonies when they manifest the "shake," augmented by "gifts" and "helps." At death, this same Spirit "takes them home." Gifts include candle holding, bell ringing, curing, interpreting the cause of sickness, baptizing, divination, shaking, and ridding a home or a room of evil spirits. Each varied "help" depends on the quality and amount of supernatural ability that a member is able to express, and, in this, most corresponds to the aboriginal possession of distinct guardian spirits. Whenever Natives join the Shaker Church, their aboriginal spirit powers convert with them, thus continuing that source of ancestral religious tradition into the new practice.

Its forms are a brilliant blend of religions. Many of its overt public gestures reflected Catholic worship—such as altars, albs, candles, and making the sign of the cross by placing fingers to forehead, shoulders, and chest. Some mirror Protestantism—such as personal salvation, local language use, hymns, and plain steeple churches. Influences from schoolrooms include the use of hand bells to accompany such hymns during circular processions. Candles for light and wood-burning stoves for heating and cooking have kept Shakers self-reliant, avoiding costly electric bills.

Overall, Shakerism is devoted to curing, temperance, and the conversion of Native people to their avowedly Christian belief. Shaker curing specifically addresses ghosting, sorcery threats, depression (feeling sorry), soul loss, and unwanted spirits. In the modern Native community its specialty is curing, especially of addictions, but unlike the ancient shamanic tradition that also continues, Shaker curing is much more universal and democratic in the sense that it is performed by all believers and is free of charge, whether in a patient's own home or a Shaker church. A basic tenet grants the truth of individual inspiration, though a continual tension exists between this autonomy and hopes for unanimity as institutionalized in the authority of the Shaker bishop and council.

Old Pierre (1860s–1946)

Old Pierre, a Katzie (Sta:lo, Fraser River) spiritual leader, most fully articulated Salishan genesis to Diamond Jenness of the National Museum of Canada in 1936. A few significant details were provided by Simon Pierre (a son born in the 1880s) to Wayne Suttles in 1952.

His mother, a spiritual practitioner herself, sent Pierre out questing from the age of three and paid three of their oldest and best informed relatives to teach him sacred epics from the age of eight. As a result, among his powerful helpers was the Father Of All Trees, the only arboreal being who could grant power. Another time, he tripped over a rock that turned out to be the pillow of the Leader of the Earth, gaining power in his hands and wrists to draw out sickness, power in his mouth to swallow it, and power to see all over the world to recover "minds" that had strayed from their bodily homes.

Pierre learned to diagnose sickness depending on its causes, either from (1) lost vitality or mind, (2) impurity or offense to a spirit or ghost, or (3) a probe shot into a victim by a hostile shaman. More important, Pierre grasped a systematic account of the Sta:lo Universe, from a Katzie perspective.

Humans were instructed to pray to deities in sequence, beginning with the Lord Above, then moving to the Sun, Khaals, Moon, and personal spirit powers. Humans owed their existence to the Lord Above, who created each of them endowed with a soul, vitality-thought, a certain talent-power, and a shadow-reflection. At death, the breath and special talent perished with the body, the soul returned to the Lord Above, and the vitality and shadow merged to produce the shade or ghost that roamed as a barely visible form in the neighborhood of its old home, feared by the surviving relatives.

Vitality, which was inseparable from thought, pervaded the entire body. Any loss of the body was accompanied by a proportional loss of vitality. The loss of a limb or the cutting of the hair, therefore, decreased its manifestation as warmth, closely linked with the sun. While it was diffused throughout the body, it was es-pecially concentrated at the heart. The Lord Above created evergreen trees at the beginning of the world so humans would have a strong source of vitality, manifested by the constant green of the foliage. During the winter, when the world is cold, ceremonials were held because they also provided warmth.

Because they were transformed from the first people, the original members of the various species were sacred and able to share their talent-power with particular humans. The more remote the home of the being was from humans, the more powerful it was. Humans needed these powers to cope with the unseen hazards and dangers that filled every life. A human without power was like a cork floating helplessly in the water, subject to all kinds of pulls, crosswinds, and undercurrents.

The Fraser River valley became a huge dish filled with food through the work of the Lord Above, who decided to send specific groups of people under a named leader to particular locales along the river. Instead of one pair, like Adam and Eve, there were many couples, each entrusted to form a set community at specific places.

Initially, the Katzie world was grim and silent, with only shellfish to feed these first people. There were no birds, animals, or winds. The Lord Above made the sun to give warmth, the moon to measure time, and the rainbow to indicate weather conditions.

In time, a leader called Swaneset emerged to "fix" the earth, marrying wives from the earth such as Sockeye Salmon and the sky such as a Star. Then the Lord Above prepared the way for humans by sending Khaals to further make things right. Through the power of thought, Khaals changed beings. Bluejay prophesied his arrival, assembling most of the beings so that Khaals, who was always just, could sort the good from the bad and make the world a better place, allowing those people who showed respect to remain human. The humans have overpopulated their world several times, suffering starvation, disease, and extermination before they were able to reform into respectful communities.

Through his work and teaching, Old Pierre provided the most detailed and systematic account of Coast Salish beliefs on record.

Native Clergy

Several Protestant churches in Canada have had Native clergy, particularly Peter Kelly (Haida), George Edgar (Tsimshian), William Henry Pierce (Tsimshian), and Edward Marsden (Tsimshian). The career of the Reverend John Kilbuck, a Delaware who helped found the successful Moravian Church among the Yup'ik Eskimo, has more human interest because he fell away for part of his career. Equally fascinating is the thwarted life of the Puyallup Reverend Peter Stanup, who lived near Tacoma, Washington.

Peter Stanup (1857–1893)

Peter Stanup was the son of Jonah, a vigorous leader who died at the age of ninety-four in 1897, and the daughter of a Puyallup chief. His parents were Roman Catholics, but he became a Presbyterian. In 1875 he started as a printer's devil for the Olympia *Daily Echo* but was the butt of many practical jokes because of his deep faith. When this press moved to Tacoma to become the *Herald,* he served as a printer. Seeking further education, he joined other Puyallups at the start of a regional federal boarding school. Later he became a reporter, describing a Skokomish Potlatch of October 22–28, 1878. During the costly Seattle/Tacoma rivalry over the name of the tall mountain often called Rainier, Stanup added that the Puyallup word *Ta-ko-ba* means "the mountain," but earlier Rainier had been called *Tu-wak-hu,* or *Twa-hwauk.* His Native terms and perspective, however, only further confused city boosters.

After he returned from school, Peter served as interpreter for the Presbyterian missionary to the Puyallups and himself studied for that ministry. Peter served in two state Republican conventions and was considered as a candidate for governor at the 1890 state Republican caucus. He married, but four of his six children died. He became involved in the sell-off of his reservation and made a financed trip to Congress in 1893. He became wealthy from these land sales, but also took to alcohol. He was preparing to take the bar and add law to his credentials when his body was found in the Puyallup River on May 23, 1893. Although no murder charge was ever made, many suspected foul play.

Petius (1904–1989)

Until 1989, the most honored shaman in the American Northwest carried the famous name of Petius, once father-in-law to the Skagit prophet and the recognized leader of the Native Samish town where Bayview now stands. Living at Lummi but with kinship ties among the Lushoosteeds, Petius and his large family served as Bible Shakers, a Pentecostal choir on radio, and lay preachers until their father led them back to Winter Dancing when he took up an expected family career as a Native doctor. Drawing on family privileges, he rapidly became successful through his use of painted power boards and an inherited ability as a medium who was able to deal with troubling ghosts.

Helped by his large family of daughters, he founded his own smokehouse and began initiating new dancers. When his older son married the daughter of another Native doctor, both their families enhanced their careers. As other children married into other reservations this network expanded, and it continues to do so.

Late in his career, Petius was given medical privileges at hospitals in Vancouver, Canada, and in several cities in Washington state. Native patients in these impersonal surroundings immediately began to improve. At his death, the eldest son assumed the mantle of his father, but has yet to enjoy the same wide fame.

Finally, the impact of other "minor" prophets should be mentioned. During the late 1800s, from the Plateau came word of the teachings of a Kootenai woman who dressed and acted like a man, of Smohallah along the Columbia River, of Jake Hunt and the Feather dance, and of the Ghost Dances of 1870 and 1890. Coquelle Thompson (1849–1946) preached an 1870 version known as the Warm House along coastal Oregon for a year after April 1877. Natives of the Oregon coast had been particularly devastated and sought succor in new faiths, including the Indian Shaker Church.

Jay Miller

See also Ceremony and Ritual, Northwest; Christianity, Indianization of; Dance, Northwest Winter Spirit Dances; Guardian Spirit Complex; Healing Traditions, Northwest; Indian Shaker Church; Missionization, Alaska; Missionization, Northwest; Religious Leaders, Alaska; *Sbatatdaq (Sqadaq)*

References and Further Reading
Amoss, Pamela. 1982. "Resurrection, Healing, and 'the Shake': The Story of John and Mary Slocum." Pp. 87–109 in *Charisma and Sacred Biography.* Edited by Michael Williams. *Journal of the American Academy of Religion, Thematic Studies* XLVIII (3/4): 87–109.
Barnett, Homer. 1957. *Indian Shakers, A Messianic Cult of the Pacific Northwest.* Carbondale: Southern Illinois University Press.
Collins, June. 1974. *Valley of the Spirits.* Seattle: University of Washington Press.
Jenness, Diamond. 1955. *The Faith of a Coast Salish Indian.* Anthropology in British Columbia Memoir 3. Victoria: British Columbia Provincial Museum.
Jilek, Wolfgang. 1982. *Indian Healing: Shamanic Ceremonialism in the Pacific Northwest Today.* Surrey, British Columbia: Hancock House Publishers.
Miller, Jay. 1999. *Lushootseed Culture and the Shamanic Odyssey: An Anchored*

Radiance. Lincoln: University of
Nebraska Press.

Ruby, Robert, and John Brown. 1996. *John
Slocum and the Indian Shaker Church*.
Norman: University of Oklahoma Press.

Suttles, Wayne. 1987. *Coast Salish Essays*.
Seattle: University of Washington Press.

———, ed. 1990. *Handbook of North
American Indians: Northwest Coast*, vol.
7. Washington, DC: Smithsonian
Institution Press.

Waterman, Thomas. 1924. "The Shake
Religion of Puget Sound." *Smithsonian
Report for 1922*: 499–507.

Religious Leaders, Plains

Bull Lodge

A spiritual leader and warrior said to
possess the ability to heal and prophesy,
Bull Lodge kept two of the central sacred
symbols within Gros Ventre religiosity:
the Feathered Pipe, or Chief Medicine
Pipe, and the Flat Pipe. Such pipes are
kept in sacred bundles, which are
wrapped in outer wrappings along with
other sacred objects.

Bull Lodge was born in 1802 and died
in 1886. He distinguished himself in his
early life as a powerful warrior, and he
sought spiritual empowerment as well,
undergoing seven different fasts in seven
different sacred spaces of the Gros Ventre
landscape. As a result he received powerful visions that aided the Gros Ventre
people through difficult eras of change
and colonization. Because of his role as
keeper of the sacred Flat Pipe and Feathered Pipe, Bull Lodge was able to influence the weather, cure illnesses, and
protect the community from danger. His

position as a healer was established
when he healed his uncle, Yellow Man,
when he was extremely ill. After having
cured nineteen people he was presented
with the Feathered Pipe, and he held the
office of Pipe Chief medicine man, a very
important honor. He died at eighty-five
years of age, having foretold his own
death. His daughter, Garter Snake, dictated his life story to Frederick Gone, a
Gros Ventre tribal member. The volume,
edited by George Horse Capture, was
published as *The Seven Visions of Bull
Lodge* in 1980.

James Blue Bird (c. 1887–?)

One of the first peyote roadmen among
the Lakota, James Blue Bird was first exposed to the peyote faith in 1902, at the
age of fifteen. Quanah Parker, a Comanche peyote roadman, led this ceremonial meeting. His father, who was an
Episcopal minister, did not protest his
son's newfound faith, seeing in it the
symbols of Christianity: the cross, the
fire, and prayer to a Great Spirit. He spent
years learning about the tradition from
John Rave and Albert Hensley in Nebraska. When James Blue Bird returned
to his community in 1916, he was quickly
acknowledged as a peyote roadman. In
1918 the Native American Church was
officially incorporated, so as to protect
its followers under the constitutional assurance of freedom of religion. Subsequently, Blue Bird organized and directed the Native American Church of
South Dakota, a position that he held for
fifty years. His church ultimately com-

prised sixteen local chapters. The year of his death is unknown.

Davéko (1818–1897 or 1898)

Davéko, an Oklahoma Kiowa-Apache who lived from about 1818 until 1897 or 1898, was a powerful healer and spiritual leader. As an adolescent, Davéko undertook the four-day vision quest, receiving the spirit-powers of turtle, owl, and snake. Davéko used a black handkerchief in his healing ceremonies; it helped him to locate the disease-causing object. He healed patients through the use of herbs, roots, songs, prayers, and through the literal sucking out of the object that was causing the disease. His success at healing, as well as his ability to find lost individuals or objects, enabled him to become a powerful spiritual leader during a tumultuous century.

Philip Deloria (Tipi Sapa) (1853–1931)

Born in 1853, Philip Deloria (Yankton Sioux) was raised in the traditional way, and he was apprenticed to his father to become a traditional spiritual leader and healer. His mother, Siha Sapewin, was Lakota of the Rosebud band. When he was three years old, while his father was away, Philip became very ill and died. When his father returned, he carried Philip to a high hill, where he prayed for his son's life. Philip was restored to life, and the next day he and his father returned to the community. When he was seventeen, Philip converted to Christianity, adopting the dress and many of the customs of Euro-Americans. In 1892, with his father's approval, he became an Episcopal priest. In 1873 he founded Wojo Okolakiciye, The Planting Society, which was later known as the Brotherhood of Christian Unity. He was elected chief of the Eight Band of the Yankton Sioux, and in 1888 he was placed in charge of the Episcopal missions of South Dakota. He served as a missionary and priest for forty years on the Standing Rock Reservation, before dying in 1931. He married Mary Sully Bordeau and had five daughters and one son, Vine Victor Deloria, Sr.

Vine Victor Deloria, Sr. (1901–1990)

Vine Victor Deloria, Sr., was born in 1901, and, following in his father's footsteps, he became an Episcopal priest. In 1926, Deloria played a key role in the government hearings at Lake Andes and Pipestone Quarry, the quarry where many Plains tribes secure the pipestone needed to carve the bowls of sacred pipes. With his assistance as a translator, the tribes were able to secure access to the quarries. Following his ordination as a priest, Deloria served for seventeen years at the All Saints Mission, and then for an additional three years at the Sisseton Mission in South Dakota. He was appointed to the Episcopal National Council in 1954 and oversaw all Episcopal Indian mission work in his position as assistant secretary for Indian Missions of the Episcopal Church of America. Later he was also appointed archdeacon of the American Indian parishes in South Dakota.

Vine Deloria, Jr. (1933–)

Vine Deloria, Jr., has been described as one of the most influential voices among contemporary American Indian authors. He has acted as an advocate for American Indian religious rights, the preservation of sacred land, and tribal sovereignty, and against the cultural assimilation of Native people. Born in 1933, he received his bachelor's degree from Iowa State University before earning a master's degree in theology from Lutheran School of Theology, Rock Island, Illinois. He decided against becoming ordained, arguing that following the white man's religion had failed to grant Indian people social or political equality, nor had Christianity succeeded in lifting the United States out of a spiritual, moral, and ecological crisis. He urged instead a return to traditional Native religiosity, and, for non-Natives, a complete change in social and theological outlook. Non-Natives as well, he argues, should return to a tribal-communal approach to life that seeks an ecologically balanced relationship with the environment.

Deloria is a founding member of the National Congress of American Indians (NCAI); he served as a professor of law and political science at the University of Arizona; and he is currently a professor of American Indian Studies, History, Law, Political Science, and Religious Studies at the University of Colorado, Boulder. His first book, *Custer Died for Your Sins: An Indian Manifesto,* published in 1969, served as an inspiration for the newly emerging American Indian Movement, and for other Indian activists of the era. Other important publications include *God Is Red: A Native View of Religion* (1973); *Behind the Trail of Broken Treaties* (1974); *American Indian Policy in the 20th Century* (1985); *Red Earth, White Lies: Native Americans and the Myth of Scientific Fact* (1997); and *For This Land: Writings on Religion in America* (1999).

Frank Fools Crow (1891–1989)

Born around 1891, Frank Fools Crow was an important spiritual leader among the Lakota. He led Sun Dances, *yuwipi* ceremonies, and was a healer (*wapiye*) for more than sixty years. In addition to maintaining his traditional faith, in 1917 he became a Catholic, and he saw no difficulty in practicing both faiths. He was faithful to both traditions until his death in 1989. A nephew of the famous Lakota spiritual leader Black Elk, Fools Crow was taught the traditional Lakota spiritual path. He was trained by his father and grandfathers, as well as by Iron Cloud, a Lakota leader, and Stirrup, a famous Lakota medicine man of the early twentieth century. During his vision quest in 1905 he received a powerful vision that would empower him in his spiritual practice. And in 1913 he received another vision while riding in the midst of a thunderstorm. His second vision quest in 1914 likewise empowered him with another powerful spirit. These visions and spiritual relationships would enable him to be a powerful leader and intercessor for the Lakota people.

Fools Crow played an important role in the American Indian Movement of the 1970s, particularly in the occupation of Wounded Knee in 1973. He blessed the efforts of the occupiers, and offered encouragement to them as a spiritual leader. He, along with other Lakota elders, also sought to achieve a peaceful reconciliation by negotiating with federal representatives. He delivered the proposed settlement to those occupying the Knee, and facilitated a peaceful conclusion. However, he himself was disappointed with the terms of the negotiation, because it failed to achieve their goals: the reinstatement of the agreed-upon treaty relationship, as established in the 1868 treaty with the federal government. Fools Crow, following instructions he received in a vision, dictated his life story to Thomas E. Mails, with the assistance of Dallas Chief Eagle. The book, *Fools Crow*, was published in 1979.

American writer Mary Crow Dog in Paris. (Sophie Bassouls/Corbis Sygma)

Albert Hensley (1875–?)

Born in 1875, Albert Hensley (Winnebago) was a peyote roadman and missionary. As a roadman, he helped to establish his particular mode of ceremony, the Cross-Fire or Big Moon ritual, throughout the northern Plains, among the Ojibwa, Chippewa, and Lakota. He also introduced the use of the Christian Bible into the ceremony, and he crafted a more Christianized expression of the peyote meeting. He was involved both spiritually and politically, writing letters to the federal government and Bureau of Indian Affairs defending the peyote religion. He was a founding member of the peyote church when the Winnebago incorporated the church, the first tribe outside of Oklahoma to do so. It was later renamed the Native American Church of Winnebago, Nebraska. The church includes both Half-Moon and Cross-Fire ceremonial traditions.

Emily Hill (1911–?)

Born in 1911, Emily Hill was a remarkable woman who worked as a spiritual leader, healer, and preserver of cultural knowledge. Hill spent nearly all her life in the Little Wind River area in Wyoming, though she briefly attended boarding school on the Wind River Reservation. Hill was the granddaughter of a Shoshone warrior woman who was well known for her bravery in battle and her fierce advocacy for mistreated women in her community. Hill herself married and had three children. After her husband's death, she lived with her half-sister, Dorothy. The two of them lived together for the remainder of their lives, supporting and caring for each other. Together they drove teams of horses, cut and stacked hay, irrigated fields, and dragged and cut large logs for firewood. After Dorothy was injured in the 1950s, Emily took care of her until her death, thirty years later.

Hill was a powerful medicine woman and healer. While at boarding school as a child, she witnessed a measles epidemic. She helped to care for the other children and gained a respect for certain aspects of Western medicine. As an adult she practiced traditional Shoshone medicine, curing people through powerful songs that she acquired within dreams and visions. She was trained by a Shoshone woman elder, who taught her traditional modes of healing and the use of herbs, as well as the procedure for procuring spirit power. Inspired by what she had seen at boarding school, Hill combined aspects of Western medicine with that of traditional Shoshone medicine, creating a unique mode of healing.

Hill and her sister were also believers in the Ghost Dance religion, and she continued to sing the sacred songs long after the dances had ceased to be held. Along with other women, she also sang at Sun Dances, supporting the efforts of young Shoshone men as they prayed and suffered for their communities. Throughout her life she continued to pray and heal using the sacred songs from the Ghost Dance, the Sun Dance, the Women's Dance, and the Wolf Dance. By singing these songs she was able to cultivate healing power and renew relationships with the powerful spirits present in the natural world. Along with four other Shoshone women, Hill collaborated with Judith Vander to produce a book, *Songprints,* which was published in 1988.

Kee'Kah'Wah'Un'Ga (Reuben A. Snake, Jr.) (1937–1993)

Born in 1937, Kee'Kah'Wah'Un'Ga (Winnebago) was an important religious and political leader. He fought throughout his adult life for religious and political freedom for American Indian people. He was a national chairman of the American Indian Movement in 1972 and national president of the National Congress of American Indians from 1985 to 1987. Kee'Kah'Wah'Un'Ga was a prayer chief and roadman of the Native American Church, as well as the elected tribal chairman of the Winnebago nation. As roadman and spiritual leader, he frequently led all-night prayer services to seek peace and justice for American Indian people. He served as a founding trustee and spiritual adviser within the American Indian Ritual Object Repatriation Foundation. He traveled throughout the country lobbying for legislation that would ensure American Indian people the right to religious freedom. It was in part due to his efforts and advocacy that the American Indian Religious Freedom Act (1978), the National Museum of the American Indian Act (1989), the Native American Graves Protection and Repatriation Act (1990), the Native Language Act (1990), and the Native American Free Exercise of Religion Act (1993) were successfully passed.

Kicking Bear (1846–1904)

Born about 1846, Kicking Bear (Lakota) was an important medicine man and warrior. He was an advocate of the Ghost Dance among the Lakota, and in 1889, along with several others, he visited the Paiute spiritual leader Wovoka. He became convinced of the truth of Wovoka's claims and returned to the Rosebud and Standing Rock reservations to teach the new religion. The Ghost Dance taught that all Native people, the living and the dead, would soon be reunited. The world would soon be remade and all white people removed from the land. The buffalo would return, and the earth would be restored. Followers were to dance in a traditional circle-dance and sing. Periodically dancers would fall to the ground and be given visions in which they were transported to the spirit world. There they were taught new songs, dances, and rituals that they were to teach to the people. The movement also called for the return to a traditional mode of life, and a

rejection of white culture and its vices, such as drinking.

Kicking Bear and his brother-in-law Short Bull received a vision instructing them to make a Ghost-Shirt. The shirts, they believed, would protect them from bullets. They brought these shirts with them to the Lakota when they taught them the Ghost Dance. The militaristic overtones that Kicking Bear inspired in the dance aroused fear in government officials, and they sought to curtail the religious practice. They attempted to arrest Kicking Bear, but he eluded them, which added to his fame and his followers' belief in the new religion. In 1890 he and his followers fled to the Badlands in South Dakota, hoping to avoid persecution.

Fearing that Kicking Bear's uncle, Sitting Bull (Tatanka Iyotake), would join them, the Standing Rock Indian agent attempted to have him arrested. In the ensuing struggle, Sitting Bull was murdered. Following that, the Minneconjou leader Big Foot (Si Tanka) decided to move his people to the Pine Ridge Reservation, to seek protection. The army however, mistakenly believed that Big Foot was on his way to join Kicking Bear and intercepted them. The next day, on December 29, 1890, the U.S. Seventh Cavalry massacred more than two hundred children, women, and men of Big Foot's band, including Big Foot himself. Afraid for their safety, Kicking Bear and his people surrendered to the army. In 1891 he was incarcerated. However, his sentence was commuted on the condition that he join

Buffalo Bill's Wild West Show for two years. He did so, returning to Wounded Knee Creek in 1892, where he lived with his family until his death in 1904.

Susan La Flesche Picotte (1863–1915)
Born in 1865 on the Omaha Reservation, Susan La Flesche Picotte was the daughter of the Omaha chief Joseph La Flesche. As a child she studied with both Presbyterian and Quaker missionaries, who facilitated her entrance into school. She graduated from the Elizabeth Institute for Young Ladies in New Jersey, the Hampton Institute in Virginia, and in 1889 from the Women's Medical College of Pennsylvania. She was the first American Indian woman to become a medical doctor trained in the European-American tradition. She worked as a reservation doctor on the Omaha Reservation and as a medical missionary to her tribe. She was an advocate for Indian rights, speaking to Congress and to many religious congregations. She lobbied for resources to end tuberculosis among Native communities, for increased access to education, and for the prohibition of alcohol on reservations. She also advocated for local, Indian control of their own lands and for the right of individual Indian people to lease or sell their land without government supervision. In 1913 she founded a hospital on the Omaha Reservation that, following her death in 1915, was named after her. While she was deeply entrenched in and able to navigate the white world of schools, congressional halls, and churches, she also remained committed to her tribal community. Her sense of communal obligation and responsibility guided her in all her actions, and she sought to improve the welfare and well-being of the Omaha people.

John Fire Lame Deer
John Fire Lame Deer was born on the Rosebud Lakota Reservation in the late nineteenth century. He was a powerful Lakota spiritual leader who received his spiritual power from the thunder beings, or *wakinyan*. At sixteen he underwent his first vision quest; he was told in a vision of his great-grandfather that he would become an important spiritual leader and instruct many more medicine men who would follow him. Throughout his adult life he was a healer, using traditional herbs as well as traditional ceremonies such as the *yuwipi* to heal his patients. He was the father of Archie Fire Lame Deer, who also went on to become an important spiritual leader in his community. Lame Deer remained a practitioner of traditional Lakota religion, preferring not to follow any Christian traditions or the Native American Church. Remaining true to the Lakota traditions, and practicing them in a faithful way as they should be done, was, he said, more than enough for him. His commitment to his community and to their traditional way of life has helped to ensure its survival through a tumultuous century.

Low Horn (Atsitsi) (1822–1846/1899)
Born around 1822, Low Horn (Blackfoot) was one of the most important spiritual

leaders of his generation, along with such individuals as Black Eagle and the medicine woman Kitsin'iki. He was a powerful healer who doctored through the spirit-powers of sparrow hawk, rabbit, thunder, and mouse. He undertook a successful vision quest at thirteen, when he acquired his first spirit-power, thunder. In a dream he was given the spirit songs of sparrow hawk, and in other visions that of jackrabbit and mouse. He was a powerful medicine man and successful warrior. In 1846 he was killed in a battle with the Cree. Fearing his great power, the Cree dismembered his body and attempted to burn the remains. A burning ember from his body flew from the fire, and where it landed a bear emerged from the ground. The bear killed five of the Cree.

Low Horn was so powerful that he was able to reincarnate himself into a young Blackfoot, named Only Person Who Had a Different Gun. When he was six, Different Gun met Low Horn's widow, and he told those around him that she had once been his sweetheart. The next day, he and his family crossed the site where Low Horn had been killed. The boy began to cry, and told his family that this was where he had been killed. To prove his identity he instructed elders in his community to find certain objects that Low Horn had hidden before his death. Eventually the community accepted Different Gun as the reborn healer and began to call him Low Horn. From that time, Low Horn was apprenticed to the spiritual leaders and healers in his community and became a powerful healer. He had the ability to cure gunshot wounds, even those that white physicians could not heal. He died in 1899.

Mon'Hin Thin Ge

Mon'Hin Thin Ge (Omaha) was born in the early 1800s, and was an important spiritual leader and keeper of the Sacred Tent of War. Three sacred tents within Omaha tradition encompasses the most important elements of Omaha spirituality: the tent for the Sacred Pole, the Sacred Tent of War, and the Sacred Tent of the White Buffalo. Mon'Hin Thin Ge was chosen to keep the Tent of War. As an adolescent, Mon'Hin Thin Ge underwent the traditional Omaha vision quest, or *No'zhi zho,* which literally means "to stand sleeping." The vision that he received empowered him in his office as spiritual leader. During and just prior to his life, the Omaha experienced a number of devastating blows: in 1802 white traders brought smallpox to the Omaha, and the resulting epidemic decimated the community. The population dropped from 3,500 to fewer than 300. The nation's cultural continuity was further threatened by the U.S. government's relocation policies, by which the Omaha were forced west of their original homeland. They were resettled on the Omaha Reservation in Nebraska in 1854. The federal government forced them to cede the northern half of the reservation in 1865, for the resettlement of the Winnebago Nation.

These devastating events brought enormous cultural changes. In 1884, Mon'Hin Thin Ge feared that the knowledge of Omaha ceremonialism would be lost with him, and with it the proper care and respect for the Sacred Tent of War. Afraid that the objects would be neglected or abused, he gave them to Omaha physician Francis La Flesche and ethnologist Alice Fletcher. The sacred objects held within the Sacred Tent of War were placed in the Peabody Museum at Harvard University. The contents of the Sacred Tent of the Sacred Pole were likewise bequeathed to Peabody Museum by their keeper, Shu'-Denaci, in 1888. Happily, since 1989 the sacred pole, which is the most sacred object of Omaha ceremonialism, as well as the objects of the Sacred Tent of War, have been repatriated to the Omaha by the Peabody Museum.

Mountain Wolf Woman (Xeháchwinga) (1884–1960)

Si'ga'xunuga (Winnebago) was born in 1884 and was a traditional healer and peyote leader. When she was three years old, she became very ill and nearly died. An Indian medicine woman, named Wolf Woman, healed her. The woman then gave Si'ga'xunuga her healing powers and a new name, Xeháchwinga, which roughly translates as Mountain Wolf Woman. She spent eight years in a Lutheran mission school and was baptized there. She left the school to enter into a marriage arranged by her brothers, and did so against her will. The experience was unpleasant, and

she determined that her own children would choose their own spouses. She left her first husband and married Bad Soldier, with whom she had eleven children. Xeháchwinga had an active faith that integrated three traditions: traditional Winnebago spirituality, the peyote religion, and Christianity.

Her father, who taught his daughters to observe certain ritual practices and prayers, introduced her to traditional Winnebago spirituality. Her grandfather, Náqiwankwa'xo'piniga, who was a medicine man and who passed on his spiritual power to her, also instructed her in traditional Winnebago healing practices. In 1908 she was first introduced to peyote, which she used during the birth of her third child. The experience was so positive that she became an adherent of the peyote faith. While attending a peyote ceremony, she had a powerful vision of Jesus. The experience was profoundly moving, and following the experience she was convinced of the sacrality of the peyote way. After that she became a peyote leader. Her reputation as a peyote leader spread widely, and people came from far away to join the meetings. She integrated Christianity within her faith in peyote and continued to believe that peyote was a holy faith, blessed by Jesus, that would help Indian people to overcome alcoholism and other destructive behavior. Throughout her adult life she continued to practice both as a traditional Winnebago medicine woman and as a peyote leader with a faith in Jesus Christ. She died in 1960, just before her life story was put to press. *Mountain Wolf Woman: Sister of Crashing Thunder,* was edited by her adopted niece, Nancy Oestreich Lurie.

Porcupine (Hishkowitz) (1847–?)

Born around 1847, Porcupine (Cheyenne) was an important healer, spiritual leader, and spokesperson for the Cheyenne nation for more than forty years. Following a visit to Wovoka at Walker Lake, Nevada, he became a believer in the Ghost Dance, and he returned to his people as an advocate for the faith. His father was Arikara and his mother Lakota, but he joined the Cheyenne nation when he married a Cheyenne woman. He is well known for his bravery as a warrior, as well as for his leadership in the Ghost Dance. He led dances until the turn of the century, when he was arrested and sentenced to hard labor for practicing a faith that the federal government had outlawed. He was a successful healer within his communities until the end of his life, and well known for his ability to cure. He healed his patients with the use of spirit-power songs, sweet grass, a sacred rattle, a sacred pipe, and medicinal teas and roots.

Pretty Shield (1857–?)

Pretty Shield (Crow) was born around 1857, and was a powerful medicine woman among her people. She was one of three sisters, all of whom married a man named Goes-Ahead. When she was sixteen, she was struck with smallpox and nearly died. A Crow medicine

woman, Sharp-Skin, healed her, and the experience left her with a sensitivity for healing the illnesses of others. As a young wife, she experienced the death of a baby girl. During her mourning period, she fasted and slept very little. She prayed for a vision that would give her comfort and also be a blessing to her community.

While in a medicine dream state, she had a vision of a spirit woman. The woman instructed her in a number of rituals that she was to perform. Once she had done them, Pretty Shield was instructed to enter a beautiful lodge that had a war eagle at its head. Following that, Pretty Shield was given the spirit-power of war eagle. Later she was also given the spirit-power of ants, a powerful spirit that enabled her to do great things. She became a wise elder and respected medicine woman. When Pretty Shield was seventy-four, she told her life story, describing the ways of the Crow people as well as traditional passages of life, such as childhood, courtship, marriage, and childbirth, to Frank Linderman. The resulting book, *Red Mother,* was published in 1932. It was reprinted in 1972 and retitled *Pretty Shield: Medicine Woman of the Crows.*

Quanah Parker (1850–1911)

Quanah Parker was born around 1850, the son of Peta Nocona, a chief of the Quahada band of Comanche, and a white woman, Cynthia Ann Parker. Cynthia Ann Parker was captured in 1836 along with her brother when she was nine years old and later married Peta No-cona. She was recaptured by a white man in 1860. She repeatedly begged to be allowed to return to the Comanche and her husband and children but was never allowed to do so. She died in 1864. Parker was known for his success as a warrior, as well as for his role in promoting the peyote religion throughout the Plains. Parker fiercely resisted white encroachment on Comanche lands, surrendering only after years of resistance. Following his surrender, however, Parker quickly adapted to the white world. He encouraged the Comanche to be educated in white schools and to learn to navigate the white world. By 1867 he was chief of the Kwahadi band of the Comanche.

The peyote faith would have been a part of Comanche culture throughout his life, as the Comanche had been using peyote since the early 1800s. But it was not until 1884, when Parker became seriously ill and was cured with the aid of peyote, that it became an important part of his life. From that time on, he defended the use of peyote against government and Christian opposition. He saw it as a means by which Native people could not merely talk about Jesus, but speak directly to Jesus. Parker went on to be a judge in the Courts of Indian Offences, which was established by Indian agents on Indian reservations. He was a chief representative for the Comanche people during the Dawes Act of 1887, and he later became a successful businessman and friend of President Theodore Roosevelt, while never aban-doning his faith in the peyote religion or his belief in the value of the traditional Comanche way of life.

Sanapia (1895–1968)

Sanapia (Comanche) was born in 1895 and was a powerful medicine woman. She attended the Cache Creek Mission School, before undertaking four years of intensive study to become an Eagle Doctor. She trained with her mother, a Comanche-Arapaho, and her mother's older brother, both of whom were Eagle Doctors. During her training she was closely observed by her mother, uncle, maternal grandmother, and paternal grandfather. When they all approved, she was accorded a blessing ceremony and granted the status of Eagle Doctor.

In her training she studied the diagnosis of illness, the use of medicinal plants, and important ritual actions and restrictions. She doctored with the use of herbal medicines; sacred songs; the spirit power of the eagle, which was called forth through her medicine songs; and by sucking the object that had caused the illness out of the patient's body. She was particularly skilled at curing Ghost Sickness, a dangerous ailment. In her religious life, she was exposed to the traditional Comanche faith by her mother and uncle, the peyote religion by her uncle and grandfather, and Christianity by her father. She incorporated elements of all these traditions within her worldview and approach to healing. Although she completed her training to be an Eagle Doctor when she was seventeen, she was not able to begin her work as a healer until after menopause. Her first healing took place in the late 1930s, when she healed her sister's child. She died in 1968.

Sitting Bull (Haná cha-thí ak) (1854–1932)

Sitting Bull (Arapaho) was born around 1854; he was an important Ghost Dance leader and prophet. One should not confuse him with the Hunkpapa Sioux principal chief Sitting Bull. Haná cha-thí ak accompanied several other men, including Kicking Bear, to visit the prophet Wovoka, who had founded the new Ghost Dance religion. He returned to the Arapaho and began teaching the songs, dance, and message of the Ghost Dance.

The Ghost Dance taught that a messiah was coming, that soon the world would be remade, that the white people would be removed from the land, and that the dead would return to life, joining their living relatives. The buffalo would return and the world would be reborn. Wovoka taught that Indians should live peacefully with whites but maintain their traditional way of life. They should abstain from alcohol, gambling, and violence. Sitting Bull received a vision that when this great event came, the whites would be removed from the land by a great wall of fire. Native people would be protected from the fire by sacred eagle feathers, and a great rain would then put the fire out.

Sitting Bull held large Ghost Dances at which thousands of people attended, including Arapaho, Cheyenne, Caddo, Wichita, and Kiowa. Participants received visions of the spirit world and communicated with departed relatives. In 1890, Sitting Bull advised the Arapaho to sell their reservation lands to the U.S. government for needed money. He firmly believed that the land would soon be restored to them with the coming of the messiah and the re-creation of the world. When the lands were not soon returned, and when the Ghost Dance movement entered into a rapid decline following the massacre at Wounded Knee, Sitting Bull lost influence and his position as spiritual leader. He died in 1932.

Tenskwatawa (c. 1775–1836) and Tecumseh (c. 1768–1813)

Born in 1775, Tenskwatawa was an important Shawnee spiritual leader who worked alongside his brother Tecumseh toward a revitalization of Shawnee culture and a political alliance with other Native people. In 1806, Tenskwatawa became ill and died. He revived suddenly, telling his people that he had had a vision from the Master of Life that showed him a beautiful country reserved for those who lived honorable lives, and a world of fiery torture for those who led wicked lives. He taught that the Shawnee should turn from drinking, intertribal violence, polygamy, intermarriage with whites, and promiscuity, and return to traditional Shawnee ways of life. He demonstrated his spiritual power by accurately predicting the total eclipse of the sun that took place on June 16, 1806.

Shawnee mystic Tenskwatawa served as a spiritual guide and inspiration for his brother Tecumseh. Early 1800s. (North Wind Picture Archives)

Tenskwatawa's religious movement served as a spiritual guide and inspiration for his brother Tecumseh's political goal of forming a pantribal confederacy. The brothers hoped to form an alliance that would prevent further expansion of white settlers. He and his brother traveled widely, from present-day Wisconsin to present-day Florida, advocating their religious and political visions. Tenskwatawa lost influence after a failed military engagement with U.S. troops. In 1813 he fled to Canada, and his religious movement came to an end.

Suzanne J. Crawford and
Karen D. Lone Hill

See also American Indian Movement (Red Power Movement); Bundles, Sacred Bundle Traditions; Ecology and Environmentalism; Ghost Dance Movement; Health and Wellness, Traditional Approaches; Missionization, Northern Plains; Native American Church, Peyote Movement; Power, Plains; Retraditionalism and Revitalization Movements; Sacred Pipe; Sweatlodge; Tobacco, Sacred Use of; Vision Quest Rites; *Yuwipi* Ceremony

References and Further Reading
Axelrod, Alan. 1993. *Chronicle of the Indian Wars: From Colonial Times to Wounded Knee.* Englewood Cliffs, NJ: Prentice Hall.
Deloria, Vine. 1969. *Custer Died for Your Sins: An Indian Manifesto.* New York: Macmillan.
———. 1973. *God Is Red: A Native View of Religion.* New York: Grosset and Dunlap.
———. 1974. *Behind the Trail of Broken Treaties: An Indian Declaration of Independence.* New York: Delacorte Press.
———. 1999. *For This Land: Writings on Religion in America.* New York: Routledge.
Fikes, J. C., ed. 1998. *Reuben Snake: Your Humble Serpent.* Santa Fe: Clear Light Publications.
Fletcher, Alice C., and Francis La Flesche. 1911. *The Omaha Tribe.* Washington, DC: Smithsonian Institution.
Grinnell, George Bird. 1962. *The Cheyenne Indians: Their History and Ways of Life.* New York: Cooper Square Publishers.
Hittman, Michael. 1990. *Wovoka and the Ghost Dance.* Carson City, NV: Grace Dangberg Foundation.
Horse Capture, George. 1980. *The Seven Visions of Bull Lodge.* Lincoln: University of Nebraska Press.
Johnson, Troy. 2002. *Distinguished Native American Spiritual Practitioners and Healers.* Phoenix, AZ: Oryx Press.
Jones, David E. 1972. *Sanapia: Comanche Medicine Woman.* Prospect Heights, IL: Waveland Press.
Lame Deer, Archie Fire, and Richard Erdoes. 1994. *Gift of Power: The Life and Teachings of a Lakota Medicine Man.* Santa Fe: Bear and Company.
Lame Deer, John Fire, and Richard Erdoes. 1972/1994. *Lame Deer: Seeker of Visions.* Reprint, New York: Washington Square Press.

Linderman, Frank B. 1972. *Pretty Shield: Medicine Woman of the Crows.* Lincoln: University of Nebraska Press.

Lurie, Nancy Oestreich. 1961. *Mountain Wolf Woman: Sister of Crashing Thunder.* Ann Arbor: University of Michigan Press.

Mails, Thomas. 1990. *Fools Crow.* Lincoln: University of Nebraska Press.

McAllister, J. G. 1970. *Davéko Kiowa Apache Medicine Man.* Austin: Texas Memorial Museum.

Neeley, Bill. 1995. *The Last Comanche Chief: The Life and Times of Quanah Parker.* New York: Wiley.

Paper, Jordan. 1989. *Offering Smoke: The Sacred Pipe and Native American Religion.* Moscow: University of Idaho Press.

Steinmetz, Paul B. 1990. *Pipe, Bible, and Peyote among the Oglala Lakota: A Study in Religious Identity.* Knoxville: University of Tennessee Press.

Stewart, Omar. 1990. *Peyote Religion: A History.* Norman: University of Oklahoma Press.

Sugden, John. 1998. *Tecumseh: A Life.* New York: Henry Holt and Company.

Tong, Benson. 2000. *Susan La Flesche Picotte, M.D.: Omaha Indian Leader and Reformer.* Norman: University of Oklahoma Press.

Vander, Judith. 1988. *Songprints: The Musical Experience of Five Shoshone Women.* Urbana: University of Illinois Press.

Religious Leaders, Plateau

Jake Hunt, Klickitat (c. 1860–1910 or 1914)

Jake Hunt founded the Waptashi, or Feather Religion. Born on the White Salmon River near Husum, Washington, in the 1860s, Hunt was raised in the Washani or Longhouse religion. He was a follower of Smohalla, the Wanapum Dreamer prophet. Following the death of his wife and son, Hunt received a vision that inspired the new religion. In Hunt's vision he saw Lishwailait, a Klickitat prophet. Lishwailait was standing in the center of a circular disk of light that symbolized an expanse of land, the earth. Lishwailait was dressed in traditional clothing, wore two eagle feathers in his hair, and carried a small drum and drumstick. Following the vision, Hunt stopped grieving for his wife and son, both of whom had died within months of each other, and built a longhouse.

The Waptashi, or Feather Religion, drew on elements of Waashat traditions and the Indian Shaker Church. Like other Dreamer Prophets of the time, Hunt advised his followers to reject white acculturation and return to Native traditions. Like the Shaker Church, the Waptashi advocate abstaining from alcohol; healing is a central part of worship, and services are held in a longhouse. Like the Waashat, Waptashi adherents continue to honor first foods ceremonies, celebrating the first salmon, berries, roots, and game of the year.

The Waptashi can be distinguished from the *Waashat,* or Seven Drums religion practiced throughout the Plateau, by its use of feathers and spinning (*waskliki*) in rituals. These elements are intended both to purify individuals and to help them attain spiritual assistance. Eagle feathers are held during services, and hand mirrors, which were also present in Hunt's vision, are used as well.

Hunt traveled widely throughout the Plateau, teaching about his new religion. When he was unable to cure a man on the Umatilla Reservation, the reservation agent banished him from the reservation and destroyed Hunt's sacred objects. He died sometime between 1910 and 1914.

Chief Joseph, Nez Perce (1840–1904)
Chief Joseph was born in the Wallowa Valley in 1840 and was named *Hin mah tooyah lat kekt,* or Thunder Rolling Down the Mountain. Chief Joseph led the Nez Perce during an era of rapid change and white encroachment on Native lands. While not an official religious leader, Chief Joseph was a central cultural and spiritual leader to his people during a time of violence, oppression, and forced relocation. His resistance to white encroachment on Native lands, and his insistence on fighting for his people's right to their Native homeland, continues to be a powerful symbol of Native strength, endurance, and commitment to their traditional spiritual values.

Throughout their history with white settlers, the Nez Perce had been cooperative and peaceful, remaining neutral or even assisting the government in their Indian wars. In 1855, Joseph's father cooperated with the territorial governor of Washington to establish a reservation for the Nez Perce, one that stretched from Oregon to Idaho, covering 5,000 square miles and including their Wallowa Valley homeland. In 1863, following the discovery of gold in the Wallowa Valley and a sudden rush of white settlers, the federal government produced another treaty. This treaty reduced the reservation to a tenth of its former size and did not in-

Chief Joseph (Hin mah tooyah lat kekt, or Thunder Rolling Down the Mountain), Nez Perce. Chief Joseph was a central cultural and spiritual leader who sought to preserve Nez Perce lands and traditions. 1900. (Gill, De Lancey/Library of Congress)

clude their homeland in the Wallowa Valley. Furious over the betrayal, Joseph's father destroyed his U.S. flag and Bible and refused to leave the valley.

Threatened with military force, Chief Joseph regretfully agreed to move to the new reservation. But on the way, a group of frustrated Nez Perce men attacked and killed several white settlers. This began the war between the Nez Perce and the U.S. Army that lasted a year and covered 1,400 miles. By the end many Nez Perce had been killed, in battle or by cold and lack of food. Joseph bitterly surrendered at the Bear Paw Mountains in 1877. In his often quoted speech, he said: "I am tired of fighting. . . . Hear me, my chiefs, my heart is sick and sad. From where the sun now stands I will fight no more against the white man" (Joseph 1995).

Despite promises that they would be returned to their reservation, Joseph and his followers were incarcerated and sent to Oklahoma, where many died of malaria and starvation. In 1879, Joseph pleaded his case in Washington, D.C., before President Rutherford Hayes. But it was not until 1885 that Joseph and the 268 remaining nontreaty Nez Perce were allowed to return to the Northwest. Even then, only half of them were allowed to go to the Nez Perce reservation. Joseph and half of his followers were sent to the Colville reservation in northern Washington, where he died in 1904.

Chief Joseph remains a pivotal character in the history and cultural identity of Native people of the Plateau. His 1879 speech before federal officials in Washington, D.C., remains a powerful statement of the ethical and spiritual position upon which he based his actions and his leadership:

> I have heard talk and talk but nothing is done. Good words do not last long unless they amount to something. Words do not pay for my dead people. They do not pay for my country now overrun by white men. They do not protect my father's grave. They do not pay for my horses and cattle. Good words do not give me back my children. Good words will not give my people a home where they can live in peace and take care of themselves. I am tired of talk that comes to nothing. It makes my heart sick when I remember all the good words and all the broken promises. If the white man wants to live in peace with the Indian he can live in peace. There need be no trouble. Treat all men alike. . . . All men were made by the same Great Spirit Chief. They are all brothers. The earth is the mother of all people, and all people should have equal rights upon it. You might as well expect all rivers to run backward as that any man who was born a free man should be contented penned up and denied liberty to go where he pleases. If you tie a horse to a stake, do you expect he will grow fat? If you pen an Indian up on a small spot of earth and compel him to stay there, he will not be contented nor will he grow and prosper. . . . I only ask of the Government to be treated as all other men are treated. . . . We only ask an even chance to live as other men live. . . . Let me be a free man, free to travel, free to stop, free to work, free to trade where I choose, free to choose my own teachers, free to follow the religion of my fathers, free to talk, think and act for myself—and I will obey every law or submit to the penalty. . . . Then the Great Spirit Chief who rules above will smile upon this land and send rain to wash out the bloody spots made by brothers' hands upon the face of the earth. For this time the Indian race is waiting and praying. I hope no more groans of wounded men and women will ever go to the ear of the Great Spirit Chief above, and that all people may be one people. *Hin-mah-too-yah-lat-kekht* has spoken for his people. (ibid.)

Kau'xuma'nupika (Kokomenepeca), Kutenai (c.1780–?)

As a prophet and religious leader, Kau'xuma'nupika sought to encourage Native resistance to white settlement and the survival of Native culture on the Columbia River. She predicted the arrival of epidemics brought by white immigrants, the imminent devastation of Indian lands, the destruction of the world, and the subsequent arrival of a golden age in which Indian peoples would be restored to their former strength and the dead would return to life. Several early written records from the early nineteenth century mention Kau'xuma'nupika. Ross Cox was one Euro-American who met Kau-xuma-nupika in person. As he recalled: "Among the visitors who every now and then presented themselves were two strange Indians, in the character of man and wife. . . . The husband, named Kocomenepeca was a very shrewd and intelligent Indian, who addressed us in the Algonquin language, and gave us much information respecting the interior of the country." Ross noted shortly thereafter that "they were both females" (Cox 1831, 92).

Kau'xuma'nupika was a Kutenai woman who had been briefly married to a white trader. She soon left her husband, declaring that she was at heart a man and would live the life of a prophet. She joined, and led, a number of war parties among the Kutenai, gaining status as a spiritual leader and warrior. Leslie Spier argued that "at length she became the principal leader of her tribe, under the designation of 'Manlike Woman.' Being young, and of delicate frame, her followers attributed her exploits to the possession of supernatural power, and therefore received whatever she said with implicit faith" (Spier 1935, 26–27). In 1811 she arrived in the Columbia River Valley with "a young wife, of whom she pretended to be very jealous" (Tyrell 1916, 512–513, 920). Kau'xuma'nupika was a powerful prophet who mobilized early resistance to white cultural encroachment and encouraged Native resistance to Christian missionization during a time of epidemic disease and the arrival of large numbers of white settlers.

Lillian Pitt, Warm Springs and Yakima (1943–)

Born in 1943 on the Warm Springs Reservation in Oregon, Lillian Pitt spent much of her life on the Columbia River Plateau. A nationally recognized artist, she now lives and runs her gallery, Kindred Spirits Gallery, in Portland, Oregon. Her work is inspired by and reflective of the living spiritual and cultural tradition of the Plateau. Her masks and sculpture are inspired by the stories, symbols, and spiritual traditions she learned growing upon the Warm Springs Reservation. She is a recipient of the Governor's Award of the Oregon Arts Commission.

Her ceramic masks and "Shadow Spirit" totem images are based on the symbolic and spiritual traditions of her Columbia River heritage. Her mixed-media installations make use of natural

materials in order to memorialize her ancestors. As she describes her approach:

> The focus of my current sculptural
> work is to combine diverse materials
> to create a rich visual context for the
> stoneware forms I hand build and fire.
> I combine beads, feathers, shells,
> strands of copper wire, stones, thread,
> and peeled or weathered wood—
> materials which allow for startling
> juxtapositions of texture and color that
> move the eye. With these materials,
> sometimes I adorn the work; at other
> times I mend or reassemble things
> that have been torn asunder. My aim is
> to heal the things of this wounded
> planet by creating a consciousness of
> the need for healing and a sense of the
> transformative magic in ordinary
> things and beings. I orient my work in
> relation to the four winds, the seven
> directions, and at times celebrate the
> ancient stories of my Warm Springs,
> Wascho, and Wishxam ancestors in the
> imagery I create. There are also times
> when new characters are born in
> response to the contradictions caused
> by remembering traditions that reveal
> the madness of current culture which
> destroys so much that has sustained
> life in our world. These characters tell
> their own stories, and new myths are
> born as I reflect on their meaning. In
> this work, I aim to create a visual
> language that will translate the stress
> on things in the natural world into a
> voice that will make everyone aware of
> the responsibility we all have to work
> inside the circle of things that supports
> life on earth. (http://www.stonington-
> gallery.com/artists/pitt.htm)

Perhaps her most famous piece, "She
Who Watches," is inspired by the well-
known Columbia River petroglyph. As she
describes the piece: "She Who Watches is
a pictograph found along the Columbia
River. She overlooked the village where
my great-grandmother lived. Because she
wanted to watch over my people forever,
Coyote changed her into a rock. Under
her watchful gaze, my people remember
her as the last woman chief of the Columbia River People" (www.lillianpitt.com).

Her work, which translates traditional
Plateau symbolic and spiritual traditions
into artistic form, is in several major col-
lections throughout the world, including
the Burke Museum at the University of
Washington, the Heard Museum in
Phoenix, Arizona, and the Sapporo City
Hall, in Sapporo, Japan.

Skolaskin (also Kolaskin), Sanpoil (1839–1922)

Skolaskin, a Sanpoil, was born around
1839 in the village of Sinakialt on the Columbia River. Like Smohalla, Skolaskin
received a vision and messages for his
people from the Creator during a near-
death experience. His message called for
an adherence to traditional lifeways, a
repudiation of private land ownership,
and a return to traditional subsistence
patterns such as salmon fishing, root
gathering, and hunting. His message
also provided a strict moral code and advocated peaceful resistance against the
encroachment of white settlers and the
U.S. government. Incarcerated on Alcatraz Island from 1889 to 1892, Skolaskin
was accused by the government of inciting reservation unrest and resistance to
white control. After his release, Skolaskin

returned to the Colville Reservation and continued to demand that the people return to traditional modes of spirituality and subsistence.

Like Smohalla and other Plateau Dreamer prophets, Skolaskin played a pivotal role in the survival of traditional indigenous beliefs and practices into the colonial era. These prophets adopted certain elements of Christianity, such as Sunday meetings in a permanent structure (the longhouse) and the occasional incorporation of Christian symbols like the bell, the cross, or the Bible. These outward symbols made the evolving tradition a viable alternative to Christianity for many Native people. These prophets also facilitated the survival of traditional lifeways, by demanding that their followers continue traditional modes of dress, subsistence food gathering, family and kinship networks, marriage, and other rites of passage. Their message of sobriety, health, and healing also came at a pivotal time, when many Native people's well-being was threatened by the importation of alcohol and disease by white settlers.

As a young man, Skolaskin suffered an injury that permanently disabled him, making it difficult for him to stand upright or walk without the assistance of a staff. It was during his recovery from this illness that he nearly died. He visited the Creator Spirit (or *Quilentsuten*), who advised him to return to his people and preach this message: the people should reject the imposition of white culture in all its forms. His authority among his people was ensured when an earthquake, which he had predicted, occurred in 1872.

On November 21, 1889, frightened by his influence over his followers and his continued resistance to non-Native encroachment on Native lands, the federal government arrested Skolaskin and imprisoned him without trial on Alcatraz Island.

In his later life, Skolaskin himself converted to Catholicism. However, the faith that he inspired and helped to set in motion, now called the Longhouse, or Seven Drums, religion, is still widely practiced on the Colville Reservation and throughout the Plateau.

Smohalla (Smowhalla), Wanapum (1815–1895)

Smohalla, a Dreamer prophet on the Columbia Plateau in the mid-nineteenth century, is often credited with having originated the Waashat religion, also known as the Seven Drums or Longhouse religion. He was born between 1815 and 1820 in Wallula on the Columbia River in Washington state and gained power through the traditional mode of a vision quest, or *wot*, when he was still young. He was given the spirit-powers of *shah* (crow), and *speelyi* (coyote). He was known by many names, including Wak'wei or Kuk'kia when he was young. When he took up his role as a prophet, he became known as Smohalla, which translates as "dreamer" or "preacher." He was also known by his people as *Yuyunipitqana,* or Shouting Mountain.

A portrait of Mourning Dove from Mourning Dove, a Salishan Autobiography. *(Courtesy of Jay Miller/University of Nebraska Press)*

On two occasions, Smohalla died and traveled to the spirit world, where he was given a vision and message to take back to his people. He called for a return to traditional Native ways of life and a rejection of efforts to forcefully assimilate Native people into white society. He taught his followers that the world would soon be made new. All faithful Native people would return to life, European settlers would be removed from the land, and the earth would be restored to its previous strength and beauty. He called

for the institution of Sunday services, seasonal holidays to celebrate the first foods (salmon, berries, roots, game), and the return to a traditionalist way of life (Hunn 1990, 253). He condemned the restriction of Native people to reservations and the loss of traditional modes of subsistence. Smohalla's message of an apocalyptic cataclysm with the return of the dead and a righteous life and strict adherence to tradition was particularly powerful because it came at a time when Native communities of the Plateau were threatened by encroaching white settlers, the U.S. military, and vast epidemics that swept through the region.

Smohalla based his community of followers at the village of P'na, at Priest Rapids on the Columbia River. When Euro-American settlers and military attempted to coerce Smohalla and his followers into a life of agriculture on reservations, he responded with a clear religious and ethical doctrine which demanded that the earth be treated with respect. "You ask me to plough the ground? Shall I take a knife and tear my mother's bosom? Then when I die she will not take me to her bosom to rest. You ask me to dig for a stone? Shall I dig under her skin for her bones? Then when I die I cannot enter her body to be born again. You ask me to cut the grass and make hay and sell it, and be rich like white men, but how dare I cut off my mother's hair?" (MacMurray 1887, 248).

During his life Smohalla interacted with and inspired many prophets throughout the Plateau, who carried similar messages of spiritual revival to their own people. These included Koti-akan, who worked closely alongside Smohalla. This Yakima Dreamer prophet taught his followers at Pa'kiut village on the Yakima River. Following a death and rebirth experience similar to that of Smo-halla, he heard a voice telling him that he was to worship the Great Spirit with song and dance, and to do so on Sundays. A Tyigh Dreamer prophet named Queah-pahmah was also active at this time, ad-vising his more than 200 followers to re-fuse the allotment of farms and annuity goods from the government and to return to traditional hunting, fishing, and gath-ering. A Umatilla prophetess Luls (also Lals) advised her own people to maintain their traditional ceremonies, celebrating the first roots, berries, fish, and game of the year. Like these other prophets, Smo-halla's central message remained a call for the preservation and veneration of the land and its eventual return to Native people; his authority came from visions received while in a ceremonial setting or near-death experience.

Smohalla and other Dreamer pro-phets were central in revitalizing in-digenous religious and cultural prac-tices during a time of intense stress. Illness brought by white settlers ran rampant among Native communities. The U.S. military and growing numbers of white settlers and missionaries placed an enormous amount of pres-sure on Native communities to assimi-late into white culture, or become wards of the state on reservations. Dreamer prophets provided an ethical code, a traditionalist way of life, and a mode of worship that enabled indigenous cul-ture and spirituality to survive through this devastating era.

Smohalla died in 1895 and was suc-ceeded by his son, Yoyonan (also Yu'yunne), who carried on the move-ment until he died in 1917. Yoyonan was succeeded by his cousin, Puck Hyah Toot, who continued as a central Washat leader well into the twentieth century. In 1989, Smohalla was selected for the state of Washington's Hall of Honor, as one of 100 people whose life had significantly influenced the state and the nation.

Suzanne J. Crawford

See also Ceremony and Ritual, Coeur D'Alene; Ceremony and Ritual, Nez Perce; Gender and Sexuality, Two Spirits; Ghost Dance Movement; Guardian Spirit Complex; Indian Shaker Church; Masks and Masking; Mourning Dove; Oral Traditions, Plateau; Retraditionalism and Revitalization Movements, Columbia Plateau.

References and Further Reading
Axtell, Horace, and Margo Aragon. 1997. *A Little Bit of Wisdom: Conversations with a Nez Perce Elder.* Lewiston, ID: Confluence Press.
Beal, Merrill. 1998. *I Will Fight No More Forever: Chief Joseph and the Nez Perce War.* Seattle: University of Washington Press.
Cox, Ross. 1831. *Adventures on the Columbia River, Including the Narrative of a Residence of Six Years on the Western Side of the Rocky Mountains, among Various Tribes of Indians Hitherto Unknown; Together With a Journey Across the American Continent.* Two Vols. London: Henry Colburn and Richard Bentley.

DuBois, Cora. 1938. *The Feather Cult of the Middle Columbia*. General Series in Anthropology 7. Menasha, WI: George Banta.

Hunn, Eugene S., with James Selam and Family. 1990. *N'ch'i-Wana, "The Big River": Mid-Columbia Indians and Their Land*. Seattle: University of Washington.

(Chief) Joseph. 1995. *That All People May Be One People, Send Rain to Wash the Face of the Earth*. Sitka, AK: Mountain Meadow Press.

Lillian Pitt Art Gallery. "About the Artist." http://www.lillianpitt.com. (Accessed September 15, 2002.)

MacMurray, Major Junius Wilson. 1887. "Dreamers of the Columbia River Valley in Washington Territory." *Transactions of the Albany Institute* 11: 248.

Mooney, James. 1965. *The Ghost Dance Religion*. Vol. 2: *Fourteenth Annual Report of the Bureau of Ethnology to the Secretary of the Smithsonian Institution, 1892–93*. Chicago: University of Chicago Press.

Relander, Click. 1956. *Drummers and Dreamers*. Northwest Interpretive Association. Caldwell, Idaho, Caxton Printers.

Ruby, Robert, and John Brown. 1989. *Dreamer Prophets of the Columbia Plateau: Smohalla and Skolaskin*. Norman: University of Oklahoma Press.

Spier, Leslie. 1935. *The Prophet Dance of the Northwest and Its Derivatives: The Source of the Ghost Dance*. American Anthropological Association. General Series in Anthropology, 1.

Stonington Gallery. "Lillian Pitt Biography." http://www.stoningtongallery.com/artists/pitt.htm. (Accessed September 15, 2002.)

Tyrell, J. B., ed. 1916. *David Thompson's Narrative of His Explorations in Western America, 1784–1812*. Toronto: The Champlain Society.

Vibert, Elizabeth. 1995. "'The Native Peoples Were Strong to Live': Reinterpreting Early Nineteenth Century Prophetic Movements in the Columbia Plateau." *Ethnohistory* 42, no. 4: 197–229.

Religious Leaders, Pueblo

Thomas Banyacya (Hopi) (1909–1999)

Thomas Banyacya was born June 2, 1909, in the Hopi village of Moencopi, Arizona, and was part of the Fox, Coyote, and Wolf clan from his mother's side. The name Banyacya refers to his father's clans, the Corn and Water clans (the name evokes the image of corn plants in a field of standing water). As a child, Banyacya attended the Sherman Indian school in Riverside, California, and in 1930 he attended Bacone College in Oklahoma. Responding to the lack of classes and resources on Native culture, language, and religion, Banyacya and his fellow students joined together to build a medicine lodge on campus and began performing ceremonies and songs.

During the 1940s, because traditional Hopi beliefs do not condone participation in war, Banyacya refused to register for the draft in World War II. As a result he spent seven years in prison. When he was released, Banyacya successfully petitioned the federal government to allow Hopi people conscientious objector status, excusing future Hopi men from registering.

In 1948 traditional Hopi leaders, the Kikmongwis, gathered to discuss the state of the world. Deeply disturbed by the events of the previous years and in particular the dropping of the atomic bomb on Japan, Hopi elders noted that their own oral traditions, prophecies, and religious traditions spoke directly to the ominous developments of the day. From this meeting, four spokespersons were appointed, of whom Thomas Banyacya was the last survivor.

Banyacya spent half a century traveling throughout the United States and the world, discussing the protection of indigenous cultures, the need to protect Mother Earth, and the dangers of contemporary consumerism and militarism. Throughout his travels in other countries, Banyacya refused to use a U.S. passport. Rather, he used a Hopi passport that he had helped to design.

Beginning in the summer of 1952, Banyacya helped to organized a series of six caravans that traveled across the United States. These caravans traveled with the intent of provoking interest and pride among Native communities in their religious and cultural heritages. These convoys traveled from reservation to reservation, and city to city, having an enormous effect on the development of American Indian retraditionalism and cultural identity in the latter half of the twentieth century. The caravans gathered together some of the most important cultural, spiritual, and political leaders in Indian Country at that time, and helped to revive Native languages, cultures, and religious practice. The caravans served as the foundations for what was in the 1960s and 1970s to become the American Indian Movement.

On December 10, 1992, Thomas Banyacya spoke to the UN General Assembly, calling upon world leaders to heal the ravages of environmental destruction, to put an end to warfare, and to feed and care for the poor and hungry. Excerpts from his speech to the General Assembly follow (*See* Hopi Prophecy):

> The traditional Hopi follows the spiritual path that was given to us by Massau'u the Great Spirit. We made a sacred covenant to follow his life plan at all times, which includes the responsibility of taking care of this land and life for his divine purpose. . . . We still have our ancient sacred stone tablets and spiritual religious societies which are the foundations of the Hopi way of life. . . . What have you as individuals, as nations, and as the world body been doing to take care of this Earth? In the Earth today, humans poison their own food, water and air with pollution. Many of us including children are left to starve. Many wars are still being fought. . . . Nature itself does not speak with a voice that we can easily understand. . . . Who in this world can speak for nature and the spiritual energy that creates and flows through all life? . . .The native peoples of the world have seen and spoken to you about the destruction of their lives and homelands, the ruination of nature and the desecration of their sacred sites. It is time the United Nations used its rules to investigate these occurrences and stop them now. (Banyacya 1992)

Juan de Jesus Romero, Deer Bird (Taos Pueblo) (1874–1978)

Born in 1874, Romero belonged to a hereditary family of *caciques*. As cacique, or spiritual leader, Romero was responsi-

Juan de Jesus Romero (center), religious leader of the Pueblo, and interpreter Paul Bernal witness as President Richard Nixon signs a bill on December 15, 1970, that gives the Taos Pueblo Indians title to their sacred Blue Lake and 48,000 acres of land surrounding it in New Mexico. Washington, D.C. (Bettmann/Corbis)

ble for carrying out the complex ceremonies and rituals of the Taos Pueblo. The ceremonial cycles, oral traditions, and rituals have existed since the Taos emerged from the underworld. This emergence, they believe, occurred at Blue Lake (Maxolo), the sacred center for the Taos people. It was there that the world was created. Because of this, it is the location of annual ceremonies celebrating the creation of the world and the Taos people.

Despite their long-lasting tie to Blue Lake, the lake was made part of the Carson National Forest in 1906. The Taos peo-

ple were allowed to occupy and use the land only with a permit, while hunters and tourists had unrestricted access. As Taos elder member Paul Bernal testified at a 1969 congressional hearing, "We are probably the only citizens of the United States who are required to practice our religion under a permit from the Government. This is not religious freedom as it is guaranteed by the Constitution" (http://www.sacredland.org/taos_blue_lake.html). Such access, the Taos people felt, violated the sacred nature of the place.

Beginning in 1906, Juan de Jesus Romero led an effort by the Taos people to regain ownership of this traditional sacred site. As he himself argued, "[If] our land is not returned to us, if it is turned over to the government for its use, then it is the end of Indian life. Our people will scatter as the people of other nations have scattered. It is our religion that holds us together" (http://www .sacredland.org/taos_blue_lake.html). He argued that in taking Blue Lake, which is inherently tied to his people's cultural traditions, the government threatened to erode Pueblo unity and their very identity. For many years he met with little success, rejecting offers from the federal government to buy the land. In 1970, at the age of ninety-six, he went to Washington, D.C., and pleaded his case before Richard Nixon. In July 1970, President Nixon endorsed legislation to return the lake to Taos ownership. Following Senate approval, Blue Lake and 48,000 acres of surrounding wilderness were returned to the Taos people in 1971, in very large part because of Romero's unceasing efforts. Romero died in 1978. He was 104 years old.

Popé, Po'pay (Tewa, San Juan Pueblo) (c. 1630–c. 1690)

Born around 1630 in San Juan Pueblo, Popé (*Po'pay*, or Ripe Squash) was raised within the traditional Tewa culture, spiritually honoring the cycles of seasons, the planting of crops, and praying with corn pollen. As a young man he was made assistant to the tribal War Captain, learning the ceremonial war dances and how to supervise them. He was soon appointed War Captain by the village leaders, and he carried out a great many social and spiritual obligations within that role. He soon became aware of the increasing threat that Spanish colonization posed to the traditional Pueblo way of life, the Spanish having first entered the area in the 1590s. Spanish settlers and the military that accompanied them coerced Indian people into forced labor. The Pueblo people were compelled to contribute their labor to building Spanish churches and were required to give food and labor to Spanish settlers. The *encomienda* system required Pueblo people to provide Spanish settlers with a portion of the pueblo's crops, as the Spanish were not able to grow enough food to support themselves. Spanish colonial authorities also exerted a system of *repartimiento,* whereby Pueblo Indians were forced to work for Spanish settlers, tending their homes, animals, and gardens without payment. Spanish missions likewise exerted enormous pressure on Pueblo people to abandon their traditional religious practice. Pueblo people were coerced into attending services, and traditional worship centers were vandalized or destroyed by Spanish militias. Priests boasted of having destroyed traditional Pueblo religious regalia and ritual equipment.

In 1675, frustrated by their lack of success in converting the Pueblo people, Spanish officials arrested forty-seven Pueblo religious leaders, charging them with sorcery. Four men were condemned to death, and the remaining forty-three, including Popé, were publicly lashed. The Pueblo people were forced to witness these punishments being carried out.

After his release, Popé began organizing the Pueblo people to resist and overthrow the Spanish colonial presence. At his direction, two messengers were sent out to all the Pueblo villages to gather support for the resistance. When colonial governor Antonio de Otermin learned of the resistance, he arrested the two messengers. In fear and anger, the villagers responded by killing a Spaniard and their padre, Juan Baptisto Pio. That day, August 10, 1680, the revolt began. Pueblo Indian warriors laid siege to Santa Fe, trapping the Spaniards inside, and blocking their water supply. After several days the city fell, and the Spanish left the area. The Pueblo once again ruled over their own land. The Spanish would not attempt to regain control over the region again until 1692.

Suzanne J. Crawford

See also Hopi Prophecy; Kachina and Clown Societies; Missionization, Southwest; Oral Traditions, Pueblo; Sacred Sites and Sacred Mountains; Spiritual and Ceremonial Practitioners, Southwest

References and Further Reading
Banyacya, Thomas. 1992. "The Hopi Message to the United Nations General Assembly" delivered December 10 (available at http://www.alphacdc.com/banyacya).
Ellis, Florence Hawley. N.d. *Anthropological Data Pertaining to the Taos Land Claim.* New York: Garland Publishers.
Geertz, Armin. 1994. *The Invention of Prophecy: Continuity and Meaning in Hopi Indian Religion.* Berkeley: University of California Press.
Mails, Thomas. 1997. *The Hopi Survival Kit.* New York: Penguin Press.
Parsons, Elsie Clews. 1996. *Taos Tales.* Dover Publications.
Sando, Joe S. 1995. *Pueblo Profiles: Cultural Identity through Centuries of Change.* Santa Fe, NM: Clear Light Publishers.
Spicer, Edward Hollard. 1982. *Cycles of Conquest: The Impact of Spain, Mexico and the U.S. on the Indians of the U.S., 1533–1960.* Tucson: University of Arizona Press.
Waters, Frank. 1942. *The Man Who Killed the Deer.* Athens: Ohio University Press.
———. 1977. *The Book of the Hopi.* New York: Viking Press.
Waters, Frank, and R. C. Gordon-McCuthan. 1991. *The Taos Indians and the Battle for Blue Lake.* Santa Fe: Red Crane Books.

Religious Leaders, Southeast

The tribes of the Southeast region of the United States had lived in the area for centuries before the arrival of Europeans, and some of those communities still exist within the region to this very day. Many others were forcibly removed from the Southeast by the U.S. government during the 1830s and 1840s and sent to the Indian Territory, which later became the state of Oklahoma. Many American Indian communities still cling to traditional religious practices, while others have either adopted one form or another of Christianity or syncretized Christian and traditional elements while maintaining their indigenous identity. In general, the traditional religions of the Southeast tribes were highly organized, and their religious practices and ceremonies were conducted by a select priesthood that perpetuated itself by training each succeeding generation, usually recruits from their own clans. The desire to guarantee the continuation of traditional practices led many religious leaders in the late nineteenth and twentieth centuries to record their knowledge in manuscript form, and also to work with ethnographers that wanted to study traditional, indigenous culture in the Southeast.

Catawbas Religious Leaders

Hagler (Arataswa, Oroloswa) (ca. 1690–1763). An important leader among the Catawba during the eighteenth century, Hagler remained a staunch British ally to his death, but he insisted that his people resist adopting Christianity and continue to practice traditional, Catawba religious beliefs.

Cherokees

Arch, John (Atsi) (?–1825). In 1820, John Arch helped found the Creek Path Mission for the Chickamauga Cherokees in Alabama after briefly working at the Brainerd Mission from 1818 to 1820. He served as an interpreter and an assistant to the missionaries and helped translate passages of the Bible into the Cherokee language. Arch died of tuberculosis on June 18, 1825.

Nancy Ward (Nan'yehi) (ca. 1738–1824). The Ghigau (Beloved Woman) of Chota, Nan'yehi, called Nancy Ward by Anglo-Americans, constantly strove to maintain peace between her people and the United States, because she believed that was the only way that the Cherokees could survive as a nation.

Born into an important clan and the maternal niece of the influential leader Attakullakulla, Ward became the Ghigau, which also means War Woman, of Chota at an early age because she picked up the musket of her husband after he was killed and helped lead the Cherokees to victory over the Muskogees at the battle of Taliwa in 1755. As Ghigau, Ward's responsibilities included deciding the fate of prisoners of war, preparing the Black Drink (a ritual, purifying tea) for ceremonies, voting in the general council of her town, leadership of her town's women's council, and a position of importance on delegations to outsiders, which included other tribes, the colonial powers in the Southeast, and eventually the United States. As the ultimate decision-maker on the fate of prisoners, Ward spared the life of a Mrs. Bean in the 1760s, and after befriending her, Ward learned many of the skills that Anglo-American women performed, including weaving and husbandry. Over time, Ward became convinced that the Cherokees needed to adopt some of the ways of Anglo-Americans to survive, and that war with the United States needed to be avoided. As the Ghigau, she used her influence to bring about some change in the Cherokee Nation. Later she married a Scots-Irish trader named Bryant Ward, and with him she began keeping an inn near Chota. After the death of her husband, Ward returned to live in Chota until she died around 1824.

Kaneeda (John Wickliffe) (ca. early 1800s). Originally a priest in the traditional Cherokee religion, Kaneeda converted to Christianity, became a Baptist missionary, and participated in the Cherokee attempt to resist removal in the 1830s.

It is not known when Kaneeda was born, but upon reaching adulthood he became a priest in the traditional Cherokee religion. He later converted to Christianity, was baptized in 1829, and was given the name John Wickliffe. Eventually Wickliffe was ordained in 1833. Also during the 1830s he became a member of the Cherokee Council and participated in the Cherokee Nation's efforts to avoid removal from their homeland in and around the southern Appalachian Mountains to Indian Territory (modern Oklahoma) by the U.S. government. After removal Wickliffe headed the congregation of the Delaware Town Church in the Cherokee Nation as its minister from 1847 to 1857.

Yonagusta (ca. 1760–1839). A prophet and peace chief among the Cherokees of North Carolina, Yonagusta successfully kept his followers from being removed to Oklahoma in the 1830s by the U.S. government.

At approximately the age of sixty, Yonagusta fell into a coma after being seriously sick, and many of his followers thought he had died. He recovered, however, and stated that he had received a vision from the spirit world. As a result of that vision, he preached a return to traditional ways and renounced the use of alcohol. In 1829, based on the provisions of an earlier treaty, Yonagusta and his followers abandoned the Cherokee Nation and became U.S. citizens on a reservation in Haywood County, North Carolina. That act along with help from his adopted son (Will Thomas), a lawyer, kept Yonagusta's band from being removed. They later became known as the Eastern band of Cherokees.

Boudinot, Elias (Galagina, Buck Watie, Stag Watie) (ca. 1802–1839). A Christian missionary to his people, Elias Boudinot is best known as the editor of the *Cherokee Phoenix* and as a leader of the Treaty Party that advocated removal to Indian Territory as an effort to preserve the Cherokee Nation.

A full-blood and born near Rome, Georgia, Galagina attended the Foreign Mission School in Cornwall, Connecticut, between 1818 and 1820. While there he took the name Elias Boudinot, after a supporter of the school. Later, from 1822 to 1823, Boudinot went to the Andover Seminary to continue his education. Upon returning home to the Cherokee Nation, he worked with Samuel Worcester in translating the Bible into the syllabary of the Cherokee language. Boudinot edited the *Cherokee Phoenix* between 1828 and 1832. Along with several other people, Boudinot signed the removal treaty of 1835. They (the treaty

Elias Boudinot, a Christian missionary to his people and editor of the Cherokee Phoenix. *Steel engraving by J. W. Paradise after painting by Waldo and Jewett. (Library of Congress)*

party) believed that eventually the United States would remove the Cherokee people to the Indian Territory anyway, and therefore they needed to get the best deal they could for the Cherokee Nation. After Boudinot moved to Indian Territory, he, along with other members of the treaty party, was assassinated on June 22, 1839, for violating the Cherokee law against giving away land.

Bushyhead, Jesse (Unaduti) (?–1844). A political and Christian missionary among the Cherokees, Jesse Bushyhead was the first ordained Baptist minister from the Cherokee Nation.

Born in the Cherokee town of Amohee at the turn of the nineteenth century, Bushyhead attended school in Tennessee, where he converted to Christianity. Beginning in 1832, he served as an assistant missionary with the Baptist Board of Foreign Missions for eleven years. Bushyhead was ordained by the Baptist Church in 1833, and over the course of his life he translated many passages of the Bible into Cherokee. On several occasions he served as a representative for the Cherokee Nation to the U.S. government in Washington, D.C. Furthermore, Bushyhead held several positions in the Cherokee national government, including a position as a justice of the Cherokee Supreme Court. After the Cherokee removal to Oklahoma, Bushyhead helped re-establish the Baptist missionary effort there and also founded the National Temperance Society within the Cherokee Nation in the West. He died on July 17, 1844.

Gahuni (?–ca. 1857). Gahuni practiced the traditional Cherokee religion as a medicine man, and he also practiced Methodism. Furthermore, he was an important informant for the ethnologist James Mooney. Gahuni recorded many sacred formulas and biblical verses in the syllabary of the Cherokee language, and after his death his family gave most of his writings to the Bureau of American Ethnology.

Tanenolee (mid-1800s). An abolitionist, Baptist missionary, and Cherokee politician, Tanenolee lived in the mid-nineteenth century, in a period of great turmoil for the Cherokee Nation during removal and the Civil War.

Tanenolee converted to the Baptist religion and most often assisted Evan Jones in his missionary work. He helped resist the removal process, and when all other options failed, Tanenolee and Jones led one of the traveling parties during the removal. After removal he was ordained as a Baptist minister and served as pastor at Taquohee, Dsiyohee, and Long Prairie. At one point he also served in the Cherokee national legislature. Because of his abolitionist views, Tanenolee may have been killed in 1862 by Cherokees that supported the Confederacy.

Downing, Lewis (Lewie-za-wau-na-skie) (1823–1872). A Baptist minister and one of the founders of the Ketoowah Society, Lewis Downing served as principal chief of the Cherokee Nation in the turbulent years following the Civil War from 1867 to 1872, and he eventually reunified the nation under one government.

Downing was born in eastern Tennessee. Like most of the Cherokee Nation, Downing and his parents, Samuel and Susan Daugherty Downing, were removed to the Indian Territory. After attending Baptist mission schools he was ordained as a minister, and in 1844 he became the minister at Flint Church in the Indian Territory. Downing spoke and wrote in the Cherokee language, and he eventually helped create the Cherokee Ketoowah Society, which was dedicated to preserving Cherokee culture and traditions. During the Civil War, Downing served as a chaplain with the rank of lieutenant colonel in the Union army. He later served as acting principal chief before being elected to the position in 1867. His primary achievement during his time as the principal leader of the Cherokees was to reunify the nation by encouraging former Confederate and Union soldiers and sympathizers to serve together in the Cherokee government.

Forman, Stephen (1807–1881). An ordained Presbyterian minister, educator, missionary, and translator, Stephen Foreman was one of the most influential leaders of the Cherokee Nation before and after the removal to the Indian Territory in present-day Oklahoma.

Foreman's mother was Cherokee and his father was a Scottish trader. Foreman was born near Rome, Georgia, before the family moved to Cleveland, Tennessee. He attended a mission school near his home in Tennessee that was run by the Congregationalist Church. Upon the death of his father, Foreman studied under the Congregational missionary Samuel Worcester in New Echota, Georgia. Later he attended the College of Richmond in Virginia and the Princeton Theological Seminary, and finally he was ordained in 1835 as a Presbyterian minister. When he returned to the Cherokee Nation, Foreman began his efforts to assist his people in their opposition to forced removal; as a result, the government of Georgia imprisoned him for his efforts. During the Trail of Tears, he headed one of the parties that set out for the Indian Territory in present-day Oklahoma.

Once there he developed a public school system for Cherokee children, and Foreman also helped Worcester translate the Bible into the Cherokee syllabary. Foreman served on the Cherokee Supreme Court beginning in 1844, and he acted as executive councilor for the tribe from 1847 to 1855. He chose to live in Texas during the Civil War, where he acted as a missionary. At the conclusion of the war, Foreman purchased Elias Boudinot's old home and converted it to a church. He preached there until his death in 1881.

Black Fox (?–1895). A conjurer, Methodist preacher, soldier, and keeper of public records, Black Fox, as well as being one of the ethnologist James Mooney's informants, created numerous records of Cherokee history, culture, and religion.

A full-blood Cherokee, Black Fox was ordained by the Methodist Episcopal Church around the year 1849, but he never abandoned traditional Cherokee ceremonial life. He kept the letters, minutes, and reports for the Echota Methodist Mission on the Qualla Boundary. During the Civil War he joined the North Carolina Infantry, in which he received the rank of sergeant. At the time of his death in 1895, Black Fox still practiced the traditional Cherokee religion. After his death, Black Fox's granddaughter gave his records and documents to James Mooney for preservation by the Bureau of American Ethnology.

Swimmer (Ayunini) (ca. 1835–1899). An Eastern Cherokee, Swimmer was a priest and healer in the traditional religion of the Cherokees, and he was an important informant for the ethnologist James Mooney.

Ayunini, known to Anglo-Americans as Swimmer, trained at an early age to become a Cherokee holy man, and by the end of his life he had become the leading authority on sacred Cherokee ceremonies and religious beliefs. He kept a record of Cherokee traditions, including folk stories, formulas, prayers, and songs written in the syllabary of the Cherokee language. Late in life, Swimmer met James Mooney, the ethnologist from the Smithsonian Institution's Bureau of American Ethnology. He was Mooney's primary informant on Cherokee tradition and ceremonies. Through Mooney, the Smithsonian purchased Swimmer's manuscripts, which continue to be valuable sources of information on Cherokee culture. Swimmer died in March of 1899.

Smith, Redbird (1850–1918). A spiritual and political leader of the Cherokees, Redbird Smith struggled his entire life to maintain the political independence and cultural persistence of his people.

The son of Cherokee parents, Smith continued their tradition of supporting the Keetoowah Society. The Keetoowahs were a resistance organization that sought to maintain Cherokee cultural and religious traditions and political independence. His father, Pig Smith, chose Creek Sam, a Natchez medicine man, to train Redbird Smith. Redbird Smith eventually became a member of the Keetoowah Society and rose in its ranks of leadership; later he helped lead Cherokee resistance to the Curtis Act and the Dawes Act, which eventually ended tribal sovereignty and gave tribal land to individuals of the tribe and to Anglo-Americans. Smith was briefly imprisoned for his resistance to the implementation of these acts. Finally the Keetoowahs withdrew from political matters, and Redbird Smith established a ceremonial grounds in 1902. In 1908, Smith became the principal chief of the Cherokee Nation, and later he established the Four Mothers Society to aid and promote communication between traditional members of the Cherokees, Chickasaws, Choctaws, and Muskogees. Redbird Smith died in 1918.

Long, Will West (Willi Westi) (ca. 1870–1947). A spiritual leader and cultural preservationist among the Eastern Cherokees, Will West Long also became an important informant for several ethnographers.

Born into a Cherokee family, Long was trained by his mother and his maternal uncle in the traditional ways of the Cherokee people. He briefly attended Old Trinity College in Randolph County, North Carolina. While he was there, a classmate taught him the Cherokee syl-labary. Later Long attended the Hampton Institute in Virginia from 1895 until 1900, and afterward he lived in New England until 1904.

In 1887, Long began a relationship with James Mooney as an informant on Cherokee culture; the relationship lasted until Mooney's death. After 1904, Long began learning as much as he could about Cherokee culture from friends and relatives. His cousin, Charley Lawson, taught him how to sing traditional songs and how to make the Booger Masks used in spiritual ceremonies. Long passed this information on to Mooney and other ethnographers such as Leonard Bloom, William H. Gilbert, Mark R. Harrington, Frank G. Speck, and John Witthoft. He died on March 14, 1947.

Choctaws

Oakchiah (ca. 1810–1849). Born a full-blood Choctaw and converting to Christianity at an early age, Oakchiah served his people as a minister and ordained deacon in the Mississippi Conference of the Methodist Episcopal Church in Mississippi before the removal of his people. Afterward he served in Indian Territory. He died at Fort Smith, Arkansas, on November 2, 1849.

Dukes, Joseph (1811–ca. 1861). Joseph Dukes served as an interpreter for several missions to the Choctaws after attending the Presbyterian mission school at Mayhew as a youth. He also played an important role in creating a Choctaw grammar book and dictionary and translating parts of the Old and New Testaments into Choctaw.

Wright, Allen (Kiliahote) (1825–1885). Allen Wright served the Choctaws in Oklahoma as a Presbyterian minister for most of his adult life and as principal chief from 1866 to 1870.

Orphaned as a child, Wright was raised by a Presbyterian minister named Cyrus Kingsbury. Kingsbury named him Allen Wright after an early missionary to the Choctaws. Initially educated at local mission schools, Wright continued his education first at a school in Delaware and later at Union College in Schenectady, New York. He graduated from Union College in 1852. Wright then attended Union Theological Seminary in New York City and graduated in 1855. Upon being ordained by the Presbyterian Church in 1856, Wright returned to Indian Territory.

After returning to the Choctaws, Wright at different periods served in the Choctaw House of Representatives, in the Senate, and as treasurer. In 1866 he represented the Choctaw Nation in treaty negotiations with the United States. Later Wright suggested the name *oklahoma* for the Indian Territory as it prepared for statehood. The word means "red people." He served as principal chief of the Choctaw from 1866 to 1870. He published a Choctaw dictionary in 1880 and translated the Choctaw and Chickasaw constitutions, legal codes, several hymnals, and portions of the Bible. He died on December 2, 1885.

Wright, Frank Hall (1860–1922). A Presbyterian minister, Frank Wright founded missions first among his own people, the Choctaws, and then to several different Indian nations in the United States and Canada during the late nineteenth and early twentieth centuries.

Wright received his initial education from local missionaries near his home at Boggy Depot in the Indian Territory (Oklahoma) and later attended Spencer Academy in the Choctaw Nation. Afterward, Wright went to Union College in Schenectady, New York, and he then attended and graduated from Union Theological Seminary in New York City (1885). He spent the rest of his life establishing missions and spreading the Christian message among various Native groups in the United States and Canada for the Women's Executive Committee of the Reformed Church. Finally, Wright was awarded his doctorate of divinity degree from Westminister College in Fulton, Missouri, in 1917. He died on July 16, 1922, in Muskoka Lakes in Ontario, Canada.

Belvin, B. Frank (b. 1914). A Choctaw by birth, B. Frank Belvin served as a missionary for the Baptist Church to the Muskogee (Creek) and Seminole nations in Oklahoma. He published *The Status of the American Indian Ministry, War Horse along the Jesus Road,* and *The Tribes Go Up.*

Muskogees (Creeks)
Francis, Josiah (Hildis Hadjo) (ca. 1770s–1818). A prophet and a leader of

the nativist Red Stick movement during the War of 1812, Josiah Francis supported Tecumseh's effort to unite all of the Eastern tribes. After the Red Sticks' defeat in 1814, he eventually moved into Spanish Florida, where he continued to resist U.S. expansion.

Although he was a mixed-blood (his mother was Muskogee and his father was white), Francis chose to follow the path of his Muskogee ancestors; throughout his life he resisted the advance of the U.S. frontier and culture into Muskogee territory. He preached a return to traditional Muskogee ways as well as armed struggle against whites. Francis's spiritual powers were reported to include his ability to disappear underwater for long periods of time and the ability to fly. He received visions from a spirit who helped him defeat his enemies.

In 1811, when Tecumseh visited the Muskogee Confederacy, Francis encouraged his people to join Tecumseh's Indian alliance against the United States, but he failed to motivate a majority of his people. Afterward he helped lead the Red Stick movement, which culminated in the Red Stick War of 1813–1814 against accommodationists within the Muskogee Confederacy and eventually against the United States. During the war, Francis founded the sacred towns of Ecunchattee (Holy Ground) as havens protected by the Great Spirit for traditional Creeks. These towns were burned during the war.

After the war Francis went to Great Britain to secure a treaty that promised the Muskogee Confederacy an independent state, but the British government chose to solidify relations with the United States instead. Upon returning to North America, Francis took up residence near St. Marks in Spanish Florida. Pursuing Natives that had been raiding the U.S. frontier in 1818, Andrew Jackson invaded Spanish Florida and burned St. Marks. He then hanged Francis on April 18 for supporting and inciting the raids on the U.S. frontier.

Winslett, David (ca. 1830–1862). Born just after his parents arrived in Indian Territory after removal, David Winslett eventually became a Presbyterian minister and an interpreter for missionaries among his people.

Winslett went to school at the Coweta and Tallahassee missions in Oklahoma, and by 1851 he had been appointed the ruling elder at the Tallahassee school. Finally he was ordained as a Presbyterian minister on September 6, 1858, and was placed in control of the Coweta Mission. Winslett served in the Confederate army during the Civil War; he became ill and died while on furlough in 1862.

Perryman, James (Pahos Harjo) (?–ca. 1882). The son of a prominent leader among the Muskogees, James Perryman was a Baptist minister and an interpreter for the missions among his people.

Perryman was educated in mission schools near his home in Oklahoma. Perryman worked as an interpreter for Presbyterian missionaries to his people, and he helped translate the first books into the Muskogee language, as well as portions of the Bible. Later Perryman switched to the Baptist faith and served his people as a minister for three decades.

Checote, Samuel (ca. 1819–1884). Samuel Checote served the Muskogee people as a Methodist minister and principal chief during the mid- and late-nineteenth century.

Born in Alabama but removed to Indian Territory with his family while he was still a child, Checote received his education in the local mission schools in the Indian Territory. In 1852 the Methodist Church licensed him to preach. After fighting on the side of the Confederates during the Civil War, Checote worked to bring together Muskogees that had fought on different sides during the war. On and off, Checote held the position of principal chief between 1867 and 1884. He died in 1884.

Perryman, Joseph Moses (1883–?). The son of Moses Perryman and the grandson of the Muskogee chief Benjamin Perryman, Joseph Perryman worked among his people as a minister in both the Presbyterian and Baptist faiths.

Perryman was educated at the Coweta Mission in the Indian Territory. After studying for a number of years, he was ordained by the Presbyterian Church. He created the North Fork Presbyterian Church and ran the local mission school for the South Presbyterian Synod. For unknown reasons, Perryman abandoned the Presbyterian faith for the Baptist denomination in 1878 and was eventually ordained in his new faith.

Perryman, Thomas Ward (1839–1903). Thomas Ward Perryman was a Presbyterian minister, political leader, and translator in the Indian Territory during the last half of the nineteenth century.

Perryman gained his early education at the Tallahassee Mission school near his home. After fighting for a time for the Confederacy during the Civil War, he switched sides and joined the Union army on December 7, 1862. He studied with the Reverend William Schenck Robertson and became a licensed minister in 1875; he was ordained the next year by the Kansas Presbytery. In addition to his religious duties, Perryman served the Muskogee people for several terms in the Creek House of Warriors, beginning in 1868; he was also a district attorney, and, in 1891 and 1896, presiding officer of the House of Kings. He later moved to Kansas City, where he died on February 11, 1903.

Smith, Stanley (ca. 1940s). From the Muskogee town of Arbika in Oklahoma, Stanley Smith traveled to Florida in 1943 at the behest of the Muskogee, Wichita, and Seminole Baptist Association to spread the gospel to Seminoles there. He delivered his sermons in the Muskogee language, and as a result of his eloquence, he began to gain converts immediately. Smith shifted his denominational affiliation to the Southern Baptist in 1945, and during that time his converts numbered almost two hundred Florida Seminoles.

Deere, Phillip (?–1985). A traditional Muskogee medicine man and tribal leader, Phillip Deere actively campaigned to improve conditions for all Native Americans throughout his life.

A descendant of participants in the Red Stick War (1813–1814) that fought to stop the infiltration of Anglo-American culture and Anglo-American seizure of Muskogee land, Deere participated in Chitto Harjo's opposition to U.S. control of Muskogee affairs in Oklahoma during the early years of the twentieth century. Deere saw himself as continuing the traditionalist movement and the resistance efforts of his ancestors into the twentieth century. He traveled extensively in the United States and Europe to lecture on the conditions confronting Native Americans in the United States. Deere acted as a spiritual advisor for the American Indian Movement in the late 1960s and early 1970s, and in 1979 he began bringing the Youths and Elders Conference to his Muskogee roundhouse to promote Native traditionalism among the generations. He was also associated with the International Indian Treaty Council, which was affiliated with the United Nations, and Deere was involved with the Circle of Traditional Indian Elders, a group consisting of elders from numerous tribal nations in the United States. Deere continued to practice the traditional Muskogee religion until his death on August 16, 1985.

Seminole

Bemo, John (1800s). A nephew of Osceola, John Bemo served the Baptist and Presbyterian churches in the mid-nineteenth century as a missionary to his people.

Captured as a youth during the Second Seminole War, Bemo was adopted by a French ship's captain. After traveling throughout his youth, he gained an education in Philadelphia. Bemo then went to Indian Territory to establish a Presbyterian mission among his people, the Seminoles. Some years later Bemo switched to the Baptist faith and continued his mission to the Seminoles as a teacher and minister.

Arpeika (Sam Jones) (ca. 1765–1860). A Seminole medicine man and war leader in the Second Seminole War, Arpeika, along with Billy Bowlegs, successfully resisted the U.S. attempt to remove him and his followers. As a young man, Arpeika was a revered *hillis hay,* or medicine man, before the three Seminole Wars. At an advanced age he became a war leader for his people because of his religious knowledge and strong spiritual power. After resettling his people in the Everglades and successfully resisting attempts to remove them to the Indian

Territory, Arpeika died of natural causes in 1860.

Jumper, John (ca. 1822–1896). John Jumper served the Seminoles as principal chief and a Baptist minister.

Descended from a long line of important leaders, Jumper was one of the first Seminoles to be removed to Indian Territory. Because he saw the value of education, he later asked the Presbyterian Church to build schools among the Seminoles. Jumper converted and became a Presbyterian in 1857. Later he switched to the Baptist Church. He aided the Confederacy during the Civil War and served in the First Seminole Mounted Volunteers as a major, eventually achieving the rank of acting colonel. After the war Jumper was ordained as a Baptist minister. Jumper died on September 21, 1896.

Billie, Josie (ca. 1887–?). Josie Billie was a medicine man and an assistant pastor among the Muskogee and Miccosukee Seminoles in Florida.

A member of the Tiger clan, Billie began his training as a medicine man at the age of fifteen when he began fasting to prepare to learn sacred information; a few years later he began an apprenticeship with Tommy Doctor. For many years Billie studied with several medicine makers, learning everything that he could from each. After some trouble in which a relative was accidentally killed, Billie moved away from his home community along the Tamiami Trail to the Big Cypress Reservation in 1943 and 1944. At the same time, he was forced to give up his medicine bundle to his brother.

Billie converted to the Baptist faith in 1943. He was heavily influenced by Stanley Smith, a Muskogee missionary from Oklahoma. Eventually the Southern Baptists licensed him as a preacher, and in 1948 he was appointed the assistant pastor at a church near the Big Cypress Reservation. Because of his extensive knowledge of Seminole culture and religion, Billie became an important informant for the ethnologist William C. Sturtevant.

Dixie Ray Haggard

See also American Indian Movement (Red Power Movement); Ceremony and Ritual, Southeast; Christianity, Indianization of; Health and Wellness, Traditional Approaches; Missionization, Southeast; Native American Church, Peyote Movement; Power, Southeast; Spiritual and Ceremonial Practitioners, Southeast

References and Further Reading
Bataille, Gretchen M., and Laurie Lisa, eds. 2001. *Native American Women: A Biographical Dictionary*. 2d ed. New York: Routledge.
Corkran, David H. 1962. *The Cherokee Frontier: Conflict and Survival, 1740–62*. Norman: University of Oklahoma Press.
———. 1967. *The Creek Frontier: 1685–1815*. Norman: University of Oklahoma Press.
Cotterill, R. S. 1954. *The Southern Indians: The Story of the Civilized Tribes before Removal*. Norman: University of Oklahoma Press.
Covington, James W. 1993. *The Seminoles of Florida*. Gainesville: University of Florida Press.
Debo, Angie. 1961. *The Rise and Fall of the Choctaw Republic*. 2d ed. Norman: University of Oklahoma Press.

Dockstader, Frederick. 1977. *Great North American Indians.* New York: Van Nostrand Reinhold.

Evans, E. Raymond. 1977. "Notable Persons in Cherokee History: Stephen Foreman." *Journal of Cherokee Studies* 2, no. 2: 230–239.

Fenton, Harold W. 1975. *Nancy Ward: Cherokee.* New York: Dodd, Mead.

Foreman, Grant. *The Five Civilized Tribes.* 1934. Norman: University of Oklahoma Press.

Hendrix, Janey B. 1983a. "Redbird Smith and the Nighthawk Keetoowahs." *Journal of Cherokee Studies* 8, no. 1: 22–39.

———. 1983b. "Redbird Smith and the Nighthawk Keetoowahs." *Journal of Cherokee Studies* 8, no. 2: 73–86.

Hirschfelder, Arlene, and Paulette Molin. 2000. *Encyclopedia of Native American Religions.* Rev. ed. New York: Facts on File.

Hudson, Charles. *The Southeastern Indians.* 1976. Knoxville: University of Tennessee Press.

Irwin, Lee. 1997. "Different Voices Together: Preservation and Acculturation in Early 19th Century Cherokee Religion." *Journal of Cherokee Studies* 18: 2–26.

Johansen, Bruce E., and Donald A. Grinde, Jr. 1997. *The Encyclopedia of Native American Biography: Six Hundred Stories of Important People from Powhatan to Wilma Mankiller.* New York: Henry Holt and Co.

Kidwell, Clara Sue, and Charles Roberts. 1980. *The Choctaws: A Critical Bibliography.* Bloomington: Indiana University Press for the Newberry Library.

Mails, Thomas E. 1992. *The Cherokee People: The Story of the Cherokees from Earliest Origins to Contemporary Times.* Tulsa: Council Oak Books.

Malinowski, Sharon, ed. 1995. *Notable Native Americans.* Detroit: Gale Research.

Malinowski, Sharon, and Anna Sheets, eds., with Jeffrey Lehmant and Melissa Walsh Doig. 1978. *The Gale Encyclopedia of Native American Tribes,* vol. 1: *Northeast, Southeast, Caribbean.* New York: Gale Research.

Martin, Joel W. 1991. *Sacred Revolt: The Muskogees' Struggle for a New World.* Boston: Beacon Press.

May, Katja. 1990. "Nativistic Movements among the Cherokees in the Nineteenth and Twentieth Centuries." *Journal of Cherokee Studies* 15: 27–40.

McClary, Ben Harris. 1962. "The Last Beloved Woman of the Cherokees." *Tennessee Historical Society* 21: 352–364.

Perdue, Theda. 1998. *Cherokee Women.* Lincoln: University of Nebraska Press.

Reeves, Carolyn Keller, ed. 1985. *The Choctaw before Removal.* Jackson: University Press of Mississippi.

Tucker, Norma. 1969. "Nancy Ward, Ghighau of the Cherokees." *Georgia Historical Quarterly* 53: 192–200.

Wells, Samuel J., and Roseanna Tubby, eds. 1986. *After Removal: The Choctaw in Mississippi.* Jackson: University Press of Mississippi.

Religious Leaders, Southwest

Hosteen Klah (1867–1937)

Hosteen Klah, also known as Azaethlin, was born on the "Long Walk Home" from Bosque Redondo at Fort Wingate. His great grandfather Narbona was also a well-known healer and leader of the Diné (Navajo). Hosteen Klah was recognized early as a traditional healer through his work with his Apache uncle, married to one of Hosteen Klah's mother's sisters. It was during this visit with the Apache uncle that it was discovered that Hosteen Klah also possessed qualities that would permit him to attain knowledge usually taught to the women of his family. Hosteen Klah's interest in healing led him to study with all of the Diné healers he knew of or heard of. At the age of forty-nine in 1917, Klah performed his first complete Yeibichai, a nine-day-long healing ceremony. That is the most complex and lengthy Diné healing process, and it established him as the most knowledgeable and powerful of all known or remembered Diné healers. In his last thirty years of life, Klah transferred his knowledge onto the visual format of rug weaving, a traditional Diné craft. Klah's weavings are known far and wide and depict many of the sacred portions of the Diné healing and religious rites.

Ruby Modesto (1913–1980)

Ruby Modesto was a member of the Desert Cahuilla tribe of indigenous peoples and known among her people as a healer. As a young child, around the age of ten, she experienced what she described as dreams, a precursor to the world of a Desert Cahuilla healer. As a member of the Dog clan, Ruby came from a long line of Desert Cahuilla healers, or *puls*. These individuals—men and women—were highly respected clan leaders capable of performing their specialties in the areas of hunting, singing for specific needs, and ceremonies. A *pul* is chosen by Umna'ah, Creator, and has a helper; in Ruby's case her helper Ahswit, Eagle, is a very powerful helper. *Puls* can heal a variety of ailments from menstruation problems to epilepsy, known as *tookisyl,* with excellent results. In Desert Cahuilla oral history, passed on by Ruby to her family, Frog is the center of negative power, or evil in Ruby's words. For the Desert Cahuilla, healers come into their source of healing power and responsibilities at approximately forty years of age and continue gathering stature throughout their lifetime.

Geronimo, Goyatholay (One Who Yawns) (1829–1909)

Chiricahua Apache of the Nednhi band and a Bedonkohe Apache (grandson of Mahko), Geronimo was an influential leader of a band of Apache who consistently refused to be bound to a specific piece of real estate known in modern times as a reservation. Because of a speech impediment, Geronimo often spoke for his brother, Juh, who was reported as being a hereditary leader. Geronimo was quoted on one occasion as saying, "I was born on the prairies where the wind blew free and there was nothing to break the light of the sun. I was born where there were no enclosures." Many of the Indian leaders of the late 1800s made statements of this nature when they and their people were rounded up and confined to reservations where they could no longer practice their sociocultural and religious way of life. Geronimo epitomized the reluctant individual who stepped up to care for and lead his people during extremely difficult times. Despite surrendering to the U.S. Army three times and leading small groups of Chiracahua back to their homeland each time, Geronimo was captured and interred in Fort Marion, Florida, in 1886.

In 1894, Geronimo and the balance of the Chiracahua who had survived were

Geronimo, Goyatholay (One Who Yawns) was a revered Chiricahua Apache medicine person and spiritual leader. 1907. (Library of Congress)

moved to Mt. Vernon in Alabama, where many more were exposed to tuberculosis and died. As a revered leader, medicine person, and spiritual and intellectual leader, Geronimo lived out the balance of his life as a prisoner of war (political prisoner) because of his ability to escape, evade, and lead his people out of government control and into what little freedom they could find in their ancestral lands. Geronimo, as a prisoner, was forced to appear in the 1904 Louisiana Purchase Exposition in St. Louis and actually rode in the 1905 inaugural parade for President Theodore Roosevelt. Geronimo was later transferred to Ft. Sill in Oklahoma, where he died near the Apache on their reservation north of Ft. Sill. Geronimo

died a prisoner of the U.S. government at Ft. Sill on February 17, 1909, and was buried in the Apache cemetery there.

Barboncito (Hástiin Dághá [Man with the Whiskers]

Bislahalani [The Orator]; Hozhooji Naata [Blessing Speaker]; Ma'ii deeshgíízhiníí [Coyote Pass People, Jemez Clan]; and Hashke yich'í Dahilwo [He Is Anxious to Run at Warriors]) (1820–1871)

Barboncito served his clan and the Diné in many capacities during his lifetime. He appears to have begun his formal responsibilities in 1860, when he joined Manuelito in a reprisal attack over the loss of a number of their horses that had been slaughtered by soldiers from Fort Defiance. In 1862, Barboncito and his brother Delgadito informed the commander of Fort Defiance, General James H. Carlton, of their intention to live peacefully with the fort. That only led to their forced movement to Bosque Redondo, at which point Barboncito and Delgadito once again joined Manuelito in rebellion. In 1864, Barboncito was captured by Colonel "Kit" Carson, a famous Indian scout during the 1863–1866 Navajo War, as a war chief. In June of 1865, Barboncito left Bosque Redondo, leading a group of 500 Diné to their ancestral lands. In November of 1866, Barboncito once again surrendered at Fort Wingate, with twenty-one of his followers.

In 1868, Barboncito was appointed as the lead signatory to the final peace treaty between the Diné and the U.S. government. Barboncito lived out his last few years after signing a peace treaty that placed the Diné back on their ancestral lands.

Dr. Lori Arviso Alvord (1958–)

Dr. Alvord, who considers herself a traditional Diné, is also a board-certified and well-respected physician. In her own words, the "words Navajo and surgeon" are rarely heard together, and never associated with each other. During the ten years between 1981 and 1991, Dr. Alvord studied and learned her surgical skills at Stanford University and in the Stanford area. From 1991–1997, Dr. Alvord plied her skills in Gallup, New Mexico, and in the process gained a new understanding of her traditional Diné healing responsibilities, working in concert with known traditional healers. It was during those ten years that Dr. Alvord was able to reconnect with her traditional early teachings and become involved with, among others, Thomas Hatathlii at the Tuba City Medical Center. She relearned the power of traditional healing, both sharing her knowledge with Hosteen Hatathlii and learning from him the power of traditional healing. Dr. Alvord credits Hosteen Hatathlii with reintroducing her to the many traditional Diné healing ceremonies, in particular Kodi's Prayer. Dr. Alvord is currently a guest lecturer at Dartmouth Medical School.

Tasiwoopa ápi

See also Ceremony and Ritual, Apache; Ceremony and Ritual, Diné; Health and Wellness, Traditional Approaches; Missionization, Southwest; Mourning and the Afterlife, Southwest; Sandpainting

References and Further Reading
Alvord, Dr. Lori Arviso, and Elizabeth Cohen Van Pelt. 1999. *The Scalpel and the Silver Bear*. New York: Bantam Books.
Barboncito. 1968. *Treaty between the United States of American and the Navajo Tribe of Indians: With a Record of the Discussions that Led to Its Signing*. Las Vegas: K. C. Publications.
Faulk, Odie. 1993. *The Geronimo Companion*. Oxford: Oxford University Press.
Iverson, Peter. 2002. *Diné: A History of the Navajo*. Albuquerque: University of New Mexico Press.
Modesto, Ruby, and Guy Mount. 1980. *Not for Innocent Ears: Spiritual Traditions of a Desert Cahuilla Medicine Woman*. Arcata, CA: Sweetlight Books.
Newcomb, Franc Johnson. 1989. *Hosteen Klah: Navajo Medicine Man and Sacred Sand Painter*. Norman: University of Oklahoma Press.

Religious Leaders, Southwest, Pueblo

See Religious Leaders, Pueblo

Religious Leadership, Alaska

See "Angalkuq"

Religious Leadership, Great Basin

Historical analyses of Great Basin American Indian religious leaders have involved profiling powerful leaders who achieved a place in Euro-American society through either fame or controversy. In this essay we depart from that model in order to examine the equally important foundations of Indian religious leadership roles in Numic society, and how those roles changed over time. We examine this issue by looking at how religious leadership manifested during four distinct historical periods—(1) traditional times, defined as being before Europeans arrived; (2) encroachment times, which include the early occupation of indigenous territories by Euro-Americans; (3) conversion times, when Europeans began to use religious conversion as a tool of conquest/salvation; and (4) multicultural times, when Indian people can choose among various religious options without fear of retribution.

Our main thesis is that the role-relationship expectations and possibilities confronting Great Basin religious leaders were seriously altered by forces beyond their control during four historical periods. Within a context of change induced by Euro-American encroachment, relationships between religious leaders and members of Indian communities were constantly renegotiated. As Numic religious leaders were exposed to other Indian religions (for example, the revitalization movement of Smohalla and the Native American Church), Western religious tenets introduced by Christian missionaries, and U.S. society at large, Numic religious leaders adapted themselves to serving the needs of their people. Basin Indian religious leaders were not victims of their times, but instead were recognized as leaders exactly because they adjusted to the times and continued to serve their people effectively.

Two concepts need to be narrowly defined in order to keep this essay within bounds. First, when talking about Basin religious leaders, this essay is restricted to those who speak the Numic language. Thus some Great Basin tribes are not considered, while certain Numic tribes residing far from the Basin are included. Numic people traditionally lived from the Sierra Nevada Mountains in California to the front range of the Rocky Mountains in Colorado. Numic groups include the Northern Paiutes in Bend, Oregon; Owens Valley, California, Paiutes and Shoshones; Western Shoshones from Wyoming to Death Valley, California; their cousins the Goshutes in Utah; Southern Paiutes in Utah, Arizona, Nevada, and California; and the Utes of Utah and Colorado. A second point is that among Numic peoples the once clear line between religious and political leadership shifted until they became indistinguishable roles, and they have once again become distinct roles only in recent times. Given the changes in role definition over time, this essay always attempts to specify what time frame is under consideration.

In view of the paucity of relevant studies of Numic religious practices, this essay is necessarily speculative. One study, however, needs to be highlighted because it informs this issue directly. It took the scholarly lifetime of Omer C. Stewart, but once he had published *Peyote Religion: A History* it became unique as a source for understanding how religious leaders in the Peyote religion (Native American Church) survived various

U.S. national polities designed either to suppress or to support that particular religion. Stewart traced the lives and shifting religious roles of hundreds of Peyote religious leaders, including many from Great Basin tribes. The book also clearly illustrates a widely shared religion and an irreversible trend toward pan-Indian cultural patterns in North America.

Traditional Times: Before 1492

Religious leadership is not usually seen in the archaeological record of the Basin, so one must guess at how Indian religious leadership functioned based on what was first observed by Europeans and the basic beliefs of Numic religion and authority. *Puha* (which glosses in English as "power" or "energy") was made as the force that causes everything to be alive and have agency. *Puha* came at the time of Creation when it, the land, and the Numic people came into being and relationship. Religion is basically an understanding of how *puha* works to keep the world in balance as it was defined at Creation, and how ceremony can be used to restore balance. Individuals, groups, plants, animals, and all else in nature can become out of balance and thus need a curative ceremony; the most common balancing ceremony is the circle or round dance.

The concept of a religious leader, which in European culture usually means a single person who is the head of a church, does not directly translate into traditional Numic culture. The closest description is a person who is primarily responsible for calling and leading balancing ceremonies that are needed by groups and nature. Persons who specialize in bringing balance back to individuals are called shamans or medicine doctors, but the process of restoring balance is fundamentally the same regardless of the problem's scale.

The power of religious leaders is not primarily their own, although they may have been especially selected as a person who will know how best to use this power, and they do bring their own power to balancing ceremonies. The term *Puhagantu,* which is often used for religious leaders and shamans, is revealing because it translates as "to have *puha*" or even "where *puha* sits." Religious leaders, like shaman, are basically windows through which power passes on the way to balance an individual, group, or aspect of nature. This power tends to arrive as spirit helpers that can be an animal, such as a mountain sheep, a mineral, such as crystal, or a spirit, such as a water baby. Places of power also add their *puha* to balancing ceremonies.

Traditionally, when religious leaders accepted the responsibility of being the window of power, they understood the risks involved. Failure to control *puha,* as evidenced by things getting worse or more out of balance, indicated that the leader/shaman was losing control over the sources of power being used to bring balance. Repeated failure eventually resulted in their friends and relatives killing them. This act has been interpreted by Euro-Americans as retribution for failure to cure or fix the world, but quite a different interpretation comes from Numic epistemology. First, when people accept the responsibility of being a religious leader or shaman, they know what they must do as the "window of *puha*." They also recognize that if they begin to fail it is because they are a broken window and they will be killed. This second point is also misunderstood because mater cannot be destroyed, it merely transforms. With reincarnation the killed leader becomes an animal, and when the animal dies it can come back as a person. In fact, there is evidence that a shaman becomes a hummingbird, and this shaman's helper can become a shaman at death.

Encroachment Times: 1776–1890
During this period Indian religion and ceremony was largely irrelevant to Euro-American society, despite the 1776 expedition of fathers Escalante and Dominguez, during which they were pleased to find friendly Southern Paiutes looking like Pueblos with rancherias and irrigated farming—and thus more easily converted than the more mobile and hostile Apaches. More important to most outsiders, however, was that Indian people not restrict the economic activities of Europeans who passed through the Basin looking for beaver furs and precious minerals. When the former were trapped out and the latter was found in California, Indian people were simply pushed back from major sources of water and away from the routes of travelers. The 1863 Treaty of Ruby Valley (Harney 1995, 193) with the Western Sho-

shone illustrates the federal policy of only taking from—not giving to—the Indian people.

As Indian people became increasingly marginalized in the Basin, they responded by working together through big balancing ceremonies. Indian religious leaders combined efforts with political leaders to organize the largest pan-Indian movement since the 1680 All-Pueblo Revolt (Nabokov 1981). Unlike that armed conflict, this was to be a religious conflict fought with *puha* instead of guns. The first well-known such ceremony was the Ghost Dance movement of 1870. Twenty years later the 1890 Ghost Dance (Dobyns 1967; Hittman 1997) was to become the largest pan-Indian joint balancing ceremony ever, because it involved up to thirty-two ethnic groups (Mooney 1991). Both ceremonies were fundamentally traditional round dances scaled up to address the greatest problem that had ever confronted Numic peoples and lands (Stoffle et al. 2000).

The federal government responded to these efforts with physical force, such as the Wounded Knee massacre among the Sioux. The safety of white society and commerce was the priority, and Indian travel and ceremony were suppressed. In many portions of the Basin, local Indians still outnumbered their non-Indian neighbors. Nevertheless, Euro-American hegemony prevailed. The famous prophet of the 1890 Ghost Dance movement, Wovoka, was put under house arrest, and a manned fence was built around Wovoka's home at Yearington,

Nevada, to restrict his travel and that of his community. Soon the federal government would add Christian missionaries to the efforts to civilize and pacify the tribes.

Conversion Times: 1890–1960

The Ghost Dance of 1890 along with an increasingly hostile boundary between whites and Indians in the Basin caused the Federal government to outlaw the practice of Indian ceremonies of all kinds (Crum 1994, 51–52). Thus the role of Indian religious leader had to be subsumed under that of a political leader or even a labor leader. Religious leaders could be jailed for public practice of ceremonies, so their activities became largely unknown to the dominant society. Indian people hid their religion within the context of social events that were legal. Ghost Dance songs continued to be sung, but they had to be buried within nonthreatening public activities (Vander 1988). Some religious leaders became the heads of Euro-American churches that permitting them to continue to serve in a modified traditional role. It is clear, however, that some of these new Indian converts to Western religions truly rejected traditional religions and ways of life. Unlike European religious practice, Indian religions permitted adding alternative approaches to understanding the world, so it is possible that an Indian religious leader could in good faith participate in both religious systems. Still, during this period, traditional religious leaders were all but invisible to the outside world.

Multicultural Times: 1960 to Today

After the Civil Rights movement achieved major successes for African Americans in the mid-1950s, many activists took heart and moved on to other issues. Some moved to the environment and became instrumental in arguing against and even stopping dams along the Colorado River, efforts that partially resulted in the passage of the National Environmental Policy Act of 1969. Others lent their voices and energies to American Indian movements of various kinds, including efforts to achieve religious freedom. After a decade of these efforts, Congress passed the American Indian Religious Freedom Act of 1979, which included both a national apology for past efforts to eliminate Indian religions and a commitment not to stand in the way of Indian religious practice in the future.

While it is impossible to characterize all of the Indian leaders who emerged during this time, it is clear that it became increasingly acceptable for Indian leaders to perform non-European religious ceremonies publicly. It is also clear that many religious leaders in the Great Basin became associated with religions that did not derive from Numic culture. Examples include most leaders of the Peyote religion, including members of the Duncan family (Utes) who served both as Sun Dance religious leaders and roadmen in the Native American Church. Many of the non-Numic religions were led by Indian people who were not Numic. Nevertheless, Numic-based religions flourished during this period as more and more situations occurred in which their religious leaders could step forward to present Numic religious principles and be positively received by both their own people and people from the general society—and even the world. An example is Corbin Harney (Western Shoshone), who was called to be a leader and eventually became a world icon; at one time he was visualized in a Sting (Gordon Sumner) concert held in honor of indigenous people.

Today Indian people still respect and follow the tenets of their traditional religions, but they are also likely to draw upon the insights of the Peyote religion and that of friends and family members from other Indian religions. Many families and all local groups contain people who share religious perspectives that originate far from the Basin. Just as the people have become multicultural, so many religious leaders practice more than one religion.

Richard W. Stoffle and Alex K. Carroll

See also Power Places, Great Basin; Ghost Dance Movement

References and Further Reading
Crum, Steven J. 1994. *Po'I Pentun Tammen Kimmappeh, The Path on which We Came: A History of the Western Shoshone*. Salt Lake City: University of Utah Press.
Dobyns, Henry F. 1967. *The Ghost Dance of 1889: Among the Pai Indians of Northwestern Arizona*. Prescott, AZ: Prescott College Press.
Harney, Corbin. 1995. *The Way It Is: One Water . . . One Air . . . One Mother Earth.* Nevada City, CA: Blue Dolphin Publishing.
Hittman, Michael. 1997. *Wovoka and the Ghost Dance*. Edited by Don Lynch. Lincoln: University of Nebraska Press.
Mooney, James. 1991. *The Ghost-Dance Religion and the Sioux Outbreak of 1890*. Lincoln: University of Nebraska Press.
Nabokov, Peter. 1981. *Indian Running: Native American History & Tradition*. Santa Fe, NM: Ancient City Press.
Stewart, Omer C. 1987. *Peyote Religion: A History*. Norman: University of Oklahoma Press.
Stoffle, Richard, et al. 2000. "Ghost Dancing the Grand Canyon: Southern Paiute Rock Art, Ceremony, and Cultural Landscapes." *Current Anthropology* 41, no. 1: 11–38.
Vander, Judith. 1988. *Songprints: The Musical Experience of Five Shoshone Women*. Urbana: University of Illinois Press.

Religious Leadership, Northeast

Native American religious leaders fulfill a multiplicity of functions, yet non-Native observers have tended to place all religious leaders in the same category. The earliest colonists and missionaries usually described them as witches or servants of the Devil. This category has transformed over time and has become identified with the term "shaman." That word comes from the Tungus people of Siberia, for whom the *saman* is a spiritual leader who can travel to the spirit world and ascertain the desires and demands of the spirits. While some Native American religious leaders are clearly engaged in similar practices, the blanket category of "shaman" for all medicine people is inappropriate. The myth of a unified, coherent religious tradition of soul travel by shamans that traveled with Arctic people over the Bering land bridge and survived in the Americas is unsubstantiated.

Religious leadership in Native American communities is almost always associated with the ability to heal. That ability can be obtained in multiple ways; it can be inherited, developed as a result of dreams or visions sent by animals or good spirits, or the person may be chosen by an actual event such as a near-fatal encounter with a dangerous or poisonous animal. In each case the medicine received cannot be used properly until the person has cultivated a familiarity with it. The spiritual medicine that a plant or animal offers tends to be aligned with its actual behavior and attributes.

The lifetime commitment to becoming a medicine person is not pursued half-heartedly. In fact it is dangerous, and some have tried to escape it. Many tribes have stories of potential medicine people who became critically ill because they refused to accept the responsibility. They describe the ultimatum given to them, of choosing to become a healer or dying. These kinds of ordeals are interpreted as tests of the individual's strength and will by the Creator or by the relevant spirit. Many healers describe a kind of death of their former self followed by a rebirth in which they take on the body and spirit of a healer.

Near-death experiences are also often the points at which a prophet has a first vision.

While the oral histories of tribes in the Northeast are no doubt full of the kind of medicine people described above, the recorded history of the Northeast is filled with the characters of Christian Indians, those who sought to bring the good news of the new, white religion to their brethren. Many Native people close to the early New England colonies were quite open to the god of the English and developed their own leadership by incorporating Christian ideas into traditional belief systems. Of course, there were also those who struggled against the intrusion of Christianity into their communities and who led movements to revitalize and reinstate the ancestral religious foundation that had sustained them for generations.

Religious leaders often fulfilled multiple roles. **Aiowantha (Hiawatha)** was one such individual who acted as a healer, prophet, tribal leader, diplomat, and orator for the Mohawk Nation in the 1500s. Aiowantha was a captivating speaker who allied with a Huron leader, Deganawida, to establish an alliance among their neighboring tribes. Deganawida preached a message of peace, and he wanted to unite the tribes to stop the cycle of revenge killing that plagued them. Aiowantha, with persuasive diplomacy, and Deganawida gathered together the Mohawk, Oneida, Onondaga, Cayuga, and Seneca nations into a confederacy known as the League of the Iroquois. When it was later joined by the Tuscarora, it also became known as the Six Nations; it became the most powerful force in the Ohio River valley region until it sided with the British during the American Revolution. When peace was attained, Aiowantha put the principles of Deganawida's vision of peace into action, developing a representative system of governance with laws and ceremonies for negotiating and settling disputes. The framers of the U.S. Constitution admired the Iroquois League's success in uniting its groups together and utilized several of the league's principles in formulating the new American government, including political equality, separation of governmental power, checks and balances, and political freedom.

Molly Ockett was an Abenaki healer and herbalist who mingled in both the world of her Native family and the white world colonizing it. Born with an Abenaki name, Singing Bird, she grew up in Pigwacket Wabanaki country in present-day Maine. While her family sought refuge in Massachusetts because of war between the French and British, she learned English and Christian religious beliefs. Because her people had sided with the French, she was taken hostage by the British and sent to live with an English family in Boston. When she was reunited with her family at about the age of ten, she had become accustomed to the white way of living, but she went back to her Native ways, learning the healing arts from her mother and others. Although her family was killed during further con-

flicts between the French and British, in 1762 she returned to her homeland and helped maintain peace between the Pigwacket band of Abenaki and the English colonists that had settled there. Her fluency in English and her commitment to her own people enabled her to help them immensely. She was a skilled healer who was known for treating anyone, white or Indian, at any time. She was also an excellent hunter and was remembered for being generous with her catch. Ockett can be understood as a peacemaker who facilitated a good relationship between two colliding cultures.

A Native American who took a different route to sponsoring good relations between whites and Indians was **Samson Occum** (1723–1792). Occum was a Mohegan who became the first Indian formally trained and ordained as a Christian minister. He was ordained by the Presbyterian Church in 1759 and began recruiting Native youths for missionary Eleazor Wheelock's educational project, Moor's Indian Charity School, which later became Dartmouth College. Occum became disillusioned with the school when it started focusing on training missionaries instead of Indians. He traveled with his family, preaching Christianity among the Algonquian peoples of New York and New England, eventually establishing a religious community called Brotherton. Occum believed that Indians should minister to Indians, and his community focused on training Native people to lead their own communities. In 1772 he published a speech, "Sermon Preached at the Execution of Moses Paul," in which he criticized white traders for bringing alcohol into Native communities. He continued preaching to the Indians at Brotherton until his death in 1792.

Another Christian Indian who fought against the exploitation of whites was **William Apess,** a Pequot born in 1798 who became a Methodist missionary to the Mashpee tribe, encouraging them to expel the corrupt white missionaries. He also fought to forbid whites to cut timber on Mashpee land. His confrontational leadership earned him the respect of Indian people and thirty days in jail. His story became well known when he published an autobiography and several other books.

Widely known as the visionary who led a successful revitalization movement among Iroquois people in the early nineteenth century, Seneca prophet **Handsome Lake** acknowledged Christian ideas but stressed a return to the traditional Iroquois ceremonies and moral ideals. Seneca land, population, and culture were being devastated by white intruders after the Revolutionary War. Without a powerful leader and a new vision, the Iroquois way of life was threatened with extinction. Handsome Lake received a vision that articulated a new religion and a new way of life for his people that combined elements of Christianity with the traditional Seneca songs, dances, and ceremonial calendar. He believed that by consciously acculturating to some American ways, the Iroquois would be better able to survive this period of white domination. Handsome Lake's grandson became the leader of the Longhouse religion after Handsome Lake's death, and it is still practiced on several reservations today.

Joseph Onasakenrat (White Feather) was a Mohawk chief and Methodist missionary in the 1860s and 1870s. He was raised in the Catholic Church in Quebec and groomed for missionary work. After attending college for three years, he was elected principal chief of the Iroquois in 1868, at the age of twenty-two. The young leader accused the Catholic Church of keeping the Natives in poverty and led a campaign to renounce them. As a result, most of his people converted to the Methodist Church, of which he became a leader. He continued to fight against the Sulpician Catholic order that controlled the Oka missionary settlement where he lived, challenging their ownership of the land in court, their wood-cutting rights, and their settlement claims. He was accused of burning down the Sulpician church in 1877, but the case was later dismissed. He spent his last years translating Scripture from French into Iroquois and preaching to Iroquois communities in Caughnawaga and St. Regis. He died in 1881.

There are few other reliable historical accounts of Native medicine people from the Northeast. Presumably, if they avoided contact with whites their stories were not recorded. Warfare destroyed many Northeastern tribes before scholars were present to record cultural information. However, beginning in the late

1960s, a religious/political faction known as the American Indian Movement (AIM) gained national attention and pan-Indian participation. **Anna Mae Pictou Aquash** was a Mi'kmaq woman from Nova Scotia who became an AIM leader in the 1970s. A tireless and productive worker for Indian rights and cultural sovereignty, Aquash helped organize the Boston Indian Council, a service agency for Indian alcoholics. She was an important "female warrior" during the FBI siege of Wounded Knee on the Pine Ridge Reservation in South Dakota in 1973. She later taught at the Ojibwa's Red School House project and was director of AIM's West Coast office in Los Angeles. In February 1976, Aquash was found dead under suspicious circumstances and became a martyr to the AIM cause.

Brian Clearwater

See also American Indian Movement (Red Power Movement); Missionization, Great Lakes; Revitalization Movements, Northeast

References and Further Reading
Johnson, Troy R. 2002. *Distinguished Native American Spiritual Practitioners and Healers.* Westport, CT: Oryx Press.
Hirschfelder, Arlene, and Paulette Molin. 2000. *The Encyclopedia of Native American Religions.* Rev. ed. New York: Facts on File.
Matthiessen, Peter. 1980. *In the Spirit of Crazy Horse.* New York: Viking Press.

Religious Leadership, Northwest

Throughout the Northwest, certain people maintained constant contact with sources of power and spirit beings that enabled them to change conditions for the better—and sometimes for the worse, if they had a selfish reason to do so. Although often called shamans or Indian doctors, they once included a range of specialists much like those of the modern medico-religious profession. With massive die-offs as a result of European diseases and dislocations, ordinary spiritual practitioners who survived began to assume more and more of the functions and practices of these specialists. Formerly, those functions included that of curer of various types, medium who communed with the dead, song master who untangled tunes, puberty preceptor, baby broker who understood babies' needs, and that of priestly figures who conducted rites such as the First Salmon and other return foods festivals.

Tsimshians

Along the North Pacific coast, for Tlingit and Haida, masks were worn by shamans while working. The neighboring Tsimshians, however, used many masks more generally as manifestations of rank and power. Tsimshian culture was imaged as a beam of light from Heaven that refracted into several branches whose emblems were positioned on the model of a head. Crests were passed through mothers and were embodied as hats; carvings of chiefly rank and power were worn on the forehead; and masks covered the face. Spiritual practitioners themselves were known as "blowers," using the mouth,

Mask used in the naxnox *dance series, which involved the dramatization of a name. The eyes have three positions: open, closed, and copper covered (shown here). The movable jaws reveal teeth or a copper band. Tsimshian culture. (Werner Forman / Art Resource, NY)*

but their power resided in their hair, which remained unkempt and uncut.

For Tsimshians, the primordial beings are called *naxnox,* and the powerful refracted light is *halaayt.* During the 1800s, *halaayt* took six manifestations. It was personalized as a blower—a curer who could be either a man or a woman who served year-round. The Tsimshian year was divided between summer activities

devoted to fishing and harvesting wild foods, followed by winter religious and communal events. A chief, as head of a cedar plank house, therefore had two guises. During the summer he coordinated dispersed food gathering, but with the onset of winter he became Smhalaayt (real *halaayt*) and took over a more priestly role that included religious duties involved with feasting, displays of heirloom art, and intertribal entertainments. Members of high rank also belonged to one of four secret orders known as Wutahalaayt (great *halaayt*), which crossed local allegiances to be international and privileged in scope.

These six roles do not exhaust the realm, however, since various groups and guilds of artists who made the crests, emblems, and embellishments also had religious functions to perform, often in private. Indeed, the penalty for stumbling upon a secluded workshop was immediate death unless the person was of high enough rank to demand immediate initiation.

The Northwest coast included this typical distinction between summer chief and winter priest for all its leaders. Most detailed information is a consequence of the length of time, personalities, and rapport that characterized any fieldwork situation. Outstanding for the coast is that for the Nuxalk (formerly Bella Coola), the northernmost member of the Salishan Language Family, which also includes Lushootseed and Tillamook. These three well illustrate the diversity once seen even among related languages.

Nuxalk

At birth, each Nuxalk person's soul or spirit took up residence in a thin bone at the back of the neck. Other spiritual aspects were located above. In the beginning, the Creator at Nusmatta (a huge house in the upper world) set up a tally post and a section in a water basin for every named person who would live. As named couples, these beings floated down to tops in the human homeland, then set up villages along waterways and began families. At death, a Nuxalk separated into corpse, shadow, and ghost. Since names were inherited, the ghost went back through an unbroken line that led back up to Nusmatta.

When a Nuxalk took seriously ill, special healers had the ability to get to Nusmatta and inspect the patient's pole and basin. If the pole leaned, the acuteness of the angle indicated the outcome of the illness. If possible, the pole was set upright again, and the water in the basin was renewed. Failing that, a doctor would sacrifice grease, bark bowls, and tiny wooden figures to the dead, who lived under the earth. With their help, a sucking cure would suddenly become effective.

Lushootseeds

For the Lushootseeds of Puget Sound, immortal beings provide career or curing abilities. Leaders had spirits, themselves leaders, that empowered them to give wise council and acquire wealth, as well as to hunt the most dangerous of animals.

The Lushootseed term for both spirits and their human allies derived from the Lushootseed for "name" or "call": in the Native system of medicine, to designate ("name") the cause of an illness correctly was to diagnose the cure. Healers and curing spirits were always at the ready, unlike career powers whose closeness varied with the seasons.

Just as European noble families sent sons into the church, into business, into banking, or into the military to widen their power base, so too did Lushootseed nobles try to have members in all positions of authority; leadership was multiplex, depending upon the task. Moreover, modern Salish families extend this strategy to include many contemporary options, particularly religious ones. Thus, while families continue to attend winter ceremonials to welcome the return of spirit partners, on Sunday they devotedly attend Protestant, Catholic, Bahai, or other services.

Lushootseed had at least four overlapping systems of power and consequent specialists concerned with guardian spirits, ghosts, dicta (word formulas, spells), and the High God. Each spirit has two aspects, as being and as song, with a third term used to personify the vision itself. The song came from the east in the fall, moved slowly north, westward, and then south during the winter; in late April or so, it headed east again.

Ghosts were the souls of the dead, who were tormented by hunger, loneliness, and nostalgia for their possessions and relatives. Those ghosts who were still in contact with the living roamed the earth between about 3:00 P.M. and 3:00 A.M. Ghosts were particularly attracted by human gatherings, especially when people were eating. A ghost was closest of all when its name was being inherited by a descendant. Certain humans once acted as mediums because they had a special relationship with a ghost, who warned of calamity. This medium conducted rituals in which food and clothes were burned in a fire to send them to the dead. While such burnings were once held separately, they have now become managed by spiritual practitioners as the first event at modern power displays, memorials, and potlatches.

Dicta were a set of enchantments (incantations and formulas) for influencing or directing the world and its inhabitants. They were passed down family lines to influence the minds and hearts of all living things.

In modern Salishan religion, the High God now features in the Indian Shaker Church and various Christian fundamental denominations. Belief in an ultimate power, however, was ancient and known as *xa'xa*—which means anything sacred and holy as well as forbidden—taboo in such a way as to provide a deification of power.

Puberty preceptors have faded out under Christian influence, yet many features from traditional puberty seclusion have been incorporated into the modern initiation of Winter Dancers. While a boy's coming of age was marked by changes in his voice and body, girls once observed great restrictions. Placed in a special hut, a girl's bed was made of fresh fir boughs. Every night, she left her hut to go to a creek to bathe and scrub with rotten cedar to make herself clean. During the day she kept very busy, weaving mats or blankets, making yarn, or coiling baskets. This effort made her industrious her whole life, and desirable as a good wife.

If it was ripe berry season, a first menstruant picked with a stick (called a "bridle") between her teeth; the stick was inspected by older women at the end of each day to see if she had stained it by eating any forbidden berries. Her strict diet included food that was allowed to cool if it was cooked. She ate very little, mostly roots, but nothing fresh or warm, using special dishes that were destroyed afterward. Fresh and bloody foods were particularly avoided.

Toward the end of her month of seclusion, her grandmother invited other old women to sing, dance, and feast to entertain the girl, who could not herself join in. Because of her supercharged condition, she was under strong taboos. She could not look at anyone or they would become sick. She never touched her own hair. She used a stick of ironwood to scratch.

Every day the girl was instructed by older women about how to conduct herself calmly when she was married, as well as techniques for drying fish, picking berries, digging clams, weaving, basketry, and keeping a household running smoothly and well. She was told to be good to her mother-in-law, other affines, and all elders, while showing kindness and compassion to everyone.

After her first seclusion a girl was regarded as dark or light for six weeks, according to the phases of the moon. On dark days, when the moon waned, her face was painted red, and on light days, when the moon waxed, she was visited by other women.

Tillamooks

Along the Oregon coast, the Tillamook once had five types of practitioner, each concerned with healing, poisons, spirits, love, and the baby (Seaburg and Miller 1990, 565). The first three wore the insignia of a braided human hair belt with its ends hanging behind like a tail. Although these specialists became wealthy by their efforts, they were generous at winter ceremonials and so never amassed a hoard.

Healers were both men and women, who would blow while curing. Only men used their hands to extract illness, while women would only suck, specializing in the removal of blood, black ooze, or white ooze, which was thrown into a fire or drowned in a basket. In severe cases, it was both drowned and burned. These women received their power from a being called Wild Woman, whose emblem was tattooed on their breasts. Male healers carved or painted their emblem on their headboard, which stood at the healer's bed until brought into use during a cure.

Poison doctors were always men, with the ability to send their own "poisons" or to extract that sent by other shamans. Their medical kit included deer hoof rattles tied on a stick layered with eagle feathers, carved humanoid poles with faces inset with abalone shell eyes, and a headdress made of fringed cedar bark or red male hummingbird scalps. A poison itself was sometimes represented as a tiny bone humanoid doll or as a fish. Their treatment went on for five nights.

Spirit doctors, always men, journeyed in human daytime to the afterworld to retrieve the souls of patients who were ill but not dead. This spirit could be returned only after human dark, when it was safe from recapture. In difficult cases, he sometimes sucked out a purplish ooze sent from the dead.

Only women served as love doctors, able to manipulate affections and sexual abilities. A baby broker was a man who could converse with babies and dream of events in Babyland, where fetuses lived until they went to be born from human mothers.

Today, throughout the Northwest, the aboriginal variety of religious functionaries now appears in the diversity of leaders of church denominations, beliefs, and spiritual practices, as elsewhere in the modern world.

Jay Miller

See also Ceremony and Ritual, Northwest; Dances, Northwest Winter Spirit Dances; Masks and Masking; Oral Traditions, Northwest Coast; Power, Northwest Coast; Religious Leadership, Northwest; Sacred Societies, Northwest Coast; *Sbatatdaq (Sqadaq)*

References and Further Reading

Miller, Jay. 1988. *Shamanic Odyssey: The Lushootseed Salish Journey to the Land of the Dead, in Terms of Death, Potency, and Cooperating Shamans in North America.* Anthropological Papers 32. Menlo Park, CA: Ballena Press.
———. 1992. "Native Healing in Puget Sound." *Caduceus* (Winter) 8: 1–15.
———. 1997. *Tsimshian Culture: A Light through the Ages.* Lincoln: University of Nebraska Press.
———. 1999. *Lushootseed Culture and the Shamanic Odyssey: An Anchored Radiance.* Lincoln: University of Nebraska Press.
Seaburg, William, and Jay Miller. 1990. "Tillamook." Pp. 560–567 in *Handbook of North American Indians: Northwest Coast*, vol. 7. Edited by Wayne Suttles. Washington, DC: Smithsonian Institution Press.
Suttles, Wayne. 1987. *Coast Salish Essays.* Seattle: University of Washington Press.

Religious Leadership, Plateau

Visions and spirit power have always been essential for religious leadership in the Plateau (Walker 1978, 1980, 1998). They are the most ancient and fundamental forms of religious belief and practice in the Plateau. The vision quest, winter spirit dances, and sweatlodge ceremony form a foundation for all other traditional belief and practice throughout the region. Before participation in any activity associated with the spirit world, people cleansed themselves in the sweatlodge, a structure used to achieve purity of body, mind, and spirit (Walker 1969).

Vision quest sites are also scattered throughout the Plateau and are especially concentrated in mountains and along rivers where stone cairns, pictographs, and petroglyphs often mark places where tutelary spirits have been encountered. Tutelary spirit power is often accompanied by a spirit sickness, and trusted healers assist in dealing with it by instructing the neophyte in the proper ways to honor and employ the power they have acquired in vision quests and dreams (Walker 1989).

Midwinter ceremonies provided opportunities not only for neophytes but especially for religious leaders to dramatize and honor their spirit power through symbolic costumes, songs, and dances. Although any person could attend, only those with spirit power would participate in these dances, while others in attendance cooked, served, and lent support in various way. The curing of illnesses of various types customarily took place in these ceremonies; in addition, ceremonial leaders officiated during both life cycle and other calendrical ceremonies associated with the changing seasons and subsistence activities—especially fishing, hunting, and the gathering of roots and berries.

The spirit powers that made a religious leader successful as a healer were also a source of potential harm. If a patient died and the healer was judged to be evil or inept, he or she might be killed. In addition to curing, some religious leaders were thought to be able to change the weather, foresee the future, impart unusual powers to inanimate objects, and possess other miraculous abilities. The primary tests for religious leadership in the traditional Plateau was the ability to heal magically and to foretell the future from visions and dreams.

Men and women occupied similar leadership roles in the Plateau religion. Each complemented the other, and they had similar spirits. Most men and women in the Plateau sought guardian spirits as children. Both genders could aspire to become healers, although in some groups there were not as many female practitioners as there were male. Both could become prophets and exercise leadership in all spheres of religious activity. Some religious leaders also specialized in ceremonies for a particular resource, such as salmon or camas roots, and would lead the first fruits ritual ceremony. This ceremony involved procuring a particular food when it first appeared, primarily during spring and summer, worshipfully carrying it back to the settlement, and conducting a public ritual over it. Each such ceremonial leader must have the proper guardian-spirit power to perform these rituals, whose principal purpose was to secure continuation of the resource.

The Prophet Dance and Religious Leadership

Most historians have assumed that the visits of early explorers such as Meriwether Lewis and William Clark in 1805–1806 marked the beginning of Plateau contact with Euro-Americans, but that assumption is open to question (Spier 1935). An increasing body of evidence points to the protohistoric (that is, the time immediately before the historical period begins: A.D. 1500–1800 in the Plateau) as a time when cultic innovations described as the "Prophet Dance" by Spier (ibid.) were already underway (Relander 1986; Walker 1969). This hypothesis is supported by the diversity of cults and prophetic figures already present in the Plateau during the early contact period, the archaeological evidence from altered burial practices, increasing non-Indian trade goods in the region, the extinction or catastrophic reduction of various groups through epidemic disease, and surviving records from oral tradition among historical and contemporary Plateau religious leaders.

The growing intensity of contacts in the protohistorical period and later during the nineteenth century created major cultural crises in Plateau religious life that brought changes in religious leadership (Stern 1993). One example is a Cathlamet Chinookan text that describes how the informant's grandfather had died during a smallpox epidemic, visited the after-world, and then returned to life bringing messages, all in good Prophet Dance fashion (Boas 1901, 247–251). This dying and reviving of religious leaders in times of cultural crisis is common in the Plateau, but it is nowhere more prevalent than among the Sahaptians of the Southern Plateau, where it has been explicitly related to population decimation and the consequent response of religious leaders such as the following account indicates:

> There was an epidemic of smallpox among the Yakima and people were dying and leaving the country. One old man, a chief, took sick and was left behind. He died. In his dream he travelled and came to a place where people were gathered eating lots of good things. He was awfully hungry.

He came to a kind of gateway and asked for food. The people turned him away and told him it wasn't time for him to come in yet. So they directed him to another place a long way off. He travelled and finally he reached there. They told him when he asked for food that they didn't eat there. They looked thin and raw boned and didn't say much. They said, "We are people called angels." They told him to go back where he came from. "We can't take you in," they said. He felt bad and went back. When he came to his place he came to life again. But his people thought he was dead. He followed them. He surprised them. The first place he went to was Hell. The second place was Heaven. (Spier 1935, 17)

Such newly inspired religious leaders typically communicated a code of worship that involved a distinctive dance, usually circular, and prophecies obtained in deathlike visions; participation in ceremonies was by whole settlements, and great emphasis was placed on a creator spirit or god who reigned above the other spirits. In some cases confession of sins was required, and prophecies of a coming world transformation were regular features of these new developments. Cult activities were periodic, with an emotional heat being generated; with a failure of prophecy, however, there was a waning of interest, only later to be regenerated (ibid.; Du Bois 1938). Spier's so-called Prophet Dance is significant in this regard and must be understood as a general term that is inclusive of various local cultural manifestations led by various "prophets" (from both the protohistorical period and the early historical period) who appeared among at least the following groups: Nez Perce, Umatilla, Spokane, Colville, Coeur d'Alene, Kootenai, Wanapam, Yakima, Klikitat, Wayampam, Palouse, Sanpoil-Nespelem, and probably certain Chinookan groups on the Lower Columbia. They included such well-known figures as Shuwapsa, Dla-upac, Spokane Garry, Kootenai Pelly, Nez Perce Ellis, Colville Kolaskin, Wiletsi, Hununwe, Jim Kanine, Shramaia, Lishwailait, Ashnithlai, the Tenino Queahpahmah, Luls, Smohalla, Wiskaynatowatsanmay, Kotiahkan, Patio, Toohoohoolsote, Jake Hunt, Martin Speedis, Yo-Yonau, and especially Puck Hyat Toot. Puck Hyat Toot was the most influential in the development of what has come more recently to be called the Seven Drum religion, the Long House religion, or the Washani/Washat religion, the dominant traditional religion now functioning widely among southern Plateau tribes (Ruby and Brown 1989; Walker 1978, 1980, 1985). It has preserved most of the earlier religious beliefs and practices of the prehistorical period, with additions emphasizing prophecy, nativism, revitalization, and some ceremonial features apparently borrowed from Christianity during the protohistorical and early historical periods. Recent leaders include Andrew George, Palouse; Clarence Burke, Walla Walla; Amos Pond, Umatilla; Gail Shippentower, Cayuse and Walla Walla; Fermore Craig, Cayuse; Armand Minthorn, Cayuse; Ron Pond, Umatilla; Steve Sohappy, Wanapum; and Dallas Dick, Wanapum, Palouse, and Nez Perce.

Indian Shaker Church leaders are closely linked to the Northwest Coastal groups first led by John Slocum and Mud Bay Louie. The Yakama and Warm Springs reservations have been centers of Shaker influence, which more recently has been extended to the Colville and Umatilla reservations. Indian Shaker leaders are often prominent both in the Shaker and the Seven Drum religion (Barnett 1957).

A more recent development in the Plateau has been the introduction of the Native American Church through such religious leaders as Leonard Crow Dog from Pine Ridge. Such leaders have been instrumental in establishing a regular presence among the Colville, Coeur d'Alene, and Yakama (Stewart 1988). Ted Strong has been a major leader in the Native American Church among the Yakama, as has David Mathesen among the neighboring Coeur d'Alene. Other leaders include Peter George, George Nanamkin, and Vance Robert Campbell on the Colville Reservation. Members of these tribes regularly assemble on various reservations for Native American Church services. There is also some ceremonial interaction among these tribes and the tribes of southern Idaho, where the Native American Church has been established much longer. Tommy Sope and Don Dunbar are principal leaders at Duck Valley and Fort McDermitt Indian Reservations, but there are many others among the Northern Paiute and Shoshone on the Wind River Reservation and the Fort Hall Reservation who, from time to time, interact with leaders of the Plateau Native American Church.

Christian Leadership

Although little reported by anthropologists, numerous Christian communities with well-known Indian leaders have developed among many Plateau tribes and date from the nineteenth century. The Catholic and Protestant missionaries of the first half of the nineteenth century have been the subject of much historical writing, but that writing rarely reveals much about Indian Christian leadership among Plateau tribes (Burns 1966; Raufer 1966; Drury 1936, 1937, 1940, 1949). Christian missionaries' programs of educating tribal pastors and priests led to large-scale conversions of tribes and the formation of permanent Christian ecclesiastical structures among such groups as the Nez Perce, Yakima, Umatilla, Coeur d'Alene, Spokane, Flathead, Warm Springs, and Colville in the Southern Plateau, as well as others in the Canadian (Northern) Plateau. Nez Perce Christian leaders include the following preachers who not only served the Nez Perce Presbyterian churches but also served as missionaries: The Reverend Archie Lawyer was pastor of the Second Kamiah Church at the time of his death in the spring of 1893. The Reverend Robert Williams, the first ordained minister, ordained in 1879, was pastor of the First Church of Kamiah at the time of his death in 1896. That was his only charge. The Nez Perce ministers were the Reverend James Hines, honorably retired be-

cause of old age; the Reverend Mark Arthur, pastor of the Lapwai Church; the Reverend Peter Lindsley, without charge; the Reverend James Hayes, pastor of the First Church of Kamiah; the Reverend Moses Monteith, pastor of the Second Church of Kamiah; the Reverend Robert Parsons, pastor of the Meadow Creek Church; the Reverend William Wheeler, stated supply of the Stites Church; the Reverend Enoch Pond, stated supply of the North Fork Church at the time of his death, March 20, 1907; and the Reverend Silas Whitman, died in June 1905 (McBeth 1908). They served in most tribes throughout the Plateau as well as among the Shoshone and Paiute of the Northern Great Basin.

Father Brown, a Blackfoot Catholic priest, is an example of the much less common Catholic tendency to train an Indian priesthood in the Plateau. Therefore, Catholic missionizing has historically been, and continues to be, primarily in the hands of non-Indian priests such as Fathers Cataldo, De Smet, O'Malley, and Connolly (Burns 1966). In contrast, Nez Perce preachers Cecil Corbett, Walter Moffett, and Mose Thomas are more recent seminary-trained missionaries who continue to operate in various tribes throughout the West and even Canada on behalf of the Presbyterians.

Small Indian-dominated Pentecostal churches have been formed and are closely tied to the Indian Shaker churches at Yakama, Warm Springs, Colville, and elsewhere. In some cases Pentecostal leaders are found as leaders in both the Indian Shaker Church and Pentecostal churches. The Pentecostal Bible and the Doctrine of the Holy Ghost have also been introduced into some Indian Shaker ceremonies. Unlike the major tests for traditional religious leadership in the Plateau—magical healing and prophecy—the Christian Indian religious leaders have depended on formal confirmation by non-Indian church authorities for legitimation. In contrast, the generally less educated Pentecostal Christian religious leaders more often establish their legitimacy by healing and visions.

Deward E. Walker, Jr.

See also Ceremony and Ritual, Coeur d'Alene; Ceremony and Ritual, Nez Perce; Oral Traditions, Plateau; Retraditionalism and Revitalization Movements, Columbia Plateau; Spiritual and Ceremonial Practitioners, Plateau; Vision Quest Rites

References and Further Reading

Barnett, Homer G. 1957/1972. *Indian Shakers: A Messianic Cult of the Pacific Northwest.* Reprint, Carbondale: Southern Illinois University Press.

Boas, Franz. 1901/1977. "Kathlamet Texts." *Bureau of American Ethnology Bulletin* 26. Reprint, St. Clair Shores, MI: Scholarly Press.

Burns, Robert Ignatius, S. J. 1966. *The Jesuits and the Indian Wars of the Northwest.* New Haven and London: Yale University Press.

Drury, Clifford M. 1936. *Henry Harmon Spalding, Pioneer of Old Oregon.* Caldwell, ID: Caxton Printers.

———. 1937. *Marcus Whitman, Pioneer and Martyr.* Caldwell, ID: Caxton Printers.

———. 1940. *Elkanah and Mary Walker, Pioneers among the Spokane.* Caldwell, ID: Caxton Printers.

———. 1949. *A Tepee in His Front Yard: A Biography of H. T. Cowley, One of the Four Founders of the City of Spokane.* Portland, OR: Binfords and Mort.

Du Bois, Cora. 1938. *The Feather Cult of the Middle Columbia.* General Series in Anthropology 7. Menasha, WI: George Banta.

McBeth, Kate. 1908/1993. *The Nez Perces since Lewis and Clark.* Reprint, Moscow: University of Idaho Press.

Raufer, Maria Ilma, Sister, O. P. 1966. *Black Robes and Indians on the Last Frontier: A Story of Heroism.* Milwaukee, WI: Bruce Publishing Company.

Relander, Click. 1986. *Drummers and Dreamers.* Seattle: Pacific Northwest National Parks and Forests Association.

Ruby, Robert H., and John A. Brown. 1989. *Dreamer-Prophets of the Columbia Plateau.* Norman: University of Oklahoma Press.

Spier, Leslie. 1935/1979. *The Prophet Dance of the Northwest and Its Derivatives: The Source of the Ghost Dance.* General Series in Anthropology 1. Reprint, New York: AMS Press.

Stern, Theodore. 1993. *Chiefs and Chief Traders: Indian Relations at Fort Nez Percés, 1818–1855.* Corvalis: Oregon State University Press.

Stewart, Omer C. 1988. "Peyotism in Idaho." *Northwest Anthropological Research Notes* 22, no. 1: 1–7.

Walker, Deward E., Jr. 1969. "New Light on the Prophet Dance Controversy." *Ethnohistory* 16, no. 3: 245–255.

———. 1978. *Indians of Idaho.* Moscow: University of Idaho Press.

———. 1980. *Myths of Idaho Indians.* Moscow: University of Idaho Press.

———. 1985. *Conflict and Schism in Nez Perce Acculturation: A Study of Religion and Politics,* 2d ed. Moscow: University of Idaho Press.

———. 1989. *Witchcraft and Sorcery of the American Native Peoples.* Moscow: University of Idaho Press.

———. 1998. "Plateau." *Handbook of North American Indians,* vol. 12. Washington, DC: Smithsonian Institution.

Repatriation, Spiritual and Cultural Implications

Today's academic disciplines of archaeology and physical anthropology share a legacy with museums rooted in desecration, sacrilege, and violations of indigenous human rights. American Indians and Native Hawaiians have battled the collective might of these imperialistic entities and won a number of important religious freedom and human rights victories in the political arena. Federal and state laws resulting from these struggles have enabled Indian nations to repatriate ancestral human remains, funerary objects, and cultural items belonging to them that were lost to the hands of others. Laws have also extended burial protections to federal lands and to some states. Museums and academics have become more receptive to Indian concerns, but this cultural war is far from having been won. Many museums, universities, and federal agencies continue to hold, and have the final say over, the disposition of items belonging to Indians and Native Hawaiians. Consequently, mistrust, fear, and doubt continue to plague this relationship. More important, the desecration of Indian graves continues in the name of progress.

Like people everywhere, indigenous peoples of the U.S. and other places have spiritual beliefs associated with the dead and the places where they are buried. These views and mortuary traditions differ in many respects from Indian nation to nation, but a common theme among them is that the dead should not be bothered except for legitimate and compelling purposes. In 1850s, Chief Seattle, responding to the U.S. government's demands that the Suquamish and Duwamish peoples of Washington cede their lands, declared, "To us the ashes of our ancestors are sacred and their resting place is hallowed ground. . . . Our dead never forget the beautiful world that gave them being. They still love its verdant valleys, its murmuring rivers, its magnificent mountains, sequestered vales and verdant lined lakes and bays, and ever yearn in tender, fond affection over the lonely hearted living, and often return from the Happy Hunting Ground to visit, guide, console and comfort them." As Seattle noted, cemeteries are sacred places. A Shasta's final words, recorded in 1877, explain the religious significance of a proper and lasting burial for many California Indians. After telling his companions not to bury him away from his home village, the dying man gave a passionate "adjuration to them not to let his body molder and his spirit wander homeless, friendless, and alone in a strange country."

Indigenous groups shared many beliefs regarding tampering with the dead. Many expect a lasting burial in which their remains would deteriorate within Mother Earth. Some believe that disinterment stops the spiritual journey of the dead, causing the affected spirits to wander aimlessly in limbo. Pawnees, Diné (Navajos), Apaches, and others assert that anyone who disrupts a grave is an evil, profane, and demented person who plans to use the dead as a means of harming the living. Sickness, emotional distress, and death are the possible effects of such activities. Many Indians stress that disinterment may occur only for a compelling reason. For example, Pawnees occasionally opened a grave of one of their deceased relatives to reposition an incorrectly placed holy object.

However, Europeans who entered the Americas had scant regard for the host population's rights. Their invasion occurred under the color of a racialized mindset that relegated Indians to the lowly position of savages and pagans. The invaders, by virtue of the "doctrine of discovery," claimed a God-given right of preeminence to the land. Graves of Indians also became fair game. English violations of Indian burials occurred shortly after the landing of the *Mayflower* at Plymouth Bay in 1620. The sacrilege escalated dramatically after the founding of the United States in 1776. Throughout the colonial and early republic periods, men of high social standing such as Thomas Jefferson disrupted Indian graves for the sake of curiosity and trophies for home display.

As the nineteenth century progressed, the looting of Indian graves became a cottage industry, an honored profession, and an undertaking sanctioned by law and public opinion. Beginning in the 1830s, Samuel G. Morton paid soldiers, federal Indian agents, and settlers to steal skulls from Indian graves. The federal policy of moving Indians westward

left thousands of Indian graves unprotected from the shovels of looters. Morton's craniometrics research sought to prove the intellectual and cultural superiority of Anglo Saxons over other races. Others used the pseudoscientific findings of Morton and his followers to write racial studies that denigrated Indians as intellectually or culturally inferior. These works supported the self-serving claim of white America that it had a God-given right to expand its borders and civilization across the hemisphere. In 1867, the Army Medical Museum (AMM) began to collect Indian remains for study. Prizing crania, field surgeons often went to the scene of battles and decapitated the bodies of fallen Indians. By the early 1890s, field surgeons and others had shipped AMM curators Indian crania and bodies representing approximately 4,000 individuals.

During the late 1800s and 1900s, professional and amateur archaeologists, joined by museum curators, joined the sacrilege in larger and larger numbers. Individuals of this bent sought to endear the work of Morton by calling him the father of American physical anthropology. University graduate programs in physical anthropology and archaeology produced scholars trained in the crafts of exhuming and studying indigenous bodies and grave contents. Amateur archaeologists scoured the countryside in search of Indian burials. Digs often drew large crowds, and some exposed cemeteries became tourist attractions and state parks. Museums acquired, displayed, and warehoused stolen skulls, bones, and grave goods for educational purposes. These profane operations gave rise to what can be termed the archaeology/museum industry. These professions shared a common value rooted in the exploitation of deceased Indians and Native Hawaiians and the taking of cultural objects under a cloud of federal oppression. The rise of professional organizations including the Society of American Archaeology (SAA) and the Association of American Physical Anthropology (AAPA) promoted scholarship involving the excavation, warehousing, study, and display of Native remains and funerary objects. Rather than telling the story of Indians from an indigenous perspective, these studies cast this history in the realm of Western intellectual thought.

The sacrilege did not stop there. Believing that Indians were a vanishing race, museums also became heavily engaged in the business of acquiring cultural objects from Indians subjected to the heavy hand of federal oppression. By the 1890s most Indian nations had been confined on reservations, where their people lived in dire poverty and faced an uncertain future. These lands often resembled prisoner of war camps, with U.S. military and Indian police forces in place to suppress Ghost Dance and other spiritual activities seen as rebellious and uncivilized. Federal agents, following a national policy committed to eradicating all vestiges of traditional Indian culture, took thousands of Indian children from their families and placed them in distant boarding schools. School personnel employed corporal punishment, education, and strict military regimentation in an attempt to force the children to forget their native languages, to accept Christianity, and to adopt white American ways. Codes of Indian offenses criminalized Indian rituals and healing ceremonies.

Facing oppression and destitution, some Indians began to sell religious objects to museum curators and private collectors who went to reservations for that purpose. The Antiquities Act of 1906 essentially turned over the ownership of indigenous graves to the federal government. Under that law, potential diggers on federal lands, including reservations, had to apply for a permit in which they agreed to turn over the fruits of their labor to public institutions for study in perpetuity. State governments followed the federal example of compelling excavators to surrender unearthed objects found on state lands to public facilities.

Through these efforts, federal and state agencies, universities, and private museums amassed enormous collections of human remains and cultural objects at the expense of Indian religious freedom and burial rights. A national mindset, complete with laws, sanctioned the desecration and oppression. The granting of citizenship rights to Indians in the late 1800s and 1900s did nothing to impede the growth of the archaeology/museum industry. It took a movement that surfaced in the 1960s to accomplish that purpose.

Indian challenges to discriminatory laws and the archaeology/museum industry emerged with the rise of the Indian movement. Along with demanding religious freedom, a return to treaty relationship with the federal government, and full sovereignty, Indian activism also focused on ending the scientific theft of indigenous graves and regaining control of the collections in museums. Members of the American Indian Movement (AIM) and others periodically disrupted digs and protested the mistreatment of their ancestors and the discriminatory laws that denied many deceased Indians a lasting burial. American Indians Against Desecration (AIAD) surfaced as an organization committed to the protection of Indian burials. In Hawaii, Hui Malama I Na Kupuna O Hawai'i Nei was founded to protect the sanctity of *iwi kupuna* (ancestral Native Hawaiian remains) and ensure their proper return to *ka 'aina* (the land) through the practice of traditional values, spiritual beliefs, and practices.

Fortunately, the message carried by AIM, AIAD, Hui Malama I Na Kupuna O Hawai'i Nei, and burial protection advocates about the disrespectful and abusive treatment of deceased Indians gradually resonated with the American public. Despite strong opposition from elements of the archaeology/museum industry, a growing number of states responded by extending burial protection laws to include unmarked Indian cemeteries. A few universities, the North Dakota Historical Society, and the Ne-braska Unicameral Legislature agreed to repatriate human remains in their collections to Indian nations.

The successes of the repatriation initiatives created a crisis in the archaeology/museum industry. Its affiliates divided, taking positions ranging from flat resistance to compromise. The American Committee for the Preservation of Archaeological Collections (ACPAC) viewed the conduct of archaeologists who participated in repatriation as treasonous. It presented its membership as victims of irrational attacks on their ability to tell the story of prehistory. Waving the banner of academic freedom, ACPAC sought to maintain professional solidarity by blackballing the "sellouts" and raising funds to support the legal defense of members accused of violating burial laws. A 1986 ACPAC newsletter declared:

> Archaeologists, your profession is on the line. Now is the time to dig deep and help ACPAC with its expenses for legal fees. Next year or next month will be too late; we have to act immediately to fight this issue. This one will be resolved in court, not by the press. We will be able to cross-examine Indians on their tribal affinities, religion, and connection to the archaeological remains they seek to destroy. We will be able to challenge anti-science laws based on race and religion. We can make a strong case, but it takes money. Send some!

Those who advocated compromise sought to continue their work by gaining the respect and trust of Indians.

As the 1980s closed, the United States became more receptive to Indian and Native Hawaiian demands for the repatriation of human remains, funerary objects, and sacred cultural objects. In 1989, American Indians and the Smithsonian Institution reached a landmark repatriation agreement. Later that year Congress implemented the agreement by enacting the National Museum of the American Indian Act (NMAIA), requiring the Smithsonian Institution to repatriate human remains and funerary objects in its collections linked to present-day Indian nations by a preponderance of evidence. The following year Congress made repatriation a national policy when it passed the Native American Graves Protection and Repatriation Act (NAGPRA). This bipartisan measure required all entities receiving federal funding to inventory the human remains, funerary objects, objects of cultural patrimony, and sacred objects in their collections. Upon receiving those inventories, Indian nations could begin the process of repatriating items linked to them. In 1996, Congress created statutory uniformity by amending NMAIA to enable Indian nations and Native Hawaiian organizations to repatriate objects of cultural patrimony and sacred objects from the Smithsonian. These laws have provided a legal avenue for Indians and Native Hawaiians to repatriate thousands of their ancestors and funerary objects. These indigenous peoples have reclaimed cultural objects that are central to their identity as a people, as well as

some that are needed for ongoing religious ceremonies.

Repatriating human remains has forced the next of kin to address the issue of how the reburials should take place. After all, Indians never before had to conduct reburial ceremonials. Does a ceremony need to be conducted? Should the remains be spiritually fed? Should non-Indians, the perpetrators, be allowed to attend the reburials? Should the press be allowed to attend, so that the reburial can be publicized for educational purposes? Indians and Native Hawaiians have devised reburial procedures that are culturally appropriate for them. Basically, reburials are often spiritual observances accompanied by reverence, prayer, and song. They are both sorrowful and joyous occasions. Those in attendance sense the disturbing history involving the disinterment and confinement of their ancestors in boxes, on public display, and on shelves. Unlike funerals for the recently departed, however, reburials evoke feelings of elation for the sacred act of returning ancestral remains to the womb of Mother Earth. These services bond the living with their ancestors in ways that are both spiritual and symbolic. Some groups exclude non-Indians from attending, while others want the occasion recorded to teach others about the shameful legacy of grave looting.

Despite these laws and the successes of the repatriation movement, serious problems continue to hamper Indians and Native Hawaiians in their quest for burial rights, repatriation, and religious freedom. First, the Society of American Archaeology, professional archaeologists, physical archaeologists, and others remain committed to preserving the privileged status they acquired through the history of scientific racism and cultural genocide. In an August 26, 1999, letter, G. A. Clark, head of the Archaeology Division of the American Anthropological Association, declared bitterly:

> I have no patience with, nor sympathy for, NAGPRA and the political correctness that underlies it. Moreover, I am deeply embarrassed for, and ashamed of, American archaeology and physical anthropology. One might've thought the various professional societies would've done a better job contesting this lunacy when it was possible to do so. Academics are not very politically adept, however, and when erstwhile Smithsonian Secretary Robert Adams agreed to repatriate the Smithsonian's skeletal collections, it knocked the pins out from under any efforts the SAA and AAPA might've undertaken to prevent it. This is what happens when politics is allowed to take precedence over rational and disinterested evaluation of the credibility of knowledge claims about the human past.

Individuals who oppose repatriation are often found in museums and federal agencies. NAGPRA assigns these people the responsibility to determine the cultural affiliation of human remains in their collections. This means that they have the ability to stop the reburial of human remains, especially the older ones such as Spirit Cave Man now coveted by the archaeology/museum industry, by rejecting evidence submitted by indigenous peoples. Additionally, SAA members comprise the majority of the staffing within the National Park Service (NPS) office responsible for NAGPRA implementation authority. Indians and Native Hawaiians feel that this arrangement constitutes a conflict of interest that allows the NPS to render administrative decisions in favor of archaeologists against native interests.

A second issue is that museums often applied deadly pesticides to masks and other cultural objects. This means that the keepers and wearers of poisoned religious objects could suffer the health consequences of contact with the toxins. Third, in some states, including Texas, legislation protecting Indian burials is missing, leaving property owners the owners of Indian cemeteries.

Finally, NAGPRA left the fate of tens of thousands of human remains up to the NAGPRA Review Committee, a body composed of Indians and academics, sometimes one and the same. This committee is supposed to submit its determination to the secretary of the interior for approval. To date, however, the committee has considered five draft recommendations without approving any of them. The last draft elevates the interests of science above those of Indians by making the repatriation of the "culturally unidentifiable" human remains voluntary.

Meanwhile, representatives of Indian nations adopted their own recommendations for consideration in a December

2002 meeting at Arizona State University's law school. The recommendations state:

1. Culturally unidentifiable Native American human remains are culturally affiliated to contemporary Native peoples, including federally recognized tribes, nonfederally recognized tribes, Native Alaskan peoples, and Native Hawaiian people.
2. All Native American human remains and associated funerary objects, including those deemed "culturally unidentifiable," shall be under the ownership and control of contemporary Native peoples.
3. All "culturally unidentifiable" Native American human remains shall be speedily repatriated to Native peoples in accordance with procedures to be determined by contemporary Native American groups.
4. All scientific study of "culturally unidentifiable" Native American human remains shall immediately cease.
5. The federal government shall be responsible for funding the costs of this repatriation. (Recommendations for Disposition of "Culturally Unidentifiable" Native American Human Remains under NAGPRA)

In closing, the repatriation movement has dramatically altered the privileged status of the archaeology/museum industry in ways that support the religious freedom and beliefs of American Indians and Native Hawaiians. Yet the repatriation battle is still raging in institutions and the courts. The fate of the so-called culturally unidentifiable human remains is still unresolved. Many indigenous peoples continue to view the archaeology/museum industry with mistrust and apprehension.

James Riding In

See also Archaeology; Identity; Kennewick Man; Law, Legislation, and Native Religion

Reservations, Spiritual and Cultural Implications

In this essay, the labels First Nations and Indigenous Peoples are used to name the Aboriginal peoples of the United States. Labels such as "Indians," "American Indians," and "Native Americans" are used only when directly quoting another source. The substitution of labels is crucial because the names Indians, American Indians, and Native Americans are "counterfeit identities" resulting from the hegemony of European American colonialism and linguistic imperialism (Yellow Bird 1999). Indigenous Peoples are "not Indians or American Indians because they are not from India. They are not Native Americans because Indigenous Peoples did not refer to these lands as America until Europeans arrived and imposed this name" (Yellow Bird 2001, 61). The change in terminology is a matter of historical and linguistic justice. Indigenous Peoples have struggled, and continue to struggle, against the oppressive paradigms of American linguistic colonialism that ignores individual tribal identities and falsely names Indigenous Peoples to serve the needs and history of the colonizer. Counterfeit labels are dan-

Entrance road sign for the Nez Perce Reservation, Idaho. (Joseph Sohm/ChromoSohm Inc./Corbis)

gerous because "they are historically entangled in American racist discourses that claim Europeans discovered a new world that needed to be settled, claimed, and civilized. This myth-making has promoted the notion that the original inhabitants were unable to settle, claim, and civilize these lands because they were nomadic, unsettled, savage peoples" (Yellow Bird 1999, 86). Therefore, this essay does not use the labels Indians, American Indians, or Native Americans.

A reservation is often defined as tract of "public" land set aside by the U.S. federal government for the "use," "possession," and "benefit" of Indigenous Peoples (*Merriam Webster's* 2000; Pevar 1992). However, this definition fails to reveal that use and possession of, and benefits from, reservation lands are largely determined and controlled by the U.S. Congress, which exercises plenary authority over those territories through the U.S. Department of the Interior and the Bureau of Indian Affairs. And in order for these lands to be declared public, a term that suggests they are open and accessible to all, control and ownership had to be first taken from the owners. Indeed, by using the force of their courts, congressional removal policies, warfare, and the violation of treaties, land-hungry, resource-starved American colonizers

A woman in a white robe symbolizes Manifest Destiny. On the ground below, Native Americans and bison run in front of her. The philosophy of Manifest Destiny, that U.S. expansion to the Pacific Ocean was inevitable and even divinely inspired, enabled Americans to justify their colonization of indigenous lands. (John Gast/Corbis)

often illegally drove Indigenous Peoples off their lands and claimed them. "Manifest Destiny," the accepted belief that U.S. expansion to the Pacific Ocean was inevitable and even divinely inspired, enabled Americans to justify their theft and colonization of indigenous lands. Missouri senator Thomas Hart Benton, a fierce proponent of this philosophy, declared that white Americans had alone received the divine command to subdue and replenish the earth, while Indigenous Peoples had no rights to the lands because they had been created for use by the white races according to the intentions of the Creator (Benton, 1846). In 1500, when Europeans began arriving in this country, Indigenous Peoples controlled billions of acres of land. By 1887 their land base was down to 140 million acres, and by 1931 it had shrunk to less than 48 million acres (Olson and Wilson 1986).

Failures by the U.S. Congress to ratify land agreements made with Indigenous Peoples also caused these groups to lose hundreds of millions of additional acres of land. The amount of land stolen from Indigenous Peoples by the citizens and governments of the United States is shocking and shameful. By 1980 the U.S. federal government held only 52 million acres of Indigenous Peoples' land in trust (ibid., 209). However, struggles for the land between Indigenous Peoples and the United States are not over, and many tribal nations continue to work for the return and protection of their aboriginal territories. Today's reservations represent the last remaining lands belonging to people who once owned and occupied all that is now the contiguous United States and Alaska (Snipp 1996, 39).

Most reservations were created by treaty, presidential order, or an act of Congress, and the majority are located west of the Mississippi River in mainly isolated, rural areas. There are two types of reservations: federal and state. These entities are referred to as colonies, communities, pueblos, ranches, rancherias, reservations, reserves, tribal towns, and villages (U.S. Census Bureau 2000). In 2000 there were 315 federal and state reservations around the nation. Reservations vary in size, "ranging from only a few acres, such as the small rancherias scattered around California, to the Navajo reservation in the four corners area, which is approximately the size of the state of West Virginia or the nation of Ireland" (Snipp 1996).

Reservations were established on some of the poorest, more remote lands in the United States and, in many in-

stances, were not regarded or intended to be places where Indigenous Peoples could reside indefinitely. In fact, many influential nineteenth-century white policy-makers believed that these groups must assimilate into white society if they were to survive, and that "the biggest obstacle to Indian assimilation was the reservation system" (Adams 1995). Over many generations, poverty, lack of opportunity, federal government neglect and relocation policies, and isolation caused many First Nations People to flee reservation life. At the inception of this system the majority of Native Peoples lived on reservations. By 1990 slightly less than 22 percent of the indigenous population resided on those lands (ibid.).

While it was asserted by white policy-makers that reservations were established to protect Indigenous Peoples from encroaching white settlers, during their early development in the mid to late 1800s, reservations were also established to serve as holding pens or concentration camps where Indigenous Peoples were detained and confined by the U.S. government. Many tribes who had resisted the American invasion into their lands were herded, often under heavily armed military guard units, onto these lands and treated as "hostiles" or prisoners of war. Whether individual tribes had been friendly or at war with the United States made little difference in these environments; most received poor treatment, such as inferior food, housing, and medical care. Reservation life took a terrible toll on the physical, emotional, psychological, and spiritual lives of the residents. Conditions were so bad that they would cause an often embarrassed U.S. Congress to launch numerous investigations to study these problems. However, little was ever done to correct or improve these environments.

When reservation life had weakened Indigenous Peoples to their lowest point of resistance, almost every social, political, and economic aspect of tribal life came under the most pointed and aggressive attack. Without any regard or respect for Indigenous Peoples' former customs and beliefs, "Bureau of Indian Affairs" superintendents, who were sometimes corrupt, and federally subsidized missionaries imposed changes in all aspects of Native life. To ensure that Indigenous Peoples could not escape from this situation and would conform to the subjugation of the reservation system, the federal government enacted harsh laws and penalties. For instance, commissioner of Indian Affairs Francis A. Walker, in his 1872 annual report, declared, "In the first announcement made of the reservation system, it was expressly declared that the Indians should be made as comfortable on, as uncomfortable off, their reservations as it was in the power of the Government to make them; that such of them as went right should be protected and fed, and such as went wrong should be harassed and scourged without intermission" (Prucha 1975, 139). Because reservations created a system of racial segregation and made

possible the political and economic discrimination and manipulation of First Nations peoples, they could, by definition, be regarded as the earliest form of government-sponsored apartheid in this nation. In fact, the reservation system was so effective at controlling Indigenous Peoples that it is believed that Nazi leader Adolph Hitler researched Indian reservations as models for his concentration camps (Means 1999).

Until the early 1970s, when a major resurgence of indigenous identity and cultural renewal occurred, the effects that reservations had upon Indigenous Peoples' religious lives were almost exclusively negative (Nagel 1997). Concentrating these groups in one area made it much easier to control and oversee their activities and made Indigenous Peoples a captive audience for missionaries. The ethnocentrism of white policy-makers and Christian missionaries caused them to look upon Native religious practices as primitive, barbaric, superstitious, and inferior, as well as preventing moral and religious development. Indigenous Peoples, it was argued, "must be taught the knowledge, values, and habits of Christian civilization" if they were to be saved (Adams 1995, 141–143). As more and more missionaries arrived on reservations for the purpose of religious conversion of Indigenous Peoples to Christianity, the spiritual lives of Indigenous Peoples faced considerable and continuing disruption.

The souls of Indigenous Peoples were divided up between various religious groups, beginning with the Quakers in 1869. By 1872 government agents had assigned 238,899 individuals from seventy-three different reservation agencies to thirteen Euro-American Christian religious groups (Prucha 1975). Family members, both nuclear and extended, were often divided between different competing religious denominations, which created spiritual conflicts and religious arguments between people where none had existed before. In fact, Lakota scholar Vine Deloria, Jr., asserts, "No de-

mand existed, however, for the people to go into the world and inform or instruct other people in their rituals and beliefs of the tribe. The people were supposed to follow their own teachings and assume that other people would follow their teachings. These instructions were rigorously followed and consequently there was never an instance of a tribe making war on another tribe because of religious differences" (Deloria 1999, 262).

Perhaps the greatest reply to the imposition of white religious beliefs upon

Leo Yellowhair stands outside his hogan on the Hopi Indian Reservation. Yellowhair and his mother, Joanne Yellowhair, live day to day along the rim of Blue Canyon about twenty miles southeast of Tuba City, Arizona. Their home is a small octagonal dirt and wood traditional Diné hogan. Living without plumbing or electricity, their life centers on tending their eighteen sheep and goats and one horse. In the summer they raise crops irrigated with water carried from Tuba City. Ca. 1996. (Kevin Fleming/Corbis)

Indigenous Peoples was delivered by Seneca leader Red Jacket, who said the following to a preacher from the Evangelical Missionary Society in 1805:

> Brother, you say that you are sent to instruct us how to worship the Great Spirit agreeably to his mind, and, if we do not take hold of the religion which you white people teach, we shall be unhappy hereafter. You say that you are right and we are lost. How do we know this to be true? We . . . only know what you tell us about it. How shall we know when to believe, being so often deceived by the white people? Brother, you say there is but one way to worship and serve the Great Spirit. If there is but one religion, why do you white people differ so much about it? We are told that your religion was given to your forefathers, and has been handed down from father to son. We also have a religion, which was given to our forefathers, and has been handed down to us, their children. We worship in that way. It teaches us to be thankful for all the favors we receive; to love each other, and to be united. We never quarrel about religion. (Wright 1992, 231–232)

More recently, Sahnish (Arikara) elder Magdalene Yellow Bird recounts as a young girl how all the people in her community would come together to pray and worship in any of the Christian churches on a given Sunday and how white religious leaders then prohibited this practice.

> It didn't matter to our people what church they attended because we were all accustomed to prayer and worship as one tribal community. It was just natural for us to all be together at this time. The church just happened to be the place we went to. After the services were over we would all sit down together in the church basement in the winter, or outside in the summer, to eat a meal and visit before going to pray at the next church. At first the ministers at the different churches didn't mind us going from place to place. I think they were just glad that they had so many of us in their congregation singing, praying, and thanking them for their good words. But it didn't take long for them to figure out what we were doing and pretty soon they began to tell us that we could not come to their services if we were not members of their church. Of course this bothered the people because they were so used to being together whenever something holy was going on. So, what happened changed how we viewed religion and it's when we started to become really divided in our spiritual beliefs. So now I'm a Catholic, one of your aunties is a Lutheran, and your grandma belongs to the United Church of Christ. Of course some still attended tribal ceremonies but didn't tell the Christian ministers about it, because they were always saying we were going to go to hell if we practiced these ways. (Interview with Magdalene Yellow Bird 1990)

Since time immemorial, "sacred landscapes, rivers, forests, stories, songs, plants (medicines), dances, and symbols have been at the center of Indigenous spirituality helping First Nations Peoples find wholeness and renew their cultures" (Yellow Bird 2001, 66). However, when

Our Lady of the Little Rockies Church, Fort Belknap Reservation, Hays, Montana. 1994. (Dave G. Houser/Corbis)

Indigenous Peoples were confined to reservations, access to these places, practices, and materials was often not possible. Holy pilgrimages to sacred sites or the collection of plants necessary for various ceremonial purposes either ceased or had to be done in secret. "Thunder Butte," a sacred landscape to the Mandan, Hidatsa, and Sahnish of the Fort Berthold Reservation in North Dakota, is located just outside the western borders of the reservation on land now belonging to a white rancher. At one time this site was located on the lands of these tribes, but it was taken away during one of the many reductions of their

territory by the federal government. For several generations the only sacred pilgrimages to this area were done in secret, under the cover of night, and at great risk to the individual. During the 1970s, tribal members who were interested in reviving their traditional religious practices approached the owner of these lands and gained permission to resume sacred use of the site. However, there often remain periods of time when the owner will not allow such visits.

The religious practices of Indigenous Peoples, who were virtual prisoners on the reservation, were continually attacked and threatened by government

A bumper sticker on a vehicle in Neah Bay, a town on the Makah Indian Reservation in the northwest corner of Washington state. (Ed Eckstein/Corbis)

Indian agents and Christian missionaries. To discourage the practice of tribal religious life, laws were imposed that banned the singing of tribal songs, dances, and religious ceremonies. Traditional religious leaders were condemned, jailed, and ridiculed by white missionaries and government agents, and they were removed from any influential position they had held among their community. Those leaders that abandoned their religious tribal beliefs and turned to white religious practices were especially useful to white colonizers.

Banned from singing songs that were an important means of transmitting

spiritual culture to younger generations, a group of prominent Sahnish leaders and chiefs petitioned the commissioner of Indian Affairs in 1913, requesting permission to be allowed to resume that practice: "Sir; Whereas the old time songs and music are being forgotten, and in order not to have them forgotten entirely, we, the undersigned do hereby respectfully request permission to meet once a month to practice the said songs, so as to give the younger generation a chance to learn them, and to let them in turn teach them to the next generation. Also we wish to perpetuate these songs to sing to Historians when they chance to come here and want to hear old time songs. Hoping that this request will be granted to us we sign ourselves" (Gilman and Schneider 1987, 224). Recognizing that the necessary degree of assimilation had taken hold among this group, the commissioner later gave his permission. However, most tribal groups that made such requests were not so fortunate.

Sharing and generosity were, and remain, important spiritual values among many First Nations Peoples. Helping others by sharing of what one has, whether it is time, resources, or knowledge, is a way in which many groups reinforce their respect and appreciation for one another. Such actions helped inspire good relationships and contributed to peace, harmony, and the well-being of all tribal members. Many Indigenous Peoples use give-away ceremonies to extend their good fortune. Items such as food, clothing, blankets, money, and cookware are shared between people. For many groups, sharing and generosity are part of their original religious tribal teachings. For instance, among the Sahnish a holy being named Mother Corn taught them "to provide for those who should be dependent upon them . . . to be generous and forbearing, to practise hospitality to strangers, to be kind to the poor" (Gilmore 1930, 108). In the past, the sharing and generosity of Indigenous Peoples were regarded as cultural defects, and many attempts were made by whites to extinguish those values (Meyer 1977). In one instance a mis-

sionary working among the Mandan, Hidatsa, and Sahnish on the Fort Berthold Reservation in the late 1800s declared that "they are a generous people and feel their responsibility toward their brother. But the mission work is gradually overcoming this" (ibid., 128).

The ceremony called the Sun Dance, practiced by many Plains tribes, was outlawed by federal authorities among the Sahnish, Hidatsa, and Mandan tribes in the early 1900s. It was considered by white missionaries to be a heathen practice of self-mutilation of the worst sort. Anyone guilty of participating in the Sun Dance had rations withheld and was jailed for a second offense. Those who were caught practicing traditional medicine were jailed for ten days (Gilman and Schneider 1987). The ban on the Sun Dance was maintained for several generations, and it was not until the 1980s that the Mandan and Hidatsa resumed that religious practice. The Sahnish did not return to the ritual until 1998, almost 100 years after the original ban.

Sahnish historian and scholar Loren Yellow Bird explains that his tribe endured many difficult trials throughout their history and that their religious traditions have lapsed; most sacred ceremonies are no longer practiced because of the impact of reservations upon Sahnish religious life (Yellow Bird 2003). However, he explains that, like many different tribal peoples, "our medicine men a long time ago in ceremonies predicted" that the "destruction of our traditions" would occur with the coming

A warning sign nailed to a tree at the edge of the Mount Currie Indian Reserve, British Columbia, Canada. The sign reads "WARNING No outside white visitors allowed because of your failure to obey the laws of our tribe as well as the laws of your own. This village is hereby closed." (Gunter Marx Photography/Corbis)

of whites who would bring with them their own beliefs. Still, he maintains, "It isn't over for us. . . . I, for one, am continuing the best that I can with the history that was passed down and look at what we need to carry on our traditions" (ibid., 13).

Although reservations were once places where Indigenous Peoples were confined against their will, for many they "have since become places whose importance cannot be overestimated." Today, for many Indigenous Peoples who reside on these lands, as well as for many who do not, the reservation remains a center of "cultural identity," "ceremonial activity," and "an essential symbol of tribal life" (Snipp 1996, 39). It is now a place where new and old sacred and secular ceremonies are being created and re-created and passed between generations of tribal peoples. However, it is important to not over-romanticize reservation life, since many continue to carry on life and death struggles with poverty, isolation, social ills, and lack of economic opportunity. In many respects, the chronically poor conditions on many reservations reinforce the feelings of many Indigenous Peoples that the U.S.

government has no more interest in the well-being of these lands, or the people that live here, than it did during the early reservation period, when these lands were used as holding pens and concentration camps.

Despite the humble environment of most reservations, Indigenous Peoples continue to reside on these lands, and many former residents return often during their lifetime. Today, many come back to the reservation from urban environments to get reconnected with their religious traditions, while others return to be buried. Many use these lands and sacred sites to overcome despair and oppression brought on by forces outside their cultures, and many come to celebrate who they are and to reaffirm their identity. For instance, a Native person living in the San Francisco area for many years returned to the reservation. "I became a Sun Dancer, a museum curator. My boys are Sun Dancers. One is a keeper of our sacred tribal pipe. . . . I brought them back to live on the reservation so they will know racism, pain, the hardcore stuff of life around here. . . . A real Indian lives in an Indian environment, learns spiritual ways, is discriminated against because of his looks, is shaped when he's young to be quiet because of racism. We pay a penalty. There's a positive aspect—the spiritual side. . . . That's what I came back for" (Nagel 1997, 191).

The reservation system has had an enormously negative effect on the religious lives of Indigenous Peoples. It has been directly responsible for much of the loss and suppression of traditional religious beliefs and practices. The reservation enabled Christian missionaries and government agents to enforce the introduction of many different white, Christian belief systems upon Native Peoples, which divided many families and communities. Despite all the divine inspiration and assistance from God given to whites, their philosophy of Manifest Destiny, and their theft of indigenous land, the reservation system was not enough to eradicate Indigenous Peoples' traditional religious lives. Today, Indian reservations remain, as do all the lands of this nation, the cultural birthright and spiritual stronghold of Indigenous Peoples.

Michael Yellow Bird

See also American Indian Movement (Red Power Movement); Law, Legislation, and Native Religion; New Age Appropriation; Retraditionalism and Identity Movements; Sacred Sites and Sacred Mountains; Termination and Relocation

References and Further Reading

Adams, David Wallace. 1995. _Education for Extinction: American Indians and the Boarding School Experience, 1875–1928._ Lawrence: University of Kansas Press.

Benton, Thomas Hart. 1846. Speech on the Oregon Question, May 28, 1846, U.S. Congress, Senate, _Congressional Globe,_ 29th Cong., 1st Sess. Washington, DC, 1846, 915–917.

Deloria, Vine, Jr. 1999. "Is Religion Possible? An Evaluation of Present Efforts to Revive Traditional Tribal Religions." In _For This Land: Writings on Religion in America._ New York: Routledge.

Gilman, Carolyn, and Mary Jane Schneider. 1987. _The Way to Independence: Memories of a Hidatsa Indian Family, 1840–1920._ St. Paul: Minnesota Historical Society Press.

Gilmore, Melvin. 1930. "The Arikara Book of Genesis." *Papers of the Michigan Academy of Science, Arts, and Letters* 12: 95–120.

Means, Russell. 1999. "Navajo Nation Jurisdictional Lawsuit." Letter to the Editor of the *Navajo Times*.

Meyer, Roy, W. 1977. *The Village Indians of the Upper Missouri*. Lincoln: University of Nebraska Press.

Nagel, Joane. 1997. *American Indian Ethnic Renewal: Red Power and the Resurgence of Identity and Culture*. New York: Oxford University Press.

Olson, James S., and Raymone Wilson.1986. *Native Americans in the Twentieth Century*. Urbana: University of Illinois.

Pevar, Stephan L. 1992. *The Rights of Indians and Tribes: The Basic ACLU Guide to Indian and Tribal Rights*. 2d ed. Carbondale: Southern Illinois University Press.

Prucha, Francis Paul. 1975. *Documents of United States Indian Policy*. Lincoln: University of Nebraska Press.

Snipp, C. Matthew. 1996. "The Size and Distribution of the American Indian Population: Fertility, Mortality, and Residence." P. 39 in *Changing Numbers, Changing Needs: American Indian Demography and Public Health*. Edited by Gary D. Sandefur, Ronald R. Rindfuss, and Barney Cohen. Washington, DC: National Academy Press.

U.S. Census Bureau. 2000. United States Census 2000. "Glossary." http://www.census.gov. (Accessed July 2003.)

United States Senate. 1989. *A Report of the Special Committee on Investigations of the Select Committee on Indian Affairs, Final Report and Legislative Recommendations*. 101st Cong., 1st Sess., Rep, 101–216.

Wright, Ronald. 1992. *Stolen Continents: The New World through Indian Eyes*. New York: Penguin Books.

Yellow Bird, Loren. 2003. "Now I Will Speak (nawah ti waako'): An Arikara Perspective on What the Lewis and Clark Expedition Missed." Paper delivered at Confluence of the Cultures: A Native American Perspective of the Lewis and Clark Expedition. May 28–30 at University of Montana, Missoula.

Yellow Bird, Michael. 1999. "Indian, American Indian, and Native Americans: Counterfeit Identities." *Winds of Change: A Magazine for American Indian Education and Opportunity,* 14 (1).

———. 2001. "Critical Values and First Nations Peoples." In *Culturally Competent Practice: Skills, Interventions, and Evaluations*. Edited by Rowena Fong and Sharlene Furuto. Boston: Allyn and Bacon.

Retraditionalism and Identity Movements

American Indians are the only Americans whose entire heritage is in the United States, has always been here, and is to be preserved here and nowhere else. While it is important to realize that the term "American Indians" is a sometimes problematic reference to a continental population actually composed of many nations, it is also true that there is a measure of collective identity to be expressed in terms of aboriginality. A common way of speaking about this is "pan-Indianism," but that term tends to gloss a plethora of interrelated issues of legal, economic, and cultural import. For some, pan-Indianism is the "pow wow culture," a broad set of practices and cultural referents, heavily influenced by Plains cultures, dubbed in the 1960s "Indians of All Tribes." For others the term is a nod to the growing cross-tribal and indeed international movement toward returning indigenous communities all over the world to a sense of self-determination. Regardless of which area of the discourse this term occupies, "pan-Indianism" has its genesis within a set of historical circumstances that opened the door for multinational communication, on this continent as well as others, regarding the current state of indigenous peoples and what the future holds for them.

One key area of this discussion is the effort being made in many contemporary Indian communities to return to a self-defined set of traditions—collective identity, worldview, spiritual practices and beliefs, etc.—that range from language revival, to seasonal ceremonies, to traditional leadership or economic views. This set of phenomena has been referred to by D'Arcy McNickle, Robert N. Wells, Jr., and Joane Nagel (among others) as "renewal," and it varies in character from group to group.

Renewal can take many forms and proceed in many directions; however, the participation level of various communities is governed by several factors. One is that there is a range of continuity experienced by these groups, with those enjoying long-term land tenure and language retention, such as the Diné, only relatively recently feeling the pressure to make concerted efforts in behalf of cultural renewal. There are other tribal groups, on the other hand, such as those in California, for whom missionization created a fairly wide cognitive rift between ancestral knowledge and contemporary Indians.

Another factor affecting levels of renewal efforts being mounted by particular communities is their current sociocultural circumstances. For some Indian nations, extreme poverty and accompanying disease remain at the forefront of communal concern. While undoubtedly most advocates, both inside and outside Indian Country, would place cultural renewal at the heart of any return to economic and social normalcy, the reality is that many communities find themselves in a veritable fight for survival that may hinder the process. One of the dirty little secrets in the United States is the level of misery experienced in some reservation communities, and indeed by individuals of Native American heritage that find themselves away from any community whatsoever in the larger cities.

In fact, the dispersal of Indian people from their communities, both geographic and human, provides a final factor in the range of successful renewal efforts among contemporary American Indians. As I will discuss in more detail below, the U.S. government made a concerted effort to strip Indian people of their culture. From the Dawes (Removal) Act, to tribal "disenrollment" and termination policies, to treaty violations, the U.S. government embarked upon, and indeed continues along, a path toward the marginalization and dissolution of separate Indian communal identities. Therefore renewal also occurs at the individual level, with many of the patterns mirroring those of the generation that W. C. Roof has called "seekers," in that a post–Viet Nam culture in the United States has raised issues of individual spirituality and religious choices to a meta level; Roof's "baby-boomer" category, of course, also includes American Indians, both reservation and urban.

American Indians are not immigrants. There are no "homelands" preserved overseas to which they may go for cultural information. The sole guardians of their languages, religions, material creations, and customs, only they are capable of preserving their ancestral cultures. American Indians have been battling attempts to obliterate their cultures from the time of the arrival of the first Europeans. The first wave of invaders, in the sixteenth and seventeenth centuries, brought military incursions that were soon amplified by the ravages of disease. The second wave, from the mid-eighteenth through the mid-nineteenth centuries, brought Euro-American populations large enough to warrant well-supported military campaigns along the series of western "frontiers." The official position of the United States during its first 150 years was articulated by the Supreme Court's chief justice John Marshall in his decision in *Johnson v. McIntosh* (1823) when he wrote: "The tribes of Indians inhabiting this country were fierce savages, whose occupation was war and whose subsistence was drawn chiefly from the forest. To leave them in possession of their country was to leave the country a wilderness; to govern them as a distinct people was impossible" (Hobson et al. 1998).

The late nineteenth century would prove to be the low point in American Indian life in many ways. According to the U.S. census website, in the 1890 census, 228,000 American Indians were recorded in the United States, less than one-tenth of the population only four centuries earlier. While the census no doubt failed to account for thousands of American Indians living independently, off of reservations, and either "passing" in some other census category or avoiding the census altogether, the substantial drop in population belied an openly racist paternalism, coupled with corruption, all over the country that often erupted into open violence against Indians. Indians were kept thoroughly ensconced in dire poverty and malnourishment, living in woefully inadequate conditions; children were forcibly taken from their parents to be kept in boarding schools, forbidden to speak their own languages or practice their religions. Mortality among Native Americans was very high, with diseases such as influenza and tuberculosis common.

The notion of cultural evolution dictated that Indians should be trained in menial labor tasks before they would be able to "progress" to higher pursuits. Western mono-crop farming was imposed upon Indians no matter the environment of their particular reservation. Any success, and there was success because of the presence of agriculture among some tribal groups for millennia, was mitigated by racist white locals or by ultimately unworkable capitalist schemes. For example, Indian small-scale cattle or pig concerns were often second-guessed by BIA managers who instructed Natives to resist taking animals to market in the fall on a gamble that prices would rise in the spring—only to have those small-production reservation outfits collapse under the weight of extra care for the animals over winter when prices dropped in the long run. While a large-scale capitalist venture might be able to play the market that way, absorbing losses or passing them on to other portions of their system, small-scale farmers like reservation-based American Indian farms would go bankrupt. That, of course, would provide both "proof" of the inadequacies of Native American farming, and cheap goods when the market enjoyed the BIA-sponsored buyout of Native concerns.

Many Indians were forced into the manual labor pool, especially as agricultural laborers, and at wages and in camp conditions that would have been unacceptable to Euro-Americans. The Indian boarding schools taught boys manual and girls domestic work, graduating young adults with an education level of eighth grade or less. One illuminating case is that of Beloit College, which between 1871 and 1884 accepted Dakota youths selected and prepared by the Riggs family of missionaries in Minnesota. Ohiyesa, called Charles Eastman in English, earned top status in mathematics at Beloit, went on to Dartmouth, and took an M.D. from Boston University in 1890. The Bureau of Indian Affairs took offense at Beloit's efforts to give such opportunities to Indians and cut off support for the program when college officials refused to limit Indian students'

academic education to manual labor and to place them in factory work.

The contemporary American Indian identity reached, in some ways, a watershed during the New Deal of Franklin Roosevelt. John Collier, commissioner of the Bureau of Indian Affairs (BIA) beginning in 1934, was in many ways as paternalistic as his predecessors, but rather than being guided by the supposed moral superiority of Christianity he romanticized Indians, seeing them as Noble Savages who should be returned to their "primitive democracy"; that notion became a large part of the national imagination with regard to Indian people. He was aided in his efforts by wealthy liberals who thought they were finally doing it right, and all federally recognized tribes were pressured into writing a constitution and electing a tribal council to govern their respective reservations. Truly traditional forms of self-government including hereditary leadership were strongly discouraged. Tribal members who opposed these ideas, including elders who made up the "library" of traditional identity, showed their disapproval by avoiding tribal elections altogether, thereby giving small minorities of "progressives" apparent victories.

Collier did, however, manage some reforms, including early legislation honoring non-Christian religious practice; supporting tribal language, arts, and manufacture programs; ending the damaging boarding school system; and reducing the role of non-Indian BIA agents in the day-to-day lives of reservation communities. Unfortunately, inasmuch as the country was in the depths of the Great Depression, many of these reforms were far less effective than they might otherwise have been, and with the onset of World War II, much of the work he began in the area of BIA reform was curtailed. The war also provided opportunities for Indians in both industry and military service, and this period can be said to have given birth to the modern Indian identity.

Much of Indian Country remained somewhat isolated, both from the events of the world in general and, more important, from each other. Nations that had become involved in Collier's reservation reforms had begun to meet regionally prior to the war, and factories, military training facilities, and the armed services all provided an opportunity for Indian people to interact on a level never before possible. At the end of World War II, it seemed to most Americans returning to a postwar society that a booming economy and progressive industrial development would provide the means for providing for their families. American Indians expected to be released from the gripping poverty of the previous century. The American government capitalized on this development, offering Natives the "opportunity" to move off of reservation land and become trained in the new industrial skills needed by U.S. companies. However, that would not prove fruitful.

Most Indians who left their ancestral lands looking for economic security found just the opposite, as factory and industrial work was occupied by white workers. Like African Americans on the so-called Northern migration, they found themselves in even more dire circumstances. Families were torn apart by the need to be mobile in order to find adequate work, and when that proved difficult, the opportunistic social diseases of poverty—depression, alcohol and other drug abuse, domestic violence, and disillusioned youth—followed quickly. Back on reservation lands poverty levels soon surpassed those of the pre-Collier years, and many who remained were forced to accept government-sponsored buyouts of land rich in mineral resources, or long-term, low-yield lease arrangements with ranchers and farmers.

The Indians' experiences during the war encouraged them to begin taking a more proactive stance. Given their newfound national identity as American Indians, they began by forming a pantribal political organization called the National Congress of American Indians (NCAI). Somewhat bolstered by familiarity with U.S. government policy and modes of civil action, acquired after Collier's Indian Reorganization Act brought many more Indians into federal employment, the NCAI persisted as a moderate but firm voice. Ironically, the mainstream presence of Indians and their newfound "noble" status resulted in intense efforts by the government to terminate Indian federal status and to force Indians out of all traditional communal practices. Laws preventing the sale of alcohol on reservations were rescinded, BIA-sponsored private land grabs were intensified, and the general sense that Native people would be better off without their traditional culture and communal practices became the guiding notion of government policy.

With the new goal of assimilation as a directive, the Eisenhower administration and Congress began enacting legislation to terminate Indian tribes. Washington began to rank federally recognized tribes according to the proportion of educated and economically independent members, on the premise that those qualities indicated adequate assimilation into mainstream American society. Following typical national politics, another large factor in termination was the desire of state politicians to disenroll particular tribes. Lobbying by state and industrial interests intent on the land that would be available to them if a given tribe were terminated intensified, stacking the deck against the relatively voiceless reservation tribes at the level of national policy-making.

At the culmination of termination in the mid-1960s, the long-term outcomes of changes begun during the New Deal began to bring about changes in American Indian identity, ushering in a sort of renaissance. During World War II, Indians, such as the famed "Navajo Code Talkers," had demonstrated their abilities and been respected. Becoming tribal leaders upon their return, they began to plan for the future of their people, including the completion of higher education that they might become lawyers,

doctors, and even U.S. government officials, in order to aid their tribal communities. The postwar generation's struggles in colleges that neither remedied poor preparation in Indian schools nor honored non-Western cultures led to programs in the 1970s assisting Indian students and bringing about new attitudes about American history, indigenous cultures, and human rights. Groups such as AIM began high-profile struggles for Native American rights, and changes in official recognition of Indian identity allowed for more people to turn to their ancestral roots to answer contemporary questions about how the universe works and what their place might be in it.

At the turn of the new millennium, much of the pan-Indian identity is tempered by a sharp return to tribal-specific themes. Many Indian people see expressing themselves culturally and spiritually in their own languages, styles, and patterns as key to their future as Indian people; there are many individual programs and processes—from language revival and education programs to traditional arts and craft cooperatives—that promise to provide the next generation with a new set of tribal memories. Rather than only struggling to survive, perhaps they will find new avenues for communication in their own languages, for traditional artistic self-expression, and for the expression of ancestral religious worldviews.

Dennis F. Kelley

See also American Indian Movement (Red Power Movement); Health and Wellness, Traditional Approaches; Identity; Native

American Church, Peyote Movement; Reservations, Spiritual and Cultural Implications; Retraditionalism and Revitalization Movements, Columbia Plateau; ; Retraditionalism and Revitalization Movements, Plains; Revitalization Movements, Northeast; Termination and Relocation

References and Further Reading

Hobson, Charles F., et al., eds. 1998. *The Papers of John Marshall, vol. 9: 1820–1823*. Chapel Hill: University of North Carolina Press.

McNickle, D'Arcy William. 1973. *Native American Tribalism: Indian Survivals and Renewals*. New York: Oxford University Press.

Nagel, Joane. 1997. *American Indian Ethnic Renewal: Red Power and the Resurgence of Identity and Culture*. New York: Oxford University Press.

Wells, Robert N., Jr. 1994. *Native American Resurgence and Renewal*. Metuchen, NJ: Scarecrow Press.

Retraditionalism and Revitalization Movements, California

California is somewhat unusual in terms of its Native history because the large variety of tribal groups that call the state home make for a rich and varied set of religious traditions. From the high desert Mojave to the coastal Chumash to the woodland Karuk, there are many traditional practices that continue today. However, owing to the state's relatively late entry into the union (1850, after the Treaty of Guadalupe Hidalgo struck between the United States and Mexico) and the fact that California was seen by most whites in the East as their ultimate destination, there was rapid and often violent change for virtually all of California's Native inhabitants with the large-scale influx of Americans.

Prior to that, of course, there had been smaller and more focused incursions into the territory, primarily by Spain and Russia. This focused immigration, forming "pockets" of non-Indians with specific resource desires, had variously severe implications, as with the Spanish mission system; there were also milder shifts, such as those surrounding the Russian fur trade and the first few gold prospectors in the Sierra Nevada foothills.

Spain's Catholic missions in Alta California began as an attempt to create pueblos—towns full of potential subjects that would populate and work the lands for the Crown. However, the process of missionization took longer than expected, and the padres' own writings at the time reflect the ongoing battle with the Indians over the residual Native religious traditions. In fact, Spain was unable, as was Mexico after the revolution, to rid the Native populations of all of their traditions, and the practice of forcing the Indians to abandon their languages in deference to Spanish actually provided the mission populations with a sort of lingua franca. In 1824, for example, the missions were caught off guard by a simultaneous revolt at several missions that began with a vision by a Chumash holy woman and the appearance of a comet in the night sky. The vision

A Hoopa basket maker shows a child how to weave baskets from straw on the Hoopa Indian Reservation in northern California, 1993. (Phil Schermeister/Corbis)

and the celestial event were taken as a sign by the people, and it surprised the padres just how well the Indians communicated between missions, and how much of the traditional belief and social cohesion remained intact.

For the Indian populations that were not under the rule of Spanish Catholicism, religious practices provided a context for cultural continuity in the face of shifting power paradigms; in the northern part of the state, there is much photographic and audiorecorded evidence of regular ceremonial participation. Unfortunately, when California became a U.S. state, the Native population went from the frying pan into the fire. U.S. systems of control were intolerant of both language use and cultural participation among Indian people, and many Natives of various tribes suffered not only bigotry and oppression but also injury and death if found to be speaking their own languages or practicing their own religions. In some areas official laws were passed barring those practices, and children were forcibly removed from their homes to be taught English, Christianity, and manual labor skills, often at the business end of a leather strap. These boarding schools and legal tactics forced Indian people in California to find innovative and even clandestine ways to maintain their cultural traditions, and in some areas many people found it necessary to abandon the overt practice of these traditions altogether.

Although many California Indians still experience bigotry toward their traditional beliefs and practices, the general cultural liberalization that occurred in this country in the post–Viet Nam era and the subsequent reinvigoration experienced by ethnic communities throughout the land had a particularly strong influence on Native cultures. Perhaps the result of equal parts cultural stimulus among Indian people and the realization of the oppressive nature of the Christian influence on American culture among non-Indians, places like California were ripe for cultural renewal. Furthermore, California in particular had the kind of political atmosphere that allowed for Indians to become much more active in the revitalization of their tribal traditions. There were two main avenues for this retraditionalism: external political activism and internal cultural awareness.

For California Indians, the nature of the "Golden State" and its place in the American economy in the latter part of the twentieth century provided one main issue to which all tribes needed to respond—the disposition of their sacred places. Developers had long been turning the state, particularly the highly desirable coastal regions, into a condominium and luxury home mecca, at the expense of Native sacred places. Burials were disturbed, springs ruined, and gathering areas paved. With little legisla-

tive ammunition with which to do battle, Indian activists set about the task of forcing local, state, and federal legislators to take this issue seriously, after many years of toe-to-toe confrontation between developers and their bulldozers and Indians and their courage. A significant shift occurred only during the Clinton administration, when the Native American Graves Protection and Repatriation Act (NAGPRA) was given additional enforcement capabilities through amendment.

It was during the battles for small victories among some devastating losses that California Indian people began to get better acquainted with their tribal traditions. In other words, there was a distinct shift in identity from the more generalized Native American to more tribal-specific self-identification. Activists sought out elders, learned their traditional languages, songs, and ceremonies, and continued to adhere to them after they had unchained themselves from the construction equipment. This cultural awareness coincided with that of Indian people who had gone a different path to the same place—a path that took the form of personal spiritual searches, art and craft skills, or both. A good example is the art form that California Native people are best known for—namely, basketry.

For most California tribal groups, basketry is not simply a practical craft (though, of course, it is that as well) but also a cultural practice. From the awareness of the plant resources, their habitats and management needs, to proper protocol for approaching basket makers for instruction and advice, making is much more than the weaving. Many tribes have very specific methods for preparing to become a weaver, with songs and ceremonies (that need to be learned from elders who are properly approached, a propriety that also needs to be learned) accompanying the plant interaction, the gathering process, the materials preparation, and the actual weaving. Weavers in some tribal groups are required to present the baskets they make to specific people for specific reasons when they first begin, and some gift baskets are accompanied by particular stories or songs devoted to that basket and its gathering and weaving. We can see, then, that an Indian person who wants to learn basket weaving learns as much, if not more, about her tribal culture and spiritual traditions as she does about baskets.

This notion can be replicated in any of a number of similar processes. Dancing and regalia, traditional foods, language acquisition, and singing are all governed by the same type of protocols described above for basketry. People who decide to "get in touch" with their Indian heritage via these or other means embark upon a journey of traditional education and spiritual development that brings them into the presence of their ancestors, connecting them not only to a time before invasion but also to the kind of spiritual traditions that enabled their people to survive that invasion.

Dennis F. Kelley

See also American Indian Movement (Red Power Movement); Ceremony and Ritual, California; Health and Wellness, Traditional Approaches; Indian Shaker Church; Missionization, California; Oral Traditions; Oral Traditions, California; Power, Barbareño Chumash; Prison and Native Spirituality; Reservations, Spiritual and Cultural Implications; Retraditionalism and Revitalization Movements, Columbia Plateau; Retraditionalism and Revitalization Movements, Plains; Termination and Relocation

References and Further Reading
Eargle, Dolan H., Jr. 1992. *California Indian Country: The Land and the People.* San Francisco: Trees Company Press.
Lowery, Chag, and Rebecca Lowery. 2003. "Original Voices." http://www .originalvoices.org/Homepage.htm. (Accessed June 12.)
Margolin, Malcolm, and Yolanda Montijo, eds. 1995. *Native Ways: California Indian Stories and Memories.* Berkeley: Heyday Press.
Nagel, Joane. 1997. *American Indian Ethnic Renewal: Red Power and the Resurgence of Identity and Culture.* Oxford: Oxford University Press.
Trafzer, Clifford E., and Joel R. Hyer. 1999. *Exterminate Them: Written Accounts of Murder, Rape, Slavery of Native Americans during the California Gold Rush, 1848–1868.* Michigan State University Press.
Vane, Sylvia Brakke, and Lowell John Bean. 1990. *California Indians: Primary Resources, A Guide to Manuscripts, Artifacts, Documents, Serials, Music, and Illustrations.* Menlo Park, CA: Ballena Press.

Retraditionalism and Revitalization Movements, Columbia Plateau

From colonial times to the present, Native revitalization and retraditionalizing

Showing some influence from Christianity, Chief Smohalla's movement, also known as the Washat, met every week on the Sabbath in longhouses that in some ways resembled churches. (Government Printing Office, 1896)

movements have been characteristic of the American cultural landscape. Ottawa chief Pontiac used teachings of the Delaware Prophet to justify military actions against British forts in the Great Lakes region in 1763. Handsome Lake, the Seneca prophet, was publicly active from 1799 to 1815. Tecumseh's brother, the Shawnee prophet Tenskwatawa, was a catalyst in the formation of an Indian alliance to drive out whites and re-establish societies based upon traditional Native ways and values. The Paiute prophet Wovoka is well known for his association with the Ghost Dance (1888–1896). Revitalization and retraditionalizing movements are well known on the Columbia Plateau as well. Washat, along with In-

dian Shaker, "Feather cult," and the Native American Church movements, are primary examples.

One of the first scholars to provide a definition of revitalization movements was Ralph Linton (1943). He described nativistic movements as "any conscious, organized attempt on the part of a society's members to revive or perpetuate neglected aspects of its culture." That, said Linton, happens when cultural groups come into contact with one another (Linton 1943, 230).

Anthony Wallace incorporated Linton's ideas into a broader framework. According to him, revitalization movements are a "deliberate, organized, conscious effort by members of a society to construct a more satisfying culture" (1956, 265). Among the wide range of social phenomena that might fit such a definition, Wallace includes "nativistic movements," "revivalistic movements," "cargo cults," "millenarian movements," and "messianic movements." Nativistic movements tend to concentrate on "alien persons, customs, values, and/or material" from the cultural fabric. Revivalistic movements generally promote ways of life and values that were once vibrant but now seem to be missing. Cargo cults are so labeled because of their characteristic importation of alien values, practices, and material culture. Millenarian movements call for societal change within the context of "an apocalyptic world transformation engineered by the supernatural." Messianic movements focus attention on single individuals understood to be divine saviors manifesting in human form. Wallace points out that these categories are not at all mutually exclusive. To the contrary, they may well act in overlapping and mutually reinforcing ways (ibid., 267).

Academic discussions about revitalization movements over subsequent decades have characterized such movements as based in conscious change. They are also understood to travel through cyclical stages: steady state, stress, cultural distortion, and revitalization, ultimately returning back to a steady state once more. Furthermore, the impetus for this is generally considered to be deprivation or oppression by the dominant society. However, evidence suggests that external pressures alone are not necessarily powerful explanatory tools, for they do not consistently produce revitalization movements. Therefore, contemporary scholarship increasingly highlights the influence of internal processes in a given group as well. Only through an examination of cultural systems already in place can a particular manifestation of revitalization "make good sense" within the larger context of deprivation or oppression (Schwarz 1997, 750–751).

Plateau Background

Dreams, visions, and guiding spirits constitute the oldest and most basic aspects of spiritual belief and practice on the Columbia Plateau. Vision quests and "medicine sings" or "winter spirit dances" are among the bedrock cultural materials upon which all other indigenous spiritual and religious convictions in the region are erected (Walker and Schuster 1998, 499).

In *Nch'i-Wana, The Big River: Mid-Columbia Indians and Their Land,* Eugene Hunn reports that powers obtained through guardian spirits supplied mid-Columbia peoples with the strength necessary for a successful life. Vision quests were solitary ventures intended, through physical deprivation and altered states of consciousness, to place a person in contact with guardian spirits. Death and revival or rebirth was a recurrent theme in achieving spiritual awareness. According to Robert Boyd, "Middle Columbia natives viewed a loss of consciousness, entry into a trance state, or recovery from a debilitating illness as potential avenues for making contact with the supernatural. . . . Many times in the ethnographic literature from the Upper Chinookan area, various forms of altered states are described by native observers as varieties of 'death'" (Boyd 1996, 119).

Spirit power was a prerequisite for participation in winter dances. At this ritual event, perhaps the most important religious occurrence of the year, individuals with new spirit guides began to experience "spirit illness." A medicine man then diagnosed the sickness and gave the individual a song. Dancing followed (ibid., 129–131). Again, ceremonial purification and death are found intertwined. Thomas Farnham's description of winter dances at Wasco in 1843 is instructive:

> Various and strange are the bodily contortions of the performers. They jump up and down, and swing their arms with more and more increases, and yelp, and froth at the mouth, till the musician winds up with the word "ugh"—a long guttural grunt; or until some one of the dancers falls apparently dead. When the latter is the case, one of the number walks around the prostrate individual, and calls his or her name loudly at each ear, at the nose, fingers and toes. After this ceremony, the supposed dead shudders greatly, and comes to life. And thus they continue to sing, and thump, and dance, and die, and come to life through the night. (quoted in ibid., 132)

Concepts and experiences involving spiritual entities, ritual purification, death, and renewal are commonly visible in Columbia Plateau revitalization movements. The first of these to come onto the scene was Washat, followed by Indian Shaker, "Feather cult," and finally the Native American Church.

Washat

Washat, also known as Seven Drum or Longhouse religion, is a nativistic movement deriving quite directly from an older tradition referred to in the academic literature as the Prophet Dance (Walker and Schuster 1998, 501–502). Leslie Spier (1935) described the Prophet Dance as a "cult" characterized by a dance, often circular, and inspired leaders who offered prophecies received through visions usually experienced during "death-like trance states" succeeded by a reviving or "rebirth." A hierarchical arrangement of spirits was ruled over by a "creator spirit." Sometimes Prophet Dance rituals prioritized the confession of group members' sins. In almost all instances, however, they revolved around prophecies of world renewal. Rituals were frequently directed toward bringing that renewal to fruition (Walker 1969, 245; Walker and Schuster 1998, 500).

The Prophet Dance has been correlated with occurrences in the Plateau during the period immediately following Lewis and Clark. Included among these events are epidemic disease, the introduction of the horse, trade, the arrival of Christianity and other "alien" beliefs and practices, and the existence of various Native prophets. However, evidence strongly suggests that the Prophet Dance was stimulated by precipitous population declines within indigenous communities before 1800 (Walker and Schuster 1998, 499–500). It appears that later forms of the dance, such as Washat, were born of such onslaughts of death as well.

In the Sahaptin language, *waashat* means "dance." This tradition is associated with the "dreamers" of the middle Columbia Plateau, known as such because of the trancelike psychological states in which their visions were obtained. By the 1830s, Washat rituals were containing distinctly Christian elements. Adherents were speaking of "the Creator," services were held on Sunday, and Longhouse leaders were using a handbell as an integral part of ritual procedures. Yet Washat maintained a very strong emphasis on older traditions. These included a reliance on guiding spirits, "shamanistic" curing, and a determination to maintain group language, behavioral expectations, ethical precepts, beliefs, values, and ways of life (ibid., 501–502).

Smohalla of the Wanapum, a people living at Priest Rapids on the Columbia River, is probably the most famous Washat leader of the nineteenth century. Speaking of events in the early nineteenth century, Smohalla commented late in his life:

> The whites have caused us great suffering. . . . Dr. Whitman many years ago made a long journey to the east [1842] to get a bottle of poison for us. He was gone about a year, and after he came back strong and terrible

diseases broke out among us. . . . The Indians killed Dr. Whitman [at the so-called Whitman massacre], but it was too late. He had uncorked his bottle and all the air was poisoned. Before that there was little sickness among us, but since then many of us have died. I have had children and grandchildren, but they are all dead. My last grandchild, a young woman of 16, died last month. If only her infant had lived. . . . I labored hard to save them, but medicine would not work as it used to. (quoted in Hunn 1990, 242)

With such death, and with the great threats it presented to family and community survival, Plateau peoples turned to dreamer-prophets. Visions were employed to shape a response to the challenges and, if possible, chart a return to a traditional way of life (ibid.). In addition to death from disease, there were also stresses induced by conflict with the U.S. military, treaty signings, and forced confinement to reservations. This was the context in which Smohalla and his contemporaries lived.

Smohalla first appears in the pubic record in 1861, when he is mentioned in a military report listing Indians hiding in a place called "Smoke Hollow." Much more is known of him through the ethnographic work of James Mooney, printed in 1896. Mooney's writings are grounded largely in talks held between Smohalla and Major J. W. MacMurray in 1884–1885 (ibid., 253). It was during the course of those conversations that Smohalla is famously quoted as denying the value of white civilization, by saying: "My young men shall never work. Men who work cannot dream, and wisdom comes to us in dreams" (ibid., 254). Further, in response to the major's exhorting the Indians to settle down and farm, Smohalla stated:

> Those who cut up lands or sign papers for lands will be defrauded of their rights and will be punished by God's anger. You ask me to plough the ground? Shall I take a knife and tear my mother's bosom? Then when I die, she will not ask me to her bosom to rest. You ask me to dig for stone. Shall I dig under her skin for her bones? Then when I die, I cannot enter her body to be born again. You ask me to cut grass and make hay and sell it and be rich like white man, but how dare I cut off my Mother's hair? It is a bad law and my people cannot obey it. (quoted in Relander 1986, 139)

Smohalla was famous across the Plateau for his ability to enter a trance and return to consciousness—after traveling to the land of spirits—with songs and messages for his followers. These were used in their ceremonial in order to quicken the coming world renewal. Smohalla is credited with prophesying earthquakes and eclipses (Hunn 1990, 253). He called for people to wear traditional clothing, adhere to time-honored means of subsistence, resist being placed on a reservation, and to be loyal to traditional forms of spiritual belief and practice. In return he guaranteed a revitalization of Native cultures in the process of which dead Indi-

ans would return to life and whites would be removed from Indian territories (Walker and Schuster 1998, 505).

Another significant figure was Skolaskin (or Kolaskin) of the Sanpoil. When he was around twenty years old, Skolaskin fell desperately ill. After two years he dropped into a coma. Burial preparations were begun, but consciousness returned the night before he was to be interred. Skolaskin had returned to life from the land of the dead. He told assembled family and friends that his illness was gone. Furthermore, he said that he had been instructed by the Creator to bring a message to the people: "All of the Indians, he had been told, must change their ways; they must no longer drink, steal, or commit adultery. But it was most important that they pray to their new god. . . . Moreover, every seventh day must be devoted to prayer and singing exclusively. . . . [A]ll were to gather together to pray and sing, and to listen to Kolaskin, prophet of their god" (Ray 1936, 68–69).

Skolaskin sought and found converts among the Spokane, Sanpoil, and Southern Okanogan. There were no dancing and no bells. His prophecies were generally apocalyptic. In one, he proclaimed

> that at the end of ten years' time the world would be enveloped in a great flood. To avoid destruction, he continued, they were to build a sawmill near the church and saw the lumber for a great boat. Before the end of ten years the boat would be completed and all followers would

gather inside at the appointed time. Also, a male and female of every animal and bird would be included. Then the rain would come and flood the earth but all those in the boat would be saved. (ibid., 71)

For approximately ten years, between 1870 and 1880, his movement had a substantial impact on the local region. Following legal trouble, however, Skolaskin embraced more traditional ways before the movement faded (ibid., 75).

There were many dreamer-prophets on the Columbia Plateau, and they were found among virtually every group. At a minimum, the Nez Perce, Umatilla, Spokane, Kootenai, Wanapum, Yakama, Klickitat, Wayampam (skin village), Palouse, Sanpoil-Nespelem, and some Chinookan groups on the Lower Columbia such as the Wishram at Celilo Falls were all represented. A list of prominent personalities would include Shuwapsa, Dla-upac, Spokane Garry, Kootenai Pelly, Nez Perce Ellis, Skolaskin, Wiletsi, Hununwe (a woman), Jim Kanine, Shramaia, Lishwailait, Ashnithlai, the Tenino Queahpahmah, Luls, the Wanapam Smohalla (smuxala), Wiskaynatowatsanmay, and the Yakima Kotiahkan (Shawaway Kotiahkan) (Walker and Schuster 1998, 499).

Washat emphasis on maintaining and promoting a nativistic vision of the world led its leaders and membership to play significant roles in wars of resistance during the 1800s. Christian missionaries and federal agents responded by acting against them on the Yakama, Warm Springs, Umatilla, and Nez Perce reservations. Collier's Indian policies in the 1930s had the effect of reducing oppressive tactics against Native American beliefs and practices. Washat expanded accordingly. By World War II its presence was very notable across the Plateau. During the 1990s Washat bloomed as a centerpiece of resistance to pressures of assimilation. It remains at the core of a neotraditionalism on the Yakama, Umatilla, Warm Springs, Nez Perce, and nearby Salishan reservations, particularly the Colville, where a number of Nez Perce and Palouse have lived since treaties were signed in 1885 (ibid., 505–506).

Indian Shaker

The Indian Shaker religion originated on the Pacific Northwest Coast and later crossed the Cascade Mountains into the Plateau. Experiences of deprivation and oppression contributed to its emergence. Even though this revitalization movement was promoted by its leaders and followers as a form of Christianity, it contained significant elements borrowed from extant local systems of Native belief.

The 1870s were difficult times for Native Americans on the Northwest Coast. In the wake of Euro-American contact, treaty signings, and confinement to reservations, many people had lost their aboriginal territories and access to vital subsistence resources. Villages were decimated by disease, and ancient ways of life and values were under assault from missionaries and federal agents. It was a period of profound change, deepening powerlessness relative to the dominant society, and great uncertainty.

John Slocum was a Squaxin (Southern Coast Salish) living near Olympia, Washington. He was exposed to Catholic teachings in his younger years. As an adult, Slocum watched eleven of his thirteen children die from disease. In 1881 he himself became quite sick and, according to available accounts, died. During the extended funeral service, Slocum awoke. After telling family and friends there that he had indeed died, he described how his soul had traveled to heaven, been met and judged by an angel, and told to return home. In consequence of leading a sinful life, he was instructed by the angel to lead other stray sheep into this new church (Barnett 1957, 5–6).

About a year after his first sickness, Slocum fell terribly ill again. Death appeared imminent. His wife, Mary Thompson, was convinced of the veracity of her husband's teachings and shaken to the core by the prospect of his passing. "[T]he crisis induced in her a hysterical seizure in the course of which she approached Slocum's prostrate body praying, sobbing, and trembling uncontrollably" (ibid., 7). Upon being touched by her, he revived. Mary and others attributed divine power to this apparently miraculous occurrence. That event marked the beginning of "shaking." Slocum soon began preaching again, and the Indian Shaker Religion was born.

Trembling or "shaking" became a distinguishing characteristic in the developing Shaker ritual, along with bell-ringing, singing, and the stamping of feet. Shaking was and is seen as a gift from God, intended to provide believers with physical and spiritual well-being (ibid., 147). Word of "the shake's" curative powers quickly spread. Congregations were soon established in Skykomish, Chehalis, Puyallup, Nisqually, Clallam, and other Native Pacific Coast communities in Washington (ibid., 7–8; Walker and Schuster 1998, 507).

John Slocum's teachings recognize the Trinity, emphasize good works, promote brotherly love, and draw from Christian eschatological visions (Barnett, 285–286). They do not typically promote Native spiritual traditions. However, Indian Shakerism does contain elements derived from Native traditions. An openness to spiritual transformation through altered states of consciousness was displayed by Mary Thompson over Slocum's body (ibid., 308). Arguably, this openness was characteristic of vision quest and other indigenous ritual practices.

Converts to the Indian Shaker religion were made on most of the reservations in Washington and Oregon, and in northwestern California and parts of British Columbia (ibid., 7–8; Walker and Schuster 1998, 507). Shakers were invited to the Yakama Reservation in 1892. A Wasco brought the religion to Warm Springs in 1893. From there it spread to the Klamath (Barnett, 70, 74). By 1908, Indian Shakerism was found throughout the

Plateau (Walker and Schuster 1998, 508). With a continuing emphasis on curing, and manifesting a strong array of Christian elements set within an ancient Native context, it remains a vibrant religion across the region.

"Feather Cult"

Unlike the Washat and Indian Shaker, the Feather cult does not seem to originate in response to external pressures, much less those related to deprivation and oppression. Instead, it was born largely from the experiences, ideas, and force of personality of one man—Jake Hunt of Husum, Washington.

Hunt was a Klickitat who was born into a Washani family between 1860 and 1870. Klickitat prophets Lishwailait and Ashnithlai, dreamer-prophets and contemporaries of Smohalla, were influential in shaping Hunt's outlook (Du Bois 1938, 16, 20; Walker and Schuster 1998, 511). In the Sahaptin language of the Plateau, the Feather cult is known as both the *waskliki* (spin) and *waptashi* (feather). In English, adherents are spoken of as the bum-bum or pom-pom Shakers. The name, says Du Bois, is a recognition of the two sources from which the Feather cult arose (Du Bois 1938, 5).

The conversion experience that led Hunt to found this "cult" in 1896 came as a consequence of his exposure to the Indian Shakers. That year his third wife and son were deathly ill from tuberculosis. On the basis of the curative powers reputedly associated with their religion,

Shakers were invited to come down to the Columbia River from the Yakama Reservation. Although resistant to Shakerism, Hunt allowed himself to be converted in the hope of saving his beloved wife and child. It was to no avail. The child died several weeks later. As the group surrounded the open grave, praying, one of Jake's nieces brought her hands together as if she had grabbed something. She reportedly said:

> My eyes were shut, yet it was as though a lighted match were held at night before my eyes. There was a large flat bright disk of light and in the center was a man. This circle was a piece of land (titcam). The man wore a buckskin shirt and trousers. In his left hand was a drum and in his right, the drum stick. . . . Jake Hunt then took the disk from her and claimed it as his own. . . . Jake . . . began to shake violently. He then seemed to seize something between his upraised hands, after which he spun rapidly in place. When Jake stopped, he announced that he had Lishwailait's soul. (ibid., 22)

Despite all their continuing efforts, Hunt's wife also died within a month. While the Shakers were in his house, one of his sisters had a vision and began to spin. At this time, in deep mourning, he lay on his wife's grave, fell asleep, and had a dream. He saw his wife and child telling him to cease grieving. He also heard the voices of his ancestors instructing him to construct a rawhide tambourine. "He saw again a disk of light . . . which was brought down from the sky by an eagle. The persons who appeared to him were singing some of the old Washani songs. He was commanded to convert people in seven lands" (ibid., 23).

Hunt built a longhouse and, with his sisters, founded the Feather cult. Its focus was primarily ecstatic healing. Ideology and rituals were borrowed from ancient Plateau beliefs, Washat, and the Shakers. Curing was undertaken through possession of spirit power. Washani elements were very similar to those associated with Lishwailait. Exposure to the Shakers provided moralistic precepts and an emphasis on curing, particularly where alcoholism was concerned (ibid., 43; Walker and Schuster 1998, 511–512).

Hunt soon began seeking converts "in seven lands." By 1905 he had won over adherents on the Yakama Reservation, and in the following year on the Warm Springs Reservation. His efforts on the Umatilla were disappointing to him, however, and afterward he spent the remainder of his life with his fourth wife at Spearfish, just upstream from Husum (Du Bois 1938, 20; Walker and Schuster 1998, 512). Some families on the Yakama Reservation were still following the Feather ways in the 1990s, and they may still be doing so today. The core of Feather cult activity, however, is located on the Warm Springs Reservation (Walker and Schuster 1998, 513).

Cora Du Bois, perhaps somewhat ungenerously, describes the Feather cult as unoriginal and artificial. Virtually all ideological and ritual aspects were borrowed. And any attempts to slow acculturation came far too late. That, she implies, is made clear in the fact that the "cult" never spread any farther than Hunt himself carried it. "The whole movement," says Du Bois, "impresses one as a one-man affair whose force was individual, appealed to no growing social need, and was correspondingly ephemeral" (Du Bois 1938, 43).

Native American Church

Peyote's use as a vehicle for spiritual or religious purposes among indigenous peoples of the Americas apparently originated in Mexico. There, as Weston La Barre explains, it played a role in an agricultural-hunting religious ceremony, preceded by a ritual pilgrimage to find the plant. Around 1870 peyote diffused to the United States. It was especially popular with Native groups living in the Plains. Following the loss of territory and with confinement to the dreary reality of reservation life, there was severe cultural fragmentation in the Plains. Kiowa, Comanche, and Caddo peoples were primarily responsible for the expansion of peyote use across the Plains and into portions of southern Canada and the Great Basin (La Barre 1975, 7). An Oto by the name of Jonathan Koshiway established a Christianized derivative of peyotism in the early twentieth century. He founded a "Church of the First-born." From that the "Native American Church" emerged (ibid., 7–8).

There was strong resistance on the part of missionaries and federal officials. However, Indian Peyotists defended their religious practices. One notable speaker was Albert Hensley, a Winnebago and graduate of the Carlisle School. By 1908, Hensley and other Winnebago understood peyote as simultaneously a Holy Medicine and a Christian sacrament. "To us," he said, "it is a portion of the body of Christ, even as the communion bread is believed to be a portion of the body of Christ by other denominations. Christ spoke of a Comforter who was to come. It never came to Indians until it was sent in the form of this Holy Medicine" (Stewart 1987, 157).

The Native American Church (see also the entry by that title) spread into the Columbia Plateau by the 1970s. While attending a peyote ritual in Arizona, a Yakama named Ted Strong had a vision of Mount Adams, a dramatic snow-capped volcanic peak that dominates the skyline of the Yakama Reservation. When he spoke of what he saw, the image was interpreted as meaning that the Native American Church would be brought to the Yakama. And in 1977 it was. Roughly contemporaneous with Strong, a group on the Colville Reservation was also seeking to found a Native American Church. They too filed articles of incorporation in 1977. Walker and Schuster state that the reasons behind incorporation were identical with those motivating Native Americans in Oklahoma in 1918: "To foster and promote religious beliefs in Almighty God . . . with the sacramental use of peyote for religious purposes" (Walker and Schuster

1998, 513). Lakota Peyotists were contacted. Leonard Crow Dog and Gilbert Steward from the Rosebud Reservation and Rufus Kills Crow Indian of the Pine Ridge Reservation came to teach the Cross Fire ceremony on the Colville Reservation. The very next year, in 1978, Paul Small and Joe Stanley, both of whom were Cree, traveled to Nespelem on various occasions to instruct people in the Half Moon ritual (ibid.).

Whether deriving from Peyote traditions found in Arizona, as in the case of Ted Strong, or from those on the Plains, as seen in the Colville example, the use of peyote as a religious sacrament has successfully spread into the Columbia Plateau in relatively recent years. Since the 1970s, Native American Church meetings have also occurred on the Nez Perce, Umatilla, Warm Springs, Spokane, Coeur d'Alene, Klamath, and Salish-Kootenai reservations, and in off-reservation places (ibid.).

Conclusions

While certainly building upon very old and culturally specific traditions in the Columbia Plateau, revitalization movements have at the same time sprung forth largely in response to external pressures of deprivation and oppression. Personal power derived from guardian spirits and practices associated with medicine men or dreamers was and is relied upon by Washat adherents, reformulated and repackaged as "the shake" by Indian Shakers, transformed into "the spin" by members of the Feather cult, and sought in various rituals by Peyotists. Continually rocked by external challenges from the dominant society and by internal social pressures resulting from a combination of prior and ongoing colonial experiences, many Native Americans on the Plateau turn to revitalization movements, just as they have since the time of Lewis and Clark.

Joel Geffen

See also Ceremony and Ritual, Nez Perce; Dance, Plateau; Dreamers and Prophets; Dreams and Visions; Indian Shaker Church; Native American Church, Peyote Movement; Religious Leadership, Plateau

References and Further Reading
Barnett, H. G. 1957. *Indian Shakers: A Messianic Cult of the Pacific Northwest.* Carbondale: Southern Illinois University Press.
Du Bois, Cora. 1938. *The Feather Cult of the Middle Columbia.* General Series in Anthropology 7. Menasha, WI: George Banta.
Hunn, Eugene. 1990. *Nch'i-Wana, The Big River: Mid-Columbia Indians and Their Land.* Seattle: University of Washington Press.
La Barre, Weston. 1975. *The Peyote Cult.* 4th ed. Enlarged. North Haven, CT: Archon Books.
Linton, Ralph. 1943. "Nativistic Movements." *American Anthropologist* 45: 230–241.
Ray, Verne F. 1936. "The Kolaskin Cult: A Prophet Movement of 1870 in Northeastern Washington." *American Anthropologist* 38, no. 1: 67–75.
Relander, Click. 1986. *Drummers and Dreamers.* Seattle: Caxton Printers.
Ruby, Robert H., and John A. Brown. 1989. *Dreamer-Prophets of the Columbia Plateau: Smohalla and Skolaskin.* Norman: University of Oklahoma Press.
Schwarz, Maureen Trudelle. 1997. "Holy Visit 1996: Prophecy, Revitalization, and Resistance in the Contemporary Navajo World." *Ethnohistory* 45: 4, 747–793.
Spier, Leslie. 1935. *The Prophet Dance of the Northwest and Its Derivatives: The Source of the Ghost Dance.* General Series in Anthropology 1. Menasha, WI: George Banta.
Stewart, Omer C. 1987. *Peyote Religion: A History.* Norman: University of Oklahoma Press.
Thornton, Russell. 1982. "Demographic Antecedents of Tribal Participation in the 1870 Ghost Dance Movement." *American Indian Culture and Research Journal* 6: 79–91.
———. 1993. "Boundary Dissolution and Revitalization Movements: The Case of the Nineteenth Century Cherokees." *Ethnohistory* 40, no. 3: 359–383.
Walker, Deward E., Jr. 1969. "New Light on the Prophet Dance Controversy." *Ethnohistory* 16, no. 2: 245–256.
———. 1968/1985. *Conflict and Schism in Nez Perce Acculturation: A Study of Religion and Politics.* Reprint, Moscow: University of Idaho Press.
Walker, Deward E., and Helen H. Schuster. 1998. "Religious Movements." Pp. 499–514 in *Handbook of North American Indians.* Edited by William C. Sturtevant. Washington, DC: Smithsonian Institution.
Wallace, Anthony F. C. 1956. "Revitalization Movements: Some Theoretical Considerations for Their Comparative Study." *American Anthropologist* 58, no. 2: 264–281.

Retraditionalism and Revitalization Movements, Northwest

See Indian Shaker Church

Retraditionalism and Revitalization Movements, Plains

The best description of Indian metaphysics was the realization that the world, and all its possible experiences, constitutes a social reality, a fabric of life in which everything has the possibility of intimate knowing relationships because, ultimately, everything is related. This world is a unified world, a far cry from the disjointed, sterile, and emotionless world painted by Western science. Even though we can translate the realities of the Indian social world into concepts familiar to us from the Western scientific context, such as space, time, and energy, we must surrender most of the meaning in the Indian world when we do so. The Indian world can be said to consist of two basic experiential dimensions that, taken together, provide a sufficient means of making sense of the world. These two concepts are place and power, the latter perhaps better defined as spiritual power or life force. Familiarity with the personality of objects and entities of the natural world enabled Indians to discern immediately where each living being had its proper place and what kinds of experiences that place allowed, encouraged, and suggested. And knowing places enabled people to relate to the living entities inhabiting it (Deloria and Wildcat 2001, 2–3).

First Peoples have always maintained varying degrees of social autonomy in their lives, in spite of powerful colonial

Scholar and writer Zitkala-Sa (Gertrude Bonnin), Dakota, ca. 1843. (Library of Congress)

forces and the consequent devastating cultural imperialism. The retention of traditional metaphysics has been central to the maintenance of that cultural autonomy. Contrary to popular misconceptions, the traditional spiritual world views and practices of Plains Indians are alive and in many cases thriving, although often still subjected to constant and significant assaults. The resistance to Eurocentric attempts to impose Christianity has not ceased since the first conversion attempts began. This ongoing refusal to be subjected to Christian imperialism can be examined during four historical eras: the initial genocide, reorganization, awakening, and renaissance.

> *I love a people who have always made me welcome to the best they had.*
> *I love a people who are honest without laws, who have no jails and no poorhouses.*
> *I love a people who keep the commandments without ever having read them or heard them preached from the pulpit.*
> *I love a people who never swear, who never take the name of God in vain.*
> *I love a people who love their neighbors as they love themselves.*
> *I love a people who worship God without a bible, for I believe that God loves them also.*
> *I love a people whose religion is all the same, and who are free from religious animosities.*
> *I love a people who have never raised a hand against me, or stolen my property, where there was no law to punish for either.*
> *I love a people who have never fought a battle with white men, except on their own ground.*
> *I love and don't fear mankind where God has made and left them, for there they are children.*
> *I love a people who live and keep what is their own without locks and keys.*
> *I love all people who do the best they can.*
> *And oh, how I love a people who don't live for the love of money!*
> *(George Catlin (1796–1872)*

The initial genocide on Turtle Island and adjacent land began with the first European contact as early as the 1400s. Cultural genocide or ethnocide began when Spanish conquistadors and other early imperialistic explorers brought with them representatives from the Catholic Church in the 1400s and 1500s. The inhumane acts of these first colonizers was justified by a religious doctrine, a Eurocentric theological justification for murder, misogyny, homophobia, and land grabs. In a papal bull of 1453, Pope Nicholas sanctioned such acts, giving clear direction to "capture, vanquish, and subdue the saracens, pagans, and other enemies of Christ," "to put them into perpetual slavery," and "to take all their possessions and property." A second papal bull, issued in 1493, gave further support to the violent subjugation of "brute animals" by "civilized conquerors." These edicts, which came to be called the Doctrine of Discovery, a legal principle rooted in a Judeo-Christian dogma, were used not only by the Spanish but also by the Portuguese, the English, the French, the Dutch, and ultimately the Euro-Americans.

Less than fifty years after the formation of the United States, in 1823, the Supreme Court quickly incorporated the Doctrine of Discovery into U.S. Law. In *Johnson v. McIntosh*, Chief Justice John Marshall used the Christian doctrine to justify the newly formed nation's further erosion of American Indian rights and the denial of First Peoples' sovereignty—thus with a sweep of his pen making them into dependent peoples because of their "heathen" condition.

From the beginning of contact, the coercive and exclusive nature of the Eurocentric religion as well as its lack of respect for women was much noted; as early as the 1600s, American Indian women, in contrast to most Indian men, resisted Christian conversion. For example, historian Carol Devens has documented how Upper Great Lakes women who resisted Jesuit control were subjected to torture and hardship. In return, these women sometimes torched the homes of Christian missionaries. Many of the descendants of these women would later be expelled into what would come to be known as the Great Plains area of the United States.

Both before and after the inception of the reservation system, Christian churches became one of the chief arms of the U.S. military and state. A significant number of the infamous Indian schools were missionary schools, funded largely by the federal government. The Department of War and later the Bureau of Indian Affairs, Department of Interior, quickly forbade the practice of traditional

spiritual ceremonies ranging from the *Inipi (*sweatlodge), the *Yuwipi* or *Lowanpi* (healing ceremonies that, like the *Inipi*, enlist the aid of holy spirits), to the *Winanayag Wachapi* (Sun Dance). For the most part, however, Plains nations were among the last of the First Peoples to have to face the ethnocide of the colonizers; thus traditional roles and cultural practices were still a vital part of Plains peoples' lives when the last of the Plains reservations were instigated in the late 1800s. During that period the well-known Ghost Dance and, in the Plains, the North American Indian Church movements emerged, while, for the most part, the practitioners of the traditional ways such as the *Inipi*, *Yuwipi*, and *Winanayag Wachapi* went underground. In reaction to the Ghost Dance Movement, Christian imperialism sparked the Wounded Knee massacre; Christian officers and soldiers killed women, children, and elders.

Young Plains people who had knowledge of the old ways and whose spirits had not been broken by the boarding schools began to return to the old ways. For example, from 1900 to 1902, Gertrude Simmons Bonnin, Zitkala-Sa (Red Bird, Yankton Sioux), who had succeeded as a scholar and writer in the Waschiu world but had chosen to return to her people and her traditional spirituality, wrote a series of essays for the *Atlantic Monthly*. One particularly poignant and telling piece, published in 1902, is entitled "Why I Am a Pagan."

The reorganization period, the second era, coincides with John Collier's political reorganization in the 1930s, through which indigenous peoples were granted more autonomy, although the limited means of self-determination were still largely dependent on Euro-American social institutions. By law, traditional practices were no longer prohibited; in fact, Christian forces still made open acknowledgment of adherence to traditional spiritualities very difficult and often impossible, if practitioners wanted employment and social acceptance. In addition, openly flouting the new laws, Christian fundamentalists continued to intrude and brazenly break up traditional ceremonies, in particular the Sun Dance. Thus many people continued to attend *Wasichu* (white) churches and secretly participate in the old ways.

The Civil Rights era, the third historical period, can be linked to a period of awakening in which empathetic postsecondary faculty, American Indian Movement members, War on Poverty workers, radical Christians, sensitive social scientists, and social service professionals began to assist medicine people in providing relatively safe environments for the open performance of traditional ceremonies and other cultural practices. Based upon oral history, experiential knowledge, and the unbiased observations of early Europeans such as artist George Catlin, who lived among the Assiniboine and other Plains peoples in the 1800s, the scholarly writings of Plains Indian intellectuals such as Henrietta Mann, Bea Medicine, and Vine Deloria, Jr., began to refute the myths perpetuated by Christians and academics about traditional spiritualities, ways of life, and the relationship to the land—in particular sacred land. During this era, Plains Indian religious rights activists, descendants of the original inhabitants as well as of those who had been forced by the colonizers into the Plains, laid the foundation for the passage of the Freedom of Religion Act in 1978, a major accomplishment albeit a rhetorical act that contained no remedies for enforcement.

The fourth period in the history of revitalization movements, the era of modern renewal or renaissance, in the Plains as well as nationally is still unfolding. New indigenous Plains writers such as Ed McGaa, Tilda Long Soldier, Mark St. Pierre, and Dan Wildcat and non-Indian allies such as Carl A. Hammerschlag have added their voices to the earlier ones, continuing to refute academic and Christian claims that traditional spiritualities have been romanticized or destroyed. In this period, the national effort to ensure the realization of First Amendment freedom of religion rights has produced a number of legal enactments, such as the National Museum of the American Indian Act of 1989, the Native American Graves Protection and Repatriation Act of 1990, and the Indian Self-Determination Act Amendments of 1994.

Such political and legal steps have helped protect the expression of traditional spirituality as well as conscious synergetic combinations of traditional metaphysics with compatible elements of Christianity. During Plains ceremonies recognition is usually given to Jesus as a holy man, albeit not as the only holy person and not as the only way to a spiritual life. A growing number of Christian denominations are also becoming more inclusive of traditional indigenous rituals. Fundamentalist Christians are now acknowledging the church's sins committed against First Peoples and permitting indigenous music and dance as part of worship. This new sensitivity may be partially explained by two influences: (1) efforts by churches to address the human rights critiques of the alliance between organized Christian religion and colonization and (2) the influence of knowledge associated with the new medical science of psychoneuroimmunology (PNI), the findings of quantum physics, and other Western scientific fields that now recognize the connections between mind, body, and spirit—an intersection that traditional spiritualities and healers have always recognized.

However, the new inclusiveness of Christian churches does not challenge its basic theology. For example, nowhere is White Buffalo Calf Woman recognized as a legitimate holy person. To do so would be Christian heresy. Given the vast differences in Eurocentric and First Peoples' world views, Deloria and Wildcat point out that an in-depth synergetic combination of American Indian metaphysics with Christian theology may never be possible.

Today Plains spiritual practices are not only blossoming again in Plains Indian Country but, in addition, the old ways have spread beyond the Plains. Diné, Apache, and others participate in the Sun Dance. Plains-style sweats are held in East Los Angeles and other urban centers throughout the United States. Recognizing a common metaphysics, the Bear Dancers in California include Plains people. And fundamentalist Christians are beginning to ask indigenous leaders for permission to preach, promising that they will not repeat the old overt name calling and condemnation practices, although most Christians have not yet reached a level of understanding at which they can make a fully informed critique of their religious imperialism, which while destroying traditional Plains spiritualities has also seeded the ground for its resurgence.

Mitakuye Oyasin (All of relations, all of my relations, Lakota).

Tsonkwadiyonrat (We are one spirit! Wyandot).

Karren Baird-Olson

See also Retraditionalism and Identity Movements; Retraditionalism and Revitalization Movements, California; Retraditionalism and Revitalization Movements, Columbia Plateau; Retraditionalism and Revitalization Movements, Southeast; Revitalization Movements, Northeast

References and Further Reading
Baird-Olson, Karren, and Carol Ward. 2000. "Recovery and Resistance: The Renewal of Traditional Spirituality among American Indian Women." *American Indian Culture and Research Journal* 24, no. 4: 1–35.
Bonnin, Gertrude Simmons (Zitkala-Sa). 1902. "Why I Am a Pagan." *Atlantic Monthly* 90: 801–803.

Great Plains

The vast region known as the Great Plains culture area stretches from the Mississippi River valley west to the Rocky Mountains and from present-day central Canada to southern Texas. Dominated by rolling, fertile tallgrass prairies in the east, where there is adequate rainfall for agriculture, the landscape shifts to short grasses in the drier high western plains. Some wooded areas interrupt these vast fields of grass, mostly stands of willows and cottonwoods along river valleys, and in some places highlands rise up from the plains and prairies, such as the Ozark Mountains in Missouri, and the Black Hills of South Dakota and Wyoming. The region is remarkable, however, for the extent and dominance of its grasslands. For thousands of years tens of millions of bison grazed the grasses of the Great Plains.

Prior to the arrival of Europeans, most occupants of the Great Plains lived along rivers in the eastern regions. Predominantly farmers, these culture groups hunted bison and other game seasonally to augment their diets with dried meat and to make use of the hide, bones, and fat of these enormous animals.

The region is known for its diverse Native cultures, some of which have resided in the Plains region longer than others. The Hidatsa, and Mandan, both speakers of Siouan linguistic dialects, as well as Caddoan-speaking Pawnee and Wichita made use of the river banks for small-plot farming and they hunted in large cooperatives once or perhaps twice a year.

More hunting-oriented peoples eventually moved into the region and developed cultural and philosophical traditions based on the bison and warfare/raiding warrior cultures. These include the Algonquin-speaking Blackfeet from the north and the Uto-Aztecan-speaking Comanche from the northwest. After, and in some cases because of, the arrival of Europeans in North America, Eastern tribal groups such as Siouan-speaking Assiniboine, Crow, Kaw, Osage, Quapaw, and the various tribal groups often incorrectly glossed as "Sioux" (Lakota, Nakota, and Dakota) from the Great Lakes region moved to the region. From the Northeast came the Algonquin-speaking Arapaho, Cheyenne, and Gros Ventre. To be certain, this is an abbreviated list. The key issues are that movement into the region coincided with

continues

Great Plains (continued)

the entrance of horses to the Great Plains and the groups that call the Plains home have all participated in a development of regional, seminomadic cultural traditions that have come to be erroneously lumped together. This tragic loss of a sense of tribal diversity on the Great Plains has been exacerbated by the "Hollywoodization" of Indian issues, itself merely a continuation of nineteenth-century dime novels about the West.

After European contact, some Great Plains peoples continued to farm, and many groups hunted a variety of game, fished rivers, and gathered wild plant foods. However, with the spread of horses as a means of transportation to follow the seasonal migrations of bison herds over great distances, bison meat became the staple food.

Most Great Plains tribes consisted of bands of related families, often with several hundred members. Tribal leadership was typically divided between a peace chief and a war chief (or several war chiefs). Peace chiefs tended to internal tribal affairs. War chiefs, usually younger men, conducted warfare and led raids on enemies. The bands lived apart in smaller family groups most of the year, coming together in the summer months for communal bison hunts, ceremonies, or councils. In opposition to the idea that Indian people never owned land, tribal groups often took responsibility for particular regions, sharing hunting lands with friendly tribes, but protecting them from enemies.

Another myth is that all Indians of the Plains lived in tepees prior to contact. The tepee is a portable shelter that served its purpose for most groups for portions of the year. Earth and grass lodges were also frequently used dwellings before Euro-American arrival, providing large communal dwellings and ceremonial structures.

Religion among the Plains peoples is as diverse as the linguistic traditions represented there, however, there are also some similarities. With the important role that bison play in the lives of these tribal groups, it is no wonder that that animal would be an important spirit being and relative, as well. In addition, the migratory nature of bison, and consequently that of the peoples who rely upon them, support a seasonal and cyclical

continues

Great Plains (continued)

philosophical system wherein the circle is a key element. Plains Indian religious culture is often represented by circles, sun-wise directional prayers, and cyclical senses of time and space.

Major ceremonies include the Sun Dance, a regular gathering of bands for communal propitiation of the spirit beings, and the more recent religious innovation known as the Ghost Dance, wherein visions and ecstatic dancing propels the tribal culture forward in the face of the difficulties arising from modernity.

The Great Plains, often viewed as the exemplary Native American culture area, is far more diverse and multilingual than popular culture depicts, and the Plains peoples have many localized and territorial traditions that represent specific regional differences.

Davenport, Frances Gardiner. 1917. *European Treaties Bearing on the History of the United States and Its Dependencies to 1648*. Vol. 1. Washington, DC: Carnegie Institution of Washington.

Deloria, Vine, Jr. 1973. *God Is Red: A Native View of Religion*. New York: Grossett and Dunlap.

Deloria, Vine, Jr., and Daniel R. Wildcat. 2001. *Power and Place: Indian Education in America*. Golden, CO: Fulcrum.

Devens, Carol. 1992. *Countering Colonization: Native American Women and Great Lakes Missions, 1630–1900*. Berkeley: University of California Press.

Hammerschlag, Carl A., M.D. 1988. *The Dancing Healers*. San Francisco: Harper and Row.

High Bear, Martin. 1983. "The White Buffalo Calf Woman as Told by Martin High Bear, Lakota Spiritual Leader." Recorded December 1983 in Pipestone, Minnesota.

Johnson v. McIntosh, 21 U.S. 543, 5 L.Ed. 681. 1823.

McGaa, Ed (Eagle Man). 1998. *Eagle Vision: Return of the Hoop*. Edina, MN: Four Directions Publishing.

———. 1990. *Mother Earth Spirituality: Native American Paths to Healing*

Ourselves and Our World. San Francisco: Harper Collins.

———. 1992. *Rainbow Tribe: Ordinary People Journeying on the Red Road*. San Francisco: Harper San Francisco.

———. 1995. *Native Wisdom: Perceptions of the Natural Way*. Edina, MN: Four Directions.

Medicine, Bea. 1980. "American Indian Women: Spirituality and Status." *Bread and Roses* 2: 15–18.

Newcomb, Steve. 1992. "Five Hundred Years of Injustice." *Shaman's Drum* (fall): 18–20.

St. Pierre, Mark, and Tilda Long Soldier. 1988. *Walking in the Sacred Manner: Healers, Dreaming, and Pipe Carriers— Medicine Women of the Plains Indians*. New York: Simon and Schuster.

Retraditionalism and Revitalization Movements, Southeast

Revitalization is a term that scholars use to describe the process whereby members of a culture perceive a loss of power and attempt to recoup it through a variety of ways, most often through religious revivals. In many ways, revitalization is a recurrent theme in the history of the Native Southeast. Cultures and societies have risen and fallen since the first people moved into the region thousands of years ago. Generally speaking, however, scholars have tended to look for Native American revitalization movements in their history after contact with Europeans. Across the American Southeast, Native societies sought to use sacred power to control the European and American invasion of their land.

Success on the deer hunt, flourishing fields of corn, and victory on the battlefield resulted from people's ability to acquire, manipulate, and deploy sacred power. When diseases introduced by Europeans decimated Native populations, when Native people came to depend on European goods for survival, and when they began to lose their land to expanding settlements, leaders across the Southeast began to question their ability to effectively wield the sacred power that for centuries had underwritten their societies' faith and power. Many Native leaders, particularly a number of self-styled prophets, proclaimed that people had to return to older ways of living in order to restore their independence, autonomy, and mastery of sacred power. Others sought to restore sacred power by reforming customary political, social, and economic relationships in ways that integrated the knowledge and power of the United States.

Tecumseh, Shawnee Chief 1768–1813. (Library of Congress)

Revitalization movements swept the Southeast in the early 1800s and followed three distinct paths. Many Creeks made common cause with prophets from the Shawnee nation of the Great Lakes region to fight the expansion of the United States. Choctaws tried to fuse American and Choctaw ways of thinking and believing in order to defend their land from settlement. And Cherokees revitalized their society by adopting a constitution based on the American one, by publishing a newspaper to advocate for their cause, and by carrying the defense of their power and sovereignty to the Supreme Court of the United States.

In the fall of 1811 the Shawnee war leader Tecumseh visited the Creeks. They welcomed him as their kin because his mother was Creek. Tecumseh had initiated a revitalization movement in the Great Lakes country and wanted Creek help to resist U.S. expansion. Some Creeks refused to support his cause, but others followed him back north to hear the vision of his brother Tenskwatawa, the prophet.

The Creeks who were sympathetic to Tecumseh's mission believed in Tenskwatawa's opposition to alcohol, his mistrust of Euro-American ways of life, and his struggle to resist American settlement. On their way back to their homeland, they killed some settlers in Tennessee. Big Warrior, a prominent Creek chief who disagreed with Tecumseh, attempted to capture the guilty warriors, many of whom were killed in a fight with their pursuers.

A number of prophets whom Tecumseh had inspired called for Big Warrior's death. Josiah Francis, Paddy Walsh, and other Creek prophets began dancing Shawnee dances and singing Shawnee songs in order to acquire the power that had strengthened their friends to the north, power that they would need to fight their enemies. They also avoided alcohol, livestock, cotton cultivation, and other facets of U.S. material culture in order to show the Great Spirit that they had taken a new path to a righteous and proper life.

In 1812 and 1813, the Creek revitalizationists, who came to be called Redsticks because of the color of their warclubs, killed livestock and tore down fences as part of their attempt to purge their society of alien influences. When they began to kill Creek opponents of their program, the Redsticks risked civil war. An assault on Big Warrior's town and followers completed the transformation of acts of sporadic violence into a full-fledged war among Creeks.

At the same time the United States was engrossed in a war against Great Britain, the War of 1812, and both British support for the Redsticks and Redstick attacks on U.S. settlements pulled the U.S. army into the Creek civil war. Forces under the command of General Andrew Jackson invaded Creek country, devastated the countryside, and crushed the Redsticks. At the Battle of Horseshoe Bend, Jackson's forces, augmented by Creeks and Cherokees who opposed the Redstick cause, crushed the remaining Redsticks. Many of the survivors fled to Florida, where they found refuge among the Seminoles and continued to resist U.S. expansion.

The Choctaws had refused to take up the hatchet that Tecumseh had extended to them when he visited as part of the tour that took him to the Creeks in 1811. The three chiefs who governed the nation preferred to side with the United States. As American settlers invaded their land and as American politicians pressured them to move to the west, they, like the Creeks, experienced a crisis of power and faith. Instead of rejecting U.S. culture and endorsing the kind of revitalization preached by Tenskwatawa,

Tecumseh, and the Redsticks, many Choctaw leaders urged their followers to incorporate agriculture, Christianity, and written laws into their lives in order to give them access to the sacred power that made the United States such a formidable opponent.

To reinforce the link between traditional forms of sacred power and new ways of life, Chief Greenwood LeFlore called a national council at the Nanih Waiya mound, the place where, Choctaws believed, the Great Spirit had created them. While standing on the mound, LeFlore issued a series of written laws that brought Choctaw life into conformity with Anglo-American law.

In addition, LeFlore embraced the message preached by American missionaries who had opened schools in the nation. He and his supporters, however, pushed the missionaries aside and began preaching that Choctaws ought to turn their prayers to the Christian god for help in their struggle. Insofar as the missionaries helped them in the cause, the Choctaws considered them to be messengers of the Great Spirit. The combination of the Great Spirit and of God in a new religious movement upset many Choctaws, and the nation teetered on the brink of civil war.

Before the two sides could begin fighting, however, the U.S. government forced the Choctaws to cede their remaining land in Mississippi and to remove to the West. Across the nation Choctaws gave up their new faith in God, began dancing old dances, singing old

Chief John Ross was among the Cherokee leaders who wrote a constitution for the Cherokee people to govern their nation in its struggles with the U.S. government. (Library of Congress)

songs, and preparing for a new life in a new land.

Like the Choctaws, the Cherokees also experienced a revitalization movement that emphasized what historians call syncretism. That is, unlike the Redstick Creeks, who rejected much of Euro-American culture, the Cherokees merged facets of U.S. and Cherokee culture in an attempt to find new sources of sacred power. Like the Choctaws, Cherokees identified written laws as a source of power in their struggle against the federal government.

European colonization and American settlement had upset the ways in which Cherokees had lived for centuries. Some

Cherokees, particularly the Chickamaugas, sided with the Shawnees and Creeks and fought the United States in the 1790s and early 1800s. Most Cherokees, however, followed a rising group of leaders who sought to revitalize their society and sovereignty by initiating a broad reform movement that focused on politics but touched equally on the spiritual foundations of the nation.

Legal and political reform began in the early 1800s. The national government created a police force to secure Cherokee property and to patrol the nation's boundaries. Eventually the government also removed the clans' authority to adjudicate legal disputes and to oversee property inheritance. Such reforms reflected leading chiefs' close relationship to the U.S. market economy and their support of missionary schools that instilled in their children U.S. values and Christian precepts.

Critics of the reforms organized a broad coalition to resist changes to Cherokee law and practice under the titular leadership of a healer named White Path. The so-called White Path's rebellion pitted shamans, clan leaders, and others who resented the degree to which chiefs had abandoned old ways for new ones and the spread of Christianity by the missionaries. Support for the rebellion, however, was too diffuse to halt the reformist and revitalizing agenda of chiefs like John Ross and George Lowry.

In 1827, Ross, Lowry, and other leaders wrote a national constitution that created a bicameral assembly, a judiciary, and elected executive to govern the nation in its struggles with the United States. Elias Boudinot edited a new Cherokee newspaper, the *Cherokee Phoenix,* to defend his nation in the popular press of the period. The reforms and Boudinot's editorials enabled the national government to defend in a more concerted fashion Cherokee land and power. They also reflected the degree to which the Cherokees hoped to appropriate sacred power from their adversaries.

The power of the new Cherokee nation alarmed its neighbors. In 1831 the state government of Georgia declared the Cherokee Nation to be null and void, so that the state could survey and sell the Cherokees' land. In response, Chief Ross launched two cases in the Supreme Court, *Cherokee Nation v. Georgia* in 1831 and *Worcester v. Georgia* in 1832. Despite the Court's finding in favor of the sovereignty and legitimacy of the Cherokee national government in the *Worcester* decision, the federal government and the government of Georgia refused to abide by the Court's decision. Unwilling to fight as the Redsticks had done twenty years earlier and thoroughly dispirited by the failure of their new sacred power to protect them and their homes, the nation acceded to the fraudulent treaty of New Echota in 1835 and embarked on the Trail of Tears four years later.

James Taylor Carson

See also Christianity, Indianization of; Dance, Southeast; Missionization, Southeast; Power, Southeast; Trail of Tears

References and Further Reading

Carson, James Taylor. 1999. *Searching for the Bright Path: Mississippi Choctaws from Prehistory to Removal.* Lincoln: University of Nebraska Press.

Dowd, Gregory Evans. 1992. *A Spirited Resistance: The North American Indian Struggle for Unity, 1745–1815.* Baltimore: Johns Hopkins University Press.

Edmunds, R. David. 1983. *The Shawnee Prophet.* Lincoln: University of Nebraska Press.

Green, Michael D. 1982. *The Politics of Indian Removal: Creek Government and Society in Crisis.* Lincoln: University of Nebraska Press.

Kidwell, Clara Sue. 1995. *Choctaws and Missionaries in Mississippi, 1818–1918.* Norman: University of Oklahoma Press.

Martin, Joel W. 1991. *Sacred Revolt: The Muskogee's Struggle for a New World.* Boston: Beacon Press.

McLoughlin, William G. 1986. *Cherokee Renascence in the New Republic.* Princeton: Princeton University Press.

———. 1994. *Cherokees and Christianity, 1794–1870.* Athens: University of Georgia Press.

Wallace, Anthony F. C. 1956. "Revitalization Movements: Some Theoretical Considerations for Their Comparative Study." *American Anthropology* 58: 264–281.

Retraditionalism and Revitalization, Northeast

One of the primary effects of colonization is that it often destroys indigenous peoples' ability to survive and thus leaves their culture and religion irrelevant. When a people's self-sufficiency has been usurped and they must rely on an occupying force for goods and services, the religious ceremonies that reaffirm traditional ways of being and celebrating abundance are inevitably seen as meaningless by some. For those, the process of religious conversion is a logical step. But for others, the loss of traditional ways is lamented. Those men and women who feel a strong connection to their cultural heritage and long for the health and balance their communities enjoyed before contact are often inspired by a dream or vision to return their people to the ways of their ancestors, which provided them with social stability and cultural vitality for generations. People are creative; they synthesize the things around them into coherent, manageable systems. It is a natural response to use the icons, ideas, and imagery of the Native religious tradition combined with an acknowledgment of the unpleasant realities caused by external forces to chart a new course. This courageous attempt by charismatic leaders to bring their communities back into traditional order by spreading a message of a new vision with a new promise for prosperity is what scholars call a Revitalization Movement. Such movements often incorporate some elements of the invading culture's ideology and are spread by prophets who tell of a vision that forebodes a great suffering and end of the world if the new message is not heeded.

One example of a Revitalization Movement among Native Americans of the Northeast Woodlands is the Seneca religious revival led by Handsome Lake around the turn of the nineteenth century. This was in response to the loss of

Iroquois culture and religion precipitated by continued exploitation by British and U.S. colonists. Handsome Lake and his followers began a new religion, one that incorporated limited aspects of Christianity into the traditional Iroquois ceremonial calendar and moral code. The revitalization of Seneca society that resulted facilitated the endurance of their cultural identity while advocating changes deemed necessary to survive reservation life. To understand fully and to interpret the meaning and value of Handsome Lake's movement, it is important to know the historical circumstances to which he was responding.

The Iroquois Confederacy, made up of the Six Nations—Mohawk, Seneca, Tuscarora, Oneida, Onondaga, and Cayuga—was founded in the 1560s and became the most powerful force in the New York region's fur-trading empire. Initially allied with the Dutch, the Iroquois later became trading partners with the British when they defeated the Dutch in 1664. Armed with Dutch and British weapons, the Iroquois attacked neighboring tribes in the mid-seventeenth century, gaining access to rich fur-trapping territory while making enemies of the French- and Algonquian-speaking peoples they defeated. When French-British competition escalated, the Iroquois, who remained allied with the British, found themselves in the center of the series of French and Indian Wars, which lasted from 1689 to 1763 with intermittent periods of peace. From 1701

to 1763 the Iroquois maintained a profitable neutrality, whereby they played the European imperial powers off against each other for their own gain. Their strategic position, considerable power, and influence over other tribes were capitalized upon by Iroquois diplomats. Although their eventual military support was pivotal in the British victory over France, the Iroquois were considerably weakened by the sustained conflict. The British now controlled all the territory around Iroquois land, which reduced their strategic importance, and the British no longer needed Iroquois men as warriors.

The Iroquois split allegiances when the American Revolution broke out in 1775. The Mohawks, Onondagas, Cayugas, and Senecas remained loyal to the British, while the Oneidas and Tuscaroras sided with the Americans. This division, along with the eventual victory of the United States, was a devastating blow to the Iroquois Confederacy. All the major Iroquois towns were destroyed by the John Sullivan expedition in 1778, and they were forced to flee to British refugee camps. With the Fort Stanwix Treaty of 1784 and later land cessions, the Iroquois were deprived of all their land with the exception of a few small reservations. By 1797 the Iroquois Confederacy was scattered; the remaining tribes were divided on relations with the new United States and whites in general. There was no effective leadership to reunite the bands that had been forced to retire to the small tracts of land available to them.

It was in this historical setting that Handsome Lake lived. He was born in 1735 to a noble Seneca family of the Allegany band, a half-brother to the famous Chief Cornplanter. Iroquois society had been ravaged by European diseases and abuse of alcohol. Handsome Lake was no exception. His life was plagued by illness and alcoholism. He spent four years as a debilitated invalid after years of drinking and intemperance. It was perhaps during this time that he had the opportunity to reflect on the entrance of European culture and religion into Iroquois society, the effects of alcohol, and the complex cultural decisions of accepting or rejecting European ways.

In 1799, Handsome Lake received the first of his visions. Although he had been sick in bed for four years, he was seen to rise and walk outside, where he appeared to collapse dead. He lay as though dead until the next day, when, surrounded by his family, he awoke. Another version is that Handsome Lake went into a coma after days of drunkenness, during which he received a vision. He immediately arose and began to preach the message sent to him by the Four Messengers, emissaries of the Creator sent to Earth to instruct the prophet of the will of the Creator. Inspired by his visions of these messengers, Handsome Lake told a new story of history; he traced the origin of the evils that the Europeans had brought to America as conceived by Hanîsse'ono, the evil one. According to the story, this devil had tricked a young preacher into supplying Columbus with "Five Things" that were to benefit the new race of people that lived across the sea. The five things were rum, playing cards, money, a violin, and a decayed leg bone. These things were carried by many ships to the Indians. According to Handsome Lake's message, they were the downfall of his people. The rum turned their minds to waste; they gambled their lands and homes away with the playing cards; the money made them greedy and dishonest, forgetting the old ways; the violin made music that made them dance and gossip idly; and the bone was the secret poison that took their lives. The Creator had pity for his people and sent the Four Messengers to tell Handsome Lake the truth and give him the vision and power to lead his people to the good religion of the longhouse.

Handsome Lake spread a teaching collected in the Gai'wiio', the Code of Handsome Lake. Every priest in this new religion memorized this code and delivers it at periodic ceremonial gatherings held in a rectangular wooden structure called a longhouse. The teachings seem influenced by Quaker ideology, which was being spread from a Quaker mission on the Allegany band's land. It indicted the Iroquois people for falling into moral ruin and espoused repentance for sins. Handsome Lake's next vision, a few weeks later, laid out a strict moral code outlawing alcohol, gambling, quarreling, gossip, and sexual misconduct, and emphasizing respect for children. He consistently expressed an extreme dislike of boasting and always stressed humility and gratitude.

The recorded message of Handsome Lake tells of a struggle between the Great Ruler, the Creator, and the evil-minded spirit for the will and minds of humans. The code also sets forth proper ways to treat one's wife, the poor, and the elderly. Handsome Lake's message was tailored to the struggles that his people were facing at the time. For example, they had less land because of their loss in the American Revolution, and the land had been overhunted for nearly two hundred years for the sale of fur. Handsome Lake's messengers advised adopting some means of survival employed by whites, such as building a permanent house, cultivating the soil for food, and keeping livestock. These practices had already been forced upon the Seneca by the United States government after the American Revolution, so Handsome Lake's message was to peacefully adapt to the current situations. He eventually endorsed the Quaker mission and recommended sending children to their schools.

The messengers told Handsome Lake that the people should return to their traditional ceremonial calendar. The penalty for noncompliance was allegedly to be the apocalypse of the world by fire. The messengers told how the world was full of sin and that if the entire world repented the world would be made new again. Handsome Lake prophesied that the world would end in the year 2100, three centuries after his

vision. At one point in his visionary travels, Handsome Lake encounters Jesus Christ, whom he regarded as the prophet of the Creator to the whites. This explicit association with Christianity, along with the analogous concepts he employed—such as the imagery of heaven and hell, confession, and abstinence—may have simply reinforced ideas already present in Iroquois belief. It is clear, however, that his message incorporated an awareness of Christian beliefs and utilized them to forge new ground upon which his followers could stand comfortably in relation to whites. He formulated a system that confirmed and revitalized the old ways while showing their compatibility with the social reforms necessary to survive in their current colonized situation.

Although it may seem that Handsome Lake was imitating or lobbying for acculturation to white ways of life, he may have been shrewdly preparing his people to survive reservation life until a stronger political situation manifested itself. To that end he accepted the reorganization of the family structure that had begun in the midcentury from strong matrilineal clans, which were instrumental in maintaining territory and trade relationships, to nuclear families, which were more conducive to farming. The traditional political power of clan matrons to nominate chiefs and lead ceremonies was not challenged, but the new economic strategy that resembled the Protestant work ethic was more easily facilitated by nuclear families, in which the man worked the fields and the woman attended to household duties.

In effect, then, Handsome Lake's movement was an attempt to revitalize the traditional religious system while adapting social life to the everyday realities of reservation life. It was a religious response to the devastation caused by colonization, but it did not take an extremist position. Rather, Handsome Lake articulated a realistic means of maintaining Iroquois cultural identity in the face of concerted, though implicit, efforts to eradicate it. His moderate path of selective acculturation paired with a revival of the old ways was successful, in that his new religion continues to function today, saving the integrity and self-respect of the Iroquois as a minority with their adherence to a foundational identity-structuring religious system.

Brian Clearwater

See also Retraditionalism and Identity Movements; Retraditionalism and Revitalization Movements, California; Retraditionalism and Revitalization Movements, Columbia Plateau; Retraditionalism and Revitalization Movements, Plains; Retraditionalism and Revitalization Movements, Southeast

References and Further Reading
Mohawk, John. 2003. "The Power of Seneca Women and the Legacy of Handsome Lake." Pp. 20–34 in *Native Voices: American Indian Identity and Resistance.* Edited by Richard A. Grounds, George E. Tinker, and David E. Wilkins. Lawrence: University Press of Kansas.
Parker, Arthur C. 1913. *The Code of Handsome Lake, the Seneca Prophet.* http://www.sacred-texts.com/nam/iro/parker/index.htm. (Accessed August 25, 2003.)
Wallace, Anthony F. C. 1956. "Revitalization Movements: Some Theoretical Considerations for Their Comparative Study." *American Anthropology* 58: 264–281.
_____1969. *The Death and Rebirth of the Seneca.* New York: Alfred A. Knopf.
_____1978. "Origins of the Longhouse Religion." Pp. 442–448 in *Handbook of North American Indians.* Vol. 15, *Northeast.* Edited by William C. Sturtevant. Washington, DC: Smithsonian Institution.

Sacred Pipe

The Sacred Pipe is so important in many American Indian religious traditions that it has become the contemporary symbol for Native religions in general, similar to what the cross is for Christianity. There are many types of pipes used ritually, but the pipe that separates into two parts— the separation and rejoining of bowl and stem itself is of ritual and symbolic significance—is preeminent in pan-Indian rituals (those rituals that bring together people from different traditions). For this reason, although all pipes used in rituals are inherently sacred, the term is often specifically applied to pipes with separable stems and is so used here.

Types of Pipes
Tubular Pipes

The original pipe was a simple tube with tobacco placed in one end and the smoke sucked out of the other; it dates to at least 4,400 years ago. This pipe type is related to tubes for sniffing tobacco snuff and for sucking sickness from an ill person's body into a tube. Tubular pipes were used throughout the Americas in the past and continue in ritual use in the western part of North America.

Tubular pipes are commonly made of stone, sometimes with a slim, round, bone mouthpiece. Pipes made from the leg bones of animals were ritually smoked in the Plains into the twentieth century by Arapaho, Cheyenne, Kiowa, Lakota, and Piegan. Bone pipes are usually wrapped with rawhide or sinew to prevent the bone from splitting as a result of the heat of the burning tobacco. Ceramic and stone tubular pipes remain in use in Pueblo rituals. The coastal California ritual pipe is a tubular one of wood, often with a stone bowl insert.

One-piece Elbow Pipes

Bending the pipe allows gravity to keep the tobacco in the bowl so that the smoker's head can remain at a normal, comfortable angle. With pottery, the tube can be bent before the clay hardens, and ceramic elbow pipes were used throughout the pottery-making regions of both North and South America.

Bending the pipe also brought the bowl into the view of the smoker, encouraging developments in decor. When Europeans sailing up the St. Lawrence River and into Lake Ontario encountered Iroquoian-speaking peoples, they found them to smoke ceramic elbow pipes in council. The tribal "flat pipe" of the Hidatsa and the Arapaho are unusually long one-piece elbow pipes, made of either wood or stone.

Pebble and "Monitor" Pipes

Besides bending the pipe, a second means of creating a pipe with an upward-directed bowl is to drill a stone from two directions, meeting in the middle, with a hollow wooden or reed stem then inserted into one of the holes. Such pipes with short stems were used over much of North America and continue in ritual use among the Pueblo peoples. About 2,000 years ago, flat stone pipes with an upright bowl in the middle began to be used throughout the Midwest, the tradition lasting about 600 years. Archaeologists termed these pipes monitor, after the Union's Civil War steel warship.

Separate-stemmed Pipes

About 1,500 years ago, pipes began to be made with a long reed or wooden stem. Bowl and stem are kept apart, save when ritually used, and both are laden with significance.

The bowls are commonly made of red stone (called "catlinite," after the artist George Catlin, the first Euro-American to describe the major quarry), symbolizing the blood of life, or black or blackened stone, symbolizing Earth. The stone itself represents Earth, and its function as a vessel for holding tobacco, as well as having a hole that is a receptacle for the stem, continues the female imagery.

A number of bowl shapes have been traditionally made. The simplest is a tubular pipe bowl with a long stem. It is an archaic shape that continues in importance among Cheyenne and some of the other Plains traditions for particularly sacred rituals, such as the Thirst Dance (Sun Dance).

Most common is the elbow shape. Many have a projection away from the stem receptacle end, either rounded or pointed. Several hundred years ago, some pipes were made with projections as long as the stem end, both ends tapering toward the bowl in the middle, with the bowl having a double taper. That is probably the basis for the T-shaped pipe bowl, common since the second half of the eighteenth century. Bowls of this last shape were made near the red-stone quarry at Pipestone, Minnesota, in a factory with drill presses for trade with Native people. (Now they are made there by local Natives, the quarry being a national monument.) The T-shape became ubiquitous; most souvenir pipes are of that type. A rare variation of the elbow pipe is a pipe with double bowls, the meaning of the two bowls varying with each pipe. A different variation of the elbow shape is for the bowl to be carved into the shape of an animal body or head, or a human head.

In ritually used sacred pipes, those with an effigy either carved on the bowl or projecting from the stem, it may be seen by the smoker when the stem is pointed toward the recipient of the smoke offering. That is because it is the prayer and offering that is the most important part of the ritual. On tourist pipes, the symbolic image often faces the smoker when the pipe is being smoked, which is but a secondary aspect of the ritual use.

Another relatively common bowl form is the keel shape. Some of the early vasiform separate-stemmed pipes had a projection at the bottom with a hole for the attachment of feathers and other sacred objects. This led to two variations, each with a flat projection at the bottom the length of the bowl, often with one to four holes for thongs to be attached. One type was common along the St. Lawrence River, in the Atlantic Provinces, and Maine. It has a tall vasiform bowl; a thong, often beaded, is tied from the bowl projection to the stem, to prevent the bowl from dropping off and breaking. A second type is common in the Northern Plains, particularly among the Blackfoot tribes. Here the bowl has a double taper, and there tend to be multiple holes on the projection.

A rare, archaic form, although common in Osage sacred bundles, is a horizontal disk shape that may be quite large, although the bowl itself tends to be shallow. The bowl may or may not have a projection away from the stem end. This shape is to be contrasted with a vertical disk, which is a variation of the elbow shape and also uncommon.

Pipe bowls have been decorated in a number of ways, some of which have been mentioned above. After contact with Europeans, bowls began to be inlaid with lead or German silver, particularly in the area of the Great Lakes. Some black bowls were inlaid with catlinite and silver. Early elbow pipes often had a flange at the top of the stem end of the bowl, of varying sizes, sometimes incised or perforated.

Stems are commonly made from wood, although early ones were made from long reeds. Stems can be round or flat and as long as a meter in length. Round stems are created by pushing out the pith, leaving a smoke channel in the center of the stem. The earliest extant stems are of that type—hence the term from the French, calumet, meaning "reed." Flat stems are generally made by splitting the wood, gouging out a channel for the smoke, and then joining the two halves together with glue, sinew, or brass tacks. The second method allows for elaborate pierced designs as well as steaming, to twist the stem into a spiral. Since the late nineteenth century, stems have also been made from catlinite, with wood inserts at both ends, particularly for the tourist trade.

A favorite wood for stems, especially round and square ones, is sumac. The pith of sumac is very soft and relatively easy to push or burn out with a thin rod.

Willow and red osier were also used for thin, round stems. Flat stems are made from a variety of hardwoods, especially ash. During the 1960s and 1970s, most of the tourist pipes made in Pipestone, Minnesota, had stems made from California redwood obtained from a local lumberyard. But the Pipestone pipemakers have since been using sumac again.

When inserted into the pipe bowl for ritual use, the stem represents male energy and creative potential. But as the channel for the smoke offering, the stem represents our voice and, as in Pawnee culture, may be decorated with black circular lines along the entire stem representing the trachea. The stem also represents the journey of life and may so be symbolized by a red line the length of the stem along its top.

The most common stem decoration is a coating of red ocher mixed with bear grease, each symbolic of life-giving spiritual energy. More elaborate stem decoration includes a variety of carvings based on individual visions, colored porcupine quill decorations, or beads obtained from trade and suspended feathers, especially of the eagle.

Sacred Pipe Ritual

There are four significant aspects to the ritual of the Sacred Pipe: that the two parts of the pipe are separable, that the purpose of the pipe is to make a smoke offering, that the pipe links the smoker and the recipients of the offering, and that the pipe is frequently used communally.

The ceremony is relatively similar in pan-Indian and in specific cultural traditions throughout North America, excluding Mexico, the American Southwest, and the Arctic. It is identical in general to the Euro-American descriptions of such rituals from the late seventeenth century to the present, and each specific contemporary action described is attested to in the ethnohistorical literature. Presumably, these rituals have remained unchanged in the main since the inception of the separate-stemmed pipe over the last millennium and a half. While a communal ceremony will be described, the ritual would be similar if only a single smoker were involved.

The ritual implements are kept either in a pipe-bag or wrapped in a bundle. The ceremony begins with the opening of the bundle or bag and the laying out of the paraphernalia. Sacred herbs are either directly lit or placed over a glowing coal from a fire. The resulting smoke is first spread in the four directions plus zenith and nadir, then the locale of the ritual—for example, the perimeter of the room in which the ceremony is being held—then over each of the implements, and finally around each of the participants. The purpose of the smudging is to purify, in the sense of removing any and all negativity. Once the purification has taken place, at any point in the ceremony sacred songs may be sung, with or without the use of hand drums or shakers.

When the preliminary laying out of the ritual paraphernalia and purification has been completed, the stem and bowl will be joined together. Only when the male stem is inserted into the female bowl, when the two major complementary spiritual forces in the universe are conjoined, is the pipe spiritually potent. This awe-inspiring act creates a sacred moment in time, a time out of time, and determines the space where the ritual is taking place to be temporarily the sacred center, the *axis mundi,* of the world. A feeling of reverence permeates the congregants.

The pipe bowl is then filled, often with the bowl resting on the sacred Earth or a symbol of Her. Each pinch of tobacco is smudged with the purifying smoke and dropped into the bowl. The first six pinches of the tobacco offering, dedicated to the sacred directions—Four Directions, Sky, and Earth—are spoken to. Other pinches may or may not be specifically dedicated, depending on the tradition, the purpose of the ceremony, and the one making the offering. A tamper is used to settle the tobacco in the pipe bowl. The filled pipe is held in both hands with the stem pointing in the direction of the primary recipient(s), and relevant prayers are spoken. At this point the filled pipe may be put aside, if the actual smoking will take place in the context of other rituals, such as during one of the breaks in a Spirit Lodge (sweatlodge) ceremony or at the completion of a vision fast.

When the pipe is smoked, traditionally the tobacco is lit with an ember from a fire, a smoldering chip of dried bison dung, a glowing braid of sweetgrass, or the glowing tip of a stick of cedar or other especially sacred wood. Nowadays some ignite the tobacco in the pipe directly with the flame of a match or a lighter.

A solo smoker, or the one leading the ritual, offers smoke through the pipe to the six directions and other spiritual recipients. This is done by taking in the smoke and blowing it in the appropriate directions. Simultaneously the stem of the pipe is usually pointed in the direction of the offering. This particular aspect of the ritual is open to a variety of variations, depending on both tradition and inspiration received directly from the spirits by the one making the offering.

In a communal ceremony the participants will be seated in a circle, usually with women and men each forming half the circle and facing each other. The pipe is passed in the direction of the path of the sun from one participant to another. Each in turn holds the pipe with both hands and takes one or four puffs. They may brush the smoke over themselves with one hand, speak the words "All my relations" in the tribal language—acknowledging their connection with the spirit realm—or turn the pipe in a circle. Participants will carry out these secondary rituals only if they have been specifically so taught by the spirits; to do so without the "right" is considered irreverent.

The pipe will continue around the circle until it returns to the one leading the ritual. If it is a large circle, the tobacco in the bowl may have become ash before the circuit is completed. But even if empty, the pipe will be taken by each participant in turn and brought to the lips. When the pipe reaches the ritual leader, if tobacco is still present the leader will smoke until all the tobacco is consumed. With further prayers and statements of thankfulness, the pipe is taken apart, the stem and bowl separated. At this point the ritual is complete, although all of the ritual paraphernalia must still be wrapped back into a bundle or returned to the pipe-bag.

Pipe rituals are carried out for a number of purposes. Because it is a major means of both offering tobacco to the spirit realm as well as communicating with the spirits, it often forms a major part of larger rituals. Indeed, there are few major rituals that do not include pipe rituals as a subsidiary part. Pipe rituals are also carried out when a simple ritual is desired to bring people together, or there is a felt need for a ritual to re-create or strengthen the relationship with the spirit realm. The pipe ritual, when carried out communally, not only makes possible communion between humans and the spirits through the medium of the shared tobacco smoke but also creates a communion among the congregants through the passing of the pipe and the sharing of the tobacco smoke.

Pipe rituals serve another important function: to allow for peaceful intertribal relationships. Long-distance trade has been a major part of Native economies for thousands of years. A mechanism was needed to allow traders to travel safely through territories of other cultures and to allow trade to take place between people of different groups. Beginning some 2,000 years ago, a common pipe shape, the monitor, continued in use for half a millennium throughout the region of the Ohio and upper Mississippi valleys, as well as in the Great Lakes. This suggests that the pan-Indian use of the separate-stemmed pipe had its antecedents hundreds of years earlier, for Sacred Pipe ceremonies served as rituals of intertribal adoption for as far back as we can trace their use. Even cultures like those in the Southwest, which do not traditionally use the separate-stemmed pipe, will carry out this ritual in intertribal contexts.

The use of a common pipe shape over virtually all of North America north of the Rio Grande River, east of the Rocky Mountains, and south of the sub-Arctic existed side by side with a common pipe ritual. Clearly, the two are intimately connected. Euro-Americans quickly learned that they could safely travel throughout this area by carrying a Sacred Pipe, a practice they often abused. The ritual smoking of the pipe as delineated above, when carried out by persons of different tribes, was understood to create a relationship among the participants; it was a ritual of adoption. By becoming a relation, one was no longer an enemy and not subject to attack.

This should not be understood to mean, however—as is often the case in the literature—that the Sacred Pipe was used only for peaceful purposes; it was also necessary for raiding and war. All activities required the assistance of the spirit realm, and the Sacred Pipe was a major means for requesting assistance for martial activities. Thus the Sacred Pipe was used to bring groups together as allies in warfare, as it also was to bring former enemies together for peace.

This ancient tradition of intertribal use of the Sacred Pipe continues in modern pan-Indian rituals. These ceremonies have often been mistaken by the dominant culture as being an ersatz modern ritual, rather than having an antiquity at least as old as, if not older than, Christianity. In contemporary intertribal meetings, as well as in prisons and hospitals, the ceremony of the Sacred Pipe is a religious ritual that can be subscribed to by virtually all the Native peoples of both Canada and the United States. As with the Spirit Lodge, the Sacred Pipe ceremony allows people of different Native religious traditions to share a common ritual and bond together meaningfully as relatives in the larger scope of "All my relations."

Jordan Paper

See also Ceremony and Ritual, Arapaho; Oral Traditions, Western Plains; Power, Plains; Sweatlodge; Tobacco, Sacred Use of; Vision Quest Rites

References and Further Reading
Blakeslee, Donald J. 1981. "The Origin and Spread of the Calumet Ceremony." *American Antiquity* 46: 759–768.
Freesoul, John Redtail, and Riverwoman Freesoul. 1984. *Breath-Made-Visible: The Pipe as Spirit, Object & Art.* Santa Fe: Freesoul Art Studio.
Hayes, Charles F., III, ed. 1992. *Proceedings of the 1989 Smoking Pipe Conference.* Research Records no. 22. Rochester, NY: Rochester Museum and Science Center.
McGuire, Joseph D. 1899. "Pipes and Smoking Customs of the American Aborigines, Based on Material in the U.S. National Museum." Vol. 1, pp. 351–645 in *Annual Report of the Smithsonian Institution, 1899.*
Paper, Jordan. 1988. *Offering Smoke: The Sacred Pipe and Native American Religion.* Moscow: University of Idaho Press.
Springer, James Warren. 1981. "An Ethnohistoric Study of the Smoking Complex in Eastern North America." *Ethnohistory* 28: 217–235.
West, George A. 1934. "Tobacco, Pipes and Smoking Customs of the American Indians." *Bulletin of the Public Museum of the City of Milwaukee* 17: 1–994.

Sacred Pole of the Omaha

Omahas are one of the five Diegha Siouan tribes. Their Sacred Pole is an emblem of tribal identity. Today the Omahas call their Sacred Pole Umon'hon'ti, the "Real Omaha." He is a physical object, a cottonwood pole—but he is also a person with a life of his own. His life touched the lives of the Omahas when they moved from a homeland east of the Mississippi to their present location on the Missouri River several hundred years ago. He continued to stand for their tribal identity during the good times when they controlled trade up and down the Missouri River. He was with the Omahas through years of war and epidemic disease. He accompanied them on the great tribal buffalo hunts of the eighteenth and nineteenth centuries. When the Omahas were forced to abandon their buffalo-hunting way of life in the 1870s, elders of the tribe were uncertain how they could continue to honor Umon'hon'ti. They knew that to avoid being forcibly removed to "Indian Territory" they would have to learn the ways of the Americans under whose jurisdiction they now found themselves.

In 1888 a young Omaha named Francis La Flesche approached the Sacred Pole's last keeper, Yellow Smoke, with a proposal. Francis was one of the first Native Americans to become a professional ethnographer. He began his study of Omaha culture in collaboration with Alice Cunningham Fletcher, a researcher and writer from Harvard's Peabody Museum. He reports his conversation with Yellow Smoke in a 660-page comprehensive ethnography, *The Omaha Tribe,* which he and Fletcher coauthored in 1911. "Why don't you send the 'Venerable Man,'" La Flesche asked Yellow Smoke, "to some eastern city where he could dwell in a great brick house instead of a ragged tent?" After thinking about the proposal, La Flesche reports, Yellow Smoke agreed. So it was that in 1888, Umon'hon'ti came into the care and keeping of the Peabody Museum in Cambridge, Massachusetts. Following the transfer, Yellow Smoke told Fletcher and La Flesche the story of the Pole's origin.

"When the Omahas still lived in wooded country near a lake," Yellow Smoke said, "their chiefs met in council to devise some means by which the bands of the tribe might be kept together and the tribe itself saved from extinction." While they were in council, a young man, the son of a chief, was hunting in the woods. At night he lost his way. He stopped to rest and to find the "motionless star" (the pole star) for his guide. Suddenly, he was attracted by a light. When he approached the light he saw that it was "a tree that sent forth light. He went up to it and found that the whole tree, its trunk, branches, and leaves, were alight, yet remained unconsumed." The young man watched the luminous tree "until with the rising of the sun the tree with its foliage resumed its natural appearance." He remained by it throughout the day. "As twilight came on it began to be luminous and continued so until the sun rose again. When the young man returned home he told his father of the wonder." The young man's father told the chiefs of all the tribes:

My son has seen a wonderful tree.
The Thunder birds come and go upon
　　this tree,
making a trail of fire
that leaves four paths on the burnt
　　grass
that stretch toward the Four Winds.
When the Thunder birds alight on the
　　tree
it bursts into flame and the fire mounts to
　　the top.
The tree stands burning,
but no one can see the fire except at
　　night.

Then they cut the tree down "and four men, walking in a line, carried it on their shoulders to the village." They made a tent for the tree and set it up within the circle of lodges. "The chiefs worked upon the tree; they trimmed it and called it a human being. They made a basketwork receptacle of twigs and feathers and tied it about the middle." They placed a large scalp lock on top of the pole for hair. "Then they painted the Pole and set it up before the tent, leaning it on a crotched stick which they called *imongthe* (a staff)." When the people were gathered, the chiefs stood up and said, "You now see before you a mystery. Whenever we meet with troubles we shall bring all our troubles to Him (the Pole). We shall make offerings and requests. All our prayers must be accompanied by gifts. This (the Pole) belongs to all the people, but it shall be in the keeping of one family in the Honga (Leader) clan."

Umo^n'ho^n'ti is a person who accumulated many stories during his long life. You can "read" some of these stories in his very appearance. He bears the signature of much devotion. For many years, people "fed" him with buffalo meat. Each year they painted him with buffalo fat mixed with red pigment. They wrapped him with a piece of leather called *a'shon-depa*, "the word used to designate the leather shield worn on the wrist of an Indian to protect it from the bowstring." Fletcher and La Flesche explain: "This name affords unmistakable evidence that the Pole was intended to symbolize a man, as no other creature could wear the bowstring shield. It indicates also that the man thus symbolized was one who was both a provider for and a protector of his people" (Fletcher and La Flesche 1992, 225).

In 1988, a century after Yellow Smoke handed Umo^n'ho^n'ti to Francis La Flesche, Omaha hands once again touched their Sacred Pole. Tribal chairman Doran Morris, who is Yellow Smoke's great-great-grandson according to the Omaha system of reckoning kinship, and Edward Cline, a former chairman, wept as they held Umo^n'ho^n'ti in prayer in a little courtyard outside the Peabody Museum. They wept because of the break in ceremonial order caused by his long absence from his people. They wept for the lack of respect that had been shown to the Pole, just as Yellow Smoke had wept more than a century before when a boy named Francis La Flesche nearly ran down the Pole and its keeper with his father's horses. They wept for the Pole's century of confinement. They wept for joy at his release. And they wept to see him refreshed by sun and wind after so many years within the walls of the "great brick house." While in Cambridge, they began negotiations for the Pole's return. Following some months of deliberation, the Peabody faculty announced a unanimous decision to approve the request.

On July 12 of the following year, 1989, Mr. Joe Johns, a Creek artist-in-residence at the Peabody, escorted Umo^n'ho^n'ti back to the Omaha tribal arena in Macy, Nebraska. Tribal chairman Doran Morris received the Pole on behalf of all Omahas in the hope that his return to the tribal circle will bring all his relations a "blessing for a long time to come." The successful completion of the transfer was not without some difficult moments. Close cooperation between Omaha tribal historian Dennis Hastings and Peabody curator Ian Brown turned out to be essential to the process. Initially the tribe had hoped to obtain temporary storage in Omaha's Joslyn Art Museum, but at the last moment that plan fell through. A resolution of the problem came when Dennis Hastings made contact with the University of Nebraska at Lincoln and requested that they provide the Pole and associated ceremonial objects with interim curatorial care on behalf of the tribe. The university agreed to house the Pole until such time as the Omahas are able to realize their long-range plan of building a tribal cultural center on the reservation.

The Omaha interpretation of these events was that the Pole had found his way to Lincoln for his own reasons—namely, that the university also held the remains of more than a hundred Omahas from the late-eighteenth- and early-nineteenth-century "Big Village" site of Ton'wontonga. By returning to Lincoln rather than to Omaha, the Pole found himself back among the people who had cared for him a century before he went to the Peabody. His return to where his people were housed also had the benefit of easing what had been a potential confrontation between the tribe and the uni-

versity over the issue of reburial. Omaha elder Lawrence Gilpin spoke to the tribe about Umon'hon'ti in 1989:

> The way I would refer to the Sacred Pole is that it is a being. This was done with God after our people realized that in the days of the beginning they talked to nature. They talked to the trees, they talked to the birds, they talked to the sky and they talked to Mother Earth. Everything here was created by what they referred to as the Holy Spirit. And they came to realize that this Holy Spirit was the Creator of all living things here on earth. He made it possible for everything that they could see on Mother Earth here. They took and cut a tree down, taking life from the ground itself, this tree. They took this tree and made it into what we today refer to as the Sacred Pole. The people made their pact, or agreement, with the Great Spirit that this tree here as they took life from it.

The Sacred Pole now has stories to tell about life in our own times. Contemporary Omahas have touched him and prayed over him. Contemporary academics have marveled at the power of motion and of life that remains strong within him. Even more than the *Twenty-seventh Annual Report of the Bureau of American Ethnology,* Umon'hon'ti offers himself as a text for reading and interpretation by people alive today. The son of an Omaha chief long ago read what was to become the Sacred Pole as "a wonderful tree." His father read the same object as "a tree that stands burning." The older man understood it as sacred, a place where "the Thunder birds come and go . . . making a trail of fire that leaves four paths on the burnt grass that stretch toward the Four Winds." Fletcher and La Flesche read him as the relic of "a past once so full of human activity and hope." Now more than a century has passed since they read the Sacred Pole as a relic of a dying culture. The Omahas have survived as a people. They still face the problem of devising "some means by which the bands of the tribe might be kept together and the tribe itself saved from extinction." In times gone by, Umon'hon'ti guided them toward that goal. If people continue to come to him in the right frame of mind, they will be gifted with what elder Clifford Wolfe called "a blessing for a long time to come."

The Sacred Pole is remarkable because he is a physical object that has survived from a distant past. He is remarkable because he is sacred and alive with meaning. He is remarkable because he is a person to members of the Omaha tribe. He is remarkable because he is a gift from Wa'konda, "a power by which things are brought to pass." He speaks to people today from a time in the tribe's past when "a great council was being held to devise some means by which the bands of the tribe might be kept together and the tribe itself saved from extinction." He was central to the tribe's ceremonies during their buffalo-hunting days. Now he has returned to the tribe as a carrier of Omaha identity.

Dennis Hastings and Robin Ridington

See also Ceremony and Ritual, Arapaho; Kinship; Missionization, Northern Plains; Oral Traditions, Western Plains; Power, Plains; Religious Leaders, Plains; Reservations, Spiritual and Cultural Implications; Spiritual and Ceremonial Practitioners, Plains

References and Further Reading
Fletcher, Alice C., and Francis La Flesche. 1911/1992. *The Omaha Tribe.* Twenty-seventh Annual Report of the Peabody Museum. Lincoln: Bison Books.
Ridington, Robin. 1992. "A Sacred Object as Text: Reclaiming the Sacred Pole of the Omaha Tribe." *American Indian Quarterly* 17, no. 1: 83–99.
Ridington, Robin, and Dennis Hastings. 1997. *Blessing for a Long Time: The Sacred Pole of the Omaha Tribe.* Lincoln: University of Nebraska Press.

Sacred Sites and Sacred Mountains

For traditional Native peoples the landscape includes not only the physical world of rocks, trees, mountains, and plains but also the spirit world. Native Americans felt obligated to protect and defend the graves of their ancestors and sacred locations where the Great Spirit both resides and communicates with them: locations such as Mt. Graham in Arizona, Bear Butte and Harney Peak in South Dakota, and Hesperus Peak in Colorado. Centuries spent living in the Great Basin or on the Great Plains brought about a deep love and understanding of the landscape in which Indians believed themselves inseparable from the land and sky.

Devils Tower, the first national monument named by President Theodore Roosevelt in 1906, is a sacred site known as Bear Lodge to many Native American tribes. (Bill Ross/Corbis)

In seeking and guarding access to sacred sites, American Indians need a guarantee of religious freedom for ceremonies, festivals, medicinal plant gathering, and pilgrimages that differ from Christian traditions. Because most Americans have not understood the uniqueness of Indian religions, we have violated their free exercise of them. We need to understand landscapes in the context of traditional Native American religion and the powerful, enduring presence of sacred geography (see Gulliford 2000).

For most tribes a sacred place is a location made holy by the Great Creator, by ancient and enduring myth, by repeated rituals such as Sun Dances, or by the presence of spirits who dwell in deep canyons, mountaintops, or hidden caves. An entire landscape may be sacred, because for thousands of years Indians migrated from place to place in search of food on seasonal rounds that took them into the high country in the summer and to lower elevations in the winter. Sacred sites remain integral to tribal histories, religions, and identities.

Indians honor oral traditions linked to specific sites such as Ribbon Falls at the bottom of the Grand Canyon, where the Zuni believe they emerged from the center of the earth as a people. A sacred site is always sacred, and human burials or village sites remain hallowed ground. If shamans carved rock art panels to evoke spirits in southern Utah or at the bottom of Echo Park in Dinosaur National Monument in Colorado, those places remain special and should not be disturbed. They are sacred sites where the living communicate with the dead or with powerful animal spirits of deer, elk, and mountain lions that the rock artist came to see in his visions.

Continuity over Time

Repetition and tradition, unbroken continuity over time—these elements define traditional Indian spirituality, whether it is a young man seeking a vision at a remote vision quest site, a tribe such as the Shoshones or the Utes at their annual Sun Dances, or Miwok leaders on a pilgrimage to collect plants for religious purposes as they visit sacred shrines in California. Indian religions—not religions in the sense of rules and dogma, but rather highly individualistic approaches to honoring the Creator—are intricately bound to a tight web of place and an intimate, subtle, even secret understanding of landscape.

For traditional tribal peoples, spirits exist and can help or hurt the living. For the Shoshone those spirits may be the elfin *NunumBi.* Different tribes have other names for spirits, but in every case the spirit world intimately links to place. What compromises are possible to protect sacred sites and to preserve a sacred landscape? How do we address significant issues of the free exercise of religion for Native peoples? To answer these questions, Native American sacred sites must first be defined by type so that they can be identified.

Religious Sites associated with Oral Traditions/Origin Stories

The first category of sacred sites would be religious sites associated with ancient myths and oral traditions that figure prominently in emergence and migration stories. To use nomenclature from the National Register of Historic Places, which is administered by the National Park Service, these sites are "traditional cultural properties" that have deep meaning for tribal identities (see Parker and King 1990). Examples would include the huge stone monoliths in Navajo Tribal Park in Monument Valley called "Big Hands," or symbolic barrels, with spouts essential in legend for storing and providing rain for the Diné (Navajo). Rainbow Bridge near Navajo Mountain has sacred qualities for Diné, because the arch comprises two beings, a male and a female, and "from their union come the rain people, rainbows, clouds, and moisture that originates here and spreads over the reservation" (see McPherson 1992; Kelley and Francis 1994).

On the 17.5 million acres of the Navajo Nation, sacred places may be associated with the origin stories of clans, the origins of ceremonies, the origin of specific customs, and the general Diné creation story. Other Southwestern tribes such as the Zuni, Hopi, and Walapai also have specific places linked to their clan migrations and creation stories.

Each tribe has its own story of emergence and migration. For the Kiowa, the story was of a long migration eastward from the headwaters of the Yellowstone River to the Black Hills and south to the Wichita Mountains. Part of that journey took the Kiowa to Devils Tower, Wyoming, which became the first national monument in the United States set aside in 1906 by President Theodore Roosevelt. More than twenty tribes have stories about Devils Tower as part of oral traditions, and Native Americans believe that Devils Tower should be renamed according to its Indian name, Bear Lodge.

Trails and Pilgrimage Routes

A second category of religious sites would be trails and pilgrimages through sacred landscapes such as the trail to Zuni Heaven or the Ute Trail. Cairns as trail markers are particularly important for migratory peoples who remembered the cairns as a place to pause and meditate, as Nez Perce guides did along the Lolo Trail with Lewis and Clark in 1806. Indians also reverently added to the cairns as each passing traveler would say a prayer and add another rock to the pile for both personal good luck and respect for their ancestors who had gone before.

Along the Columbia River in Washington, tall cairns of basalt represent kinship and family lineage for the Yakama, as well as fishing boundaries for different Plateau bands of Indians. Native peoples believe that cairns contain the essence of the builder and must be approached with care, because they offer comforting proof that ancestors passed through the area generations earlier.

Traditional Gathering Areas

A third category of religious sites would include gathering places for fish, wildlife, sacred plants, and materials to quarry, such as mineral deposits that provide sources for face and body paint. Crucial to religious ceremonies, Great Plains paint mines would be neutral territory, and warring tribes could gather red, yellow, and black clay in peace. Sacred paint sources include the Paint Mines near Calhan, Colorado, and in Wyoming at Sunrise and Rawlins. Shield Cave in Colorado represents a rare site that contains every clay color needed in Ute religious ceremonies.

Diné gather hematite and special dirt and sand for sand paintings used in healing ceremonies. Most Southwestern tribes also have sacred places where men gather salt. There are sacred gathering areas at which clans gather special roots and herbs, as well as family-use sites.

There are gathering areas for willows to be used for baskets, wild tea for medicinal purposes, and places to retrieve special water from sacred springs or snowmelt from high elevations. For their *Jish*, or medicine bundles, Diné medicine men may also collect projectile points and pieces of petrified wood. The gathering of such items is always done with gratitude and prayer.

Because Native peoples use plants in religious ceremonies, traditional gathering areas for sacred sage, sweetgrass, and other herbs must be protected. Tribal sacred sites include these traditional cultural property areas where for generations tribes have gathered food, whether it be salmon among the Plateau Indians, bitterroot among the Shoshones, camas roots among the Nez Perce, or huckleberries among the confederated tribes of Warm Springs and the Yakama Nation. These sites retain their sacredness, because they bring the people together each year at harvest time to gather plants for the first feasts and to initiate young girls as women and young men as hunters or fishermen. Indians in the Northwest are acutely conscious not only of their reservation lands but also of lands ceded by treaty, lands that guaranteed Natives the perpetual right to hunt and fish in their "usual and accustomed places." Tribal members exercise those rights yearly. Gathering roots and berries in the old way keeps the people physically strong and knitted together by social tradition.

Offering Areas: Altars and Shrines

Native peoples also make offerings either privately or within ceremonial cycles when they gather sacred materials. At certain times of the year, American Indians offer prayer sticks and special foods to the Creator to keep the people in harmony, to heal the sick, and to provide general balance and prosperity. Offerings are also left for powerful animals like bears and buffalos. Archaeologists sometimes consider such offering sites prehistoric, assuming that they are no longer used, but Native peoples consider such time distinctions irrelevant. Altars are never abandoned; they represent active conduits to the spirit world.

Vision Quest and Other Individual Use Sites

A fifth category of religious sites would be sites used by single individuals, such as vision quest sites. These sites are often composed of stones 18 to 24 inches high, placed in a horseshoe or circular shape. The young man or woman seeking a vision enters the earth or stone enclosure, remaining without food or water until the arrival of the animal or bird spirit, which then becomes the source of his or her personal power or medicine. Indians built most vision quest sites on high precipices with panoramic views, sites that "are among the most common forms of sacred geography in North America," according to Deward Walker (1998). Small, individually used sweatlodges or wooden tree platforms used by medicine men for meditation and healing exist in deep canyons or on mountain ridges.

Vision quest sites can be found at remote locations throughout the Rocky Mountains, and Indians who visit them today often leave offerings of sacred sage, tobacco, or water to placate the spirits. An Indian might reuse the site for a modern vision quest or leave it undisturbed, but in either case a seeker of visions has made it a sacred place.

Group Ceremonial Sites: Sweatlodges, Dances and Sings

Ceremonial dance sites such as Sun Dance, Bear Dance, or other dance sites are also sacred places, and usage may date back for decades or centuries. Plains Indians erect the Sun Dance lodge at the same spot in a lengthy ritual that includes a virtuous woman selecting the forked aspen or willow tree for the central lodge support.

Once the dance has been completed, prayers have been offered, and people have been healed, the dancers leave the lodge by midafternoon of the last day. A permanent Sun Dance structure is not the traditional Shoshone, Ute, or Arapaho way. The Sun Dance lodge loses its religious purpose, because after the dancers have left the space is no longer hallowed. Their sacrifice over, the cosmic spell has been broken. What endures is the process, the community ritual, and the repetition of the Sun Dance, with each group of committed dancers sacrificing themselves at the same sacred place. Ten months out of the year, no one visits the sites (see Jorgensen 1972).

Just as with the routes taken by the Shalako spirits at Zuni or the Deer Dancers at Taos Pueblo plaza, what is sacred is the reconstruction of tradition through meditation and performance. Building the Sun Dance lodge anew brings people together. Ancient ceremonial sites include Serpent Mound National Monument in Ohio and Pueblo Bonito at Chaco Canyon in Chaco Culture National Historic Park in New Mexico. Men's societies still actively use kivas in the Southwest to initiate young boys, and, on the high mesas—such as the village of Walpi on First Mesa at Hopi—ancient plazas still reverberate with the dance steps of the Katsinas.

Ancestral Habitation Sites

Another category of sacred sites to be respected and protected would include ancient Puebloan ruins, as well as tepee rings where Plains people once set up large seasonal encampments. Brush shelters, or wickiups, for Great Basin tribes or Utes in Colorado would also qualify as sacred village sites. Zuni tribal leaders closed to visitors the ancient site of Hawikuh, which is now protected by the Zuni Preservation Department, although other ancestral Puebloan sites—such as those at Mesa Verde National Park or Canyons of the Ancients National Monument—are open to respectful visitation.

Petroglyphs and Pictographs— Ceremonial Rock Art

Many petroglyphs, pictographs, and pictograms qualify as sacred. The Eastern Shoshone believe that petroglyphs represent messages from the spirit world and that only properly trained medicine men or shamans can decipher them. Ceremonial rock art often illustrates origin and creation stories and can be found on the tops of mountain peaks, on boulders in the bottom of drainages, and along pilgrimage routes—anywhere, in fact, the rock surface can be incised down to the desert patina under ledges protected from weathering.

The Spanish priests Fray Francisco Atanasio Dominguez and Fray Silvestre Velez de Escalante, traveling north from Santa Fe, New Mexico, in 1776, encountered a variety of Fremont-era and Ute rock art south of present-day Rangely, Colorado, in a canyon that they named Canyon Pintado because of the colored drawings. In their journals they specifically noted the famed *kokopelli*, or flute player, represented in stylized form throughout the Southwest. Much rock art symbolism has been analyzed and described, and distinct motifs vary among cultural and geographical regions. Petroglyphs and colored pictograms also represent living tribal traditions, and some examples of historical rock art may help to validate tribal claims to ceded lands.

Individual Burials and Massacre Sites

As with all cultures, human remains are sacred to tribal peoples, and with the passage of the Native American Graves Protection and Repatriation Act of 1990, unmarked graves found on public lands now come under federal protection. While some tribes find every individual burial sacred, for the Diné in the Southwest, burials are to be protected, also being places to avoid out of respect.

In addition to Indian burials, another sacred category includes massacre sites and mass burials such as the Marias River Massacre site in Montana; Sand Creek in eastern Colorado; Washita River in Oklahoma; the Camp Grant Massacre site in Arizona; and Wounded Knee at Pine Ridge, South Dakota. These sites of shame, where armed military forces attacked sleeping Indian villages, rarely receive protection or interpretation. Without question these sites are sacred to Native Americans who feel an obligation to tell the living about past atrocities.

Observatories and Calendar Sites

Massive stones atop Fajada Butte at Chaco Canyon National Historical Park in New Mexico functioned as a solar and lunar calendar, designed by ancient Puebloan peoples to mark the passage of time and the seasons. Throughout the Southwest, stone alignments and concentric circles on rock art indicate solstice markers. For the Fremont people who once lived near Rangely, Colorado, a ridgetop observatory may have helped determine their very limited agricultural season at high elevations on the northern boundary of the Colorado Plateau. In southern Colorado, Chimney Rock near the Southern Ute Reservation is high in elevation and was used as a solstice marker. In the South, the misnamed Old Stone Fort near Manchester, Tennessee, represents a sacred earthen enclosure from the Mississippian period with an entrance to the east constructed to admit maximum sunlight on June 21, the longest day of the year.

One of the most powerful sites in North America is the Medicine Wheel in northern Wyoming, which is aligned to both the summer solstice and to the rising of the summer stars Aldebaran, Rigel, and Sirius, though the wheel has been periodically altered over the centuries. The Medicine Wheel must be considered as an entire religious complex including vision quest sites, sacred trails, and even stone cairns in the shape of an arrow pointing to the site from more than 40 miles away across the Big Horn Basin. According to Fred Chapman, Native American liaison with the Wyoming State Historic Preservation Office, the Medicine Wheel represents an "archetypal form of religious architecture" (Chapman 1993).

Sacred Mountains

A special landform sacred to Native peoples is mountains, which have important meanings because they represent diverse ecological niches in which a variety of plants and animals can be found, depending upon the elevation. Desert peoples understood that mountain snows and summer storms created their main source of water, and spirits reside in mountain springs, adjacent canyons, crystal blue lakes, and on the tops of peaks. Mountains in the Appalachians and Adirondacks had meaning for tribes east of the Mississippi, but because President Andrew Jackson forcibly relocated many tribes after 1830, case studies will be drawn from Western mountains still accessed today by Native peoples.

San Francisco Peaks: Home of the Katsinas

The highest peaks in Arizona rise to the west of the Colorado Plateau and stand as silent sentinels, catching the morning sun and reflecting the last light of day near Flagstaff. Sacred to the Hopi and the Zuni, the San Francisco Peaks are also revered by the Diné, whose traditional homeland is bounded by four mountains with the San Francisco Peaks as the boundary mountains to the west. Solitary volcanic mountains, the peaks can be seen 80 miles away by the Hopi who live on high mesas and who for centuries have made annual pilgrimages back to the peaks to leave offerings for the Katsinas who dwell there. Former Hopi chairman Vernon Masayesva writes that the peaks are "the shrine we look to because it is the home of ancient Katsina spirits, emissaries of life. Sometimes we felt we could touch the mountain near Flagstaff" (Masayesva 1998).

Attempting to utilize both the National Historic Preservation Act of 1966 and the American Indian Religious Freedom Act of 1978, the Hopis filed suit against the U.S. Forest Service in 1982 to

Aerial view of Serpent Mound National Monument in Ohio, which is an ancient ceremonial site. (Richard A. Cooke/Corbis)

prevent the expansion of a ski resort that would alter ancient shrines, religious ceremonial sites, and gathering areas held sacred by Hopi clans. The tribe lost in court. Frustrated by a judge who determined that ski area expansion and more parking spaces would have little impact on religious sites, Hopi cultural officer Leigh Kuwanwisiwma found that "there is no final, absolute protection under either act." Equally grating to the Hopis, who, according to Kuwanwisiwma, "once used to go to the mountains unhindered," is the demeaning requirement for a special-use permit to gather the sacred plants they have collected for millennia. The permit is required be-

cause under U.S. Forest Service rules, such gathering is now subject to federal jurisdiction.

Leigh Kuwanwisiwma explains: "It bothers me because I have been assigned by my clan to lead pilgrimages to the peaks. The last time I led a pilgrimage we were supposed to get a permit, but a Hopi goes where his heart tells him to—not where he is told to gather spruce branches." He adds that there are numerous trails from Hopi villages to the San Francisco Peaks, and though some trails are no longer used, "ceremonial activities deified the trails that then came into disuse with better maintained roads into Flagstaff. Now when pilgrimages are made we think of the trails and offer special prayers so that the trails do not lose their significance." Pilgrims originally came to the mountains on foot and then by burro, horse, and horse-drawn wagon. Now the clans come in pickup trucks, but their purpose is the same as it has been for centuries.

Leigh Kuwanwisiwma argues: "Regardless of its use or not, in our prayers and ceremonies the trails still have integrity because you always have a spiritual element. Clans have living memories and hold specific place names for ancestral sites." Offering areas are associated with the sacred peaks, and on the ancient trail from Oraibi to Wupatki National Monument, formal shrines with distinct characteristics mark the route for male Hopi travelers. Because of the prominent San Francisco Peaks, an entire sacred landscape exists across the Colorado Plateau.

California's Mount Shasta

Visible from much of northeastern California, 14,162-foot volcanic Mount Shasta glitters white with snow half of the year and is considered sacred to northern California Indians including the Shasta, Modoc, Pitt River, Hupa, Karuk, and Wintu. Because Californians brutally exterminated Indian tribes in the nineteenth century, and the California legislature even considered legalizing Indian slavery, several tribes interested in protecting Mount Shasta are not federally recognized: today they are few in number and have only a tiny land base

compared with their aboriginal territory of hundreds of square miles. Mount Shasta was an important feature in the mythology of all groups whose territories bordered the mountain, and today's use of the mountain is rooted in traditional practices and values.

The Wintu have maintained the closest ties to the mountain, and they believe, along with the Pitt River Indians, that Mount Shasta is the home of the "little people" who reside inside the peak. A powerful Pitt River spirit called Mis Misa is said to live inside the mountain and has served to keep the universe in balance. Some tribes bury their dead toward the mountain because it points the way toward the spirit world, and when the Wintu dance and pray they always face Mount Shasta. Pitt River Indians believe that spirits of the deceased fly on the backs of eagles to the top of the mountain as a way station before leaving for the Milky Way.

Wintu spiritual leader Florence Jones, who is in her mid-80s, still conducts ceremonies and teaches tribal culture on the mountain, as did her great-great-grandfather. An important ceremony is held at Panther Meadow because of the healing power of its spring, which forms the headwaters of the McCloud River, which flows through original Wintu tribal lands.

Indian tribes and the Save Mount Shasta Citizens' Group wanted Mount Shasta in its entirety listed on the National Register of Historic Places as a National Register Multiple Property, which would include Panther Meadow, a small subalpine meadow that is a spiritual quest/ceremonial site, and the top of the peak. There are twenty-three associated sites, including Coonrod Flat on Pilgrim Creek, where Wintu camp, visit, and entertain as part of a four-day spiritual preparation prior to ascending to upper Panther Meadow Spring. Debate has swirled around exactly how much of Mount Shasta is sacred in the context of the legal boundaries necessary for designation on the National Register of Historic Places. The development of a ski area has sparked a debate and pitted tribes with centuries of occupation and use against developers and local residents.

The 1994 designation of the entire mountain as a sacred site pleased the Indians and New Age religious users but infuriated non-Native locals and a California congressman. The Mount Shasta listing has since been cut to a 40-acre site at Panther Meadow and a 19,000-acre "Native American Cosmological District" within a preexisting 38,000-acre wilderness area reaching from the 8,000-foot contour at timberline to the 14,000-foot summit. Only the top of the mountain has been totally preserved. These new boundaries reflect the original proposal by the California State Historic Preservation Office and the Shasta-Trinity National Forest, although other types of cultural properties are not included and have not yet been evaluated for their archaeological or ethnographic importance.

Gloria Gomes, secretary of the Wintu Tribe of Shasta County, explains: "Mount Shasta is the most sacred area to our people. Our creator lives there, and that's where our spiritual leader receives her power." Merely to preserve the mountain's summit dissatisfies local tribes as well as Gomes, who says, "Declaring only the top of the mountain significant is like considering only the steeple of the church. Why not respect the whole church?"

Taos Pueblo Blue Lake

High in the mountains above Taos, New Mexico, at nearly 14,000 feet in elevation, a lake rests between granite stones and tall spruce trees. Sacred to the Taos people who have lived at their pueblo since at least A.D. 1300, Blue Lake and its watershed symbolize cultural continuity for the tribe and the source of all their health and spiritual well-being. It is from this sacred lake that the tribe emerged, and the lake is the source of their origin as a people. Taken by the U.S. Forest Service as public land and incorporated into the Carson National Forest in 1906, the Blue Lake area has stood as a symbol of the denial of Native American religious freedom. As novelist Frank Waters explained, "The quest for Blue Lake brought Indian religion to the forefront of national consciousness. And it was crucial to the Indians' success that they convince the general public that religion lay behind their claim."

The pueblo's cacique, or religious leader, worked for more than sixty years

Mount Shasta in the Cascade Range is considered sacred to northern California Indians. ca. 1992–1994. (David Muench/Corbis)

to have legal title to the sacred turquoise lake, *Ba Whyea,* restored to Taos Pueblo. The cacique is responsible for the tribe's spiritual life, and he knows all the rituals and mythic stories that begin with tribal emergence from their sacred lake. According to the religious leaders, Blue Lake and the surrounding area "is an ancient place of worship. It is where our ancestors dwell, the source of our life giving water and the heart of Taos Pueblo religion and life."

The pueblo proclaimed: "Our tribal government is responsible to this land and to the people. We have lived upon this land from days beyond history's records, far past any living memory deep into the time of legend. The story of my people and the story of this place are one single story. No man can think of us without also thinking of this place. We are always joined together." Each year the August Ceremony took place at Blue Lake, and tribal members of all ages made their annual 25-mile-long pilgrimage to its deep blue waters, which flow through the pueblo as Blue Lake Creek, or Rio Pueblo de Taos.

Believing that a U.S. Forest Service designation would help protect their property, especially from rampant overgrazing, Taos Pueblo acquiesced to the U.S. government's incorporation of the Blue Lake area into the Carson National Forest in 1906. But the agency's mandate of multiple use of forest resources soon distressed pueblo leaders, who came to regret the inclusion. Serious disagreements arose between local Indians and Forest Service personnel who demanded visitation permits and treated Native Americans condescendingly. Taos people increasingly felt as if they were trespassing on their own sacred lands, but in fact it had been non-Natives who had trespassed and squatted on pueblo land.

Tribal leader Seferino Martinez explained: "We don't have beautiful structures and we don't have gold temples in this lake, but we have a sign of a living God to whom we pray—the living trees, the evergreen and spruce, and the beautiful flowers and the beautiful rocks and the lake itself. We have this proof of sacred things we deeply love, deeply believe."

Taos Indians could visit the lake, but so could tourists, hunters, campers, lumberjacks, and cattlemen. Their sacred area—and the source of water for the Taos village—was no longer under the pueblo's control as it had been for centuries before recorded history. Cacique Juan de Jesus Romero feared that "[if]

our land is not returned to us, if it is turned over to the government for its use, then it is the end of Indian life. Our people will scatter as the people of other nations have scattered. It is our religion that holds us together" (quoted in Brookover 1996).

After years of political delays, in 1969 Congress finally reintroduced the Blue Lake Bill, or House Bill 471, which recommended passage of the law as the cornerstone of a new Indian policy of self-determination. President Richard M. Nixon signed the bill into law on December 15, 1970, returning 48,000 acres of forest land known as the Blue Lake Wilderness Area to federal trust status for Taos Pueblo and granting an exclusive-use area, making the lake and adjacent mountains off-limits to anyone not an enrolled member of Taos Pueblo. At the symbolic signing of the bill, President Richard Nixon said, "Long before any organized religion came to the United States, for 700 years, the Taos Pueblo Indians worshipped in this place. We restore this place of worship to them for all the years to come." As it has since time immemorial, the War Chief's Office patrols Blue Lake and associated sacred shrines and pilgrimage trails.

A major legislative accomplishment without parallel in Indian history, the return of Taos Blue Lake could not have been accomplished without the steadfast support of tribal members, tribal leaders, non-Native attorneys, and sympathetic outsiders who respected Indian religious beliefs and felt that Taos Pueblo had clearly been wronged. Frank Waters noted that the return of Blue Lake "was the first land claims case settled in favor of an Indian tribe based on the freedom of religion."

Although the Blue Lake area is restricted to enrolled Taos Pueblo members, the ancient village is not, and Taos Pueblo welcomes tourists to enjoy "a thousand years of tradition." It is this openness to the larger society that created the necessary coalition to achieve the return of Blue Lake. The sixty-year struggle resulted in an enormous burden, but there was never any hesitation about the effort or the goal. By protecting Blue Lake and their sacred watershed, the people of Taos Pueblo are protecting themselves and ensuring that future generations will be firm in their identity and rooted in a special sacred place. As Cacique Juan de Jesus Romero said, "It is our religion that holds us together" (quoted in Brookover 1996).

Mount Graham: Telescopes and the Big-Seated Mountain

The failure of Apaches to stop the construction of two telescopes high atop 10,720-foot Mount Graham in the Pinaleno Mountains of southeast Arizona represents a critical defeat for Native Americans and environmentalists, and a resounding victory for the University of Arizona, expensive lobbyists, and Washington, D.C., lawyers willing to play hardball to protect their clients. A small tribe of Apaches challenged the Mount Graham International Observatory and its as-

sociated Angel Mirror Laboratory, which is considered one of the most important astrophysical projects in the world.

The Apaches lost by providing too little cultural information, too late, on the mountain known to them as "Big-Seated Mountain," or Dzil Nchaa Si An. Indians claimed that the mountain is one of four sacred Apache mountains, and that it contains the burial sites of medicine men, the homes of spiritual beings including Gaan Dancers, and that it is a sacred pilgrimage site for the collection of plants and medicines. "There are songs about Mount Graham that are an important part of our religious practice," stated Apache medicine man Franklin Stanley. "There are herbs and sources of water on Mount Graham that are sacred to us. Some of the plants on Mount Graham that we use are found nowhere else." He explained: "The mountain is part of spiritual knowledge that is revealed to us. Our prayers go through the mountain, through and to the top of the mountain. Mount Graham is one of the most sacred mountains. The mountain is holy. It was holy before any people came, and in the mountain lives a greater spirit." Eighteen varieties of plants and animals are found there that live nowhere else.

A formidable environmental alliance to stop the telescopes included Defenders of Wildlife, Earth Island Institute, Greenpeace, National Audubon Society, National Wildlife Federation, the Sierra Club, and the Wilderness Society. Other opposition came from the National Council of Churches, the Unitarian Universalist Association of Congregations, and tribal groups including the Apache Survival Coalition and Apaches for Cultural Preservation. Commentators argued that environmentalists sought Indian alliances only after earlier attempts to stop the construction on environmental grounds had failed.

In a June 1991 letter to the U.S. Forest Service, the San Carlos Apache Tribal Council demanded that construction of the telescopes be stopped because of Mount Graham's "vital importance for maintaining the integrity of our Apache culture and tradition." The council argued, "Any permanent modification of the present form of this mountain constitutes a display of profound disrespect for a cherished feature of the Apache's original homeland as well as a serious violation of Apache traditional religious beliefs." Along with the Zunis, for whom Mount Graham is also a sacred site, the San Carlos Tribal Council called for an assessment of the mountain under Section 106 of the National Historic Preservation Act, but construction permits had already been approved.

Apache silence about their religious traditions did not help in this legal battle. Because Native Americans had previously not objected to change on the mountain and had not discussed or described their sacred sites, federal officials had assumed that no important sites existed; they acted accordingly. The U.S. Forest Service sent letters to the tribal council after locating two rock cairns and a shrine on the mountain, but they received no written response. The University of Arizona and other institutions involved with the telescopes do not deny Apaches their religious beliefs; instead, this is the familiar dilemma of restricting access to sacred sites on public land. James Welch, historic preservation officer for the Fort Apache Reservation, argues that non-Apache "experts" should not decide issues of cultural significance for Apaches, and that Native oral traditions must be recognized on a par with academic findings.

Colorado's Hesperus Peak, or Dibe'nsta

Hesperus Peak in the La Plata Mountains is one of the four sacred mountains in Diné cosmology; it represents the northwest boundary of the Diné cultural area. In 1868, when the Diné were incarcerated at Bosque Redondo, chief Barbacito said that they would do anything if only they could go home and not be sent to Oklahoma. In his speech to General William Tecumseh Sherman, he described the boundary areas including Hesperus Peak as one of the Four Sacred Mountains.

Hesperus Peak, 13,232 feet high, figures in Diné lore not only from the treaty's nineteenth-century date but also much earlier in Diné myth and legend. One of the most important of all Diné ceremonies, the Yei Bi Chai, or Nightway Ceremony, is performed only certain times of the year; it is one of two major healing ceremonies held only during the winter months, when the snakes are hibernating and there is no danger of lightning. This ceremony is performed for eight days and nine nights, being initiated when a patient first seeks the help of a hand trembler, who can sense and feel symptoms of a certain nature.

By midafternoon of the second day of the ceremony, sand is used to make figures on the four sacred mountains, and the sand is placed in all directions beginning with the east, south, west, and finally north. Talking God enters the hogan where the ceremony is being performed, and he rotates himself around the patient four times in a clockwise motion, beginning with the east and finishing in the north.

Diné medicine men go to the area to gather sacred dirt and special plants for their medicine bundles, because the heart and soul of the Diné start with the four sacred mountains. Diné medicine man George Blueeyes explains, "These mountains and the land between them are the only things that keep us strong. . . . We carry soil from the sacred mountains in a prayer bundle that we call *dah nidi-ilyeeh*. Because of this bundle, we gain possessions and things of value: turquoise, necklaces, and bracelets. With this we speak, with this we pray. This is where the prayers begin."

A small church and cemetery with white crosses for grave markers stands in the desert below Black Mesa in New Mexico. ca. 1980–1990. (Macduff Everton/Corbis)

According to legend, the sacred mountains were the pillars that held up the sky; thus as pillars they had to be fastened down. The sacred north mountain, or Hesperus, was tied down with a rainbow, black beads, and mist; many plants and animals were added. A dish of black beads, *paszini*, held two blackbird eggs under a cover of darkness, and on Dibentsaa lived Pollen Boy and Grasshopper Girl. Because of the sacred nature of Hesperus, "sacred mountains should not be climbed unless it is done in a proper way through prayer and song, and they should be returned to by medicine men every twelve years to renew their Blessingway prayers," wrote Robert S. McPherson (see McPherson 1992).

Sacred Sites Today

If the term "sacred site" has multiple meanings for tribal peoples, it is a term that is generally misunderstood by non-Indians, who do not easily comprehend how Native Americans value their lands and landscapes. Perhaps through the use of the term, despite its ambiguity, Indian sites can be better protected. Certainly Presidential Executive Order No. 13007 on Indian Sacred Sites (May 1996), signed by President William Clinton, provides new protections to special areas and helps to accommodate American Indians in the free exercise of their religions. As Deward Walker has noted, "Clearly sacred geography is a universal and essential feature of the practice of American Indian religions" (Walker 1998).

After centuries of religious oppression and denial of Indian religious freedom, it is time to respect tribal traditions. Former Hopi Chairman Vernon Masayesva explains, "If an Indian says a rock contains the spirit of God, courts and judges must not dismiss this as a romantic description. Keep in mind, to a Catholic consecrated bread is no longer bread but the very physical body of Christ." He adds, "No court would challenge the Catholic belief in that regard." Masayesva concludes, "And no court should challenge as romantic overstatement that places or things contain the spirit of God either."

Andrew Gulliford

See also Ceremony and Ritual, Diné; Ecology and Environmentalism; Hopi Prophecy; Identity; Mother Earth; Oral Traditions; Religious Leadership, California; Religious Leadership, Southwest, Pueblo; Reservations, Spiritual and Cultural Implications; Sacred Sites and Sacred Mountains, Black Hills; Termination and Relocation

References and Further Reading
Brookover, Linda. 1996. "Desert Claims." *OneWorld Magazine.* *http://www.oneworldmagazine.org/focus/deserts/pueblo2.htm.* (Accessed February 14, 2005)
Chapman, Fred. 1993. "The Medicine Wheel: Tourism, Historic Preservation, and Native American Rights." *Wyoming Annals* 65, no. 1 (spring).
Gulliford, Andrew. 2000. *Sacred Objects and Sacred Places: Preserving Tribal Traditions.* Boulder: University Press of Colorado.
Jorgensen, Joseph G. 1972. *The Sun Dance Religion: Power for the Powerless.* Chicago: University of Chicago Press.
Kelley, Klara B., and Harris Francis. 1994. *Navajo Sacred Places.* Bloomington: Indiana University Press.

Masayesva, Vernon. 1998. "We Have Electricity, Jobs, and Clean Air." *High Country News* 30: 6.

McPherson, Robert. 1992. *Sacred Land, Sacred View: Navajo Perceptions of the Four Corners Region.* Provo: Brigham Young University.

Parker, Patricia, and Thomas King. 1990. "Guidelines for Evaluating and Documenting Traditional Cultural Properties." In *National Register Bulletin no. 38.* Washington, DC: U.S. Department of the Interior, National Park Service, Interagency Resources Division.

Walker, Deward. 1998. "American Indian Sacred Geography." *Indian Affairs: Special Supplement—American Indian Religious Freedom,* no. 116 (summer).

Sacred Sites and Sacred Mountains, Black Hills

The Black Hills, which cross the borders between western South Dakota, northeast Wyoming, and southeast Montana are sacred spaces for the Oceti Sakowin (the peoples collectively referred to as Sioux), particularly the Lakota, as well as the Northern Cheyenne and Omaha.

According to the Lakota Sioux, they have always lived in the northern Great Plains area. Any migration was purely localized, they say, outward from the Black Hills into the regions surrounding them. For the Oceti Sakowin, the Black Hills are profoundly religiously and spiritually significant. The Lakotas are the chosen protectors and caretakers of the Black Hills—largely because the Black Hills are recognized as their birthplace.

According to Lakota oral tradition, the Oceti Sakowin first emerged from the Black Hills. The traditional story tells of a time when the people lived beneath the earth. This place beneath the earth had been their home for thousands of years. They emerged through Wind Cave, which is located in the southern Black Hills. Once they emerged, they were no longer able to return to their ancestral home. The people had left their leader behind, underground. He foresaw the hardships that his people would soon encounter, the cold and the hunger. Sacrificing his secure and comfortable existence, the leader emerged through Wind Cave. As he did so, he took on the form of the buffalo. The buffalo would then sustain the Oceti Sakowin during their first years on the earth and for generations to come, providing food, shelter, clothing, tools, and all the other necessities of life.

The Black Hills are known to the Oceti Sakowin as Paha Sapa, or "the heart of everything that is." The hills contain all the curing elements necessary for the psychological and physical well-being of the people. Sites within the Black Hills of particular importance are Harney Peak, Devils Tower, and Bear Butte. Lakota oral traditions tell of the creation of these places, and of their importance in Lakota religious life. Ceremonies are conducted at these sites. Their timing is in accordance with the movement of the constellations, beginning in the spring and continuing throughout the summer.

The Oceti Sakowin first encountered Euro-American settlers in the eighteenth century, and trade with Euro-American traders reached its peak between 1825 and 1839. A struggle with the U.S. government began in earnest in the mid–nineteenth century, as the United States began to seize land through treaties. These documents set boundaries for tribal lands, constraining the Natives' freedom and traditional ways of life. A series of treaties with the Oceti Sakowin set the boundaries of the so-called Great Sioux Reservation, which encompassed the western half of present-day South Dakota.

However, when gold was discovered in the Black Hills, which were within the agreed-upon boundaries of the Great Sioux Reservation, the U.S. government sought to convince the Oceti Sakowin to sell the Black Hills. The Oceti Sakowin were unconvinced. Without a legal agreement, the U.S. government pushed a treaty through a gathering representing only 10 percent of the adult male population, removing the Black Hills from the Great Sioux Reservation. The government seized the land, resulting in a long and bloody war. Since that time the Oceti Sakowin have continued to protest the seizure of their sacred lands, and to refuse any monetary compensation.

In 1980 the Court of Claims, the Indian Claims Commission, and the Supreme Court acknowledged the illegality of the seizure. Instead of ordering that the land be returned, the Lakota were offered a monetary sum: the value of the land in 1877 plus interest: $570 million. Arguing that a people cannot sell sacred land, the Oceti Sakowin refused to accept the sum.

The Black Hills have been subject to logging, mining, and recreation, despite protests from the Lakota. Gold, coal, and uranium mining have polluted the water with cyanide and left open pits throughout the hills. Very often, companies are permitted to leave sites without any efforts at environmental clean-up.

Today, Bear Butte (Mato Paha) and Devils Tower are popular tourist destinations for hikers and climbers. For tens of thousands of years, Bear Butte has been the site of tribal gatherings, vision quests, and ceremonies. Hikers have been requested to stay on designated trails and to avoid ceremonial areas. However, restrictions are not enforced.

The American Indian Religious Freedom Act has failed to protect these sites from incursions and to preserve them as ceremonial and sacred places. Politicians continue to permit the violation of sacred places in the Black Hills, allowing mining companies to abandon depleted mines without restoring the land. Only 0.8 percent of the Black Hills are protected from logging, and the U.S. Forest Service permits logging throughout the region.

Suzanne J. Crawford and
Karen D. Lone Hill

See also Ceremony and Ritual, Lakota; Kinship; Oral Traditions, Western Plains; Oral Traditions, Lakota; Reservations, Spiritual and Cultural Implications; Sacred Sites and Sacred Mountains; Termination and Relocation; Vision Quest Rites

References and Further Reading
Brown, Brian Edward. 1999. *Religion Law and Land: Native Americans and the Judicial Interpretations of Sacred Land.* Westport, CT: Greenwood Press.
Gulliford, Andrew. 2000. *Sacred Objects and Sacred Places: Preserving Tribal Traditions.* Boulder: University Press of Colorado.
Neihardt, John G. 2000. *Black Elk Speaks: Being the Life Story of a Holy Man of the*

Oglala Sioux as Told through John G. Neihardt. Lincoln: University of Nebraska Press.

Walker, James R. 1991. *Lakota Belief and Ritual.* Lincoln: University of Nebraska Press.

Sacred Societies, Great Lakes

Sacred Societies (sometimes known as Medicine Societies) were formed by Iroquoian and Anishnabeg nations in the Great Lakes region to convey the blessings of a particular Spirit to members of their communities. Members of both groups believed that humans shared the universe with powerful beings who, although occupied with concerns of their own, sometimes helped humans. Sacred Societies, which owned particular songs and dances and followed certain rules, were devoted to serving and pleasing various spirits. The societies attended annual festivals as a group to appease discontented Spirits and to honor beneficent ones. While the entire community benefited from the intervention of the societies, individuals could also ask them for special healing, though some payment for the rite was usually required to fulfill obligations to the Spirit. The Sacred Societies continue today and are especially prominent in Minnesota and on Manitoulin Island, where their members guard the teachings and rituals of the societies from the view of nonmembers.

Most studies of the religion of First Nations concentrate either on details of the rituals or on the social value of the societies. What the rituals meant to individuals within the societies, rather than to the community as a whole, is difficult to uncover. Furthermore, the historical development of the societies is also difficult to determine, as the documentary record, which began in the seventeenth century, contains only the impressions of observers who were not usually privy to the meaning of the ceremonies. Iroquoian Sacred Societies were certainly active from the early seventeenth century, and the Anishnabeg from at least the middle of the seventeenth century. Scholars and First Nations communities, however, disagree among themselves and with each other over when the societies actually began.

The Iroquois Confederacy was and continues to be served by many medicine societies, including the False Faces, the Bear, the Buffalo, the Chanters for the Dead, the Eagle, the Husk Face, the Little People, the Otter, and the Society of Women Planters. Most of these societies have procured special abilities from their patrons. The Husk Faces, for example, received agricultural skills and shared them with the community. Other societies served a protectionist role. The Little People Society protected their community by ensuring that their potentially malevolent patrons received enough attention. Anishnabeg First Nations, on the other hand, developed only two major societies: the Midéwiwin, or Grand Medicine Society, and the Wabeno, or People of the Dawn. In the

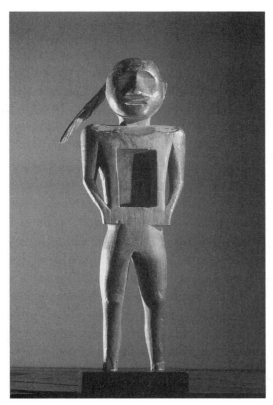

Carved wood figure with rectangular opening in the chest, used by the Midéwiwin secret society. From Leech Lake, Minnesota. (Werner Forman/Art Resource, NY)

nineteenth century, Anishnabeg communities incorporated the Drum Dance and Peyote rituals from other First Nations into their rituals. Alongside the societies, the Anishnabeg maintained less structured personal networks between people who had dreamed of the same Spirit. Dependants of the powerful Bear Spirit, for example, shared a sweatlodge ceremony renowned for its brutal temperatures. The Anishnabeg also had a visionary religious tradition in which indi-

viduals spontaneously took on spiritual leadership after receiving Spirit dreams.

Most of the Iroquois and Anishnabeg societies told stories about the origins of their society. One of the most famous is the Iroquoian story about False Face and his Creator brother. When the Creator was busy making the world, his brother False Face grew annoyed and began to follow him around, taking things apart after his brother had made them and adding unpleasant animals to the growing collection of useful ones. Eventually, when the world was complete, the two brothers got into a fight about who had actually made it. The Creator suggested a duel of power. Each would try to move a mountain. Whoever succeeded clearly was the creator. False Face tried first and failed. His brother then told False Face to turn his back. Being by far the more powerful, the Creator moved the mountain up behind False Face's back, and when False Face turned around he smashed his nose on it.

False Face admitted that he was the weaker and asked his brother to allow him to live. The Creator assented but insisted that in return for his life, False Face should take care of humans. False Face agreed to give humans the power to manipulate hot coals, to survive the cold, and to fight disease, witches, and bad weather, so long as they demonstrated their respect and affection for him by giving him tobacco and corn mush. The False Face Society in turn took as its first responsibility the creation and maintenance of Masks with which they could act out the relationship between humans and False Face prescribed in the origin story.

The story of the two brothers demonstrates a common perception of the relationship between humans and Manitous in the Great Lakes area. False Face was motivated to become the guardian of his society by circumstances foreign to the human Iroquois. The Society accepted his help with the knowledge that it was offered, not out of affection or inclination, but as part of a bargain; it would continue only as long as they fulfilled their half of the agreement.

Not all Iroquois became members of the False Face Society. But those who did reflected their patron's combination of hostility and helpfulness while spreading the protection of False Face to their community at the Midwinter festival. The Society members, themselves called False Faces, ritually purged their community of the malevolent power of both unseen Mysteries and antisocial humans. In one dramatic ritual the False Faces organized themselves into two groups at opposite ends of the village. Each group began to walk toward the center, entering every house on their path. Inside the homes the False Faces yelled to frighten malevolent spirits away and shook rattles into the darkest corners to eradicate all dangerous human and spiritual forces. The False Faces also jostled sick people to their feet and teased layabouts. When the houses were all visited the Faces met in the center, where a representative of the villagers quickly thanked the Faces

and offered gifts of tobacco and corn soup to prevent the False Faces from becoming resentful and turning on the village. Thus the relationship between the villagers and the False Face Society who served them mirrored the relational structure of reciprocal obligations between humans and Manitous.

In the twentieth century, many of the False Face Masks were photographed; others were displayed in museums for the amusement and education of non-Iroquois people. Some Iroquois leaders charged that such actions abused the Spirits associated with the Masks, and a number of scholars lost the support of their Iroquois informants. Museums holding Masks and other religiously significant pieces were forced to begin the long, slow process of self-examination that has led to the return of some religious objects. However, some Iroquois believe that the people who gave the Masks to the museums will be deprived of Spirit blessings until the Masks are returned.

Like the False Face Society, the Anishnabeg Grand Medicine Society, or Midéwiwin, offered spiritual protection to members and nonmembers alike. However the Midéwiwin incorporated a broader cross-section of society into its general membership than did the False Faces. Possibly that was because the Midéwiwin helped people to live well in order to prepare them for death. In one version of the Midéwiwin origin story, a human named Cutfoot had a vision of terrified Anishnabeg being turned away from *Ishpeming,* the land of the dead, because they were not at peace. Nanabozho, the trickster Spirit credited with creating the earth and the Anishnabeg, gained permission from the other Spirits to give Cutfoot birch bark scrolls containing knowledge of herbal healing, rituals, and teachings that would enable the Anishnabeg to approach death with equanimity and enter *Ishpeming.* Members of the Midéwiwin learned and passed on the wisdom given to the Anishnabeg by Cutfoot.

Joining the Midéwiwin entailed either purchasing a curing ritual from the Mide leaders or undergoing an initiation ceremony. Mide curing ceremonies lasted for several days and featured an incremental recitation of the Mide origin story. The Anishnabeg believed that telling stories about the Manitous promoted healing because the Manitous visited people who spoke about them. Once cured, the patient became a member of the first order of the Midéwiwin. Through initiation into the Midéwiwin, even children could gain the general blessings of the Society. Mide initiation ceremonies began with the construction of a Mide lodge, or a *Midewagamig,* a rectangular tent built with doors opening toward the east and west. In the middle of the tent stood one or two poles hung with figures of humans ready to be filled with medicine.

To open the ceremonies the gathered community shared a large feast. When the meal was over, the Mide leaders went into the woods alone to sing. At night the people entered the lodge and sat down between fires lighted at each entrance. Mide leaders played drums and led the assembly in singing and dancing. Eventually the adolescent initiates walked to the center, where a Mide leader charged them to remember to fast faithfully. Then the assembled Mide took out their medicine bundles, or *Kahshkekeh mahahkemoot,* and circled the lodge. The leaders passed by the initiates, shooting *migis* shells into the initiates' bodies by touching them with their medicine bundles. The shells were believed to have come from the Great Ocean and to contain the power of life. At each touch the children fell, overwhelmed by the power suddenly in their bodies.

After each fall the initiates stood again, ready for the next. When the last of the Mide leaders had passed by, the children remained prone on the ground until a woman who was standing behind them throughout raised them by singing in their ears and drawing their attention to the four directions and then to the earth. Once the initiates were raised, the head Mide distributed pieces of medicine from his own bag to the Mide leaders. The Mide leaders all chewed their medicine, then spat the juice onto the initiates' chests, necks, and backs, transferring their power to the initiates. Finally each leader addressed the children, identifying them as members of the Mide and welcoming them to all of the ceremonies of the Mide.

Leadership in the Midéwiwin fell to men and women known for having dreams of powerful beings. Such people received instruction in the meaning of birch bark scrolls marked with detailed line drawings, like the ones given to Cutfoot by Nanabozho. The scrolls contained teachings corresponding to four degrees of initiation. Higher degrees of the Midéwiwin included instruction in herbal remedies, in curing victims of witchcraft, and in traveling over distances without physical bodies. The first two degrees of the Midéwiwin were associated with the earth and water Mysteries, Otter and Weasel. The more powerful Mysteries, Bear and Mink, watched over the second two degrees, known as the sky degrees. As students progressed through the levels of the Midéwiwin, their powers both to heal and to harm others grew. As a result, people known to have achieved the third and fourth degrees could easily become suspected of sorcery. Like the False Faces, high-level Mide priests could never be uniformly beloved by their community.

Scholars are divided over the origins of the Midéwiwin. Several, drawing on the work of anthropologist Harold Hickerson, have concluded that the Midéwiwin began as a spiritual revival motivated by cultural changes resulting from the arrival of European traders and settlers. Such scholars argue that before the advent of the Midéwiwin, small kin groups, each with local spiritual leaders, observed ritual practices according to directions they received personally from the Manitou. When

the fur trade began, increased centralization allowed influential leaders to establish a priestly order. While the reasoning is sound, the initial argument rested on the presence of a cross figure in Midéwiwin scrolls. However, other scholars have pointed out that in the context of Anishnabeg beliefs, the cross symbolized the four directions and the four wind Manitous who presided over them. Later scholars have argued that the Anishnabeg received the Midéwiwin before the arrival of Europeans in North America, independent of outside influence.

Catherine Murton Stoehr

See also Ceremony and Ritual, Anishnabe; Dreams and Visions; Manitous; Masks and Masking; Sacred Societies, Northwest Coast; Sacred Societies, Plains; Sweatlodge; Tricksters

References and Further Reading
Angel, Michael. 1997. "Discordant Voices, Conflicting Visions: Ojibwa and Euro-American Perspectives on the Midéwiwin." Ph.D. diss., University of Manitoba.
Danford, Joanne. 1989. "Will the 'Real' False Face Please Stand Up?" *Canadian Journal of Native Studies* 9, no. 2: 253–272.
Landes, Ruth. 1968. *Ojibway Religion and the Midewiwin*. Madison: University of Wisconsin Press.
Mogelon, Alex. 1994. *The People of Many Faces: Masks, Myths and Ceremonies of the Iroquois*. Lakefield, Ontario: Waapoone Publishing and Promotion.
Vecsey, Christopher. 1983. *Traditional Ojibwa Religion and Its Historical Changes*. Philadelphia: American Philosophical Society.
Wallace, Anthony. 1969. *The Death and Rebirth of the Seneca*. New York: Vintage Books.

Sacred Societies, Northwest Coast

Sacred, or secret, societies were common throughout the Northwest coast, with the exception of the far northern reaches of the Alaska panhandle and among some of the more southerly groups. Gatherings of these societies invariably took place in winter. The Kwakwak'wakw (Kwakiutl) viewed the world as a disk that was flipped over in the winter, revealing a dark underside. This was the natural milieu of superhuman spirits that were often threatening, although who also offered important gifts. This world was fundamentally hostile to humans. It was dark, especially in the higher latitudes, and stormy; the resources upon which humans relied were either absent or difficult to obtain. During this period humans relied upon stored food, especially dried salmon, which was eaten in large quantities at feasts and potlatches associated with the sacred society dances. Late winter, after the conclusion of the ceremonies, was a period of hunger, even famine, as well as ritually prescribed fasting. Not until the first run of salmon or oolichan (a common, oily fish species; also spelled "eulachon") in the spring did life return to a normal, human-centric routine of food procurement. The unifying theme of sacred societies, and thus their diagnostic criterion, is the dramatic representation of possession by spiritual power and the ability of the group and individual to overcome that possession.

Regional Variations

Many features of Northwest coast culture run along a north-south axis. In the case of sacred societies, the northern tribes tended to practice a more communal and highly structured type of performance, while in the southern region it tended to be more individualistic. In the south, winter performances fade into a type of generic guardian spirit complex, where at some point they cease being "societies" at all. In the north, not only are the dances organized communally but, in addition, they represent communal themes. The source for many of the dances performed in the northern coast region is the north-central region, especially the Heiltsuk, who apparently invented flesh-eating dances and other dances that are found regionally. This area is also the richest in terms of a number of distinct societies. It is likely that the idea of sacred societies itself originated in this area and diffused south and north, reaching limits in what is now southern Washington and southern Alaska.

Southern Region

In the southern half of the Northwest coast—from southern Oregon through southern British Columbia—sacred societies were a rather loose organization of individuals holding superhuman power, usually from zoomorphic donors. That was the basic pattern of the southern Salish Spirit Dances, in which dancers displayed evidence of the powers bestowed upon them by a guardian spirit.

Only people of chiefly lineage were eligible to take the role of a Hamatsa, or Cannibal Dancer. To indicate his hunger for human flesh, his costume had carved wooden skulls attached. The depicted skull on the wooden arc would have been carried by Kinqalalala, his female attendant. With this she would subdue Hamatsa. (Werner Forman/Corbis)

They did so in an organized fashion that superficially resembled the more communal societies of the central and northern Northwest coast. However, the individual spirits "sung" were unique to the holder, and thus they did not constitute series or subgroups within the dance.

Adolescent boys and girls obtained spirit power of their own accord through vision quests, and they displayed it in public for the first time at winter dances. These dances were ultimately therapeutic, in that they were sponsored by someone suffering from the effects of spirit power.

Spirit powers were used to cure the sufferer. However, spirit powers were equally capable of inflicting harm, and they could in fact become an instrument of sorcery. One function of Spirit Dances was thus to channel the spirit power toward positive ends. The performances varied by group and according to the type of power, but for many Coast Salish it involved the rhythmic shaking of deer hoof rattles and beating of roof planks, the use of "spirit boards" to represent the guardian spirit power (which became animated during the course of the dance), and some degree of bodily mutilation, often the piercing of flesh with a knife. Certain tricks, such as bleeding in the mouth and hanging from ropes, were performed. Specific ceremonies were performed to retrieve souls from the land of the dead.

In the region of the central Coast Salish, the dances took on a more communal form. Rather than acquiring power through vision quests, initiates were "grabbed" by veterans of the society and taken away for seclusion and training. During this period the initiates were thought of as dead, and thus their return represented a rebirth. A song revealed to the initiate in a vision is a mark of power, and the initiate is classed according to the type of power revealed in the song. Elaborate costumes and face paint, but no masks, were worn by the initiates. They danced for the remainder of the winter season, while remaining secluded and engaging in frequent bathing and other purificatory practices.

Among the northern Coast Salish, masked dancing was practiced. There, the basic principle of the sacred society transformed from an individually acquired guardian spirit to an inherited privilege, although among some local groups the characteristic southern form persisted. Groups such as the Comox of Vancouver Island practiced the Sxwayxwey masked dance, which represents cultural diffusion from the neighboring Kwakwak'wakw.

Northern Region

In the north, a number of separate dance societies were typically incorporated into the Winter Ceremonial. The highest-ranking and best-known dance society in this region was the Hamatsa, or Cannibal Dance. This originated with the Heiltsuk and was acquired by the Kwakwak'wakw in the nineteenth century. It epitomized the theme of spirit power as threatening to humans. Initiates were "grabbed" and taken to the bush for training. They were said to be dead, to have been eaten by the cannibal spirit. Upon return they demonstrated their possession by biting people, appearing to cannibalize a corpse, and other "wild" behavior. Although theatrical tricks were used, there was undoubtedly some eating of human flesh. Since the initiates were believed to be possessed by the cannibal spirit, they were not considered human at the time. Over several days initiates were "tamed," becoming more manageable. For the remainder of the winter season, initiates fasted, drank seawater, and otherwise purified themselves in order to reenter human society.

Other similar dance societies involved sickness, war, predation by animals, and death. With the exception of the Hamatsa, who was minimally clothed in cedar bark, these were all masked dances. As a rule, these most powerful dances entailed existential threats to humanity. These threats were, in a sense, brought into human society, where they were ultimately defeated. In the Heiltsuk version of the Winter Ceremonial, two distinct series, called the Tsaika (meaning "shamans") and the Dluelaxa (meaning "second down"—that is, from heaven) were opposed as forces of destruction and restoration of order. The threatening dances were generally in the former; the latter allowed hereditary chiefs to use their power to bestow blessings and to "heal" the community. The Kwakwak'wakw had these two series as well; the latter was sometimes called the Weasel Dance, referring to fur-decorated headdresses worn by the chiefs (rather than masks).

Among the Tsimshian a similar opposition pertained, although dances were organized into four separate societies. A Dog-eating Dance took the place of the Heiltsuk Cannibal Dance. Among the Nuxalk (Bella Coola), two dance series were held, although not all of the dances were derived from the neighboring Heiltsuk. The Haida of Queen Charlotte Islands performed Winter Ceremonial dances, but they apparently simply borrowed them directly from the Heiltsuk. They had more the quality of entertainment than dances on the mainland. The Nuu-chah-nulth (Nootka) of western Vancouver Island and their Makah cousins to the south had a community masquerade called the Tlukwana, or Wolf Ritual. This reenacted events from the mythical age, involving the acquisition of supernatural power by human ancestors. Most male members of the community would be involved. In addition, central and southern Nuu-chah-nulth and Makah possessed a second "shamans" series, the Cayiq. This was influenced by both the Heiltsuk and Kwakwak'wakw Tsaika (the names are

Kwakwak'wakw man kneeling on one knee dressed in skins, hat, and other garments, 1910. (Edward Curtis/Library of Congress)

cognate) and northern Coast Salish Spirit Dancing. Like the latter, it focused more on actual healing, rather than on the defeat of existential threats to human existence.

One commonality among all these dance societies is the notion of transformation. This was more evident in the masked dances, but it pertained as well in unmasked versions of Spirit Dancing and performances such as the Hamatsa. With masking, the effect is more obvious—the dancer is no longer human, or at least no longer his or her "normal" self—but other features make it obvious that even unmasked dancers are psychologically and spiritually in an altered state. With most dances—the spiritually more potent ones, especially—an initiate is not thought to be impersonating a spirit but rather possessed by that spirit. The dance is thus a performance of liminality—of a person moving in and out of a social identity.

Such transformation is a cosmological principle. The very seasonality that provides the backdrop for sacred society performances is itself an example. Moreover, living things transformed themselves, both originally in the myth age and through reincarnation. Humans and their prey are likewise transformations of one another, as salmon, for instance, are thought to live in societies much like those of humans. In one sense, the Cannibal Dance represents the completion of this transformation, in which humans become prey. A class of Kwakwak'wakw masks, called "transformation masks," illustrates this principle visually. An animal mask may open up and turn into a spirit, and then into another species; likewise, benevolent and malevolent beings may appear in the same mask. This represents a high form of religious thought, in which seemingly contradictory ideas may be held simultaneously. It stands, moreover, as a metaphor for the interconnectedness of the human and natural worlds.

Historical Variations

These traditional sacred societies were themselves subject to historical processes, such as diffusion and, later, prohibition by colonial authorities. Additional dances were invented in response to European contact, and certain dances (for example, those dealing with disease and death) became more important. Additionally, influences from outside the culture area led to the development of indigenous religious societies. Most important was the influence of the widespread Ghost Dance, which, in the Northwest, became the Warm House cult in Oregon and the Prophet Dance in the Plateau. Syncretistic religious movements, such as the Indian Shaker Church, had their origins in indigenous sacred societies.

Most sacred societies were discouraged or, especially in Canada, prohibited from the late nineteenth through the mid-twentieth century. Since the 1960s, many of these performances have been revived, or, in some cases, have become public again after decades of secrecy. These undeniably are continuous with the precontact societies, although they have undergone considerable change as well. Gone are even theatrical renditions of anthropophagy in the Hamatsa, as well as, generally, the bloody aspects of all dances. At the same time, they have adapted to changed circumstances—for example, Spirit Dances have been used to treat substance abuse and behavioral problems in Salish youth.

Michael Harkin

See also Ceremony and Ritual, Northwest; Dances, Northwest Winter Spirit Dances; Guardian Spirit Complex; Masks and Masking; Oral Traditions, Northwest Coast; Power, Northwest Coast

References and Further Reading

Boas, Franz. 1966. *Kwakiutl Ethnography.* Chicago: University of Chicago Press.

Drucker, Philip. 1951. *The Northern and Central Nootkan Tribes.* Bulletin 144. Washington, DC: Bureau of American Ethnology.

Elmendorf, William. 1948. "The Cultural Setting of the Twana Secret Society." *American Anthropologist* 50: 625–633.

Harkin, Michael. 1996. "Carnival and Authority: Heiltsuk Cultural Models of Power." *Ethos* 24: 281–313.

———.1997. *The Heiltsuks: Dialogues of Culture and History on the Northwest Coast.* Lincoln: University of Nebraska Press.

Jilek, Wolfgang G. 1982. *Indian Healing: Shamanic Ceremonialism in the Pacific Northwest Today.* Surrey, British Columbia: Hancock House.

Lévi-Strauss, Claude. 1982. *The Way of the Masks.* Seattle: University of Washington Press.

Mauzé, Marie, Michael Harkin, and Sergei Kan, eds. 2004. *Coming to Shore: Northwest Coast Ethnology, Traditions and Visions.* Lincoln: University of Nebraska Press.

McIlwraith, Thomas F. 1992. *The Bella Coola Indians,* 2 vols. Toronto: University of Toronto Press.

Seguin, Margaret, ed. 1984. *The Tsimshian: Images of the Past, Views for the Present.* Vancouver: University of British Columbia Press.

Suttles, Wayne. 1987. *Coast Salish Essays.* Seattle: University of Washington Press.

———, ed. 1990. *The Handbook of North American Indians: The Northwest Coast,* vol. 7. Washington, DC: Smithsonian Institution Press.

Sacred Societies, Plains

Acquiring supernatural power through spiritual intermediaries was an individu-alized process throughout nineteenth-century, prereservation Plains communities, although those who possessed similar powers usually convened in sacred societies: doctors' societies performed curing rituals, and medicine bundle societies maintained tribal spirituality through shared rites of intensification. United by spirit-derived powers obtained spontaneously and involuntarily, or through the vision quest, members of sacred—and usually secret—societies guarded their collective esoteric knowledge from outsiders (Irwin 1994, 78–79). Other societies, less sacred in nature, were associated with a common feature of Plains Indian social organization: the formation of non-kin groups, or associations. Plains peoples lived as semisedentary horticultural villagers, or as equestrian bison hunters. Tribal kinship patterns varied from unilineal descent—patriclans, matriclans, moieties, and phratries—to bilateral descent—bands and villages—crosscut by men's age-graded or nongraded military societies (sodalities) and women's age-graded or nongraded societies. Whether membership was voluntary or restricted to collective powers, societies shared common animatistic/animistic beliefs pertaining to the acquisition and accumulation of spiritual power and its connection to success in warfare, hunting, curing, and social activities. Steeped in these principles, Plains societies, even those labeled "secular," had sacred components.

Medicine bundle societies among the horticulturalist Plains Village Tradition

Six men participate in the Arikara medicine ceremony, the Bears. 1908. (Edward Curtis/Library of Congress)

peoples consisted of priests and ceremonial leaders representing clans, bands, or villages. In the Upper Missouri region, villages of northern Siouan-speaking Mandan and Hidatsa were subdivided into exogamous matrilineal clans and moieties. Keepers of personal and sacred tribal bundles belonged to different clans, conducting important tribal ceremonies connected with their bundles (Wood and Irwin 2001, 357; Stewart 2001, 335–336). Characterized by patrilineal clans, the Dhegiha Siouan-speaking Omaha, Ponca, Kansa, Osage, and Quapaw and the Chiwere Siouan-speaking Iowa and Oto/Missouria also had ritual specialists and keepers of sacred clan or village bundles (see DeMallie 409, 423, 470, 480–481, 502, 439, 448–449). Unique for villagers, the Caddoan-speaking Arikara and Pawnee reckoned bilateral kinship and organized at the village level; each autonomous village had an origin myth and a sacred bundle owned by a priest who maintained the spiritual integrity of the community. Pawnee and Arikara cultures were stratified, so priests and leaders derived from the upper class (Parks 2001a, 373, 375; Parks 2001b, 530–532, 534). In all these cultures, rituals conducted by village and clan leaders spiritually unified exogamous kin groups, and on a larger level, the tribe.

Among equestrian peoples there were priestly keepers of Sun Dance and other sacred bundles, but most tribes lacked the medicine bundle societies typical of the predominantly clan-based villagers. The Crow, linguistically related to the Hidatsa, were unusual for equestrians because of the formation of matrilineal clans, which perhaps explains medicine bundle societies uniting those with similar powers: the Tobacco, Sacred Pipe, and Horse Dance societies (Voget 2001, 707). In contrast, their Siouan-speaking Northwestern Plains neighbors, the Assiniboine, had six to eight Holy Men— ceremonial leaders, diviners, dream interpreters, and practitioners of malign shooting magic—who did not form a society (DeMallie and Miller 2001, 578). Also unique among equestrians were the Kiowa-Tanoan-speaking Kiowa, distantly related to the Taos Pueblo peoples of the Southwest; tribal unity and spiritual well-being were maintained by a priestly society of ten men, keepers of the sacred Split Boy or Boy Medicine bundles, who met periodically to renew the bundles (LaBarre et al. 1935). Shield societies linked to power visions also existed, a trait shared with their linguistically unrelated Southwestern Plains allies, the Athabascan-speaking Plains Apache (Levy 2001, 913–915; Foster and McCollough 2001, 931). Two of the four important tribal ceremonies of the Algonquin-speaking Cheyenne were related to the Medicine Hat and Sacred Arrows bundles, protected by full-time priests; the Sacred Arrow Renewal was the most important Cheyenne ceremony (Moore, Liberty, and Straus 2001, 873–875).

Doctors' societies comprising individuals sharing common shamanic curing powers were widespread throughout the Plains. Such secret societies existed among the Arikara and their Caddoan Pawnee and Wichita relatives. Below chiefs and priests in status among the Arikara were doctors, particularly the leaders of the eight doctors' societies— Ghost, Black-Tailed Deer, Shedding Buffalo, Cormorant, Duck, Owl, Din of Birds, and Bear—which coalesced in the medicine lodge during important tribal ceremonies held in mid-August (Parks 2001a, 381–382). Similar distinctions acknowledging priests as bearers of sacrosanct bundles pertaining to tribal welfare, and shamans as the recipients of curing powers, were found in Pawnee culture, where an amorphous association of doctors was superseded in importance by the Doctors' (or Medicine) Lodge, which held two-day ceremonies in the spring and summer, followed by a month-long early fall ceremony conducted by leaders who publicly displayed their magical powers (Parks 2001b, 532).

Semisecret, open-membership societies related to various aspects of tribal well-being existed among the Wichita. Notable was the Deer Dance—extinct after 1871—led by a Deer shaman, which ensured overall good health and prosperity for the tribe. Possible use of the mildly hallucinogenic mescal bean (*Sophora secundiflora*) enhanced visions from power animals (Newcomb 2001, 558). Doctors' societies also existed among the Omaha, Ponca, Quapaw, and Osage (DeMallie 2001, 410, 424, 502; Bailey 1995, 45–48). The Iowa Medicine Dance and the Medicine Lodge of the Oto/Missouria were similar to the Central Algonkin Midéwiwin Society: curing through sacred bundles, ceremonial song and dance, and herbal medicines characterized the former, whereas the elite members of the Medicine Lodge employed sorcery to control deviant behavior (Wedel 2001, 440; Schweitzer 2001, 451–452).

Siouan equestrian tribes with doctors' societies included the Assiniboine, Santee, Yankton, Yanktonai, Teton, and Crow. Assiniboine Horse Society rites pertained to doctoring people and horses, and Fool Society ceremonies held during the summer Sun Dance included a special healing ceremony for people with vision problems (DeMallie and Miller 2001, 579). The Santee Midéwiwin Society conducted curing and renewal ceremonies and held feasts for the dead (Albers 2001, 769). Another version of the Central Algonkin Midéwiwin, the Yanktonai (and perhaps Yankton) Medicine Dance, involved curing performances by Tree-Dweller dreamers (DeMallie 2001a, 789–790). Teton doctors' societies were loosely organized groups of individuals who had received power visions from certain animals (ibid., 808). Although Crow medicine bundle societies had specific medicine powers related to victories against enemies, acquisition of horses and wealth, and longevity, they also functioned like doctors' societies in their emphasis on curing and well-being (Voget 2001, 706–707).

Other equestrian groups with doctors' societies included the Kiowa (Levy 2001, 915) and Plains Apache (Foster and McCollough 2001, 931); their comrades the Uto-Aztecan-speaking Comanche had a number of "medicine societies" composed of up to twelve individuals sharing the same power (Wallace and Hoebel 1952, 165; Kavanagh 2001, 892), such as the Eagle doctors (Jones 1972, 27–30). One of the four major ceremonies of the Cheyenne, the Massaum, or Crazy Lodge, was performed by shamans dressed like the animals from which their powers derived (Moore, Liberty, and Straus 2001, 874). The Arapaho were linguistically related to their Cheyenne confederates; near the end of the nineteenth century, Southern Arapaho doctors' societies were created by shamans sharing the same powers, although they could belong to several societies (Fowler 2001, 844). Perhaps the last tribe to emerge onto the Plains, the Algonquin-speaking Plains Ojibwa, bison and moose hunters organized into patrilineal clans, maintained numerous Woodland traditions including the Midéwiwin, or Medicine Lodge ceremony (Albers 2001, 650).

Most common among doctors' societies were those related to curing powers received from animals, particularly, Buffalo, Bear, and Black-Tailed Deer. Buffalo societies existed among the Ponca, Omaha, Iowa, Oto/Missouria, Quapaw, Mandan, Pawnee, Teton, Arapaho, and Kiowa. The Plains Cree, a transitional Plains culture linguistically related to the Plains Ojibwa, practiced a Buffalo Dance unrelated to curing, unique for Plains tribes. Tribes with Bear societies and Grizzly Bear Doctors included the Ponca, Omaha, Iowa, Quapaw, Arikara, Pawnee, Wichita, Teton, and Arapaho. Black-Tailed Deer societies were found in the Arikara, Pawnee, Mandan, and Teton cultures (DeMallie 2001, 360, 381–383, 410, 424, 440, 451–452, 502, 538, 647, 808, 844, 915).

That Plains cultures recognized women as eminent healers was evident by several doctors' societies with female membership. The Buffalo Doctors' Lodge of the sedentary Oto/Missouria and the Buffalo Society of the Iowa included male and female shamans (Schweitzer 2001, 451–452; Wedel 2001, 440), as did the Deer Dance of the Wichita (Newcomb 2001, 558), and the Medicine Dance of the Yanktonai (DeMallie 2001a, 789–790). Both genders likewise participated in the Cheyenne Massaum Ceremony dressed like the animals representing their shamanic powers (Moore, Liberty, and Straus 2001, 874), and men and women belonging to the Assiniboine Horse Society specialized in doctoring horses and humans (DeMallie and Miller 2001, 578).

Some tribes even had exclusive women's societies. Prior to coalescence in Like-a-Fishhook Village in 1845, the Hidatsa and Mandan inhabited matrilineal, clan-based villages crosscut by age-graded men's and women's societies, largely secular in function but with some spiritual elements. Since Mandan and Hidatsa women had access to supernatural power, each culture had four age-graded women's societies: post-menopausal Mandan women formed a shamanistic healing society, the White Buffalo Cows, and members of the powerful Hidatsa Holy Women Society, including berdaches, participated in all important tribal rituals (Stewart 2001, 337, 344; Wood and Irwin 2001, 360). The Wichita, Arikara, and Ponca each had three women's societies; membership in the Ponca Tattooed Women society consisted of the daughters of chiefs and affluent men (Newcomb 2001, 558; Parks 2001a, 378; Brown and Irwin 2001, 424).

Among the equestrian tribes, the Kiowa were represented by women's societies (Levy 2001, 912). The Plains Apache had the Izuwe, a secret society comprised of twenty elderly women who prayed for sick people and departing warriors (Foster and McCollough 2001, 930–931); the Blood and Northern Blackfoot divisions organized the Women's Society (Ewers 1982, 61, 106). Presided over by elderly women, the Assiniboine Dance without Robes—similar to the Old Women's Society dance of the Kiowa—included male dancers, and the sacred Female Elk Society performed yearly fertility dances (DeMallie and Miller 2001, 579; Kracht 1989, 183–188). More secular women's societies included quilling societies that emphasized decorative sewing skills, as found among the Kiowa, Cheyenne, and Teton (Kracht 1989, 247; Grinnell 1923, 159–169; DeMallie 2001b, 808).

Men's military and dancing societies existed in at least twenty of the semisedentary and equestrian Plains tribes, and they were all similar in form and function, notwithstanding variations of age-grading. Age-graded men's societies were present among the equestrian Blackfoot, Arapaho, Gros Ventre, and Sarcee, whereas the six Kiowa sodalities were loosely graded (DeMallie 2001, 615, 633, 683, 844, 846, 912). Among semisedentary peoples, Mandan and Hidatsa societies were age-graded; when young boys formed a new cohort, the other grades advanced in rank (Wood and Irwin 2001, 360; Stewart 2001, 334–335). When the Arikara joined Like-a-Fishhook Village in 1862, they differed from the Mandan and Hidatsa because they were subdivided into nongraded men's societies (Parks 2001a, 375, 383). Besides the Arikara, nongraded men's societies were found among the Pawnee, Omaha, Ponca, Iowa, Assiniboine, Stoney, Plains Cree, Plains Ojibwa, Crow, Teton, Cheyenne, Comanche, and Plains Apache (DeMallie 2001, 411, 423–424, 440, 532, 579, 597, 645, 704, 802–803, 876, 893–894, 931).

Plains military societies possessed distinctive songs, dances, staffs, lances, and other distinguishing regalia. Although some societies were sacred, most were secular organizations that sponsored social dances featuring variant performances of the War Dance following the safe return of war expeditions, or during summer Sun Dances and other tribal ceremonies. Societies were often called upon to safeguard tribal encampments or to police the summer bison hunts to prevent individual hunters from scattering the herds preceding the departure of organized hunting parties; optimal control ensured the maximal gain of buffalo meat for the community. In certain tribes there were elite fighting societies composed of men with outstanding combat records and suicide warriors with no-retreat rules compelling them to fight rearguard skirmishes with their flowing sashes staked to the ground: the Assiniboine No Flight Society (DeMallie and Miller 2001, 579); the Teton Lance Bearers (DeMallie 2001b, 802–803); the Comanche Lobo Society (Kavanagh 2001, 893–894); the Plains Apache Klintide Society (Foster and McCollough 2001, 931); the Cheyenne Dog Soldiers (Moore 1996, 112, 126–127, 132); and the Kiowa Principal Dogs (Levy 2001, 912; LaBarre et al. 1935). Crow men losing the will to live became exalted Crazy Dog Wishing to Die warriors (Lowie 1935, 331–332).

The following is a brief sketch of sacred societies among the prereservation Kiowa of southwestern Oklahoma, largely based on the ethnographic field notes of James Mooney (1891–1904) and

Weston LaBarre (et al. 1935), located in the National Anthropological Archives, Smithsonian Institution. Kiowa orthography is consistent, wherever possible, with Merrill (et al. 1997).

Nineteenth-century Kiowa religious beliefs centered on the Sun Dance held in mid-June to unite the coalesced Kiowa bands spiritually and socially. It was believed that successful performances of the ceremony regenerated the Kiowa people and the bison herds on which they depended. The *Taimek'i,* or "Taime Man," was the full-time priest who cared for the Taime Sun Dance bundle and directed the ceremony. Equal in importance to the sacrosanct Taime were the ten *zaidethali* "Split Boy" or *talyi-da-i* "Boy Medicine" bundles—also known as the Ten Medicines—created in mythological times when the culture hero Sun-Boy, the son of Sun, and one of the Split Boys transformed himself into the eucharistic bundles (Mooney 1979, 239). The Ten Medicines sometimes were referred to as *adalbehya,* "lots of hair, or scalps," because people offered enemy scalps and other gifts to the bundles along with prayer requests. Human-shaped figurines inside the bundles were the principal source of *dw'dw',* or "power," of the bundles, respectfully treated as if they were people. Strict taboos accompanied the bundles: only a keeper's wife could erect the twenty-four pole tepee that housed his bundle, which hung suspended on the west side of the lodge; transported bundles were carefully fastened over the back and to the left side of the horse. Since the bundles disliked disturbances from playing or crying children, the tepees were pitched outside village limits; only the wives of the keepers or Mexican captives were allowed to handle the bundles, because their powers were greatly feared.

Revered as holy men, the Ten Medicines keepers were expected to be pleasant, peaceable, nontruculent, patient, and helpful. Taboos followed by the keepers included the avoidance of bear meat, hides, or any part of the bear, since the bundles allegedly contained bear claws—but mostly because the Kiowa have always been brothers and sisters to the bear. Eldest sons or other close relatives inherited the bundles, but if a keeper died without naming a successor, the other nine convened to select an heir. Until a new recipient was named, the deceased keeper's widow or daughter cared for it. New owners did not necessarily possess *dw'dw',* though they could seek it through the vision quest or through transferal sweatbaths.

Individually, Ten Medicines keepers served as civil servants who settled disputes within the villages by offering lighted, long-stemmed pipes to the aggrieved parties. These were expected to smoke together and resolve their differences, as witnessed by the spirit world and connected by the rising tobacco smoke. Individually and collectively, the keepers prayed for the well-being of the Kiowa people, especially after first Thunder in the spring signaled the new year. Power existed equally in the ten bundles, so offerings to one bundle symbolized the power of all ten; supplicating the bundles with gifts that included scalps, meat, horses, and blankets put *dw'dw'* in prayer requests, which typically related to good fortune on war expeditions, recovery from illness, the birth of a child, or infertility. In most instances sweatlodge ceremonies were held for individual bundles; during emergencies or epidemics, bringing together at least four keepers provided powerful enough prayers to protect the entire tribe. Ten Medicines keepers aspired to attend annual sweatlodges, and every two to three years the ten bundles were brought together in the Sun Dance encampment inhabited by the aggregated Kiowa bands, the Plains Apache, and visitors from other tribes. Pledges to sponsor the sacred sweat for the ten bundles were made well in advance, often during austere times of illness or near annihilation by enemies. During the four-day performance of the Sun Dance proper, the keepers assisted the *Taimek'i.*

Recognizing Buffalo as the most powerful terrestrial animal, about twenty Kiowa shamans formed a powerful doctors' society, the Buffalo Society, or the Buffalo Medicine Lodge, inspired by the power vision of Etda-i-tsonhi, "Old Woman Who Has Medicine On Her," sometime between 1750 and 1770. According to the myth, Etda-i-tsonhi and another woman, fleeing from Pawnee warriors, encountered a bear that ate her companion, and she barely escaped, using a cedar tree to climb a large rock;

later that night she slipped away by walking on buffalo chips to cover her tracks. The next day she crawled under the rib cage of a decomposing buffalo bull carcass, then while dozing received an involuntary power vision. Since Kiowa women could not possess dream shields, Etda-i-tsonhi manufactured a shield from buffalo bull hide and presented it to her husband, who eventually passed it to their son, Pa-gyato, "Buffalo Old Man," who made seven shields for his sons and three for his brother's sons based on the original shield design. The Buffalo Medicine Society originated with the ten buffalo shields.

War parties departing south into Texas and Mexico seeking captives and livestock typically recruited one or more buffalo doctors. Prior to battle, the buffalo doctors made medicine by painting the left sides of their bodies red and the right sides white while singing a buffalo song. They fought like other warriors but assisted fallen comrades by spewing red paint (clay) on open wounds to stanch the bleeding. Although they often worked alone, up to fourteen buffalo doctors worked together on emergency cases, each doctor applying his own special healing technique. Until recovery, patients were expected to assume the taboos of the doctors, including the avoidance of "wounded meat" and other animal parts. Like other bundle owners, the buffalo doctors prayed daily to their bundles, but they also assembled during the Sun Dance to conduct sweatlodge ceremonies. Every few years they congregated to renew the bundles, repair old ones, or create new ones. Attendance was mandatory at these assemblies.

Like the buffalo shields, several dream shield societies existed that were linked to original power visions and inheritance of replica shields. Notable were the Sun Dance shields: seven Taime shields introduced after 1834 and carried by the *demguk'o,* "yellow breasts," shield keepers; the seven Kowde shields resulting from Poor Buffalo's 1839 vision; and the five Hotoyi shields derived from the vision of Hotoyi, or Akopti, "Timber Mountain," and introduced in 1869. These shields were carried by the owners, who danced during the Sun Dance proper. Other dream shields included eagle shields, fish-hawk shields, and others that were forgotten following the Kiowa surrender at Fort Sill in May 1875 and the confiscation of weapons and war regalia by the U.S. Army. Shield societies died out shortly afterward because of the attenuation of their power.

Virtually every Kiowa male belonged to a warrior society, since possessing *dw'dw'* or war honors was not a prerequisite for membership. Sodalities were founded in the principle of *kom,* "bloodbrothers," friends who paired off for life upon initiation into a society. All boys able to walk belonged to the Polanyup, or "Rabbits" Society, and attended feasts at which they were taught Kiowa virtues. After boys reached the age of twelve, they were "kidnapped" by other societies, except the K'oitsegun, the highest ranked.

Many advanced to the second society, the Adaltoyui, "Young (Wild) Sheep," where they spent a brief time prior to being kidnapped by a higher-ranked society, perhaps the Tsentanmo, "Horse Headdresses," the Tonkonko, "Black Legs," or the T'anpeko "Skunkberry People." Tonkonko membership was restricted, its high status represented by a no-retreat staff, and the equally important T'anpeko Society owned several no-retreat sashes. Not to be outdone, the K'oitsegun, "Real Dog" or "Crazy Dog," Society, representing the most outstanding and oldest warriors, owned ten suicide sashes. As in other Plains cultures, societies above the rank of Rabbits were frequently called upon to police tribal encampments, monitor communal hunts, enforce decisions concerning domestic disputes witnessed by the Ten Medicines keepers, and to assist during the Sun Dance—a period when the societies held social dances inside large tepees with the flaps rolled up so that female supporters could join the ceremonial song and dance.

Several women's societies also existed. Defunct after 1905, the Bear Society, supposedly connected to the Ten Medicines, conducted clandestine meetings greatly feared by men. More popular was the Old Woman's Society, whose membership was extended to postmenopausal women renowned for their great *dw'dw'* and obscene dances because they had "no shame." Warriors departing on war expeditions vowed feasts for both societies upon the procurement of scalps, whereas individuals sought the help of the Old Woman's Society when family members were sick, especially since this society was related to the power of Taime. Finally, the Industrious Women Society, composed of five or six middle-aged women acclaimed for their tanning skills, made the suicide sashes for the K'oitsegun Society; they were also known as skilled midwives.

Unfortunately, the passing of the horse and buffalo culture of the nineteenth century brought about the demise of most Kiowa societies. The Sun Dance has not been performed since 1887, although Taime is still cared for, as are the Ten Medicines, even though there is no formal society. Only two warrior societies remain, the T'anpeko, known today as the Kiowa Gourd Clan, and the Tonkonko, or Kiowa Black Leggings Society. These societies have been kept alive by the warrior spirit that continues in Kiowa veterans and soldiers serving in the armed forces.

Benjamin R. Kracht

See also Bundles, Sacred Bundle Traditions; Dreams and Visions; Power, Plains; Spiritual and Ceremonial Practitioners, Plains; Vision Quest Rites

References and Further Reading

Albers, Patricia C. 2001. "Santee." Pp. 761–776 in *Handbook of North American Indians: Plains*, vol. 13. Edited by Raymond J. DeMallie. Washington, DC: Smithsonian Institution Press.

Bailey, Garrick A. 2001. "Osage." Pp. 476–496 in *Handbook of North American Indians: Plains*, vol. 13. Edited by Raymond J. DeMallie. Washington, DC: Smithsonian Institution Press.

———, ed. 1995. *The Osage and the Invisible World: From the Works of Francis LaFlesche.* Norman: University of Oklahoma Press.

Brown, Donald N., and Lee Irwin. 2001. "Ponca." Pp. 416–431 in *Handbook of North American Indians: Plains*, vol. 13. Edited by Raymond J. DeMallie. Washington, DC: Smithsonian Institution Press.

DeMallie, Raymond J. 2001a. "Yankton and Yanktonai." Pp. 777–793 in *Handbook of North American Indians: Plains*, vol. 13. Edited by Raymond J. DeMallie. Washington, DC: Smithsonian Institution Press.

———. 2001b. "Teton." Pp. 794–820 in *Handbook of North American Indians: Plains*, vol. 13. Edited by Raymond J. DeMallie. Washington, DC: Smithsonian Institution Press.

DeMallie, Raymond J. ed. 2001. *Handbook of North American Indians*, vol. 13. Washington, DC: Smithsonian Institution Press.

DeMallie, Raymond J., and David Reed Miller. 2001. "Assiniboine." Pp. 572–595 in *Handbook of North American Indians: Plains*, vol. 13. Edited by Raymond J. DeMallie. Washington, DC: Smithsonian Institution Press.

Ewers, John D. 1982. *The Blackfeet. Raiders on the Northwestern Plains.* Norman: University of Oklahoma Press.

Foster, Morris W., and Martha McCollough. 2001. "Plains Apache." Pp. 926–940 in *Handbook of North American Indians: Plains*, vol. 13. Edited by Raymond J. DeMallie. Washington, DC: Smithsonian Institution Press.

Fowler, Loretta. 2001. "Arapaho." Pp. 840–862 in *Handbook of North American Indians: Plains*, vol. 13. Edited by Raymond J. DeMallie. Washington, DC: Smithsonian Institution Press.

Grinnell, George Bird. 1923. *The Cheyenne Indians: Their History and Ways of Life*, vol. 1. New Haven: Yale University Press.

Irwin, Lee. 1994. *The Dream Seekers: Native American Visionary Traditions of the Great Plains.* Norman: University of Oklahoma Press.

Jones, David E. 1972. *Sanapia: Comanche Medicine Woman.* New York: Holt, Rinehart, and Winston.

Kavanagh, Thomas W. 2001. "Comanche." Pp. 886–906 in *Handbook of North American Indians: Plains,* vol. 13. Edited by Raymond J. DeMallie. Washington, DC: Smithsonian Institution Press.

Kracht, Benjamin R. 1989. "Kiowa Religion: An Ethnohistorical Analysis of Ritual Symbolism, 1832–1987." Unpublished dissertation, Southern Methodist University, Department of Anthropology.

LaBarre, Weston, Donald Collier, Jane Richardson, William Bascom, Bernard Mishkin, and Alexander Lesser. 1935. "Notes on Kiowa Ethnography." Washington, DC: National Anthropological Archives, Smithsonian Institution.

Levy, Jerrold E. 2001. "Kiowa." Pp. 907–925 in *Handbook of North American Indians: Plains,* vol. 13. Edited by Raymond J. DeMallie. Washington, DC: Smithsonian Institution Press.

Liberty, Margot P., W. Raymond Wood, and Lee Irwin. 2001. "Omaha." Pp. 399–415 in *Handbook of North American Indians: Plains,* vol. 13. Edited by Raymond J. DeMallie. Washington, DC: Smithsonian Institution Press.

Lowie, Robert H. 1935. *The Crow Indians.* New York: Rinehart.

Merrill, William L., Marian Kaulaity Hansson, Candace S. Greene, and Frederick J. Reuss. 1997. *A Guide to the Kiowa Collections at the Smithsonian Institution.* Smithsonian Contributions to Anthropology, no. 40. Washington, DC: Smithsonian Institution Press.

Mooney, James. 1891–1904. "Kiowa Heraldry Notebook: Descriptions of Kiowa Tipis and Shields." Washington, DC: National Anthropological Archives, Smithsonian Institution.

———. 1979. *Calendar History of the Kiowa Indians.* Washington, DC: Smithsonian Institution Press.

Moore, John H. 1996. *The Cheyenne.* Cambridge, MA: Blackwell Publishers.

Moore, John H., Margot P. Liberty, and Terry Straus. 2001. "Cheyenne." Pp. 863–885 in

Handbook of North American Indians: Plains, vol. 13. Edited by Raymond J. DeMallie. Washington, DC: Smithsonian Institution Press.

Newcomb, William W., Jr. 2001. "Wichita." Pp. 548–566 in *Handbook of North American Indians: Plains,* vol. 13. Edited by Raymond J. DeMallie. Washington, DC: Smithsonian Institution Press.

Parks, Douglas R. 2001a. "Arikara." Pp. 365–390 in *Handbook of North American Indians: Plains,* vol. 13. Edited by Raymond J. DeMallie. Washington, DC: Smithsonian Institution Press.

———. 2001b. "Pawnee." Pp. 515–547 in *Handbook of North American Indians: Plains,* vol. 13. Edited by Raymond J. DeMallie. Washington, DC: Smithsonian Institution Press.

Schweitzer, Marjorie M. 2001. "Otoe and Missourai." Pp. 447–461 in *Handbook of North American Indians: Plains,* vol. 13. Edited by Raymond J. DeMallie. Washington, DC: Smithsonian Institution Press.

Stewart, Frank Henderson. 2001. "Hidatsa." Pp. 329–348 in *Handbook of North American Indians: Plains,* vol. 13. Edited by Raymond J. DeMallie. Washington, DC: Smithsonian Institution Press.

Voget, Fred W. 2001. "Crow." Pp. 695–717 in *Handbook of North American Indians: Plains,* vol. 13. Edited by Raymond J. DeMallie. Washington, DC: Smithsonian Institution Press.

Wallace, Ernest, and E. Adamson Hoebel. 1952. *The Comanches: Lords of the Southern Plains.* Norman: University of Oklahoma Press.

Wedel, Mildred Mott. 2001. "Iowa." Pp. 432–446 in *Handbook of North American Indians: Plains,* vol. 13. Edited by Raymond J. DeMallie. Washington, DC: Smithsonian Institution Press.

Wood, W. Raymond, and Lee Irwin. 2001. "Mandan." Pp. 349–364 in *Handbook of North American Indians: Plains,* vol. 13. Edited by Raymond J. DeMallie. Washington, DC: Smithsonian Institution Press.

Sacred Societies, Southwest

See Kiva and Medicine Societies

Salishan Shamanic Odyssey

See Sbatatdaq

Sandpainting

Sandpaintings—or drypaintings—are sacred ephemeral paintings made of dry, pulverized materials strewn onto a level surface primarily for medical and religious ceremonies that include divination, disease diagnosis, and curing. Powerful gifts of deities, sandpainting are also referred to as sand altars, sand mosaics, ground paintings, earth pictures, and sand pictures. They also serve as mnemonic devices used for teaching and are always made under the direction of a religious specialist. Many groups throughout the world, including Native peoples living in Australia, Africa, Central America, India, and North America, make some form of sacred drypainting. A few also use them for secular purposes, including birthday greetings, personal blessings, and maps.

Use of drypaintings in the Americas predates European contact and continues to the present. Cheyenne and Arapahos, for example, use them during the Sun Dance, and Native American Church leaders paint sand designs on their altars. In southern California, sandpaintings are made as part of initiation ceremonies and puberty rites. The designs are abstract renditions of the universe and astronomical phenomena. Sacred sandpaintings appear extensively among Uto-Aztecan speakers from Guatemala north to California; as an art and religious form, however, they are most developed in the American Southwest, where the designs and the technique are highly valued by Puebloan, Apachean, O'Odham, and Cahitan peoples. Materials used to make the sacred drawings include pulverized sandstones, ocher, sand, corn pollen, and pulverized flower petals and leaves. Designs center on important symbols and include depictions of deities required by ritual.

The group that has the richest repertoire of sandpaintings, as both a religious act and a secular art form, are the Diné or Navajo. Drypaintings, or *iikaah*, which means "the place where the gods come and go," are the gifts of the Holy People to Earth Surface People. How each of the more than 1,200 designs was given to Earth Surface People and the rules that accompany their appropriate use is recorded in the sacred texts that accompany each Navajo ceremonial cycle (see Ceremony and Ritual, Diné).

In general the first sandpaintings were said to be "sewings" (*naskha*) composed of five or six kinds of materials. These included buckskin, unwounded deerskin, cotton, black or white clouds, sky, or spider webs. The Holy People unrolled these materials during a prototype ceremony

Hataali Gray Squirrel ritually blends the sands of a sandpainting, as part of a four-day ritual to bring rain. Two children then rest atop sheepskins spread over the blended sands during the ensuing three days of the ritual. Each summer, Gray Squirrel does one or two full ceremonies to bring rain. Farmington, New Mexico, 1978. (Ted Spiegel/Corbis)

recounted in the sacred texts of each chantway. They showed the paintings to the protagonist following his or her adventures who memorized it and took the knowledge of the design and how it must appropriately be used to invoke healing back to Earth Surface People. After the ceremony the Holy People rolled up each *naskha* and carried them away to their homes. Because of the delicacy, value, and sacredness of the *naskha*, the Holy People decreed that Earth Surface People should use ephemeral sandpaintings made of powdered rock and similar materials, and that they should produce them anew for each ritual use. The other reasons given for this decree were that the *naskha* might be stolen, soiled, overused, damaged, lost, or quarreled over. Paintings might also become material possessions that outsiders could steal and evil beings (including witches) could misuse to the detriment of the Diné. To further ensure that the sacred designs depicted in a sandpainting were safe and that the powers within them would not be misused, the Holy People decreed that misuse would lead to blindness, illness, and death to the individual and disaster and drought to the People.

Sandpaintings are simultaneously the place where ritual behavior is carried out and symbolic representations of powerful supernaturals used in many curing ceremonies. They serve as a temporary holy altar and a means of attracting the Holy People who are invoked to cure and bless. Each of the approximately 1,200 paintings used in fifty-six different Holyway and Blessingway ceremonial cycles is a visual, mythical statement and mnemonic device. A specific painting has a specific name, generally based on the main theme symbol—for example, Arrow People from Female Shootingway. The paintings all use similar symbolic and artistic conventions yet are specific to a song ceremonial that in turn is related to a particular set of etiological factors and supernatural powers. The specific painting chosen by a *hataatli* (a highly trained religious specialist who chants or sings during ceremonies and oversees the curing process), in consultation with a patient's family, depends on the nature of the illness, the sex of the patient, seasonality, when the painting was last used, the length of the total ceremony, and the *hataatli*'s ability to control the use of powerful symbols.

Subject matter in Diné sandpaintings consists of symbolic representations of powerful supernaturals who are invoked to cure the patient and restore *hozho*—restore balance, goodness, beauty, and harmony and bring those things that causes sickness under ritual control—and of portrayals of beings or powers who assist this process. Figures in the paintings symbolize humanlike portrayals of protagonists of the origin myths that accompany each ceremonial, figures of the Holy People (Diyin dine), *yeis* (a special class of Holy People who help humans), and various personified beings, animals, and plants whom the protagonist met on his or her travels. These may also be the etiological factors that cause illness, for like can cure like. Holy People are the most common power and are depicted as personified plants, animals, anthropomorphic beings, natural or celestial phenomena, mythological creatures, or natural objects. Animals and plants may be painted in the different manifestations of their power, either naturalistically or as Holy People. They are also made in a semistylized form as subsidiary figures; the most common plants are corn, beans, squash, and tobacco.

Sandpaintings also symbolically portray an episode in the sacred text that accompanies each curing ceremony. The action is played out in Dinétah, the traditional and sacred homeland of the Diné, which is bounded by the four sacred mountains. These are shown in sandpaintings as colored circles placed in the corners between the main theme symbols. Mountains as a generic landscape feature are black ovals on which Holy People stand. Reading location symbols is like reading a mythological road map. In the center of radial paintings is a local symbol representing water, a mountain, a house, or a *hajinaí*, the place of emergence. In linear compositions, the locality symbol is the bar placed to the west, beneath the feet of the Holy People. Location, rain, symbols of movement, and other critical features are used to place the painting in mythological and historical time and space. Locations can be any place in the Diné (Navajo) sacred geography or cosmology. While sandpaintings are illustrative of events occurring in the sacred texts, few are narrative or realistic in their figurative style, in the Western sense of the term. Also, while they are depictions of past events and episodes, they re-create these events in the present, thereby visualizing Diné concepts of cyclical time as well as sacred settings.

Gifts of the Holy People, sandpaintings are to be used only under the direction of the *hataatli* and treated with respect because of their inherent power. They are very dangerous if misused. They must be made perfectly in order to be efficacious; they are destroyed at the end of a ceremony because they are full of transferred sickness. The paintings are blessed by the *hataatli* using pollen and cornmeal offerings when complete. In addition, large and elaborate paintings are used to cast out illness, to prevent evil from intruding into a person's life, for blessing, and for harmonizing a person and the community with nature.

Sandpaintings can be viewed as the ceremonial membrane that allows the transference of goodness for evil to take place during a Holyway ceremony; they help the patient identify with the healing powers. This ritual process has been likened to a spiritual osmosis in which the evil and sickness in an Earth Surface Person and the goodness and holiness in Holy People penetrate the sandpainting from both directions. During the process sickness is neutralized by holiness, but only if the exact conditions for the transfer have been fulfilled. Universal rules of reciprocity govern this exchange. If the sandpainting is made flawlessly, the Holy People are drawn irresistibly to their pictures; they view the gifts and offerings of the participants and then become the beings depicted in the paintings. They are then compelled to come to the sacred site and cure in exchange for the appropriate gifts. Because of this ability to take on supernatural power or holiness, sandpaintings are considered living entities when consecrated, and hence they are revered as beautiful in the sense of *hozho*. They are not, however, considered "art" in the strictly Euro-American sense of the term: something to be simply looked at and admired.

A sandpainting ceremony is performed once during a two-night chant and successively on the last four days of a five- or nine-night ceremonial cycle. One painting is made each day during Holyway ceremonies in order to receive the sun's blessing. For exorcistic rituals the paintings are made at night. A different design, representative of a group of Holy People and events, is used on each occasion; the same design is never used twice in the same ceremonial round. Male relatives of the patient, assistants of the *hataatli,* and any other men in the community with the requisite skill and knowledge produce the painting under the direction of the *hataatli*. Women seldom help unless they are curers or apprentices. Although women are not barred from painting, they are usually reticent to participate if they are of childbearing age, for fear of inadvertently harming an unborn baby. All assistants should have previously been patients in a ceremony; that means they have some ritual preparation for being around the concentrated power residing in a sandpainting.

At the beginning of the sandpainting ceremony, a sandpainting setup is erected in front of the hogan door. This setting-out ritual occurs at dawn and notifies both Earth Surface People and Holy People that sacred portraits are about to be made. To the accompaniment of prayers, the bundle prayer sticks from the *hataatli*'s *Jish* are stuck in an upright position in a small mound outside the hogan to the east of the door. The hogan has already been cleaned and the central fire moved to one side. Next the floor is covered with clean riverbed sand and smoothed with a weaving batten. Colored pigments—which have been collected by the family sponsoring the ceremonial and previously ground with a mortar and pestle on the northwest side of the hogan—are placed in containers near the central area. These colored pigments include pulverized sandstones, mudstones, charcoal from a hard oak hit by lightning, cornmeal, powdered flower petals, and plant pollens. No adhesive is used, because the painting will be ritually destroyed at the end of the ceremony. A sandpainting is made freehand, except for the occasional use of a taut string to make guidelines straight and to ensure that the main figures will be the same size. Extreme coordination and speed are necessary to make a thin, even line of sand.

Although paintings vary in size from a foot in diameter to more than 12 feet square, most are approximately 6 by 6 feet, the floor area of the average hogan. The typical sandpainting requires the labor of three to six men and takes roughly four hours to complete. The more elaborate the composition, the more time it takes to construct; the most complex and powerful require as many as forty painters each working ten hours. Larger paintings are preferred because supernatural power is increased by the repetition of figures, but smaller and simpler compositions are also effective. The factors determining the size of the sandpainting include the amount the sponsoring family can afford to spend on gifts for the painters, the number of people available to paint, and finally, the chant in which the painting is used.

Construction, placement of figures, composition, and the use of ritualized artistic designs are strictly prescribed by the Holy People for each painting. These rules must be followed explicitly in order for the cure to be effective. The painting is begun in the center, with the painting's location symbol, and constructed outward in a sunwise sequence (east, south, west, and finally north). Next the main figures and secondary figures are painted. Finally an encompassing guardian figure (often a rainbow) is painted around the entire composition but left open at the east. This ensures that the concentrated power in the painting is protected from evil and that the painting has a boundary. The eastern opening allows for the transference of power during the ceremony. To future help the *hataatli* control the transference process, the paired guardians (messengers of the Holy People) are constructred at the east opening. The same construction sequence is used for each figure in the composition: when a picture of a Holy Person is made, the entire torso is painted first in one color. Then the figure is clothed by means of a technique called overpainting. Finally, decoration—masks, headdresses, symbols—are added. All of these designs, figures, and symbols must be perfect (that is, made as the Holy People have taught) in order for the ceremony to be effective. The only allowable individual artistic deviations are in the kilt design and the decoration of the medicine bags that hang from the waist of Holy People.

When completed, the painting is reviewed for mistakes, which will be covered over with clean background sand and the figure begun again. After the *hataatli* is satisfied that the painting is error-free, he intones a Blessingway prayer to neutralize any unknown errors that could be harmful to the makers or inadvertently invalidate the ceremony. He will also bless and consecrate the painting by sprinkling sacred pollen on the composition in the specific order in which it was made, ending with the protective guardian.

After the painting is blessed the patient enters the hogan and reconsecrates the painting. He or she sits on a specified portion of the painting, facing east. While praying and chanting, the *hataatli* touches parts of the painting with herb medicine on his palm and then the corresponding part of the patient's body, matching parts of the body. Usually he works from the feet to the head, and from right to left, emulating the growth of plants and the rotation of the sun. This procedure is repeated four times, along with other ritualistic acts and prayerful chanting. The healing *hozho* in the painting moves through the *hataatli* into the patient while the illness in the patient is simultaneously transferred into the painting. The painting in effect absorbs the sickness.

These procedures identify the patient with the deities represented in the paintings. Their supernatural strength and goodness are transferred via the *hataatli* to the patient. The patient becomes like the Holy People, for he or she has been able to partake of the nature of their divinity and *hozho.* As a result the patient is made strong and immune from further harm but also becomes potentially dangerous to anyone who is not similarly ritually prepared to come into contact with concentrated supernatural power. The patient must follow a number of prescriptions, including using special eating utensils, for four days before returning to society. Violations of these requirements may reinfect the patient or injure other people.

Upon completion of the sand application the patient leaves, and relatives may hastily apply some of the painting to their own bodies. After the women leave the hogan, the *hataatli* erases the painting in the opposite order from which the figures were laid down. The sand is deposited north of the hogan under a lightning-struck tree, where it becomes a barrier against the evil and sickness that has been driven away. The use of the sandpainting usually takes less than an hour.

Like other religious paraphernalia that can be imbued with sacredness, such as masks and medicine bundles (*jish*), sandpaintings must be treated with respect. They are feared as well as revered (Reichard 1950). The painting never remains in a pristine form unattended; the longer it remains intact, the greater the possibility that someone will make a mistake in its presence and cause unintentional harm.

During the twentieth century, however, permanent forms of sandpainting have been developed to both preserve Diné sacred designs and as a form of secular art. At first, reproductions were made by religious specialists and anthropologists to ensure that the knowledge contained in the designs is preserved for future generations. Based on technological changes in the backing and adhesive, artistic sandpaintings have been made for the regional and international ethnic art market since the 1960s. Originated by Fred Stevens, Jr., a Diné Nightway *hataatli*, and Luther A. Douglas, an Anglo artist, Diné secular sandpaintings—which are permanent paintings made of pulverized dry materials glued onto a sand-covered wood backing—have become an established art tradition. While not as extensive an industry as weaving or silversmithing, several million dollars worth of paintings have been sold each year since the 1980s; more than six hundred Diné men and women have been or are painters. While primarily men or women past childbearing age make the sacred sandpaintings, Diné artistic sandpainting is a Diné art form that is produced equally by both sexes.

While artistic sandpaintings developed from sacred sandpainting designs, they are not conceptualized as the same thing, although both are beautiful. They are felt to be art in the Western sense and are made intentionally for sale to non-Diné. A process of secularization has resulted in this new category of art. The singers and artists intentionally make the paintings imperfect, by changing symbolism through simplification, elaboration, transposition, and several other symbolic devices to accomplish this transformation. The design symbolism is changed so that the resulting composition does not call the Holy People, and so the Holy People will recognize that the designs are not intended for a curing ceremony. The paintings, however, are clearly recognized as deriving from sacred templates and therefore as containing *hozho*.

Nancy J. Parezo

References and Further Reading
Griffin-Pierce, Trudy. 1992. *Earth Is My
    Mother, Sky Is My Father: Space, Time and
    Astronomy in Navajo Sandpainting.*
    Albuquerque: University of New Mexico
    Press.
Haile, Berard, Maud Oakes, and Leland
    Wyman. 1957. *Beautyway: A Navajo
    Ceremonial.* New York: Pantheon Books.
Joe, Eugene Baatsoslanii, Mark Bahti, and
    Oscar T. Branson. 1978. *Navajo
    Sandpainting Art.* Tucson: Treasure
    Chest Publications.
Newcomb, Franc Johnson. 1964. *Hosteen
    Klah, Navaho Medicine Man and Sand
    Painter.* Norman: University of
    Oklahoma Press.
Newcomb, Franc Johnson, and Gladys A.
    Reichard. 1975. *Sandpaintings of the
    Navaho Shooting Chant, 1937.* New York:
    Dover Publications.
Parezo, Nancy J. 1983. *Navajo
    Sandpainting: From Religious Act to
    Commercial Art.* Tucson: University of
    Arizona Press.
Reichard, Gladys A. 1939. *Navajo Medicine
    Man: The Sandpaintings of Miguelito.*
    New York: J. J. Augustin.
———. 1950. *Navaho Religion: A Study of
    Symbolism.* New York: Pantheon Books.
Wyman, Leland. 1960. *Navaho
    Sandpainting: The Huckell Collection.*
    Colorado Springs, CO: Taylor Museum.
———. 1970. *Sandpaintings of the Navajo
    Shootingway and the Walcott Collection.*
    Smithsonian Contributions to
    Anthropology, no. 13. Washington, DC:
    Government Printing Office.
———. 1983. *Southwest Indian
    Drypainting.* Albuquerque and Santa Fe:
    School of American Research and
    University of New Mexico Press.
Wyman, Leland, and Clyde Kluckhohn.
    1938. *Navajo Classification of Their Song
    Ceremonials.* Memoirs of the American
    Anthropological Association, no. 50.
    Arlington, VA: American Anthropological
    Association.

Sbatatdaq (Sqadaq)

Distinctive of Puget Sound, *Sbatatdaq
(Sqadaq)* was a symbolic journey undertaken by cooperating spiritual practitioners who traveled to the spirit world to recover the soul of a sick person.
Erroneously called Spirit Canoe Ceremony, *Sbatatdaq* involved a space defined by planks and effigies to provide a
vehicle to the land of the dead. There the
ceremonialists regained some vitality, depending on the severity of the illness (variously a lost guardian spirit, soul, or
mind), and returned it to their patient.
During the entire ritual, the patient rested
unobtrusively on a cedar mat at the rear
of the house. *Sbatatdaq* was last held in
full form in 1900, though a more personal
version still occurs today. To add to the
confusion, local pioneers often called this
ritual the Ghost Dance, though it has no
relation to the national spiritual revivals
of 1870 or 1890 that originated in Nevada.

Each occasion of the rite was cus-
tomized to local conditions of that patient, community, dwelling, drainage, and
current events. Each rite was therefore
distinctive, though each relied on common beliefs about the reversed conditions
between the worlds of the living and that
of the dead. When it was summer there, it
was winter here; day was night; low tide
was high tide; and what was whole was
broken. This public ceremony, therefore,
was set during the coldest, wettest months
of the year, often in January.

Originally, the cedar plank house was
either owned by the patient or loaned for

Plateau

The native people of the Plateau are linguistically and culturally diverse. Many aspects of their lives are unique adaptations to the mountains and valleys in which they live. However, these people were strongly influenced by the Plains people to the east and the Northwest Coast people to the west prior to Euro-American contact. Most of the Plateau people lived in small villages or village clusters, with economies based on hunting, fishing, and wild horticulture.

The Plateau culture area is an upland region that encompasses the Columbia Plateau and the basins of the great Fraser and Columbia Rivers. The Columbia Plateau is surrounded by the Cascade Mountains to the west, the Rocky Mountains to the east, the desert country of the Great Basin to the south, and the forest and hill country of the upper Fraser River to the north.

The mountains bordering the Columbia Plateau catch large amounts of rain and snowfall. This precipitation drains into a great number of rivers and streams, many of which feed the Columbia River on its way to the Pacific Ocean. The mountains and river valleys have enough water to support forests of pine, hemlock, spruce, fir, and cedar, while the land between the mountain ranges consists of flatlands and rolling hills covered with grasses and sagebrush. The climate varies greatly depending on proximity to the ocean and the altitude. Game animals are generally small, except in the mountain areas. However, nutritious plant foods such as tubers and roots can be found in meadows and river valleys. Seasonal runs of salmon in the Columbia, Fraser, and tributary rivers significantly enhanced the region's available food supply, providing both a staple food and a key sacred symbol.

The Plateau was not as densely populated as the Northwest Coast culture area to the west before contact, yet many different tribes have called the region home. Two language groups are dominant: Penutian speakers such as the Cayuse, Klamath, Klickitat, Modoc, Nez Perce, Palouse, Umatilla, Walla Walla, and Yakama in the interior portions, and Salishan speakers, the Columbia, Coeur d'Alene, Flathead, Kalispel, Shuswap, and Spokane to the northwest.

continues

Plateau (continued)

More than two dozen distinct tribal groups inhabited the Columbia Plateau at the time of European contact. Ancestors of peoples speaking languages of the Penutian linguistic family probably settled the area more than 8,000 years ago. Over the centuries these groups have been influenced by the landscapes of the Plateau region in the development of their religious cultures, often centering on the sharing of the salmon runs. First Salmon ceremonies are fairly typical in the region, wherein the people celebrate and give thanks for the new salmon run with a religious ritual prior to partaking in the resource. This activity, while displaying an appreciation for the gift from the sacred beings that salmon represent, also ensures that adequate numbers of fish get to villages farther upstream, and that the strongest fish arrive at the spawning grounds, maintaining a strong genetic line for the future.

Localized variations on this ceremony abound, as well as region-specific rituals and ceremonies of thanksgiving and propitiation appropriate to localities. The extended-family group nature of the tribal system, along with the numerous tribes in the region, also point to the need for extended cooperative trade relationships and intermarriage.

The Plateau cultural area, like all of the cultural regions used to discuss Native American peoples, is really a diverse and varied one with linguistic, cultural, and religious differences from area to area within the region. However, there is enough ecological similarity in the region to inspire some common traits among the tribal groups. Groups of the region often sacralize these commonalities in regular intertribal gatherings for trade and intermarriage.

the occasion. Its floor space was cleared so that a middle aisle was bordered by paired planks. These handmade cedar boards, shaped and painted, were stood up so that carved effigies of each practitioner's Little Earth could be placed between them. These Little Earths conferred the ability to go to the land of the dead and return safely, because they were the "owners" of the earth itself. Because they were of the earth, they could draw the doctors back to it.

What was unique about this enactment was that, while doctors usually worked alone, here several doctors worked simultaneously. To balance the depicted vehicle an even number of practitioners, usually four or six, co-officiated during the rite, although one of them took the lead. In addition to their power from Little Earths, their other spirit allies were also called upon periodically to help, so that the doctors could safely go to the afterworld and return. Almost all of the doctors were men. Women were not prohibited from joining the rite, but very few female spiritual practitioners had the necessary spirit helpers. Only two such women are still recalled.

Everyone in the community was involved in the preparations. Meanwhile, the practitioners, or that practitioner associated with the house, went into the woods and selected a large cedar tree, which was hauled or floated to a convenient location near the community. There it was split into planks, each shaped into a particular tribal (river-specific) form, particularly with a top that had either a curve, a snout, or a disk. Every drainage had its own style of plank. For example, the Snohomish cut out the snout because they traced descent from a legendary marine mammal.

Each plank was coated with a chalky, white layer of paint to provide a background before thick black outlines were drawn along the edges. The day before the ceremony, each doctor was assigned a plank on which he painted an image of his primary power in the middle in red, white, and black. Sometimes dots in red or black surrounded the figure to represent the song that linked doctor and spirit. Since humans were alien in the afterworld, doctors felt as though they were traveling through an engulfing viscosity. Whenever they sang or talked, their breath escaped as bubbles, represented as these painted dots, moving through this thickness. Poles were also made for or by the doctors to serve multiple purposes during the rite—as bows, punts, probes, spears, paddles, or place markers.

Every spiritual practitioner possessed a carved humanoid figure about a yard high representing his Little Earth. Before an odyssey, this figure was cleaned, repainted, and dressed, as appropriate, to look its best. When the Little Earths, primordial male and female spirits who lived in forest marshes, heard the practitioners singing as they departed for the afterworld, they rushed into the house to help out by lodging within their carved effigies. According to common belief, these earthlings actually made the voyage that was merely depicted by the doctors.

While helpers readied the room for the ritual, often digging up the floor to make it loose enough to implant artifacts, spectators had to keep very still, since these actions were fraught with danger. Much could go wrong, because worlds were about to be breached, and that might lead to fatal consequences.

When all was prepared, practitioners and their human helpers lined up outside, ready to march in and set up the paraphernalia so that they could start their odyssey. Engulfed by drumming and singing, this procession entered the house. The doctors were wearing special cedar-bark headbands and face paint.

Long strips of woven cedar bark were sometimes draped around the neck like scarves. At the very start, each curer carried his Little Earth, with an assistant carrying the painted plank. Sometimes the planks were held so that they appeared to peek inside the door, making their power seem more lifelike. Each doctor placed his figurine in a line down the center aisle of the outfit and sat down on the side.

Helpers arranged the planks in pairs so that each spiritual practitioner could face the image on his centrally painted spirit power. The boards at the ends were painted on only one side, while those in the middle were painted on both. When the schematic vehicle had been constructed in the middle of the floor, the practitioners stood in the cubical spaces between each board and acted out their departing. They had to hurry, because in Lushootseed belief, any illness was a prelude to death, not a brief disability. Their patient was wasting away, without any obvious cause, because the dead were sapping the patient's vitality. At this point, the Little Earths occupied the aisle. Later, during various stops and activities, the figures and doctors switched places.

At the first stop, doctors visited a place filled with the spirits of artifacts, each of which sang its song. Moving among them, these healers learned and repeated these songs to help people to use tools more efficiently. Tools and foods were attracted to people, just as spirit-powers and kin yearned for their relatives.

Since this was the initial encounter with the "other side," everyone was reminded that it was the spiritual (and sung) aspects of existence that were the most important, a logical beginning place for any such journey, and for life in general.

After some time the trip continued, until they got to a berry thicket where bird-size berries were hopping about in the shape of human babies. Spiritual practitioners tried to pluck a berry or two with their poles, and their clumsy antics created much humor for the audience. If they managed to get just one, there would be a plentiful berry harvest the next fall.

Continuing on, the practitioners next came to a lake where their vehicle was reconfigured into a flat-water canoe. A practitioner with a lake-dwelling spirit like Otter called out its name to speed the canoe across this water.

Next, they came to a wide prairie where the practitioners used their poles as bows and seemed to hunt meat. If they were successful, there would be plenty of game in the fall.

Fifth they came to Mosquito Place, where they were attacked by these insects, the size of birds, fighting them off with their poles. Any sting would be fatal. Mosquitoes were doctors in the spirit world because of their ability to suck out blood. Moving on, the doctors came to Beaver Den, where they hunted using their poles as spears. If they killed a beaver, furs would be of high quality the next year.

Afterward, the doctors braced to meet the Dawn after they had been traveling most of the night. The curers had to "lift the daylight" by passing their poles over their heads. Because Dawn had increasing intensities, they had to lift it several times to safely move on. What was dawn for the spiritual practitioners was sunset for the ghosts. After their exertion, the practitioners rested all day, since it was night in the land of the dead, preparing to resume the next evening. Sometimes the lead practitioner, if he had great power, would make a quick trip to this afterworld to plan the final assault.

During the next day's journey, the major difficulty was a raging river with collapsing banks and rolling boulders. The doctors quickly conferred and decided to tip up one end of a plain cedar plank to serve as a ramp to help them jump across the river, using their poles to vault. A doctor was most vulnerable at the moment when he was suspended in the air, supported only by his spirits. If a doctor slipped or fell, he was expected to die within the year.

By now the crew was close to the town of the dead, whose physical setting sometimes became the nearest human graveyard. The vehicle was beached. While a few spiritual practitioners reversed the enclosing planks and figures so they could head back home, the rest went along the trail to the town. They sometimes encountered a ghost, played by a member of the audience, who was out picking berries. A ghost walked by crossing and recrossing the feet. Pretending that they too were ghosts, they asked for news and learned the quality and name of the newest occupant and where it dwelled. This newcomer was the soul, mind, or spirit of the patient. Then the practitioners quickly killed the ghost and buried it in a shallow grave. Such ghosts went to other lands of the dead until all memory of them faded away.

Having learned from the ghost what they were after, the doctors planned for visiting the town. Sometimes they created a diversion by having one of their spirit powers appear in front of the town as an elk, deer, or beaver. Every ghost rushed to the river to hunt that animal. Acting like a ghost, the most powerful doctor entered the deserted house to lead out the patient's vitality. Other doctors protected the retreat as they rushed to the vehicle. Once aboard, a doctor "threw his meanness" at the ghosts, who swarmed to fight for the vitality. Apparently, by successfully fighting for the lost spirit, doctors were able, in fairness, to keep it.

In some towns, this final battle was enacted with long flaming splinters shot at the doctors by youngsters acting the part of the ghosts. Any doctor hit or burned died within the year. Since the enactment took place at night, often inside a house, these flames were both dramatic and dangerous inside the old wooden buildings.

The spiritual practitioners paddled hard, with their Little Earths providing heightened protection. Sometimes they took a short cut used by those who died suddenly that brought them back in a few hours instead of days. The practitioners arrived, each quivering with power. Their leader came forward with the missing vitality and acted as though he was pouring it into the head of the invalid. Slowly at first, then with renewed vigor, the victim began to sing his or her power song.

Sometimes, while away, doctors retrieved the souls of other "healthy" people, carried back in a shredded cedar scarf, and restored it to the owner. These unintended patients liberally compensated their healer.

Once the vessel returned safely, everyone in the house heard about future conditions. Any artifacts, berries, or meat brought back were given out to families who might need them. Predictions were also made, both to delight or to warn everyone.

Although the doctors might rest briefly, the used paraphernalia had to be dismantled to close off the route to the afterworld. Planks were left in a remote area of the woods to rot, returning to their elements. The poles may have also been abandoned, but some seem to have been reused in later rites.

Kept for a lifetime career, Little Earth figurines were carefully washed, losing much of their paint, and hidden in special places in the woods, often in a hollow tree. There each awaited the next ceremonial use by its spiritual practitioner partner. Only after the practitioner died was the Little Earth left forever in the forest to rot away.

In Puget Sound, intertribal contacts enhanced local social, political, and religious complexity. Important leaders fostered these interchanges by hosting feasts, namings, marriages, funerals, cult initiations, and winter dances. These activities in turn engendered the larger environment that made possible the international spiritual connections basic to this complex odyssey.

Jay Miller

See also Ceremony and Ritual, Northwest; Dances, Guardian Spirit Complex; Health and Wellness, Traditional Approaches; Healing Traditions, California; Healing Traditions, Northwest; Masks and Masking; Missionization, Northwest; Northwest Winter Spirit Dances; Oral Traditions, Northwest Coast; Potlatch; Religious Leadership, Northwest; Sacred Societies, Northwest Coast; Vision Quest Rites

References and Further Reading
Jilek, Wolfgang. 1982. *Indian Healing: Shamanic Ceremonialism in the Pacific Northwest Today.* Surrey, British Columbia: Hancock House Publishers.
Miller, Jay. 1988. *Shamanic Odyssey: The Lushootseed Salish Journey to the Land of the Dead, in terms of Death, Potency, and Cooperating Shamans in North America.* Anthropological Papers 32. Menlo Park, CA: Ballena Press.
———. 1992. "Native Healing in Puget Sound." *Caduceus* (Winter) 8: 1–15.
———. 1999. *Lushootseed Culture and the Shamanic Odyssey: An Anchored Radiance.* Lincoln: University of Nebraska Press.
Suttles, Wayne. 1987. *Coast Salish Essays.* Seattle: University of Washington Press.
———, ed. 1990. "Northwest Coast." In *Handbook of North American Indians,* vol. 7. Washington, DC: Smithsonian Institution Press.

Waterman, Thomas. 1930. "The Paraphernalia of the Duwamish 'Spirit-Canoe' Ceremony." *Indian Notes* 7, no. 2: 129–148, 295–312, 535–561.

Scratching Sticks

Extensive ethnographic studies on indigenous girls' puberty rites have identified a number of "marginal survival traits" that are distributed throughout North and South America. The theory of "marginal survivals" was first used by Erland Nordenskiold in 1912 to explain distribution traits occurring throughout the Western Hemisphere (Driver and Riesenberg 1950, 1–31). The most readily identifiable ritual object in rites of menarche is the widespread use of deer hoof or dew-claw rattles. However, culture-element surveys frequently overlook the field of meaning in various forms of scratching sticks, scratching stones, or scratchers used in puberty rites and menstruation seclusion practices. Typologies of women's ritual objects are invariably catalogued and identified as symbols of subsistence, fertility, power, influence, and privilege (Maschio 1995, 131–161). Less studied have been the ways in which material ritual objects attend to aspects of self-oblation, privacy, autonomy, and transcendence while women are in ritual seclusion. A comparative analysis of archival data and field research reveals the extent to which scratching implements are common in both puberty and menstrual seclusion rites.

The earliest archival reference to scratchers comes from the ethnographic work of Leslie Spier, who in 1930 identified four types of Yurok "head" scratchers (*sado'ktcuts*) used by girls in puberty rites (Spier 1930). Spier's illustration shows four oblong-shaped bone pendants that are strung by a cord and "tucked under the left wristband or hung about the neck" (ibid., 69). His illustrations indicate a plain scratcher and three elaborately decorated ones. I contend that they represent two distinct versions of the same thing—a private and a public scratcher. The cross-hatching designs may not be merely decorative but may in fact elaborate how many times a woman has participated in menstruation seclusion rites. I base my theory on Janet Spector's (1991) study of similarly incised, cross-hatching designs on Sioux women's sewing awls (Gero and Conkey 1991, 389). In Spector's analysis, each incised line on the awl was a record of the material goods produced in seclusion; it was proudly worn as a public record of women's diligence to ritual and material production.

In 1942, Harold Driver's "culture-element distributions" for girl's puberty rites in Western North America provided a broad survey of ritual objects used by California Indians; the survey includes a description of shell scratchers used by Southern California Diegueños and Luiseños. Unfortunately, Driver did not provide an illustration, and he failed to elaborate on the function or religious significance of the oblong scratchers he describes (Driver 1942, 59).

The Tlingit of Alaska used scratchers made of bone or stone. Frederica de Laguna identified "mouth stones" and "body scratchers" that were used by men in hunting rites and by women during puberty rites (De Laguna 1972, 521, 538, 598, 666, 689–690). The stones were used to symbolically scratch the inside of an initiate's mouth as a reminder never to gossip maliciously about another human being. They were quickly buried after ritual use, so that "ugly thoughts" would be buried along with them. De Laguna also described "a long thin stone" that was used while a girl was in seclusion "to scratch herself, apparently to avoid self-contamination from her fingers" (ibid., 521).

Taking a different form and different material are the scratchers used by Chumash women in puberty ceremonies. Chumash scratchers were made from the outer rim of an abalone shell and worn like a pendant. Using a standard anthropological approach, Travis Hudson and Phillip Walker record that a menstruating girl was "not allowed to touch her head directly with her fingers and was required instead to use a pendant made from the rim of an abalone shell to scratch herself" (Hudson and Walker 1993, 104). Hudson and Walker do not determine where the "pendant" fits into the ritual symbolic system, other than to add that restrictions associated with menstruation were "intended for the good health and well-being of the entire household" (ibid.).

In New Mexico, contemporary Mescalero Apache puberty ceremonies of Isánáklèsh Gotal also include a scratching stick (*tsibeecichii*) as one of the ritual objects used by young girls during their eight-day initiation process. Willetto Antonio, the ritualist who "sings" the young girl through her transformation from girlhood to deity and back to womanhood, tells us that the young girl is never allowed to scratch herself, because if she touches her skin it will wrinkle prematurely; if she scratches her head, her hair will turn gray (personal communication, June 1991, May 1992). The Mescalero Apache scratching stick is carved by the initiate's father and is made from sycamore, oak, or cottonwood. She wears it suspended from the right side of her leather-fringed blouse and uses the scratching stick only when scratching is necessary. The Lipan and Chiracahua Apache of Arizona also use a similar scratching stick in rites of passage ceremonies known as "Changing Woman" or "White Shell Woman" (Basso 1966, 145).

Interpretation of the symbolism or "form meaning" of scratching sticks calls to mind what Victor Turner identified as "the smallest units of ritual which still retain the specific properties of ritual behavior; it is a 'storage unit' filled with a vast amount of information" (Turner 1967, 19, 50–52). What this study reveals is that scratching sticks are more than just simple tools that satisfy a bodily itch, or an amulet to ward off evil or contamination. Scratching sticks are seen to assist women in regenerating and actualizing a transcendent mode of consciousness. A concept that has not been fully explored in cross-cultural context to any extent, nor has its implication for religious studies theories been developed, is the idea that while scratching sticks may represent a worldly and mundane tool, their use in women's rites serves to remind women of Creator's presence.

Avoiding the extreme objectivity characteristic of Boasian descriptions, which tend to discard exegetical (the indigenous interpretation), operational (the way they are utilized within ritual context), and positional (the position in the total symbolic system) meanings entirely, I prefer a descriptive schema that can elaborate on the religious dimension of scratching sticks in the context of what women hope to achieve or enjoy in the rituals they celebrate. Dominant interpretations concerning ritual objects are that they are either all psychological or sociological in nature (as in Victor Turner's model). But can the meaning of ritual objects extend beyond the representational or symbolic, or the psychological or sociological? How are moments of transcendent experience and regenerative action achieved through the use of scratching sticks? Cultural anthropologist Thomas Buckley illustrates the religious dimension of scratching sticks as they are used by Yurok women in the context of a communicational transaction between sacred and profane worlds when he states that "a woman must use a scratching implement, instead of scratching absentmindedly with her fingers, as an aid in focusing her full attention on her body . . . by making even the most natural and spontaneous of ac-

tions fully conscious and intentional. 'You should feel all of your body . . . exactly as it is . . . and pay attention'" (Buckley 1988, 190).

According to this description, the scratching stick may be seen as a tool that allows a participant to maintain the proper liminal space while in focused meditation. Scratching sticks incorporate vital energy, and they reflect their role as "energizing nodes." A scratching stick is a "tool for making the intangible concrete" (Rubin and Pearlstone 1989, 16). Used in ritual meditation, the proper function of the scratching stick becomes a method by which to suppress the unconscious response to the mundane act of satisfying a bodily itch while in mindful prayer. Meditation is the moment-to-moment awareness of self within the cosmos. To scratch the body or head unconsciously would automatically break the conscious connection with the divine in nature. Once a participant had achieved a state of unusual mental calm, she would very consciously pick up the scratching stick and very consciously scratch that discomforting itch, remaining conscious of each moment and each movement. The practice of "mindfulness" and the pattern of meditation, bathing, and ritual scratching are foundational for the regeneration and reformation of spiritual and moral action that can than be carried back into everyday life.

The persistence of ancient traditions, and moral and aesthetic values, are embodied in the nascent revivalism of traditional gender religious practices that require ritual scratching sticks. The values of the past have evolved and changed, yet they continue. It is hoped that these values may be seen and admired, appreciated, and even understood. In Native American culture, women are honored as the central site of creation, and they are highly esteemed for their acts of piety and devotion to community well-being. For Native American women, scratching sticks help to maintain a purposeful and conscious contact with the divine.

Mary V. Rojas

See also Ceremony and Ritual, Apache; Female Spirituality; Female Spirituality, Apache; Female Spirituality, Dakota; Feminism and Tribalism; Menstruation and Menarche; Women's Cultural and Religious Roles, Northern Athabascan

References and Further Reading
Basso, Keith H. 1966. "The Gift of Changing Woman." In *Anthropological Papers*. Bureau of American Ethnology Bulletin no. 76. Washington, DC: U.S. Government Printing Office.

Buckley, Thomas. 1988. "Menstruation and the Power of Yurok Women." In *Blood Magic: The Anthropology of Menstruation*. Edited by Thomas Buckley and Alma Gottlieb. Berkeley: University of California Press.

De Laguna, Frederica. 1972. "Under Mt. St. Elias." In *Smithsonian Contributions to Anthropology*, vol. 7. Washington, DC: Smithsonian Institution Publications.

Driver, Harold E. 1942. "Culture Elements Distributions: XVI Girls' Puberty Rites in Western North America." *Anthropological Records* 6, no. 2.

Driver, Harold E., and S. H. Riesenberg. 1950. "Hoof Rattles and Girls' Puberty Rites in North and South America." *National Journal of American Linguistics* 16, no. 4.

Gero, Joan M., and Margaret W. Conkey, eds. *Engendering Archaeology: Women and Prehistory*. Oxford: Basil Blackwell.

Hudson, Travis, and Phillip Walker. 1993. *Chumash Healing*. Banning, CA: Malki Museum.

Maschio, Thomas. 1995. "Mythic Images and Objects of Myth in Rauto Female Puberty Ritual." In *Gender Rituals: Female Initiation in Melanesia*. Edited by Nancy C. Lutkehaus and Paul B. Roscoe. New York and London: Routledge.

Rubin, Arnold, and Zena Pearlstone. 1989. *Art as Technology*. Beverly Hills, CA: Hillcrest Press.

Spector, Janet D. 1991. "What This Awl Means: Toward a Feminist Archaeology." In *Engendering Archaeology: Women and Prehistory*. Edited by Joan M. Gero and Margaret W. Conkey. Oxford: Basil Blackwell.

Spier, Leslie. 1930. "Klamath Ethnography." *University of California Publications in American Archaeology and Ethnography* 30.

Turner, Victor. 1967. *The Forest of Symbols: Aspects of Ndembu Ritual*. Ithaca: Cornell University Press.

Song

Music and dance remain at the center of how Native Americans maintain ceremonies and traditions of all kinds. To sing to the Creator or to guardian spirits is to bring the past into the present. Performing religious Native music almost always requires employing techniques and evoking sounds that are distinctly Native, so that a given song is both sacred in function and an important marker of tribal or general Native identity. It is true that most Native Americans enjoy—and some perform—recreational music that matches or draws heavily on white or black genres, such as country music, types of rock music, and the like. In addition, the music of Christian churches that Native Americans attend (as a minority or majority) may sound much like the church music of their neighbors of other ethnic groups, though some words and meanings will likely have been modified for Native purposes. Further, there are a few distinctively Native genres of music that are explicitly secular—for instance, courting songs played on the flute or social dance music that is fiddle-based in certain cultures. Nevertheless, substantial bodies of Native religious song remain in use. In fact, most Native song that remains distinctively Native in sound is sacred, and the composition of songs, formerly often done during vision quests, still frequently involves prayer.

Evidence of the importance of music to Native Peoples reaches back millennia. And despite the great variety in all aspects of Native culture over the centuries, there has been considerable unity too. Inasmuch as North America was long a land of seminomadic or entirely nomadic populations, with anything resembling cultural borders in constant flux, cultural interaction of all types was common. In fact, songs seem to have crossed from one Native group to another fairly often, whether bringing associated performance characteristics with them or not. Later on, when tribal boundaries were imposed by outside forces, those artificial boundaries re-

mained fluid in terms of culture. With the considerable outmigration from reservations during the twentieth century, music has become a tool of ever-increasing importance both for marking specific Indian populations and for allowing Native peoples to express shared experiences in a shared way. It has proved to be easier to mark Native culture as distinctive through music and dance than in any other way.

The uses of music in ritual or in ceremonies with any kind of sacred connection are legion. In fact, the overarching function of song in Native American culture is to mediate between man and his spiritual and physical universe. Songs record myths and legends. Parts of the life cycle may be marked through singing, and most funeral traditions include music. Songs often invoke celestial aid in hunting and placate the spirits of the harvested animals. Many animal dances involve considerable pantomime. Activities loosely associated with hunting need songs, too. For instance, in sub-Arctic Canada, singing specific songs eases the considerable labor involved in moving the massive carcasses of whales. Songs are the principal means of communication with spirit helpers, are integral to curing ceremonies, and may help to foretell the future. The Inuit use songs to influence the weather. From California to the Great Basin to the Southwest, song helps men maintain or renew harmony with nature. Song is integral to all religious ceremonies, new and old, public and private.

And even song-driven ceremonies that may seem relatively secular to outsiders may be infused with religion. In particular, the powwow may not appear to be religious to the casual outsider observer, but its purely secular moments—snake dances and 49s and such—are in the minority. Flag songs and ceremonies to retrieve fallen important feathers are clearly religious, and some participants—particularly in the North and East—speak of the meat-and-potatoes intertribals (war dances) as having religious overtones.

The musical details of the many Native song styles tend to be differentiated, as are the broad culture areas in general; in fact, the anthropological definition of the term "culture area" was based to some extent on those musical styles. More recently, styles have come into being that span culture areas—in order of appearance, the music for the Ghost Dance, for the Native American Church, and for powwow culture. There is not enough room here for a meticulous listing of musical traits according to culture area; the interested reader can best explore these details in the many articles on Native music in the third volume of the *Garland Encyclopedia of World Music,* the volume covering the United States and Canada. What follows is a summary description.

The principal sound source in Native music is the voice, generally the male voice. (While there are a very few types of songs that women sing alone, most performance of sacred Native song is either entirely by men or by men supported by women singers, who generally double the men's melody at the octave.) The unit of performance is the individual song, generally of five minutes or less in length, so that many ceremonies consist of a mosaic of songs.

Men may sing alone or as a group in unison, or they may take turns singing (either one man's voice alternating with another, or a soloist to whom a chorus responds); alternatively, in a texture common today and well known through powwow style, a soloist may start a song or section of a song, with a group of other men joining in within a few seconds. Most songs also include the sounds of percussion instruments, ranging from bells attached to dancers' feet, to rattles or small hand-held drums, to the large drum of the modern powwow. The word "drum" refers both to the instrument itself and to the ensemble, the few to a dozen or so men striking the instrument in unison. (The formal umbrella term for this array of textures is monophony—that is, melody lacking any sort of harmonizing accompaniment, either explicit or implied.)

Most songs either remain steady in tempo or, more often, gradually speed up, and they may also become gradually a bit louder. Subdivisions of a given song are marked by accents in the percussion accompaniment or in the volume of the voice(s), or, also frequently, by repetitions in the contours of pitches that the melody traces. These contours—that is, the broad sweep of melody—tend to start high and end low, though certain styles found in parts of California and elsewhere in the Southwest feature the "rise," portions of a song that reach up in pitch level for a few moments here and there. Nearly all song forms contain plenty of repetition of patterns of pitches. When these repetitions seem about as long as a verse of a song, we call the form strophic. Forms can be literally strophic, as in powwow songs: one extended section of music repeats several times to make up the song, whether that section has new words each time or not. Other basically strophic forms can be more complicated, as in the involved forms of the Southeast. And forms that cannot reasonably be called strophic still contain much repetition. For instance, songs of the Northwest coast contain short patterns that recur, and both Great Basin and Peyote songs contain some paired phrases.

Most songs that have any words at all have just a few phrases of them, though those few phrases are very carefully chosen. In fact, many songs are made up mostly or entirely of vocables—of sounds made by the voice but that do not have a specific concrete meaning that is known at this time. In many cases we may think of the voice singing vocables as an instrument. In rarer instances, sounds that the voice emits once bore more specific meanings, but those have been forgotten. But patterns of vocables often retain a more general meaning, that of tribal or regional identity markers, since a given array of vocables will

have emerged naturally from a certain Native language or group of languages. When there are specific words in a song, these often come at predictable places in a given musical form. For instance, in the Plains-style singing of powwow music, the forms are strophic, with each verse (strophe) first descending in a terraced contour, then proceeding in what is called an incomplete repetition. That is, when the voices get to the bottom of the range of the song, and go high again within the verse, they do not go quite all the way back to the beginning. In most powwow songs that have words, those words occur only in that section of incomplete repetition.

While pitch sets employed in Native songs may be diatonic (like the major scale, having seven different pitches per octave), most styles and individual songs use fewer pitches, from four to six pitches per octave. Since seven-pitch diatonic scales permeate the art music most familiar to the musicologists who coined Western musical terminology, the sorts of scales employed in Native music have come to be called "gapped" scales. Such scales allow more room in some Native styles for a very wide vibrato and for pulsations of various kinds. Indeed, while the usual performance forces can be thought of as tightly circumscribed—only male voices and a few percussion instruments—the amazing range of techniques that the voice employs makes it an unusually versatile and expressive sound source. The voice may be relatively relaxed (as in much of the music found on both coasts), or, more often, nasal or tight, which are qualities that allow sound to carry far without amplification. Interjections of moans or gasps infuse a few styles, and pulsations of many kinds can either permeate a performance or be employed to mark the formal divisions of a song.

Native American song is now in a period of expansion and diversification. More and more newly composed powwow songs have relatively involved contours, and more and more are word songs. And Native populations that have lost much of their expressive culture are working actively to recover, acquire, or create materials to replace what has been lost. For instance, the Occaneechi-Saponi of central North Carolina, a population of about five hundred, are rebuilding their music and dance repertoire in several ways. While they are a woodlands people, they have the gift of Plains-style powwow music, and they arrange several traditional powwows each year. In addition, tribal leaders have acquired woodland songs from tribes with which they share some parts of their history, such as the Cayuga (a group now geographically distant); they are also seeking the help of the Creator to compose new songs. Even among this tiny Native population, just as throughout Native America, sacred Native song is thriving today.

Chris Goertzen

See also Dances, Great Basin; Dances, Northwest Winter Spirit Dances; Dances, Plains; Dances, Plateau; Dances, Southeast; Drums; Kiowa Indian Hymns

Song, Kiowa

See Kiowa Indian Hymns

Sovereignty

The idea of sovereignty is typically understood in the European sense of worldly rights or powers deriving from the Deity, a matter most clearly expressed in the medieval assertion that monarchs rule by divine right. All Western constructions of the concept have evolved directly from this basic premise. Hence, at a number of levels, it matters little whether modernist depictions of sovereignty frame it in accordance with the Hegelian proposition that it consists of certain prerogatives naturally vested in the state, or, as Jean-Jacques Rousseau, Thomas Jefferson, and Karl Marx alike insisted, as a property inhering exclusively in "The People." Within the parameters of mainstream discourse, the concept of the sovereign ultimately devolves, as nazi legal theorist Carl Schmitt rather famously observed during the 1920s, upon questions of political theology. Self-described postmodernist thinkers, given their recent propensity to swallow Schmitt more or less whole, would appear to have little to add.

Given the Eurocentrism with which the word "sovereignty" has been both conceived and applied, as well as the fact that no known indigenous language evidences a terminological equivalent, it has been widely believed—indeed, actively contended—that American Indians possessed no true conception of sovereignty, at least until such time as it was inculcated among them by Europeans. A closer, and perhaps more honest, inspection of Native belief systems reveals the falsity of such conclusions, however. Merely because something is not seen or appreciated for what it is by an observer or group of observers hardly means it is therefore nonexistent. Put most simply, the indigenous notion of sovereignty has been, and for the most part remains, incomprehensible or invisible to those of the Western tradition, largely because it tends to reverse the polarity of that which presumptively inheres in the sovereign.

As Onondaga faith-keeper Oren Lyons once responded to a young Euro-American New Ager demanding that he respect what she considered her right to acquire the innermost secrets of Onondaga spirituality, "We Haudenosaunee have no conception of rights. Our tradition gives us only an understanding of our responsibilities." (Haudenosaunee refers to the Six Nations Iroquois Confederacy—of which the Onondagas are part—situated in upstate New York and southern Ontario.) In other words, this time paraphrasing the late Oglala Lakota principal chief Frank Fools Crow, that which the Creator—or Great Mystery, as the Lakota approximation of Deity is usually known—endows the people, individually and collectively, is more properly viewed as a divine responsibility rather than a right of any sort. To the extent that something resembling a right may be said to exist, it amounts to an expectation that both the individual and the group will remain unfettered in their fulfillment of their obligations to the Creator.

The theme is recursive, resounding throughout the oral teachings of virtually every people native to North America and endlessly committed to paper from the point European stenographers first began to record the statements of indigenous leaders. While the range of specific applications of the principle at issue is at least as great as the number of cultures applying it, it nonetheless forms what may be accurately portrayed as a fundament of indigenous law, irrespective of variations (real or apparent). At base, this is always and everywhere an injunction that the group—and, by extension, each individual within it—must conduct their affairs in ways allowing them to pass along the creation as they encountered it to their posterity several generations in the future (just as their ancestors did for them). From this flows the oft remarked Native preoccupation with apprehending and preserving the natural order and the placement of a high social value on personal attributes such as humility, respectfulness, and generosity (for example, absence of material covetousness).

Taken as a whole, every formulation of tribal law embodies a bedrock insight that only through the conscious protection of nature by each generation can there be assurance that it will remain sustaining in coming generations. In practical terms, for any people to comport themselves in the manner indicated, they must enjoy what amounts to complete control vis-à-vis other human groups over the geography comprising their environment. Such control adds up, regardless of the name assigned it, to the exercise of sovereign prerogatives. Assertion by another culture of control over or ownership of the land base of a given people is by definition preemptive of the ability of the usurped people to meet the range of responsibilities dictated by their spiritual tradition to the land itself and thus abridges their sovereignty in the most elemental way conceivable. This is all the more true when the usurping culture is, as has been the case with European Christendom in its invasion and continuing occupation of the New World, one that takes transformation of nature into the form of consumable commodities as the cardinal signifier, not only of virtue and value, but of its intrinsic superiority to the culture(s) upon whose land it settles.

Contemporary Native Americans are thus presented with an unfathomable dilemma. To assert their sovereignty within the paradigm of Eurocentric understanding is to nullify themselves in terms of their own traditions and identities as distinct peoples. At the same time, failure to advance such assertions, insofar as it allows Euro-America's devastation of the land to go unchallenged, is guaranteed to produce essentially the same result. Since both routes lead to the continuing dissolution and eventual disappearance of indigenous cultures and societies, the choice appears to be between acceptance of their own genocide on the one hand and an autogenocidal participation in the eradication process. Whether there is a way out of this particular box remains to be seen, but, all things considered, the prognosis is exceedingly grim.

Ward Churchill

See also American Indian Movement; Identity; Law, Legislation, and Native Religion; Retraditionalism and Identity Movements

References and Further Reading
Armstrong, Virginia Irving. 1971. *I Have Spoken: American History through the Voices of Indians*. Chicago: Swallow Press.
Deloria, Vine, Jr. 1973. *God Is Red*. New York: Grosset and Dunlap.
Fowler, Michael Ross, and Julie Marie Bunck. 1995. *Law, Power, and the Sovereign State: The Evolution and Application of the Concept of Sovereignty*. University Park: Pennsylvania State University Press.
Means, Russell. 1995. "For the World to Live, Europe Must Die: Fighting Words on the Future of Mother Earth." Appended to Russell Means and Marvin J. Wolf, *Where White Men Fear to Tread: The Autobiography of Russell Means*. New York: St. Martin's Press.
Schmitt, Carl. 1988. *Political Theology: Four Essays on the Concept of Sovereignty*. Cambridge: MIT Press.
Vecsey, Christopher, and Robert W. Venables, eds. 1980. *American Indian Environments: Ecological Issues in Native American History*. Syracuse: Syracuse University Press.

Spirit Canoe Ceremony

See Sbatatdaq

Spirits and Spirit Helpers, Great Lakes

See Manitous

Spirits and Spirit Helpers, Plateau

The role of Spirits or Spirit Helpers in an individual's life is a relationship of great significance within the Plateau region. The association between an individual and his or her Guardian Spirit is remarkably intimate and ever present. An individual's Helper is not held in reserve only to be called upon as needed, but is consistently used as a powerful ally embodied within its holder throughout the day.

For Indian people, the Spirit world is not something to explain, prove, or deconstruct. The Spirit world and its power is alive, real, and encompassing. Spirits are not viewed as foreboding but are accepted as part of the life circle. Spirit is the glue that binds all circles together, the circles shared by the animal world, physical world, Spirit world, and humans.

The varied tribes on the Plateau believe that one would lead an unsuccessful or unproductive life without the aid of one or more Spirit Helpers. Spiritual power is used or needed for essentially every domain of life; consequently, lacking the assistance of a Spirit Helper is considered a grave predicament.

Within Plateau cosmology, animals, plants, and particular inanimate objects are believed to have a spiritual aspect or quality. Visions, Spirits, and power are shared by those entities in the forms of song, dreams, or visitations. Through such sacred connections, these entities or Spirit Helpers might provide an individual with enhanced and physical or mental abilities. Spirit Helpers may bestow gifts of knowledge, spiritual power, or medicine.

Song is the primary medium through which Spirit Helpers communicate a particular power. Within the Plateau, Spirit and song are so closely identified with each other that they are often described by the same word. Song is considered the embodiment of the Spirit, and a person rarely exists apart from it. Among the Klamath, *Swis*, or song, is also the term for the Spirit who imparted the song. The bestowal of *Swis* by the Spirit Helper establishes the relationship between the individual and the Guardian Spirit.

Spirits and spiritual powers are referred to by diverse terms specified by each cultural group and location within the Plateau region. Various Salish peoples tend to refer to Spirit powers as *suumesh*. Within the ethnographic literature there are several different spellings of the term *suumesh*, including *somesh*, *sumex*, and *sumi'x*. *Suumesh* is the most common currently. Among the Wishram the term *Walu'tk* is used to describe life, Spirit, wind, and breath. The Kootenai refer to Spirits as *Nupik'a* (Spier and Sapir 1930). Guardian Spirits and the powers bestowed to their holders are termed *Wéyekin* by the Nez Perce, *Taax* by the Umatilla, and *Sukat* by other Columbia River Sahaptin people.

The concept of the Guardian Spirit or Spirit Helper among Plateau Peoples is a multidimensional complex that goes beyond simply acquiring a particular

Spirit Helper on a quest. Schuster (1998) articulated the Guardian Spirit complex among the Yakama as consisting of the Sweatlodge, Vision Quest, and the Winter Spirit Dance. The Sweatlodge is used by both men and women and is considered one of the most powerful of the Guardian Spirits because it possesses the ability to protect and restore one's spiritual power and purity (ibid.). Additionally, Spirits might come to an individual during a Sweat to deliver a message or offer a particular power. The Vision Quest was practiced by prepubescent or pubescent boys and often girls. During the Vision Quest, neophytes would attempt to obtain a Spirit Helper. The Winter Spirit Dances, held at the beginning of each year, provided individuals an opportunity to give thanks and to honor their Guardian Spirits, cure illness, ask for protection, and gain good fortune for the upcoming year. The composition of the Guardian Spirit complex consisting of the Sweatlodge, Vision Quest, and Winter Spirit Dance was common throughout the Plateau region.

The Quest for Spirits

Children had close contact with the Spirits from an early age. Turney-High documented that, among the Kootenai, even a very young child could be sent from the lodge if he was disobedient, in the hope that some Spirit might correct him (1941). A parent, in his old age, may teach a song to a young child and then dance with the child upon his

back to transmit the Spirit power (Stern 1998a).

Before and during puberty, male and often female children were sent on a Vision Quest. It was important for a child to gain a Spirit Helper while still young. If a child failed to gain the power of a Spirit Helper in time, the opportunity to gain that power vanished, and the individual was to live without the protection of a Spirit forever (Spier and Sapir 1930). Very early in a child's life, he or she learned that "a successful Spirit experience is indispensable to any valued achievement as an adult, indeed to avoid complete social insignificance" (Ray 1939, 68).

Verne Ray describes a Sanpoil shaman's first vision experience as a young boy:

> A young boy was often sent down to the river at night. He did not know what he was to do on these ventures. He wandered aimlessly along the banks of the river. One evening he met a handsome young fellow who spoke to him and asked him where he was going. The boy answered that he did not know. The stranger said, "Well, you had better listen to me. I'm not a friend of yours now but I will be. I'm not who you think I am. I'm going to tell you something. When you grow up you will be lucky. If you take something from someone else you will not be caught. You will be able to get food easily. You will be favored by women. You will be sharp eyed. You will be able to see (know) what is going on at night. When you are in danger I will warn you." He gave him a song and left. It was Wood Rat. (Ray 1932, 183–184)

Among the Yakama, it is documented that Guardian Spirit power could be sought on a Vision Quest, or it could be inherited from another person. There was a tendency for similar powers to be found within the same family (Schuster 1998). The Kootenai, Cayuse, Umatilla, Walla Walla, and Yakama believed that an individual usually had no choice which Spirit powers he or she obtained. Nevertheless, individuals attempted to influence the type of power they would receive by engaging in activities to attract a particular Spirit, such as taking a token from a relative's Spirit bundle who possessed the desired power (Burnton 1998; Stern 1998a). In all cases, the Spirit bestows the power, as Spiritual Helpers or Powers cannot be bought or obtained unless the Spirit is willing to bestow it upon the individual (Schuster 1998).

In some tribes it is believed that the Spirits have no specific dwelling place. Among the Klamath and other Salish peoples, children would be sent to traditional places where a Spirit might appear or where specific spiritual powers would be found: on mountaintops, near streams, in whirlpools, or in caves (Ray 1939; Stern 1998a).

The novice must enter upon a Vision Quest with proper intentions and attitude. Walker (1998) identified that if the child was hostile or jealous he might be visited by an undesirable Spirit, who could bestow powers that may be used for malicious purposes.

Typical Vision Quests lasted one night, although some quests lasted five days or longer. Among the Kootenai, the quest was rarely longer than a single night. If the child was unsuccessful on the first night, the quest was prolonged until success was achieved. One of the single most important aspects of obtaining the power of a Spirit Helper and being successful was acquiring a song imparted by a Spirit during the quest. During a quest, a Spirit, taking the form of an animal, insect, or object, might take pity upon the child and bestow a song with instructions on how to use the power the song conveyed or what taboos to observe (Schuster 1998).

Spirit Helpers can appear to their holder in various forms. A Spirit may come in the physical form of an animal, plant, or tree, or in the nonphysical form of a ghost, heavenly body, or act of nature such as lightning, floods, or ice (Walker 1998).

Spirits are specialized and grant powers that vary considerably. A man may be given special hunting powers, fighting powers, medicine powers, fishing powers, the power to move stealthily, hide readily, the power of invulnerability, or the capacity to win at gambling or attract women. Women may be given special root digging, berry picking, or medicine powers (French and French 1998; Spier and Sapir 1930; Walker 1998). Having more than one spiritual power is possible, and often Coeur d'Alene and Flathead adolescents would go on multiple quests to obtain greater spiritual power.

A lad on a quest met Magpie, who said, "My nest is built high in a tree. It is of brush. Once my enemies were shooting arrows at me. But the arrows went right through the nest and didn't hurt me. It will be the same for you." Then the boy saw Flint Rock. He said, "Arrows and bullets can hit me but they don't go through me. It will be that way with you." Then he saw Grizzly Bear. "You will be like me," Grizzly Bear said: "strong, brave and quick tempered." So he got three powers at one time. (Ray 1932, 184)

Holders of particular Spirit powers could use their powers for extraordinary purposes. Some may change the weather or the outcome of battles, help plants grow, create love magic, end a famine or bring a famine to an enemy, heal terminal illness, or maliciously create an illness.

> For clairvoyant powers, Klamath shamans relied upon the Spirits such as Bear; to find lost objects, Dog was useful. A shaman with Eagle or Weasel power could predict the outcome of an impending battle. To abate cold weather, the aid of tutelaries such as West Wind, Rain, and Thunder was invoked. Appropriate tutelaries might, upon appeal, bring snow upon enemies. During the Modoc War, a shaman acted to bring down a shielding fog against the army's advance (Stern 1998, 460).

It is documented that men kept various representations of their Guardian Spirits, including claws, feathers, bones, and roots. For the Nez Perce, an essential aspect of spiritual power was possession of a collection of sacred objects. This collection needed proper care and appropriate use, since they possessed great

power (Walker 1998). Medicine bags among the Nez Perce, as well as among other Plateau tribes, were often carried into battle, and the skins or feathers of a Spirit Helper were frequently affixed to an individual's clothing or hair (Walker 1998).

The quests to gain a Spirit Helper ended after puberty, and the *Suumesh* or *Wéyekin* was not to be recalled or revealed. The manifestation and exhibition of one's Spirit Helper did not occur until adulthood, when the Spirits reappeared to the individual. An exception to this practice is the Kootenai, which did not have a pattern of "forgetting" one's Spirit Helper until maturity (Ray 1939).

When the Spirit Helper returned to the individual, he or she would fall ill with Spirit sickness, often feeling an overall sense of despondency. Among the Sanpoil this Spirit illness was called *Kélem-sasumixu* (Ray 1932). During this time the Spirit Helper would sing the power song and instruct an individual to sponsor or sing at a Winter Spirit Dance, thus helping the individual overcome the Spirit sickness. The Winter Spirit Dance and the curing of Spirit sickness are closely linked. The Okanogan referred to the Winter or Guardian Spirit Dance as the *Snixwam*, which means "to take sickness and drop it down" (Kennedy and Bouchard 1998).

It is documented that, among the Nez Perce, when a child obtained a Spirit Helper the public came to know the nature of his Spirit Helper for the first time when the child sang a new song at the

Guardian Spirit Dance (Spinden 1908). James Teit, in his invaluable ethnography of the Okanogan, reported that during the Guardian Spirit Dance the individual would sing the song that he acquired, show his powers, and imitate his Guardian Spirit while dancing, yet not announce who his Guardian Spirit was (1928).

Within the Colville, Okanogan, and other Plateau tribes, the exact nature of one's Spirit Helper was not announced during the annual Winter Spirit Dance. Hunn (1990) documented that among the Sahaptin peoples it was essential that young persons not reveal their visions to anyone. If the Spirit Helper was revealed, sickness, spiritual loss, or death might occur. It was not until the point of death that the individual could reveal the mysteries of his or her Spirit Helper. This practice was common among Salish peoples as well, where—as among the Klamath—individuals were free to discuss their Spirit Helpers in public (Spier and Sapir 1930; Teit 1928).

The Winter Spirit Dances were occasions for those with Spirit power to sing their Spirit songs and to dance. The purposes of the Winter Spirit Dances were to give thanks, honor one's Guardian Spirit, cure illness, ask for protection and healing, and gain good fortune for the upcoming year. During the Winter Spirit Dances those with Spirit Helpers would often renew their connection with their Spirits, as well as provide an opportunity for validating the Spirit power of novices.

Throughout life, the strength of one's spiritual power could become inconsistent and fluctuate. Spiritual powers had to be used to remain effective, although excessive use of one's power could diminish its strength. If the Spirit Helper's power were neglected, it could not provide the necessary protection or guidance. Ray (1932) illustrated by explaining that if an individual possessing arrow immunity were wounded by an arrow in combat, his wound could be attributed to the individual's not thinking of his protective power when struck.

The use of the Sweat Lodge ceremony continues as the primary means of maintaining communication with one's Spirit. Tobacco is also utilized to show gratitude and to honor the Spirits. It is believed among the Kootenai that when the Indians took over the land, the Spirits could no longer gather tobacco. Since the spirits needed tobacco, they provided tobacco seeds and taught man how to grow it (Turney-High 1941).

In healing, doctors cured illness by extracting malignant Spirits that invaded the person's body. Among the Wishram, however, a shaman could cure an individual bewitched by a Spirit only if his own Spirit Helper was more powerful (Spier and Sapir 1930). Among the Klamath, the curing procedure involved searching for the Spirit responsible for causing the illness. Multiple Spirits might be invoked in an attempt to find the culpable Spirit (Kroeber et al. 1930).

Spiritual powers were not always used for a good cause. The Nez Perce believed that spiritual power could be used by most individuals to cause sickness or disasters (Walker 1998). It was believed that Rattlesnake and Spider could give an individual the power to kill others (Stern 1998). A Wishram man with a Snake Spirit could have the ability to send his Spirit to bite someone (Spier and 1930).

Contemporary Indian people of the Plateau still go into the mountains in search of a Spirit Helper, but the number of those with a Guardian Spirit has decreased significantly in modern times. It is apparent that "with the traditional context largely destroyed, young people are no longer able to benefit from the guidance, assistance, and powers of their elders in their own search for meaningful spiritual links to their social and natural environment" (Hunn 1990, 239).

Although many traditional ways of living have disappeared, many Plateau people still seek out and obtain Spirit Helpers and powers much like those of yesteryear. The Spirits today are just as powerful as the Spirits of the past. A Coeur d'Alene consultant remarked that for him, "Spirit is still the core of life itself." Spirits and Spirit Helpers are very real to Plateau Indian people. The American Indian might have changed in appearance, but Spirit Helpers still play the same quintessential role they did during precontact times (personal interview, June 2002).

The Spirit world is something greater than human beings. We are just small little things. We don't try to question it; we simply accept it. As you lie there and listen to the wind blow through the trees, you begin to see how small we are, how pitiful we are as human beings. We need the power that Spirit put into our circle.

The Spirit is what lights the fire in the middle of our circle. "A small little tiny ant might come to me, turn around and dance, and a song would come. He'd give me a song, that tiny little ant; just a speck. It doesn't have to be a big grizzly bear, a big moose, or a mountain lion. It is the Spirit that is in the heart, which is found in the smallest little thing" (ibid.).

Aaron Denham

See also: Ceremony and Ritual, Nez Perce; Dances, Plateau; Song; Spiritual and Ceremonial Practitioners, Plateau; Vision Quest Rites

References and Further Reading
Boas, Franz, and James Teit. 1996. *Coeur d'Alene, Flathead, and Okanogan Indians.* Fairfield, WA: Ye Galleon Press.
Burnton, Bill B. 1998. "Kootenai." Pp. 223–237 in *Handbook of North American Indians: Plateau,* vol. 12. Edited by Deward E. Walker, Jr. Washington, DC: Smithsonian Institution.
French, David H., and Kathrine S. French. 1998. "Wasco, Wishram, and Cascades." Pp. 360–377 in *Handbook of North American Indians: Plateau,* vol. 12. Edited by Deward E. Walker, Jr. Washington, DC: Smithsonian Institution.
Frey, Rodney. 2002. *The World of the Schitsu'umsh (Coeur d'Alene Indians): Landscape Traveled by Crane and Coyote.* Seattle: University of Washington Press.
Hunn, Eugene S. 1990. *Nich'i-Wana: The Big River.* Seattle: University of Washington Press.
Kennedy, Dorothy I. D., and Randall T. Bouchard. 1998. "Northern Okanagan, Lakes, and Colville." Pp. 238–252 in *Handbook of North American Indians: Plateau,* vol. 12. Edited by Deward E. Walker, Jr. Washington, DC: Smithsonian Institution.
Ray, Verne F. 1933. *The Sanpoil and Nespelem.* Seattle: University of Washington Press.
———. 1939. *Cultural Relations in the Plateau of Northwestern America.* Los

Angles: Southwest Museum Administrator of the Fund.

Schuster, Helen H. 1998. "Yakima and Neighboring Groups." Pp. 327–351 in *Handbook of North American Indians: Plateau*, vol. 12. Edited by Deward E. Walker, Jr. Washington, DC: Smithsonian Institution.

Spier, Leslie. 1930. *Klamath Ethnography.* Berkeley: University of California Press.

Spier, Leslie, and Edward Sapir. 1930. *Wishram Ethnography.* Seattle: University of Washington Press.

Spinden, Herbert Joseph. 1908. *The Nez Perce Indians.* Lancaster, PA: American Anthropological Association.

Stern, Theodore. 1998a. "Cayuse, Umatilla, and Walla Walla." Pp. 395–419 in *Handbook of North American Indians: Plateau*, vol. 12. Edited by Deward E. Walker, Jr. Washington, DC: Smithsonian Institution.

———. 1998b. "Klamath and Modoc." Pp. 446–466 in *Handbook of North American Indians: Plateau*, vol. 12. Edited by Deward E. Walker, Jr. Washington, DC: Smithsonian Institution.

Turney-High, Harry Holbert. 1941. *Ethnography of the Kutenai.* Mensha, WI: American Anthropological Association.

Walker, Deward E., Jr., ed. 1998. *Handbook of North American Indians: Plateau*, vol. 12. Washington, DC: Smithsonian Institution.

Spiritual and Ceremonial Practitioners, Alaska

See Angalkug

Spiritual and Ceremonial Practitioners, Basin

See Puhagants

Spiritual and Ceremonial Practitioners, California

The vastness of the California aboriginal cultures and the variety of traditions within them make a comprehensive accounting of all ceremonial practitioners virtually impossible here. As a result, broad comparisons will be drawn utilizing specific information from three distinct regions: the communities along portions of the Klamath River, the Karuk and the Hupa; the high desert–dwelling Chemehuevi; and the south coastal villages in Chumash country.

The role of ceremonial leader varies in most Native communities by what kind of ceremony it is that they are leaders of. California Indian religious ceremonies can be general community events that occur on a regular schedule, or they can be smaller, more specific rituals such as those that accompany physical healing or birth/death ceremonies.

Villages along the Klamath River and its tributaries are linked by a cyclical ritual system referred to by anthropologists as "World Renewal" ceremonies. The cycle consists of several ceremonies held every year encompassing a wide range of ritual performances including the White Deerskin and Jump Dances, which, among other things, afforded opportunities for wealth display and costuming. These are all presided over by particular Native practitioners, whose authority is tied to their knowledge of the particular aspects of the ceremonies, as well as to their timing. The leaders of these ceremonies take responsibility for arranging the date and time of

Sam Lopez, wearing Tolowa costume including a redheaded woodpecker scalp headdress and strings of dentalia shell beads. He holds a traditional painted bow and an obsidian blade, a sign of wealth. ca. 1923. (Library of Congress)

each ritual performance, as well as for assembling the proper personnel and seeing that all materials are gathered properly and readied for the ceremony. Thus, for World Renewal rituals, the leader convenes, emcees, and provides authority both prior to and during the ceremony. These roles are often passed from father to son, but initiates into the leadership roles all apprentice with an expert for some time before they are considered competent enough to lead a ceremony.

World Renewal rituals also include various "first fruits" ceremonies tied to an annual cycle and to specific locations. These elaborate rituals are intended to show respect for the gifts of the earth, thus ensuring their regular arrival. Although each ceremony is different from the others, and there exist multiple variations in ceremonial detail, all tend to include two parts: a private part followed by a public performance of one or both of two distinct rituals, the Jump Dance and the White Deerskin Dance. In the private part, the ritualist visits sacred sites and recites "formulas"—a sort of incantation/prayer that acknowledges the first performance of the ceremony in sacred time and its benefit to the people, thereby establishing the logic of its continuity. The sacred history of the people is thus invoked in virtually all such ceremonial situations. This requires that the priest/ritualist can be trusted by the community to perform these functions properly, in order to ensure the efficacy of the ceremony.

Following the private rituals, the dancing begins and goes on every day for up to ten days or more, when possible. Modern life often requires a change in this pattern, and it is the ceremonial leader who makes that decision and announces the schedule after consulting with the participants. The Karuk dance regalia is fairly standardized by custom, and it is also up to the ceremonial leader to ensure that all participants are within compliance. Dancers in the White Deerskin Dance wear regalia of deer hide or wildcat skirts and dentalium shell necklaces; wolf fur and woodpecker scalps form the headdress. The name of the dance derives from the fact that all dancers carry poles from which hang white deerskins, complete with the head of the deer at the point.

The Jump Dance regalia consists of a headdress made from woodpecker scalps and white feathers along the forehead. Dentalia are also worn, and a skirt of deerskin. The ceremonial leader is responsible for seeing that all of this takes place according to custom, and the leader makes the proper speeches and invocations during the ceremony. He will often invite honored attendees to speak to the assembly, and see to it that singers, dancers, and musicians are all paid for their participation. The feast that follows these ceremonies is also organized by the key leader, though the food itself is usually sponsored by another person.

Other, less elaborate observances, are also held in this region. Among the Hupa, an Acorn Feast is held in the autumn, when the nuts begin to fall from the oaks, and a First Salmon ceremony takes place when the spring run of fish begins. The acorns or salmon are carefully obtained, especially for these rituals, and various prayers are said and sacred acts performed. Until these procedures are completed no one eats the food, and the harvesting and fishing cannot continue until the ceremonies are held. The leaders for these ceremonies are often village elders and important family members who will also oversee the season's take for that area. Extended families possess rights to certain areas along the river and in oak groves, but with those rights come the responsibilities to the larger community that proper respect be paid and all members of the community be cared for.

For the Chemehuevi, the seasonal arc differs from that of the riverine environs of the Karuk and Hupa. Clearly, the environment plays heavily into the ceremonial cycle of any traditional community; the available resources and topography associated with the Mojave Desert are best managed via small extended-family groups through much of the year, with regular, seasonal gatherings of larger scale. For the Chemehuevi, day-to-day religious life takes on a particularly personal quality, and one can seek the assistance of a Spirit Helper to aid one in the navigation of the world; each person has particular ritual obligations to that helper.

In terms of broad religious leadership, those roles are either inherited, as with the lineage's "head man," who presides over the larger seasonal ceremonies having to do with observances of the solstices and equinoxes by several lineages in a region, and smaller, intralineage rituals for hunting, water control, or healing. In the former, the captain of a lineage is chosen to preside over a regional ceremony and is in charge of all the details, much like the Karuk World Renewal ceremonial leader. For the latter, the designation as ritualist is most often derived from dreams, but such dreams can be brought on from the ceremonial use of the Jimsonweed plant. These are most often male, but female healers and water priests are not uncommon. Hunter priests, as can be inferred from the title, perform certain rituals to ensure success in hunts. Water priests can either "dowse" for springs and oases, or invoke spiritual help to start or stop the rains. Healer priests are able to manipulate spiritual and medicinal factors for purposes of physical healing, and they oversee birth and death ceremonies as well. Their power is concentrated in cane staffs that are used in all ritual situations.

The Chemehuevi's use of Jimsonweed, in some respects, mirrors that of the final exemplary tradition, the coastal Chumash. For the grouping of loosely interconnected and independent villages that have come to be known as Chumashan, the key cultural aspect that helps to define ceremonial leadership is the extensive trade relationships that were central to Chumash life prior to the influence of Spanish missionaries. These trade partnerships, partnerships that crossed language groupings within Chumash country, were maintained via a series of guilds that oversaw the material and cultural products of the villages. From basket weavers to ritualists, the guilds served to unite what would have otherwise been a disparate cultural region. The priesthood tended to fall into several categories: ceremonial presider, often the role of the presiding village's political leader (whose membership in the priestly guild was assumed); astronomers, who were charged with keeping constant the people's awareness of seasonal changes and celestial events via extensive knowledge of the cosmos and its movement; and the ubiquitous healers, whose specialties ranged from treating snake bites to broken bones. The most typical healing priest in California, the suck doctor, tends to have a "general practitioner" approach in Chumash country, in that she or he sucks the illness-causing agent from the person's body, either directly or through a hollow reed or tube.

Initiation into the priesthood that oversees the spiritual aspects of these ritualists involves, as with the Chemehuevi, consumption of a concoction derived from the Jimsonweed plant. The result of this ceremonial consumption is a mild coma, during which the initiate receives his or her Spirit Helper and the songs associated with the particular ceremonial role.

As can be seen from these brief descriptions, ceremonial leaders throughout California are in their positions because of their ability to do what is needed for the overall health of the people. Whether that means keeping track of the proper ritual protocols from season to season so that they are always performed properly, or enduring potentially deadly initiation ceremonies so that their Spirit Helper may put them at the service of their communities, ritualists among most California Indian peoples approach their role as a "vocation": to be in the role of ceremonial leader means a lifelong commitment to proper maintenance of the power invested in them by the universe on behalf of the people.

Dennis F. Kelley

See also Ceremony and Ritual, California; McKay, Mabel; Oral Traditions, California; Parrish, Essie; Power, Barbareño Chumash; Religious Leaders, California; Retraditionalism and Revitalization Movements, California

References and Further Reading
Arnold, Mary Ellicott, and Mabel Reed. 1980. *In the Land of the Grasshopper Song: Two Women in the Klamath River Indian Country in 1908–9.* Lincoln: University of Nebraska Press.
Blackburn, Thomas C., ed. 1980. *December's Child: A Book of Chumash Oral Narratives.* Berkeley: University of California Press.
Blackburn, Thomas C., and Kat Anderson, eds. 1993. *Before the Wilderness: Environmental Management by Native Californians.* Menlo Park, CA: Ballena Press.
Dixon, R. B., and A. L. Kroeber. 1971. *The California Indians: A Source Book.* Berkeley: University of California Press.
Eargle, Dolan H., Jr. 1986. *The Earth Is Our Mother: A Guide to the Indians of California, Their Locales and Historic Sites.* San Francisco: Trees Company Press.
———. 1992. *California Indian Country: The Land and the People.* San Francisco: Trees Company Press.
Forbes, Jack. 1982. *Native Americans of California and Nevada.* Happy Camp: CA: Naturegraph Publishing.
Laird, Carobeth. 1976. *The Chemehuevis.* Banning, CA: Malki Press.
Sarris, Greg, ed. 1994. *The Sound of Rattles and Clappers: A Collection of New California Indian Writing.* Tucson: University of Arizona Press.
Vane, Sylvia Brakke. 1990. *California Indians: Primary Resources: A Guide to Manuscripts, Artifacts, Documents, Serials, Music and Illustrations.* San Francisco: Ballena Press.

Spiritual and Ceremonial Practitioners, Northwest Coast and Southeast Alaska

Northwest coast religious practitioners may be divided into roughly a half-dozen categories by function. The one factor that links them all is contact with and use of some type of supernatural power. Although these functions are discrete, individuals may have carried out more than a single one. The categories are: first fruits/hunting and fishing magic practitioner; domestic cult leader; shaman;

witch/sorcerer; winter ceremonial dancer; and artist. Considerable variation occurs along a north-south axis, from southeastern Alaska, through coastal British Columbia, to the Oregon coast. Within this area there exist ten major ethnolinguistic group, and scores of "tribal" groupings. Thus any discussion of the area in general terms necessarily involves simplification and abstraction.

First Fruits/Hunting and Fishing Magic

This function was often fulfilled by a hereditary chief in his role as owner and steward of productive territories. Occasionally, other high-ranking persons might fill the role of priest. However, individual hunters and fishers usually practiced some rituals in preparation for their endeavors, and consumers observed certain rules of food preparation, eating, and disposal. First fruits rituals had the dual function of honoring the species, usually and most importantly salmon, and of effectively opening the season on that species. Salmon were universally thought to be a sentient being whose existence paralleled that of humans. The five species of salmon provided the main staple for all coastal groups. Thus the question of how they were taken was of fundamental importance. Salmon knew and communicated to others whether they were treated well or badly by particular local groups. If they were ill treated, they would absent themselves in future years, thus withdrawing that group's sustenance. The

Nuu-chah-nulth man taking a ceremonial bath before a whale hunt. Clayoquot, Vancouver Island, British Columbia. 1843. (Library of Congress)

appearance of the first salmon of a given species was of the greatest importance to a group; it often gave rise to a "first salmon" ritual, in which the fish was ceremonially prepared and served. In addition to first fruits rituals, which honored the collective "run" of fish, individual salmon were treated with respect by having their bones returned to the water, which, it was believed, ensured their regeneration.

Hunters and certain types of fishers (generally, those who fished from boats) practiced a variety of ritual preparations. These usually involved multiple abstinences—from food (especially of the same type as that to be pursued) and sexual intercourse. In addition, bathing and other purificatory practices were adopted. This may have had a practical effect of making the hunter less easily detectable by keen-scented land animals, and certainly was connected to cultural ideas about purity. By appearing as purely human, as opposed to human mixed with the nonhuman essences of foodstuffs, the hunter appeared in an unambiguous form, facilitating exchange, the basis of all hunting and fishing. Fish and game animals willingly gave themselves up to humans as part of a cosmic exchange that was imagined differently in different cultures but that generally viewed humans as one among many communities of sentient and social beings. In addition to abstinence, prayer was commonly employed both before and after the kill. Hunters and fishers attempted to ensure not only their immediate success but also the long-term welfare of their community.

The most elaborate example of hunting magic comes from the Nuu-chah-nulth (Nootka) of the west coast of Vancouver Island. In preparation for open-sea whaling (which only they and their southern kinsmen the Makah engaged in), a hereditary chief, who was also the leader of whaling expeditions, would bathe, pray, and fast in secret places, including special shrines erected away from the village. These shrines contained human remains, as well as carved representations of humans and whales. When the chief and his party embarked,

the chief's wife or other noblewomen would carry on the ritual in the shrine. This was considered essential to the success of the hunt and to fending off disaster. The woman, who had ritually prepared herself for this, remained immobile in the shrine. At this point she was explicitly identified with the whale. If she moved, the whale moved, making it more difficult to catch; in addition, this was an action that could, if it occurred at the wrong moment, capsize the canoe and kill the crew.

Domestic Cult Leader

Most religious practice was connected with the domestic unit. These units varied in composition and organizing principles, but they were composed minimally of a household of persons related by blood and through marriage. Larger groupings, such as extended lineages and clans, brought multiple households together into a single structure. For illustrative purposes, I will here discuss the Kwakwak'wakw (Kwakiutl) *numaym*, or "house," a cognatic or bilateral descent group. Leadership in the *numaym* (as in other such groups) was vested in a senior male and his close kin. Senior position was determined by primogeniture, with a patrilineal preference; thus, eldest sons of eldest sons of eldest sons, and so on back into the genealogical depths, were preferred as chiefs. However, matrilineal descent was also considered. The head chief was also the steward of the *numaym*'s symbolic property, which included religious paraphernalia, knowledge of origin stories (both genealogical and mythological), the use of certain crest designs (which appeared on houses, poles, button blankets, and movable property), and the right to perform certain dances during the winter ceremonial. As the guardian of this property, the head chief was responsible for displaying it under proper circumstances. The most important such context was the potlatch, a great giving-away feast to which other *numaym*s were invited. Other occasions included weddings, funerals, and naming ceremonies. The prosperity and prestige, as well as the health and spiritual power, of the group was considered a direct result of the effectiveness of the head chief in his role as domestic cult leader.

Shaman (Spiritual Healers)

Shamans, or spiritual healers, were ubiquitous on the Northwest coast. They operated independently of both the secular and religious structures of society. In some extreme cases, healers did not dwell with others in a village but lived alone in the bush, where they kept shrines. Many healers were peripatetic. Spiritual healers possessed one or more "helpers," usually the spiritual form of animals such as bears, wolves, and killer whales. Shamans constituted a sort of guild that transcended tribal and community boundaries. Intergroup competitions were held, in which elaborate sleight-of-hand techniques were practiced and judged. The primary function of shamans, at least from the standpoint of nonshamans, was to heal illness, especially illness caused by taboo violations or witchcraft. The job of the healer was thus to diagnose the spiritual cause of the disease and to restore the patient's soul, the loss of which was the proximate cause of the illness. More powerful spiritual practitioners could, however, use their ability to cause illness, or to "throw" power into enemies. In some cases shamans worked for chiefs, and carried out warfare by other means. In other cases shamans became powerful sorcerers who could use their powers to obtain what they wished. Such spiritual practitioners were frequently wealthy, since few would refuse them payment. Ironically, these individuals were also the persecutors of witches and sorcerers, whom only they could detect. In the north especially, the persecution and torture of persons suspected of witchcraft and sorcery was commonplace. Among the Tlingit of southeastern Alaska, such spiritual practitioners are remembered today. They were especially active during the disease pandemics of the late nineteenth century, which most Tlingits blamed on sorcery.

Witch/Sorcerer

Witchcraft and sorcery—a distinction that rests on whether or not spells and esoteric knowledge are used (sorcery), or whether it is merely a type of spiritual malevolence (witchcraft)—was widespread on the Northwest coast. It was not considered a religious practice by most

Northwest coast people, but it certainly fits within our definition. Moreover, as we have seen, shamans, who were the most powerful religious practitioners, might "turn" and become sorcerers. Power over the victim is increased if one has access to objects associated with that person, such as clothes, or, even better, body parts, such as hair or nail clippings. For this reason, such items were usually disposed of carefully. Although generally malevolent, with the intent to cause disease, misfortune, or death, some witchcraft took the form of love medicine. This form at least is still practiced today in areas of the Northwest coast.

Winter Ceremonial Dancer

The winter was the sacred season on the Northwest coast. The pervasive darkness, bad weather, and relative lack of food made it a poor time for productive activity. The Kwakwak'wakw envisioned the world's turning over during the winter, with an effect similar to that of turning over a rock and finding slugs and worms. The spirits likewise came out in the winter, and humans impersonated them or were, in some cases, possessed by them. Most adolescent and adult males of respectable but not necessarily noble lineage participated in winter dances; in some groups women likewise participated. A wide variety of dances and dance types existed among different groups. Many involved masks and elaborate theatrics. The Kwakwak'wakw were especially well known for constructing masks weighing a hundred pounds or

more that had moving parts and could even change appearance. These "transformation" masks illustrated the concept of the interconnection between the human, spirit, and animal worlds. Other dances were performed with little costume; these tended to emphasize a state of spiritual possession or the inherent sacredness of the dancer.

A further distinction between dances was between those that were shamanistic in character and those that were closely related to the domestic cult. The shamanistic series of dances, called by groups such as the Kwakwak'wakw and the Heiltsuk (Bella Bella) by the word for "shamans," replicated in collective form the spiritual encounter of practicing shamans. This did not make the participants any more than "honorary shamans," however. The most powerful such performance was the Hamatsa, or "Cannibal Dance," which employed theatrical and perhaps actual anthropophagy. Other dances appeared closer to the themes of the domestic cult and were often led by hereditary chiefs. Such dances invoked supernatural ancestors and other heavenly beings and asked for blessings upon the community. Groups such as the Heiltsuk and Nuxalk (Bella Coola) kept the two types of dances entirely separate, while other groups mixed them together.

Artist

The role of artist was an explicitly sacred one throughout the Northwest coast. On the one hand, artists were in contact with the sacred as they manufactured ritual objects, including masks, and decorated even utilitarian surfaces with the crests of the clan. More than that, though, artists were masters of a special type of power akin to shamanism. Like shamans, their ability to "see" the spirit world enabled them to operate on a spiritual plane, apart from normal humans. The Tsimshian of northern British Columbia called artists *gitsontk,* people with secret power. The Northwest coast world was a profoundly aesthetic one; house interiors were suffused with objets d'art. Since each such design represented—in a literal sense—spiritual beings, the artists could be seen as one important way in which humans and nonhuman spiritual beings were brought into contact. Even the most utilitarian of objects, such as cedar storage boxes, which were the universal container for everything from preserved food to masks, were decorated with sacred designs. And yet these were no mere designs; the box was thought to become the spirit represented on its front, and thus to look over and protect the contents. Similarly, the ancestral crests on the fronts of houses sheltered the occupants as much as did the roof and walls.

Almost all important artwork was done with wood, usually a type of cedar or alder. The artist thus stood at the nexus of several streams of spiritual power: that of the tree, that of the tools (traditionally made of stone or bone before the advent of metal), and that of the entity represented—in addition to the frequently powerful personage commissioning the work. Many surfaces were painted, and that too involved potent forces. Paint—red and black were the main colors employed—was made from elements such as charcoal and red ocher, which were themselves not devoid of power. For certain powerful masks, menstrual blood—an immensely potent and dangerous substance—was sometimes used.

Michael Harkin

See also Ceremony and Ritual, Northwest; Dances, Northwest Winter Spirit Dances; Guardian Spirit Complex; Masks and Masking; Oral Traditions, Northwest Coast; Power, Northwest Coast; Sacred Societies, Northwest Coast

References and Further Reading
Boas, Franz. 1966. *Kwakiutl Ethnography.* Chicago: University of Chicago Press.
Harkin, Michael. 1997. *The Heiltsuks: Dialogues of Culture and History on the Northwest Coast.* Lincoln: University of Nebraska Press.
Jonaitis, Aldona. 1999. *The Yuquot Whalers' Shrine.* Seattle: University of Washington Press.
Kan, Sergei. 1989. *Symbolic Immortality: The Tlingit Potlatch of the Nineteenth Century.* Washington, DC: Smithsonian Institution Press.
McIlwraith, Thomas F. 1992. *The Bella Coola Indians,* 2 vols. Toronto: University of Toronto Press.
Seguin, Margaret, ed. 1984. *The Tsimshian: Images of the Past, Views for the Present.* Vancouver: University of British Columbia Press.
Suttles, Wayne. 1987. *Coast Salish Essays.* Seattle: University of Washington Press.
———, ed. 1990. *The Handbook of North American Indians: The Northwest Coast,* vol. 7. Washington, DC: Smithsonian Institution Press.

Spiritual and Ceremonial Practitioners, Plains

To this day, spiritual and ceremonial practitioners—possessors of supernatural powers linked to magical protection, good fortune, success in warfare, and curing—maintain, to varying degrees, the metaphysical integrity of Plains Indian communities. Although prereservation, nineteenth-century Plains peoples were semisedentary, horticultural/bison-hunting villagers or were equestrian, nomadic hunters and gatherers, they shared the common belief in an animatistic power force permeating the universe, obtainable by humans through the assistance of animistic, spiritual beings represented by animals or natural forces. Individuals receiving "power" through dreams, visions, inheritance, or purchase typically possessed sacred "medicine" bundles representing personal, clan, band, village, or tribal powers; these healers or spiritual leaders were frequently summoned to mediate on behalf of their brethren.

Sacred power, often associated with a creator, was identified by Dhegiha Siouan-speaking peoples—Omaha, Ponca, Kansa, Osage, and Quapaw—as a variant of *wakkanda* or *wakanda* (Liberty, Wood, and Irwin 2001, 408; Brown and Irwin 2001, 423; Bailey and Young 2001, 469; Bailey 2001, 480; Young and Hoffman 2001, 503). The Chiwere Siouan-speaking Iowa and Oto/Missouria also believed in *wakanda* (Blaine 1979, 192; Schweitzer 2001, 450), as did the Northern Siouan Mandan and Hidatsa, albeit they employed different terms (Wood and Irwin 2001, 357; Stewart 2001, 335). The Caddoan-speaking villagers, the Arikara, Pawnee, and Wichita, also identified a supreme being and a hierarchy of power (Parks 2001a, 381; Parks 2001b, 536; Newcomb 2001, 557).

Among the nomadic equestrian tribes, the Athabascan-speaking Sarcee and Plains Apache acknowledged an all-powerful creator—Maker of the Earth—and the Uto-Aztecan Comanche referred to their creator—sometimes identified with Sun—as Niatpo, "My Father" (Dempsey 2001b, 633; Foster and McCollough 2001, 931; Kavanagh 2001, 892). Algonkin tribes likewise recognized a creator as possessor of the greatest powers: Napi, or "Old Man" (Blackfoot); a non-personified spirit creator (Plains Cree); The One Above Thought (Gros Ventre); Maheo (Cheyenne); and Pipe Person (Arapaho) (Dempsey 2001a, 616; Darnell 2001, 646; Fowler and Flannery 2001, 682; Moore, Liberty, and Straus 2001, 873; Fowler 2001, 843). Conversely, the Siouan-speaking Assiniboine, Santee, Yankton/Yanktonai, and Teton recognized the animatistic powers connected with variant forms of the Lakota *wakan* "holy," the "common denominator of oneness," and *wakan tanka*, "big holy," or the totality of everything (DeMallie and Miller 2001, 578; Albers 2001, 768; DeMallie 2001a, 790; DeMallie 2001b, 806). To the Crow, also Siouan speakers, Sun, or "father," was the most important

The site of a Crow Sun Dance Circle. Crow Agency, Montana. 2001. (Marilyn "Angel" Wynn/ Nativestock)

spirit power (Voget 2001, 706), a conception similar to the Kiowa belief that Sun possessed the strongest *dw'dw'*, "power" (Kracht 2000, 237).

Despite different etymologies, power was attainable through inheritance, dreams and visions, or purchase. Among the Hidatsa, the Mandan, and the Dhegiha and Chiwere tribes, clan bundles were inherited according to unilineal descent rules—some bundles were tribal, others were personal (Stewart 2001, 335; Wood and Irwin 2001, 357; Liberty, Wood, and Irwin 2001, 409;

Brown and Irwin 2001, 420, 423; Schweitzer 2001, 449–450; Bailey and Young 2001, 469–470; Bailey 2001, 481; Young and Hoffman 2001, 502). Pawnee and Arikara social organization centered on endogamous villages unified by origin myths and bundles that passed from father to son (Parks 2001a, 373; 2001b, 530). The equestrian Cheyenne and Kiowa, keepers of Sun Dance bundles and other sacred tribal icons, chose sons or close male relatives to maintain the medicines after their death. Cross-culturally, Plains peoples believed that the continuation of individual power was contingent on heirs who assumed responsibility for bundles, songs, techniques, and sacred knowledge; otherwise, power died with its owner.

Throughout the Plains, power was informally obtained through "involuntary or spontaneous visions" initiated by spiritual forces, and formally through the institutionalized vision quest, a near pan-Plains phenomenon (Irwin 1994, 78–79). Vision quests usually involved self-sacrifice by fasting and thirsting an average of four days and nights in remote, often elevated locations by young male supplicants who offered prayers to the spirit world, accompanied by wisps of tobacco smoke drawn from long-stemmed pipes. Mandan, Crow, and Hidatsa seekers often took self-sacrifice to extremes, by severing finger joints as offerings (Wood and Irwin 2001, 357; Voget 2001, 706; Stewart 2001, 335). If fortunate, novices gained pity from animal— or other—spirits and were bestowed with power visions. Afterward, it was not unusual for new ecstatics to seek further knowledge from experienced individuals in the community, especially those with similar powers.

Becoming understudies to power keepers, providing them with gifts, and replicating their power symbols, bundles, and related ceremonies was another way in which individuals gained access to power. Perhaps the most unusual form of power transference, practiced by the Mandan, Hidatsa, Arikara, Gros Ventre, and Crow, involved ritual intercourse between a seeker's wife and a bundle keeper (Wood and Irwin 2001, 357; Stewart 2001, 337; Parks 2001a, 383; Fowler and Flannery 2001, 684; Voget 2001, 706–707). Regardless of its source or strength, acquired power could ensure successful hunting, lucrative raiding and horse-stealing, warrior prowess over enemies, longevity, and overall well-being; however, the strongest power belonged to shamans, the principal Plains healers (Irwin 1994, 72–73).

Power was largely male-dominated, although Hidatsa, Mandan, and Crow women deliberately sought visions. Among the Santee Sioux, Gros Ventre, Lipan Apache, Arapaho, Assiniboine, Blackfoot, Cheyenne, Kiowa, Comanche, Pawnee, Teton, and Dhegiha tribes, women gained power, often through involuntary spontaneous visions. Moreover, male shamans could not function properly without their primary assistants—their wives; husband-wife shaman pairs existed among the Crow, Cheyenne, Blackfoot, Gros Ventre, and Comanche (Stewart 2001, 337; Wood and Irwin 2001, 361; Frey 1987, 77; Albers 2001, 768; Irwin 1994, 80–81, 176–177). Healers, male or female, usually derived their powers from spirits represented by certain animals, especially Bear, Black-Tailed Deer, and, notably, Buffalo. Bear and Buffalo doctors existed among the Omaha, Ponca, Iowa, Oto/Missouria, Quapaw, Pawnee, Wichita, Santee, Teton, Arapaho, and Kiowa (Liberty, Wood, and Irwin 2001, 410; Brown and Irwin 2001, 424; Wedel 2001, 440; Schweitzer 2001, 451–452; Young and Hoffman 2001, 502; Parks 2001a, 537–538; Newcomb 2001, 558; Albers 2001, 768–769; DeMallie 2001b, 808; Fowler 2001, 844; Levy 2001, 915; Kracht 2000, 239). Other power animals related to healing powers were Panther, Elk, Beaver, Owl, and Snake.

In the ensuing sketch, the concept of power and its use by spiritual and ceremonial practitioners—shamans and tribal bundle keepers—among the pre-reservation Kiowa of southwestern Oklahoma is described. This reconstruction is largely based on the ethnographic field notes of James Mooney (1891–1904) and Weston LaBarre (et al., 1935), housed in the National Anthropological Archives, Smithsonian Institution. Kiowa orthography is consistent, wherever possible, with Merrill (et al. 1997).

Nineteenth-century Kiowa religious beliefs were centered in the notion of *dw'dw'*, "power," an impersonal spirit force permeating the universe, including plants, animals, the sun, moon, stars, earth, water, and rocks. *Dw'dw',* largely obscure to humans, was sometimes revealed in lightning, thunder, tornadoes, directional winds, and other natural phenomena, as well as in animals, birds, and reptiles. In a hierarchical spirit world in which greater and lesser powers coexisted, Sun was recognized as the principal life force because everything else depended on its *dw'dw'* in order to live. In Kiowa cosmology, the combined powers of Sun and Wind brought rain, causing the grasses to grow, which fed the bison upon which the Kiowa depended. Sun was also linked to the creation of the sacred *thali-da-i,* "boy medicine" bundles, known today as the Ten Medicines. As father to the bison and grandfather to the Kiowa, Sun was presented buffalo meat offerings and petitioned for good health and well-being with personal sacrifices of human flesh. Young male recipients of Sun-inspired visions acquired war power, developed into great warriors, and often became band leaders of the ten to twenty Kiowa bands. Sun power provided invulnerability, so warriors painted solar designs on their bodies, war shields, and war ponies. Sacred shields and dancers were also adorned with sun motifs during the Sun Dance, the most important tribal ceremony, performed to regenerate the bison herds and the Kiowa people.

Living in the upper level of the universe with Sun were the lesser powers, represented by Moon (female) and other stars. Beneath them dwelled Wind, the authority of the middle realm who physically supported Sun and his retinue and controlled the movements of rain clouds and the stars. Thunder, Whirlwind, Tornado, or *tseigudl,* "Red Horse," and the four directional winds dwelled in Wind's domain, as did Eagle, Hawk, and Falcon, symbols of war power, and Crow, whose powers included the ability to dodge bullets. Feathers from these and other birds were used in most Kiowa rites, including curing rituals. *Dom,* "Earth," addressed in prayer as "mother," dominated the lower level of the universe, inhabited by surface, underground, and underwater creatures coexisting in a predator-prey hierarchy. Among the terrestrial beings, Buffalo Bull was dominant because he received his power directly from Sun and could endow male vision seekers with war power from Sun. Otherwise, Buffalo had great medicine powers transferable to men who became buffalo doctors, or buffalo medicine men. Other earthbound power animals included Elk, Antelope, Deer, Prairie Dog, Beaver, Wolf, Mountain Lion, Badger, Wolf, and Horse. Snake and Snapping Turtle represented healing power. Power animals feared by the Kiowa included Owl, the messenger of death; Coyote, whose howling implied sickness; Gopher and Mole, diggers of poisonous burrows; Underwater Monster; and Bear, still regarded by the Kiowa with ambivalence.

Regardless of how power was obtained—purchase, inheritance, or the vision quest—the Kiowa believed that a man received war power or curing power—two distinct, mutually exclusive categories of *dw'dw'*. For those who attained either type of power, public disclosure was considered improper because of the conviction that newly acquired power would manifest itself at the appropriate time: for instance, a warrior returning from a fierce battle unscathed, or a novice shaman called in as the last resort to cure a patient.

Notably, shamans, as doctors, had the ability to accumulate different powers; powerful shamans often specialized in several specific disorders—for instance, a shaman who treated fevers and battlefield wounds.

Those who acquired curing *dw'dw'* and became shamans were obligated to live according to the dictates of their helping spirits, who imposed stringent taboos on their particular medicine powers. Dietary and behavioral taboos included the avoidance of bear, mole, and fish meat, and certain animal parts, such as brains and marrow; some shamans could not use knives as eating utensils. Each shaman also adhered to specific behavioral taboos: prohibiting people from walking behind them while they were eating, or disallowing visitors whose feet touched the ground while doctoring. Breaching these and other taboos could result in sickness and, ultimately, the death of the shaman, who also did not treat his own family members because of the concern that he would become sick instead.

Magical doctoring powers, *gietso* (meaning "unknown"), resided in the shaman's torso, ready to be coughed up, on demand, in the form of stones, paint (colored clays), moles, lizards, snakes, toads, pieces of buffalo horn, and hide. Osonte, "No Voice," possessed the ability to spit out a miniature bison as part of his magic. During healing episodes, shamans discharged *gietso* from their mouths to demonstrate the strength of their particular *dw'dw'*, and likewise spewed *gietso* at the end of the session highlighted by the "sucking" technique, the magical extraction of disease agents from the patient's torso. This was a practice founded in the notion that sickness was caused by supernatural beings or human sorcerers who selected victims, then discharged foreign objects into their bodies; the objects could be retracted only by shamans and spat out with their medicine. When a shaman died, *gietso* shot out of his mouth and was lost forever, unless an apprentice was there to receive a mouth-to-mouth transference.

Curing ceremonies in behalf of sick persons were initiated by any male relative who lit a long-stemmed pipe before approaching a shaman; the shaman respectfully listened to the problem and asked appropriate questions about symptoms. If the shaman felt his powers could help, he accepted the pipe, smoked, and prayed to his spirit powers for assistance in curing the patient. Prior to examination, the shaman purified his hands in sweetgrass smoke, then took a black handkerchief, or perhaps a buffalo calfskin, and placed it over his eyes while scanning the patient's torso to locate the "poison."

Once the source of affliction was determined, the shaman took sharpened flint, incised the skin, and began sucking the wound, although each practitioner had his own eccentricities: some shamans did not make incisions, others placed hot embers in their mouths beforehand, used hollowed-out bison horns for sucking, or applied feathered fans smudged in cedar smoke to the smitten area. Patients screamed from excruciating pain as the entity was extricated and spat out for display to the assembled family members supporting the healing process. The object, perhaps a stone, a piece of deerskin or black handkerchief, or exuviae from human corpses, including hair, skin, teeth, and fingernail pairings, was displayed to show that the shaman had successfully removed the entity. Afterward, family members rewarded the shaman with horses, blankets, or other gifts, unless the patient's condition worsened, upon which nothing was said. A shaman lost prominence, however, after repeated failures. Convalescing patients were expected to adhere to their practitioner's personal taboos until the completion of a ritual feast sponsored by the shaman.

Notable among Kiowa shamans were the buffalo doctors. The power of Buffalo resides in the cud, or in the hair balls in its stomachs coughed up and swallowed during the digestive process, as symbolized in the magical healing rite of buffalo doctors who spewed Indian paint or colored clay on the torsos of their patients. Buffalo doctors usually accompanied war parties because of their talents for treating arrow and bullet wounds. Before skirmishes with enemies, those buffalo doctors in attendance sang a buffalo song while painting their bodies red and white to symbolize the power of Buffalo, derived from rolling in the dirt. Buffalo doctors usually worked alone to assist fallen warriors by spewing red paint (clay) on open wounds to stanch the bleeding; in severe cases, as many as seven or eight worked together. Most buffalo doctors employed the sucking technique, though other treatments involved rubbing buffalo tails, fur, or even buffalo bundles across the patient's body. After successful treatment ceremonial paint was applied to the patient, accompanied by the healing power of buffalo songs. The patient was expected to follow the taboos of the buffalo doctors: they could not eat "wounded" meat—the location of the fatal wound—raw livers, kidneys, and gizzards, raw meat, or uncooked blood. Nobody was allowed to break bones in their vicinity, nor could they place buffalo tails, horns, or hooves into fires. Violating these taboos was considered dangerous to patient and practitioner alike.

Another group of shamans, the owl doctors, received their *dw'dw'* from that dreaded bird and understood Owl language, permitting them to communicate with deceased spirits using owls as mediums. The so-called owl prophets sometimes conducted nighttime seances by summoning owl spirits into miniature tepees placed at the western end of a special tepee pitched for a divination rite designed to find lost comrades and horses, or to predict the future outcome of a war expedition. Owl doctors typically treated individuals bewitched by owls and ghosts, responsible for facial twisting or paralysis. Other healers were those with Snake power, including women, who treated snake and spider bites.

Besides healing episodes, shamans often displayed their *dw'dw'* in power contests, a practice that continued well into the twentieth century. Such public expositions typically were performed by men who possessed their own unique powers and did not belong to medicine societies: Tsodltoi, "Spotted Wing," a snakebite doctor, could magically spew four large rattlesnakes from her mouth; Pododlte (meaning unknown), one of the intermittent Owl doctors, kept a spider, centipede, turtle, butcher knife, and pistol in his stomach; and the remarkable Tonakwt, "Turtle," a recipient of Turtle and Underwater Monster powers, withstood a point-blank rifle shot to the face—a story that survives in oral traditions today.

Most Kiowas feared these individuals, a fear founded in the belief that medicine powers could be used for good or evil, and that shamans who did not belong to medicine societies had a penchant for sorcery. Anyone foolish enough to offend such a person expected to get sick and possibly die. A sorcerer, using

the restrictive taboos of an adversary to his advantage, sketched an outline of the intended victim on the ground; then, based on the principle of sympathetic, or image, magic, placed a blade of grass, needle, small feather, or other object into a pipe stem and blew it into the desired area. Sorcerers could also "shoot" bones into the bodies of their victims, or cause harm by pointing and chanting in the person's direction. These practices were consistent with Kiowa etiology that illness was caused by intrusive supernatural entities, oftentimes sent by shamans practicing sorcery. The well-documented deaths of Kicking Bird in 1875 and Joshua Given in 1893 under mysterious circumstances have been attributed to shamans punishing them for allegedly betraying the Kiowa people.

Once smitten by malign magic, part of the cure involved identifying the culprit, who might avoid the victim, or treat him especially well to cover his sorcery. If the perpetrator was unknown, certain shamans were hired to perform divination ceremonies involving the placement of black handkerchiefs over their eyes while examining the patient's body. The hope was that a suspect would be named, his poisonous *gietso* sucked out, spat into a fire, and destroyed. After the sorcerer's identity was revealed, there were several options: he was stalked and forced to rescind the spell at gunpoint; or the services of a more powerful shaman were engaged to bewitch him. To this day, the Kiowa believe that those engaging in sorcery would eventually succumb to malevolent powers, bringing about their own demise.

Unlike shamans, who possessed curing *dw'dw'* and employed individualized healing techniques, keepers of the eleven tribal bundles offered spiritual assistance and intervention in personal and tribal affairs; individually and collectively, they performed sacred rituals in behalf of the Kiowa people. Keepers of the ten "boy medicine" bundles, or Ten Medicines, were holy men who prayed for everyone's welfare, especially in the early spring, when Thunder first appeared. Individual keepers were often summoned to pray for sick persons being doctored by shamans, and in the winter encampment, people brought offerings of scalps, tobacco, calico, blankets, beads, dried meat, buckskin, or sticks symbolizing horses to an owner's tepee and placed them on the bundle with prayer requests. Sick persons were then allowed to inhale the contents of the inner bundle, after loosening the outer covering. The next morning, the keeper kept some of the offerings or gave them to relatives, and summoned children to eat the meat for well-being and longevity. Symbolically, gifts to one bundle were inclusive to all ten, so a popular offering was ten balls of meat.

Ten Medicines keepers also served as tribal civil servants, because their services were solicited to facilitate conflict resolution. Whenever disputes arose in the encampments, relatives of one of the aggrieved parties dispatched a gift-bearing relative to find the nearest keeper.

Leading several horses, or carrying presents for the opposing party, the kinsman pleaded for the keeper to fill his long-stemmed pipe with tobacco, seek out the disputing factions, and offer them the lighted pipe—a request impossible to refuse, because smoking together symbolized the agreement to resolve their differences, as witnessed by the spirit world that was contacted by the smoke carrying the prayers of the Ten Medicines keeper.

The keeper of the sacred Taime Sun Dance bundle, the *Taimek'i*, "Taime man," prayed for the people, as did the Ten Medicines keepers. Likewise, gifts and prayer requests were brought to Taime, and sometimes Taime was invited to sweatlodge ceremonies for one of the Ten Medicines. Most important were pledges to erect medicine lodges for Taime, signifying a forthcoming Sun Dance in mid-June. The Sun Dance—not necessarily an annual ceremony because of extraneous factors such as drought, bison availability, and the presence of enemies—was performed to regenerate the buffalo herds and the Kiowa people. During the six-week period following the aggregation of the dispersed Kiowa bands into a single encampment and concluding with the three-and-a-half-day Sun Dance proper, the *Taimek'i* became the high priest overseeing all activities. Under his authority violence was prohibited, based on the belief that any bloodshed would attenuate the ceremony. In addition, only communal bison hunting was permitted, since solitary hunters dispersed the bison herds before enough animals could be dispatched to feed the assembled bands.

The Kiowa Sun Dance has not been performed in its entirety since 1887, although the Taime bundle still exists, as do the Ten Medicines, which are still consulted with prayer requests. Indeed, Kiowa belief systems have changed over the last century, with the advent of Christianity, the Native American Church, and other religious movements filling the void following the demise of the Sun Dance. Today, *dw'dw'* assumes many guises as spiritual and ceremonial practitioners—whether shamans or ministers—continue ministering to people's needs.

Benjamin R. Kracht

See also Bundles, Sacred Bundle Traditions; Dreams and Visions; Power, Plains; Sacred Societies, Plains; Vision Quest Rites

References and Further Reading

Albers, Patricia C. 2001. "Santee." Pp. 761–776 in *Handbook of North American Indians: Plains*, vol. 13. Edited by Raymond J. DeMallie. Washington, DC: Smithsonian Institution Press.

Bailey, Garrick A. 2001. "Osage." Pp. 476–496 in *Handbook of North American Indians: Plains*, vol. 13. Edited by Raymond J. DeMallie. Washington, DC: Smithsonian Institution Press.

Bailey, Garrick A., and Gloria A. Young. 2001. "Kansa." Pp. 462–475 in *Handbook of North American Indians: Plains*, vol. 13. Edited by Raymond J. DeMallie. Washington, DC: Smithsonian Institution Press.

Blaine, Martha Royce. 1979. *The Ioway Indians*. Norman: University of Oklahoma Press.

Brown, Donald N., and Lee Irwin. 2001. "Ponca." Pp. 416–431 in *Handbook of North American Indians: Plains*, vol. 13. Edited by Raymond J. DeMallie. Washington, DC: Smithsonian Institution Press.

Darnell, Regna. 2001. "Plains Cree." Pp. 638–651 in *Handbook of North American Indians: Plains*, vol. 13. Edited by Raymond J. DeMallie. Washington, DC: Smithsonian Institution Press.

DeMallie, Raymond J. 2001a. "Yankton and Yanktonai." Pp. 777–793 in *Handbook of North American Indians: Plains*, vol. 13. Edited by Raymond J. DeMallie. Washington, DC: Smithsonian Institution Press.

———. 2001b. "Teton." Pp. 794–820 in *Handbook of North American Indians: Plains*, vol. 13. Edited by Raymond J. DeMallie. Washington, DC: Smithsonian Institution Press.

DeMallie, Raymond J., and David Reed Miller. 2001. "Assiniboine." Pp. 572–595 in *Handbook of North American Indians: Plains*, vol. 13. Edited by Raymond J. DeMallie. Washington, DC: Smithsonian Institution Press.

Dempsey, Hugh A. 2001a. "Blackfoot." Pp. 604–628 in *Handbook of North American Indians: Plains*, vol. 13. Edited by Raymond J. DeMallie. Washington, DC: Smithsonian Institution Press.

———. 2001b. "Sarcee." Pp. 629–637 in *Handbook of North American Indians: Plains*, vol. 13. Edited by Raymond J. DeMallie. Washington, DC: Smithsonian Institution Press.

Foster, Morris W., and Martha McCollough. 2001. "Plains Apache." Pp. 926–940 in *Handbook of North American Indians: Plains*, vol. 13. Edited by Raymond J. DeMallie. Washington, DC: Smithsonian Institution Press.

Fowler, Loretta. 2001. "Arapaho." Pp. 840–862 in *Handbook of North American Indians: Plains*, vol. 13. Edited by Raymond J. DeMallie. Washington, DC: Smithsonian Institution Press.

Fowler, Loretta, and Regina Flannery. 2001. "Gros Ventre." Pp. 677–694 in *Handbook of North American Indians: Plains,* vol. 13. Edited by Raymond J. DeMallie. Washington, DC: Smithsonian Institution Press.

Frey, Rodney. 1987. *The World of the Crow Indians: As Driftwood Lodges.* Norman: University of Oklahoma Press.

Getty, Ian A. L., and Erik D. Gooding. 2001. "Stoney." Pp. 596–603 in *Handbook of North American Indians: Plains,* vol. 13. Edited by Raymond J. DeMallie. Washington, DC: Smithsonian Institution Press.

Irwin, Lee. 1994. *The Dream Seekers: Native American Visionary Traditions of the Great Plains.* Norman: University of Oklahoma Press.

Kavanagh, Thomas W. 2001. "Comanche." Pp. 886–906 in *Handbook of North American Indians: Plains,* vol. 13. Edited by Raymond J. DeMallie. Washington, DC: Smithsonian Institution Press.

Kracht, Benjamin R. 2000. "Kiowa Religion in Historical Perspective." Pp. 236–255 in *Native American Spirituality: A Critical Reader.* Edited by Lee Irwin. Lincoln: University of Nebraska Press.

LaBarre, Weston, Donald Collier, Jane Richardson, William Bascom, Bernard Mishkin, and Alexander Lesser. 1935. "Notes on Kiowa Ethnography." Washington, DC: National Anthropological Archives, Smithsonian Institution.

Levy, Jerrold E. 2001. "Kiowa." Pp. 907–925 in *Handbook of North American Indians: Plains,* vol. 13. Edited by Raymond J. DeMallie. Washington, DC: Smithsonian Institution Press.

Liberty, Margot P., W. Raymond Wood, and Lee Irwin. 2001. "Omaha." Pp. 399–415 in *Handbook of North American Indians: Plains,* vol. 13. Edited by Raymond J. DeMallie. Washington, DC: Smithsonian Institution Press.

Merrill, William L., Marian Kaulaity Hansson, Candace S. Greene, and Frederick J. Reuss. 1997. *A Guide to the Kiowa Collections at the Smithsonian Institution.* Smithsonian Contributions to Anthropology, no. 40. Washington, DC: Smithsonian Institution Press.

Mooney, James. 1891–1904. "Kiowa Heraldry Notebook: Descriptions of Kiowa Tipis and Shields." Washington, DC: National Anthropological Archives, Smithsonian Institution.

Moore, John H., Margot P. Liberty, and Terry Straus. 2001. "Cheyenne." Pp. 863–885 in *Handbook of North American Indians: Plains,* vol. 13. Edited by Raymond J. DeMallie. Washington, DC: Smithsonian Institution Press.

Newcomb, William W., Jr. 2001. "Wichita." Pp. 548–566 in *Handbook of North American Indians: Plains,* vol. 13. Edited by Raymond J. DeMallie. Washington, DC: Smithsonian Institution Press.

Parks, Douglas R. 2001a. "Arikara." Pp. 365–390 in *Handbook of North American Indians: Plains,* vol. 13. Edited by Raymond J. DeMallie. Washington, DC: Smithsonian Institution Press.

———. 2001b. "Pawnee." Pp. 515–547 in *Handbook of North American Indians: Plains,* vol. 13. Edited by Raymond J. DeMallie. Washington, DC: Smithsonian Institution Press.

Schweitzer, Marjorie M. 2001. "Otoe and Missourai." Pp. 447–461 in *Handbook of North American Indians: Plains,* vol. 13. Edited by Raymond J. DeMallie. Washington, DC: Smithsonian Institution Press.

Stewart, Frank Henderson. 2001. "Hidatsa." Pp. 329–348 in *Handbook of North American Indians: Plains,* vol. 13. Edited by Raymond J. DeMallie. Washington, DC: Smithsonian Institution Press.

Voget, Fred W. 2001. "Crow." Pp. 695–717 in *Handbook of North American Indians: Plains,* vol. 13. Edited by Raymond J. DeMallie. Washington, DC: Smithsonian Institution Press.

Wedel, Mildred Mott. 2001. "Iowa." Pp. 432–446 in *Handbook of North American Indians: Plains,* vol. 13. Edited by Raymond J. DeMallie. Washington, DC: Smithsonian Institution Press.

Wood, W. Raymond, and Lee Irwin. 2001. "Mandan." Pp. 349–364 in *Handbook of*

North American Indians: Plains, vol. 13. Edited by Raymond J. DeMallie. Washington, DC: Smithsonian Institution Press.

Young, Gloria A., and Michael P. Hoffman. 2001. "Quapaw." Pp. 497–514 in *Handbook of North American Indians: Plains,* vol. 13. Edited by Raymond J. DeMallie. Washington, DC: Smithsonian Institution Press.

Spiritual and Ceremonial Practitioners, Plateau

The physical landscape among the Plateau people is a world deeply imbued with spiritual qualities. Spiritual life is not separate from mundane existence, as all entities, actions, and phenomena occurring within the physical world have a spiritual connection. These close relationships are often recognized through ceremonies utilized to facilitate life transitions and offer necessary prayers.

Because of the rich physical and spiritual landscape the Plateau people embodied, spiritual and ceremonial practitioners were involved in the numerous realms of their existence. The ceremonial practitioners were responsible for conducting or facilitating the diverse number of ceremonies within the Plateau region. In addition to using their powers for curing, spiritual practitioners conducted individual or communitywide ceremonies including the first food ceremonies, Winter Spirit Dances, love rituals, war ceremonies, and gambling rituals. "The weather is controlled, fish are made to run, lost articles and thefts discovered, the fate of a war party is foreseen, and the community is protected against malignant spirits" (Spier and Sapir 1930, 118). There often were several practitioners within each particular band or cultural group, specializing in a particular domain. Because they possessed only select specialties, most spiritual practitioners did not practice all the above ceremonies. Only those with the proper spiritual powers were allowed to conduct specific ceremonies.

Ray (1939) reported that the quest to obtain Spirit Helpers and become a doctor was identical to that of a layperson's spirit quest, except that the doctor is distinguished by his amount of power and the results that power was able to obtain. Men and women doctors, known as *twatima* within the Western Columbia River Sahaptin, were recognized as possessing "extraordinary spiritual powers by virtue of numerous and particularly powerful spirit allies gained through a charismatic calling and repeated vision questing" (Hunn et al. 1998, 388).

Despite the strength of a practitioner's power or how many Guardian Spirits he may possess, other attributes must be present to differentiate a doctor from a layperson. An individual was not considered a capable practitioner unless he had received a specific spirit, had been commissioned by the spirit during a vision quest, or had received the power by heredity (Ray 1939, 93).

An individual's spiritual powers were known to most members of the community. Often practitioners gave performances to demonstrate the strength of their powers during community events or ceremonies such as the Winter Spirit Dances. Occasionally, rivalries would develop between doctors, and claims of superior power were made. Tricks would be played against other doctors, attempting to usurp or undermine their power.

At times, doctors might be accused of causing sickness, a serious accusation that could result in the death of the offending doctor. Spiritual practitioners that were known to have intentionally used their powers to kill were called *wataytam,* or sorcerers, among Western Columbia River Sahaptin (Hunn et al. 1998). Unnatural illnesses or events caused by magical poisoning are called *ptax* by the Lillooet. The power of *ptax,* practiced by women of postmenopausal age, can be used to alter events for both good and evil ends (Kennedy and Bouchard 1998).

Healing Practitioners
It was commonly accepted that illness was caused by natural or supernatural causes, although most illness among the Plateau people was considered spiritual in origin. Principal explanations for illness could include spirit or soul loss, intentional or unintentional spirit intrusion, object intrusion, moral transgressions, or spirit possession (Hunn et al. 1998; Ross 1998).

In the event of an illness, curing practitioners, known as *Idiaxi'lalit* among the Wishram (Spier and Sapir 1930) or *twati* by the Yakama, were called upon to provide diagnosis, prognosis, and treat-

ment. A curing practitioner would consult with his or her Spirit Helper to determine the cause of the illness or the sorcerer responsible for causing it. Treatment could include manipulation, sucking at the site of illness, sweating, smudging, dancing, singing, giving the patient medicine to drink, massaging the area of illness, and extracting the foreign substance from the body and plunging it into water to render it harmless (Ross 1998; Schuster 1998, Spier and Sapir 1930; Walker 1998). Ross (1998) characterizes the curing rituals as psychodramas in which practitioners employed ventriloquism, hypnotism, legerdemain, and demonstrated their power through glossolalia, various dramatic and even painful proofs of ordeal, or by transformation (280).

An enormous amount of pressure was placed upon the healer. "Because a medicine doctor has the potential to help or cause harm, a great deal of ambivalence surrounded his role" (Schuster 1998, 342). An unsuccessful doctor could be accused of being a sorcerer or be judged as being careless or inept. Such an individual could be killed by the patient's family (Schuster 1998).

The most important ceremonial practitioner among the Nez Perce, the *tiwét,* was known to cure illness (Walker 1998). Among the Umatilla the most feared of spiritual practitioners were the *isxipin,* whose powers derived from the tutelary of a dead shaman or from his own ghost. Their powers were very dangerous.

Through their powers of divining, an *isxipin* was able to locate lost objects and foretell future or distant events (Stern 1998a, 411).

Among the Nez Perce the *'isxíipit* was highly respected and played a role that involved several complex attributes. Walker (1998) notes that "this shaman was temperamental, much opposed to disorder, and very desirous of property. If an *'isxíipit* shaman commented on the attractiveness of an object belonging to another, it was advisable that it be given up immediately. Otherwise, he would become offended and sick, sometimes going into a tantrum in which he might lose control, cutting himself and cursing the object's possessor" (426).

Lewis and Clark encountered an *'isxíipit* while passing through Nez Perce country. William Clark wrote in his journal: "Tuesday October 9th . . . The Indians and our party were very mery this after noon a woman faind madness &c. &c. Singular acts of this woman in giving in Small potions all She had & if they were not received. She would Scarrify her Self in a horid manner &c. . . ." (Clark 2001).

Members of the expedition concluded that this woman was crazy because she started giving away all her possessions, went into incantations, slashed herself, and passed out. A Nez Perce consultant discusses the nature of *'isxíipit.*

> And what this is, is that you want to increase your knowledge of something or some people or some person and the way to do that is to confront them and make yourself humble and try to increase your knowledge of a particular thing or human being. This is what she was doing and to see if Lewis and Clark were really the people they really said they were. Are they bringing peace, are they bringing these good things to us and are they going to treat us well? This is what she was trying to find out. There is a reason why she did that. She wanted to gain knowledge about these strange people and that's the way she was doing it. (http://www.L3-lewisandclark.com)

Food-Related Ceremonies

It is believed that the spiritual and ceremonial practitioners' most important task lay in maintaining the series of seasonal, religious ceremonials (Walker 1998). Ceremonies often followed or were structured upon the seasonal round. Among the Coeur d'Alene, the people would come together to celebrate the first gathering of berries, roots, or salmon of the year. Spring marked the first salmon and roots ceremony. During the summer, the ceremonial gathering of the first fruits was celebrated. Autumn often marked various hunting ceremonies. The nature of these specific ceremonies embraced and reflected the essential teachings of the first people.

Gathering of the particular fruit or root was not allowed until the first fruits ceremony had been held. Before any hunting, fishing, berry-picking, or root-digging season was initiated, a prayer was offered giving thanks to the Creator as well as the plant or animal and asking for a plentiful harvest. A simple ceremony called *skpu'tenem* among the Sanpoil and Nespelem was performed during the initial gathering of the first fruits and roots. All were called together for an offering of thanks and for a feast of the particular food (Ray 1932).

The Kootenai celebrated the Grizzly Bear Dance. Held at the beginning of the berry-picking season, this three-night dance served as a prayer for plenty. The power of the Grizzly Bear was called upon because berries are its primary source of food. A special spiritual practitioner, known as the Grizzly Bear shaman, facilitated the ceremony (Turney-High 1941).

The salmon season was initiated with the first salmon ceremony, known as *snxa'wi'lem* among the Sanpoil. This multiday celebration brought many people together to feast and celebrate the arrival of the salmon. A ceremonial headman, known as the Salmon Chief, or *xa'tu's*, was in charge of the selection of materials for the traps and the collection, proper butchering, and distribution of the salmon. It was the duty of the *xa'tu's* to see that no salmon were taken before the *snxa'wi'lem* ceremony had been performed. It was also his responsibility to ensure that all fish were distributed equally (Ray 1932).

The Southern Okanogan believed that Coyote taught the First Salmon Ceremony to their ancestors. It is believed that "Coyote said the ceremony should be done so, and so it is" (Cline 1938, 17). Throughout the Plateau, the First Salmon Ceremony is necessary to guarantee the salmon runs. If the First Salmon Ceremony is not observed the salmon might not return in the future: Salmon traveled a long distance for the Indian people, and recognition of the Salmon's sacrifice is essential (Cline 1938).

Additional ceremonies included songs and rituals associated with hunting and the various stages of butchering. When food was scarce, ceremonial practitioners with the proper powers would lead specific ceremonies to bring game, particularly deer, to their people.

War Ceremonies

A war dance or ceremony was held to seek supernatural protection during battle, to predict success, to enlist recruits, or as a procession before battle or after victory. An individual with specific war powers would pray and sing for the success of the war party. Depending on the cultural group, those going on the war party would join in with the same song, or sing their own Guardian Spirit song. A war shaman did not have to be the leader of the war party to lead a war-related ceremony (Ray 1932).

Stick or Hand Game Practitioners

The Stick Game is a widespread game of skill and chance that has been played since precontact times. Games can take place in any location, often occurring whenever there is a large gathering of people, such as at first food ceremonies or at powwows. The game consists of two teams sitting in a row and facing each other. The object of the game is to guess in which hand an opposing team member is hiding the striped bone or stick. A correct guess wins a stick from the opposing team. The winning team is the one that acquires all the opposing team's sticks. As play commences, songs are sung and other personal rituals are practiced so as to bring forth one's power in guessing or deceiving the opposing team. Stick game players often possess distinct powers or songs specific to bone handling or guessing. For the Plateau, "all material manifestations are mirrored in spirit. It is thus understandable that the stick game is not merely a material event. The ideas of spirit and power are as much a part of the game as is strategy" (Brunton 1998, 579).

Winter Spirit Dance

The Winter Spirit Dances were occasions for those with spirit power to sing their spirit songs and dance. The purposes of the Winter Spirit Dances were to give thanks, honor one's Guardian Spirit, cure illness, ask for protection and healing, and gain good fortune for the upcoming year. During the Winter Spirit Dances, those with Spirit Helpers would often renew their connection with their Spirits, as well as provide an opportunity for validating the Spirit power of novices.

Each midwinter, individuals attending the Winter Dances would sing their power songs and dance in honor of their Spirit Helper. The various spiritual and ceremonial practitioners, such as healers and the hunting and salmon leaders, would sing their particular power songs during curing ceremonies and ask for a successful deer hunt or salmon catch (http://www.L3-lewisandclark.com).

Spiritual leaders sponsored Winter Spirit Dances, acted as masters of ceremony, and helped those with new Spirit Helpers express their spirit powers in dance and song (Hunn et al. 1998; Kennedy and Bouchard 1998). Among the Yakama, the *twati* helped the neophyte bring out the power he or she had received and express it at the Winter Spirit Dance (Schuster 1998).

Aaron Denham

See also Ceremony and Ritual, Nez Perce; Spirits and Spirit Helpers, Plateau; Vision Quest Rites

References and Further Reading
Brunton, Bill B. 1998. "Kootenai." Pp. 223–237 in *Handbook of North American Indians: Plateau,* vol. 12. Edited by Deward E. Walker, Jr. Washington, DC: Smithsonian Institution Press.
Clark, William. 2001. *The Journals of Lewis and Clark,* vol. 5. Edited by Gary Moulton. Lincoln: University of Nebraska Press.
Cline, Walter. 1938, "The Subsistence Quest." Pp. 9–34 in *The Sinkaietk or Southern Okanagon of Washington.* Edited by Leslie Spier. Menasha, WI: George Banta.
Frey, Rodney. 2002. *The World of the Schitsu'umsh (Coeur d'Alene Indians): Landscape Traveled by Crane and Coyote.* Seattle: University of Washington Press.

Kennedy, Dorothy I. D., and Randall T. Bouchard. 1998. "Northern Okanagan, Lakes, and Colville." Pp. 238–252 in *Handbook of North American Indians: Plateau*, vol. 12. Edited by Deward E. Walker, Jr. Washington, DC: Smithsonian Institution Press.

Life Long Learning Online. "The Lewis and Clark Rediscovery Project." http://www .l3-lewisandclark.com/ShowOneObject .asp?SiteID=34&ObjectID=139. (Accessed July 28, 2002.)

Ray, Verne F. 1932. *The Sanpoil and Nespelem: Salishan Peoples of Northwestern Washington.* Seattle: University of Washington Press.

———. 1939. *Cultural Relations in the Plateau of Northwestern America.* Los Angeles: Southwest Museum Administrator of the Fund.

Ross, John A. 1998. "Spokane." Pp. 271–282 in *Handbook of North American Indians: Plateau*, vol. 12. Edited by Deward E. Walker, Jr. Washington, DC: Smithsonian Institution Press.

Schuster, Helen H. 1998. "Yakima and Neighboring Groups." Pp. 327–351 in *Handbook of North American Indians: Plateau*, vol. 12. Edited by Deward E. Walker, Jr. Washington, DC: Smithsonian Institution Press.

Spier, Leslie. 1930. *Klamath Ethnography.* Berkeley: University of California Press.

Spier, Leslie, and Edward Sapir. 1930. *Wishram Ethnography.* Seattle: University of Washington Press.

Stern, Theodore. 1998a. "Cayuse, Umatilla, and Walla Walla." Pp. 395–419 in *Handbook of North American Indians: Plateau*, vol. 12. Edited by Deward E. Walker, Jr. Washington, DC: Smithsonian Institution Press.

———. 1998b. "Klamath and Modoc." Pp. 446–466 in *Handbook of North American Indians: Plateau*, vol. 12. Edited by Deward E. Walker, Jr. Washington, DC: Smithsonian Institution Press.

Turney-High, Harry Holbert. 1941. *Ethnography of the Kutenai.* Mensha, WI: American Anthropological Association.

Walker, Deward E., Jr., ed. 1998. *Handbook of North American Indians: Plateau*, vol. 12. Washington, DC: Smithsonian Institution Press.

Spiritual and Ceremonial Practitioners, Southeast

Whether one uses the term medicine man, shaman, healer, conjurer, or priest—all have been rejected, both by scholars and practitioners themselves— the Southeast presents a dizzying variety of traditional spiritual specialists. To take but one culture, some labels in the Cherokee culture are *adawehi* ("one who goes about freely," magician, conjurer, counselor, wiseman), *kuniakati* (wound doctor; lit.: "he follows the arrow"), *uku* (priest; lit.: "owl"), *nunnehi* (Little People, fairies, immortals, and those who communed with them—for example, Beloved Woman Nancy Ward [Nanyehi, Ghigau, or Tsitunagiski, ca. 1738–1824]), *dinadanu(n)wiski* (conjurer, healer, curer), and *(a)tskili* (witch, owl, shapeshifter, sorcerer). All healers ascribe their powers and any success they may have to a gift from the Creator. There were also some highly specialized practitioners, such as eagle-feather gatherers (Cherokee) and bone pickers (Choctaw Buzzard Cult).

The most powerful practitioner in the prehistoric Native world was a Southeastern woman. Big Jar (Ko-ke-lus), queen of the Calusa Indians in Spanish

Florida, was reputed to know the secrets of the ages. She was summoned by the Natchez Indians to cure unfamiliar diseases introduced by the French, died at the age of 110, and is buried in a mound built for her palace on the Tennessee River, near Hurricane Mills, Tennessee.

Until the American Indian Freedom of Religion Act became law in 1979, the practice of Native religion and ceremonies was illegal in the United States. Traditional healers and seers were trained secretly, often under the guise of learning card tricks. Apprenticeship could last seven years or more, and enormous feats of memory were required. Today many practitioners are dying without having trained a follower.

Chief Billy, a Seminole healer, was employed as a consultant by the pharmaceutical industry because of his vast range of knowledge concerning herbal drugs. However, by the time his pharmacological virtuosity was tapped in the mid-1990s, the majority of the plants known to him were no longer to be found growing anywhere.

Southeastern tribes are credited with having introduced tobacco (a Cherokee monopoly, used extensively as an antiseptic until the last century), goldenseal (which grows best in the Blue Ridge Mountains), ginseng (traded to the Chinese since the Han dynasty), and echinacea (the term is thought to derive from the Cherokee language). Southeastern tribes also understood the concepts of hygiene and holistic, diagnostic, and preventive medicine.

Herbs were not named or classified as in Western science, nor were they thought to have only one beneficial principle or to operate on just one part of the body. Most uses were regulatory, systemic, and restorative. Herbs were divided into men's and women's medicine. Confusingly to modern people, the same name might be used for a dozen different species; only an herb walk with the practitioner will sort them out. For instance, in Cherokee, *tsoliyusti* can refer to mullein or any tobacco-like plant.

The difference between a spiritual healer (shaman) and herbal healer (often "root doctor") lies in their respective tool chests. The former invoke spiritual forces and helpers to defeat the spiritual and material causes of disease, often traveling to the upper or lower world and suffering a symbolic death. Varieties depend on the different spirit guides, helpers, powers, experience, training and divining abilities. For instance, there might be a spirit healer with spider medicine. All are trained as the sole successor of a master healer and are usually chosen early in life. Herbalists drew on their knowledge of plants, prescribed in the form of smudges, teas, tinctures, topicals, and powders, and often chewed, applied with spittle, blown through a tube, or otherwise applied in a hands-on fashion. Significantly, their knowledge is proprietary and hereditary, often commanding handsome fees.

Dhyani Ywahoo (Etowah Band Cherokee) claims to be the twenty-seventh of her lineage to practice her particular philosophy of spiritual wellness. According to her book, she was instructed by her grandfather, Eonah Fisher, who received the teachings from his father-in-law, Eli Ywahoo. Vernon Cooper, a Lumbee "faith doctor" alive in 1995, is a good example of the combination of the two types of practice with Bible Belt Christianity. Many traditionalists became ministers of the Gospel, whether out of sincerity or subterfuge. For instance, Black Fox (Enola) of Wolftown, North Carolina, became a Methodist minister in 1848.

Conventionally, a diagnosis is first performed, the traditional fee being one dressed deerskin. Later this was commuted to a blanket. Most scrupulous practitioners operate on the basis of permission. If they do not have spiritual permission to heal, or the treatment is not within their scope of activities, the deerskin is returned. A diagnosis may take several days. The traditional answer to repeated queries is "I have taken it to the spirit lodge." The religious basis of all Native medicine is thus apparent. Moreover, treatments work in the original (sacred) Native language only, though some would say they work *best* that way.

Every nation, tribe, clan, band, and family maintained its own specific remedies. In this respect, Southeastern Indian society was egalitarian and nonspecialist. The woman was usually the guardian of a family's nostrums. Every individual knew the virtues of a handful of herbs for self-medication. Nearly everyone carried a medicine pouch with at least some tobacco, a protector stone or fetish, and a snakebite cure. The occupation of healer was rarely pursued as one's sole livelihood but rather combined with being a farmer, hunter, and warrior.

Nicolas Chiviliu Tacaxoy, the Tzutujil Mayan shaman described in Prechtel's *Secrets of the Talking Jaguar* (1998), ran many businesses in his hometown of Santiago Atitlan in Guatemala, becoming a principal chief and one of its richest citizens. Typical of his profession, he was said to have been a high liver, not particularly saintly or even honest, and with many enemies.

A certain degree of showmanship or magic went with the turf. To keep a parrot, even among northern Indians, was a medicine man's privilege, equivalent to hanging out a shingle. In prehistoric villages, the shaman's lodge was often on the edge of town; he was regarded as irascible and antisocial. Sequoyah was disliked. Yet the practitioner's standing in the eyes of the village could rise very high. In many tribes, the roles of priest and king were united. One of the time-honored duties was purifying young men for the warpath and conferring military decorations upon their return. European soldiers had standing orders to shoot the "medicine men" and "witch doctors" first, the effect proving most demoralizing.

Shamanism is international, and there appears to be a silent code of recognition and cooperation among its practitioners. You might have a convention of shamans from Africa, South America, and Siberia, and they would all understand each other. Mooney notes conjurers' exchange of secrets, mercenary interests, and competitive tensions. When Cherokee medicine men learned that the Potawatomi had lost their lands and possessions, they set out from the Tennessee mountains to bring herbs, formulas, and ceremonial objects. By the same token, Indians in the Southeast were open to revivalists from other tribes. The Plains Ghost Dance religion popularized among the Cheyenne and Sioux by Wovoka, a Paiute, can be traced to Cherokee antecedents in the age of Dragging Canoe and White Path. Native religion was thus ecumenical and synthesizing.

The range of an old-time Cherokee shaman was large. In 1887, Mooney's principal informant, Swimmer (Ayunini, d. 1899), had a 240-page book of old prayers, songs, and prescriptions covering the following subjects: herb gathering songs, medicine preparation songs, divination, worms, chills, rheumatism, frostbites, snakebites, black and yellow bile, childbirth, wounds, bad dreams, witchery, love charms, fishing charms, and hunting charms (for which he charged patients $5 apiece), as well as prayers to make corn grow, to frighten away storms, to drive off witches, to destroy life, to help warriors, to know one's place of death, for long life, for safety among strangers, and for acquiring influence in council and success in the ballplay.

A Muskogee medicine man from modern-day Oklahoma, Marcellus Williams (Bear Heart), was able to produce snow for a Colorado ski resort and cause choking fits from a distance in those with evil intentions. Rolling Thunder (John Pope, Cherokee, 1916–1996), a brakeman for the Southern Pacific Railroad during most of his life, cured a woman of multiple sclerosis; acted as spiritual advisor to pop singer Bob Dylan, the Grateful Dead rock band, and Muhammad Ali; and caused it to rain on several Western Indian reservations. Jamake Highwater (probably Cherokee, foster name Jay Marks, ca. 1932–2001) was a prolific artist, crossing many boundaries, from poetry and philosophy to dance, music, and film.

Paul Russell (Two White Feathers, Tihanama-Potawatomi-Shawnee-Cherokee, b. Saginaw, Michigan, 1938), an elder of the Thunderbird Clan of the Tihanama people of middle Tennessee and southern Florida, is a spiritual healer, herbalist, principal chief (since 1990), storyteller and teacher, ceremony chief, conjurer, traditional grass and straight dancer, keeper of seer traditions, amateur astronomer and geophysicist, painter, leather worker, jeweler, mechanical engineer, computer programmer, third-level Midéwiwin Lodge priest, flute and drum maker, songwriter, singer, composer, recording artist, stone carver, potter, mask and mandela maker, knife maker and gunsmith, bow and arrow maker, and woodworker/carpenter. His wife, Penny Russell (Ojibwa-Seminole, b. Isabella Indian Reservation, 1939), is a Bear Clan mother, women's spiritual workshop leader, weaver, jeweler, bead-work artist, dreamcatcher maker, and dream consultant.

Space forbids describing divination processes among seer-healers or the paraphernalia used by them. However, one might mention crystals, cowry shell beads (which came from the Pacific), stargazing, snake handling, rattles (of gourd for men, tortoiseshell for women), drums (always one-sided for a shaman), mad stones, medicine sticks, protector stones, spirit brushes, tobacco, and greenstone pipes. Clients today are most interested in knowing about love matters, dream interpretation, and where they will die, most indigenous people being convinced that the time and place of their death is fixed and unalterable.

Donald Panther-Yates

See also Ceremony and Ritual, Southeast; Health and Wellness, Traditional Approaches; Oral Traditions, Southeast; Power, Southeast; Religious Leaders, Southeast; Spirits and Spirit Helpers, Plateau

References and Further Reading
Arden, Harvey, and Steve Wall. 1994. *Wisdomkeepers: Meetings with Native American Spiritual Elders.* Hillsboro, OR: Beyond Words Publishing.
Bear Heart (Marcellus Williams). 1996. *The Wind Is My Mother: The Life and Teachings of a Native American Shaman.* New York: Clarkson Potter.
Boyd, Doug. 1974. *Rolling Thunder: A Personal Exploration into the Secret Healing Powers of an American Indian Medicine Man.* New York: Random House.
Cabeza de Vaca, Alvar Nuñez. 1550. *Naufragios de Alvar Nuñez Cabeza de Vaca y Relación de la Jornada que hizo a la Florida con el Adelantado Panfilo de Narvaez.* English translation by Fanny Bandelier (1922): *Alvar Nuñez Cabeza de Vaca and His Companions, from Florida to the Pacific 1528–1538.* New York: Allerton Book Co.
Eliade, Mircea. 1964. *Shamanism: Archaic Techniques of Ecstasy.* Translated by Willard R. Trask. Princeton: Princeton University Press.
Gattuso, John, ed. 1993. *A Circle of Nations: Voices and Visions of American Indians: North American Native Writers and Photographers.* Hillsboro, OR: Beyond Words Publishing.
Halifax, Joan. 1980. *Shamanic Voices: A Survey of Visionary Narratives.* New York: Dutton.
Mails, Thomas E. 1992. *The Cherokee People: The Story of the Cherokees from Earliest Origins to Contemporary Times.* Tulsa, OK: Council Oaks Books.
Mooney, James. 1972. *Myths of the Cherokee and Sacred Formulas of the Cherokees.* Nashville, TN: C. Elder Bookseller.
Prechtel, Martin. 1998. *Secrets of the Talking Jaguar: Memoirs from the Living Heart of a Mayan Village.* New York: Penguin Putnam.
Swan, Jim. 1987. "Rolling Thunder at Work: A Shamanic Healing of Multiple Sclerosis." Pp. 145–157 in *Shamanism: An Expanded View of Reality.* Edited by Shirley Nicholson. Wheaton, IL: Theosophical Publishing House.
Ywahoo, Dhyani. 1987. *Voices of Our Ancestors: Cherokee Teachings from the Wisdom Fire.* Edited by Barbara Du Bois. Boston: Shambhala.

Spiritual and Ceremonial Practitioners, Southwest

The topic of spiritual and ceremonial practitioners in the American Southwest covers a broad range of cultures, practices, concepts, and beliefs. Historically, the "Southwest" is taken to mean the areas of Arizona and New Mexico, though many of the cultures in those states are also represented elsewhere to the immediate north and south. Perhaps the best-known cultures are the various "Pueblo" cultures, such as Hopi, Zuni, and the southern Athabascan groups of the Apache and Diné (Navajo). However, many other cultures are found within this region as well. Because of the great cultural diversity, this short essay cannot be a comprehensive study of the Southwest. Instead, the focus here will be a comparative overview of spiritual and ceremonial practitioners in the southern Athabascan cultures of the Apaches and Navajos.

Anthropological works on spiritual and ceremonial practitioners in the Southwest make use of a variety of indigenous terminology, titles, concepts, and names. However, equally as common are the uses of such generic terms as "shaman," "medicine man/woman," "healer," "singer/chanter," and even "priest." One of the goals of anthropology and the comparative study of cultures and religion has been to develop and employ non–culture specific terminology to facilitate general understanding and to ease the process of comparative research. Yet the use of such generic terms can obfuscate as much as it can educate, for in the process of rendering Native terms and concepts in generic terminology, the indigenous subtleties and nuances are often glossed over. In an effort to highlight the specific over the general, this essay will emphasize in-digenous concepts and how they might be glossed in English and related to more generic terms.

To begin, it is important to recognize that there is not simply one "Apache" culture within the Southwest, and that Navajo culture, while somewhat more uniform, also has wide latitude for variations and regional practices and understandings. Historically, "Apache" cultures, or *Inde*, "The People," have been grouped in the Southwest into "Western Apache"—such as the Cibecue Apache, White Mountain Apache, and San Carlos Apache in Arizona—and the "Eastern Apache"—such as the Chiricahua Apache, Mescalero Apache, Lipan Apache, and Jicarilla Apache. While Apache cultures share many aspects of ceremonial practices and oral tradition, each culture is unique. Some of the Eastern Apache, such as the White Mountain Apache, have been described as being somewhat closer to Navajo ceremonial practices than other Apache cultures, with their use of sand-paintings, while the Jicarilla Apache have been described as being more influenced by Pueblo ceremonialism than the Chiric-ahua or Mescalero. Among the Navajo, or *Diné*, "The People," families are grouped according to regional clans in which different ceremonial repertoires may be emphasized. Thus it is important to understand that diversity and variation are the norm and not the exception.

Several of the ceremonial practitioners in these Athabascan cultures, and Pueblo cultures as well, have been referred to as "priests" by many anthropologists—a

Little John, a revered Diné medicine man. Monument Valley, Arizona, 1994. (Arne Hodalic/Corbis)

concept that has been contrasted with "shamans" or "medicine people." This anthropological distinction has been made on the basis that certain ceremonies, such as Navajo "chants" or "chantways," and Navajo and Apache puberty ceremonies, are conducted by trained specialists who do not necessarily possess any particular spirit "power." Instead, such practitioners rely on codified bodies of knowledge, oral traditions, song repertoires, and ritual practices. In contrast, "medicine people" and "shamans" are those whose practice is more individualized and based on the practitioner's personal connection to some source of "power" or "spirit helper."

In both Apache and Navajo contexts, those who are classified as "priests" are almost always referred to as "singers" or "chanters" in the indigenous languages. Singers are identified as *gutaal'n* among the Chiricahua and Mescalero, *gokaalii* among the Jicarilla, and other linguistically related terms in the other Apache groups—all of which can be glossed in English as "one who sings/chants" or a "singer" or "chanter." Among the Navajo this same designation is found with the term *hataatli*. Such singers are generally contrasted in Apache cultures with *diyin,* or "holy people," commonly called "medicine people" or "shamans" in English and anthropological literature.

Diyin are individuals who have a personal connection with some source of spiritual power outside of themselves; they base their ceremonial or spiritual practices on this direct spiritual connection. The concept of *diyin* in Apache cultures should not be confused with the *Diyin Dine'é,* "Holy People," of the Navajo, which term refers to sacred personages in Navajo oral tradition.

Apache and Navajo singers perform preestablished ceremonials that often combine elements of recitation of oral traditions, the singing of a designated corpus of songs, and engaging in particular ceremonial activities such as the construction and use of sandpaintings, directing ceremonial dancers, and performing puberty ceremonials for young women. The overall emphasis in such ceremonial acts is on precision and correctness. Navajo "chantways," which are numerous, and Navajo and Apache puberty ceremonies are understood by Native practitioners to be re-creations of ceremonies that were originally established by sacred beings. To be considered authentic leaders of these ceremonies, individuals must apprentice themselves to experienced singers. During that apprenticeship, the novice is instructed on the proper procedures, oral traditions, songs, and ceremonial activities that are to take place within the ceremonial.

Such an apprenticeship is often a long and difficult process that requires an extreme dexterity of oral memory and recitation as well as, among the Navajo and some Western Apache, intricate memorization of the proper construction and use of highly elaborate sandpaintings and tradition-specific symbolism. Once that is mastered, the new singer is given the right to perform his (singers are most often males) new ceremony. He need not be inspired or directed by a spiritual power and does not generally enter into altered states of consciousness, though intense concentration is required. Furthermore, ceremonies performed by singers are not considered to be open to personal change or innovation. Singers should perform the ceremony as taught, for the ceremony is passed down in a lineage from the original "Holy People" to the contemporary practitioners. Such ceremonies are highly conservative, and any introduced change is widely regarded as improper, potentially invalidating of the ceremony and practitioner; it is also dangerous for practitioners and insulting to the spiritual powers.

In contrast to the "priestly" function of singers and chanters, Apaches use the designation of "holy person," or *diyin,* to indicate a practitioner who operates from individual spiritual inspiration. This term has most often been glossed as "shaman" or "medicine person" in the literature. When speaking English, many Apaches will use the term "medicine man/woman" when speaking of a *diyin,* and, in fact, that is a fairly reasonable gloss. *Diyi* has been translated as "power," "holy," "medicine," and so forth, depending on the context and the writer. A *diyin* is therefore "one who has power/medicine" or "one who is holy," and therefore "medicine person" is somewhat accurate. However, both Navajo and Apache ceremonial singers are often called "medicine men" as well, with Navajo singers currently forming the "Navajo Medicine Men's Association." The fact that such singers are also called "medicine men" can be a source of some confusion, especially when there is a contrasting indigenous term.

In Apache cultures, a *diyin* is someone who has had, and may continue to have, direct contact with spiritual forces, such as through dreams, visions, auditory experiences, and so forth, and who may be initiated either intentionally, such as through a vision fast, or through spontaneous spiritual experience. While a singer in the girl's puberty ceremonial or the Mountain Spirit ceremony may be *diyin*, that is not a necessity.

The practices of *diyin* tend to be highly individualized, as each practitioner follows his or her own spiritual inspiration. Even when two different practitioners claim to have a similar spirit power, it does not mean that their powers, abilities, or ceremonial actions and songs will be the same. It is widely understood that the power itself will instruct the individual in his or her practices, and thus those can be highly individualized. Even when a novice *diyin* apprentices himself to a more established *diyin*, which is common, the novice will introduce many personalized elements into his or her own practice, according to how the spirits and powers instruct. The abilities of *diyin* also vary greatly—from healing to diagnosing illness, performing protective ceremonies, finding lost objects, performing blessings, and so forth. Some *diyin* may emphasize treatment through herbs and roots, ceremonial procedures, or various healing practices such as sucking, blowing, removal of witchcraft objects, or any number of other culturally significant practices. Just as with doctors in the mainstream medical profession, *diyin* are understood to have specialties and primary interests. It should also be noted that there is a great deal of intercultural exchange in the Southwest, and that medicine people and singers commonly perform for people outside their specific culture.

The "medicine people" of the various Apache cultures tend to play more prominent roles within their cultures than the spiritually inspired practitioners in Navajo culture. Apache medicine people perform ceremonies, healings, and other common practices, whereas inspired practitioners in Navajo culture tend to perform more limited diagnostic functions. In English, such Navajo practitioners are referred to as "crystal" and "star gazers," "hand tremblers," and generically as "diagnosticians," such as those who use the vision-inducing datura plant. These practitioners tend to find lost objects and diagnose diseases according to indigenous disease etiology. The diagnostician will consult with spiritual forces or manipulate symbolic and spiritual elements to determine the cause and course of treatment for a disease. He or she then informs the patient of what ceremonial repertoire or chantway is required to bring about the restoration of balance and harmony, known as *hozho* in Navajo. Thereby the patient is referred to a singer or chanter who can perform the requisite ceremonial procedure to effect restoration.

Another highly significant aspect of Navajo and Apache ceremonial practice is the use of masked dancers. In Navajo culture, masked dancers often play a part in the performances of the various chantways. All chantways have sacred oral traditions to which they are related wherein the deeds and actions of various *Diyin Dine'é* are described and recounted. At specific portions of the chantways, masked dancers such as "Talking Gods" and "Calling Gods" and other personages may make a ceremonial appearance. Such dances are always performed by men, even when the personage represented is understood to be female.

One such Navajo masked dancer type is referred to as *hasch'ééh*, which has been compared to the Apache "Mountain Spirits" or "Mountain Gods." Terms for these figures vary in Apache cultures, with Western Apaches using the terms *gan, gaan,* and *ga'an;* Mescalero and Chiracahua tend to use *gaahe.* However, at times *hastchin, hactcin,* and *haastch'i* are also used by Apache cultures to indicate the Mountain Spirits. Each Apache culture has its own oral traditions describing the origins and natures of these

spiritual beings, and their visual appearance and ceremonial actions vary greatly from one Apache culture to the next. However, like Navajo masked dancers, the Mountain Spirits are danced by men and are commonly understood to possess the ability to bless, heal, and protect those for whom they dance.

While anthropologists have tended to associate both Apache and Navajo masked dancers with Pueblo influences, it is important to recognize that they should not be classified as "kachinas," as Pueblo masked dancers are generically designated; Pueblo masked dancers tend to be grouped into spiritual societies. Among the Apache, for example, Mountain Spirit dancers are separated according to dance group, led by a singer or medicine person, and generally not according to specific spiritual societies. Furthermore, whereas anthropologists have referred to both Navajo and Apache masked dancers, as well as Pueblo kachinas, as "impersonators" of mythological figures, the indigenous understandings emphasize embodiment of spiritual forces whereby the dancers are understood to directly manifest the powers of the spirit embodied in the dancer. In this sense, dancers are themselves transformed during the ceremonials into spiritually powerful beings.

Martin Ball

See also Art (Contemporary), Southwest; Bundles, Sacred Bundle Traditions; Ceremony and Ritual, Diné; Ceremony and Ritual, Pueblo; Clowns and Clowning;

Herbalism; Kachina and Clown Societies; Kiva and Medicine Societies; Masks and Masking; Oral Traditions, Pueblo; Religious Leaders, Southwest; Sandpainting; Vision Quest Rites; Yoeme (Yaqui) Deer Dance

References and Further Reading

Ball, Martin. 2000. "Sacred Mountains, Religious Paradigms, and Identity among the Mescalero Apache." *Worldviews, Environment, Religion, Culture* 4: 264, 282.

Basso, Keith H. 1970. *The Cibecue Apache.* New York: Holt, Rinehart and Winston.

Farella, John R. 1984. *The Main Stalk: A Synthesis of Navajo Philosophy.* Tucson: University of Arizona Press.

Farrer, Claire R. 1991. *Living Life's Circle: Mescalero Apache Cosmovision.* Albuquerque: University of New Mexico Press.

Goodwin, Grenville. 1938. "White Mountain Apache Religion." *American Anthropologist* 40: 24, 37.

Griffin-Pierce, Trudy. 1992. *Earth Is My Mother, Sky Is My Father: Space, Time, and Astronomy in Navajo Sandpainting.* Albuquerque: University of New Mexico Press.

Kelley, Klara Bonsack, and Harris Francis. 1994. *Navajo Sacred Places.* Bloomington: Indiana University Press.

Mails, Thomas E. 1974. *The People Called Apache.* Englewood Cliffs, NJ: Prentice Hall.

McNeley, James Kale. 1981. *Holy Wind in Navajo Philosophy.* Tucson: University of Arizona Press.

Opler, Morris Edward. 1941. *An Apache Life-Way.* Chicago: University of Chicago Press.

———. 1969. *Apache Odyssey.* New York: Holt, Rinehart and Winston.

Sandner, Donald. 1991. *Navaho Symbols of Healing.* Rochester: Healing Arts Press.

Witherspoon, Gary. 1977. *Language and Art in the Navajo Universe.* Ann Arbor: University of Michigan Press.

Sun Dance

The Sun Dance is a ceremony of community solidarity and renewal that is found among many Native American peoples of the Plains, Prairie, and Great Basin regions of North America. Dancers enter into a sacred structure in which they undergo ordeals that draw together personal resolve, community welfare, and cosmic spirits. The primary purpose for participation in this ceremonial is to acquire sacred power for the community. Generated through the sufferings of the dancers, this power is not simply personal. Rather, the creative potential of the Sun Dance flows throughout the community just as material wealth flows from redistribution rituals during and after this ceremonial. These traditional concepts of sacred power evoked in the Sun Dance relate to religious, economic, and social ideas and practices that are not separate from each other. Rather, religion, trade, and subsistence activities mutually interact as a lifeway that orbits around an axis of sacred power. Currently, some Native Americans associate the Sun Dance with resistance to the cultural dominance of mainstream America. Commercial exploitation of the phrase "Sun Dance" by non-Indians concerns traditional American Indians. In recent times Native Sun Dance leaders have brought non-Indians into this ceremony in both reservation settings and nontraditional locations such as Arizona, Oregon, Mexico, and Europe.

Great Plains Sun Dance lodge. Rocky Boy, Montana. 2003. (Marilyn "Angel" Wynn/Nativestock)

The tribal ceremonies referenced by the phrase "Sun Dance" are actually quite different, but there are several striking similarities—namely, they are communally based, cosmologically comprehensive, and personally transformative. Sun Dances are performed in particular seasons of the year, such as the full moon of late spring or early summer. Particular ceremonies were used as pictographic markers on buffalo robe calendars in the nineteenth century to record historic events. During the Sun Dance a sequence of rituals over a multiday period builds solidarity by evoking sacred powers to renew the community of all living beings. One such ritual is the discovery and capture of the cottonwood tree that becomes the center of the Sun Dance structure. The tree is addressed as a living person and often treated as an honored enemy. Among some people a ritual apology is offered to the birds that nest in the tree before it is cut down. The tree is then placed upright at the center of the designated Sun Dance grounds, where a lodge, corral, or arbors will be built. The center tree becomes the focus of prayer and the place for the experience of transformative power.

A redistribution of goods begins with extensive giveaways and feasts before and after Sun Dances, involving the participation of extended families, clans, and often the larger band or village community. Individuals who have had dreams or other experiences vow to dance in the ceremonial. Dancers undertake instruction by intercessors regarding the completion of their vows. Dancers determine to undergo bodily deprivation or physical pain as acts of commitment to the community and as the means to bring about visionary experiences. Typically, dancers attend sweatlodge ceremonies before the Sun Dance for purification and as a way to focus on the challenges they face.

The dancers' commitments parallel the distributive giving of the community, as well as the community's intentions to evoke those cosmological forces that created the world and sustain life. Such a spiritual presence is embodied in a buffalo skull or hide placed on the center pole or at its base as part of an altar. The lodge, moreover, is charged with cosmological symbolism in the number and arrangement of the timbers used in the structure. The dynamics of groups both within and without the lodge interweave, contest, and coordinate their spiritual roles to augment the power of the ceremonial. Families outside the lodge stand as witnesses to the sacrifice of the participants. Elders may sit at the entrance of the Sun Dance lodge in silent support of the dancers. Announcers may also be found at the eastern-facing entry of the Sun Dance lodge, calling out to the participants in encouragement and with instructions. Singers gathered around the drum sing personal power songs as well as traditional Sun Dance songs. The dancers themselves often coalesce in groups to care for one another physically, share tobacco in sacred pipe rituals, and provide the setting for the narration of personal experiences. At the back of the lodge or in designated arbors or teepees the sponsor, leaders, and healers at the Sun Dance form a special coterie of wisdom keepers and guides for the ceremony. Dancers often have face and body painting on different days of the Sun Dance that has clan and individual visionary significance. The roles and activities of all the participants and the attendant community manifest an exceptional religious intensity that is strikingly beautiful and deeply moving.

The phrase "Sun Dance" is first reported in a memoir of the trader Jean-Baptiste Trudeau. In 1794–1796 he noted that this ceremony was found among Sioux, Cheyenne, Arapaho, and neighboring tribes on the upper Missouri River. George Catlin also used the term in 1833 for a ceremony named *wiwanyang wacipi,* or "gazing at the sun." Catlin saw this ceremony at the mouth of the Teton River, held by a division of the Sioux (Lakota). In 1849, Mary Eastman described a ceremony of the Santee Dakota as a Sun Dance (Archambault 2001, 983). Since that time, the term has been used as a classificatory name for these diverse ceremonies. However, among the approximately thirty tribes known to have practiced such a ceremonial dance, few concentrated on the Sun or even referenced it during their ceremony.

The Sun Dance can be understood as having three historical phases. First, from the precontact period into the 1880s, different Native groups performed Sun Dances that manifested distinct tribal lifeways. These ceremonials undoubtedly changed with migratory pressures related to the early contact period with Euro-Americans. Intertribal warfare flared in response to the movements of peoples westward. Different Sun Dances display characteristics associated with clan revenge, warrior initiations, and renewal of the living world that accord with those dynamic and troubled centuries. Among the Crow and Kiowa, for example, obtaining a warrior vision revenging a clan death was a primary motivation for the dance. Among the Cheyenne, Lakota, and Arapaho, the Sun Dance was more of a community vision quest and initiation of warriors. Among the Shoshone, healers often competed during the ceremonial, both to demonstrate and to augment their curative powers. The Sun Dance definitely stands in continuity with established tribal understandings of creative powers associated with animals located in land, waters, sky, and adjacent realms of the cosmos.

From 1883, both the Canadian and U.S. governments suppressed the Sun Dances. For example, in 1883, Secretary of the Interior H. M. Teller wrote Commissioner of Indian Affairs Hiram Price, condemning the Sun Dance, medicine men, and traditionalists who supported them. The U.S. commissioner of Indian affairs sporadically acted in league with missionaries, Indian agents, and the military to ban all Indian ceremonials throughout this period.

In 1934 the Sun Dance was publicly revived with the passage by Congress of the Indian Religious Freedom and Indian Culture act. Revitalization was possible because several peoples, such as the Shoshone, Lakota, Cheyenne, and Arapaho, had taken the Sun Dance underground, performing it far from Indian police, government agents, and resident Christian missionaries.

While legislative action and more accepting attitudes eased pressures on the Sun Dance, it did not entirely eliminate the "Christianizing" and "civilizing" agendas that had suppressed the Sun Dance. Native leaders took the lead in reestablishing confidence in the public performance of the Sun Dance. From traditional dances among the Canadian Blackfeet/Blood, the Plains Cree, and Plains Ojibwa, the Sun Dance was restored to many Canadian tribes. Two indigenous restoration moments were primary in the resurgence of the Sun Dance. This first pulsation reverberated from the turn of the twentieth century, when several tribes resisted the suppression of Native American religious life by performing the Sun Dance and other ceremonials in remote areas. The second restorative pulse came in the 1960s, from intertribal political and religious movements on the Plains often associated with the American Indian Movement (AIM). The Sun Dance revival signaled a political renewal of Indian identity that attracted both Indian youth and non-Indians disaffected from the dominant society.

In 1870 at least nineteen groups were practicing the Sun Dance—namely, Blackfoot, Northern and Southern Cheyenne, Northern Arapaho, Gros Ventre, Plains Cree, Plains Ojibwa, Arikara, Sarcee, Kiowa, Hidatsa, Crow, Ponca, Assiniboine, Santee (Sisseton and Canadian Sioux), and Teton in the Plains; as well as the Eastern Shoshone and Ute in the Great Basin. The Omaha *Hedewachi,* the Pawnee "Four Pole" ceremony, and the Mandan *Okipa* are considered closely related ceremonies. It was reported by Margot Liberty in 1965 that Sun Dances among twelve of these groups were extinct. However, by the end of the twentieth century all but the Ponca, who held their last Sun Dance in 1908, had recovered their traditional dance or adopted a modified form of the ceremony from another tribe when their own original Sun Dance was lost. In addition, tribes like the Comanche, Kootenai, Mandan, Arikara, and Pawnee, which may not have practiced a traditional Sun Dance, obtained the ceremony from nearby Indian religious leaders.

Some of the names for the Sun Dance among tribal groups give some indication of the different perspectives on this ceremony. For example, the English phrase among the Ute, Shoshone, Plains Cree, and Plains Ojibwa is "thirsting dance" or "thirst lodge"; the Sioux and Ponca say "sun-gazing dance." The Assiniboine call this ceremony "lodge-making dance," whereas the Cheyenne name it the "new life lodge" or "medicine lodge ceremony." The Gros Ventre say "sacrifice lodge" or "prayer lodge," while the Arapaho call it "sacrifice lodge" or "offerings lodge." The old Crow Sun Dance, which is no longer practiced, was called the "fringed ankle dance" or "miniature lodge," whereas the ceremony acquired from the Shoshone in 1941 is called "imitation lodge." The Arikara call their ceremony "house of whistling." The Sioux and Ponca definitely reference the Sun in their name for their ceremony, but for other nations the Sun has little or no overt mention in their name for the ceremony. The Sun, however, is a major symbolic presence at Sun Dances that have a dawn greeting ritual.

Despite the ambiguity of the term "Sun Dance" in academic usage, the sheer volume of the literature on the Sun Dance warrants consideration and use of the term. Even more important, the pan-Indian movements of the twentieth century have led many Native American elders to emphasize the intertribal, and for some, the interracial foundations of their particular version of the Sun Dance (Yellowtail 1991, 177–183). It can be stressed, however, that the religious and spiritual dimensions of the Sun Dance are central and take precedence over any social or political interpretations. The religious aspects of the Sun Dance can be said to refer to the interwoven cultural, organizational, and logistical concerns whereby the ceremony is conducted. Spiritual dimensions suggest more personal and experiential interpretations that transmit the intentions and purposes of participants. The following sections explore these dimensions, especially in communal, cosmological, and personal expressions.

Communal Basis

The communal nature of the Sun Dance is evident in the following statement of Lakota elders in 1896: "The Sun Dance is the greatest ceremony that the Oglalas do. It is a sacred ceremony in which all the people have a part. It must be done in a ceremonial camp. It must be conducted by a shaman who knows all the customs of the people. He must know all the secret things of the shamans. He is chief and *wakiconza* [intercessor] of the ceremonial camp. Other shamans should help him as his council" (Walker 1980, 181). While the shaman has a special role, traditionally everyone in the local village or band community would be connected to preparations for a performance of a Sun Dance. Such defined positions as the Thunder-men among the Ponca led the ceremonial after they had been invited to dance four times. Among the Blackfeet a Sacred Woman is the sponsor and the one who initiates the ceremonial. Other roles at the Sun Dance include mentors for the candidates, the Sun Dance chief, and shamans who might join him in the lodge. Along with the participants as dancers, there are singers and others who maintain the fire during the nights of the ceremonial. There are those who police the campground, maintaining order. There are usually camp criers or announcers. Some people still have sacred clowns at their Sun Dances who bring humor into the dramatic settings of the ceremonial. Through these diverse roles and varied responsibilities, a community unites in the performance of a Sun Dance, manifesting communal solidarity as a conduit for sacred benefits.

From the late nineteenth century, Native American Sun Dance communities have been affected by the introduction of Christian denominations on reservations and an increasing secularization brought on by the dominant society's consumer individualism and scientific worldviews. Changes in traditional Sun Dance patterns can result from employment. Thus the Sun Dance is often held now over weekends to accommodate work schedules. Moreover, Christian values may intrude into traditional interpretations of the Sun Dance. However, the Sun Dance as a means for bringing benefits for the whole community of living and nonliving beings continues to be a central purpose of this ceremony. The Crow elder and Sun Dance chief Thomas Yellowtail expressed it this way: "In the Sun Dance way, the individual benefits from his prayers, but this is not all. The entire tribe benefits from the Sun Dance, because one part of our prayers is especially for the tribe and for all creation. Without these prayers from all of the different Indian tribes, the world might not be able to continue" (Yellowtail 1991, 103). This statement reflects the changing character of the Sun Dance from a communal exchange with sacred powers and a major ceremonial redistribution of goods to an intertribal prayer for the continuation of the world as a whole. Communal motivations for the Sun Dance are exemplified in the preparations prior to the Sun Dance.

Preparations for the Sun Dance include instruction of the candidates who have made vows, gathering of the material necessary for constructing the lodge, and organizing pledges from clan and village groups (for example, *tiospaye*) of food and assistance during the ceremony and afterward at the feasts. These preparations for the Sun Dance are often coordinated at rituals of smoking tobacco with sacred pipes and the opening of sacred bundles. Medicine bundle openings are conducted many times (typically four) over the months before the actual dance. Usually at the full moons before the Shoshone-Crow Sun Dances, a sequence of "outside dances" are held at which pledgers gather to witness the sponsor and a family member dance in full regalia. The return of the buffalo hunt as a preparatory feature of the Sun Dance has resulted from the development by many tribes of private buffalo herds. Moreover, the close association of the buffalo with most tribal Sun Dances marks continuity with traditional practices. The buffalo as the major symbolic presence of abundance, fertil-

ity, and strength is central to the cosmology of the Sun Dance. In the older Sun Dances the buffalo hunt and collection of buffalo tongues were central events leading up to the actual dance.

Cosmological Context

On or near the central cottonwood tree of the Sun Dance lodge a rawhide effigy of a buffalo is hung, or a buffalo skull altar is prepared, or the head of a buffalo is mounted on the tree. The dancers draw inspiration from the buffalo. A stuffed eagle may also be placed in the fork of the central tree where the rafter poles will rest. Such animal and bird figures are not presented as symbols of absent spiritual agents. Rather, they make present the sacred powers that originally gave the Sun Dance to the people. These cosmological powers are named and evoked by the shamans in their healing rituals in the lodge during the Sun Dance. Thus the Sun Dance becomes at times a healing ceremony, and at other times it appears to be a communal vision quest. At times the ordeal of an individual pledger seems central in his or her effort to break free of personal problems and to be restored to the larger cosmos of power.

These cosmological concerns are evident in the ceremonial speech of Pete Catches, a Lakota healer and Sun Dance intercessor. Addressing those at a Sun Dance, he said,

> My relatives, this Sun Dance is a very great ceremony. . . . The Sun Dance is

the greatest of all, the highest of the Lakota prayers which they direct toward *Tunkasila* [Grandfather] *Wakan Tanka* [the Presence of Mystery]. For this they [those to be pierced] select the ropes they will need on that day. They attach the selected ropes to the selected trees and they lay them down on a buffalo robe or a bear robe which is painted red; and pregnant women pass by, singing and speaking a prayer for generation; and then in the morning they gather to pray, and the children touch the tree at each direction as they walk around it. And they pray, to *Wakan Tanka* they pray. Then that tree around which *Wakan Tanka* will cause them to dance, is here set in the ground. There the people come in and make the ground smooth, for they have come together to pray to *Wakan Tanka,* they have been waiting to show themselves to *Wakan Tanka.* The people burn sweet grass, and they pray for the poor, and they clear a space on the ground. (Rice 1989–1990, 68)

Here a powerful picture emerges of those who will submit themselves to the sacrifice of the Sun Dance by being pierced and attached by ropes to the central tree. They, like their ropes, are laid down on buffalo robes, pierced, and attached to the tree. They will be "burned" away like the sweet grass; they will be wiped smoothe like the ground that the people have prepared for them. With the people they will show themselves to the sacred powers who are one and many, and this showing is in prayerful hope of re-creating the people, of renewal and fertility as pregnant women and children pass by. These pledgers continue the old Sun Dance ethos of warriors who protect the people by entering into the sacrifice of themselves for the good of the people. Their sacrifice is the culmination of the space of the Sun Dance lodge, which joins with cosmological reflections on time.

The number of days of the Sun Dance ceremonies varies a great deal. Some Plains Ojibwa have been described as having three days of dance. The Cheyenne speak of four or eight days, the Shoshone-Crow of four nights, the Comanche and Kiowa of twelve preparatory days and four actual dance days. No definite length united the different tribal groups, although each Sun Dance complex shows a concern for multiples of four. This numerical symbolism makes present cosmological thought of the four directions so prevalent in Plains religious ideas. The correspondence of colors, animals, winds, stones, and virtues with the four directions varies within and among the Plains peoples in their Sun Dances. In a related symbolism, the dancers walk into and out of the lodge in a sunwise (clockwise) direction, to place themselves correctly in relation to the cosmological powers.

Personal Transformation

From that moment when the participants enter the Sun Dance lodge in a sunwise direction they begin a test of their endurance. Participants take a vow (either publicly or privately) to undertake the suffering involved in the ceremony so as to help others. The vow to enter the Sun Dance includes fasting from food and water at the same time as participating in strenuous dancing to and from the center pole. This fast from food and water may last for two, three, four, or even five days among the Crow, Kiowa, and Shoshone.

Among the Lakota and Cheyenne who practice piercing of the body during the Sun Dance, a vow may be taken by a male dancer to have an incision made on his chest, skewers inserted, and ropes attaching the skewers to the center tree. The dancer then exerts himself until the flesh tears and he breaks free of the attached line. A vow may also be made to pierce the shoulder area and drag buffalo skulls until the flesh tears. Vows also may be made by women to cut pieces of skin from their arms in support of dancers or in fulfillment of their own promises to assist others. Women dancers regularly dance at the Crow Sun Dance and at some Fort Hall Shoshone dances. In Sun Dances related to the American Indian Movement, especially on the Pine Ridge and Rosebud reservations of the Teton Sioux, women have begun to play a more active role in dancing and piercing.

Participation in the Sun Dance brings to completion the dream injunction or invitation to dance from elders, ceremonial organizers, or spiritual beings. Personal transformation relates to both the older Sun Dance ideal of the warrior who sought a vision for revenge or for acquiring military abilities, and the contemporary quest for personal power in the face of the powerlessness created by dominant societies. Behind both ideals is a commitment to the larger community within which one's personal transformations find their deepest meanings.

John A. Grim

See also Ceremony and Ritual, Arapaho; Dances, Plains; Oral Traditions, Lakota (Teton); Oral Traditions, Plateau; Oral Traditions, Pueblo; Oral Traditions, Western Plains; Spiritual and Ceremonial Practitioners, Plains; Sun Dance, Crow; Sun Dance, Kiowa; Sweatlodge; Vision Quest Rites

References and Further Reading
Amiotte, Arthur. 1992. "The Sun Dance." Pp. 135–136 in *Native American Dance: Ceremonies and Social Traditions.* Edited by Charlotte Heth. Washington, DC: National Museum of the American Indian.
Archambault, JoAllyn. 2001. "Sun Dance." Pp. 983–995 in *Handbook of North American Indians: Plains,* vol. 13, pt. 2. Edited by Raymond DeMallie. Washington, DC: Smithsonian Institution Press.
Brown, Joseph Epes. 1987. "Sun Dance." In *Encyclopedia of Religion,* vol. 14: 143–147. Edited by Mircea Eliade. New York: Macmillan.
Dorsey, George Amos. 1903. *The Arapaho Sun Dance: The Ceremony of the Offerings Lodge.* Field Columbian Museum Publications, no. 75. Chicago: Field Museum of Natural History.
———. 1905. *The Cheyenne: II, The Sun Dance.* Field Columbian Museum Publications, no. 103. Chicago: Field Museum of Natural History.
Gill, Sam D., and Irene F. Sullivan. 1992. *Dictionary of Native American Mythology.* Santa Barbara, CA: ABC-CLIO.
Harrod, Howard L. 1987. *Renewing the World: Plains Indian Religion and*

Morality. Tucson: University of Arizona Press.

Hirschfelder, Arlene, and Paulette Molin. 1992. *The Encyclopedia of Native American Religions.* New York: Facts on File.

Hoxie, Fred E., ed. 1996. *Encyclopedia of North American Indians.* New York: Houghton Mifflin.

Jorgensen, Joseph G. 1972. *The Sun Dance Religion: Power for the Powerless.* Chicago: University of Chicago Press.

Lowie, Robert H. 1915. "The Sun Dance of the Crow Indians." Pp. 1–50 in *Anthropological Papers of the American Museum of Natural History,* vol. 16, pts. 1–5. New York: The Trustees.

Mails, Thomas E. 1978. *Sundancing at Rosebud and Pine Ridge.* Sioux Falls, SD: Center for Western Studies, Augustana College.

Markowitz, Harvey, ed. 1994. *American Indians,* vol. 3. Englewood Cliffs, NJ: Salem Press.

Pettipas, Katherine. 1994. *Severing the Ties that Bind: Government Repression of Indigenous Religious Ceremonies on the Prairies.* Manitoba Studies in Native History, no. 7. Manitoba: University of Manitoba Press.

Powell, Peter John. 1969. *Sweet Medicine: The Continuing Role of the Sacred Arrows, the Sun Dance, and the Sacred Buffalo Hat in Northern Cheyenne History,* 2 vols. Norman: University of Oklahoma Press.

Rice, Julian. 1989–1990. "Words for the Sun Dance: Pete Catches, 1969." *Melus* 16, no. 1 (spring): 59–76.

Spier, Leslie. 1921. "The Sun Dance of the Plains Indians: Its Development and Diffusion." Pp. 449–527 in *Anthropological Papers of the American Museum of Natural History,* vol. 16, pt. 7. New York: The Trustees.

Voget, Fred W. 1984. *The Shoshoni-Crow Sun Dance.* Norman: University of Oklahoma Press.

Walker, James. 1980. *Lakota Belief and Ritual.* Edited by Raymond J. DeMallie and Elaine A. Jahner. Lincoln: University of Nebraska Press.

Yellowtail, Thomas. 1991. *Yellowtail: Crow Medicine Man and Sun Dance Chief.* As told to Michael O. Fitzgerald. Norman: University of Oklahoma Press.

Sun Dance, Crow

The Crow (Apsaalooke) name for the traditional Sun Dance is Baaiichkiisapili-olissuua, "fringed ankle dance," and the contemporary ceremony is called Ashkisshilissuua or Ashkisshe, "Big Lodge." The traditional Crow and contemporary Shoshone-Crow and Sioux-Crow forms, like Sun Dances of other tribes, are ceremonial prayer rituals of intensification and renewal for individual worship and the general welfare of the tribal community. Prayer, sacrifice, and suffering are involved through fasting, effort, and traditionally by sacrificial piercing. During the nineteenth century, it took place at the time of tribal reunion, hunting, feasting, and visiting, when the tribal bands came together between early summer and early fall.

Some Crow consider the Big Horn Medicine Wheel in the mountains of northern Wyoming to be "the Sun's Lodge"; it is associated with spirit people who had no iron or fire, called "the Little People" in popular writing. One story is of Red Feather, who fasted at the Medicine Wheel and was instructed by them. The early Kiowa and Crow Sun Dances appear to have been related from the time in the 1700s when the two tribes were allies. The Taime (Sun Dance doll)

Apsarokee man, with strips of leather attached to his chest and tethered to a pole secured by rocks, all part of the piercing ritual of the Sun Dance, 1908. (Edward Curtis/Library of Congress)

of the Kiowa was obtained from the Crow. The Wind River Shoshone received the Sun Dance about 1800 from a Comanche, Yellow Hand, who in turn had been familiar with the Kiowa Sun Dance.

During the nineteenth century, the Crow Sun Dance was a prayer for group welfare including food, raising of children, health, freedom from disease, and protection from enemies. Gradually it became more related to warfare as a ceremony to test and prove individual bravery and fortitude, and a prayer for vengeance against the enemy tribes that surrounded them. It might be held every

three or four years, or several times a year. It was done when a man sponsored it, usually following the death of a relative, based on the need for spiritual understanding, power, and revenge. In the 1860s young people liked it, and some older people were distressed by it.

Following the 1868 Fort Laramie Treaty, the Crow were located on a reservation, and in 1875 they were relocated to another agency. The government stressed farming rather than hunting as a way of life, and there was discouragement of traditional ceremonies by the Bureau of Indian Affairs. The Crow discontinued the Sun Dance "voluntarily," but they continued other ceremonies such as the vision quest, sweatlodge, and Tobacco Planting and Adoption ceremonies. Sun Dances remained in the people's hearts, and in some tribes they were held in secret or modified so as to obtain permission of the U.S. government to perform them (for example, by discontinuing piercing and adding Christian elements). Some Crow participated in the Sun Dance ceremonies of other tribes. A twenty-four-year-old Crow rebel named Wraps His Tail, or Sword Bearer, participated in a Cheyenne Sun Dance about 1887. A Shoshone form of the Sun Dance on the Wind River Reservation in Wyoming integrated a number of Christian elements between 1890 and 1905, and a number of Crow attended during the following decades.

Following the 1934 change in Bureau of Indian Affairs policy, to no longer interfere with Indian religion, there was a revival of Sun Dances. In the summer of 1941, a Sun Dance was sponsored on the Crow Reservation with an invited Shoshone leader to guide it. It was the fulfillment of a prayer by the sponsor for survival of his young son, who had been sick. The entry of the United States into World War II led to sponsorships with an emphasis on prayers for safety by soldiers preparing themselves to enter the service or by their relatives, or vows to sponsor a Sun Dance if they returned safely. The 1955 Sun Dance at Crow Agency was dedicated to Korean War veterans and preservation of the peace. During and after the Vietnam and Desert Storm wars, the Crow and other tribes continued to pray for safety or give thanks for the successful return of soldiers by sponsorship or participation in Sun Dances.

Sun Dances are given when a sponsor makes a pledge (vow) for a specific purpose, such as aid for the sick, health, good luck in finding work, peace for mankind, or gratitude for a previous healing. Dancers make their own decisions about participation. Preparation begins during the winter and continues into early summer with four Medicine Bundle ceremonies: four Outdoor Dance Prayer services, obtaining lodgepole pine, aspen, fir trees, and the sacred forked cottonwood tree center pole. The lodge is constructed the day of the dance, which begins in the evening. A buffalo head and cloth offerings are placed on the center pole; in the fork is the nest of the eagle. Participants fast

and exert themselves by praying with tobacco cigarette smoking and by charging toward and backing away from the center pole with sincerity and determination (*diakaashe*). The goal is to worship, encounter, and receive sacred power (*xapaaliia*), a vision, or adoption by a Medicine Father (*Iilapxe*). A dance usually lasts three days, and sometimes four. Attire is a combination of traditional and contemporary clothing: skirts (kilts) for men and dresses for women, along with sheets and Pendleton blankets, beaded belts, chokers, eagle bone whistles, and finger plumes. Face and body painting is done on the third day.

Between 1941 and the 1960s, at least two dances were usually held each summer on the Crow Reservation. Since the mid-1970s there have been from 85 to 120 dancers in each ceremony; there have sometimes been more than one each year in different communities. Women began to participate within the lodge itself during the 1950s. The majority of participants in the Crow Sun Dance are members of the tribe. Indians from other tribes and non-Indians sometimes participate, however. Both young and old attend, as well as people from every social stratum. As many as a thousand people might camp and provide support for a Sun Dance. In 1991, the Golden Anniversary Sun Dance was sponsored by the son of the 1941 sponsor.

There are variations and controversies about the Crow Sun Dance and other spiritual practices. In the theology of some, interpretations of symbols are traditional. Others accept Christian interpretation, such as lodge rafters equated with the disciples of Christ and the center pole with the cross. Still others believe that each religion (for example, Sun Dance, Peyote, Catholic, Baptist) is like the spoke of a wheel: each separate, distinct, and not to be mixed, but all connected to the hub. Most participants are tolerant of syncretism. There has been debate into the twenty-first century between those who feel that the Crow Sun Dance should be held only on the reservation by formally accepted leaders and those who feel that Sun Dances can be sponsored and held anywhere they might be desired. Crow people visit and participate in Sun Dances and other rituals of other tribes. By the mid-1980s, relationships between Crow and Sioux, partly through involvement with the intertribal political American Indian Movement, grew strong, and some Crow sponsored a Sioux (Lakota) (or Sioux-Crow) piercing version of the Sun Dance on the Crow Reservation. Other Crow turned to an individual vision quest/Sun Dance with piercing. The first off-reservation Shoshone-Crow Sun Dance was held in Arizona for a group of counselors involved with troubled youth. Another was held in the East, led by an off-reservation Crow man. About 1990 a variation of the Crow Sun Dance was held in England. There have been increasing numbers of visitors from Germany and other countries to the Sun Dances held on the Crow reservation. Most visitors do not partici-pate in the ceremonies within the lodge, but rather witness or help with building the lodge and other activities.

Such ceremonies as the Sun Dance serve to express and maintain both specific Crow tribal and intertribal identities. Involvements with Sun Dances and other spiritual activities are a symbolic commitment to the adaptation to everyday stresses and modern life, as well as persistence, revival, and renewal of tradition and community survival.

The Sun Dance of the Crow and other tribes has been portrayed in literature, photography and film, and on stage. During the 1950s, several Crow traveled to Europe, where scenes of the Sun Dance were performed on stage along with other dance exhibitions. Hyemeyohsts Storm's controversial novel *Seven Arrows* (1972), a popular book among Indian and other American counterculture/New Age adherents, is a fictionalized story incorporating ideas from the medicine wheel, from Crow and Cheyenne Sun Dances, shields, and teaching stories, as well as Jung and Oriental thought.

Key works on the Crow Sun Dance include Lowie (1915), Voget (1984), and Frey (1987). There is a biography of the prominent Sun Dance leader Thomas Yellowtail (1991). Documentary works include the videos "The Gift of the Big Lodge" (1989) and "The Crow/Shoshone Sun Dance, A Traditional Ceremony" (1992), and Crummett's (1992) Sun Dance photographs and commentary.

C. Adrian Heidenreich

See also Christianity, Indianization of; Kinship; Missionization, Northern Plains; Oral Traditions, Western Plains; Power, Plains; Retraditionalism and Revitalization Movements, Plains; Spiritual and Ceremonial Practitioners, Plains

References and Further Reading
Crummett, Michael. 1993. *Sun Dance: The 50th Anniversary Crow Indian Sun Dance*. Helena, MT: Falcon Press.

Frey, Rodney. 1987. *The World of the Crow Indians: As Driftwood Lodges*. Norman:University of Oklahoma Press.

Lowie, Robert H. 1915. "The Sun Dance of the Crow Indians." Anthropological Papers of the American Museum of Natural History no. 16. New York: American Museum of Natural History.

Old Coyote, Lloyd G. "Mickey," director. 1992. (video recording) *The Crow/Shoshone Sun Dance: A Traditional Ceremony*. New York: Thunderous Productions.

Old Elk, Dan, director. 1989. *The Gift of the Big Lodge*. Rotterdam, The Netherlands: Blue Horse Productions.

Storm, Hyemeyohsts. 1972. *Seven Arrows*. New York: Ballantine Books.

Voget, Fred W. 1984. *The Shoshoni-Crow Sun Dance*. Norman: University of Oklahoma Press.

Yellowtail, Thomas. 1991. *Yellowtail: Crow Medicine Man and Sun Dance Chief, An Autobiography*. Norman: University of Oklahoma Press.

Sun Dance, Kiowa

The Kiowa Sun Dance was the tribe's most important ceremony until its suppression by federal authorities in the late nineteenth century. Like the Sun Dance complex widely shared by Plains people, the Kiowa version brought the entire tribe together for the only time during the year; it was the occasion for ritually and symbolically important ceremonies that ensured good health, prosperity, good hunting, success in war, and happiness (Kracht 1989, 258–265). "This was a dance of thanksgiving," writes Maurice Boyd. "For those who had been spared in battle, had survived a serious illness, or had been rewarded with good hunting, the dance was an expression of gratitude. For those whose family members needed to be healed, whose women desired the blessing of children, whose camps needed food, or whose tepees sought revenge . . . the Sun Dance ritual . . . offered strength for the fulfillment of sacred vows for the new year" (Boyd 1981, I: 37).

The Kiowas called their dance Skaw-tow. The first scholars to work with the Kiowas, however, often failed to hear the softly pronounced "s" at the beginning of the word, and it was subsequently recorded as "Kaw-tow," or as James Mooney and Hugh Lennox Scott put it, "ka'do," or "kado" (Mooney 1898, 237, 242–244; Scott 1911, 345). The original meaning of the word is unclear, but according to Billy Evans Horse, it means "We're building an abode, a house, or dwelling that we all meet in" (Lassiter 1998, 91). Kiowas also called the dance Daw-s'tome, or "procession-entering-the-lodge," an interpretation that echoes Billy Evans Horse. The Kiowas associated their dance with Pahy, the sun, because it was Pahy that entrusted the Kiowas with the care of the "Taime," a two-foot-long figure representing a female human that is central to the Kiowa Sun Dance rituals. Tribal historians have described the ritual as "a dance of thirst and self-denial," and they note that it is related to the sun "only at the moment of sunrise and sunset, when certain songs in the ceremonial ritual coincided with the action of the sun. Although the ritual was not concerned primarily with the sun, the dancers did stare incessantly at the sun or the medicine bundles at the top of the center lodgepole" (Boyd 1981, I: 35; Mikkanen 1987, 6–7).

Kiowas say that both the Tai-may and the Sun Dance came to them through the Crow people, among whom the Kiowas lived before acquiring horses in the early eighteenth century and migrating onto the Plains. James Mooney estimated that they learned the dance around 1765, as did the tribal historians who assisted Maurice Boyd on *Kiowa Voices* (1981). Based on his conversations in the early twentieth century with elderly Kiowas, Hugh Scott believed that the Kiowas obtained the Tai-may and Sun Dance a century earlier, in 1670 (Mooney 1898, 241; Scott 1911, 369–372). In any case, tribal historians give several accounts of its origin. In one, a poor Shoshone man attended a Crow Sun Dance and prayed with great sincerity before the Tai-may. Taking pity on the man, the Crow Sun Dance priest gave him the Tai-may, an act that brought the man great spiritual powers and wealth. Angered, other Crows stole the Tai-may back. The Shoshone man made a copy of the Tai-may, later married a Kiowa woman, and

gave the Tai-may and Sun Dance to her people. Recognizing Tai-may's power, the tribe "adopted it as our most sacred medicine, and regarded it as the most important symbol used in our great Skaw-tow . . . ceremony." According to tradition, the keepers of the Tai-may are the descendants of that Arapaho man and Kiowa woman (Boyd 1981, I: 31–32; Mooney 1898, 240–241).

In an alternative version, Scott's consultants told him of an elderly Arapaho couple who accompanied the Kiowas on a visit to the Crows but were too poor to make the return trip. Out of kindness, a Crow chief gave them the Tai-may, and when the Kiowas returned on a subsequent visit, the Arapaho couple went with them and gave them the Tai-may and Sun Dance. As in the first version, their descendants became the traditional keepers of the Tai-may bundle, which became the mediator between the Kiowas and the power of the sun (Scott 1911, 350, 368–369).

The Tai-may was maintained in a sacred bundle by a hereditary keeper who determined the year's Sun Dance site, usually during midwinter, to give ample time to those who had made vows to dance or otherwise assist with the ceremony. (By some accounts, he could also appoint an honored warrior to make the decision.) The timing of the dance was determined by one of several signs, including the appearance of downy white fluff on the cottonwoods, or when the sage grass was about a foot high and the ponies were fat. The site had to be within four days of the most distant Kiowa camps, and it had to provide enough water and pasture for the tribe as well as its large pony herds (Kracht 1989, 265; Scott 1911, 349; Boyd 1981, I: 37–38; Mikkanen 1987, 5–9).

The date usually fell near the summer solstice, but that was not a strict requirement. In 1873, for example, the dance began on June 16; in 1874 it began on July 3 (Scott 1911, 349). Although every effort was made to hold the dance, in some summers it proved impossible. In 1833, for example, the Osages stole the Tai-may and prevented the dance from being held again until the Tai-may was returned in 1835. In another example, Mooney's consultants told him that because the tribe was constantly on the move in the summer of 1841, no dance was held. There was no dance in 1852 or 1860, or in 1871, 1872, 1880, 1882, 1884, 1886, or between 1888 and 1892, when federal authorities finally suppressed the ceremony. Conversely, two Sun Dances occurred during the same summer in 1842 and again in 1878 (Mooney 1898).

Once the site and time were known, the Kiowa bands gathered in one large encampment for about two weeks. In a typical year, the ceremony required four to six "getting ready days" and another four "dancing days." The "getting ready days" began with the search for the tall, forked cottonwood tree that served as the center pole in the Sun Dance lodge, and also for an appropriate campsite for the assembled Kiowa bands. Two men from a warrior society who had been rit-

ually cleansed in the sweatlodge led four bands of mounted warriors on the search. Once the tree—which needed to be about twenty feet tall—and campsite were identified, the bands set up their lodges, each claiming a designated place as part of a large circle, in the center of which would stand the Sun Dance pole and lodge (Kracht 1989, 275–311; Boyd 1981, I: 38–42).

On the second day, a young buffalo bull was killed and its hide brought to the Sun Dance lodge. Protocol dictated that a man with war honors kill the bull with no more than two arrows. Moreover, the animal had to be chased in such a way that when it died it faced east and fell on its belly. Finally, the shot had to be into the heart, to prevent bleeding from the animal's nose or mouth, something that was considered an ill omen and a harbinger of illness. The bull was skinned, and a wide strip of skin from the tail to the head (including the hide around the entire head) was taken to the Tai-may keeper, who took it into the sweatlodge and blessed it prior to placing it at the Sun Dance pole (Boyd 1981, I: 38–43; Scott 1911, 356–360; Meadows 1999, 71).

On the third day, an elaborate sham battle, or "laugh fight," was held between warriors on foot and on horse around the sacred tree, which had not yet been cut. After a series of charges by the mounted riders, the tree was surrendered by the warriors on foot. A woman—often a captive, to ensure that any miscues in the felling would not affect any Kiowas—cut it down and limbed it, and the tree was tied to the mount of a warrior, who dragged it to the center of the camp. As with many other Plains tribes, the warriors ritually charged the tree and counted coup on it as it was moved. Members of the Calf Old Woman Society dug a hole, members from the warrior societies raised the tree, and then the women danced (Boyd 1981, I: 43–46).

The fourth and fifth days were for the construction of the Sun Dance lodge. On the fourth day, a large circular arbor of cottonwood trees twelve to fifteen feet in height was built around the center tree, and brush was dragged to the camp circle to cover the walls of the Sun Dance lodge. During this time, young men and women were allowed to mingle unchaperoned, and social regulations about courting practices were relaxed (ibid., I: 47; Scott 1911, 352; Meadows 1999, 74–76). On the fifth day the walls and roof of the lodge were completed and covered with brush, and a cedar screen was erected close to one side of the lodge on a north-south axis behind which the dancers and officials would rest during the ceremony. The Calf Old Woman Society and children from the Rabbit Society cleaned the arbor and covered its floor with sand. The Rabbits' job for the remainder of the Sun Dance was to keep the lodge clean, a practice that is carried on to this day at the annual meeting of the Tiah-piah, or Gourd Dance Society. The Sun Dance shields were hung on the cedar screen, two earthen censers for burning cedar were erected at either end of the screen, and the Tai-may and other ceremonial objects were prepared (Boyd 1981, I: 47; Scott 1911, 350).

On the sixth day, the "Mud Head" ceremony was held, during which men disguised under mud-coated buckskin masks rode through the camp teasing people and acting out practical jokes. This was followed by a symbolic buffalo hunt, during which men covered in buffalo robes were herded into the Sun Dance lodge, which they circled four times before lying down as if they had been killed. Members of the Buffalo Medicine cult then searched under the buffalo robes for the man who had the most war honors. His name was announced to the assembled tribe, and the entire affair was repeated four more times to honor the four greatest Kiowas "who had struck their enemies the greatest number of times during the past year." The preparations for the dance were now almost complete, and the Tai-may keeper unwrapped the Tai-may from its bundle, tied it to a six-foot-long pole, covered it, and prepared it to be placed in the center of the Sun Dance lodge (Boyd 1981, I: 48–49).

At sunset, the Tai-may keeper and his assistants entered the lodge, circled it four times, and placed the Tai-may to the left of the center pole and in front of the cedar screen. The first of the four dancing days began at sunset and continued until midnight. The next three dancing days began at dawn and continued to midnight, except for the final day, when dancing ended at sunset. The dancers, who were under the command of the Tai-may keeper and his assistants, were men who had made vows the previous year to dance. Bareheaded, with their torsos and arms painted white, dancers wore white-painted buckskin shirts and blue aprons that reached to the ground. Standing in a line facing the Tai-may, they danced in a bobbing motion, blowing eagle bone whistles with outstretched arms. Dancers moved about the arena, and could perform more or less freely. This continued from noon to sundown, when there was a brief break. Dancing resumed until midnight, when spectators retired to their lodges while the dancers and officials remained in the Sun Dance lodge. Dancers fasted during the entire ceremony but were given water lilies to cool their bodies. Unlike other Plains Sun Dances, the Kiowa version strictly avoided bloodshed, scarification, and piercing. Bloodshed of any kind was an ill omen and could bring the entire ceremony to a halt (ibid., I: 50–52; Scott 1911, 353–354).

The second and third dancing days featured several acts of symbolic death. In one instance, a middle-aged man wearing a buffalo robe entered the lodge and reenacted the death of the buffalo killed on the second getting ready day. Staring at the sun, he danced more and more rapidly until he collapsed and fell on his stomach, facing eastward as in the actual hunt. In another instance, a dancer was symbolically killed, usually once each afternoon, after being chased by the Tai-may keeper until he collapsed

and fell unconscious. With luck, the dancer would have a vision that he would later share. Dancers chosen for the honor of the "feather killing" were expected to have a long life and good health (Boyd 1981, I: 52–53).

Near the end of the fourth dancing day, spectators piled goods around the base of the Sun Dance pole in order to gain protection and power from the ceremony. Dancing ended just before sunset; the Tai-may was packed into its bundle, and clothing and other goods were tied to the Sun Dance pole as offerings. A large social dance was held that night, and raiding parties were organized to leave the next morning, when camp was broken and the bands went their separate ways. Just prior to departing on the raids, the men would perform the Buffalo Dance "in hopes of receiving strength and courage from the Buffalo Guardian Spirit" (ibid., I: 53; Kracht 1989, 341–342). With that, the Skaw-tow ended, and as Billy Evans Horse put it, "Every society felt renewed through the prayers that they offered and the dances they did. They rejuvenated their spirit, so to speak, and they were ready to go wherever. And they knew that the following year they were going to have it again" (Lassiter 1998, 91).

The Skaw-tow ended in the late nineteenth century, when federal authorities suppressed it (Kracht 1989, 725–733). As noted above, for example, between 1871 and 1892 the Kiowas failed to hold the dance on at least eleven occasions. And in years when they did hold it in that era, they were increasingly under the scrutiny of federal troops and several times had to resort to buying the buffalo bull whose hide they needed for the ceremony. When the dance was suppressed, however, its songs and rituals were not forgotten but were folded into surviving ceremonies, most notably those of the Tiah-piah Society (also called the Taimpego Society, which means "Gourd Dance Society" or "Gourd Clan"), a men's warrior society that had a prominent role in the old Sun Dance. Tiah-piah members began to hold dances in 1912, and they continued to do so until 1938. When members revived the society in 1957, they did so by including some of the old Sun Dance's most meaningful practices, including the timing (July 4, which coincides roughly with the traditional timing of the old dance), dancing for four days, using Sun Dance song traditions such as Brush Dance Songs, having members of the Rabbit Society clean the arena, and performing the Buffalo Dance at the end of the Gourd Dance (Lassiter 1998, 119; Meadows 1999, 136–139). Since the 1970s, Gourd Dancing has become one of the most important expressions of identity in the Kiowa community; it also enjoys nationwide popularity as part of the pan-Indian powwow complex (Ellis 1990).

In 1997 an attempt to revive the Kiowa Sun Dance produced strong objections from tribal elders. When Vanessa Jennings, a Kiowa, announced plans to invite a Crow-Shoshone Sun Dance priest to her home in Ft. Cobb, Oklahoma, to hold a Sun Dance in June 1997, tribal elders opposed her. Harding Big Bow noted that when Kiowas put away the dance in the nineteenth century, they agreed never to speak of it again. Big Bow noted that the prayers and rituals had been lost, and that the dance could be performed only when all of the bands were camped together. "We respect our ancestors," he said. "Our society depends on it." In a resolution that passed by a vote of 178 to 173, Kiowa elders criticized "the continued stripping of culture by . . . ambitious individuals . . . creating an evil humiliation of tribal customs and religions." Jennings rejected the resolution, saying it wasn't "a case of . . . tradition, of respect—it's male domination" ("Tribal Elders Fight Resurrection" 1997; Brinkman 1997). The dance was not held, and there have been no subsequent attempts to organize another attempt.

Clyde Ellis

See also Bundles, Sacred Bundle Traditions; Ceremony and Ritual, Arapaho; Christianity, Indianization of; Kinship; Kiowa Indian Hymns; Missionization, Kiowa-Comanche-Apache Reservation; Oral Traditions, Western Plains; Power, Plains; Sacred Pipe; Sun Dance

References and Further Reading
Battey, Thomas C. 1875/1968. *The Life and Adventures of a Quaker among the Indians.* Reprint, Norman: University of Oklahoma Press.
Boyd, Maurice. 1981. *Kiowa Voices: Ceremonial Dance, Ritual, and Song,* vol. 2. Ft. Worth: Texas Christian University Press.
Brinkman, Lillie-Beth. 1997. "Kiowas Ban Dance, Veto Land Lease." *Daily Oklahoman,* November 18.

Ellis, Clyde. 1990. "'Truly Dancing Their Own Way': Modern Revival and Diffusion of the Kiowa Gourd Dance." *American Indian Quarterly* 14: 19—33.

Kracht, Benjamin. 1989. "Kiowa Religion: An Ethnohistorical Analysis of Ritual Symbolism, 1832–1987." Ph.D. diss., Southern Methodist University.

———. 1994. "Kiowa Powwows: Continuity in Ritual Practice." *American Indian Quarterly* 18: 321–348.

Lassiter, Luke Eric. 1998. *The Power of Kiowa Song: A Collaborative Ethnography.* Tucson: University of Arizona Press.

Mikkanen, Arvo Quoetone. 1987. "Skaw-Tow: The Centennial Commemoration of the Last Kiowa Sun Dance." *American Indian Journal* 9: 5–9.

Mooney, James. 1898. *Calendar History of the Kiowa Indians.* Seventeenth Annual Report of the Bureau of American Ethnology. Washington, DC: Government Printing Office.

Nye, Wilbur. 1934. "The Annual Sun Dance of the Kiowa Indians: As Related by George Hunt." *Chronicles of Oklahoma* 12: 340–358.

Scott, Hugh Lennox. 1911. "Notes on the Kado, or Sun Dance of the Kiowa." *American Anthropologist* 13: 345–379.

Spier, Leslie. 1921. "Notes on the Kiowa Sun Dance." *Anthropological Papers of the American Museum of Natural History* 16: 433–450.

———. 1967. "The Kiowa Sun Dance." Pp. 503–513 in *The North American Indians: A Sourcebook.* Edited by Roger C. Owen, James J. F. Deetz, and Anthony D. Fisher. New York: Macmillan.

"Tribal Elders Fight Resurrection of Long Banned Ceremony." *Ojibway News.* May 30, 1997.

Sweatlodge

The sweatlodge ritual is found among a wide variety of Indian groups in North America. It entails prayer, physical and spiritual cleansing, preparation for other sacred events, healing, and social and spiritual interaction. Participants are exposed to high temperatures in a dark, tightly enclosed structure for significant amounts of time. In wide use before European contact, this ceremony was deliberately suppressed by civil and religious authorities in the 1800s and early 1900s, along with other rituals, but it has come out from hiding, has revived, and continues to be important to a wide variety of Native groups. The structure of the lodge and the ceremony itself varies according to the cultural group, the time period, and the inspirations of specific spiritual leaders. Despite cultural, temporal, and personal variations, the ceremony itself has remained fairly consistent over time. The greatest flexibility and variability for this ritual lies in the purposes for which it is performed.

Scholars have distinguished two types of sweats used by Native North Americans: direct heat and steam. Direct fire baths are found primarily among Natives in Alaska, California, and the Plateau. Steam baths are found in the rest of North America. There are a few groups in the Southeast and Southwest as well as Mesoamerica who did not use this ritual, or about whom we know too little to be sure if they used the ritual or not.

Sweating is a circumpolar phenomenon; it is found in other parts of the world as well. Russians, Latvians, Estonians, Finns, and Swedes all utilize saunas.

Luna Harrington, a Pima Medicine Man, in a sweatlodge during a purification ceremony. Monument Valley, Arizona. 1994. (Arne Hodalic/Corbis)

be material artifacts, such as spears and canoes, or social customs such as marriage rules or kinship terms. Rituals are an important category of culture, and the sweatlodge is thus a trait (or feature) within that larger category. In this encyclopedia, elements of Native culture are identified as traits for ease of interpretation and to focus each article on different elements of Native religions. Note, however, that in contemporary religious and anthropological studies, the focus on studying a ritual is on how it relates to other elements within that culture—such as the social order, kinship, politics, health and healing, economics, history, folklore, and, indeed, other rituals. While we can analytically separate the sweatlodge from its cultural nexus, in reality it is always part of a complex social whole.

Studying Rituals

Native peoples and scholars often differ in their interpretations of and interests in this ritual. Native people focus on proper (respectful) use of the sweat and its power, while scholars often focus on ritual structures and procedures, changes in the ritual over time, as well as the distribution and diffusion of this ceremony. For example, anthropologists suggest that the sweat may have originally come from Asia or from Europe, while Native peoples often explain that their ancestors were taught the ritual by a divine entity, or that the ritual was given to someone through a dream or vision to improve the life of the people or to heal or revivify someone.

What is distinctive about Native American sweats is that they have retained their religious orientation; except in the case of neopaganism and Jewish purification baths, contemporary European sweating is secular, although in places such as Russia sweating was once a religious practice.

Traits and Trait Analysis

Nineteenth-century anthropology called for the analysis of cultures by their "traits" or component parts. Traits could

The Nature of the Ritual

Today, ritual sweating according to a Native tradition is becoming more prevalent, both on reservations and in urban areas. Non-Natives will sometimes join Native people for sweats, and, at times, non-Natives will conduct their own sweat rituals. This has caused much controversy in Native communities as they try to protect their spiritual traditions from exploitation by outsiders as well as from other Natives.

Because of its increasing prominence and popularity, the sweat has become a very important ritual, though not as central a ritual as the Sun Dance or vision quest (to use the Plains tribes as an example). It acts as a transitional or boundary ritual, allowing people to move from one state (profane) to another (sacred), and, indeed, to be transformed and to transform the social order. Outsiders may be invited to participate if they have a connection with the group who are sweating and are "respectful." Respect includes being in the proper ritual disposition (there are certain restrictions on when one may sweat and how one prepares), acting properly, and following directions.

Writing about the sweat, as in writing about anyone's religious belief, also requires respect. The author of this article is a non-Native who has been honored to be invited to many sweat rituals and has attempted, to the best of his ability, to be respectful in his writings. Many Native people have stressed that outsiders should have an understanding of their rituals and beliefs so that they may be appreciated and respected, and so that they not again suffer the suppression imposed upon them both by the U.S. government and by Christian churches. So I gratefully acknowledge my welcome to the sweats, and I seek to use my own scholarly work to make appropriate information known for the sake of understanding and tolerance on all sides. I ask in advance for forgiveness for any shortcomings or omissions in this article. I do not speak for Natives, nor do I define their ritual practice. Rather, I seek to share what I have learned from Native practitioners of the sweat, as well as research that shows the wide variety of sweat practices. I seek also to highlight the importance of these ritual procedures, to consider controversies surrounding the sweatlodge today, and to let Native and other voices speak through my own work.

Historical Descriptions of the Sweatlodge

One source of our knowledge of early sweatlodge ceremonies derives from observations of the ritual by European explorers, diplomats, missionaries, military personnel, government agents, fur traders, and, much later, anthropologists. Europeans, and especially missionaries, had an ambivalence about this ritual. They were interested in its physical and curative properties, but they rejected its use in worship and belief; the early missionaries were quite intolerant of non-Christian belief, worship, and ritual practices. The descriptions that these individuals left are one source for a broader knowledge of the ritual. Another source of information has been oral literature that was generally kept within tribal groups, although sometimes it is shared with sincere and interested outsiders.

Native people have been engaged in recovering their past through accessing both local oral historians and more remote non-Native archival and published descriptions of their cultures. While descriptions by outsiders are often partial and in some ways flawed, Native peoples make use of non-Native archival and published descriptions of their cultures. A blurry photograph of a loved one taken by a photographer not known to you is better than no photograph at all. While the imprecise image is not the person, the picture can be added to the heart and mind along with memories, oral reports, and other knowledge to create a better composite picture of the past.

We will look at sweating in three different geographical areas during three different eras, through the eyes of a variety of non-Native observers. This will help us to appreciate the historical depth and variety of forms of this ritual, which some Native societies date to the foundations of their cultural orders. This will also help us to understand the goals and biases of various collectors of this information and how their viewpoints color their descriptions and understandings. Finally, it will give the reader a method for studying sweatlodge practices of other groups in the future.

The Jesuit Relations: Hurons and Montagnais

One of the first groups to interact intensively with Native peoples for an extended period of time, in what they referred to as New France, were the Jesuits, members of a Roman Catholic religious order that came to spread their faith and culture. They became students of Native languages and cultures both with a genuine interest and sometimes to refute their beliefs and replace them with Catholicism. Jesuit priests wrote detailed accounts of Native custom and behavior as reports for their superiors and as guides for others in their order who would take up their work.

Jesuit Father François Joseph Le Mercier, S.J., quotes a letter from fellow missionary Fr. Pierre Pijart, who describes a sweatlodge ceremony he observed in 1637 while among the Hurons:

Here is something quite remarkable: Towards evening of the 26th (of May), they prepared a sweat, which was followed by a feast. I never saw anything like it in my life; 20 men entered, and almost piled themselves upon one another. Even the sick man dragged himself thither, though with considerable difficulty, and was one of the troop; he also sang for quite a long time, and in the midst of the heat of this sweat he asked for water with which to refresh himself,—a part of which he drank, and the rest he threw over his body. An excellent remedy, forsooth, for a sick man on the verge of death! So the next day I found him in a fine condition; indeed it was a fine condition for him, since God then gave to him the grace to conceive the importance of the concerns of his salvation, and to me to put into my mouth the words to explain to him our principal mysteries.

Le Mercier pays most attention to the medicinal efficacy of this ritual; he seems less aware of its spiritual dimensions. When a cure is effected, the Jesuit interprets it through his own cultural lens as the result of his preaching of Christianity rather than the efficacy of the Native prayer ritual. Note the other elements of the sweat—specifically Huron—that are revealed: singing, drinking water, and feasting afterward are important elements of the sweat. The sweat is also social: a large number of people crowd in with the sick man. Finally, Le Mercier reveals his European fascination with this "odd" ceremony, a fascination with the exotic that continues to hold many Europeans to this day.

Father Le Jeune, S.J., writes a very detailed description of the sweatlodge of the Montagnais in his report of 1634:

> They sing and make these noises also in their sweating operations. They believe that this medicine, which is the best of all they have, would be of no use whatever to them if they did not sing during the sweat. They plant some sticks in the ground, making a sort of low tent, for, if a tall man were seated therein, his head would touch the top of this hut, which they enclose and cover with skins, robes, and blankets. They put in this dark room a number of heavy stones, which they have had heated and made red-hot in a good fire, then

they slip entirely naked into these sweat boxes. The women occasionally sweat as well as the men. Sometimes they sweat all together, men and women, pell-mell. They sing, cry and groan in this oven, and make speeches; occasionally the sorcerer beats his drum there. I heard him once acting the prophet therein, crying out that he saw Moose; that my host, his brother, would kill some. I could not refrain from telling him, or rather those who were present and listened to him as if to an oracle, that it was indeed quite probable that they would find a male, since they had already found and killed two females. When he understood what I was driving at, he said to me sharply, "Believe me, this black robe has no sense." They are so superstitious in these uproars and in their other nonsense, that if they have sweats in order to cure themselves, or to have a good hunt, or to have fine weather, [they think] nothing would be accomplished if they did not sing, and if they did not observe these superstitions. I have noticed that, when the men sweat, they do not like to use women's robes with which to enclose their sweat boxes, if they can have any others. In short, when they have shouted for three hours or thereabout in these stoves, they emerge completely wet and covered with their sweat.

We learn a lot about Fr. Le Jeune here as well as about the sweat. He has no tolerance for Native religious practices, equating them with superstitions and nonsense. He is not above interfering with the spiritual leader, denigrating his predictions as obvious. Jesuits were trained in debate throughout their philosophical and theological studies, to use refutation in verbal combat not only with Native Americans but also against European Protestants. Nevertheless, we learn some more important elements about the sweatlodge. Singing is vital to the process. In addition to healing, there is supplication and prognostication. Drums are sometimes used. Women and men sometimes sweat together. Le Jeune also provides a detailed description of the construction of the sweatlodge enclosure. He tells us that there are multiple uses for the sweat: curing, success in hunting, predicting where game will be found, and to bring about good weather. Other Jesuits point out that the Natives used the sweat to get knowledge of a patient's disease, to gain the help of spiritual forces (referred to at that time as "demons"), to make the medicine more effective, and to predict future events such as occurrences in warfare and to diagnose illness.

While the Jesuits were sometimes tolerant of Native social customs, they were most intolerant of their ritual life. They set about refuting these practices among the Natives and making enemies of the traditional spiritual leaders, and proscribing their use by converts to Christianity. Nevertheless, the missionaries did recognize some natural curative efficacy to these baths. Contemporary Native Christians also make accommodations and transferences as they enter this new religion, continuing prayer and recitation in the sweat, but in Christian metaphor. Fr. Lalemant describes an early instance of this phenomenon in 1640:

> This good Christian,—having returned some months ago from a journey that he had made to the Khionontateronons (the Tobacco Nation), whither he had gone to assist our Fathers in the preaching of the Gospel,—seeing himself wearied with travel, took a sweat (this is a certain kind of bath which these Savages use, with which to refresh themselves). Having entered this bath, it was a pleasure to hear him,—not singing of dreams, and war songs, as all his fellow countrymen do on this occasion, but animating himself to a new combat; resolving to die for the defense of the Faith; promising God to scour the whole country, and announce everywhere his holy name. In a word, what is deepest in the heart is the most ordinary subject of his conversation, of his songs, of his most affectionate intercourse.

Like many other Europeans, Jesuits demonstrated an interest in the medical practices of the Indians. Jesuits were generalists and particularists, describing the specific details of local customs among specific tribes but also sometimes generalizing for all Natives they encountered.

The study of primary documents, despite the limitations of their authors, is essential to reconstructing early sweat ceremonies. The more different sources one can use in the reconstruction (Native and non-Native, textual and oral, written, drawn, and photographed), the fuller a picture we can derive.

Explorers and Ethnographers: Mandan and Hidatsa

The explorer-artist George Catlin visited the Mandan Indians in 1832, when he noted the use of sweatlodges among those people. The baths were located near villages along the banks of the river. Inside the lodge, there was a double row of rocks about three feet apart on which rested a "crib" in which the bather sat. Outside the lodge, a woman heated rocks and brought them in, placing them under the bather and then dashing cold water on the rocks to produce an abundance of steam. The lodge was sealed tight during this process. Catlin further describes the process:

> He [the bather] is enveloped in a cloud of steam, and a woman or child will sit at a little distance and continue to dash water upon the stone while the matron of the lodge is out preparing to make her appearance with another heated stone. He will sit and dip from a wooden bowl, with a ladle made of the mountain-sheep's horn, and throw upon the heated stones, with his own hands, the water which he is drawing through his lungs and pores. The steam distills through a mat of wild sage and other medicinal and aromatic herbs, which he has strewed over the bottom of his basket, and on which he reclines.

Catlin reports that the sweater made a verbal utterance, the door was opened, and the occupant plunged himself into a river. He considered this a rather satisfactory remedy for about every disease known to the Mandan.

The explorer Maximilian, Prince of Wied, spent the winter of 1833–1834 with the Mandan and the culturally related Hidatsa, whom he referred to as the Manitarie. He concurs with Catlin on the extensive medical use of the sweatlodge. He provides more extensive data for uses of the Hidatsa sweatlodge:

> When a man intends to undertake anything, and to implore by medicine the aid of the higher powers, he builds a small sudatory of twigs, which is covered all over with buffalo hides. Before the entrance is a straight path, forty feet long and one broad, from which the turf is taken off and piled up in a heap at one end opposite the hut. Near this heap a fire is kindled, in which large stones are made red hot. Two rows of shoes, sometimes, thirty or forty pair, are placed along the path. As soon as the stones are hot, they are borne into the hut, where a hearth has been dug, on which the hot stones are laid. The whole population sits as spectators on either side of the path, where are placed a number of dishes with provisions, such as boiled maize, beans, meat, &c.

Maximilian points out that a medicine man conducted the ceremony. He walked to the sweat on top of the shoes. The supplicant for whom the sweat was created lamented in front of the sweat. The older men then went into the sweat,

Sweat lodge frame. Chief Plenty Coups State Park, Montana. 2001. (Marilyn "Angel" Wynn/ Nativestock)

and women covered it tightly. Inside, the men sang, using a rattle for an accompaniment. When the door was opened a buffalo head was carried over the row of shoes and placed on the mound in front of the lodge. Offerings were put on a pole behind the sweatlodge. The sweat itself was located outdoors, but in winter sweats were constructed within the earth lodges.

Maximilian noted the religious import of this ceremony, which included self-torture to ensure spiritual help and success from "higher powers" that Maximilian, in his ethnocentric view, unfortunately described as "superstition."

When we move to anthropological texts, we get a fuller picture of the religious dimension that Catlin missed in his description. Anthropologist Alfred Bowers, who worked with Mandans and Hidatsas from the 1920s to the 1940s, provides a Mandan story about a young man named Black Wolf, who was brought into a sweatlodge by Black Bear and a group of animals. They sang in the sweat, prayed to the animals, poured water on themselves, and then came out. Black Wolf was told that the sweat was a place to refresh oneself as well as to heal people who were sick. Note that prayer is an essential element of the sweat in the story and should not be separated from healing, as both are integral to a successful cure in Native understanding. The Hidatsa held that the sweatlodge could bring blessings, good fortune, new life, good homes, health, success against enemies, and material wealth. Sweats were also used in ceremonial preparation for catching eagles, according to ethnomusicologist Francis Densmore, who worked with the Mandans and Hidatsas in 1912, 1915, and 1919.

Missionaries, Explorers, and Anthropologists: Yup'ik

The Yup'ik of Central Alaska traditionally used the *qasegiq*, or men's house, for sweating. This structure is also known as the *kashim*. This building was also used for religious ceremonies such as the Great Feast to the Dead and the Bladder Festival, for recreation, and as a living space for men.

Edward William Nelson, meteorologist, explorer, and part-time ethnographer, lived from 1877 to 1881 among the Bering Strait Eskimo. He provides an early account of their sweats:

> In these buildings (the kashim) sweat baths are taken by men and boys at intervals of a week or ten days during the winter. Every man has a small urine tub near his place, where this liquid is saved for use in bathing. A portion of the floor in the center of the room is made of planks so arranged that it can be taken up, exposing a pit beneath, in which a fire of drift logs is built. When the smoke has passed off and the wood is reduced to a bed of

coals, a cover is put over the smoke hole in the roof and the men sit naked about the room until they are in profuse perspiration; they then bathe in the urine, which combines with the oil on their bodies, and thus takes the place of soap, after which they go outside and pour water over their bodies until they become cool. While bathing they remain in the kashim with the temperature so high that their skin becomes shining red and appears to be almost at the point of blistering; then going outside they squat about in the snow perfectly nude, and seem to enjoy the contrasting temperature. On several occasions I saw them go from the sweat bath to holes in the ice on neighboring streams and, squatting there, pour ice water over their backs and shoulders with a wooden dipper, apparently experiencing the greatest pleasure from the operation.

The author also describes how bathers protect themselves from the intense heat by using a cap of waterfowl skins, and respirators:

> Throughout the region visited the men, while taking their sweat baths, are accustomed to use a cap made of the skin of some water fowl, usually the red- or black-throat loon. The skin is cut open along the belly and removed entire, minus the neck, wings, and legs; it is then dried and softened so as to be pliable and is fastened together at the neck in such a way that it can be worn on the head. Owing to the intense heat generated in the fire pit, the bathers, who are always males, are obliged to use respirators to protect their lungs. These are made of fine shavings of willow or spruce bound into the form

of an oblong pad formed to cover the mouth, the chin, and a portion of the cheeks. These pads are convex externally and concave within; crossing the concave side is a small wooden rod, either round or square, so that the wearer can grasp it in his teeth and thus hold the respirator in position.

John Henry Kilbuck, a Moravian missionary of Mohican and Delaware Indian descent, worked among the Yup'ik from 1885 to 1922. He wrote this description of the direct fire bath:

> The heat is sometimes so intense as to blister the ears—before perspiration takes place. When the wood is dry and piled properly—there is quick combustion with a minimum amount of smoke, and the bathers in the midst of such enjoyment—set up a lamentation which is so like the howling of a pack of huskies or wolves. This lamentation is for the dead because they are missing such a luxurious sweat-bath.
>
> From experience the Eskimos have learned which embers and partially burned pieces of wood produce distressing headaches—and these are carefully put out—before the window is replaced.—Boys are not permitted to take these sweatbaths.—After the sweat—the men go out into the open air—and roll in the snow in wintertime—or plunge into the nearby stream in summer.

Anthropologist Chase Hensel worked in this region in the 1980s and 1990s. He describes how the *qasegiq* fell into disuse by the early 1990s because of radical changes in social and religious life, but shows how sweating continues to be an important hygienic and social activity and serves as a marker of cultural identity. Men still sweat together, but there are also family sweats and sweats with outsiders, Native and non-Native. There is joking, and challenges are thrown out to cosweaters to endure the heat. Men engage in the sweat and sweating is an important topic of discussion. Note that the sweat is a highly flexible social and religious institution, adjusting to shifts in family structure and gender relations. Sweats, like other rituals, are transformed by contemporary need in dialogue with structures of the past. Tradition does not invalidate but rather guides present practices, as we will see in looking at more contemporary sweatlodge phenomena.

Personal Experience: Lakota

Eber L. Hampton is a Chickasaw and Euro-American from Oklahoma. He grew up in California, and his primary teacher in traditional ways is a Kiowa. Hampton writes of the respect necessary in learning about the sweat, analyzing it, and representing it in textual form, but he also stresses that the sweat is primarily an event, not a description: "The learning, the transformation takes place at a level deeper than words. Everything related to the sweat has a purpose and an effect. Its reality is not a symbol with a meaning. It is real at all levels and works with our actions to have real effects."

As I have learned from my own teachers, one should speak one's opinion about spiritual matters. So this article will shift from formal academic research to a reflection on my own participation in the sweat. I have sweated and continue to sweat primarily with Lakota people, mostly on the Pine Ridge Reservation. I want to be careful to speak only from my experience, understanding, and what I was taught. I do not universalize my own experience into a "standard sweat"; nor do I claim any authority over what is right or wrong practice. Each sweat I have attended was structurally the same, involving prayer, song, intense heat, and intense emotions, from sorrow to joy. Each sweat was also unique.

What strikes me most about the ceremony is its intensity, not only in terms of heat but also in terms of religious and social experience. The ceremony forges close spiritual and social bonds among participants. People come together to form sweat groups for various needs and concerns: personal, tribal, and even cosmic. The sweatlodges that I have attended are primarily places of prayer, whether it be petition or thanksgiving. In Christian churches, one recites a creed to establish a harmony of belief; the sweatlodge provides for a harmony of practice—all undergo the same difficult ritual, regardless of how they pray or what they believe. While anthropology often focuses on the social and cultural elements of this ritual, at root it is essentially religious.

Lakota sweats generally have four rounds, periods marked by closing and then opening the single door. Rocks are heated outside the sweat and brought in by a doorkeeper, who may or may not join the rest of the group for the sweat. The sweatlodge itself is a dome-shaped frame of willow or cherry branches covered with tarps and blankets so as to be airtight. The entrance faces a specific direction, usually west or east. Sage and sometimes carpets are placed on the seating area. A pit in the center of the lodge holds the hot rocks, and there is an exterior fireplace in line with the pit and the entrance outside. Sometimes an altar is formed outside of the lodge in line with the door from the stones excavated from the interior pit.

People are expected to be in good relationship with each other when entering the sweatlodge together. Negative thoughts or feelings are amplified in the sweat, as are positive ones, so one should not bring negativity into the lodge, according to my teachers. The Lakota ask that women who are menstruating exclude themselves from the sweat, for they have a different power at that time. The people with whom I work are quick to point out that this means nothing negative or judgmental, but that the mixing of powers is dangerous.

Everyone enters the lodge before the rocks are brought in. The first six or sometimes seven rocks are arranged in a special way, with prayers and incense. Sometimes a sacred pipe is touched to each rock. The rest of the rocks are then brought in, and a bucket of water and a ladle are also introduced. Singers bring hand drums with them. Once the water is blessed, the door is shut and the first round is begun. The leader of the sweat welcomes the participants, tells what the sweat is being "put up" for, and sometimes mentions his or her qualifications for leading the sweat—always in a humble and self-effacing way. The four rounds are conducted with prayers, singing, sometimes talks between rounds, and the pouring of water to create an intense steam heat. Leaders are careful not to scald anyone, and they encourage people to say "*Mitakuye Oyasin*" ("all of my relatives") if it becomes too uncomfortable, so that someone can open the door. People in the sweat open their hearts and lives to each other. What is said and prayed about during a specific sweat is kept confidential. Intimate prayer sharing amid the physical suffering in the lodge brings participants release from their sufferings and intensifies spiritual and communal support. Between rounds, water is drunk, speeches may be given, and people sometimes converse and joke. Humor is an essential part of every Lakota ritual, and it certainly has its place in the sweat.

At the same time, the sweatlodge is a place where Natives encounter not only spiritual reality in an intense way but also social reality. Many sweats are gatherings of family members, voluntary associations, veterans, or people enhancing their own sobriety. The sweat is also a place where outsiders, non-Indians, can meet and pray with Native people *if they are invited* and properly prepared. Thus the sweat can be a place of reconciliation. I have often heard Lakota people re-

mind participants that in the sweat we are all equal: we have no color in the darkness, and we are all humbled and reborn. This is not merely rhetoric, but reality in the sweatlodge. Others respect the universality of the ritual but ask outsiders to honor their own traditions in their own ways, rather than to participate in Native rituals.

There are any number of published works describing different forms of sweats; each has unique elements as well as a consistent format. The Lakota sweat is sometimes cited as the most prevalent type. It endured when other groups ceased sweating and then was learned by those groups. But other Native groups also continue their own precontact sweat rituals, all incorporating both past practice and contemporary needs. Both on and off reservations, there is wide interest in the ceremony.

Simply learning about the sweatlodge ceremony does not entitle one to participate in the ritual, nor does it give a person the authority to construct or conduct a sweat. Different tribes have different criteria for who may lead a sweat, who may be taught how to do so, and who may participate. I have always entered the sweat as a participant, sometimes called upon to pray in a special way or to speak between rounds—but I have always been an invited participant, not the one who conducts the ritual.

Contemporary Uses

Historical accounts teach us that the sweatlodge was used for a variety of purposes: spiritual, medical, and social. Native societies did not necessarily consider these to be separate categories, as modern Western cultures do. Thus it is not surprising that Natives continue to adapt the ceremony for additional purposes. On the Pine Ridge Reservation, where I sweat, some of the uses of the lodge include healing family crises, consoling mourners, preparing people who will engage in other rituals such as the Sun Dance or vision quest, honoring veterans and healing the traumas they may have encountered, consulting with spirits for guidance, healing people physically and emotionally, and incorporating new group members from the reservation or, depending on the group, sometimes from off-reservation. Lakota not raised in traditional ways sometimes use the sweat as the first step toward reincorporating themselves into traditional ritual practice.

Beyond the boundaries of the reservation, the sweatlodge can be found today throughout North America and in Europe. Natives from cities and rural areas make use of this ceremony. The sweatlodge ceremony is practiced by Natives in many prisons as well as in drug and alcohol treatment centers, personal growth and therapeutic programs, and in men's and women's groups. The controversy arises when non-Natives appropriate the sweatlodge for their own purposes, or sometimes when Natives actively spread the use of this and other rituals among non-Natives.

Abuses and Protests

The Lakota I have met have a broad acceptance of people who sincerely seek a spiritual path. Hospitality is valued in ritual as well as in social life. Problems over ritual participation are likely to arise when people force themselves into situations, begin taking over, or exploit what they have been privileged to experience. Mistrust of outsiders is justified. Both the U.S. government and Christian churches once vigorously opposed and suppressed Native religious practices. A series of people, non-Native and Native, have exploited Native religion for personal gain. Memories of abuse are long. Healing is sometimes slow.

Some Lakota cite the four colors used to designate the sacred directions—red, white, yellow, and black—as evidence of the inclusivity of the sweatlodge ritual, both symbolically and ethnically. Others stress that the whites have taken everything from the Lakota, and that their religion is the last thing they have left. Understandably, they and other tribal groups are very guarded about non-Indians participating in the sweat, and they distrust some of their own people who misuse spiritual ways. Red Cherries, a Northern Cheyenne Sun Dance/Arrow Priest and Elk Society Headman, had this to say about the exploitation of Native ceremonies, specifically the sweatlodge:

> The sweat lodge was given by the Creator: we have oral history as well as ceremonial proof and testimony, that it ascended from certain Tribes.

Although there are similar forms of sweat lodges in other tribes, it is the Plains Warrior Sweat of the Cheyenne and Lakota Nations that seems to be the most often exploited, he said.

The Plains ceremonies are imitated and exploited by non-Native, and at times Native, New-Age shamans who are self proclaimed priests or priestesses molding it to there [sic] wild agendas.

I have heard of sweats termed as new moon sweats and solstice sweats, somewhere this non-sense must be challenged. I don't think our elders who fought so hard and paid the ultimate price with their blood and lives so that we could continue to carry on our ceremonies have ever heard of these types of sweats.

Non-Natives have been charged with misappropriating the sweatlodge for financial gain and with conducting unauthorized ceremonies, or with abuse of the ceremony itself through inappropriate innovations. Different tribes and individuals within tribes have various views and opinions about this issue. Some allow non-Natives to participate in sweats, or even to conduct them, while others more strictly regulate who may conduct and participate in sweats and restrict those privileges to members of their own group. Some groups allow one to lead a sweat based on his or her personal spiritual experiences, while others regulate leadership socially, by passing down the right to conduct the ceremony—sometimes referred to as pouring water—among members of the group.

On reservations, sweats and other ceremonies are regulated through community approbation or nonattendance at rituals. With the expanded use of the sweatlodge ceremony off reservations and, in some cases, out of local Native control, new modes of regulation of the sweat ceremony and protection of sacred ceremonies have arisen. Lists of proscribed leaders, newspaper articles, documentaries, books, the Internet, and even legal action in tribal or non-Indian legal systems have been resorted to.

There is a large and growing literature on the appropriation of Native religious culture. Some Non-Natives hold that they have a right to spiritual practice and that it cannot be owned culturally. Some Natives hold that non-Natives be completely restricted from any Native ceremony—either to observe, participate, or lead. It is safe to say that all Natives would agree that ceremonies such as the sweatlodge should be conducted properly. The proper role of non-Natives is currently being settled in many places and in many different ways. Just as there is no single, simple answer from the variety of Native communities to the question of whether non-Natives can engage in sweats and other ceremonial activities, there is no one opinion from the non-Native scholarly, professional, and practicing communities.

Conclusion

The sweatlodge is a uniquely universal example of Native ritual. Practiced widely among tribal groups in the past, and now again in the present, the ceremony is easily replicated. As a boundary or transitional ritual, it is ideal for moving people between profound and sacred worlds—and, when appropriate, between Native and non-Native realities. The ritual is transformative, and many have found physical, spiritual, and even cultural healing in its warm embrace. In the past, geography, language, dress, and custom allowed for clear boundaries between groups, Native and non-Native. Religion remains one of the unique identifiers for Natives. Despite the ravages of colonialism, the sweatlodge allows Native people to establish and recognize boundaries, both sacred and profane, to control those boundaries, and to cross them—and sometimes allow others to cross, as well.

Raymond A. Bucko, S. J.

See also Academic Study of American Indian Religious Traditions; Architecture; Ceremony and Ritual, Lakota; Ceremony and Ritual, Yup'iq; Christianity, Indianization of; Health and Wellness, Traditional Approaches; Identity; Kinship; Law, Legislation, and Native Religion; Menstruation and Menarche; Mother Earth; New Age Appropriation; Oral Traditions; Prison and Native Spirituality; Reservations, Spiritual and Cultural Implications; Sacred Pipe; Spirits and Spirit Helpers, Plateau; Symbolism in Ritual and Ceremony; Vision Quest Rites; Warfare, Religious Aspects

References and Further Reading
Aaland, Mikkel. 1978. _Sweat: The Illustrated History and Description of the Finnish Sauna, Russian Bania, Islamic Hammam, Japanese Mishi-Buro, Mexican Temescal and American Indian and Eskimo Sweatlodge._ Santa Barbara, CA: Kapra Press.
Bowers, Alfred W. 1950. _Mandan Social and Ceremonial Organization._ Chicago: University of Chicago Press.
———. 1992. _Hidatsa Social and Ceremonial Organization._ Lincoln: University of Nebraska Press.
Brown, Joseph E. 1953. _The Sacred Pipe: Black Elk's Account of the Seven Rites of the Oglala Sioux._ Norman: University of Oklahoma Press.
Bruchac, Joseph. 1993. _The Native American Sweat Lodge: History and Legends._ Freedom, CA: Crossing Press.
Bucko, Raymond A. 1998. _The Lakota Ritual of the Sweat Lodge: History and Contemporary Practice._ Lincoln: University of Nebraska Press.
Catlin, George, ed. 1975. _Letters and Notes on the North American Indians._ New York: Clarkson N. Potter.
Clements, William M. 2001. "The New Age Sweat Lodge." Pp. 143–162 in _Healing Logics: Culture and Medicine in Modern Health Belief Systems._ Edited by E. Brady. Logan: Utah State University Press.
Densmore, Frances. 1972. _Mandan and Hidatsa Music._ New York: Da Capo Press.
Driver, Harold E. 1975. _Indians of North America,_ 2d ed. Chicago: University of Chicago Press.
Fitzhugh, William W., et al. 1982. _Inua: Spirit World of the Bering Sea Eskimo._ Washington, DC: Smithsonian Institution Press.
Hampton, Eber L. 1981. "The Sweat Lodge and Modern Society." Dissertation qualifying paper, Harvard University.
Hensel, Chase. 1996. _Telling Our Selves: Ethnicity and Discourse in Southwestern Alaska._ New York: Oxford University Press.
Henshaw, Henry. 1971. "Sweating and Sweat-Houses." Pp. 660–662 in _Handbook of American Indians North of Mexico, part 2._ Edited by Fredrick W. Hodge. New York: Rowman and Littlefield.
Kilbuck, John. 1988. "Something about the Inuit of the Kuskokwim River, Alaska." In _The Yup'ik Eskimo: As Described in the Travel Journals and Ethnographic Accounts of John and Edith Kilbuck who served with the Alaska Mission of the_

Moravian Church 1885–1900. Edited by A. Fienup-Riordan. Kingston, Ontario: Limeston Press.

Krickenberg, W. 1939. "The Indian Sweat Bath." In *Ciba Symposia,* 19–26. Summit, NJ: Ciba Pharmaceutical Products.

Lalemant, Jerome. 1898. "Relation of 1640." In *Jesuit Relations and Allied Documents,* vol. 19. Edited by R. G. Thwaites. Cleveland: Burrows Brothers.

Le Jeune, Paul. 1897a. "Relation of What Occurred in New France in the Year 1636." In *Jesuit Relations and Allied Documents,* vol. 10. Edited by R. G. Thwaites. Cleveland: Burrows Brothers.

———. 1897b. "Relation of What Occurred in New France on the Great River St. Lawrence, in the Year 1634." In *Jesuit Relations and Allied Documents,* vol. 6. Edited by R. G. Thwaites. Cleveland: Burrows Brothers.

Le Mercier, François Joseph. 1901a. "Relation of What Occurred in New France in the Year 1637." In *Jesuit Relations and Allied Documents,* vol. 14. Edited by R. G. Thwaites. Cleveland: Burrows Brothers.

———. 1901b. "Relation of What Occurred in New France in the Year 1637." In *Jesuit Relations and Allied Documents,* vol. 13. Edited by R. G. Thwaites. Cleveland: Burrows Brothers.

Lopatin, Ivan. 1960. "Origin of the Native American Steam Bath." *American Anthropologist* 62: 977–993.

Maximilian, Prince of Wied. 1905. *Travels in the Interior of North America,* 3 vols. Translated by H. E. Lloyd. Volume 2. Cleveland: Arthur H. Clark Company.

Nelson, Edward William. 1899. "The Eskimo about Bearing Strait." Pp. 19–518 in *Eighteenth Annual Report of the Bureau of American Ethnology to the Secretary of the Smithsonian Institution 1896–1897.* Edited by J. W. Powell. Washington, DC: Government Printing Office.

Norrell, Brenda. 2002. "Fake Lakota Medicine Men Hold Sun Dance Ceremonies: Cheyenne Headsman Calls for Bear Butte Meeting." *Lakota Journal.* Rapid City, SD.

Quinn, William J., and Thomas E Smith. 1992. "The Sweat Lodge Ceremony in Challenge/Adventure Programming." In *Celebrating Our Tradition, Charting Our Future: Proceedings of the International Conference of the Association for Experimental Education.* Banff, Alberta, Canada. ERIC Document Reproduction Service ED 353121.

Stolzman, William, S.J. 1986. *How to Take Part in Lakota Ceremonies.* Pine Ridge, SD: Red Cloud Indian School.

Sturdevent, William, ed. 1978. *Handbook of North American Indians.* Washington, DC: Smithsonian Institution Press.

Vecsey, Christopher. 1988. "The Genesis of Phillip Deere's Sweat Lodge." Pp. 206–232 in *Imagine Ourselves Richly: Mythic Narratives of North American Indians.* Edited by C. Vecsey. New York: Crossroad.

Welch, Christina. 2002. "Appropriating the Didjeridu and the Sweat Lodge: New Age Baddies and Indigenous Victims?" *Journal of Contemporary Religion* 17, no. 1: 21–38.

Yellowtail, Thomas. 1991. "Sweat Lodge." Pp. 106–114 in *Yellowtail: Crow Medicine Man and Sun Dance Chief: An Autobiography as Told to Michael Oren Fitzgerald.* Norman: University of Oklahoma Press.

Symbolism in American Indian Ritual and Ceremony

Symbolism connects rituals and ceremonies to the sacred stories of the people and to the kinship systems told about in the stories. These kinship relations include plant and animal relatives, along with human relatives and spirit relatives who are other-than-human. Rituals and ceremonies are chiefly concerned with the renewal and maintenance of these kinship connections, which are fundamental for the survival of every people. Rituals and ceremonies establish and orient a people in relation to (1) their place in the world by means of the sacred directions, and (2) the important personages in their kinship network by means of appropriate reciprocities.

The meaning of any symbolism depends on the sacred stories underlying the symbols. All ritual life and ceremonial traditions are based on the stories that the people hold as sacred, so that rites and ceremonies are a sort of replay of, or re-engagement with, the experiences related in those sacred stories. Sacred stories originate from (1) unusual dreams or visionary experiences of individuals that may be described as prophetic, revelatory, mystical, or shamanic, or (2) unusual group experiences that dramatically transform the communal life of the group. In either case, a sacred story relates the experience as an oral narrative of an encounter with nonordinary reality that establishes a relationship with other-than-human beings who possess power over life and death. The primary narrative features in these sacred stories are shaped and reshaped by the people through an ongoing process of remembering and recounting these narrative elements as they relate to the day-to-day existence of the people. In this way, a set of signifiers is formed from the stories that estab-

lishes the people's way of looking at the world, at the whole of existence, and at the meaning of life and death. This set of signifiers functions as a symbolic system, and the power of symbols can come into play through ritual words and acts that (1) recall and renew the formative relationships with the primordial spirit-persons as told about in the sacred stories, and (2) call forth the protective and regenerative forces of those relationships to be operative in behalf of the people in the circumstances of the present moment.

The symbolic systems of American Indian peoples differ from those of European-derived cultures because of the difference in the stories. The sacred stories of any people will include creation stories that tell of the origin and structuring of the universe. Each story about the origin of the universe always includes, either explicitly or implicitly, an account of the cosmology of the universe, which is a narrative that tells how the universe came to be structured as an orderly, functioning cosmos. While each indigenous people has its own distinctive creation stories that result in a particular cosmology which shapes the signifying system of that people, there are similarities among these indigenous cosmologies that mark them collectively as distinct from the European-derived cosmology. In modern times that European cosmology has taken the form of a scientific story of creation (the big-bang theory) and of cosmology (a sought-after unified field theory). A scientific cosmology too often dismisses all forms of human consciousness and experience other than a cognitive perception of an objectified world, so that it includes no respect for dreams and visions or for transformative moments in communal self-perception. Because the cosmology of a people governs the signifying system of that people, the discourse or accepted way of communicating in a European-derived culture will function differently from the discourse of an American Indian culture. For this reason, it is vital that our understanding of symbolism as it functions in the rites and ceremonies of indigenous peoples be clearly derived from indigenous cosmologies and avoid the discourse patterns of the dominant culture.

Cosmologies of American Indian peoples commonly feature systems of kinship relations that give priority to inclusiveness and interconnectedness, so that all oppositions and separations are secondary to the fundamental relatedness of all beings. Kinship-centered symbolism influences the symbolic role of places and of persons in indigenous ritual and ceremony. In symbolizing place, this world is not seen as an impersonal landscape where the physical processes of nature play out in a closed system of cause and effect; instead, this world is characterized by a sacred geography in which all places are related in one way or another to episodes in the sacred stories about the ongoing relationships connecting human persons to their plant and animal relatives, their deceased ancestors, and the other-than-human

spirit persons. Each place is a location that is symbolically tied to the special kinship interactions "taking place" (whether past, present, or future) in some intimate association with that location. In symbolizing persons, an individual person is not seen as a subjectively separate self whose existence is cut off from, and incapable of, any intimate identification with other humans, plants and animal relatives, or sacred beings. Instead, indigenous symbolism includes sacred systems of metamorphosis by which a mask, a song, or a dance introduces you to stunning shifts in identity; momentarily, but authentically, you become the face, voice, and persona of an other-than-human person, thus affirming in the face of all evidence to the contrary that such a person is your very real kin.

It is virtually universal among indigenous peoples of North America to orient the symbolism of place around four sacred directions. These four directions would be misunderstood if we equated them to the four cardinal points of north, east, south, and west in the manner of mere coordinates. Instead, these four should be understood in the personal mode of kinship as the four sacred winds, or the four sacred mountains, or whatever set of four is known in a people's stories as the four distinctive forces that give all places their own particular features and that empower places with possibilities for encountering significant others when they are invoked in ritual and ceremony.

In Lakota tradition the west wind has priority in ritual status, so that prayer will be directed first to the west, followed by ritually facing and addressing in sequence the north, east, and south, and completing the cycle by once again facing the west. Lakota people pay kinship respect to fellow beings of all four quarters of the cosmos by saying the ritual words *mitakuye oyasin,* commonly expressed in English as "all my relations," and by ritually making a full turn of the body so that all relatives of the four quarters are acknowledged. This cycle of fourness is so formative in indigenous cosmologies that it may be extended symbolically to designate four seasons of the year, four stages in a human life, or other ways of periodizing time by fours—such as the four openings of the doorway to a sweatlodge, marking the four stages of the ceremony or the four days of a contemporary Sun Dance. The fourness that permeates indigenous stories signals that temporality as well as location is framed by the personalizing considerations of kinship.

Beginning with the ubiquity of sets of four throughout North American traditions, the complexity of indigenous cosmologies typically moves beyond this basic fourness to embrace two additional directions, for a total of six. The kinship quality of these six is memorably evident in the well-known vision-story of the Lakota holy man Nicholas Black Elk, in which he reports a shamanic or out-of-body journey to a cloud-tepee in the sky. Within this imposing tepee he finds six old men and is told: "Your Grandfathers are having a council" (Neihardt 1932, 24). He realizes that "these were not old men, but the Powers of the World" (ibid., 25). Each of these "Grandfathers" addresses him in turn, beginning with "the Power of the West." Each gives him a gift that represents a specific power, and each subsequently leaves the tepee and undergoes metamorphosis into an animal form, the sixth transforming into a likeness of Black Elk himself. These six sacred persons empowering the Lakota universe are described with the kinship term of "grandfather," and the gifts they give and the forms of their metamorphoses symbolically indicate their specialized powers. These six "grandfathers" include, besides the standard four, two "grandfathers" named "the Spirit of the Sky" and "the Spirit of the Earth" (ibid., 29–30). The ritual sequence for the six begins with the four representing the horizontal plane of existence and shifts to the vertical by including the sky above and the earth below as the fifth and sixth sacred directions, thus encompassing the whole of the real world.

While all six sacred beings are gendered as male in Black Elk's story, Lakota tradition customarily treats the sixth of these as female, as "grandmother," and other traditions also commonly identify the sky, the sun, and the realms above as male and the earth, its navel, and the realms below as female. Both the above and the below are considered to be sacred realms that are off-limits for ordinary human existence, though accessible to individuals through dreams and visionary journeys. Ordinary people may relate to these sacred realms symbolically in ceremonies in which a sacred mountain, a sacred tree, a lightning bolt, or a falling star may represent an access route for relations with sacred beings from above, and a sacred spring or a sacred cave may represent an access route for relations with sacred beings from below. The sacred realms of both the above and the below may be represented as multilayered. Stories about human emergence from a series of worlds below our present middle world characterize the Pueblo traditions of the Southwest, whereas stories about human origin through a woman falling from the world above can be found among Iroquoian peoples of the Northeast. Other traditions identify sacred realms existing at the extreme perimeter of the middle world, marking a domain normally inaccessible to humans in a way similar to the above and the below. Kwak'wak'wakw people of the Northwest coast expect Baxbakwalanuxsiwae, the Man-Eater Spirit from the North End of the World, to fly in bird-form from the extreme north in order to make a ritual appearance at the *tsetseqa* (winter solstice ceremony). That ceremony symbolizes the renewal of life and all of its relationships, when the power of winter is reversed and the birthing light once again defeats darkness.

While indigenous symbolism of place and time conveys a sense of the wholeness of the created order and its kinship network by way of the six sacred directions, some traditions highlight the importance of a seventh "direction," which functions as a focal point for the set of six. The Zuni story of the water strider identifies its six legs as signifying the four horizontal and two vertical directions and specifies that the *itiwana* (center) of the universe lies at the place where the six vectors of the water strider's legs converge, which is the water strider's own middle, or "heart." The water strider revealed to the Zunis the location of the sacred middle place of the universe, thus concluding their migration history. They had been searching for this convergence point where all true orientation of place and time begins and where life is engendered and empowered. This seventh "direction" becomes the most propitious location for ritual acts, since it is the true convergence place of relatedness for each of us to the whole range of our cosmic kin.

The seventh "direction," as the focal point for renewing ritual relations on a cosmic scale, can be a specific geographic location, or it can be ceremonially construed as the center of the universe by addressing and invoking in turn each of the six winds or mountains or cosmic forces—thus making that specific place of ceremony an empowered location where the six powers of the universe converge. When the cosmic powers of the six sacred mountains are invoked in Diné (Navajo) ceremony through sacred chants and replications of sacred mosaics (called sandpaintings) on the floor of the ceremonial hogan (the traditional Diné dwelling), ordinary space and time are opened up to the nonordinary realities acknowledged in Diné sacred stories. When the person to be healed enters the sacred mosaic and sits in the center of that ritual space, he or she is understood to have stepped into an ancient world of story in which the principal powers of this world are enacting or re-enacting creative moments of balancing the life-and-death factors that connect all relationships and that bring order to ordinary existence. Sitting at the center of things, where the sacred world momentarily impinges on the ordinary realm, is to be at the ritual place where the fundamental relationships that shape all life are specifically engaged. These relationships possess the intimacy and reciprocity characteristic of kinship, while also conveying the profound capacity to extend beyond the boundary of the human so as to embrace those other-than-human beings who transcend ordinary space and time.

Besides telling about the beginnings of the universe and the shaping of place and temporality, sacred stories include narratives about hunting and fishing and the harvesting of plants. Food is fundamental to survival, and all food is understood in these stories as given and re-ceived within the mutual reciprocities of a kinship system. When you eat animal or plant foods, you are eating your relatives and incur an obligation to them that you discharge by respectful treatment and ritual acts of giving back to your plant and animal relatives so that your kinship ties with them are maintained and renewed.

Contemporary Lakota communities celebrate the annual Sun Dance in which the male dancers are pierced so that wooden or bone skewers are inserted through the flesh of the upper chest or of the upper back (there are alternative modes of piercing available to contemporary female dancers). Thongs are attached to the skewers and the thongs are connected to a rope tied to the central tree (when piercing the chest) or to one or more buffalo skulls (when piercing the back). To dance until the flesh gives way was understood by the dancers to be a voluntary act of sacrifice by which reciprocity with your buffalo relatives was carried through. The buffalo people had given away their lives to their relatives; these hunters were obligated to emulate their buffalo relatives with similar acts of generosity. The give-away of the buffalo brought life-sustaining food to the human relatives, and the give-away of the Sun Dancers is understood by contemporary Lakota people to bring life-enhancing benefit to the entire kinship system of the dancers, while recognizing that such a system extends not only to the buffalo people but also to all the beings of the universe.

In one of his dream-vision episodes, Black Elk describes how the camp of people he is leading transforms into "buffalo and elk and even fowls of the air" (DeMallie 1994, 126). In an aside to his narrative, Black Elk explains to John Neihardt that this metamorphosis means "that the Indian generations have dreams and are like unto the animals of this world. Some have visions about elks, birds, and even gophers or eagles. People will be like the animals—take the animals' virtues and strengths" (ibid., 127). Because all humans dream, the universality of dreaming consciousness with its characteristic signature of metamorphosis fosters the recognition that our kinship relations extend well beyond the strictly human community. By engaging these kinship reciprocities, Sun Dancing and other rituals open the door of dreaming consciousness to a psychic and symbolic depth beyond the merely human.

Black Elk's narrative of his visionary journey to the realm of the Six Grandfathers includes instances of his being given plants (herbs) with extraordinary powers. Plants play a variety of symbolic roles in indigenous ritual and ceremony. The "four smokes" of Great Plains traditions include the protective and purifying roles of sage and cedar, along with the roles of sweet grass and tobacco in attracting, pleasing, and propitiating spirit relatives. Some of the plants revealed to Black Elk possessed power to heal illness when used in a ritually appropriate manner, which would include a respectful acknowledgment of kinship reciprocity with those plant persons possessing medicine power.

Among peoples who cultivate food plants, there are stories that tell how we are related to Corn Mother. There is a common storyline to these stories, claims George Tinker, that "involves the willing self-sacrifice (vicarious suffering) of the First Mother (Corn Mother) on behalf of her children" (Tinker 1998, 150). Tinker notes that this implies "the sacramental nature of eating. Corn and all food stuffs are our relatives," and he points out our reciprocal obligation—that is, "[O]ne can never eat without remembering the gift of the Mother" (ibid., 151). Tinker wishes to emphasize the symbolic role of gender in the ritual acknowledgment of Corn Mother's give-away, admonishing us "to pay attention to the inherent valuing of female gifts and wisdom in our communities. We are to remember forever that healing in the form of both food and spiritual sustenance has come to us traditionally not through men but through a woman" (ibid., 152). Tinker also acknowledges that the example of the White Buffalo Calf Woman among the Lakota people establishes the importance of the feminine within the rituals of kinship among a hunting people (ibid., 149). She functions as the Buffalo

Mistress, the one who looks after the welfare of the buffalo people and mediates between them and the human community by providing the Lakota with a set of appropriate kinship rituals, including the Sun Dance.

Another powerful plant being has come to play a prominent role in contemporary indigenous ritual and ceremony, based on stories with relatively recent origins. The peyote cactus is featured in traditions beginning in the 1870s and 1880s on the Southern Plains. Not only are the stories linked with peyote of more recent origin than most sacred stories; they also differ from the norm by the pantribal reach of their symbolism and by the openness to inclusion of elements borrowed from the Christian stories of Euro-Americans. By providing an alternative symbol system for American Indian peoples whose traditional rituals and ceremonies were rapidly disappearing in the face of a cultural destruction that included geographical displacement and military suppression, in addition to the loss of the kinship reciprocities with the vanishing buffalo and other increasingly scarce game, peyote represented a way of spiritual survival. The new symbolic structures of peyote ritual included much that was familiar, such as the healing and wisdom-giving powers of a plant relative and the reciprocal kinship obligations toward such a relative. In a time of cultural distress, the Peyote Spirit offered stabilizing forms of story, symbol, and ceremony.

All sacred stories, all symbolic systems, and all ritual and ceremony exist in time and, therefore, within the processes of change from generation to generation. Recent decades have been times when various American Indian peoples have taken the opportunity to reclaim ritual practices once suppressed or reduced to clandestine observance. Recovery of traditional ways can function as a renewal of the force of the old stories and the symbol systems vested in those stories, and this cultural and religious renewal can serve to differentiate a people's identity from the imposed stories and symbols of the dominant culture; it can even mark a political resistance to the globalizing interests of the world's governing elite, who are living by their own, quite different story, a story that values commodities instead of kinship. However, the old stories and their symbolic meanings will survive only if they serve the actual life of their communities, and this matter of surviving always faces practical realities and requires a process of both validating and adapting the stories and symbols in order for the rituals and ceremonies to continue to be powerful and true.

Dale Stover

See also Dreams and Visions; First Foods and Food Symbolism; Hunting, Religious Restrictions and Implications; Kinship; Masks and Masking; Native American Church, Peyote Movement; Sandpainting

References and Further Reading
Bucko, Raymond A. 1998. *The Lakota Ritual of the Sweat Lodge: History and*

Contemporary Practice. Lincoln: University of Nebraska Press.

DeMallie, Raymond J. 1984. *The Sixth Grandfather: Black Elk's Teachings Given to John G. Neihardt.* Lincoln: University of Nebraska Press.

Neihardt, John G. 1932. *Black Elk Speaks: Being the Life Story of a Holy Man of the Oglala Sioux.* Lincoln: University of Nebraska Press.

Niezen, Ronald. 2000. *Spirit Wars: Native North American Religions in the Age of*

Nation Building. Berkeley: University of California Press.

Stover, Dale. 2001. "Postcolonial Sun Dancing at Wakpamni Lake." *Journal of the American Academy of Religion* 69, no. 4 (December): 817–836.

Tinker, George. 1998. "Jesus, Corn Mother, and Conquest: Christology and Colonialism." Pp. 134–154 in *Native American Religious Identity: Unforgotten Gods.* Edited by Jace Weaver. Maryknoll, NY: Orbis Books.

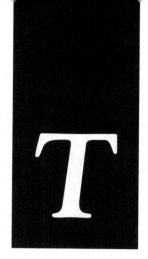

Tekakwitha, Kateri (1656–1680)

(Spiritual leader/Mohawk)

Kateri Tekakwitha, also known as Kateri Tegaquitha, Catherine Tekakwitha, Catherine Tegahkouita, La Sainte Sauvagesse, and the Lily of the Mohawks, was born in 1656 in the Mohawk village of Ossernenon near present-day Auriesville, New York. Tekakwitha was the daughter of an Iroquois chief and an Algonkin Christian mother. Her parents and younger brother died of smallpox when she was four, and she was left crippled, with poor eyesight, and horribly disfigured by pockmarks. Her name, Tekakwitha, has variously been translated as meaning "she-pushes-with-her-hands," "who walks groping for her way," "hard-working woman," or "gathering-things-in-order"(Vecsey 1997).

After the death of her immediate family, Tekakwitha lived with an uncle, Iowerano, an ally of the Dutch and a critic of the Catholic Church and of Catholic conversions. He was particularly critical of Tekakwitha for taking an intense in-terest in conversion when, in 1675, Jesuit father Jacques de Lambertville started a mission in Kateri's village. Father de Lambertville started to prepare Tekakwitha for baptism into the Catholic faith, and a year later, on Easter Sunday, 1676, she was christened and named Kateri (Catherine). As her conversion was not accepted by her extended family, de Lambertville suggested that she relocate; in a heroic escape she fled north to the St. Lawrence Jesuit reduction, Sault St. Louis/Kahnawake, near Montreal, Quebec.

Tekakwitha became a central figure in the Christian community and persevered in trying to live a life of Christian perfection. Although she was ineligible to become a nun because she was Indian, she observed the life of hospital nuns in Montreal, which increased her desire to take a vow of chastity and to get closer to her self-avowed spouse, Jesus Christ. After much instruction she was allowed to take the long-desired vow and was indeed the first Iroquois to take the vow of chastity. She subjected herself to extreme mortifications, such as flagellation, exposure to the elements, fasting, and sleeping on thorns. Although her confessors urged her to reduce her mortifications, she continued with more extreme asceticism and became mortally ill. As she weakened, she received last rites and died on April 17, during the Holy Week, in 1680. She was twenty-four. It is documented by her confessors that within half an hour of her death her pockmarks disappeared and her beauty overcame those around her.

Within a few weeks of her death, Tekakwitha's confessors, Jesuits Pierre Cholenec and Claude Chauchetiere, wrote Tekakwitha's biography as hagiography. Those writings contain most of the information that is known about Tekakwitha today. Shortly after the hagiographies were written, Tekakwitha was transformed from a Mohawk girl whom few knew to a symbol, Kateri Tekakwitha, the first Iroquois virgin and a saint-in-the-making. She became a symbol for the Jesuit mission's success in Catholic conversion. Her story grew over time, and in 1884 the Jesuits petitioned for her canonization, the first step on the road to becoming a saint. In 1932 her dossier was presented to the Vatican, and after careful deliberation Pope Pius XII declared her Venerable in 1943. In 1980 the Vatican beatified her, and she officially became the Blessed Kateri Tekakwitha, with her feast day being July 14. At present she is one miracle away from becoming a saint. The Vatican is carefully weighing evidence of her intercessions and miracles that have happened in her name, but they are awaiting one more confirmed miracle before she can be elevated to sainthood.

Tekakwitha, over time, has functioned as a healing force for Native Americans within the Catholic Church. Many Native Americans find her identity as Indian particularly appealing. The annual Tekakwitha Conference began in 1939. Initially it was an advisory group of non-Native priests looking for ways to incorporate Native American spirituality with Christianity. Over time the conference embraced a board of both Native Americans and non-Native clergy. The mandate is now to unify Native American Catholics while accepting and nurturing tribal differences. They also pray for Tekakwitha to be elevated to sainthood. Out of the conference has developed so-called Kateri Circles. These are independent, local gatherings of Native Catholics who focus on Kateri's virtuous example and pray for her canonization. Pragmatically, these circles also do good works within the community, helping the infirm, the poverty-stricken, and the dying.

Donna Cameron-Carter

See also Christianity, Indianization of; Missionization, Northeast; Religious Leadership, Northeast

References and Further Reading
Bechard, S.J., Henri. 1992. *Kaia'tano: ron: Kateri Tekakwitha*. Khanawake, Quebec: Centre Kateri.
Greer, Allan. 2000. *The Jesuit Relations: Natives and Missionaries in Seventeenth-Century North America*. Boston: Bedford/St. Martin's.

Koppedrayer, K. I. 1993. "The Making of the First Iroquois Virgin: Early Jesuit Biographies of the Blessed Kateri Tekakwitha." *Ethnohistory* 40, no. 2: 277–306.

Vecsey, Christopher. 1997. *The Paths of Kateri's Kin*. Notre Dame, IN: University of Notre Dame Press.

Termination and Relocation

Federal termination and relocation policies profoundly influenced the religious beliefs of American Indians during the 1950s and 1960s. Even after those two efforts were replaced during the 1970s with a new federal Indian policy called Indian self-determination, their effects continued for the remainder of the twentieth century. The results have netted a polarized situation in many Indian communities between old ways and new ways of life. The dilemma of the new and old originated with the arrival of Columbus and the introduction of new ideas and values to Native peoples. This continuous binary situation was accelerated because of termination and relocation.

The 1950s

The world witnessed great changes following World War II as the United States positioned itself as the leading industrial power. This modern transition involved undertaking new ideas and considering new values as America launched the atomic age. American leaders envisioned a standard way of life involving suburban living in an ideal nuclear family, paying a mortgage on a ranch-style house in a democratic, industrialized society. As the rise of the Soviet Union challenged U.S. democracy with the launching of Sputnik in 1957 and nuclear testing, many American Indians felt more a part of the mainstream, since an estimated 25,000 Indian men served in the armed services of the United States in World War II. That tradition of Native patriotism was repeated with another 10,000 who served proudly in the Korean War. An estimated 43,000 Indian men served in Vietnam, and the Native tradition continued with the Persian Gulf conflict and the war with Iraq. This Native tradition in the armed services convinced bureaucrats and congressmen that Native Americans were ready to leave reservations to join the American mainstream by living and working in cities where jobs were plentiful.

Goals of Termination and Relocation

Termination of tribal status had a finality about it, and its implication had serious results. Termination had several versions that included liberating American Indians from the constraints of federal trust restrictions. Policy-makers in the Bureau of Indian Affairs claimed that Indian people had changed and that a termination would lift the trust restrictions by relocating eighteen- to forty-five-year-old adults with their children to cities with federal assistance. Additionally, termination worked with federal action in 109 cases to permanently nullify the special minority status that American Indians held because of their 389 treaties and agreements made with the United States between 1778 and 1871.

Those responsible for introducing termination and relocation proved to be congressmen from Western states motivated by their interests in the natural resources on reservations. Senator Arthus Watkins of Utah, Congressman E. Y. Berry of South Dakota, Senator Patrick McCarran of Nevada, and Congressman William Harrison of Wyoming introduced House Concurrent Resolution 108 in the House of Representatives, and Senator Henry Jackson of Washington sponsored the bill in the Senate. Commissioner of Indian Affairs Dillon S. Myer, formerly of the War Relocation Authority, which relocated Japanese-Americans to camps farther within the United States during World War II, came into the BIA to initiate the relocation program.

Essentially, Myer and other government officials believed that reservations could not support a postwar economy for tribes and that it was time for American Indians to join the mainstream society. In addition to assistance from the government, churches and civic groups helped Indians to adjust to urban life in large cities such as Chicago and Los Angeles. More than 100,000 Native Americans participated in the relocation program from 1951 to 1973. As a part of their new lives in cities, American Indians found themselves attending churches and starting their own in urban Indian areas, such that an Indian church of Baptist, Methodist, or Lutheran belief was a part of the focal point in urban Indian areas alongside the typical American Indian Center.

The newness of living in cities and its urban culture threatened the nativism of American Indians. Indian values, distinct for each tribe, became vulnerable, including American Indian religious beliefs. Many American Indians adopted urban values and began to attend churches of various denominations in cities, while others joined the Native American Church (NAC), based on the Southwestern sacrament of peyote. Federal government action continued termination and relocation until the early 1970s, when President Richard Nixon declared a halt to termination. In 1970, President Nixon signed over 45,000 acres to the Pueblo, the Sacred Taos Blue Lakes located in New Mexico. This important land return included three other instances of the federal government's returning land to Native peoples.

The early 1970s saw the rise of the American Indian Movement (AIM), which began in the summer of 1968 in Minneapolis as an urban Native effort to stop police brutality against Indian people. By the mid-1970s, the federal government had begun to recognize American Indian religious rights with the passage of the American Indian Religious Freedom Act in 1978 during the Jimmy Carter administration. Federal court decisions followed to support American Indian religious practices, but legislation and court battles focused mainly on cultural and treaty rights.

As mentioned, other Indians joined the Native American Church. The history of the NAC began with the introduction of peyote in the Southwest and became increasingly popular in the 1880s. Two versions of the Native American Church, the Half Moon and Big Moon (also called Cross Fire), developed as the NAC became widely recognized in the early twentieth century. By 1922, the NAC had 22,000 members. As more Indians searched for belief in something relevant to life, this modern Indian religion grew with a membership currently estimated at 250,000.

Christianity made a great impact on urban Indians. One survey in 1950 of Christian Missions indicated thirty-six Protestant denominations housing 39,200 Indian Christians. By the early 1990s there were several hundred ordained Christian ministers of American Indian descent. In 1974 the United Presbyterian, Protestant Episcopal, United Methodist, American Baptist, United Church of Christ, and Reformed and Christian Reformed indicated 452 Indian parishes operating with a staff of 177 missionaries.

By the end of the twentieth century, at least seventeen states had major Indian Christian organizations: the Alaska Native Brotherhood in Alaska; American Indian Bible College, Chief Inc., and United Indian Missions, Inc., in Arizona; American Indian Liberation Crusade, Inc., and the Native American Ministry Project in California; Four Corners School of the Bible in Colorado; Bureau of Catholic Indian Missions and Friends Committee on National Legislation in the District of Columbia; Commission for Multicultural Ministries of ELCA Native American Program in Illinois; Associated Executive Committee of Friends in Indiana; Mennonite Indian Leaders' Council in Kansas; Council for American Indian Ministries (CAIM)/United Church of Christ in Minnesota; Assemblies of God/Division of Home Missions in Missouri; Tekakwitha Conference National Center in Montana; American Indian Bible Missions, Inc., in New Mexico; American Bible Society, Episcopal Council of Indian Ministries, Interreligious Foundation for Community Organizations (IFCO), National Council of the Church of Christ in the United States of America, Native American International Caucus/United Methodist Church, and Native American Ministries, United Presbyterian Church USA in New York; National Native American Ancestral Religion in North Carolina; American Baptist Indian Caucus and Native American Field Office of the Episcopal Church in Oklahoma; American Friends Service Committee in Pennsylvania; Church of Jesus Christ of Latter Day Saints Indian Committee in Utah; and North American Indian Mission (NAIM) Ministries in Washington.

Since the introduction of Christianity to American Indians, many Native peoples have converted from their Native beliefs, as noted by the famous conversion of Black Elk of the Oglala to Catholicism. Since termination and relocation, an increasing conversion among American Indians has occurred to establish their own kinds of Christianity, such as Hopi Catholics, Choctaw Methodists, Muskogee Creek Baptists, and the like, while many Indian people have converted to the mainstream way of Episcopalians, Lutherans, and Pentecostals. Such conversions are too numerous to estimate. However, many scholars and community members have continued to argue that American Indians frequently have more than one religious belief, practicing Native religions and Christianity simultaneously and without apparent contradiction, a dual mode that most non-Native people would see as a clash of religious ideologies.

Traditionalism of tribal beliefs has persisted in spite of the mainstream influence on Native Americans. Various individuals such as Sanapia of the Comanche, Philip Deer of the Muskogee Creek, and Willie Lena of the Oklahoma Seminole have carried forward the traditional beliefs and cultural practices of their people. While it is typical that elders of a community practice the old cultural ways of the people, new generations of Indians are finding it increasingly difficult to know what is traditional. A renaissance began during the 1970s to increase the knowledge about tribal histories, family genealogies, and cultural traditions. Relocated Indians in cities found it increasingly difficult to maintain connections with those on the reservations.

With each generation of American Indians becoming more urbanized and adopting mainstream values, tribal languages are spoken less all the time and cultural ways are being lost. Specifically, fewer American Indians are learning the languages of their people or practicing traditional ways. At the end of the twentieth century, an estimated 210 tribal languages were spoken among the 562 federally recognized tribes in the United States.

Borrowing the ways of other people has been an effective means of cultural survival for Native peoples in the United States. Adopting the technologies of others to better meet the needs of daily life, such as hunting, has enhanced Indian life while introducing new material items to Native cultures.

As American Indian people live adjacent to and within the American mainstream, their identities as Native people are held intact. They have changed many of their cultural ways to adjust to modern times, but they are still American Indians. Religion remains an integral part of their lives.

Donald L. Fixico

See also Black Elk; Christianity, Indianization of; Law, Legislation, and Native Religion; Religious Leadership, Plains; Reservations, Spiritual and Cultural Implications

References and Further Reading
Burt, Larry W. 1982. *Tribalism in Crisis: Federal Indian Policy, 1953–1961.* Albuquerque: University of New Mexico Press.
Fixico, Donald L. 1986. *Termination and Relocation: Federal Indian Policy, 1945–1960.* Albuquerque: University of New Mexico Press.

———. 2000. *The Urban Indian Experience in America*. Albuquerque: University of New Mexico Press.

Irwin, Lee. 2000. *Native American Spirituality: A Critical Reader*. Lincoln: University of Nebraska Press.

LaGrand, James B. 2002. *Indian Metropolis: Native Americans in Chicago, 1945–75*. Urbana: University of Illinois Press.

Smith, Houston, and Reuben Snake, eds. 1995. *One Nation under God: The Triumph of the Native American Church*. Santa Fe: Clear Light Publishers.

Weibel-Orlando, Joan. 1991. *Indian Country, L.A.: Maintaining Ethnic Community in Complex Society*. Urbana: University of Illinois Press.

Tobacco, Sacred Use of

The single feature unique to American Indian religions is the ritual use of to-bacco smoke (a variety of tobacco is chewed but not smoked by Native Aus-tralians). Elsewhere in the world one can find such relatively common aspects of American Indian religion as the ritual use of sweat ceremonials, fermented beverages, dog sacrifice, shamanic trance, and so forth. The focus on to-bacco as the primary sacred plant is ubiquitous throughout the Americas save for the Arctic and the southern tip of South America.

The word "tobacco" comes from a lin-guistic misunderstanding by Christo-pher Columbus, who thought that a Carib word for a *Y*-shaped inhaling in-strument meant the plant itself. The early French explorers used *petun*, a Brazilian Tupi word for the plant.

Tobacco is classified botanically as the genus *Nicotiana* Linnaeus, named after a sixteenth-century French ambassador to Lisbon, Jean Nicot; it belongs to the nightshade family (*Solanaceae*), which includes the potato and eggplant. Most of the sixty-four species in the genus are native to the Americas.

Although it is questionable whether tobacco is technically a psychoactive substance, it is used in healing practices among Native peoples in Central and South America in ways similar to their use of powerful psychoactive plants. Nicotine liberates the neurohumor nor-epinephrine, which is chemically related to mescaline, and it releases the hor-mones epinephrine, dopamine, and serotonin.

Euro-American domestic tobacco is derived from *N. tabacum* L. from the Caribbean; in eastern North America, the native plant is *N. rustica* L. In the Plains, three other varieties were grown, and several yet different varieties were cultivated on the West Coast.

N. rustica L. is an attractive plant that varies in height from two to four feet, de-pending on climate and soil, and has medium-size leaves and small, yellow blossoms. Both the dried leaves and the blossoms are smoked. The leaves dry green, the preferred color, in shade. The plant is hardy and self-seeding. The seeds are quite tiny, similar to mustard seeds in size.

In discussing tobacco in Native reli-gion, one is considering not only vari-eties of the genus *Nicotiana* but also

A medicine bundle belonging to the weasel chapter of the Crow Tobacco Society. During ceremonies the bundle is opened and women dance with the weasel skins to obtain supernatural powers that ensure the fertility of the sacred tobacco and so the growth of the Crow tribe as a whole. (Werner Forman/Corbis)

other substances either mixed with *Nicotiana* or smoked in its place when it was not available. Those alternatives include the inner bark of certain trees of the genus *Cornus,* such as red osier, the leaves of one of the sumacs (*Rhus glabra*) when they have turned red in the autumn, and the leaves of bearberry (*Arctostaphylos uva-ursi*). All these plants have an association with red, symbolizing blood, the essence of life: the outer bark of red osier is red; sumac leaves turn brilliant red in autumn; and bearberry has red berries and the dried leaves are similar to the green of shade-dried tobacco leaves. The Algonquin language word *kinnikinnick* is applied to smoking mixtures as well as individual elements.

Tobacco is the oldest domesticant in the Americas, dating to more than 8,000 years ago in central South America. It probably reached the middle of North America some 4,000 years ago. The cultivation of tobacco is generally quite distinct from the growing of plant foods. In some Plains cultures only tobacco is grown, and it is cultivated by men; plants for food, with few exceptions, are everywhere traditionally grown by women. Frequently, tobacco is but sown and allowed to develop with no further human assistance or allowed to self-seed. Tobacco horticulture requires special rituals and is an especially sacred act; those who grow it often belonging to ritual societies.

The purpose of offering tobacco, either directly or as smoke, is for communication with the spirits. The primary mode of offering tobacco is to place the leaves directly in or on the earth, water, sacred stones and plants, and the remains of animals/spirits. Whenever herbs, trees, animals, or stones are taken for use, especially sacred use, tobacco is placed by the requested substance as it is asked to offer itself for human needs.

Other nonsmoking uses of tobacco include snuffing the powdered leaves into the nasal passages, chewing the leaves, ingesting the powdered leaves mixed with other substances, as enemas, and imbibing liquid infusions from the leaves, often as a purifying emetic. Snuff was common to a number of areas of the Caribbean and South America, where a forked pipette was used to facilitate the inhaling of the powdered leaves or a liquid infusion. Chewing tobacco or placing powdered tobacco in the mouth, usually mixed with lime, was practiced from California south through much of South America.

The most common means of offering tobacco smoke to spirits is the most direct: throwing the leaves on fire or placing them on coals. Other methods involve those making the offering bringing the tobacco smoke into themselves and then blowing it toward the spiritual recipient. The sharing of the smoke between the one making the offering and the spirit receiving it creates communion between the two.

In being thrown on fire or coals, tobacco in North America becomes similar to the sacred fumigants. These include cedar leaves in the East, sweetgrass in the Central region, sage in the Plains, and juniper and pine needles in the Southwest; presently, the use of these substances is not limited to specific geographic areas. This smoke is used to purify the place, participants, paraphernalia, and offerings used in ceremonies.

There are several methods of smoking, often indicating regional preferences. The simplest is to place one's head over burning leaves and inhale. Next in order of complexity is the cigar, a roll of leaves ignited at one end, with the smoke drawn into the mouth through the other. This was the most common method of smoking in the Caribbean and Mesoamerica, and cigars are still used ritually by the highland Maya. Next in complexity is the placing of shredded tobacco in a tubular, combustible container as a reed or rolled corn husk. This method of ritually smoking tobacco is found from the American Southwest through much of South America. Finally, there are manufactured smoking devices—that is, pipes—that are the most common form of containing tobacco for smoking in North America.

Jordan Paper

See also Bundles, Sacred Bundle Traditions; Healing Traditions, California; Health and Wellness, Traditional Approaches; Herbalism; Sacred Pipe

References and Further Reading

Haberman, Thomas W. 1984. "Evidence for Aboriginal Tobaccos in Eastern North America." *American Antiquity* 49: 269–287.

Linton, Ralph. 1924. *Use of Tobacco among North American Indians.* Natural History Leaflet 19. Chicago: Field Museum.

Lowie, Robert H. 1919. "The Tobacco Society of the Crow Indians." *Anthropological Papers of the American Museum of Natural History* 21: 2.

Paper, Jordan. 1988. *Offering Smoke: The Sacred Pipe and Native American Religion.* Moscow: University of Idaho Press.

Robicsek, Francis. 1978. *The Smoking Gods: Tobacco in Maya Art, History and Religion.* Norman: University of Oklahoma Press.

Wilbert, Johannes. 1987. *Tobacco and Shamanism in South America.* New Haven: Yale University Press.

Totem Poles

One of the most frequently illustrated and commonly photographed types of Northwest coast art is the totem pole, which has become the stereotypical Northwest coast artwork. It turns out that the totem pole as we think of it today—a tall, elaborately carved and painted crest monument erected outdoors—is a relatively recent development in Northwest coast art history, emerging from the coalescence of several different aboriginal artistic traditions. In 1791, John Bartlett, a seaman on the ship *Gustavus III,* drew the earliest known depiction of a totem pole, a 40-foot-high frontal pole in the Haida village of Dadens on Haida Gwaii. While that was the first recorded image of a totem pole, two years earlier, John Meares had sighted and briefly mentioned an exterior pole on North Island. Before that time no traveler had described or illustrated exterior poles. By 1829, Skidegate had thirty to forty poles in what was clearly a proliferation of that type of carving. By the 1880s, Haida villages boasted forests of poles.

The Northwest coast totem pole as we now know it appears to have developed, shortly after contact, out of several aboriginal types of art: interior house posts that depicted esteemed crests stacked one atop the other, free-standing funerary sculptures that stood outside houses, and painted house facades that illustrated crests to all who passed the structure. With metal tools artists could carve larger and more complex works of art, and commercial paints could facilitate their decoration. The wealth that poured in as a result of the fur trade contributed to the production of these status sym-

A totem pole carved by members of the Haida Nation in the village of Skidegate, British Columbia. (Christopher Morris/Corbis)

bols, which became among some groups increasingly abundant as the century progressed. By the second half of the nineteenth century, totem poles—which combined the form of the housepost, the freestanding exterior sculptures of the funerary monuments, and the public declaration of crest imagery of the house front—had become significant cultural features of the Haida, Tsimshian, and some southern Tlingit villages.

Totem poles were not uniformly favored throughout the Northwest coast during the nineteenth century. Unlike the Haida, whose every village had an abundance of poles, the Tlingit to the north had relatively few poles. Only the southern Tlingit included totem poles as part of their cultural landscape, presumably because of their proximity to the Haida. In contrast, residents of Klukwan, one of the most conservative Tlingit communities, considered poles foreign and thus limited their heraldic carvings to house posts, such as those from the Whale House (*see* Art [Traditional and Contemporary], Northwest Coast). The Wakashan-speaking Kwakwak'wakw and the Nuu-chah-nulth as well as the Nuxalk also had relatively few totem poles at this time. Among the Nuu-chah-nulth, most were simple poles surmounted by birds. By the first decade of the twentieth century, however, the Kwakwak'wakw produced numerous poles, perhaps as defiant expressions of cultural sovereignty.

During the early twentieth century, both the Canadian and U.S. governments recognized the value of totem poles as tourist attractions, and they supported projects for their restoration. Between 1926 and 1930 the Canadian government collaborated with the Canadian National Railway to restore thirty Tsimshian poles along the railroad's Skeena River route. Although during the first few years the restorations were carried off relatively successfully, by 1927 antagonism toward the project began to develop. Some Tsimshian were particularly incensed that the government, which just a few years earlier had

Tsimshian Indians use guide ropes to put a totem pole into place at a gathering of three clans in Metlakatla, Alaska. (Bob Rowan/Progressive Image/Corbis)

strongly discouraged totem pole carving, now spent money on their preservation.

Across the border in southeast Alaska, another totem pole project got underway a few years later. In 1933, President Roosevelt had approved the founding of the Indian Civilian Conservation Corps (CCC). In Alaska the first projects under this New Deal program, such as construction of housing for teachers and nurses in Hoona, were intended to improve the social conditions of the Natives. By 1938 the Indian CCC had moved into the more aesthetically oriented activity of restoring totem poles. That project, managed by the Forest Service, sup-

ported the retrieval of poles from abandoned villages, their restoration by Native artists, and their erection along the ferry route.

By around 1940 museums had begun to play increasingly larger roles in totem pole salvage. In 1957 an effort to salvage some Haida totem poles from Ninstints brought some exquisite artworks to Victoria for safekeeping. Unlike those who had earlier shown no sensitivity toward the Natives whose cultural treasures they were collecting, Wilson Duff of the British Columbia Provincial Museum (now the Royal British Columbia Museum) first approached the Skidegate Band to obtain their permission for the project. Only after receiving their approval did Duff and a crew including artist Bill Reid and Harry Hawthorne of the University of British Columbia Museum of Anthropology travel to the southernmost tip of Haida Gwaii and remove poles to be preserved in museums.

In addition to salvage projects, museums have become involved in sponsoring totem pole restoration or carving. The two major British Columbia museums, the Royal British Columbia Museum in Victoria and the Museum of Anthropology on the University of British Columbia campus in Vancouver, were innovative in this respect. In 1947, Kwakwak'wakw master Mungo Martin began restoring some old poles and carved some new ones for the University of British Columbia's Museum of Anthropology. Five years later Martin went to the British Columbia Provincial Museum in Victoria as the chief carver in that museum's totem pole restoration program. Martin's legacy at the Royal British Columbia Museum is impressive, for his successors there include Kwakwak'wakw artists Henry Hunt, Tony Hunt, and Richard Hunt, and Nuu-chah-nulth Tim Paul.

Mungo Martin's Big House and Dzoonokwa totem pole in Thunderbird Park, outside the Royal British Columbia Museum at Victoria. 1993. (Gunter Marx Photography/Corbis)

Today totem poles flourish, with expert carvers of every group creating new monuments. Many Native villages up and down the coast have poles declaring the cultural strength of their inhabitants. Recently carved poles stand in cities and towns in Alaska, British Columbia, and Washington state, having been commissioned by museums, municipalities, and private donors. One can find contemporary Northwest coast totem poles throughout the United States and Canada, as well as in Europe, Asia, and the Pacific.

Aldona Jonaitis

See also Art (Traditional and Contemporary), Northwest Coast; Ceremony and Ritual, Northwest; Healing Traditions, Northwest; Oral Traditions, Northwest Coast; Power, Northwest Coast; Religious Leaders, Northwest; Sacred Societies, Northwest Coast

References and Further Reading
Darling, David, and Douglas Cole. 1980. "Totem Pole Restoration on the Skeena, 1925–30: An Early Exercise in Heritage Conservation." *BC Studies* 47: 29–48.
Drucker, Philip. 1948. "The Antiquity of the Northwest Coast Totem Pole." *Journal of the Washington Academy of Sciences* 38: 389–397.
Garfield, Viola, and Linn Forrest. 1948. *The Wolf and the Raven*. Seattle: University of Washington Press.
Halpin, Marjorie. 1981. *Totem Poles: An Illustrated Guide*. Vancouver: University of British Columbia Press.
Jonaitis, Aldona. 1999. "The Northwest Coast Totem Pole." In *Unpacking Culture*. Edited by Ruth Phillips and Christopher Steiner. Los Angeles: University of California Press.
Wright, Robin. 2001. *Northern Haida Masters*. Seattle: University of Washington Press.

Trail of Tears

The Trail of Tears, in its most commonly used meaning, refers to the 1838–1839 forced migration of the Cherokee people from their traditional homeland in Georgia, North Carolina, and Tennessee to "Indian Territory" west of the Mississippi River—territory that later became Arkansas and Oklahoma. Because approximately one in four of the more than 16,000 Cherokee people who began the journey died as a result of the ordeal, the Cherokee came to call their removal *Nunna-da-ul-tsun-yi*, "The trail where we cried"—hence the English name, Trail of Tears.

Taken more broadly, the term "Trail of Tears" refers to the larger experience of Indian Removal set in motion by the Removal Act, which passed the U.S. Congress in 1830. In particular, the five tribes that resided in the Southeastern states—the Choctaw, the Muskogee (Creek), the Chickasaw, and the Seminole, as well as the Cherokee, collectively known to the people of the United States as the "Five Civilized Tribes"—have all used the term "Trail of Tears" to refer to their forced removal. While the actual name "Trail of Tears" was said to have been first used by the Choctaw during their removal ordeal in 1831, more than likely each tribe removed used some name for their experience that could warrant the expression, whether or not that name is known to us today. Certainly the number of deaths that each tribe endured must have left behind a trail of tears for every mile the

Cherokee Trail of Tears memorial overlooking the Arkansas River, Cadron Settlement Park, Conway, Arkansas. (North Wind Picture Archives)

people traveled. The impact of the Trail on the peoples who walked it, and on their religious and spiritual traditions, lingers to haunt their tribes and descendants even in the present day.

The Election of Andrew Jackson and the Beginnings of Removal

Andrew Jackson was elected president in 1828 on a platform of Indian removal, and in his inaugural address he called for the removal of all Indians remaining east of the Mississippi. Moreover, contradicting what had been federal policy since the passage of the Non-Intercourse Act of 1791, Jackson called for states to design and enforce their own Indian policies, without consultation with the federal government. In Georgia, where gold was discovered in the same year that Jackson took office, state legislators moved with great speed to write laws claiming jurisdiction over Cherokee lands and resources. They began to survey Cherokee lands and divide them into sections to distribute to incoming settlers.

The U.S. Congress followed Jackson's program by passing the Removal Act of 1830, mandating federal negotiations with tribes to exchange all remaining Indian lands east of the Mississippi for equivalent portions of land west of the Mississippi, in what would be called "Indian Territory." While the terms of the Removal Act directed only that there be negotiations, President Jackson proceeded as though Congress had mandated forced removal, with or without a legally negotiated treaty. Every tribe with holdings remaining in the east—but particularly those in the Southeast, who still lived almost entirely in their original homelands—would be affected by these developments.

Removal of the "Five Civilized Tribes": The Choctaw and the Chickasaw

The Choctaw and the Chickasaw were the tribes of the Southeast with the westernmost locations; each of their homelands already extended to the shores of the Mississippi River. The Chickasaw were a relatively small tribe, numbering in 1830 approximately 4,000 persons. They occupied the northern part of Mississippi, from the great river eastward, extending slightly north into Tennessee and as far as a few miles into Alabama. The 25,000 Choctaw held a much larger territory extending from the river eastward, bordering the Chickasaw on the north and occupying much of the rest of Mississippi into Alabama. Like most tribes, both the Choctaw and the Chickasaw already had ceded large portions of land in treaties made with the United States between the end of the Revolutionary War and the time of forced removal; they had hoped that by cooperating with the new government and by giving up part of their land they could

keep the rest. But the Removal Act demanded all land east of the Mississippi, and the negotiators from Washington would no longer accept partial results.

On September 27, 1830, foreshadowing what would happen later with the Cherokee, a minority of Choctaw elders and chiefs signed the Treaty of Dancing Rabbit Creek, agreeing to exchange 11 million acres of land east of the Mississippi for 15 million acres north of the Red River, extending across the southern half of what would later become the state of Oklahoma. A larger contingent of elders, chiefs, and common people had initially come to the meeting with Jackson's secretary of war John Eaton and his favorite nephew-by-marriage and fellow Indian fighter, General John Coffee, but they had left in disgust after two weeks of negotiations. Those who remained were the chiefs most willing to sign if enough money changed hands, and thus the treaty was made. To the U.S. Senate, one signed Indian treaty looked like any other; if no one told them it was fraudulent within its own nation, the senators, even those disposed to giving the Indians justice, had no way to know they were being presented with a problematic document. Thus the Treaty of Dancing Rabbit Creek was ratified and enforced.

Between 1831 and 1839 the Choctaw peoples, moving in waves, attempted the trip to Indian territory. Some 6,000 perished along the way from cholera, shipwreck, starvation, exposure, or a variety of other diseases. Approximately 7,000 remained in Mississippi or left the trail and found their way back home, hiding in the woods and swamps or blending in with slave communities that already contained mixed-blood Indians. Those who survived the journey settled along the Red River, just north of the boundary with the independent Republic of Texas. There they faced the double challenge of rebuilding themselves as a nation and bringing harmony between those who had signed the treaty and those who had not. That same challenge would face their neighbors, the Cherokee, for very similar reasons.

The Chickasaw, on the other hand, made their move under more favorable conditions and with much less loss of life. Both they and the federal government had learned from the Choctaw disaster, and better provisions were made for health and safety along the Chickasaw's trail. By the end of 1838 almost all the Chickasaw people had relocated west of the Choctaw area in Indian Territory.

The Muskogee (Creek) and the Seminole

Like the Choctaw and the Cherokee, the Muskogee (Creek) people, located east of the Choctaw and south of the Cherokee, were divided over issues of assimilation and removal, but the Muskogees' most profound crisis had come long before the U.S. Congress became involved in removal. A portion of the Muskogee warriors known as the Red Sticks had sided with the British in the War of 1812. The split engendered by those events contin-

ued into what would come to be known as the Creek Wars of 1813–1814. In reality, the 1813–1814 events are more correctly seen as a Creek civil war, with the United States and the Cherokee siding with the more assimilated Creeks against the more traditional Red Stick Creeks. Joel Martin has described the event as a "sacred revolt" by the traditionalists in a last effort to preserve culture and spiritual tradition against the onslaught of "civilization." Even after the "progressives" won the wars, the culture battles continued. Ultimately, with the memory of the bloody Creek Wars still in the white settlers' memories and with the Muskogee peoples still deeply divided among themselves, removal of the Muskogee became a nightmarish reality. By 1837, 15,000 Muskogee had reached Indian Territory alive, but at least 3,500 were dead from disease, starvation, accident, exposure, or heartbreak.

An uncertain number of Muskogee resisted removal by fleeing toward Florida to live with relatives among the Seminole. The Seminole, unlike the other southeastern tribes, resisted the Removal Act militarily. They too, however, ultimately were divided over removal, and some did move west after years of fighting to save their homelands.

The Cherokee

With the most northern location of the five tribes, the Cherokee had experienced the longest period of contact with whites and the most positive history of intermarriage and cultural mingling.

Many Cherokee had adopted white styles of dress, were bilingual, and were well educated in both the white and the Cherokee sense. A large number of "promising" young men had been sent by the missionaries to be educated in New England schools, and some had married young ladies of New England. Among the gifts of civilization they had adopted, none perhaps was as strong as the belief and trust in American democracy. Indeed, feeling empowered to marry whomever they wished and being blind to race and class demonstrated not merely love of a young lady but also faith in the ideals of equality for all under the law. Although the Cherokee were related to the Iroquois people, who had given the early colonists many of their ideas about democracy and who had provided much of the substance of the constitutional law the colonists finally adopted, the Cherokee themselves had not been functioning under a written constitution. Still, they were familiar with democracy from their practice of giving everyone, both men and women, voice in the tribal councils, and they quickly came to believe in the constitutional version of democracy that their New England education had taught them governed the United States. By the Cherokee's understanding of U.S. democracy, Georgia could not do what it was trying to do, and the United States could not do what it was threatening to do when it passed the Removal Act. Thus, in accordance with democratic principles, the Cherokee brought suit in the courts.

In their first suit, *Cherokee Nation v. Georgia* (1831), the Cherokee people argued that the Cherokee Nation had a legal relationship with the United States as a nation, not with Georgia as a state. Thus state law could not be forced on them apart from federal law. Chief Justice John Marshall declined to take the case as such, saying that the tribe was neither a foreign nation nor composed of U.S. citizens but, rather, was a "domestic dependent nation." Marshall implied that he would be willing to rule in a case involving a U.S. citizen, and within a year the Cherokee had such a case to bring him. Through all of the legal efforts, the most "civilized" and "progressive" of the Cherokee leaders held to their faith that justice and democracy would surely triumph.

The Role of Christian Missionaries

In the several decades before and for nearly a century after removal, colonial opinion, followed by official U.S. government policy, held that civilization and Christianization for the Indian went hand in hand. The overall goal of both was assimilation. Being considered "civilized" meant, in part, that the southeastern tribes had become receptive to the overtures of Protestant missionaries. While the proportion who accepted Christianity never approached a majority in any tribe, the numbers were large enough, and their impact great enough, that the story of removal cannot be told apart from the story of the missionaries.

A unidimensional view of missions would see them as simply one more point of pressure toward the assimilation that was threatening the continued existence of Indians as culturally distinct peoples in every part of the continent. From that viewpoint, one might expect the missionaries to have worked hand in hand with federal agents to dispatch the peoples to Indian Territory as rapidly as possible, since their souls could be saved just as well out of view of the white settlers. Such an analysis would be quite incomplete, as the case of the Cherokee missions exemplifies.

Several groups of missionaries were laboring in Cherokee country at the time of the Removal Act, but the key figures with regard to removal were the Baptist Evan Jones and the Congregationalist Samuel Worcester. Both men had learned to speak Cherokee fluently, and both were engaged in projects to translate the Bible into Cherokee, using the syllabary script developed by Sequoyah and read by nearly all speakers of the language. Like most missionaries, both Jones and Worcester took the side of the people to whom they ministered when threats to the land came from Washington.

Evan Jones, in particular, is remembered for teaching the Cherokee people that God sided with the oppressed of the world. Just as he had looked with compassion on the Hebrew slaves, so God would look with compassion on the Cherokee who were threatened by the might of the United States. To recognize how radical this missionary theology would have sounded to many white citizens of the United States, particularly to those settlers waiting to take Cherokee land as soon as it was vacated, one need only think of the theology implicit in the soon-to-be-proclaimed doctrine of Manifest Destiny, already incipient in American political realities. From William Bradford and Plymouth Plantation to Andrew Jackson and beyond, white Christians would say quite directly that God had ordained for them to take over the North American continent, that God had prepared the land for their arrival, and that their rights to the New World paralleled the rights God gave to the children of Israel, to whom Christ Jesus had made them the rightful heirs.

The colonists saw their journey to the shores of the New World and from those shores on to the frontier, wherever that frontier might lead, as paralleling the migration of Abraham to the land where God directed, or the exodus of the Hebrew slaves into the promised land. Now America was their promised land. God could not intend the "pagan savages" to continue on the land, preachers in the settlers' churches taught, for the savages were not among the "chosen people" and were not subduing and dominating the earth as God had commanded in Genesis 1:28. The theology of most of white America and the theology of the missionaries differed so radically that chiefs of both the Creek and the Cherokee were reported to have questioned whether the other Christians were even reading the same Bible as the one the missionaries had translated. Chief Junaluska, a great

Eastern Cherokee warrior who saved the life of Andrew Jackson at the Battle of the Horseshoe Bend (a kindness he later regretted), made a typical comment upon hearing the first reading of the Gospel of Matthew in his own language: "Well, it seems to be a good book—strange that the white people are not better, after having had it so long" (Mooney 1992, 163).

The Bible as the missionaries presented it to the people did seem, for the most part, to be a good book. Evan Jones, more than the other missionaries, asked that the people accept Jesus but did not demand that they reject all of their traditional beliefs and practices. While most missionaries were not as tolerant of traditional Cherokee culture as Jones, all looked for elements of the peoples' old beliefs onto which Christianity could be grafted, hoping that in that way the new faith would take better root and flourish.

Those Protestant groups that had become successful by the 1830s owed their success in large part to their missionaries' having become a part of the communities in which they labored. Integrated into the peoples' lives, the missionaries felt that their homes were threatened by removal, just as the homes of the Indians were threatened. Thus Samuel Worcester maintained he was simply following his calling as a minister when he went to jail in Georgia rather than follow the new state ordinance that compelled all white people living in Cherokee territories to register with the state. The other missionaries preached on the civilly disobe-

dient Daniel going to the lion's den and the apostles Paul and Silas going to jail to explain what Worcester was doing. Worcester's long imprisonment provided the Cherokees with the opportunity they needed to return to Justice Marshall's court.

In the lawsuit that Worcester brought on behalf of himself and the Cherokee Nation, *Worcester v. Georgia* (1832), Marshall ruled in the missionary's behalf, saying that the "Cherokee Nation . . . is a distinct community, occupying its own territory, . . . in which the laws of Georgia can have no force, and which the citizens of Georgia have no right to enter, but with the assent of the Cherokees" (Perdue and Green, 1995). Thus the Supreme Court nullified all of Georgia's laws against the Cherokees and supported the long-standing doctrine of a national Indian policy, not a state-by-state policy.

The bringing of the suits, the support of the missionaries, and the decision of the court were all closely watched by Indian peoples and their supporters throughout the country. Marshall's ruling was welcomed with rejoicing and thanksgiving and was seen as validating the ideal of Christian democracy that the missionaries, both religious and cultural, had been preaching to the Indians. It supported the idea that red people and white people could live side by side on the land as children of the same great Father in Washington as well as the same great Father in Heaven. But even while the missionaries were leading their Indian converts in praising God for the blessings of democracy, the great Father in Washington, President Andrew Jackson, the Indian fighter and champion of removal, was telling the states to ignore Justice Marshall's ruling.

The Double Tragedy of Cherokee Idealism: John Ross vs. John Ridge

Several small groups of Cherokee had removed to Indian Territory on their own, even before the lawsuits were settled, to avoid being forced to move later. But the failure of *Worcester v. Georgia* to secure Cherokee title to the lands led to the final split within the Cherokee nation. The group of Cherokee led by Major John Ridge, mostly mixed bloods and often called assimilationists, who had been most closely allied with Worcester and with the publication of the Cherokee *Phoenix* newspaper, became known as the Treaty Party. They argued that removal was now inevitable and that the best thing for the people would be to negotiate a favorable treaty and make the move on their own terms. Principal Chief John Ross, also a mixed-blood Cherokee, and also assimilated in many ways, who was closer to the Baptist missions and Evan Jones, continued to believe that the ideals of democracy would win out. The vast majority of the Cherokee people supported their chief and formed what would be called the Patriot Party.

Viewing the split as simply one between assimilationists and traditionalists ignores the complexity of the issues: cultural, political, and also spiritual. Both groups had accepted a part of the American dream, and yet both believed deeply in the preservation of their people. Both John Ridge and John Ross thought what they were doing would best ensure the survival of the Cherokee. Both were themselves wealthy plantation owners who served their nation politically because of their deep love for their people. John Ross was principal chief, while John Ridge was the eminent speaker of the Tribal Council. Both were considered by the whites to be pro-Christian progressives, truly "civilized" Indians.

For Ross, survival of the people meant survival on the land. For Ridge, survival meant survival intact as a people, in as healthy a condition as possible and with the resources needed to start a new life. On December 29, 1835, while Chief Ross was in Washington, D.C., trying to see the president, Major Ridge and other members of his party signed a treaty at the Cherokee capital of New Echota agreeing to move the Cherokee people to Indian Territory. The sale of lands without tribal consent, according to the Cherokee constitution adopted only a few years before, was punishable by death; Major Ridge hoped that he could persuade the rest of the people that the move would be their best chance for survival. Even as he signed he said, "Today I am signing my own death warrant."

Happenings in the Cherokee Nation were news all over the United States, especially in the nation's capital. John Ross traveled again to Washington and demanded that the president, by then Van

Buren, investigate the fraudulent treaty, presenting a petition to the Senate signed by 15,665 Cherokees—ostensibly every man, woman, and child who had not signed the Treaty of New Echota. Ralph Waldo Emerson wrote to Van Buren, saying, "A crime is projected that confounds our understandings by its magnitude, a crime that really deprives us, as well as the Cherokee, of a country." Emerson, along with other New England intellectuals, understood the philosophical importance of what was occurring and saw clearly that a juncture was about to be crossed from which the new nation could never return. Either equality under the law applied to all, or in reality it applied to none. Eminent statesmen including Henry Clay and Davy Crockett spoke passionately against ratification of the Treaty of New Echota. In the end the treaty was ratified by the U.S. Senate, but by only one vote.

After ratification, one group of about five hundred and another of nearly four hundred Cherokee set out west. But even as hope for a legal remedy was vanishing, the rest of the Cherokee remained on their land until they were rounded up by soldiers and forced into stockades to await removal. In 1839, after the removal was complete, the signers of the Treaty of New Echota were executed by assassination in Indian Territory, as they knew they would be. John Ridge died a villain and a traitor, while John Ross died years later in old age as a patriot and hero. Both men died believing in the ideals of democracy that were their blood heritage as Cherokee but that they had learned in their education as "civilized" Indians. Although only John Ross traveled the officially named Trail of Tears, the Ridges, like all who were removed, traveled their different trail with their own measure of grief, their progressive hope in the ideals of civilization and American democracy shattered.

Religious and Spiritual Implications of Removal

In focusing on the political intrigues of removal, its profound impact on the religious and spiritual lives and traditions of the peoples easily can be overlooked. As matrilineal and matrilocal peoples, the nations of the Eastern Woodlands, north and south, as well as of the Atlantic Coast, practiced spiritual traditions organized around the agricultural seasons. Like most Native American peoples, they conducted their ceremonies in long-revered sacred locations. These ancient religious traditions, unlike those of the Christian Euro-Americans now controlling the peoples' homelands, were not thought of as "portable." Whereas the Christian god had begun his relationship with his "chosen people" by commanding Abraham to migrate west to an unknown land, the creators of the Indian peoples had rooted each of them in a particular land and made corn grow there to sustain them. In their land they had birthed their children, buried their dead, and received their original instructions on how to live in the world. Removal from their traditional homelands provoked for Indian peoples a profound spiritual crisis that served to make the obvious political and personal crises even more acutely felt, both by individuals and by each nation as a whole.

Although the Christian and pro-Christian groups in each tribe played key roles in the leadership of both proremoval and antiremoval parties, the majority of people in each tribe were religious traditionalists. Even many of the pro-Christian progressives accepted missionaries for what they could offer in education, not for what they brought in religion. Until removal, ceremony and ritual, as well as traditional healing arts, continued to be practiced much as they had been in the peoples' lands since time before memory.

Both Christian missionaries as well as traditional healers and ritual leaders accompanied the peoples on their various trails. In addition, by the time of removal each denomination had trained and ordained Native preachers to work alongside of the missionaries. Evan Jones, who with a handful of missionaries of other denominations stayed with the Cherokee while they were confined to internment camps awaiting removal, was gratified to report that "the Christians, the salt of the earth, are pretty generally distributed among the several detachments of prisoners" (McLoughlin 1994, 100). Many converts were won, Jones reported. The same was true among the Choctaw, where the Bible was read each night along the trail and hymns were sung as the people walked, led as often by Choctaws who had served as interpreters for the missionaries as by the few missionaries who remained with the Choctaw at removal (Noley 1998).

At the same time the Christians were finding a place of ministry in the midst of the removal tragedy, a revival of traditional religion was occurring. The ancient ceremonies and dances led by the *adonisgi* were as popular in the Cherokee camps as the Christian services of the missionary and Native preachers. As McLoughlin comments: "What was remarkable was the lack of friction between the two religious groups. Each allowed the other the consolations of the religion of his or her choice" (1994, 101).

Once Indian Territory was reached, however, the lack of sacred sites and the press of the tasks of reconstituting themselves as peoples gave advantage to the Christians in continuing the practices of their faith. Although they had not known it when they first believed, the Christians had in fact embraced a portable faith, one that had stories of removals, exiles, and migrations that could comfort them in their grief. Like the Jews in Babylon, the Native peoples who had been removed learned that they could still sing the creator's song in a new land.

The Impact of the Trail of Tears on Its Contemporary Survivors

Those who made it to Indian Territory knew they were the survivors. For reasons unknown, they were alive while many they loved had been buried along the Trail. As they raised children who barely remembered another land, and as they birthed new children in new homes, those who survived taught their children that they too would be survivors. The experience of surviving the Trail continues to be formative on its descendants as parents continue to say to their children: "But we are survivors." Journalist Sarah Vowell explained on National Public Radio's *This American Life* that she knows she is alive only because her great-grandparents survived the Trail of Tears. Although she knows herself and her twin sister to be "typical American mutts" with blood of several nations, "only the Cherokee and the Swedish really mattered. . . . Here's what we knew about ourselves [as children]," she says: "Ellis Island. Trail of Tears. . . . Even the youngest child knows what tears mean" (Vowell 1998).

In 1987, the National Park Service designated 2,200 miles of land and water routes traveled by the Cherokee as a National Historic Trail. Since that time, the Trail has become something of a pilgrimage path for survivors. As they traveled the Trail in 1998, seeking to understand the stories they had been told as children, Sarah Vowell and her sister Amy experienced for themselves some of the conflicted feelings that beset their Cherokee ancestors in the 1830s. "The nausea we suffer standing on the broken promises at Ross's Landing are peculiar to a democracy, because in a democracy we're all responsible for everything our government does," Sarah explained. "The more I learn, the worse I feel, and

the more hatred I feel toward this country that I still love, and therefore the more conflicted" (ibid.).

As Sarah Vowell's statement indicates, the conflicted feelings that divided John Ridge and John Ross continue to plague the survivors of the Trail into the contemporary age. Anyone who is today a survivor and an Indian is a citizen, unlike their ancestors who walked the Trail. Many, but still not most, survivors today are as educated as the people's leaders were at the time of removal. But the full-bloods and mixed bloods are still suspicious of each other. The racism that is the legacy of slavery often divides black Indians from white Indians and both from full-bloods. Those trying to revive long-forgotten or barely remembered religious and spiritual ceremonies are suspicious and resentful of Christian Indians who also want to be a part of tradition. The Identity Wars are not as bloody as the old feuds, but the pain may be even more intense because it does not produce an early death.

Portions of the removed tribes that fled from the Trail along the way, or who hid from its beginning, have gained strength and been re-recognized as Indian. They too are survivors, without a doubt, but their formative influences differ from those of Trail descendants; thus a new conflict within the peoples has been born.

When descendants of survivors walk the Historic Trail thinking they are tourists, often they realize, like Sarah and Amy Vowell, that without intending to they have become pilgrims. They speak of not knowing they had such feelings within them, of wondering where the feelings came from and whether they have always been with them. Often they are angry and want to tell the story again and again. They wonder if the spirits of those who did not survive still linger on the Trail. They say they have become somehow "more Indian" (personal conversations of author with Historic Trail walkers, October 1998, Nashville, Tennessee). The historical event of the Trail of Tears concluded in 1839. But history has demonstrated that the Trail of Tears as an identity-forming event will continue as long as its survivors tell their stories.

Pamela Jean Owens

See also Beloved Women, Beloved Men, Beloved Towns; Missionization, Southeast; Oral Traditions, Southeast; Power, Southeast

References and Further Reading
Anderson, William L., ed. 1991. *Cherokee Removal: Before and After*. Athens: University of Georgia Press.

Carson, James Taylor. 1999. *Searching for the Bright Path: The Mississippi Choctaws from Prehistory to Removal*. Lincoln: University of Nebraska Press.

Champagne, Duane. 1992. *Social Order and Political Change: Constitutional Governments among the Cherokee, the Choctaw, the Chickasaw, and the Creek*. Stanford: Stanford University Press.

DeRosier, Arthur H., Jr. 1970. *The Removal of the Choctaw Indians*. New York: Harper and Row.

Ehle, John. 1988. *Trail of Tears: The Rise and Fall of the Cherokee Nation*. New York: Doubleday.

Foreman, Grant. 1972. *Indian Removal: The Emigration of the Five Civilized Tribes of Indians*. Norman: University of Oklahoma Press.

Kidwell, Clara Sue. 1995. *Choctaws and Missionaries in Mississippi, 1818–1918*. Norman: University of Oklahoma Press.
———. 2002. "The Effects of Removal on Indian Tribes." Website of the National Humanities Center/Teacher Serve/Nature Transformed/Native Americans and the Land/Indian Removal. http://www.nhc.rtp.nc.us: 8080/tserve/nattrans/ntecoindian/essays/indianremoval.htm. (Accessed February 16, 2005.)

McLoughlin, William G. 1984. *Cherokees and Missionaries, 1789–1839*. New Haven: Yale University Press.
———. 1986. *Cherokee Renascence in the New Republic*. Princeton: Princeton University Press.
———. 1993. *After the Trail of Tears: The Cherokees' Struggle for Sovereignty, 1839–1880*. Chapel Hill: University of North Carolina Press.
———. 1994. *The Cherokees and Christianity, 1794–1870: Essays on Acculturation and Cultural Persistence*. Athens: University of Georgia Press.

Mooney, James. 1992. *James Mooney's History, Myths, and Sacred Formulas of the Cherokees: Containing the Full Texts of Myths of the Cherokee (1900) and The Sacred Formulas of the Cherokees (1891) as published by the Bureau of American Ethnology*. Asheville, NC: Historical Images.

Noley, Homer. 1998. "The Interpreters." Pp. 48–60 in *Native American Religious Identity: Unforgotten Gods*. Edited by Jace Weaver. Maryknoll, NY: Orbis Books.

Perdue, Theda, and Michael D. Green, eds. 1995. *The Cherokee Removal: A Brief History with Documents*. Boston: Bedford Books of St. Martin's Press.

Sturm, Circe. 2002. *Blood Politics: Race, Culture, and Identity in the Cherokee Nation of Oklahoma*. Berkeley: University of California Press.

Trafzer, Clifford E. 2000. *As Long as the Grass Shall Grow and Rivers Flow: A History of Native Americans*. Fort Worth, TX: Harcourt College Publishers.

Vowell, Sarah, commentator. 1998. Radio program *This American Life,* episode 107, "Trail of Tears." Hosted by Ira Glass. July 3. http://www.thislife.org/.

Wallace, Anthony F. C. 1993. *The Long, Bitter Trail: Andrew Jackson and the Indians.* New York: Hill and Wang.

Woodward, Grace Steele. 1963. *The Cherokees.* Norman: University of Oklahoma Press.

Tricksters

Tricksters are mythic characters found in every region of Native North America. Although their names, shapes, and specific meanings vary from culture to culture, tricksters are everywhere an important source of laughter. Trickster stories provide critical cultural teachings, including stories about the creation of the earth, the shape of the cosmos, as well as the origins of significant religious and ceremonial observances. Mixing comic trickster stories with sacred religious teachings may seem profane to those accustomed to the strict separation of religious from secular materials, but as Peggy Beck and Anna Lee Walters point out, "Most Native American sacred traditions have a common belief that humor is a necessary part of the sacred" (Beck, Walters, and Francisco 1977, 31). They observe that Native religious traditions are not caught up with questions of "good" and "evil" but are rather concerned with issues of balance and imbalance. Being too powerful or too serious, Beck and Walters note, could upset the balance of life in a community or environment. Humor, such as that provided by tricksters, is there to "teach us . . . not to take ourselves too seriously. This means, not to make ourselves too important" (ibid.). Overlooking the importance of humor in Native religious conceptions denigrates tricksters to the status of comic relief. Trickster stories provoke sacred laughter as they offer insight into human foibles and weaknesses, as well as providing (as all mythic stories must) opportunities to "envision the possibility of things not ordinarily seen or experienced" (ibid., 61).

Tricksters around North America

The continental landmass we speak of as North America holds many geographic variations, ranging from wetlands to mountains to plains; no single word, definition, or idea captures the range and variety of geographic experiences in North America. So it is with the tricksters who are remembered in the words and imaginations of the Native people of the continent; no single idea or definition adequately captures the variety of tricksters found in different tribal traditions. Perhaps the most famous of Native tricksters is Coyote, who appears in the oral literatures of many Plains, Great Basin, Plateau, West Coast, and desert Southwestern tribal cultures. In other tribal cultures, tricksters have other forms. Raven, Bluejay, and Mink are found in the Pacific Northwest; Spider is found on the Plains (where the Lakota call him Iktomi and the Cheyenne call him Wihio); Hare or Rabbit is spoken of as a trickster in Southeastern North America (where, combined with African trickster stories, he inspired the tales of B'rer Rabbit); Hare also features in the tales among the Native cultures in the Northeast, the Great Lakes, and Plains regions; elsewhere in the Northeast, Wolverine, Raccoon, Fox, and Turtle are the tricksters. While all of these tricksters have animal names, not every Native culture follows this practice. Tricksters such as the Nanabozho (or Waynaboozhoo, depending on the dialect of Ojibwe being spoken), Wakdjunkaga, Napi, the Old Man, Wisakedjak (anglicized as "Whiskey Jack"), and Glooscap are clearly presented as human in form.

When we think about tricksters and we encounter an animal name such as Raven or Coyote, we might tend to think that the trickster is literally that animal. That is not always so, though it may be. There is no hard and fast rule. An animal name is no guarantee of an animal form. Thus Coyote may be spoken of as an animal by one storyteller, as an animal in man's clothing by another, or as a man named for the animal by yet another—and all three storytellers may be from the same tribal culture. Likewise, though tricksters are almost always male, they may, if the situation demands it, become female, or a baby, or a tree stump. Generally speaking, tricksters throughout North America have the ability to shapeshift. The watchword with tricksters is fluidity. They can move fluidly between the states of animal and human, human and plant, as well as between male and female. Their fluidity also allows them to shift easily between spiritual and material realities; in this ability they reflect or inspire a medicine person's ability to effect the same kind of movement (see Grim 1983, 85–92). Tricksters move beyond all the boundaries that the material world imposes on humanity.

The power of this fluidity has led many non-Indian scholars to wonder if tricksters are best understood as men or as gods. In tribal expression, tricksters are an active presence in cultural life and are treated as neither men nor gods. (Early in the twentieth century, the anthropologist Clark Wissler wrote: "Whenever [I] asked if the Old Man [the trickster] was ever prayed to, the absurdity of the question provoked merriment" among his Blackfeet informants [Wissler and Duvall 1908, 9].) It is perhaps better to regard tricksters as spirits. The Ojibwe refer to their trickster, Nanabozho, as a manitou, a word that translates as "spirit" or "mystery." The Ojibwe ethnologist Basil Johnston notes that "manitou" refers "to realities other than the physical ones of rock, fire, water, air, wood, and flesh—to the unseen realities of individual beings and places and events that are beyond human understanding but are still clearly real" (Johnston 1995, xxi–xxii). Like Nanabozho, tricksters from other tribal traditions benefit from being conceived in terms of the "unseen realities" of mysteries and spirits.

A trickster then can be animal or human while simultaneously male but sometimes female; a trickster is also a spirit that comes from realities other than the familiar reality of the material world, as well as being a mystery that is "beyond human understanding" yet is "still clearly real." All these things and more, tricksters express and help people imagine what is possible and desirable in the world.

Tricksters in Native Mythic Traditions
Mythic stories—stories full of power and teaching—suspend the familiar reality of the material world, in order to help Native people understand their responsibilities to the ongoing task of creation. Such stories are intrinsically religious, as they reflect on the sacred origins of the world. While trickster stories often seem foolish or whimsical, they too offer important religious or ethical lessons. To understand how a story about the Cheyenne trickster losing his eyeballs contains religious instruction, we need to understand, generally speaking, that there are two types of stories in Native North America.

The first type of story is often spoken of as "mythological," and it offers the important narratives of origins. The second type of story is often referred to as "folklore" or "legend," and here are found tales of adventure and love as well as humorous anecdotes. Terms like "mythological," "folklore," and "legend" often implicitly judge a story, denigrating it as somehow false or unworthy of serious consideration (see Doty 1986, 6–9). A Native story about the battle at Little Big

Horn might thus be referred to as a "legend" rather than as an oral history; likewise, a Native story conveying important cultural knowledge might be spoken of as "mythological" rather than as a sacred text. The terms "mythic" and "myth" should not be equated with "false," but rather should be recognized as positive terms that describe the sacred stories and teachings of a people.

Tribal cultures have their own means of distinguishing between these two significant types of stories. The Inuit people refer to stories as being either "old" or "young," as a means of distinguishing between the stories of a prehuman mythic age and the human era we now live in (Bierhorst 1985, 5). Old stories deal with creation and the events of sacred time, while young stories recount events and encounters from human experience. The ethnographer Wendy Wickwire explains the distinction between the two types of stories. Old stories, she writes, are those "which explain how and why the world and its creatures came to be. They come . . . from a prehuman mythological age when the [Native] people were not yet fully human, but partook of both animal and human characteristics" (Wickwire 1989, 16). Young stories, Wickwire writes, "come from the more recent period, the world as we know it today. . . . Some of these stories occurred long ago . . . before the white man, but after the time of the animal-people" (ibid.). While other tribal languages will use other words to distinguish between the types of stories, the pattern of "old" stories and "young" generally holds across Native America.

These distinctions are crucial to understanding the religious significance of tricksters. Gregory Cajete observes that "stories about the time following creation [but before the human era] are filled with metaphorical tales about transgressions" against the order established in creation. He writes: "Unless one understands his/her place in the whole, there is always a tendency to move beyond, to glorify, to self-aggrandize" (Cajete 2000, 38). Tales of transgression are, in part, cautionary tales, examples of how *not* to behave—which returns us to tricksters.

Trickster stories are often lessons about transgression. When the Cheyenne trickster, Wihio, sees a man who can send his eyes out of his head high up into a tree and then call them back, he wants to learn the trick. The man teaches Wihio but warns him not to do it more than four times a day. Wihio disregards the man's warning, and on the fifth time his eyes do not come back. Punished for his transgression, Wihio is left blind. Shortly thereafter he receives two new eyes, one from a mouse, the other from a buffalo. "But the [buffalo] eye did not fit the socket; most of it was outside. The other was far inside. Thus he remained" (Thompson 1929, 63). We are left with an image of a curiously eyed trickster who, though punished for his misdeed, will not learn from his mistake and will proceed in other stories to transgress other warnings.

The purpose of such stories might seem merely cautionary—that is, from Wihio's example people learn not to misbehave and to heed the instructions offered by other members of the community. While the story has clear religious importance (offering, as it does, guidance to good ethical behavior by the example of what happens when Wihio misbehaves), to focus solely on the "moral" of the story is to overlook other crucial religious elements in such comic stories of transgression.

When the folklorist Barre Toelken asks about the foolish things Ma'ii (as Coyote is named in Diné) does, the Diné storyteller Yellowman answers, "If he did not do all those things, then those things would not be possible in the world" (Toelken and Scott 1981, 80). Toelken understands this to mean that Coyote is more "an enabler whose actions, good or bad, bring certain ideas and actions into the field of possibility" (ibid., 81). The stories about tricksters may be funny and offer simple and direct moral lessons, but they offer more as well. As Yellowman tells Toelken, "Many things about the story are funny, but the story is not funny. . . . Through the stories everything is made possible" (ibid., 80).

Trickster stories then are about possibility: indirectly or directly, tricksters make new things possible. In making things possible, trickster stories deal with the sacred powers of creation. Stories of creation—the "old" stories of a prehuman mythological era—"explain [the] origins of animals, or tribes, or objects, or ceremonies, or the universe itself" (Thompson 1929, xvii). Just as they are present in the postcreation stories of transgression, tricksters also live in the stories of the creation times. For instance, the Crow people tell how the Creator began making the world with the help of some ducks, erecting mountains, creating grasses, plants, food, and humans and then encountered Cirape, the coyote. Cirape tells the Creator that he had done well in making this world, only there should be more animals than just ducks. The Creator agrees and calls all the other animals into being. Cirape the coyote then points out that the people the Creator has made are not living well and that they need tepees, bows and arrows, and fire to enrich their lives. While it is the Creator who makes these good things, it is Cirape who points out their necessity (Erdoes and Ortiz 1984, 88–93). The trickster is possessed of the natural reason to see what the world needs, and he makes it possible by helping the Creator realize what is missing.

Tricksters help create the world, inspire critical religious practices, and express an uninhibited, often immoral, sexuality, among their many other traits. This variety of abilities and characteristics may be found in differences between two tribal traditions. For instance, the Ojibwe people speak of how Waynaboozhoo created this world from a grain of earth after the great flood (Benton-Banai 1988, 29–35); the Crow people tell of a time when Old Man Coyote disguised his penis as a strawberry in the hope that some young woman would, in her berrying, satisfy him with the touch of her hand (Erdoes and Ortiz 1984, 314). While such variations in behaviors between tricksters from differing traditions might be expected, it is even more crucial to note what might not be expected. That is, tricksters may exhibit this range of characteristics—from the generosity of creation to the obscene pranks of an adolescent—within a single tribal tradition. The Blackfeet people tell how Napi (also known as the Old Man) created the earth, established social roles for men and women, and made the mountains of the Blackfeet homeland on the Northern Plains (Wissler and Duvall 1908, 19–23). His power though is seductive, and he becomes obsessed with using it to get food and entice women. Eventually the people abandon Napi, and he turns into a lone pine tree that can still be seen, according to Percy Bullchild, on the bank of the Highwood River in Alberta, Canada (ibid., 25–39; Bullchild 1985, 127–228).

While many Native cultural traditions allow their tricksters ambiguously to be both creator and transgressor (as is the case with Napi), other traditions will make a distinction between two types of tricksters. Thus there may be, as Bierhorst notes, "two kinds of Coyote or two kinds of Spider." For example, the Cheyenne tell tales of "low comedy and violence" about Wihio (the spider or wise one), while in their stories of creation and origin Heammawihio (wise one above) is spoken of. In other Native cultures "there is a tendency to give the trickster a companion, so that we have stories about Coyote and Skunk, Coyote and Wolf, or Coyote and Fox" as a means of distinguishing between the admirable character and the less than worthy one (Bierhorst 1985, 14).

The Problem with "Trickster"

Using the word "trickster" to describe Native mythic characters raises a problem. Trickster is a non-Native word, and it carries many connotations, some of which are less than flattering. These unflattering connotations come out of the emphasis that the word "trickster" puts on "trick." As a word, "trick" carries with it associations of deceit, cheating, duplicity, and treachery that describes the actions of the trickster characters in many stories. Furthermore, as the linguist Edward Sapir points out, the suffix "-ster" is a structural feature of language that no longer has a "productive life," and, he states, "it cannot be said to really exist at all" in modern English (Sapir 1921, 141). The suffix "-ster" then suggests an archaic remnant from an era that has now passed into irrelevance (or perhaps an attachment to some outmoded and irrelevant values, as is the case with a word like "hipster"). In the history of Native and white relations, Native cultural values, including those of a religious or spiritual nature, have often been assumed by non-Natives to be outmoded, irrelevant, and archaic. In its etymology the word "trickster" connotes this sense of archaic and outmoded, and, placed in the context of Na-

tive-white relations, we have to wonder if the word "trickster" connotes a denigration of these powerful Native cultural figures.

The nineteenth-century anthropologist Daniel Brinton has been credited as the first to use the word "tricksters" to describe this category of characters found within Native mythic traditions (Gill and Sullivan 1992, 308). While there is no evidence to suggest that Brinton had these belittling connotations in mind when he used the word, his analysis of the Algonkin trickster, Michabo, clearly shows that he regarded "tricksters" as something less than edifying. In his analysis, Brinton argues that Michabo began as a "Great God of Light" but that, over time, the Algonkin people lost this meaning and the stories of Michabo devolved into the vulgar tales of the trickster (Brinton 1868, 161–169).

Recognizing such connotations as a shortcoming in the word, many scholars have sought to honor the trickster's creative power by referring to him as a Culture Hero or Transformer. A Culture Hero is a figure "who inhabits the earth throughout the myth age, preparing it for the day-to-day needs of humans" (Bierhorst 1985, 15). A Transformer is a hero who, as the name suggests, transforms the beings of the myth age into the useful creatures and objects of this world. The activities of Culture Heroes and Transformers are also activities that tricksters engage in, but these names fail to embrace the full range of situations that tricksters create, leading some scholars to redress the problem by stringing the words together in awkward, though perhaps accurate, hyphenated collages such as Trickster-Transformer or Trickster-Transformer-Culture Hero.

In recent years, Native writers and scholars such as Tomson Highway and Gerald Vizenor have engaged in an effort to reclaim tricksters from such rigid categorical definitions. They assert that tricksters are meaningful only when approached from the perspective of Native cultures. Their work suggests that the word "trickster" is neither denigrating nor descriptive, and so debates about its meaning (or about what best to call these characters) distract from the trickster stories, which Highway asserts are "the core of Indian culture" (Highway 1989, 13). Vizenor's work suggests that as long as all attempts at finding a definite categorical meaning of "trickster" are suspended, trickster stories will liberate people to a fuller realization of what Native cultures mean and simultaneously liberate the word "trickster" from denigrating connotations (see Vizenor 1989, 187–211). According to Native intellectuals such as Vizenor and Highway, "tricksters," as a word, should not be understood as an anthropological category (like "Culture Hero" or "Transformer") but as an idea or a spirit in the stories that tells Native people who they are, where they came from, and how they should live. Everyone who engages tricksters in this spirit comes to a richer appreciation of what Native cultures value.

Contradictions

The characteristics of tricksters, ranging from the greatest kind of benevolence to the basest kind of "vile pranks" (Wissler and Duvall 1908, 11), strike many non-Native peoples as contradictions. Such seeming contradictions struck many early European writers as evidence that Native peoples had a debased and degenerate religion (see Le Jeune 1954, 52). Later, non-Native scholars latched on to such contradictions, arguing that they are conundrums that can be resolved—made logical and rational—through the careful application of various linguistic, psychological, and anthropological theories (see Brinton 1868; Jung 1956; and Radin 1956). The problem with such responses—no matter how benign the intent—is that in settling on an emphatic definition of what tricksters should be, they undo what tricksters are. Looked at logically tricksters are nefariously illogical and contradictory in their nature, and, paradoxically, it is their very contradictions that make them so potent in Native cultural traditions. Tricksters are an unseen reality that is clearly real. Embodied in the words and stories of the Native peoples of North America, tricksters return the people to the sacred times of creation and remind them what may happen when the order of creation is transgressed. Unseen realities, creation, transformation, transgression, and compassion are subjects that all great religious traditions explore. Native tricksters stand in the middle of all these noble abstractions, arousing the laughter that reminds everyone that humor is a sacred thing.

Carter Meland

See also Clowns and Clowning; Emergence Narratives; Literature, Religion in Contemporary American Indian Literature; Oral Traditions

References and Further Reading

Beck, Peggy V., Anna Lee Walters, and Nia Francisco. 1977. *The Sacred: Ways of Knowledge, Sources of Life*. Tsaile, AZ: Navajo Community College Press.

Benton-Banai, Edward. 1988. *The Mishomis Book: The Voice of the Ojibway*. Hayward, WI: Indian Country Communications.

Bierhorst, John. 1985. *The Mythology of North America*. New York: William Morrow.

Brinton, Daniel G. 1868/1992. *The Myths of the New World*. Reprint. Baltimore: Clearfield Company.

Bullchild, Percy. 1985. *The Sun Came Down: The History of the World as My Blackfeet Elders Told It*. San Francisco: Harper and Row.

Cajete, Gregory. 2000. *Native Science: Natural Laws of Interdependence*. Santa Fe, NM: Clear Light Publishers.

Doty, William G. 1986. *Mythography: The Study of Myths and Rituals*. Tuscaloosa: University of Alabama Press.

Erdoes, Richard, and Alfonso Ortiz, eds. 1984. *American Indian Myths and Legends*. New York: Pantheon Books.

Gill, Sam D., and Irene F. Sullivan. 1992. *Dictionary of Native American Mythology*. Santa Barbara, CA: ABC-CLIO.

Grim, John A. 1983. *The Shaman: Patterns of Religious Healing among the Ojibway Indians*. Norman: University of Oklahoma Press.

Highway, Tomson. 1989. *Dry Lips Oughta Move to Kapuskasing*. Calgary, AB: Fifth House Publishers.

Johnston, Basil. 1995. *The Manitous: The Supernatural World of the Ojibway*. New York: HarperPerennial.

Jung, C. G. 1956. "On the Psychology of the Trickster Figure." Translated by R. F. C. Hull. Pp. 195–211 in *The Trickster: A Study in American Indian Mythology*. Edited by Paul Radin. New York: Schocken Books.

Le Jeune, Paul. 1954. "Relation of What Occurred in New France in the Year 1634." In *The Jesuit Relations and Allied Documents*. Edited by Edna Kenton. New York: Vanguard Press.

Radin, Paul. 1956. *The Trickster: A Study in American Indian Mythology*. New York: Schocken Books.

Sapir, Edward. 1921. *Language: An Introduction to the Study of Speech*. New York: Harcourt, Brace, and World.

Thompson, Stith. 1929. *Tales of the North American Indian*. Bloomington: Indiana University Press.

Toelken, Barre, and Tacheeni Scott. 1981. "Poetic Retranslation and the 'Pretty Languages' of Yellowman." Pp. 65–116 in *Traditional Literatures of the American Indian: Texts and Interpretations*. Edited by Karl Kroeber. Lincoln: University of Nebraska Press.

Vizenor, Gerald. 1989. "Trickster Discourse: Comic Holotropes and Language Games." Pp. 187–211 in *Narrative Chance: Postmodern Discourse on Native American Indian Literatures*. Edited by Gerald Vizenor. Albuquerque: University of New Mexico Press.

Wickwire, Wendy. 1989. "Introduction." Pp. 9–28 in *Write It on Your Heart: The Epic World of an Okanagan Storyteller*. Edited by Wendy Wickwire. Vancouver: Talonbooks/Theytus.

Wissler, Clark, and D. C. Duvall. 1908/1995. *Mythology of the Blackfoot Indians*. Bison Book Edition. Lincoln: University of Nebraska Press.

Tuunrilría

See Angalkuq

Vision Quest Rites

The concept of the "vision quest" has long been identified with the peoples of the Great Plains, where the rite of seeking special dreams is an old traditional practice. However, many communities outside the Plains have also practiced dream-seeking rites, such as most Native communities of the northeastern and central Canadian woodlands, the South, the West and Northwest coast, as well as the northwest-central Plateau area. Only among the Southwest Pueblo people and Diné (Navajo) is vision seeking less central (though dreams are still noted and regarded as important). In the 1920s, the anthropologist Ruth Benedict (1922, 1923) wrote several descriptive articles on dream seeking, as a result of which the concept of the "vision quest" was popularized. Subsequently the term "vision quest" has tended to overwrite the fact that every Native community has its own terms and language for the rites involved. These Native language terms rarely refer to a "quest" and most often refer to prayer and to supplications made by the seeker—for example, as the Lakota term for the rite, *hanblecheya* ("crying for a dream") or the Omaha term, *nozhinzhon,* which means "to stand sleeping."

The traditional Omaha rite was carried out, as it was in a majority of other Native communities, at adolescence when the mind of the child "had become white"—that is, clear, pure, and open to the spirit world and "able to know suffering." The rite was carried out in the spring. The face of the young man was covered with white clay, as a symbol of the creation, and a special fasting prayer was taught: "Wakonda, here in poverty I stand." The seeker had to fast for as many days as he stood praying outside of the village away from the people. He would repeat the prayer and appeal to the greater (Wakonda) and lesser (sun, moon, stars, animals and so on) powers for a visionary dream. Out of *i'thaethe,* "compassion or pity" for the innocence and sincerity of the faster, a spirit power would appear while the seeker was

Teton Sioux man performing vision Cry Ceremony through fasting and chanting to the Great Mystery, 1907. Edward Curtis. (Library of Congress)

nozhinzhon. The visionary would then receive a gift of power in the form of a dream rite, a song, a certain medicine, or specific actions (or prohibitions) to be done to solicit the power of the dream. Then the faster would return to the village, rest for four days, then seek an older man whose vision experience was similar to receive instructions on how to develop the power given in the dream (Fletcher and La Flesche 1911, 128–131).

The basic purpose of this rite among most Native peoples is for a seeker to experience a certain type of dream, one that is recognized as powerful and useful to the dreamer beyond the normal dreams of ordinary sleep. The majority of dreams in ordinary sleep are not usually classified as dreams of power, because dreams of power are regarded as enhancing human abilities and success in the world. Dreams of power may come in a spontaneous manner, but more often they are sought in various types of fasting and ritual. The contents of such dreams are not predetermined or prescribed in specificity, but they are interpreted within the context of the community and worldview of the dreamer (see "Dreams and Visions," this volume). Each Native community has its own criteria for determining the value and significance of a powerful dream based on the experience of successful elder dreamers and ritual leaders. Overall, dreams are highly valued, and vivid, powerful dreams have long been regarded as a primary means of communication with the spiritual world. Dreamers who have such "big" dreams often become spiritual leaders, teachers, and advisers to the people of their communities; often their spiritual role is defined by the dream.

As Benedict notes, the vision fasting rite is commonly described as a ritual that marked the transition to a new maturity and social identity based on the contents of the dream or vision. Among the Plateau Salish, the Winnebago, and central Algonkin nations such as the Shawnee and Kickapoo, children as young as five to seven years of age would train for the more rigorous prayer-fasts and might have a vision during, or they might fast periodically until marriage, which often ended the dream seeking period. Among many Plains groups, conversely, men and women might seek visions throughout their entire lifetimes, and some Northern Plains peoples such as the Cheyenne and Lakota used extreme means of self-inflicted pain (like piercing) and suffering to summon a pitying dream spirit. Benedict also makes an important distinction— namely, that the vision fasting rites were not always based on the search for a specific "guardian spirit," by which she means an animal or other spirit guide or helper (1922, 2–3, 13–14). Acquiring such a helping spirit was not regarded as the most powerful form of dream or vision; the "big dream" was most respected and sought after to attain spiritual knowledge and techniques for healing, war, hunting, or spiritual guidance that would benefit the life of the community in times of crisis or need. The vision experience cannot be accurately reduced to a search for an animal guide or helping spirit, and, in fact, the more significant visions have no mention of acquiring such a spirit (Benedict 1923, 29). Instead, the visionary receives guidance or instructions that may be unique for a particular practice and may not involve calling upon any individual spirit but only following the dream instructions. Conversely, "guardian spirits" may be acquired without dreams or visions through inheritance, purchase, or ritual transfer.

Later writings on the dream fast have described a richness in ritual practice, preparation, and interpretation that far exceeds any one ideal model or example. One debate on the subject has been over the significance of the fasting rite as producing dreams and visions that conform to a particular "culture pattern" (ibid., 41–43). While early anthropology was preoccupied with reducing complex religious phenomena to manageable schemata, the actual ethnography of vision seeking does not simply show conformity to specific cultural patterns. Such a reduction not only masks the complexity of the phenomena but also conceals visionary differences and diversity within a single culture. Dreams do not simply conform; they lead to creative transformations and innovation in culture as primary direction and guidance from the highest sources of religious empowerment (Albers and Parker 1971, 208). Vision seeking is not an isolated pattern within a general cultural milieu, but a specific religious activity closely linked to aspects of cosmology, ritual, shamanic roles, leadership, kinship, and social identity with significant degrees of variability. Understanding the dream-seeking rite also requires a thorough knowledge of the worldview and practices of the seeker's religious community.

Visions are a primary source for cultural innovation as recorded from the very earliest ethnographies into the present and are by no means simply a mechanism for maintaining a static culture. Because dreams were regarded as a form of communication with primary sources of spiritual knowledge and empowerment, they became a natural basis for cultural innovation and change. The vision seeking rite was often a means for confirming an existing social role, or claims to various types of power, or membership in ritual groups, such as dream societies. However, "big dreams" were often sent for the good of the community and prescribed change and innovation in cultural and religious practices, or in meeting and adapting to cultural oppression such as during colonialization (Irwin 1994, 189, passim). Successful visionaries often introduced radical changes and new directions based on visions, such as those of the Seneca visionary Handsome Lake or Kenekuk, the Kickapoo visionary leader. Changes in ritual or the sponsorship of rituals, or bringing back old rituals, new technologies, the discovery of sacred places, and so on were all based in visionary experiences. A failure to dream or to have visions in fasting rites was interpreted as a lack of creative power and an inhibition of social development; unsuccessful dreamers were seen as "ordinary people" rather than outstanding leaders or spiritual teachers (Irwin 2000).

Vision seeking is also not reducible to a fixed ritual pattern. Rituals of vision seeking are highly diverse, some very structured with careful directions by highly qualified advisers, others more spontaneous and often with no direct supervision by elders or religious professionals. Further, visions that occur spontaneously often signify to the community a special election by spirits and therefore might hold an outstanding value in the life of the individual. The Lakota holy man Black Elk had several spontaneous visions, including a great vision at the age of twelve without fasting or seeking a vision; later, when he fasted for a vision, his great vision was repeated (DeMallie 1984, 11–124). This vision was then the template for his healing and medicine work. Many traditions of dream seeking for women are far less structured than those for men. Women fasted for visions during quiet seclusion for menstruation, while mourning for their dead relatives, or when grief stricken because of the loss of a child or mate, as well as in times of famine or difficulty when separated from the community. Women visionaries are often founders of sacred rites, and a majority of these were based in spontaneous visionary encounters rather than in visions obtained during structured rites. Many groups did have structured rites for women, often near the family dwelling, in the gardens, or while sleeping on the drying racks for corn and squash. Nevertheless, spontaneous visions are more common for women in the general ethnography than for men (Irwin 1994, 83–97; Irwin 2001).

A typical contemporary and pantribal vision fasting rite, for both men and women, usually begins by gaining the permission of a medicine person or other elder to supervise the rite through an offering of tobacco or other gifts.

Closely resembling some Plains Nation traditions, the one to fast is often required to make a series of tobacco ties, each made of a small 6 by 6 inch piece of colored cloth tied up to enclose tobacco and other contents, while the maker prays for a successful vision as he or she makes each one. Often hundreds of these are made, in four colors, and then are tied in a long string—long enough to create a circle on the ground in which the faster will carry out the fasting rite. After all the preliminary rites have been preformed, the faster and the guide, often with some singers, will take a sweat in a special lodge, usually before or at dawn. The faster, purified, will then be taken to a high butte where he or she will lay down the tobacco tie circle (about 6 to 8 feet in diameter, with the four directions marked by small, 2-foot red painted forked sticks) under the supervision of the medicine person. Then, often carrying a pipe, he or she will enter the circle with minimal clothing on, with a blanket but no food or water, and then spend four days and nights fasting and praying for a vision. After the fast ends, the medicine person will escort the faster back to the sweatlodge, and another sweat will be taken during which the faster will narrate his or her vision observations, experiences, and impressions during the fast. Often the medicine person will then interpret the vision or possibly tell the faster to wait for more dreams. Such a fasting rite is considered a preliminary rite to the Sun Dance in some Plains groups. A classic description of the Lakota *hanblecheya* rite was recorded by Walker in the 1890s (see DeMallie and Jahner 1980, 129–132).

The visions given in the rites of fasting are highly variable. Often they have a material or symbolic content that results in the visionary's fashioning ritual objects as seen in the vision. This includes feather fans, rattles, hoops, shields, paint, various animal or plant items, and often, in the Plains traditions, a pipe and tobacco, as well as specific herbs or medicine used in carrying out the vision ritual. The dream is thus encoded into various symbolic forms that are considered to be directly connected to the sacred powers of the vision. The vision forms may be painted on walls or teepees, on the body, on horses, or carved in wood or stone as in the Northwest; certain objects, such as crystals, may be embedded in the physical body of the visionary by the dream spirits, as among the California Shasta. Often the dream spirits are thought to reside in the body and to leave it only at death. The various objects, or their representations, are then collected and placed into a bundle and kept by the visionary to be opened only on special occasions for the performance of the vision rite. These rites have traditionally been rites of healing, hunting, fishing, war, or planting and care of sacred gardens. In contemporary times, these rites have been more oriented to community healing and empowerment. Usually there is a set of songs given, and these are generally sung when the ritual is performed. The vision is only rarely narrated, and there is a belief that telling the vision will exhaust or give away the power. Sometimes the rites are communal ceremonies and other times they are individual practices, but both are usually for the good of the community (Irwin 1994, 211–236). Some powers of the visionary world can be harmful, and those dream rites are kept secret and rarely discussed or even mentioned.

Most vision seeking results in a demonstration of the power or gift of the dream that was given. Often this demonstration is not given for many years as the visionary continues to seek additional dreams or a deeper core of the vision and its relationship to the ritual and social life of the community before enacting it. Alternatively, a vision may be a specific call for a change in ritual patterns or for initiating new cycles of ritual. As a call for ritual or as ritual changes, the dream or vision is more often spontaneous, whereas the vision of a specific, individual practice is more often part of a vision seeking rite. In some traditions there is a period of waiting, often signified by four dreams that further empower the individual. Or the visionary may not understand how to enact the vision and may wait for further instructions. When the visionary reaches maturity, he or she will then announce to the community the rite or demonstration. A special time will be chosen, and the individual will then perform the dream rite, opening the bundle and singing the appropriate songs while performing actions seen in the vision, with the expec-

tation that he or she will demonstrate some unusual or remarkable ability that comes only through the vision. Failure to produce this demonstration will discredit the vision. Only when the person can truly demonstrate the power of the dream is it considered real and valid (ibid., 163–184).

A contemporary interpretative concern has been to highlight the alternative paradigm of knowledge that the vision seeking rite has institutionalized. In Native theory, visions are based in an epistemology that maintains clear connections between the dreaming and waking states, and vision seeking is seen as a means for increasing contact with tangible sources of both spiritual and practical knowledge. Vision questing is not, therefore, interpreted by Indian people in terms of psychological or psycho-physiognomic responses to stress, sensory deprivation, changes in body chemistry, and the like, as is usually the case in Western interpretations of these phenomena. In the Native context, vision fasting is seen as a means to access various planes of reality, through sacred vision sites, which requires a special capacity to enter the dreaming state. Understanding vision quest rites also requires grasping the epistemology of dreaming, as well as the discourse frames for interpretation within the religious context of the vision seeker, as well as the preformative genres that provide a social arena for the enactment of the dream or vision (Tedlock 1987, 23–25). Vision seeking is inseparable from a religious cosmology and theories of knowledge that ground the vision seeking rite and the dream experience in the narrative landscape of the visionary. This epistemology necessarily includes concepts of personhood, self, social roles, and communal responsibilities—all of which are linked to the vision seeking process. It also includes a wide range of visionary states, paranormal abilities, out-of-body narratives, and various types of trance or altered states of awareness. Native traditions have a rich phenomenology of the vision rite, its symbolism, social application, and semiotic context that is inseparable from the interpretation of the vision or dream.

In contemporary Native culture, vision seeking is still widely practiced in many communities, particularly among the north-central Plains peoples. While often part of traditional practices, it is also linked to the general development of an increasing ecumenical Native spirituality in which certain rites, such as the sweatlodge and Sun Dance, have been borrowed and readapted within many communities other than the Plains as a means for affirming Native spiritual identity. This is true for women as well as for men (St. Pierre and Long Soldier 1995). Unfortunately, many non-Native people have also appropriated the vision fasting rite and offer it as a token experience to non-Natives without proper training or understanding of the deep connection of the fast to the larger religious context of traditional Native communities. This decontextualized, usually stereotyped borrowing has resulted in a "spirituality for sale" mentality that pays little or no attention to the authentic practice and its role in community life and development (Jocks 2000). In most cases the vision fast has been a means for strengthening communal ties to a sacred view of the world, in Native language and in the context of a rich and complex spirituality. It has never been seen as an isolated, separate practice, remote from community, but always taken as a means for deeper engagement with the full complexity of communal religious life.

Lee Irwin

See also Ceremony and Ritual, Nez Perce; Ceremony and Ritual, Northwest; Ceremony and Ritual, Southeast; Datura; Dreamers and Prophets; Dreams and Visions; Female Spirituality; Kinship; Native American Church, Peyote Movement; New Age Appropriation; Power, Northwest Coast; Power Places, Great Basin; Power, Plains; Power, Southeast; Sweatlodge; Warfare, Religious Aspects

References and Further Reading
Albers, Patricia, and S. Parker. 1971. "The Plains Vision Experience." *Southwestern Journal of Anthropology* 27: 203–233.
Benedict, R. F. 1922. "The Vision in Plains Culture." *American Anthropologist* 24: 1–23.
———. 1923. "The Concept of the Guardian Spirit in North America." *American Anthropological Association Memoirs,* no. 29. Menasha, WI: George Banta.
DeMallie, Ray, and Elaine Jahner. 1980. *Lakota Belief and Practice.* Lincoln: University of Nebraska Press.
———, ed. 1984. *The Sixth Grandfather: Black Elk's Teachings Given to John G. Neihardt.* Lincoln: University of Nebraska Press.
Fletcher, Alice, and Francis La Flesche. 1911. "The Omaha Tribe." *Bureau of American Ethnology, 27th Annual Report.*

Washington, DC: Smithsonian Institution Press.

Irwin, Lee. 1994. *The Dream Seekers: Native American Visionary Traditions of the Great Plains.* Norman: University of Oklahoma Press.

———. 2000. "Freedom, Law and Prophecy: A Brief History of Native American Religious Resistance." In *Native American Spirituality: A Critical Reader.* Edited by Lee Irwin. Lincoln: University of Nebraska Press.

———. 2001. "Sending a Voice, Seeking a Place: Visionary Traditions among Native Women of the Plains." Pp. 93–110 in *Dreams: A Reader on the Religious, Cultural, and Psychological Dimensions of Dreaming.* Edited by

Kelly Bulkeley. New York: Palgrave Press.

Jocks, Christopher. 2000. "Spirituality for Sale: Sacred Knowledge in the Consumer Age." In *Native American Spirituality: A Critical Reader.* Edited by Lee Irwin. Lincoln: University of Nebraska Press.

St. Pierre, Mark, and Tilda Long Soldier. 1995. *Walking in a Sacred Manner: Healers, Dreamers and Pipe Carriers— Medicine Women of the Plains Indians.* New York: Simon and Schuster.

Tedlock, B. 1987. "Dreaming and Dream Research." Pp. 1–30 in *Dreaming: Anthropological and Psychological Interpretations.* Edited by Barbara Tedlock. Cambridge: Cambridge University Press.

Warfare, Religious Aspects

Since the publication of Prussian general Carl von Clausewitz's famous treatise in 1832 entitled *Vom Kreig,* or *On War,* making war has been considered a political rather than a religious act. Historically, however, more wars have been fought for religious beliefs and institutions than for any other cause. Indeed, warfare was, particularly in the Western mind, thought of as a category of religious obligation. The Western conception of the "just war" was often explained in terms of religious conviction and the adherence to a specific creed.

In a broad overview, pre-Colombian Native American warfare had its religious aspects, but for the most part it was not viewed as a creedal conflict. Native Americans were not usually out to change or destroy an enemy's religious precepts or to further a particular ideology. War in Native North America had many ceremonial implications to be sure, and it was certainly more of an individual spiritual experience than a state-sponsored institution. Native Americans fought for economic gain, to take captives, to give valued status to young men, and to guard territorial boundaries. The Native peoples of North America also fought to satisfy certain religious responsibilities and to maintain a healthy relationship with the spirit world.

One of the best examples of making war for the sake of fulfilling religious obligations was the so-called Flower War of the Aztec empire of central Mexico. The Aztecs had created an empire, using war as a political tool. Once they had established both political efficacy and religious orthodoxy, the Aztecs constructed a hegemonic-tributary imperial system as opposed to one that was based on military occupation or the plantation of colonies. Non-Aztecs forced into the Aztec empire paid tribute to the central government but for the most part were not deliberately colonized.

The Aztec Flower War was fought to obtain captives for ritual execution and sacrifice to the Aztec deities. After ritual

Piegan man in a war bonnet, holding a feathered coup-stick, 1910. (Edward Curtis/ Library of Congress)

purification, an Aztec army issued a challenge to and took the field against a traditional enemy that had not yet been incorporated into the empire. Aztec military culture—indeed the military culture of all of central Mexico—emphasized taking prisoners over killing the enemy. The principal hand-to-hand weapon, for example, was a flat club lined with obsidian blades. This swordlike weapon was designed to inflict shallow wounds or to incapacitate a foe without killing. The most honored Aztec warriors were those who had captured the most prisoners in combat.

One form of Aztec ritual sacrifice emphasized the spiritual relationship between combatants, captives, and captors. A captive was adopted by his captor and taken in as a favored son for a period of about a year. The captive knew full well that he was to become a victim of ritual sacrifice—he was shown where and told how he would die—yet he stayed on with his adoptive family. After a year the son/captive was taken to the temple of the war god, tethered to a raised platform, and forced to fight representatives from the various Aztec regiments. The victim was armed with a feathered war club, while his opponents carried their usual obsidian-bladed swords. He was never killed outright but wounded over and over again with cuts from the extremely sharp obsidian blades until finally he dropped from exhaustion and loss of blood. He was sacrificed in this condition and his body flayed. The captor, who was an important witness to the ritual slaying and attended the ceremonies, was given the victim's skin, which he wore on his own person until it literally rotted away.

The macabre but intensely religious act of human sacrifice was not limited to the Aztecs. Several of the Native nations of the eastern woodlands practiced what has been called "mourning war." Among these peoples grief was understood to be a disruptive and nearly uncontrollable force. The mourning wars amounted to the raiding of traditional enemies in order to replace dead relatives, physically and spiritually. The Native nations of the Haudenosaunee, or League of the

Iroquois, practiced this type of warfare in its purest form.

A widow or clan mother who sought to replace a deceased relative usually instigated the mourning war. An experienced war leader might then raise a party of warriors to raid a traditional enemy. If the raid were successful the party would return with a few captives to be handed over to the women of the clan who had sustained the loss of a loved one. The women, in turn, would decide whether a captive was a suitable replacement for the deceased. Children and female captives were most often adopted into a clan. The clan took on the responsibility of assuming the cost of an adoption ceremony, providing for the welfare of and eventually assimilating the captive. Indeed, the constitution of the Haudenosaunee provided unambiguous directions for the adoption of captives. Quite often the adopted captive would take on all of the honors and titles of the deceased person being replaced. Gender was not especially important in the adoption ritual, and consequently young female replacements might even receive male names or war honors that had been awarded to a dead clansman.

Adult male captives, although often adopted, were occasionally tortured, slain, and ritually cannibalized in an act of spiritual substitution or sacrifice. The victim, like those of the Aztec sacrifices described above, was often a complicit partner in the entire process. While being tortured by the women, armed usually with burning torches or sharp sticks, the victim defiantly sang songs and downplayed the women's attempts to cause him pain. When the victim grew weary or collapsed from blood loss or pain, the women spoke to him in kinship terms—brother, son, grandson—and gave him water and food to revive his strength. Finally, when the captive could endure no more, he was killed. If he had been especially brave in his defiance of their efforts, parts of his body would be cooked and eaten so that his captors could literally ingest his spiritual essence.

Ultimately, the sacrifice was a victory for both captors and captive. The captive had demonstrated extreme courage and had gained a spiritual triumph. The captors, on the other hand, had demonstrated ascendancy over traditional enemies and had shared this triumph with those who had directly participated in the raid that resulted in the enemy's defeat. Clan grief had been diverted and even assuaged. Overall, the mourning war was a deeply religious act that counteracted the deleterious effects of grief, renewed the bonds of kinship, restored order, and maintained beneficial relations with the spirit world.

In one form or another, virtually all Native nations practiced mourning war. The widespread "scalp dance" was usually performed by Native women who either paraded with war trophies or used enemy scalps literally to "dry their tears." In raids, Apaches habitually took captives to replace lost relatives. On the Great Plains, numerous Native nations

American veterans saluting during D-Day anniversary celebrations at Omaha Beach, Normandy, France.1994. (Owen Franken/Corbis)

engaged in the practice of "counting coup" in battle. Often associated with a system of graded war honors, counting coup took the form of a spiritual battle. It was widely understood that the acts of coup in battle were ranked in order. First and foremost was touching an enemy in battle with a special "coup stick," lance, bow, or even the hand. Of secondary importance was stealing an enemy's favorite horse, which might be tethered close to his tepee, or taking an enemy's shield or weapons, or running off a village's entire horse herd. The lowest form of coup was killing the enemy. The idea of humiliating the enemy, or "capturing

his spirit" and leaving him alive to suffer his defeat, was certainly involved in this type of highly ritualized warfare.

But on occasions an enemy might be humiliated without even knowing it—thus reinforcing the notion that coup was "spiritual warfare." One of the most famous coup stories ever recorded concerned a Comanche warrior, who on a previous raid had stolen a Ute enemy's special blanket. One night this warrior, accompanied only by a young man to hold the horses, donned the blanket and strode into a Ute village. The Utes were involved in a hand game, and nearly the entire populace was in a particular place. The Comanche warrior went unnoticed and was able to move around secretly touching every Ute participating in or watching the hand game. He exited the encampment without incident and returned to his own village able to count more than fifty coups. His daring and stealth were honored, and the entire Comanche village from which he came viewed his exploit as a great defeat for the Utes. That the Utes themselves did not know of their defeat at the hand of a single Comanche warrior mattered not at all. By deception and courage their spirits had been captured.

Compared with that of most Western societies, life in a Native American society was nonconfrontational and markedly pacific. By definition a tribe is a society based on kinship. An ethos of cooperation and the give and take of well-defined relationships between each member of society are constantly reinforced through story, song, sacred history, ritual, language, and even economic practices. Violence was normally directed toward other groups, most notably traditional enemies. Having traditional foes in many ways strengthened the internal cooperative ethos of tribal groups and made war an act that was considered the very opposite

Female Diné army soldiers. Shiprock Navajo Fair, Shiprock New Mexico, 2004. (Marilyn "Angel" Wynn/Nativestock)

of normal behavior. Most Native peoples did not have a specific word for war as it is defined in the Western world. In the O'odham language, for example, war is the equivalent of chaos. In consequence, most Native peoples devised specific war ceremonies intended to convey individual warriors as well as entire societies from normality to abnormal circumstances and behaviors and back again.

Before a war expedition was undertaken, medicine people were called upon to perform purification and protection ceremonies to ensure the safe return of warriors. They were also consulted to interpret signs and omens regarding a forthcoming conflict. Special prayers and songs were used to call upon the spirits in order to guarantee the success of a war party. Cherokee warriors were secluded for a period of time, then took part in a series of dances intended to inspire them to victory. Upon their return from a successful raid or pitched battle, Cherokee warriors handed over captives or booty to their female relatives and again went into seclusion. When properly cleansed of the taint and trauma of battle, they often donned masks and danced in a victory celebration.

Like the Cherokees, most tribes devised ceremonies that honored returning warriors and attempted to heal them both physically and emotionally of the trauma of battle. Because conflict was viewed as an extraordinary and disruptive activity, it was often treated very much like any other serious illness. The Diné (Navajo) Enemy Way, for example, is usually a four- to seven-day ceremony during which a medicine man and his helpers utilize sand paintings, songs, and particular symbols to restore the individual warrior to health. Diné medicine, like Western medicine, functions to cure the body, mind, and spirit of the individual. But Diné medicine, like that of most other tribal forms, also seeks to restore the harmony of the individual's environment. In other words, Native American medicine, especially that connected with warfare, recognizes that an individual's trauma spreads across an entire community, disrupting the balance of life. Nearly every tribal society has a particular word to describe the goal of a balanced, orderly, harmonious existence within a particular landscape. Loosely translated, the terms mean the "peace," the "way," or the "path."

Each tribe's sacred history usually includes stories about how and why a ceremony to cure a particular illness is used. Most often, holy people, heroes, or the spirits give a ceremony to the people so that they will have the power to restore health and harmony to their particular world. The Diné Enemy Way ceremony is a recitation of the story of Monster Slayer, who slew the monsters of the world in order to provide a safe place for human beings to dwell. After he had accomplished that formidable task and had abused his special powers to do so, he fell ill. Another Holy Being recognized that Monster Slayer's illness had been brought on as a result of the death and destruction he himself had wrought. The Holy Being devised the Enemy Way to purge Monster Slayer of the trauma of seeing so much death and to restore the beauty of the natural world. The teachings of the Diné sacred history are thus applied to certain curative processes, in this case warfare.

Although Native Americans went to war for many different reasons, they all recognized it as an extraordinary, perhaps even mysterious, event. Warriors often sought spiritual powers to aid them in combat; they also sought supernatural assistance in returning them to peace. War, among some peoples, may have been a spiritual experience or a way of serving the deities to ensure a prosperous and happy life. All Native peoples, however, understood that because war was a terrible and terrifying experience it absolutely required religious comprehension and sacred attention.

Tom Holm

See also Ceremony and Ritual, Diné; Oral Traditions, Pueblo; Oral Traditions, Western Plains; Power, Plains

References and Further Reading
Beck, Peggy V., et al. 1995. *The Sacred: Ways of Knowledge, Sources of Life.* Tsaile, AZ: Navajo Community College Press.
Holm, Tom. 1995. *Strong Hearts, Wounded Souls.* Austin: University of Texas Press.
———. 2002. "American Indian Warfare." In *A Companion to American Indian History.* Edited by Philip J. Deloria and Neal Salisbury. Malden, MA: Blackwell Companions to American History.
Hultdrantz, Ake. 1980. *The Religions of the American Indians.* Berkeley: University of California Press.
Jennings, Francis. 1976. *The Invasion of America: Indians, Colonialism and the Cant of Conquest.* New York: W. W. Norton.
Turney-High, Harry Holbert. 1971. *Primitive War: Its Practice and Concepts.* Columbia: University of South Carolina Press.
———. 1993. *Way of the Warrior.* Alexandria, VA.: Time-Life Books.

Whaling, Religious and Cultural Implications

Makah and Nuu-chah-nulth Whaling Traditions

Coastal peoples throughout the Pacific Northwest and the Arctic have relied heavily on success in whale hunting for their livelihood. Whaling traditions formed a central aspect of cultural life and religious practice, as well as subsistence materials. Complex ritual and ceremonial practices arose throughout the millennia to ensure communities success in their hunting endeavors. For all of these communities, success in the hunt is believed to be dependent upon a good relationship between the human community and the whales. Whales are not caught but rather give themselves willingly to a community that has earned their respect and affection through proper ritual preparations and respectful treatment of the whale after it is killed.

Today, many Native communities seek to continue their traditional whaling practices, arguing that they are central to their religious and cultural existence as a people. This has resulted in political protests and confrontations between

Native communities and some environmental groups. Native communities argue that such protestors do not understand the sacred nature of indigenous whaling, its religious and cultural significance, or the ritual practices that accompany it. In order to understand these cultural dynamics more fully, it is helpful to look at particular tribal traditions, as well as the religious and cultural traditions that structure their approach to whaling and their relationship with whales. This essay focuses on the whaling traditions of the Makah and Nuu-chah-nulth peoples of the Pacific Northwest coast.

The Makah and Nuu-chah-nulth peoples' traditional territory is in the central Northwest coast, the Makah in the Cape Flattery area at the northwestern tip of the Olympic Peninsula in Washington State, and the Nuu-chah-nulth on the west coast of Vancouver Island in British Columbia. The Makah refer to themselves as the Kwih-dich-chuh-ahtx, "People who live by the rocks and the seagulls." They received the name Makah from their Clallam neighbors, a word meaning "generous with food." The name was adopted by U.S. officials in the 1850s, and since then it has been used both internally and externally to refer to the tribe (Taylor 1974, 15).

The Nuu-chah-nulth were originally known as the Nootka (also spelled Nutka) people, a name given to them by Captain Cook in 1778. Although they are separated into specific tribal groups, they share linguistic and cultural ties

and maintain a collectivity. In 1978 they changed their name to Nuu-chah-nulth, which means "all along the mountains." Topographically, the traditional territory of the Makah and Nuu-chah-nulth consists of steep and rocky terrain with mountain ranges—the Coast Range in British Columbia and the Cascades in Washington and Oregon—acting as natural dividers, cutting off those seafaring, maritime peoples from the inland hunter and gatherer societies. These natural boundaries surrounding the various indigenous groups resulted in a large number of small, autonomous, coastal indigenous societies (Kehoe 1981, 403–406).

The Makah and Nuu-chah-nulth are among the Wakashan-speaking peoples, sharing linguistic ties, cultural patterns, and a tradition of hunting whales. The Nootkan language is separated into three dialectic divisions: Nootka proper, spoken from Cape Cook to the east shore of Barclay Sound; Nitinat, used by the groups of Pacheena and Nitinat Lake; and Makah, spoken by the Cape Flattery people. These dialects seem to differ through a few fairly simple and consistent phonetic shifts, so that although they are at first mutually unintelligible, a person who speaks one form can soon understand the others and make himself understood (Drucker 1955, 16; Taylor 1974, 37). The Makah are the only tribe in the United States who have a right to hunt whales secured and affirmed in a treaty, signed in 1855. The Nuu-chah-nulth are presently negotiating a con-

A family views the body of a whale. Many Native communities seek to continue their traditional whaling practices, arguing that they are central to their religious and cultural existence as a people. This has resulted in political protests and confrontations between Native communities and some environmental groups. Neah Bay, Washington. 1999. (Anthony Bolante/Corbis Sygma)

temporary treaty with the government of Canada.

Archaeological discoveries in the Makah and Nuu-chah-nulth traditional territories provide material evidence that whaling has been central to the two groups' cultures for more than 2,000 years. An archaeological excavation in 1970 in Makah territory uncovered an ancient whaling village, reaffirming Makah's oral histories, in which they clearly had an entrenched whaling tradition. Whaling villages have been marked by shell middens in both Makah and Nuu-chah-nulth territories (Kirk 1991, 171). A Nuu-chah-nulth whaler's shrine was removed from their territory in 1904 and is now housed in the American Museum of Natural History. The shrine not only proves the existence of whaling among the Nuu-chah-nulth people but also shows the importance that was placed on the whaling tradition through spiritual rituals that were performed in these holy places. Nuu-chah-nulth artist Art Thompson says that the legends explain, document, and affirm the importance and centrality of the whale to both the Makah and Nuu-chah-nulth people.

I was told by my elders that our thunderbird headdresses used in our ceremonial dances are the most important things for our people. The thunderbird, the serpent, and the whale are significant symbols of our culture and are maintained in our songs, dances, and artistic expressions. The thunderbird used the serpent to catch the whale. He would wind the serpent around his waist and go out to sea to look for the whale. When he spotted a whale he took the serpent and threw it down at the whale, hitting and stunning it. This made it easier for the whale to be caught, because while it was stunned it remained floating on top of the water. The thunderbird took the whale and brought it to the people for all of them to eat. (Personal communication with Nuu-chah-nulth artist Art Thompson from the Diditaht tribe, November 28, 2001)

Whaling was clearly inherent to both tribes' cultural systems at the time of contact and was well documented by early explorers, Indian agents, and ethnologists. One of the first documentations of Nuu-chah-nulth whaling was in 1792 by explorer Jose Mozino, who also documented the physical and cultural similarities between the Nuu-chah-nulth and Makah peoples (Mozino 1991). The tradition noticeably set the Makah and Nuu-chah-nulth apart from the other tribes along the coast, as they were the only groups that whaled. There is evidence that other tribal groups (Quileute, Quinault, Clallam, and Chemakum) along the Olympic Peninsula did whale, but it was believed that they learned the art from their Makah and Nuu-chah-nulth neighbors. Writers have theorized about the peculiarity of Makah and Nuu-chah-nulth whaling and why they were the only tribes in the area that whaled. Archaeological evidence led anthropologist Philip Drucker to suggest a linkage between the Nuu-chah-nulth whaling complex and Eskimo-Aleut whaling in Alaska—that at one time there had been close contact between the two cultures,

even though today they are separated by hundreds of miles (Drucker 1955, 198–206). Boas and Lantis also found striking similarities in the ritual aspects of the Nuu-chah-nulth, Makah, and Alaskan whale cults, leading them to suggest a connection between those indigenous societies (Lantis 1938).

Whaling was an important component of Makah and Nuu-chah-nulth cultures and was entwined in the complex web of social interactions that constructed their identities. Whaling served important social, subsistence, and ritual functions. "The unity and interaction of the various activities surrounding whaling worked to form an elaborate and interconnected mesh of economic, ritual and redistribution prerogatives" (Reaveley 1998, 3). Whalers underwent months of cleansing and purification before the whale hunt commenced. To become successful whalers these men needed to go through a rigorous and lengthy training period that included fasting, swimming, and purification. The whalers abstained from their normal food, abstained from sexual intercourse, and in most cases lived apart from their wives during their whaling preparation. They ceremonially washed their bodies during the morning, afternoon, and evening and rubbed their skin with twigs. "It was during whaling rituals that chiefs implored supernaturals for assistance in the hunts" (Jonaitis 1999, 5; Jewitt 1996, 130–131).

"The belief that human beings could get power from individual entities in the nonhuman world underlay much of the belief system of the Northwest Coast" (Suttles 1990, 4). The guardian-spirit complex was integral to many of the tribal cultures along the coast. The practice of abstinence, fasting, bathing, and rubbing was needed to seek out the "guiding and protecting spirit" that the Makah and Nuu-chah-nulth called *tumanos* (Gunther 1942, 66). The guardian spirit is also spelled *tamanawas*, which is the Chinook jargon word that is used to describe the supernatural. Many ceremonies in Makah and Nuu-chah-nulth cultures included the spiritual quest of obtaining a guardian spirit.

> For success in hunting, fishing, and other pursuits, or for health and long life, Nuu-chah-nulth men and women sought to obtain spirit power through prayer and through special preparations, usually *uusimch* (a cleansing, bathing ritual). This could involve fasting, continence, bathing in cold water, cleansing oneself with bundles of twigs and plants, singing, and more. Each family had its own set of inherited ritual practices and sacred places that are closely held family secrets. (Huu-ay-aht First Nations 2000, 41–42)

It was believed that the intense purification rituals were needed to attain a guardian spirit, and that the individual would be "protected from harm by his ritual purity" (Drucker 1965, 86). The most important and significant religious observances were connected to the Makah and Nuu-chah-nulth whaling tradition. The guardian spirit was considered a strong spiritual power that the whaler sought out during his strenuous months of whaling preparation. If the preparation were done properly, the whaler would secure a guardian spirit that would not only protect him and his crew during the hunt but also make the hunt successful (Densmore 1972, 47). The whaler, the one who actually harpooned the whale, was a person of high rank and status, inheriting his chief's position from his father's lineage. Thus whaling was strictly an inherited privilege, and it was seen as one of a "noblest calling" (Arima and Dewhirst 1990, 395).

In Makah and Nuu-chah-nulth cultures "intermediate spirits" were believed to "guard the destinies of individuals," and they manifested themselves through visions, signs, and dreams (Swan 1964, 61). The great Mowachaht (Nuu-chah-nulth) chief Maquinna was believed to have received his "valuable secret knowledge about whaling" from a guardian spirit (Drucker 1965, 134).

During his time held captive by the Nuu-chah-nulth, British sailor John Jewitt observed Maquinna's whaling preparation. He noted how in the months leading up to the hunt Maquinna continually said prayers "to his God" asking him for success in the upcoming whale hunt. Jewitt noted how Maquinna, as well as the whaling crew, observed a fast a week before whaling commenced. They would daily bathe, "singing and rubbing their bodies, limbs and faces with bushes" (Jonaitis 1999, 8).

The Southeast

The Southeast culture area is a region north of the Gulf of Mexico and south of the Middle Atlantic–Midwest region, extending from the Atlantic coast west to what is now central Texas. Semitropical in nature, the area is humid and wet. The terrain and vegetation of the Southeast culture area consists of a coastal plain along the Atlantic Ocean and Gulf of Mexico, with saltwater marshes, grasses, and large stands of cypress. Rich soil can be found in what are now Alabama and Mississippi, as well as along the Mississippi River floodplain. The region also includes the vast swamplands, hills, and the high grass of the Everglades in present-day Florida, as well as mountains of the southern Appalachian chain. At the time of early contacts between Native Americans and Europeans, much of the region was woodland, with southern pine near the coasts and more broadleaf trees further inland.

European incursion, initiated by the French from the Mississippi Valley, then the Spanish after the eighteenth century, found a region of the United States that was bordered by the Atlantic Ocean, the Gulf of Mexico, the Trinity River, and the Ohio River. The cultures of this region include the Catawba, Chickasaw, Choctaw, Creek, Cherokee, and Seminole Nations. Influenced by the earlier Mississippian cultures, characterized by monumental mound building and corn cultivation, later tribal groups tended toward sedentary village-based cultures, regional trade, diplomatic systems, and religious traditions that supported the agrarian lifestyle. Much of this lifeway is characterized by sacred activities oriented toward seasonal plant growth patterns.

One example of such sacred activity is the renewal festival, an annual ceremony oriented toward fertility of the soil in the coming year, recognition of the passing of the annual celestial cycle, and especially thanksgiving for the bounty of the previous year. Like many regional ceremonies throughout Native America, these festivals played important diplomatic roles because status issues were an important part of the process of planning and celebrating these festivals. The festivals provided opportunities for young people to meet potential mates outside their familial lineage group.

continues

The Southeast (continued)

In addition to agricultural production of corn, beans, and squash, pre-contact Southeastern tribal groups hunted game to augment the plant foods in their diet, and this practice also gave rise to certain rituals. Hunters all over Indian country are aware of the sacred nature of their endeavor, and this is certainly true among the peoples of the Southeastern United States. The propitiation of animal spirits and the need for respectful treatment of the physical beings associated with them require hunters to hunt in a respectful way; failure to do so runs the risk of going hungry.

Another aspect common throughout the region is the important role that games play in both the leisure and religious realms. Most notable among these is the ball game, in which a small leather ball is thrown, kicked, or advanced with playing sticks (depending on the tribal area) by two teams intending to score by advancing the ball past the opponent's goal, as in a combination of field hockey, soccer, and American football. This game has sacred as well as entertainment value.

Many traditions have similar regional manifestations, owing to the relatively unified early cultures extant before European inculcation, far too many for this brief introduction. Suffice it to say that, although the tribal cultures that call the Southeastern United States their place of origin differ greatly one from another, the tendency to maintain similar traits such as sedentary village life, clan and sacred society membership, and regular, important religious festivals remind the student of these cultures that the tribal differentiation which is now of great import in these communities developed out of a regionally aware collection of autonomous villages with much intervillage interaction and intellectual discourse prior to the arrival of Europeans.

The village served as the primary form of social organization among Indians of the Southeast prior to contact, and political organization also began at the village level. The people governed the affairs of a specific area, and village leaders, often led by a headman, met regularly to discuss matters of import to the entire community, such as the cultivation of fields owned by the community, or providing for defense of the village.

continues

The Southeast (continued)

Some Southeast tribes are organized into chiefdoms, defined as a society with an ultimate ruler with social rank often determined by birth. Some earlier Southeast chiefdoms encompassed many villages, and these tended to have powerful priesthoods, leading to stratification in those societies. The Natchez, Chickasaw, and the Creek Confederacy had well-developed hierarchies until the Euro-American political system undermined the authorities within them. Other Southeastern tribes such as the Cherokee and Choctaw, tended to be more democratic in their political organization and were less likely to be inundated with efforts by religio-political American authorities. Today, the village orientation continues in the region, albeit within the imposed Indian Reorganization Act (1934) system.

Astronomy played a significant role in whaling preparation. It was believed that the supernatural power came to a whaler "with the changing year," so strict observances were made in regard to the phases of the moon in determining when the training would commence (Curtis, in Waterman 1920, 40). According to Sapir the training period would begin "when the moon is waxing," thus being carried out during the winter months (Sapir 1991, 312). Drucker noted how the Mowachaht whaler would bathe nightly for "eight waxing moons" (Jonaitis 1999, 5). The whale hunt would begin with the sighting of the first new moon in May (Waterman 1920, 40).

Anthropologist Edward Curtis's research on the Nuu-chah-nulth in the early 1900s provided extensive details on the rituals and religious observances attached to their whaling tradition and how the whalers believed they needed to possess this "medicine" or "spiritual" power in order to whale. Curtis noted that to obtain this medicine the whaler would go out in the early morning and bathe in a freshwater lake or pond. He submerged himself four times and after each time rubbed himself with hemlock (ibid., 39). The bathing in cold water and scrubbing with hemlock were used to cleanse the whaler's body of human odor, which, it was believed, "the spirits found most unpleasant" (Jonaitis 1999, 5). He would begin on his left side, vigorously rubbing his body with the branches, sometimes drawing blood. When the branches eventually wore away the whaler would go ashore and take new branches to begin the same process on the right side of his body (Waterman 1920, 38). *"Osimch,"* ritual bathing, was done by many coastal people throughout the year to gain luck and general well-being. However, for whaling preparation, *osimch* was more rigorously performed and for longer periods at a time (Arima 1983, 10).

The whaler's rituals included imitative elements, performing certain movements in the water as if copying a whale. As the whaler emerged he emulated the whale by blowing mouthfuls of water toward the center of the lake or pond. The whaler's movements were always "quiet and slow," believing that his actions would induce the whale to act in the same way (Waterman 1920, 39). The whalers had secret sites and shrines where they performed their special rituals asking the supernatural for power and assistance in capturing a whale. The rituals and sites were closely guarded family secrets. Despite that, in 1905 a whaling shrine from the Nuu-chah-nulth village of the Mowachaht people was removed from their territory by anthropologist Franz Boas and placed in the American Museum of Natural History (Jonaitis 1999). Families also held rights to specific plants that were used in the cleansing rituals and to certain songs and prayers. Even the techniques utilized by the whalers were connected to the spirit world. It was understood that "certain spirits had instructed an ancestor on the proper rituals to be conducted in a specific secret location," and those methods would be closely followed by the next generation of whalers (ibid., 8).

Prayers were made at night asking the "four chiefs" (the Moon Chief, the Mountain Chief, the Sea Chief, and the South Chief) for luck, success, and guidance during the whale hunt (Jonaitis 1999, 8). The chiefs were also known by the names the Above Chief, Horizon Chief, Land Chief, and Undersea Chief. They also prayed to the whale, this taking place before and during the whale hunt and after the whale was caught and killed. Much emphasis was placed on the prayers and the seeking of the *tumanos,* as it was implicit that the whaler had to "have more than human strength" to capture a whale. During the hunt the whalers in the canoes chanted in the attempt to lure the whale to the shore and to their canoes. Once speared, the whale headed toward the open sea. But, if the whaler had obtained a good *tumanos* and had sung his songs correctly, the whale would calmly turn around and go toward the shore (Densmore 1972, 48).

It was believed that if a canoe capsized or was damaged by the whale, the whaler and his "crew had failed in their preparatory offices" (Sproat 1868, 227). Anthropologist Philip Drucker interviewed one of the last Nuu-chah-nulth whalers, Aliyu, from the Ahousaht village. Aliyu told Drucker that the loss of a whale during the hunt was seen as being directly caused by the "laxness" of the crewmembers in observing the ritual preparation. But a whaler's success "was regarded as proof that he acquired a powerful guardian spirit" to help him capture the whale, and, that from there on he would be "endowed with supernatural power" (Colson 1953, 5). Drucker noted how ritual behavior "was considered essential for all sea hunting . . . but because of the importance of whaling in native eyes its ceremonial requirements were more elaborate and more rigid than those for any other quest" (Drucker 1936, 47).

"Although all crew members were subject to many taboos and intense training, it was only the whaler and his wife who went through the complicated ritual of ceremonial bathing designed to influence the whale spirit and to induce the whales to allow themselves to be captured" (Province of British Columbia 1966, 35). The whaler's wife was intricately involved in the whale hunt and followed preparation and rituals similar to that of her husband. During the whaling season the whaler and his wife abstained from sexual intercourse and slept away from each other. If the wife was menstruating during the hunt, she could not touch any of the whaling equipment.

The wife also underwent months of preparation before the hunt and followed strict taboos during the hunt to ensure the success and safety of her husband. The wife "had to observe great care in her actions because of the underlying concept of imitative magic"—meaning that her behavior affected her husband and his ability to catch a whale, and also affected the whale he was hunting (Lantis 1938, 461). Curtis described one of the rituals performed by the whaler's wife during the preparation period: she held a rope tied to her husband's waist, which represented the harpoon line. As the man sang whaling songs he would walk slowly around the woman. In turn the woman sang during the ritual, repeating over and over again, "This is the way the whale will act" (Waterman 1920, 39; and Curtis 1970).

After the whaler left the shore to pursue the whale, the wife would return to her home, lie down in a dark room, and stay very still. "A significant symbolic connection existed between the whale and the 'noblewoman' in that during a hunt the harpooner's wife would *actually* become the whale" (Drucker in Jonaitis 1999, 8). If she moved it would make the whale unruly and difficult to catch. The wife was not allowed to comb her hair because it was thought that if the comb broke it would cause the husband's whaling harpoon line to snap. She was not allowed to eat or drink anything until 2:00 p.m. the following day (Gunther 1942, 67–68). Many of the whaling songs focused on the position and importance of the wife in the Nuu-chah-nulth and Makah whale cult, and some even suggest that "the wife really is the power" that brings in the whale because of its attraction to her (Lantis 1938, 461). Drucker suggested that the wife exerted a "special influence over the whale" and could "call it" to the shore (Drucker 1936). Elder Stanley Sam says that this aspect of the whaling custom displays the "power of our spirituality" by showing how the whaler's and his wife's power were intrinsically connected (Nuu-chah-nulth Elder's Whaling Workshop, Campbell River, B.C., December 4–5, 1998).

Prayers were also expressed during the hunt when the whale was harpooned. According to Curtis the whaler would speak to the whale, enticing it to give itself up to the whalers. This prayer was told to Curtis by a Yuquot (Nuu-chah-nulth) whaler:

> Whale, I have given you what you wish to get—my good harpoon. And now you have it. Please hold it with your strong hands. Do not let go. Whale, turn towards the fine beach . . . and you will be proud to see the young men come down . . . to see you; and the young men will say to one another: What a great whale he is! What a fat whale he is! What a strong whale he is! And you, whale, will be proud of all that you hear them say of your greatness. (Waterman 1920, 39)

When the whale was captured and killed it was brought ashore, with the whaler's wife being the first person to greet the whale. With her arms outstretched the wife "extended a special welcome to the animal's anthropomorphic spirit, which resides in its dorsal fin. In order to make that spirit feel at home, the dorsal fin was cut off first and treated to four days of ritual songs and prayers" (Jonaitis 1999, 9). Following this ceremony the whale was divided up among all the tribal members according to tribal rank and status, with the whaler retaining the prize parts of the carcass.

The Makah and Nuu-chah-nulth tribes stopped whaling in the 1920s as a result of the commercial whaling industry, which had depleted the whale stocks to near extinction. As a result international rules and regulations banned whaling, and the gray whale was placed on the Endangered Species List. In 1994, following its population increase, the gray whale was removed from the list, and the Makah (and a few years later the Nuu-chah-nulth) stated their intentions to resume their whaling practices. In 1999 the Makah captured and killed a 30-foot California gray whale. The whaling crew went through months of preparation, with spiritual observation still a main component of the contemporary whale hunt. The harpooner, Theron Parker, said that the crew was "spiritually in tune with everything and then we asked (the whale) to come home with us; and it did" (personal interview with Theron Parker, June 17, 2000).

It is evident from the documents and literature on Makah and Nuu-chah-nulth whaling that the guardian spirit complex was a central and important component of their whaling tradition. Ritual cleaning, purification, and specific taboos were all followed carefully so that the whaler could acquire a guardian spirit that would guide and protect him before and during the hunt. Even today, with the revival of Makah and Nuu-chah-nulth whaling practices, spirituality and guidance from the spirit world remain important elements of this tradition.

Charlotte Coté

See also First Food Ceremonies and Food Symbolism; First Salmon Rites; Fishing Rights and First Salmon Ceremony; Guardian Spirit Complex

References and Further Reading
Arima, Eugene Y. 1983. *The West Coast (Nootka) People: The Nootkan of*

Vancouver Island and Cape Flattery. British Columbian Provincial Museum, Special Publication no. 6. British Columbia: Province of British Columbia.

Arima, Eugene, and John Dewhirst. 1990. "The Nootkans of Vancouver Island." Pp. 391–421 in *Handbook of North American Indians: The Northwest Coast,* vol. 7. Washington, DC: Smithsonian Institution Press.

Colson, Elizabeth. 1953. *The Makah Indians: A Study of an Indian Tribe in Modern American Society.* Minneapolis: University of Minnesota Press.

Curtis, Edward S. 1970. "The Nootka." Pp. 3–112 and 177–186 in *The North American Indian,* vol. 2. Reprint, New York: Johnson Reprint Corporation.

Densmore, Frances. 1939/1972. *Nootka and Quileute Music.* Smithsonian Institution, Bureau of American Ethnology, Bulletin no. 124. Reprint, New York: Da Capo Press.

Drucker, Philip. 1936. *Diffusion in Northwest Coast Culture Growth in the Light of Some Distributions.* Ph.D. dissertation, Newcombe Collections, Victoria Provincial Archives.

———. 1955. *Indians of the Northwest Coast.* New York: Published for the American Museum of Natural History by McGraw Hill.

———. 1965. *Cultures of the North Pacific Coast.* San Francisco: Chandler Publishing.

———. "Nootka Whaling." 1951, 1966, 1989. In *Indian Tribes of the North Pacific Coast.* Edited by Tom McFeat. Ottawa, Canada: Carleton University Press.

Gunther, Erna. 1942. "Reminiscences of a Whaler's Wife." *Pacific Northwest Quarterly* 1, no. 1: 65–69.

Huu-ay-aht First Nations. 2000. "Kiix in Agenda Paper." In *Nuu-chah-nulth Voices: Histories, Objects, and Journeys.* Edited by Alan L. Hoover. Victoria, British Columbia, Canada: Royal British Columbia Museum.

Jewitt, John R. 1854/1996. *The Captive of Nootka or The Adventures of John R.*

Jewitt. Reprint, Washington, DC: Ye Galleon Press.

Jonaitis, Aldona. 1999. *The Yuquot Whaler's Shrine.* Seattle: University of Washington Press.

Kehoe, Alice. 1981. "The Northwest Coast." In *North American Indians: A Comprehensive Account.* Englewood Cliffs, NJ: Prentice-Hall.

Kirk, Ruth. 1991. *Tradition and Change on the Northwest Coast: The Makah, Nuu-chah-nulth, Kwakiutl, and Nuxalk.* Ottawa, Canada: Canadian Museum of Civilization.

Lantis, Margaret. 1938. "The Alaskan Whale Cult and Its Affinities." *American Anthropologist* 40: 438–464.

Mozino, Jose Mariano. 1970/1991. *Noticias de Nootka: An Account of Nootka Sound in 1792.* Translation and introduction by Iris Higbie Wilson. Reprint, Seattle: University of Washington Press.

Nuu-chah-nulth Elders Whaling Workshop. 1998. Campbell River, British Columbia. Audiotape held at the Nuu-chah-nulth Tribal Council, Port Alberni, B.C., December 4–5, 1998.

Parker, Theron. 2000. Personal interview. June 17, 2000.

Province of British Columbia. 1966. *Nootka: Our Native Peoples, Series 1, Volume 5.* British Columbia Heritage Series. Province of British Columbia, Department of Education.

Reaveley, Travis. 1998. "Nuuchahnulth Whaling and Its significance for Social and Economic Reproduction." *Chicago Anthropology Exchange Graduate Journal of Anthropology* 28 (spring).

Sapir, Edward. 1991. "Sayachapis, The Nootka Trader." In *American Indian Life.* Edited by Elsie Clews Parsons. Lincoln: University of Nebraska Press.

Sproat, Gilbert M. 1868. *Scenes and Studies of Savage Life.* London: Smith, Elder and Co.

Suttles, Wayne. 1990. *Handbook of North American Indians: The Northwest Coast,* vol. 7. Washington, DC: Smithsonian Institution Press.

Taylor, Herbert C. 1974. "Anthropological Investigation of the Makah Indians

Relative to Tribal Identity and Aboriginal Possession of Lands." In *American Indian Ethnohistory: Indians of the Northwest.* Edited by David A. Horr. New York: Garland.

Thompson, Art. 2001. Personal communication. November.

Waterman, T. T. 1920. *The Whaling Equipment of the Makah Indians.* Seattle: University of Washington Publications in Anthropology, vol. 1, no.1.

Winnemucca, Sarah (c. 1844–1891)

(Activist/orator/writer, Paiute)

Sarah Winnemucca (ca. 1844–1891) was a controversial Paiute activist, orator, and writer who worked to sustain tribal communities in the Great Basin amid increased pressure on American Indians to give up their traditional practices and beliefs. The results of her work were mixed. One of relatively few Paiute people during the mid-nineteenth century to be educated among whites, Winnemucca challenged corrupt Indian agents for their abuses of the reservation system and traveled widely (often dressed as an "Indian princess"), commanding large audiences with her lectures on Paiute culture and concerns. In 1883 she became one of the first Native American women to publish an autobiography, *Life among the Piutes.* Toward the end of her life, she started a school near Lovelock, Nevada. Unlike the government-run boarding schools that sought, in the infamous words of Carlisle

School founder Richard Henry Pratt, to "kill the Indian and save the man," the Lovelock school proceeded from bilingual instruction and an emphasis on Paiute community. But Winnemucca has also angered many Paiute people, in her own day and since, especially for her work as a scout for the U.S. Army. The tribal museum at the Pyramid Lake Reservation tells visitors that, alongside all of her successes and contributions, Winnemucca may also have unwittingly abetted the forced removal of many Paiute people north to the Yakima Reservation in 1878.

Winnemucca's book appears more overtly concerned with Christianity than with traditional indigenous religious life. That is not surprising, since *Life among the Piutes* was geared toward (and, many believe, heavily edited by) white women reformers who called for the assimilation of indigenous peoples into Euro-American ways of life. Moreover, Winnemucca's own experience was a complicated blend of Native and Christian traditions. She makes several references to the Paiutes' belief in a power like God or Jesus, suggesting that she did not see Christianity and Paiute beliefs as mutually exclusive—as did U.S. policy of that time—but as mutually sustaining and continuous. This does not mean that she accepted Euro-American theology or institutions uncritically; on the contrary, she openly excoriated the hypocrisy she saw in self-professed Christian Indian agents and settlers. While many critics have assumed that Winnemucca was a

Sarah Winnemucca Hopkins, as princess.
(Nevada Historical Society)

straightforward assimilationist, asking for help in "improving" her race, it is also possible to understand her life and writing as insisting on Paiute self-determination and humanity. Like many Native Christian intellectuals of her day, she may have seen participation in Christian practice as a way to continue tribal community and belief.

The anthropologist Catherine Fowler has described earlier forms of Paiute spirituality as deeply personal, seldom ritualized in large groups or even discussed among family members, so it is possible that Winnemucca simply had little reason to detail such beliefs and practices in her book. Still, she does offer some insights into her family's religious experience and their syncretic embrace (or rejection) of given Christian practices. She begins her autobiography with a story told by her grandfather, Captain Truckee. In it, the original parents of humankind separate their four quarreling children, banishing the two "white" ones "across the mighty ocean"; "by-and-by the dark children grew into a large nation; and we believe it is the one we belong to, and that the nation that sprang from the white children will some time send some one to meet us and heal all the old troubles" (Winnemucca 1994, 7). The book's readers, in 1883, might well have interpreted this narrative as a panacea for the guilt of colonialism and justification for their "reform" agenda. At the same time, though, Winnemucca seems to be indicating a cosmology that encourages peaceable and reciprocal relations between groups, as well as radically underscoring the fact of Paiute nationhood.

Collective Paiute ritual in precontact times, as the historic record paints it, combined dance and prayer, the spiritual and the material. Winnemucca describes an antelope hunt, for example, as beginning in much sacred preparation and drumming by a group of women, men, and young boys. Her father was an antelope charmer, who had powers and dreams that gave him access to both material and spiritual sustenance for the group. Old Winnemucca, as he was called, had other dreams: he reportedly predicted that dead Indians would one day be resurrected to eliminate the white people. Apocalyptic visions of this kind have helped drive many acts and movements of resistance among oppressed peoples. While Winnemucca's book does not make much of such visions, nor of shamanism or other Paiute curative and prophetic practices, such practices may well have informed her life and actions.

At the end of the nineteenth century, Jack Forbes has argued, the Paiutes and other indigenous people in Nevada shifted away from more military forms of resistance to those based more explicitly on religiosity. Wodziwob and Jack Wilson helped promulgate the Ghost Dance, giving many Native people an immediate and profound means of community regeneration. Peyotism has also sustained others in the region with its own healing and moral functions. And, true to Winnemucca's vision, many Paiutes and neighboring peoples have found in Christianity ways to continue their tribal beliefs and practices. Sarah Winnemucca is among the best-remembered nineteenth-century Paiute leaders largely because of her significant accomplishments, but also because she was one of the few to write and publish. A more fully balanced understanding of her role in Paiute religious and political life still needs to be supplemented by Paiute oral histories.

Siobhan Senier

See also Christianity, Indianization of; Female Spirituality

References and Further Reading
Canfield, Gae Whitney. 1983. *Sarah Winnemucca of the Northern Paiutes.* Norman: University of Oklahoma Press.
Forbes, Jack. 1967. *Nevada Indians Speak.* Reno: University of Nevada Press.
Fowler, Catherine, and Sven Liljeblad. 1986. "Northern Paiute." Pp. 435–465 in *Handbook of North American Indians,* vol. 11, *Great Basin.* Edited by Warren d'Azevedo; general editor, William Sturtevant. Washington, DC: Smithsonian Institution Press.
Scott, Lalla. 1966. *Karnee: A Paiute Narrative.* Reno: University of Nevada Press.
Winnemucca, Sarah. 1994. *Life among the Piutes.* Reprint. Reno: University of Nevada Press.

Women's Cultural and Religious Roles, Great Lakes

Aboriginal Nations of the Great Lakes Area belong to a variety of Algonquin language–speaking groups: Ojibway, Potawatomi, Odawa, and Algonquin. Prior to contact, the Woodland Cree also utilized the northern Great Lakes. The southern shores of the Great Lakes were occupied by Iroquoian-speaking groups. The northern nations were nomadic, traveling in an area that provided seasonal hunting and gathering. Plants were available for food and medicine, and they hunted deer, moose, and birds. Women gathered plants, which were dried for teas and poultices. They also hunted for small game that was necessary when the men went on hunting trips and were absent for a period of time. In northern groups, women were treated as equals in the pre-reserve period. In the southern nations living on the Great Lakes, Iroquoian women (who included Mohawks and Cayugas) of the original five nations possessed a high political status within their longhouses. They may not have been in the forefront of the community meetings, but they would advise their clan leaders from behind the scenes; their advice, especially that of the elder women, carried great weight. Women could also be dream interpreters and visionaries for their clans.

The religious structures of the hunting and horticultural groups were different because of the emphases on subsistence patterns. In the hunting-oriented northern groups, property was not owned. Families lived in small family groups in wigwams (birch bark, dome-shaped dwellings) and traveled often. Southern groups were matrilineal in their ownership of longhouses and in social/political structure. Maize, tobacco, beans, and squash were staples of the horticultural southern groups. Deer and birds were also hunted, but maize was considered a staple. Both northern and southern groups operated on a clan system signified by animal identifications that included the bear, eagle, wolf, deer, martens/otters, and sometimes a type of fish or another bird. Northern groups referred to the spirits of plants, rocks, animals, water, earth, and birds as spiritual entities or as manitous, or "other-than-human-persons." The manitou or spirit could be called upon for everyday tasks as well as for pivotal life events and dangerous activities such as war. For instance, one could ask for assistance with tasks that needed to be completed, such as securing a particular plant for medicine or catching fish or game for the family's meal.

The four sacred medicines of the Great Lakes are tobacco, cedar, sage, and sweet grass. These plants were grown or harvested by women in many areas of the region. Tobacco was a smaller and stouter plant than the commercial tobacco that is grown today. It did not grow well in the shorter summer season of the northern areas but was more plentiful within the Iroquoian groups, where it was cultivated and harvested. Cedar was available around the Great Lakes. It could be utilized to line the floor of a sweat or fasting lodge or boiled for its medicinal properties. Sage was a stocky plant and could be easily dried. Sweet grass grew on the shorelines of lakes and could be picked when still green and braided. The grass represented the hair of Mother Earth, which could be braided, dried, and burned. It has a sweet, pleasant aroma and typically was used for burning or hanging in the dwelling, rather than for tea or medicinal purposes.

All of these medicines would be dried and burned separately or all together to create an aromatic smoke or "smudge," which would be used to offer prayers to the Grandmothers and Grandfathers (human ancestors or manitous).

Smudging would involve burning one or more of the sacred medicines and "washing" or wafting the smoke over the head and then the upper and lower body to purify the body and mind and to ask for blessings or guidance. Depending on women's menstrual cycles, sometimes only sweet grass or female sage could be used if a woman was on her "moon time."

Berries were also an essential plant product for women and would be eaten or abstained from, depending on the type of berry and the growing season. For example, a feast might be held in early spring to recognize the importance of the strawberry. All nations of the Great Lakes recognized the importance of the strawberry as a source of food, and it was seen as having healing properties.

There are some precontact, plant-related activities that are still carried on today. For example, if a family member is ill or has died in a house, cedar branches are immersed in a pot of boiling water, and the branches are taken out of the water and brushed over the bed and curtains as a disinfectant. The oil in the cedar needles is dispersed from the branches onto surfaces. Although this is a practical hygienic activity, the practice is also considered a purifying ritual that usually only women perform. In addition, the use of flower motifs seems to be a common thread between all Great Lakes Aboriginal Nations. Flowers and plants seem to be accepted as having a decorative as well as a religious value, possessing "powers" to heal.

There were ceremonies that benefited both women and men. Both young women and men participated in puberty fasts. Each faster made a specific request for a vision for purpose in life, a spiritual name, and a guide, as well as for assistance with purpose and place within the community. Women and men took part in sweatlodges, which were built in a style similar to that of a home dwelling. A pit was dug in the middle of the structure, and red-hot stones were deposited into the pit. Water would be poured over the rocks, and the steam would rise, filling the structure. Participants would ask the spirits for assistance with health matters, a quest, or direction in life.

Women could also become leaders and spiritual visionaries. They regularly served not only as elders and teachers but also as medicine people. In this last role they often emphasized their skills as herbal healers in conjunction with the spiritual power attained through relationship with manitous or spirit helpers. In addition, given the desire, competence, and a legitimating vision, a woman could also go to war and receive the title of "brave."

Women's spiritual practices differed from those of men because of their ability to bear children and their menstrual cycles, and therefore the moon played an important role in the religious practices of women. Grandmother Moon is the overseer of the menstrual cycle, and women are empowered spiritually with the onset of menses. The connection between Mother Earth and Grandmother

Moon is especially powerful for women on account of their life-giving qualities. In northern groups, women were secluded at the onset of menses. They would be separated from the rest of the community and stay in a wigwam. The power of women's menstrual cycles is still misunderstood to the present day. Women are at their highest point of power at the time of their menstrual cycle, and they have the spiritual power to interfere with or draw power from men's ritual objects. Even today women are asked not to join a pipe ceremony in case the pipe bowl breaks or the spiritual balance and connection between the conductor and the ancestors is disconnected. This is not a case of "contamination" but rather a respect for women at their time of highest spiritual power. It is interesting to note that in most communities, approximately one-quarter of the women are on their "moon-time" during the same period each month. It is practical to consider that someone needed to look after the children if a ceremony were taking place. Also, because the women were secluded, they did not have to take care of their households while they were separated. It could be viewed as a time to recharge spiritually. Today women continue to refrain from certain activities during their menstrual periods. It is common, for example, for women to withdraw from powwow dances when on their moons.

The impact of the fur-trade and Christianity was pervasive in the Great Lakes. For the northern groups, the participation in the fur trade was extensive. Being nomadic, families would often travel with French fur traders. Later, Aboriginal women married fur traders and had children—hence the term "Metis," or mixed-blood children. During the reservation period men lost their roles as providers for their families, and many turned to alcohol. The hunting land-base was diminished, and men did not hunt and trap as extensively once they were living on reserves. Catholicism spread among the northern groups, while the Protestant faiths settled into the Iroquoian groups as a result of the influence of the English in the south. As more Aboriginal women became Catholic they gave up prior forms of birth control and started having large families, becoming more sedentary and attending church services. Traditional practices were repressed by Christianity and some were forgotten, but a few older people preserved the women's ceremonies, which have been recently revived.

Women have performed primarily the same societal and religious roles as they always have, from the prereservation period to the present. Typically women have borne children, and cared and provided for them. Overall, women from the Great Lakes area revered plants, in particular the ones that provided spiritual and medicinal qualities. Women were visionaries, herbalists, and sometimes warriors for their people. The primary difference in approaches to the spirits was determined by membership in either a hunter-gatherer or agricultural group. Women were respected for their abilities in the prereservation period, lost some of their spiritual rituals during the last several decades, but are regaining their status as healers and visionaries in present-day society.

Marilyn E. Johnson

See also Female Spirituality; Feminism and Tribalism; First Food Ceremonies and Food Symbolism; Herbalism; Menstruation and Menarche

References and Further Reading
Buffalohead, Priscilla K. 1983. "Farmers, Warriors, Traders: A Fresh Look at Ojibway Women." *Minnesota History* 48, no. 6: 236–244.
Densmore, Frances. 1928/1987. *Indian Use of Wild Plants for Crafts, Food, Medicine and Charms*. Smithsonian Institution Bureau of American Ethnology, 44th Annual Report. Reprint, Oshweken, Ontario: Iroqrafts.
Hallowell, Irving A. 1960. "Ojibwa Ontology, Behavior, and World View." Pp. 19–52 in *Culture in History: Essays in Honour of Paul Radin*. Edited by Stanley Diamond. New York: Columbia University Press.
Landes, Ruth. 1938. *The Ojibwa Woman*. New York: Columbia University Press.

Women's Cultural and Religious Roles, Northern Athabascan

Northern Athabascan customs regarding gender emerge from religious theories specific to important women's life cycle events, including the beginning and end of menses, maternity, widowhood, and in the contemporary world, social hardships related to colonialism. Because the sub-Arctic environment rarely makes life easy for northern Athabascans, their natural world plays a dominant role in forming their spiritual thought and narrating gender roles.

The northern Athabascan region takes up a large portion of the land in the Alaskan and Canadian sub-Arctic. Except for the Dena'ina, northern Athabascan nations are landlocked, dependent on rivers and mountains for subsistence resources. Life, ever harsh in the precolonial era, has been rendered somewhat more comfortable by the use of contemporary technology, particularly in transportation; however, even in the twenty-first century people die of hypothermia and frostbite. Typical of Native North Americans, northern Athabascan cultures teach that all things in nature are alive and aware of each other, including the forces of wind and ice.

Traditional life in every northern Athabascan nation requires close working relations between men and women, boys and girls. Their subsistence resources used to require constant seasonal moving, from spring muskrat lakes to summer fish camps, then on to fall moose or caribou hunts, and finally to winter dwellings for midwinter celebrations. For precolonial northern Athabascans, this kind of life worked best when a brother and sister along with their respective spouses teamed together for those journeys, a custom emerging from a fluid matrix of matrilineal kinship relations. Housing forms varied with the type of activity, but all shared one common element—a single cramped room for each nuclear family of five, and often far more, people. Rules regarding behavior between brothers and sisters were strictly enforced. Chief among them was absolutely no eye contact and minimal conversation between members of the opposite sex. These customs persevere among northern Athabascans of today, albeit in a more lenient form.

Life changes in women had a considerable impact on these small communities. For instance, blood flow during menses attracts predators, so women had to take precautions that kept the flow under control, disguised the odor, and protected their clothing from permanent damage. One of the consequences of these concerns was consignment of women to isolation huts in some cases, separate chambers in others. The entire family had to be conscious of the danger women in menses represent and respond accordingly.

Northern Athabascan religious traditions provided the logic by which people behaved toward women in menses. Theories about spiritual power follow gender lines. Women, because of their ability to become pregnant and give birth, as well as their power to attract destructive predators, are considered to have stronger spiritual power than men. By contrast, men's spiritual or medicine power, usually thought of as hunting luck and defined by the gift of prophetic dreaming to know where game will be at any given time, must be developed and sometimes never emerges. Women occasionally have the same kind of power or

luck as men. A northern Athabascan tradition holds that women can destroy a man's luck by touching him or his hunting gear. Thus northern Athabascan women learned to avoid their brothers, fathers, uncles, and later their husbands during menses.

The end of menses, or menopause, heralds a time when women can safely develop and be known for their medicine powers. The traditional method involves the Athabascan religious traditions of dream interpretation. According to many sources, menopausal women often reveal dreams that indicate the strength of their hunting luck or other prophecies. If women knew they had such power earlier in their lives, they made use of it by learning the healing arts of northern Athabascans, especially midwifery. Other medicinal skills that both men and women learned were eye surgery, dental surgery, blood letting, bone setting, and herbal remedies. Those men and women whose medicinal skills are facilitated by medicine power are constantly sought for their expertise. Not surprisingly, precolonial women learned to identify, harvest, and prepare medications that helped alleviate menstrual cramps, morning sickness, nervous tension, and discomfort in childbirth. Some also learned which preparations could abort a fetus. All of these skills were highly prized in precolonial Alaska, and contemporary Athabascans recite stories about the healers in their families.

One of the most conflictual areas in northern Athabascan gender relations arises from the rules about men's and women's work. The cultural ideals suggest that men were expected to hunt big game, while women were expected to raise the children, prepare food for immediate and long-term use, and prepare hides for clothing. The realities of the sub-Arctic climate, long-distance hunting trips either with or without the entire family, and uneven volumes of work have always made these ideals inefficient. Women must always be prepared to become widows. Likewise, children must also be prepared to be orphaned, and men must always be prepared to cook, sew, and raise their children alone. Nothing short of this works in extreme environments.

Conflicts arise between the ideal northern Athabascan paradigms and actual life circumstances, and they are perpetrated by the very religious traditions that provide comfort and information in other contexts. The overriding cultural norm of autonomy usually resolves the tension. Gwich'in author Velma Wallis, in her 1993 novel *Two Old Women*, provides a complex articulation of the conflictual roles older women play in a subsistence economy. The story features two elderly women who are cast out of their community because they no longer perform work. The spiritual underpinning to the abandonment of the elderly is an Athabascan theory that all people should be both self-sufficient as well as aware of how to receive guidance from spiritual sources. Otherwise they pose a hazard to the rest of the community. In *Two Old Women* the elders survived.

In the colonial era, northern Athabascan peoples face new forms of hardship such as alcoholism, drug abuse, domestic conflicts, and sexual abuse. Other problems particular to Canada's and Alaska's colonial histories have caused cultural and domestic upheaval in Athabascan communities. Primary among these is enforced mainstream education, which sometimes takes children away from their homes and communities for months and even years at a time. The consequences of these changes to women include the foundering of traditional cultural models of gendered behavior for motherhood, which are in direct conflict with very different behaviors seen in movies, heard in popular songs, and witnessed in cities. Circumstances are more harsh for mothers or women who are heads of their households. Athabascan women throughout the region desperately seek solutions. Northern Athabascan oral traditions provide models for women in times of upheaval. In many stories women are featured as very intelligent people, often medicine women, who are full participants in solving their own problems. One example occurs in an ancient Gwich'in Athabascan narrative, "She Who Is Ravished," as reported by Émile Petitot (1886) and the late Gwich'in elder Julia Peter.

Two key figures dominate the narrative. They are L'atpa-tsandia (also known as "celle que l'on ravit de part et d'autre," "she who is ravished," and the "Prize Woman") and her husband, Ko'ehdan ("l'homme sans feu," or the "man without fire"). Both of these mythic figures are common in Canadian Athabascan oral traditions. They fit into an ongoing discourse about starvation, interethnic warfare, and revenge. L'atpa-tsandia symbolizes Athabascan women of precolonial times who were captured, deemed by their Athabascan husbands to have been raped by the enemy, and taken to parts unknown. L'atpa-tsandia also symbolizes a far older theme that situated the Gwich'in in a continuum of interethnic warfare and trade with their northern neighbors, the Inuit (Inupiat in Alaska). Petitot also described her as "cette femme, quoique vieille, était parfaitement belle, c'est pourquoi on la pillait san cesse" ("this woman, no matter how old, was perfectly beautiful, that is why they pillaged her without end") (Petitot 1886, 51; translation by author). L'atpa-tsandia, thus, symbolizes something of immense value to both Gwich'in and Inuit—women of beauty as a source of strength and intelligence. In a twentieth-century version collected by Slobodin (1975) she is called "Prize Woman." As Slobodin (ibid., 293–299) reported, there are many Gwich'in accounts of women who were routinely taken captive by one or the other of the Gwich'in or Inuit and then restored to their alternate homes in the other community. Slobodin wasn't sure if the accounts were about actual people or merely the perpetuation of a cultural ideal about the importance of

women in the northern indigenous trading partner complex. In any event, the way that L'atpa-tsandia is stereotyped fits into both Gwich'in ideals of paradigmatic, autonomous women as well as the Inuit custom of wife exchange.

Does "She Who Is Ravished" provide a model for northern Athabascan women in the contemporary world? Yes and no. The answer is yes for the Gwich'in women who tell the story often and praise each other for being able to act alone, make successful decisions without consulting others, and use their ingenuity to find ways out of bad situations. The answer is no in that not many northern Athabascan women know about the story, and even fewer relate the symbols inherent in the tale to contemporary situations. In terms of spirituality, traditional narratives like "She Who Is Ravished" are viewed as proof of survival skills, as well as evidence of how medicine men and women use their abilities to communicate, find others, and survive. However, stories like "She Who Is Ravished" provide little solace when viewing the body of a child who has died of a drug overdose or an alcohol-related accident, something that many contemporary Athabascan women find themselves doing all too often.

Where are the spiritual paradigms or solutions for contemporary malaise? Most Northern Athabascan women often find answers in prayer; others find them in music or other art forms. Many have remarked that Athabascan people seem to be intensely spiritual. Women as well as men have adopted Christian faiths and traditions, often exploring various Christian denominations in an effort to find their own mode of spiritual thought. There are several northern Athabascan women who have become ministers, deacons, lay readers, as well as taking other positions of authority in Christian churches. Quite a few such women have also been known as traditional medicine women or healers. One Dena'ina Athabascan woman said about herself that she resolved the conflict by following her Russian Orthodox priest's advice. She had to accommodate both roles in her own way. In other words, in the contemporary religious environment of the sub-Arctic, neither the church nor the people in the community considered that either religious tradition excluded the other.

Northern Athabascan women in the contemporary world follow a spiritual path that is complex and without hardened rules. As caregivers, givers of life, and witnesses of cultural upheaval, most seek haven in a combination of traditional Athabascan religious values and those from other cultures.

Phyllis Ann Fast

See also Female Spirituality; Feminism and Tribalism; Menstruation and Menarche; Missionization, Alaska; Scratching Sticks

References and Further Reading
Carlo, Poldine. 1978. *Nulato, an Indian Life on the Yukon.* Published by author. Fairbanks, Alaska.
James, Sarah. 1995. "We Are the Caribou People." Pp. 221–229 in *Messengers of the Wind: Native American Women Tell Their Life Stories.* Edited by Jane Katz. New York: Ballantine Books.
Petitot, Émile. 1886. *Traditions Indiennes du Canada Nord-ouest.* Les Litteratures polulaires de toutes les nations 23. Paris: Maisonneuve freres et C. LeClerc.
Slobodin, Richard. 1975. "Without Fire: A Kutchin Tale of Warfare, Survival, and Vengeance." Pp. 259–301 in *Proceedings: Northern Athapaskan Conference 1971,* vol.1. Canadian Ethnology Service Paper, no. 27. Edited by A. McFadyen Clark. Ottawa: National Museum of Canada.
Wallis, Velma. 1996. *Bird Girl and the Man Who Followed the Sun.* Fairbanks, AK: Epicenter Press.
———. 1993. *Two Old Women.* Fairbanks, AK: Epicenter Press.

Women's Spirituality

See Female Spirituality

Women's Spirituality, Great Basin

See First Menses Site

Yoeme (Yaqui) Deer Dance

The Yoeme Deer Dance is the central religious ceremonial dance performed by Yoeme boys or men. The Yoeme people reside in both northwestern Mexico and southern Arizona. The dance is accompanied by the music and songs of deer singers of this indigenous people, usually during all-night ceremonies called the *pahko*. According to oral histories, during ancient times prior to Spanish contact, the person known to the Yoeme as *Yevuku Yoleme,* or Wilderness Person, secretly learned this tradition from a father deer as he taught his own children. Since then, the Yoeme have used the ceremony as a spiritual way for deer hunters to ask for forgiveness from this special animal, whom the Yoeme often refer to as *saila,* or little brother, prior to hunting (Evers and Molina 1987). Despite the end of their reliance on deer hunting as a means of subsistence, deer dancing and singing continues throughout the year in contemporary Yoeme communities as a critical element of Yoeme ceremonial tradition, with a respite from public dancing and singing during the Catholic Lenten season.

While the deer songs and dances are often performed for their beauty in homes and other social settings, deer dancing and singing is performed for the most part during the *pahko*. Many Yoeme religious societies—such as the *pahkola* dancers and musicians, who are also usually men; the Cantora Society, the majority of whom are women who sing Catholic prayers in Spanish, Latin, and Yoeme; and the Matichini Society, a men's religious society whose members also dance to the musical accompaniment of the violin and guitar—as well as spectators and sponsors of the *pahko* join to create the communal ceremony in which deer dancing and singing take place. The *pahkola* dancers dance in tandem with the deer dancer. Acting as hosts, clowns, and historians, the *pahkola* dancers often mimic and poke fun at the deer, as well as entertaining the *pahko* audience (ibid.).

The deer dance is the physical representation of the animal that the Yoeme

Native American dancers perform a Deer Dance at a pueblo in Santa Fe, New Mexico, ca. 1980s–1990s. (Chris Rainier/Corbis)

fondly refer to as *Saila Maso*, little brother deer, "a term [that] emphasizes the kin relation Yoeme believe exists between themselves and the deer" (ibid., 47). The little brother deer, the Yoeme believe, comes to the people from a place of great spiritual power called the Seyewailo, or Flower World. The Seyewailo is always located in the east, beneath the dawn (Evers 1978). The little brother deer also emerges from a place of spiritual power located in the Sonoran Desert called the Yo Ania, or Enchanted World, "an ancient world, a mythic place outside historic time and space . . . yet present in the most immediate way" (Evers

and Molina 1987, 62). With the dancing of the deer and the singing of the deer songs, the *ramada* ceremonial structure—with a reed cane roof and mesquite tree trunks for posts—is transformed into the Huya Ania, or Wilderness World, the place that surrounds the Yoeme villages in the Sonoran desert and that "encompasses a rich poetic and spiritual and human dimension" (ibid., 44). All of these worlds collectively form the spiritual worlds of the Sonoran desert, where Yoeme, like many Plains indigenous nations, travel to gain spiritual power by praying, fasting, or seeking spiritual guidance through meditation.

The deer dancer himself dances to honor all living things, especially those that provide the Yoeme with sustenance. The deer head he wears on his head and the hooves attached to the belt worn around his waist, or *rijutiam,* represent the thousands of deer who have died so that the Yoeme could live. The two gourd rattles filled with tiny pebbles represent the plant world that provides nourishment as well as medicines to the people. The moth cocoons attached to the dancers' ankles represent the insect world (Evers and Molina 1987). As Yoeme deer singer and teacher Felipe Molina narrates in the film *Seyewailo:* "Even though the moth is dead, he knows that his house is still occupied." A brightly colored fuchsia or red scarf decorated with embroidered flowers is gracefully wrapped around the antlers of the deer head to represent the Flower World as well as to bless the deer dancer. In the Yoeme tradition, flowers represent sacredness, spiritual power, and protection.

Together, the deer dancer and deer singers bring spiritual blessings from the Yo Ania, Huya Ania, and the Sea Ania of the desert world to the village ceremonies. But while the deer dancer embodies the deer spirit, the deer singers vocalize the deer's relationship with the natural world. Composed of usually three to four men and boys, the deer singer group verbalizes "the most ancient form" of the Yoeme language (ibid., 7). The deer songs tell of the different stages of the deer's life. The first series of songs to begin the *pahko,* that usually starts in the early to late afternoon, tell about the fawn who is just born and "does not have enchanted legs" (ibid., 101). After the "world turns" at midnight, the deer singers sing about the adult deer who has grown mature with "a crown of antlers" but is also playful and sways his antlers back and forth to the words of the songs (ibid., 160). During the early morning, the deer singers sing for the elder deer, the "flower person," who travels back to the "enchanted flower wilderness" of the Seyewailo (ibid., 123). In songs that reflect both the personal perspective of the deer's life as well as his surrounding environment, the deer singers sing both to the deer and for the deer. According to Yoeme elder and deer singer Miki Maso of the Rio Yaqui Valley, Sonora, Mexico, this is the way that the "Enchanted World speaks to itself" (Evers and Molina 1987). Thus, the deer dance and singing tradition is one way that the Yoeme actively relate and communicate with the natural and spiritual world.

The survival of this tradition in Yoeme communities of both Sonora, Mexico, and Southern Arizona, where about 25,000 and 10,000 Yoeme, respectively, reside, is astounding given the history of physical genocide and cultural ethnocide that the Yoeme people endured from the late 1890s to the beginning of the Mexican Revolution in 1911 (Spicer 1980). At the height of the Mexican government's campaign to clear the Yoeme traditional lands from indigenous resistance, about 6,000 Yoeme (or about one-fourth of the population) were forcibly removed from their homes by relocation and forced labor, government-sponsored murder, and political persecution. In order to attain freedom hundreds of Yoeme fled north to Arizona Territory and into the surrounding Mexican populations (ibid.). The Yoeme came closest to realizing their dream of maintaining their homelands free of Mexican control in 1939, when Mexican president Lazaro Cardenas established the first "Indigenous Community" and set up protected boundaries by presidential decree for the Yoeme (ibid.).

Juan A. Avila Hernandez

See also Kachina and Clown Societies; Oral Traditions, Pueblo; Termination and Relocation

References and Further Reading
Evers, Larry, producer. 1978. *Seyewailo/The Flower World.* Tucson: University of Arizona.
Evers, Larry, and Felipe Molina. 1987. *Yaqui Deer Songs/Maso Bwikam: A Native American Poetry.* Tucson: Sun Tracks and University of Arizona Press.
Maaso, Miki. 1992. "The Elders' Truth: A Yaqui Sermon." Transcribed, translated, and annotated by Felipe S. Molina and Larry Evers. *Journal of the Southwest* 35, no. 3 (autumn): 225–317.
Spicer, Edward H. 1980. *The Yaquis: A Cultural History.* Tucson: University of Arizona Press.

Yuwipi Ceremony

Contemporary variants of the *yuwipi* ceremony are performed by the Lakota Sioux yuwipi *wica'sa,* or "yuwipi man," and there are still several yuwipi men residing at the Pine Ridge (Oglala division) and Rosebud (Sicangu, or Brule division) reservations in southwestern South Dakota. Recognized as *wica'sa wakan,* "sacred person[s]," yuwipi men are conjurers who consult their spirit helpers during nighttime yuwipi ceremonies held in darkened rooms to treat "Indian sickness," give family advice, and find lost persons and objects. Perhaps the oldest Lakota ritual apart from the sweatlodge and vision quest, the yuwipi (meaning "wrapped up," or "they wrap him up") refers to binding the yuwipi man at the beginning of the ceremony. Undoubtedly the most popular Lakota ceremony during the reservation period, yuwipi also flourished in the post–World War II era, although there are fewer yuwipi men today as compared to one hundred years ago. Similar divination rites were performed in nineteenth-century Plains communities by Crow men and women with ghost power, Kiowa owl doctors, and in Yankton conjuring ceremonies.

Exactly where yuwipi originated is the source of some debate. While some scholars claim that it is derived from the Shaking Tent ceremony performed by Woodland Algonkin-speaking peoples, and others suggest westward origins from the Algonquin Blackfoot and Arapaho, the genesis of the Oglala yuwipi at Pine Ridge traces historically to the old man Horn Chips, or Chips (1836–1916), who became Crazy Horse's brother through a pipe smoking ritual. Chips gave Crazy Horse his protective medicine, a small *tunkan* ("stone") related to yuwipi powers that he carried under his left arm during combat. Chips had two sons connected to yuwipi: James Moves Camp (1869–1949) and Charles Chips (1873–1946). Without his father's help, the former received supernatural power through a vision quest, then assisted his younger brother, Charles, in obtaining his own vision. Their father, however, imparted personal power to his grandson, James's son Sam Moves Camp (1897–1973), who then passed it to his own grandsons, Sam Moves Camp, Jr. (b. 1948) and Richard Moves Camp (b. 1956). Charles Chips transferred power directly to his son Ellis Chips (b. 1909), who then passed it to his son Godfrey Chips (b. 1954). Throughout the years, the Chips/Moves Camp family has presided over yuwipi ceremonies in Wanblee and other eastern districts of Pine Ridge Reservation. Well-known yuwipi priests in recent times include the now-deceased George Plenty Wolf of the Pine Ridge community, who taught anthropologist William K. Powers about the ceremony (Powers 1984, xi), and Frank Andrew Fools Crow of Kyle, a very powerful yuwipi man who conducted yuwipi ceremonies for physician Thomas H. Lewis (1987, 179ff.). Fools Crow, Plenty Wolf, John Iron Rope, and other yuwipi men also worked closely with Jesuit scholar Paul B. Steinmetz.

Elderly Oglalas at the turn of the last century referred to the yuwipi men as Rock dreamers, in conjunction with the Oglala belief in *Inyan*, "Rock," as one of the four superior *Wakan Tanka* "big holy"—the totality of everything incomprehensible in the universe—with a material body; Sun, Sky, and Earth are the other three. Yuwipi also refers to small, spherical, translucent stones found near anthills that are imbued with sacred power because they come from the underworld, where everything is pure. These sacred stones each contain a *šicun* "spirit" that assists the yuwipi men, and are addressed in sacred language as *tunkasila* "grandfather," derived from *tunkan* "stone." During yuwipi "spirit meetings," or "seances" held in the darkness, the collective *tunkan wašicun*, "spirit of the stone," of the *yuwipi inyan*, "yuwipi stone," untie the bound yuwipi man and assist him in healing, foretelling the future, and finding lost objects. Nonbelievers attending ceremonies are struck by the stones. Prior to yuwipi ceremonies, 405 *canli wapahte*, "tobacco bundle," offerings are made by placing a pinch of tobacco in small one-inch-square cotton cloths and tied; the offerings represent the 405 different types of *šicun* in the universe, and those in attendance take the tobacco offerings to smoke with the other *šicun* of the universe.

Yuwipi stones are connected to the *tunkan* (hot rocks) used in the sweatlodge, as exemplified when Horn Chips—the Stone dreamer—performed divination rites during sweatlodge ceremonies by sending out his yuwipi stones to find lost objects or persons. Sweatlodges, often conducted as independent rites without accompanying rituals, normally precede the *wapiya lowanpi*, or "curing sing," and the *wopila lowanpi*, or "thanksgiving sing," whereas they are not required for emergency sings such as the seldom-performed *okile lowanpi*, "hunting sing," to find stolen property—without identifying the thief—and the *Inktomi lowanpi*, "Spider sing," to acquire a *tunkan* invested by a *šicun*. Inktomi the Spider is related to yuwipi because Spider is the offspring of Inyan the Rock and *Wakinyan Oyate*, "Thunder-Beings," manifested in nature as Thunder and Lightning; hence the connection between yuwipi stones and Inktomi. Individuals seeking *tunkan* to carry for personal protection from harm and sickness often find smooth, circular stones near creek beds, then place them in specially made buckskin pouches, or they request the yuwipi man to find one for them. During the Spider sing, the stone is invested by a protective spirit, then named.

Yuwipi is also connected to the vision quest because the Rock dreamer experiences esoteric visions that are coherent only to another Rock dreamer, also referred to as the *iyeska*, "interpreter" or "medium," who understands spirits and communicates with them. Once a dream recipient realizes that his role in life is to become a yuwipi man, he begins an apprenticeship under a senior yuwipi *wica'sa*, although the information received in the vision—songs, prayers, and ritual items—specifically belongs to him. If the Rock dreamer's father was a yuwipi *wica'sa*, then his destiny is to "walk with the pipe," acquire his father's ritual paraphernalia, and undertake an apprenticeship; otherwise, a yuwipi man's regalia are burned or placed in his grave following death. Since yuwipi power derives from visions, a yuwipi *wica'sa* must constantly renew his power through the vision quest at least once a year. But more critically, to ensure his own well-being a yuwipi man must not offend the powerful *šicun*. Mishandling the sacred pipe made of "red stone" or catlinite, and proximity to menstruating women are particularly offensive to the spirits. Over the years, yuwipi men get weaker from the cumulative effects of giving their spirits away by naming stones, eventually losing their clientele to younger yuwipi men.

When the need arises, such as illness in the family, financial difficulties, or other family and personal troubles, contemporary Lakota find solace by smoking and praying with *cannunpa wakan*, the sacred pipe, to the Four Winds, the Sky, the Earth, and the Spotted Eagle that carries prayers to Wakantanka, the Great Spirit, Creator, and Provider. An individual desiring to sponsor a yuwipi ceremony solicits the yuwipi man with the sacred pipe—or cigarette—addressing him respectfully as *tunkasila*, "grandfather." If the yuwipi *wica'sa* decides to accept the case and conduct a yuwipi ritual, he takes the pipe and they smoke together with the stipulation that the sponsor must follow up with a *wopila lowanpi*, or thanksgiving feast, within a year. The following is a generalized description of a yuwipi meeting for curing.

On the afternoon of the yuwipi ceremony, the sponsor arrives at the home of the yuwipi *wica'sa* with the requested items for the ceremony: cotton cloth, groceries, and meat from a slaughtered dog for the ensuing feast. While a fire is prepared to heat the hot rocks for the sweatlodge rite, the cotton cloth is cut into 405 one-inch-square tobacco bundles tied off with string, then attached to a longer string used to mark off the *hocoka,* "camp circle," or sacred space inside the yuwipi man's house. By sundown, when the sweatlodge rocks are white hot, the sponsor, yuwipi man, and several others depart into the sweatlodge while the women prepare the ritual meal and other men prepare the house—either a one-room house or one room in a large house—for the yuwipi ceremony by removing furniture, metal, glass, and objects representing Anglo culture and sealing off windows and entrances so that the inside is pitch black when the ceremony begins. Star quilts and pillows are set around the periphery of the room for singers and spectators, sage is placed on oversize furniture to appease the yuwipi spirits, and the space in the middle is left for the yuwipi altar.

Once the interior of the house is prepared, the participants enter the room through the east door, then assume their respective positions around the perimeter of the room: men on the south side, women on the north side, and singers on the west side. All attendees are given a sprig of sage to wear behind the right ear so the "spirits may know them" during the ceremony. Then the paraphernalia for the altar is brought in by an assistant, including four to seven three-pound coffee cans filled halfway to the top with earth, then topped off with colored cloth *wanunyanpi,* "offerings," affixed to willow canes, and the long string containing the 405 tobacco bundles. The cans are set up in the northwest, southwest, northeast, and southeast quadrants—in the four-can variant—then the *hocoka,* or ritual space, inside is delineated by winding the stringed tobacco bundles around the willow canes. While the ritual space is prepared, the yuwipi man enters and constructs an earthen altar in the center—often out of gopher or mole dirt—decorated with symbols of Sun, Moon, Thunder-Beings, and other sacred beings. Next to the earthen altar is a bed of sage, yuwipi rattles filled with 405 stones, tobacco, the sacred pipe and pipe bag, yuwipi stones, an eagle bone whistle, and other regalia connected to his vision.

After the lights have been turned off to test the darkness, a single light is turned on and the ceremony begins with the now shoeless and shirtless yuwipi man sitting in the middle of the ritual space facing west. First he explains his powers, then, accompanied by the *opagipi olowan,* "filling the pipe song," the yuwipi *wica'sa* fills the sacred pipe with seven pinches of tobacco for the Four Directions, Earth, Sky, and Spotted Eagle. When the pipe is filled with tobacco and topped off with sage, the assistant and a singer wrap the yuwipi man in a star quilt, bind him with rope, and then lay him face down on the sage altar. Once that is done the light is turned off again, the room is plunged into darkness, and the singers and drummers sing the powerful *wicakicopi olowan,* "they call them song," to summon the spirits of the universe, followed by three *wocekiye olowan,* "prayer song[s]." The spirits usually arrive on the fourth song, making their appearance known by the sounds of shaking rattles, the striking of floor and walls, and *peta,* or blue sparks. The next set begins with another *wicakicopi olowan,* followed by an extensive conversation between the patient and other attendees; at this time the yuwipi man is consulting with his yuwipi spirits. A fourth song set features *wapiye olowan,* "curing song[s]," for patients seeking a cure by standing in the darkness with their backs to the altar while the rattles touch them. Following is the fifth song set of *cehohomni olowan,* "around the kettle song[s]," sung only when ritual dog meat is served following the meeting. Then two *wicayujujupi olowan,* "they untie him song[s]," are performed, succeeded by a dance song for the attendees, and another for the spirits to take the tobacco offerings. During the sixth set sparks emanate from the seven sage-adorned intersections of the rope binding the yuwipi man and from the tobacco bundle string around the circumference of the sacred space. Finally, the seventh set features two songs for the withdrawing spirits: *wanagi kiglapi olowan,* "spirits go home song," and the *inkiyapi olowan,* "quitting song."

Once the spirits have embarked on their journey to the west where they live between the Earth and Sky, the light is turned on, revealing a disheveled altar, although the yuwipi *wica'sa* is sitting in the middle of the altar with the star quilt, rope, and tobacco bundle placed neatly next to him. The packed pipe is smoked by all present, including women and children, who may merely touch the pipe if they so desire, then water is passed around for everyone to drink; upon receiving the pipe and water, each recipient utters *Mitakuye oyasin,* "All my relations." Afterward, the food is brought into the house by the women who prepared it, everyone eats, and any leftovers are taken home. The tobacco offerings are often given to the patient, and the star quilt that bound the yuwipi man is sometimes put over the patient's head while the patient inhales medicines. When the ritual meal concludes, the individual at the south side of the entryway says "*Mitakuye oyasin,*" followed in turn by the participants, then finally the yuwipi man, marking the end of the ceremony.

Even though variations of the yuwipi ceremony continue to this day, there is considerable controversy associated with the ritual. Not all Lakota condone the ritual, particularly those who have converted to Christianity following the teachings of the Christian clergy, who historically have condemned the ritual as satanic. Nevertheless, the yuwipi ceremony still represents the performance of ritual to unify the Lakota spiritually.

Benjamin R. Kracht

See also Bundles, Sacred Bundle Traditions; Dreams and Visions; Power, Plains; Sweatlodge; Vision Quest Rites

References and Further Reading

DeMallie, Raymond J. 2001a. "Yankton and Yanktonai." Pp. 777–793 in *Handbook of North American Indians,* vol. 13, *Plains.* Edited by Raymond J. DeMallie. Washington, DC: Smithsonian Institution Press.

———. 2001b. "Teton." Pp. 794–820 in *Handbook of North American Indians,* vol. 13, *Plains.* Edited by Raymond J. DeMallie. Washington, DC: Smithsonian Institution Press.

Grobsmith, Elizabeth S. 1981. *Lakota of the Rosebud: A Contemporary Ethnography.* New York: Holt, Rinehart and Winston.

Lame Deer, John (Fire), and Richard Erdoes. 1972. *Lame Deer: Seeker of Visions.* New York: Washington Square Press.

Levy, Jerrold E. 2001. "Kiowa." Pp. 907–925 in *Handbook of North American Indians,* vol. 13, *Plains.* Edited by Raymond J. DeMallie. Washington, DC: Smithsonian Institution Press.

Lewis, Thomas H. 1987. "The Contemporary Yuwipi." Pp. 173–187 in *Sioux Indian Religion.* Edited by Raymond J. DeMallie and Douglas R. Parks. Norman: University of Oklahoma Press.

Powers, William K. 1977. *Oglala Religion.* Norman: University of Oklahoma Press.

———. 1984. *Yuwipi: Vision and Experience in Oglala Ritual.* Lincoln: University of Nebraska Press.

Steinmetz, Paul B. 1990. *Pipe, Bible, and Peyote among the Oglala Lakota: A Study in Religious Identity.* Knoxville: University of Tennessee Press.

Voget, Fred W. 2001. "Crow." Pp. 695–717 in *Handbook of North American Indians,* vol. 13, *Plains.* Edited by Raymond J. DeMallie. Washington, DC: Smithsonian Institution Press.

Walker, James R. 1980. *Lakota Belief and Ritual.* Edited by Raymond J. DeMallie and Elaine A. Jahner. Lincoln: University of Nebraska Press.

Indian Entities Recognized and Eligible to Receive Services from the United States Bureau of Indian Affairs

Absentee-Shawnee Tribe of Indians of Oklahoma

Agua Caliente Band of Cahuilla Indians of the Agua Caliente Indian Reservation, California

Ak Chin Indian Community of the Maricopa (Ak Chin) Indian Reservation, Arizona

Alabama-Coushatta Tribes of Texas

Alabama-Quassarte Tribal Town, Oklahoma

Alturas Indian Rancheria, California

Apache Tribe of Oklahoma

Arapahoe Tribe of the Wind River Reservation, Wyoming

Aroostook Band of Micmac Indians of Maine

Assiniboine and Sioux Tribes of the Fort Peck Indian Reservation, Montana

Augustine Band of Cahuilla Mission Indians of the Augustine Reservation, California

Bad River Band of the Lake Superior Tribe of Chippewa Indians of the

Bad River Reservation, Wisconsin

Bay Mills Indian Community, Michigan (previously listed as the Bay Mills Indian Community of the Sault Ste. Marie Band of Chippewa Indians, Bay Mills Reservation, Michigan)

Bear River Band of the Rohnerville Rancheria, California

Berry Creek Rancheria of Maidu Indians of California

Big Lagoon Rancheria, California

Big Pine Band of Owens Valley Paiute Shoshone Indians of the Big Pine Reservation, California

Big Sandy Rancheria of Mono Indians of California

Big Valley Band of Pomo Indians of the Big Valley Rancheria, California

Blackfeet Tribe of the Blackfeet Indian Reservation of Montana

Blue Lake Rancheria, California

Bridgeport Paiute Indian Colony of California

Buena Vista Rancheria of Me-Wuk Indians of California

Burns Paiute Tribe of the Burns Paiute Indian Colony of Oregon

Cabazon Band of Cahuilla Mission Indians of the Cabazon Reservation, California

Cachil DeHe Band of Wintun Indians of the Colusa Indian Community of the Colusa Rancheria, California

Caddo Indian Tribe of Oklahoma

Cahuilla Band of Mission Indians of the Cahuilla Reservation, California

Cahto Indian Tribe of the Laytonville Rancheria, California

California Valley Miwok Tribe, California (formerly the Sheep Ranch Rancheria of Me-Wuk Indians of California)

Campo Band of Diegueno Mission Indians of the Campo Indian Reservation, California

Capitan Grande Band of Diegueno Mission Indians of California:

    Barona Group of Capitan Grande Band of Mission Indians of the Barona Reservation, California

    Viejas (Baron Long) Group of Capitan Grande Band of Mission Indians of the Viejas Reservation, California

Catawba Indian Nation (also known as Catawba Tribe of South Carolina)

Cayuga Nation of New York

Cedarville Rancheria, California

Chemehuevi Indian Tribe of the Chemehuevi Reservation, California

Cher-Ae Heights Indian Community of the Trinidad Rancheria, California

Cherokee Nation, Oklahoma

Cheyenne-Arapaho Tribes of Oklahoma

Cheyenne River Sioux Tribe of the Cheyenne River Reservation, South Dakota

Chickasaw Nation, Oklahoma

Chicken Ranch Rancheria of Me-Wuk Indians of California

Chippewa-Cree Indians of the Rocky Boy's Reservation, Montana

Chitimacha Tribe of Louisiana

Choctaw Nation of Oklahoma

Citizen Potawatomi Nation, Oklahoma

Cloverdale Rancheria of Pomo Indians of California

Cocopah Tribe of Arizona

Coeur D'Alene Tribe of the Coeur D'Alene Reservation, Idaho

Cold Springs Rancheria of Mono Indians of California

Colorado River Indian Tribes of the Colorado River Indian Reservation, Arizona and California

Comanche Nation, Oklahoma (formerly the Comanche Indian Tribe)

Confederated Salish and Kootenai Tribes of the Flathead Reservation, Montana

Confederated Tribes of the Chehalis Reservation, Washington

Confederated Tribes of the Colville Reservation, Washington

Confederated Tribes of the Coos, Lower Umpqua and Siuslaw Indians of Oregon

Confederated Tribes of the Goshute Reservation, Nevada and Utah

Confederated Tribes of the Grand Ronde Community of Oregon

Confederated Tribes of the Siletz Reservation, Oregon

Confederated Tribes of the Umatilla Reservation, Oregon

Confederated Tribes of the Warm Springs Reservation of Oregon

Confederated Tribes and Bands of the Yakama Indian Nation of the Yakama Reservation, Washington

Coquille Tribe of Oregon

Cortina Indian Rancheria of Wintun Indians of California

Coushatta Tribe of Louisiana

Cow Creek Band of Umpqua Indians of Oregon

Cowlitz Indian Tribe, Washington

Coyote Valley Band of Pomo Indians of California

Crow Tribe of Montana

Crow Creek Sioux Tribe of the Crow Creek Reservation, South Dakota

Cuyapaipe Community of Diegueno Mission Indians of the Cuyapaipe Reservation, California

Death Valley Timbi-Sha Shoshone Band of California

Delaware Nation, Oklahoma (formerly Delaware Tribe of Western Oklahoma)

Delaware Tribe of Indians, Oklahoma

Dry Creek Rancheria of Pomo Indians of California

Duckwater Shoshone Tribe of the Duckwater Reservation, Nevada

Eastern Band of Cherokee Indians of North Carolina

Eastern Shawnee Tribe of Oklahoma

Elem Indian Colony of Pomo Indians of the Sulphur Bank Rancheria, California

Elk Valley Rancheria, California

Ely Shoshone Tribe of Nevada

Enterprise Rancheria of Maidu Indians of California

Flandreau Santee Sioux Tribe of South Dakota

Forest County Potawatomi Community, Wisconsin (previously listed as the Forest County Potawatomi Community of Wisconsin Potawatomi Indians, Wisconsin)

Fort Belknap Indian Community of the Fort Belknap Reservation of Montana

Fort Bidwell Indian Community of the Fort Bidwell Reservation of California

Fort Independence Indian Community of Paiute Indians of the Fort Independence Reservation, California

Fort McDermitt Paiute and Shoshone Tribes of the Fort McDermitt Indian Reservation, Nevada and Oregon

Fort McDowell Yavapai Nation, Arizona
(formerly the Fort McDowell Mohave-
Apache Community of the Fort McDowell
Indian Reservation)
Fort Mojave Indian Tribe of Arizona, California
and Nevada
Fort Sill Apache Tribe of Oklahoma

Gila River Indian Community of the Gila River
Indian Reservation, Arizona
Grand Traverse Band of Ottawa and Chippewa
Indians, Michigan (previously listed as the
Grand Traverse Band of Ottawa and
Chippewa Indians of Michigan)
Graton Rancheria, California
Greenville Rancheria of Maidu Indians of
California
Grindstone Indian Rancheria of Wintun-
Wailaki Indians of California
Guidiville Rancheria of California

Hannahville Indian Community, Michigan
(previously listed as the Hannahville Indian
Community of Wisconsin Potawatomie
Indians of Michigan)
Havasupai Tribe of the Havasupai Reservation,
Arizona
Ho-Chunk Nation of Wisconsin (formerly
known as the Wisconsin Winnebago Tribe)
Hoh Indian Tribe of the Hoh Indian
Reservation, Washington
Hoopa Valley Tribe, California
Hopi Tribe of Arizona
Hopland Band of Pomo Indians of the
Hopland Rancheria, California
Houlton Band of Maliseet Indians of Maine
Hualapai Indian Tribe of the Hualapai Indian
Reservation, Arizona
Huron Potawatomi, Inc., Michigan

Inaja Band of Diegueno Mission Indians of the
Inaja and Cosmit Reservation, California
Ione Band of Miwok Indians of California
Iowa Tribe of Kansas and Nebraska
Iowa Tribe of Oklahoma

Jackson Rancheria of Me-Wuk Indians of
California
Jamestown S'Klallam Tribe of Washington
Jamul Indian Village of California

Jena Band of Choctaw Indians, Louisiana
Jicarilla Apache Nation, New Mexico (formerly
the Jicarilla Apache Tribe of the Jicarilla
Apache Indian Reservation)

Kaibab Band of Paiute Indians of the Kaibab
Indian Reservation, Arizona
Kalispel Indian Community of the Kalispel
Reservation, Washington
Karuk Tribe of California
Kashia Band of Pomo Indians of the Stewarts
Point Rancheria, California
Kaw Nation, Oklahoma
Keweenaw Bay Indian Community, Michigan
(previously listed as the Keweenaw Bay
Indian Community of L'Anse and
Ontonagon Bands of Chippewa Indians of
the L'Anse Reservation, Michigan)
Kialegee Tribal Town, Oklahoma
Kickapoo Tribe of Indians of the Kickapoo
Reservation in Kansas
Kickapoo Tribe of Oklahoma
Kickapoo Traditional Tribe of Texas
Kiowa Indian Tribe of Oklahoma
Klamath Indian Tribe of Oregon
Kootenai Tribe of Idaho

La Jolla Band of Luiseno Mission Indians of the
La Jolla Reservation, California
La Posta Band of Diegueno Mission Indians of
the La Posta Indian Reservation, California
Lac Courte Oreilles Band of Lake Superior
Chippewa Indians of Wisconsin (previously
listed as the Lac Courte Oreilles Band of
Lake Superior Chippewa Indians of the Lac
Courte Oreilles Reservation of Wisconsin)
Lac du Flambeau Band of Lake Superior
Chippewa Indians of the Lac du Flambeau
Reservation of Wisconsin
Lac Vieux Desert Band of Lake Superior
Chippewa Indians of Michigan
Las Vegas Tribe of Paiute Indians of the Las
Vegas Indian Colony, Nevada
Little River Band of Ottawa Indians of
Michigan
Little Traverse Bay Bands of Odawa Indians,
Michigan (previously listed as the Little
Traverse Bay Bands of Odawa Indians of
Michigan)
Lower Lake Rancheria, California

Los Coyotes Band of Cahuilla Mission Indians of the Los Coyotes Reservation, California
Lovelock Paiute Tribe of the Lovelock Indian Colony, Nevada
Lower Brule Sioux Tribe of the Lower Brule Reservation, South Dakota
Lower Elwha Tribal Community of the Lower Elwha Reservation, Washington
Lower Sioux Indian Community in the State of Minnesota (previously listed as the Lower Sioux Indian Community of Minnesota Mdewakanton Sioux Indians of the Lower Sioux Reservation in Minnesota)
Lummi Tribe of the Lummi Reservation, Washington
Lytton Rancheria of California

Makah Indian Tribe of the Makah Indian Reservation, Washington
Manchester Band of Pomo Indians of the Manchester-Point Arena Rancheria, California
Manzanita Band of Diegueno Mission Indians of the Manzanita Reservation, California
Mashantucket Pequot Tribe of Connecticut
Match-e-be-nash-she-wish Band of Pottawatomi Indians of Michigan
Mechoopda Indian Tribe of Chico Rancheria, California
Menominee Indian Tribe of Wisconsin
Mesa Grande Band of Diegueno Mission Indians of the Mesa Grande Reservation, California
Mescalero Apache Tribe of the Mescalero Reservation, New Mexico
Miami Tribe of Oklahoma
Miccosukee Tribe of Indians of Florida
Middletown Rancheria of Pomo Indians of California
Minnesota Chippewa Tribe, Minnesota—Six component reservations:
    Bois Forte Band (Nett Lake)
    Fond du Lac Band
    Grand Portage Band
    Leech Lake Band
    Mille Lacs Band
    White Earth Band
Mississippi Band of Choctaw Indians, Mississippi
Moapa Band of Paiute Indians of the Moapa River Indian Reservation, Nevada

Modoc Tribe of Oklahoma
Mohegan Indian Tribe of Connecticut
Mooretown Rancheria of Maidu Indians of California
Morongo Band of Cahuilla Mission Indians of the Morongo Reservation, California
Muckleshoot Indian Tribe of the Muckleshoot Reservation, Washington
Muscogee (Creek) Nation, Oklahoma

Narragansett Indian Tribe of Rhode Island
Navajo Nation, Arizona, New Mexico and Utah
Nez Perce Tribe of Idaho
Nisqually Indian Tribe of the Nisqually Reservation, Washington
Nooksack Indian Tribe of Washington
Northern Cheyenne Tribe of the Northern Cheyenne Indian Reservation, Montana
Northfork Rancheria of Mono Indians of California
Northwestern Band of Shoshoni Nation of Utah (Washakie)

Oglala Sioux Tribe of the Pine Ridge Reservation, South Dakota
Omaha Tribe of Nebraska
Oneida Nation of New York
Oneida Tribe of Indians of Wisconsin (previously listed as the Oneida Tribe of Wisconsin)
Onondaga Nation of New York
Osage Tribe, Oklahoma
Ottawa Tribe of Oklahoma
Otoe-Missouria Tribe of Indians, Oklahoma

Paiute Indian Tribe of Utah
    Cedar City Band of Paiutes
    Kanosh Band of Paiutes
    Koosharem Band of Paiutes
    Indian Peaks Band of Paiutes
    Shivwits Band of Paiutes
Paiute-Shoshone Indians of the Bishop Community of the Bishop Colony, California
Paiute-Shoshone Tribe of the Fallon Reservation and Colony, Nevada
Paiute-Shoshone Indians of the Lone Pine Community of the Lone Pine Reservation, California
Pala Band of Luiseno Mission Indians of the Pala Reservation, California

Pascua Yaqui Tribe of Arizona

Paskenta Band of Nomlaki Indians of California

Passamaquoddy Tribe of Maine

Pauma Band of Luiseno Mission Indians of the Pauma and Yuima Reservation, California

Pawnee Nation of Oklahoma

Pechanga Band of Luiseno Mission Indians of the Pechanga Reservation, California

Penobscot Tribe of Maine

Peoria Tribe of Indians of Oklahoma

Picayune Rancheria of Chukchansi Indians of California

Pinoleville Rancheria of Pomo Indians of California

Pit River Tribe, California
    Big Bend
    Lookout
    Montgomery
    Creek and Roaring Creek Rancherias
    XL Ranch

Poarch Band of Creek Indians of Alabama

Pokagon Band of Potawatomi Indians, Michigan and Indiana (previously listed as the Pokagon Band of Potawatomi Indians of Michigan)

Ponca Tribe of Indians of Oklahoma

Ponca Tribe of Nebraska

Port Gamble Indian Community of the Port Gamble Reservation, Washington

Potter Valley Rancheria of Pomo Indians of California

Prairie Band of Potawatomi Nation, Kansas (formerly the Prairie Band of Potawatomi Indians)

Prairie Island Indian Community in the State of Minnesota (previously listed as the Prairie Island Indian Community of Minnesota Mdewakanton Sioux Indians of the Prairie Island Reservation, Minnesota)

Pueblo of Acoma, New Mexico

Pueblo of Cochiti, New Mexico

Pueblo of Jemez, New Mexico

Pueblo of Isleta, New Mexico

Pueblo of Laguna, New Mexico

Pueblo of Nambe, New Mexico

Pueblo of Picuris, New Mexico

Pueblo of Pojoaque, New Mexico

Pueblo of San Felipe, New Mexico

Pueblo of San Juan, New Mexico

Pueblo of San Ildefonso, New Mexico

Pueblo of Sandia, New Mexico

Pueblo of Santa Ana, New Mexico

Pueblo of Santa Clara, New Mexico

Pueblo of Santo Domingo, New Mexico

Pueblo of Taos, New Mexico

Pueblo of Tesuque, New Mexico

Pueblo of Zia, New Mexico

Puyallup Tribe of the Puyallup Reservation, Washington

Pyramid Lake Paiute Tribe of the Pyramid Lake Reservation, Nevada

Quapaw Tribe of Indians, Oklahoma

Quartz Valley Indian Community of the Quartz Valley Reservation of California

Quechan Tribe of the Fort Yuma Indian Reservation, California and Arizona

Quileute Tribe of the Quileute Reservation, Washington

Quinault Tribe of the Quinault Reservation, Washington

Ramona Band or Village of Cahuilla Mission Indians of California

Red Cliff Band of Lake Superior Chippewa Indians of Wisconsin

Red Lake Band of Chippewa Indians, Minnesota (previously listed as the Red Lake Band of Chippewa Indians of the Red Lake Reservation, Minnesota)

Redding Rancheria, California

Redwood Valley Rancheria of Pomo Indians of California

Reno-Sparks Indian Colony, Nevada

Resighini Rancheria, California (formerly the Coast Indian Community of Yurok Indians of the Resighini Rancheria)

Rincon Band of Luiseno Mission Indians of the Rincon Reservation, California

Robinson Rancheria of Pomo Indians of California

Rosebud Sioux Tribe of the Rosebud Indian Reservation, South Dakota

Round Valley Indian Tribes of the Round Valley Reservation, California (formerly known as the Covelo Indian Community)

Rumsey Indian Rancheria of Wintun Indians of California

Sac and Fox Tribe of the Mississippi in Iowa

Sac and Fox Nation of Missouri in Kansas and Nebraska

Sac and Fox Nation, Oklahoma

Saginaw Chippewa Indian Tribe of Michigan (previously listed as the Saginaw Chippewa Indian Tribe of Michigan, Isabella Reservation)

St. Croix Chippewa Indians of Wisconsin (previously listed as the St. Croix Chippewa Indians of Wisconsin, St. Croix Reservation)

St. Regis Band of Mohawk Indians of New York

Salt River Pima-Maricopa Indian Community of the Salt River Reservation, Arizona

Samish Indian Tribe, Washington

San Carlos Apache Tribe of the San Carlos Reservation, Arizona

San Juan Southern Paiute Tribe of Arizona

San Manual Band of Serrano Mission Indians of the San Manual Reservation, California

San Pasqual Band of Diegueno Mission Indians of California

Santa Rosa Indian Community of the Santa Rosa Rancheria, California

Santa Rosa Band of Cahuilla Mission Indians of the Santa Rosa Reservation, California

Santa Ynez Band of Chumash Mission Indians of the Santa Ynez Reservation, California

Santa Ysabel Band of Diegueno Mission Indians of the Santa Ysabel Reservation, California

Santee Sioux Tribe of the Santee Reservation of Nebraska

Sauk-Suiattle Indian Tribe of Washington

Sault Ste. Marie Tribe of Chippewa Indians of Michigan

Scotts Valley Band of Pomo Indians of California

Seminole Nation of Oklahoma

Seminole Tribe of Florida
    Dania Reservations
    Big Cypress Reservations
    Brighton Reservations
    Hollywood Reservations
    Tampa Reservations

Seneca Nation of New York

Seneca-Cayuga Tribe of Oklahoma

Shakopee Mdewakanton Sioux Community of Minnesota (previously listed as the Shakopee Mdewakanton Sioux Community of Minnesota (Prior Lake))

Shawnee Tribe, Oklahoma

Sherwood Valley Rancheria of Pomo Indians of California

Shingle Springs Band of Miwok Indians, Shingle Springs Rancheria (Verona Tract), California

Shoalwater Bay Tribe of the Shoalwater Bay Indian Reservation, Washington

Shoshone Tribe of the Wind River Reservation, Wyoming

Shoshone-Bannock Tribes of the Fort Hall Reservation of Idaho

Shoshone-Paiute Tribes of the Duck Valley Reservation, Nevada

Sisseton-Wahpeton Sioux Tribe of the Lake Traverse Reservation, South Dakota

Skokomish Indian Tribe of the Skokomish Reservation, Washington

Skull Valley Band of Goshute Indians of Utah

Smith River Rancheria, California

Snoqualmie Tribe, Washington

Soboba Band of Luiseno Indians, California (formerly the Soboba Band of Luiseno Mission Indians of the Soboba Reservation)

Sokaogon Chippewa Community, Wisconsin (previously listed as the Sokaogon Chippewa Community of the Mole Lake Band of Chippewa Indians, Wisconsin)

Southern Ute Indian Tribe of the Southern Ute Reservation, Colorado

Spirit Lake Tribe, North Dakota

Spokane Tribe of the Spokane Reservation, Washington

Squaxin Island Tribe of the Squaxin Island Reservation, Washington

Standing Rock Sioux Tribe of North and South Dakota

Stockbridge Munsee Community, Wisconsin (previously listed as the Stockbridge-Munsee Community of Mohican Indians of Wisconsin)

Stillaguamish Tribe of Washington

Summit Lake Paiute Tribe of Nevada

Suquamish Indian Tribe of the Port Madison Reservation, Washington

Susanville Indian Rancheria, California

Swinomish Indians of the Swinomish Reservation, Washington

Sycuan Band of Diegueno Mission Indians of California

Table Bluff Reservation—Wiyot Tribe, California

Table Mountain Rancheria of California

Te-Moak Tribes of Western Shoshone Indians of Nevada—Four constituent bands:
    Battle Mountain Band
    Elko Band
    South Fork Band
    Wells Band

Thlopthlocco Tribal Town, Oklahoma

Three Affiliated Tribes of the Fort Berthold Reservation, North Dakota

Tohono O'odham Nation of Arizona

Tonawanda Band of Seneca Indians of New York

Tonkawa Tribe of Indians of Oklahoma

Tonto Apache Tribe of Arizona

Torres-Martinez Band of Cahuilla Mission Indians of California

Tule River Indian Tribe of the Tule River Reservation, California

Tulalip Tribes of the Tulalip Reservation, Washington

Tunica-Biloxi Indian Tribe of Louisiana

Tuolumne Band of Me-Wuk Indians of the Tuolumne Rancheria of California

Turtle Mountain Band of Chippewa Indians of North Dakota

Tuscarora Nation of New York

Twenty-Nine Palms Band of Mission Indians of California (previously listed as the Twenty-Nine Palms Band of Luiseno Mission Indians of California

United Auburn Indian Community of the Auburn Rancheria of California

United Keetoowah Band of Cherokee Indians in Oklahoma (previously listed as the United Keetoowah Band of Cherokee Indians of Oklahoma)

Upper Lake Band of Pomo Indians of Upper Lake Rancheria of California

Upper Sioux Community, Minnesota (previously listed as the Upper Sioux Indian Community of the Upper Sioux Reservation, Minnesota)

Upper Skagit Indian Tribe of Washington

Ute Indian Tribe of the Uintah and Ouray Reservation, Utah

Ute Mountain Tribe of the Ute Mountain Reservation, Colorado, New Mexico and Utah

Utu Utu Gwaitu Paiute Tribe of the Benton Paiute Reservation, California

Walker River Paiute Tribe of the Walker River Reservation, Nevada

Wampanoag Tribe of Gay Head (Aquinnah) of Massachusetts

Washoe Tribe of Nevada and California:
    Carson Colony
    Dresslerville Colony
    Woodfords Community
    Stewart Community
    Washoe Ranches

White Mountain Apache Tribe of the Fort Apache Reservation, Arizona

Wichita and Affiliated Tribes, Oklahoma:
    Wichita
    Keechi
    Waco
    Tawakonie

Winnebago Tribe of Nebraska

Winnemucca Indian Colony of Nevada

Wyandotte Tribe of Oklahoma

Yankton Sioux Tribe of South Dakota

Yavapai-Apache Nation of the Camp Verde Indian Reservation, Arizona

Yavapai-Prescott Tribe of the Yavapai Reservation, Arizona

Yerington Paiute Tribe of the Yerington Colony and Campbell Ranch, Nevada

Yomba Shoshone Tribe of the Yomba Reservation, Nevada

Ysleta Del Sur Pueblo of Texas

Yurok Tribe of the Yurok Reservation, California

Zuni Tribe of the Zuni Reservation, New Mexico

Source: Department of the Interior, Bureau of Indian Affairs. 2002. *Federal Register* 67 (134):46328–46331.

Index

Note: Page numbers in **boldface** indicate major discussions in the text.

About the Editors

Suzanne J. Crawford received her Ph.D. in Religious Studies from the University of California at Santa Barbara. She is the author of *Native American Religions* (Prentice Hall and Lawrence King, 2005). She is currently assistant professor of Religion and Culture at Pacific Lutheran University, and lives in Seattle, Washington.

Dennis Kelley is a visiting lecturer at the University of Missouri–Columbia. He lives in Columbia, Missouri, with his wife, Kate, and their son, Seamus Bear.